Learn to Program Objects with Visual Basic 6

John Smiley

Active Path Ltd. ®

Learn to Program Objects with Visual Basic 6

First published December 1999

activepath

Published by Active Path Ltd,
Arden House, 1102 Warwick Road, Acocks Green,
Birmingham, B27 6BH, United Kingdom

Printed in USA

ISBN **1-902745-04-3**

Trademark Acknowledgements

Credits

Author
John Smiley

Development Editor
Andy Corsham

Technical Editors
Andy Corsham
Daniel Walker

Layout and Production Team
Tom Bartlett
Mark Burdett
William Fallon
Jonathan Jones
John McNulty

Technical Reviewers
Humberto Abreu
Monica Atkinson
Kieron Conway
Eddie Correia
Antoine Giusti
Emma Morgan
Lonnie Moseley

Index
Alessandro Ansa

Cover
Chris Morris

About the Author

John Smiley, a Microsoft Certified Professional in Visual Basic, is the President of John Smiley and Associates, a computer consulting firm located in South Jersey, which serves clients both large and small in the surrounding Philadelphia Metropolitan area. John is also an adjunct professor of computer science at Penn State University in Abington, the Philadelphia College of Textiles and Science, and Holy Family College, and has been teaching computer programming courses for nearly 20 years. He teaches a number of very popular online courses at SmartPlanet and Ziff Davis University (ZDU).

On the writing front, John is the author of *Learn to Program with Visual Basic 6*, *Learn to Program with Visual Basic Examples*, and *Learn to Program Databases with Visual Basic 6*, all published by Active Path. He has also done technical editing on a number of Wrox Press and Que Visual Basic titles. You can find a case study he wrote in *Beginning Visual Basic 6* by Wrox Press.

Feel free to visit John's web site at

`http://www.johnsmiley.com`

or contact him via email at `johnsmiley@johnsmiley.com`. He'd love to hear from you, and he answers all of his emails religiously.

Dedication

This book is dedicated to my wife Linda – none of this would be possible without you.

Acknowledgments

First and foremost, I want to thank my wife Linda for her love and support. Thank you.

A fourth book is no easier on the family of the author than the other three – so, thanks again to my three wonderful children, Tom, Kevin and Melissa, who each contributed something to the book in his or her own way – even if it was nothing more than putting up with my pleas for some quiet time! I've told you all many times that none of this would be possible without you all, and I really mean that.

Many thanks go to the great people at Active Path. Once again, I want to thank Dave Maclean for continuing to give me the opportunity to pursue my dream of writing innovative books on computer programming. I want to thank Andy Corsham and Daniel Walker, my editors at Active Path, for their dedicated hard work in getting this book ready for publication. Thanks go to my other friends at Wrox Press and Active Path for their kind words and encouragement, too.

As I've said before, books aren't produced in a vacuum. Behind the scenes there are reviewers, technical editors, artists, layout specialists, copy editors, indexers, and a group of marketing experts – all working towards the goal of making the book a success. Special thanks to Burt Abreu, Monica Atkinson, Antoine Giusti, Kieron Conway, Eddie Correia, Emma Morgan, and Lonnie Moseley for reviewing the book. Thanks also go to Chris Morris for the beautiful cover, and to Tom Bartlett, Mark Burdett, William Fallon, Jonathan Jones, and John McNulty, who all worked on the layout and production.

Many thanks also go to the thousands of students I've taught over the years for your tireless dedication to learning the art and science of computer programming. Your great questions and persistent demands to get the most out of your learning experience truly inspired me, and you've contributed significantly to my books. Many of you dragged yourself to class after a long, hard day of work, or rose early on your Saturday day off to learn Visual Basic and the other programming languages I've taught. You have my greatest respect and admiration and, if you look carefully, you can see your spirit reflected in the students in my books.

I want to thank the thousands of readers of my first three books who've taken the time to write to me and tell me what a difference they've made to you – I truly appreciate hearing from you and your success stories. I publish my email address intentionally – feel free to use it.

I want to thank all the members of my family for their belief in and support of me over the years, in particular my mother, who has patiently waited for this book. Special thanks to Bob and Pat for giving my books priority placement in bookstore windows whenever you can!

Finally, I want to acknowledge my father who, although not physically here to see this book, is surely flicking through its pages right now. It's been nearly twenty-five years since I last saw you, but your role in the writing of this and my first three books can never be understated – you and mother have been great inspirations and role models for me. As I've said before, I know that the God who made us all will someday permit us to be together again.

Learn to Program Objects with Visual Basic
Bullina's
China

Table of Contents

Learn to Program Objects with Visual Basic
Bullina's
China

Read this First!

The fact that you've picked up this book and started reading it is a testimony to how important objects are in the world of Visual Basic programming. Of all the topics I teach in my programming classes, perhaps none makes students tremble as much as objects. But, by the time we're finished, most of them report that objects are actually an exciting way to develop high-quality programs which – most importantly – have an internal strength and logic that's clear to the programmers who use and maintain them.

What this Book is about

Newcomers often regard **object-orientated programming** (OOP) as something overly abstract and complicated, but it's really not at all! Even that phrase – object-oriented programming – can sound daunting and formal, until you realize that it just means 'programming that's done using lumps of code called objects'. If you say 'OOP' instead (to rhyme with 'scoop') it's even less scary.

You've programmed with Visual Basic before, haven't you? Well, you might be surprised to find that you've been using objects all along!

Like the Scarecrow, who traveled to meet the Wizard of Oz in the hope of gaining a brain, only to find that he already had one, Visual Basic programmers are often surprised to find they're already employing the enormous power that object-oriented design offers: objects are actually built into the way that the designers at Microsoft developed and delivered the Visual Basic language and application. Whenever you've been firing up VB and adding controls to a form, you've been using objects implicitly. Now it's time to empower yourselves by learning how to use these OOP techniques *explicitly* in your own programs.

During the course of this book, I'll talk about why objects are a fundamental part of the modern programming world. I'll introduce you to some objects that are indispensable to Visual Basic, and show you what goes on behind the scenes of these objects – objects that you've actually already been using in your Visual Basic programs. In the rest of the book, I'll show you how to create and use your own objects. We'll also see how we can 'borrow' the objects from standard programs like Word and Excel and use them to add power and elegance to our programs.

At the end of the book I hope that you too can say – like the students in my classes – that objects aren't so terrifying, after all. When you finish the book, you'll be equipped to explore the world of object-oriented programming with real confidence.

The Learn to Program Approach to Teaching

For those of you unfamiliar with the *Learn to Program with Visual Basic* approach to learning, this book will place you, the reader, in a classroom setting. As you sit in on my university class, we'll modify an existing program (included on the book's CD) to use Visual Basic objects. This gives us the opportunity to ask all of those questions that you'll have, but which other books don't give you the opportunity to ask and have answered. Follow along with us, and have fun at the same time!

Who is this Book for?

This book is aimed at the reader who's already got an essential grounding in Visual Basic, and who's keen to learn about how to use object-oriented programming principles in their code. We expect that you know your way around the Visual Basic IDE, and that you've written a few simple programs of your own, and that you're familiar with fundamental Visual Basic elements like forms, controls, loops, and variables.

So, you need to be comfortable discussing core VB terminology and code. If you've read John Smiley's previous books and want to build on what you've already learned, you should be able to take this book in your stride. If, on the other hand, you've climbed the VB tree a different way – by reading another text or taking a course, maybe – and you can work your way through a VB problem without having to ask too many questions, you'll be comfortable with this book, too. Most of all, you'll want to learn about objects and get a sense of how they can make your programming life richer and more rewarding.

> **If you aren't confident about your VB skills, consider working through John's previous books, *Learn to Program with Visual Basic 6* and *Learn to Program with Visual Basic Examples.***

What will you Need?

Well, you'll need to be running some edition of Visual Basic 6. If you don't already have Visual Basic, you might like to think about buying *Learn to Program with Visual Basic 6,* which actually includes the Visual Basic **Working Model Edition**. Almost everything in this book (the exception being some of the more advanced material in Chapter 9) works fine with this stripped-down version of VB.

The code in some of the chapters also interacts with Excel and Word, so you should have those available on your PC too, if you want to get the full benefit from this book.

What's Covered in this Book?

This book teaches you the essentials of using objects in Visual Basic. As in the previous *Learn to Program with Visual Basic* titles, we aim to focus on **depth** rather than breadth. So, what we cover, we cover in detail, so that you'll absorb and understand it properly.

We don't pretend that this book is the only one you'll need in your programming career if you're going to work successfully with objects: there are hundreds of books available about programming with objects, and one of the reasons for that is that the field is large and complex the higher you go. We suggest that this book is the best one to start with, because it gives you the foundations that you need, explained in language that you can understand and absorb.

With the foundation established, you can look into each more specialized area of object-oriented programming with confidence, and with a mental framework to fit your new learning into.

Essentially, what we show you in this book is this:

- Why objects are so important in the programming world
- The advantages of doing programming the object-oriented way
- Using Visual Basic's built-in objects
- Designing and creating your own objects
- Binding objects together in your code
- Using objects from other applications
- Getting other programs to use *your* objects

How's the Book Structured?

A lot of people think that if something's hard, they can't do it. That's just not true – it just takes a little more work, and a little more help. This book takes object-oriented programming out of the realms of 'too hard'.

Structurally, this means that we want to give you a consistent project to relate your learning to. Here, we use an existing program – the China Shop program – that John Smiley and his students built in a previous book. The China Shop program was designed and built to cater for the computing needs of a small store selling fine china pieces.

And don't worry if you haven't got John's original book – we supply the project as it stands at the start of *this* book on the CD inside the back cover, so you're ready to pick it straight up and run with it. If you *did* build the China Shop project already, you can continue working with your own version.

> **For instructions on getting the China Shop project up on your PC, please refer to Appendix B.**

We'll familiarize you with the functions of the existing China Shop program before we move on to looking at how the owner of the China Shop store – a guy called Joe Bullina – wants the program modified. The rest of the book teaches you how to do this in an object-oriented context. We talk through the theory in my class, work through some code examples, and then apply these principles to the China Shop program. This approach is designed to give you plenty of practice, and to make sure that you absorb the theoretical material.

What's on the CD?

The CD in the back of this book contains all of the code to get the China Shop installed on your machine as it stood at the end of the previous *Learn to Program with Visual Basic 6* book.

> **If you didn't read our previous title, you'll need to copy across the China Shop program from the CD before you can get started on this book – see Appendix B for how to do this properly.**

The CD also has folders containing the project at various stages of modification as we add to it in *this* book. We've supplied this pre-built code so that you have a backup version if your own code gets lost, destroyed, or corrupted.

However...

We really do recommend that you create your own enhanced, object-oriented version of the China Shop program by keying **all** the code yourself rather than copying the 'built-in-stages' versions that we've supplied on the CD. The whole point of the *Learn to Program* series is that you *learn by doing*, building your skills and expertise through practice. You *owe it to yourself* to build the code in this book for yourself.

Do I Get any Support?

What do you do if you get stuck in a book?

You're not alone, OK? Just remember that. The Active Path website at `www.activepath.com` is there as a resource for you to use. There'll be the opportunity to ask the book's editors questions and give us feedback (positive or negative – we can take it). Just email us at `feedback@activepath.com` if you have a question or suggestion about the book. Please don't ask us about general VB questions, though, unless they're really related to the books – we'd love to be able to help you out individually but there just isn't enough time in the day to do that *and* bring out the great books you want to see from Active Path.

What is Active Path?

Active Path is a publishing house with a fresh attitude to learning about computer programming. As a publisher, we understand your need to have the most up-to-date, cutting-edge information about the computing world around you. We also understand that the computing world is full of jargon, and awash with unhelpful books that either treat you like an idiot or talk over your head, making no attempt to help you learn and build your skills.

So what makes Active Path different? Well, books from Active Path start at your level. There'll always be an entry-level book, for which there's no previous experience required – guaranteed. We're not going to blindly show you everything about a subject in one massive brain-dump; we'll present the concepts when they become relevant to the problem. We don't believe anything is too complicated to learn; but we do believe that if you can imagine the problem, we should be able to illustrate the solution in terms you can understand.

We like detailed examples, and giving you the chance to work out your own solutions to problems designed to get you thinking and applying your knowledge. Most books try to cover everything, but end up leaving you baffled. We think that if you can pick it up and use it yourself, you're well on the way to thinking it's not so hard after all.

Basically, we believe that you should be able to learn what you want, how you want, when you want, and at a pace you feel comfortable with. All we do is write books to let you do that.

What about Text Styles?

To help you pick out important pieces of information and distinguish a piece of code in a paragraph of text, we've used certain fonts and styles throughout the book. We've kept it simple, so we don't distract you from the content, which we believe is the key here. Here are examples of each kind of style we use:

Since this book is about programming, there are quite a few times when we need to point out pieces of code. There are three ways of doing it, but they all look similar, so you can easily pick them out of a crowd. Sometimes we'll use `this style` to refer to a `procedure` or `code-related thing` in the middle of the text.

```
When we describe a new chunk of code, it'll be displayed on a gray
background like this

If you see this twisted arrow symbol in a code listing,
  ↳ it means that you should type all the code on one line,
  ↳ leaving out the twisted arrow.
  ↳ Don't try to find this symbol on your keyboard -
  ↳ it's not there!
```

```
Code that has already been explained won't usually have the gray background.
   ↳ Quite often it will be a chunk of code you've seen before,
   ↳ and we've
   ↳ changed one line of it, or added something.
   ↳ So the new part looks like this, with a gray background.
```

[By the way, if the line's *really* big, you might want to use the VB line continuation character, the underscore (_).]

Important **terms** and **new phrases** will be bolded like this.

Text from a Menu or on command buttons that you see on your computer screen appears like this, much as it does on the screen.

> **If we want to point out something important that you really need to know and remember, it will stand out in a chunky gray box like this.**

And if John's scribbling merrily away on his wipe board in the classroom, or showing slides on the projector, it'll show up like this.

OK – let's **Learn to Program Objects with Visual Basic 6**.

Learn to Program Objects with Visual Basic
Bullina's
China

Chapter 1
The Return of the China Shop

Object-oriented programming techniques help us build better programs – programs that do the job that their buyers want them to do, and that are delivered on-schedule, and on-budget. The ultimate motivation for learning about objects is the desire to create higher-quality programs.

In this chapter, we'll prepare the ground for our examination of **objects** in Visual Basic. The story of Visual Basic objects is a vital and important one for any VB programmer to know, and we'll set about it in a gradual fashion to ensure that we tell it right.

Firstly, we'll refresh your memory about the China Shop project that we developed in my previous book. After that, we'll discover some new requirements that the owner of the China Shop has identified for the existing system, and then we'll discuss how object-oriented programming can help us address these requirements, and why the object-oriented approach is becoming an industry standard. Next, we'll meet up with the students in my Visual Basic Objects class and outline the sequence in which we'll learn about objects together. Then we'll agree how to approach the problem of modifying and re-engineering the China Shop.

This first chapter will give us the background we need to work through the object-related modifications to a real-world application.

Let's begin our study of Visual Basic objects by looking afresh at the program that was developed and written in my first book, ***Learn to Program with Visual Basic 6***. This program, the **China Shop Project**, will be the vehicle that we use to put our knowledge about objects into practice.

A Brief History of the China Shop

For those of you unfamiliar with the story so far, here's an update. During the **Introduction to Visual Basic Programming** course that I taught at Penn State University in the previous fall semester, my students and I designed and programmed a price quotation system for Joe Bullina, the owner of the Bullina China Shop. Joe's China Shop specializes in selling fine china – plates, soup bowls, cups and saucers, and so on. Customers can buy individual China items in various combinations, or they can buy the china pieces that make up a **complete place setting**, which consists of one each of all the available china pieces – all the cups, saucers and plates that a person would need for a really good dinner!

Joe had approached me in my capacity as a computer consultant, and he'd explained that when customers came into his store wanting to check prices, they sometimes got frustrated that a member of staff wasn't immediately available to serve them – Joe's store is pretty successful, and it's invariably crowded. What Joe wanted was a computer system that would let customers select the china pieces that they were interested in buying, and then display a price quotation on the screen. The customer could then make a note of the quotation, and wait for a member of staff to become available if they still wanted to make the purchase.

Working as a team, my class and I designed and coded the China Shop program. This is what the completed program looks like now that it's installed on a PC in Joe's store:

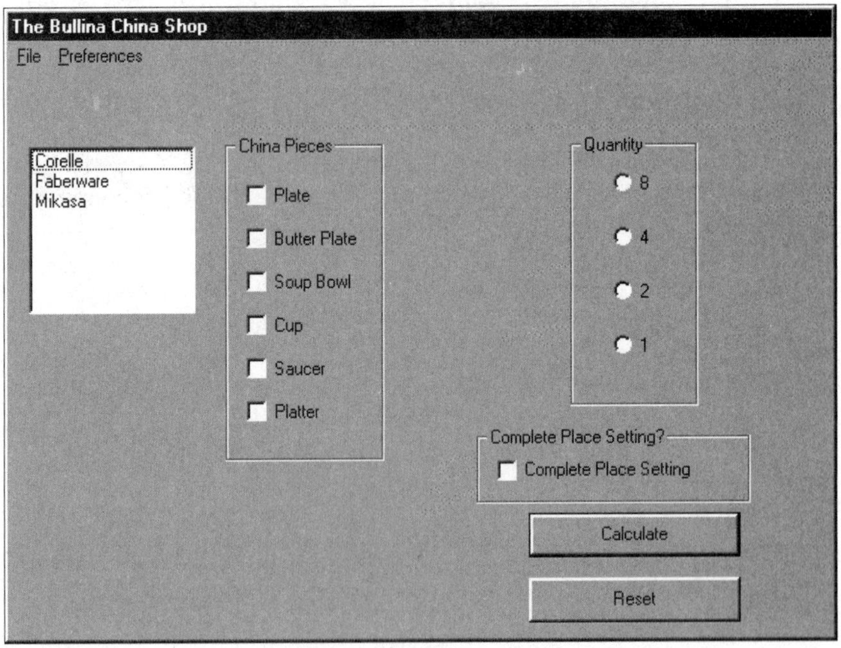

As you can see, this is a single form, with a number of controls on it – mostly option buttons, check boxes, and command buttons, plus some frames to group things together. Let's take a look at how the program is used in-store.

> **Now would be a good time to install the existing China Shop program on your PC. Full instructions on what you need to do to get the China Shop up and running can be found in Appendix B of this book.**

A Walk around the Store

When a customer uses the system to get their quotation, the first thing they do is use the mouse to select a brand of china from the list box on the left-hand side of the form. There are three different brands of china to choose from – Corelle, Faberware, and Mikasa:

By the way, Corelle is the most inexpensive brand, and Mikasa the most expensive. Anyway, let's continue our tour.

Say that a customer comes into the shop to use the program. Let's imagine him as a dignified, gentleman of mature years – we'll call him Gil. He goes to the computer to see how it works. After a few moments, he selects the Mikasa brand of china by clicking on it. When he does this, his selection is highlighted in the list box, and a picture of the Mikasa pattern appears in the image control on the form:

Now let's assume that Gil wants to buy all of the china pieces that make up a complete place setting. To get a quotation for a complete place setting, he simply clicks on the Complete Place Setting check box. When he does this, five check marks appear in the China Pieces frame, next to the china items that, together, comprise a complete place setting:

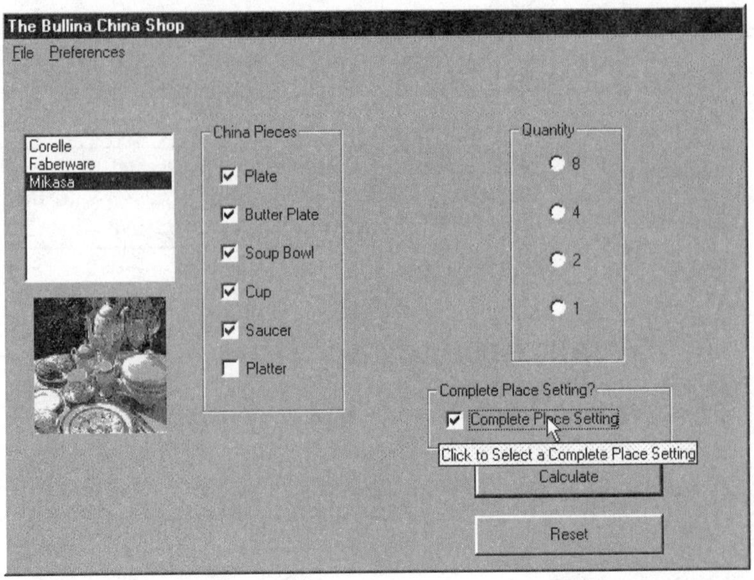

Now that Gil has selected the types of china pieces that he wants, the next step is to say *how many* complete place settings he wants to buy – he doesn't want any of his dinner guests to feel that they've got less china than the person sitting next to them! He specifies the number of complete place settings by clicking on one of the option buttons in the Quantity frame:

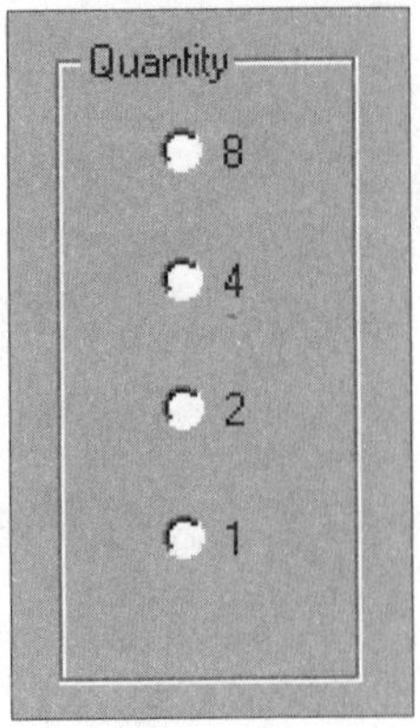

Note that – for business reasons – the user can only choose quantities of 8, 4, 2, or 1.

Let's imagine that Gil is feeling affluent, and that he decides to choose a quantity of 8 complete place settings:

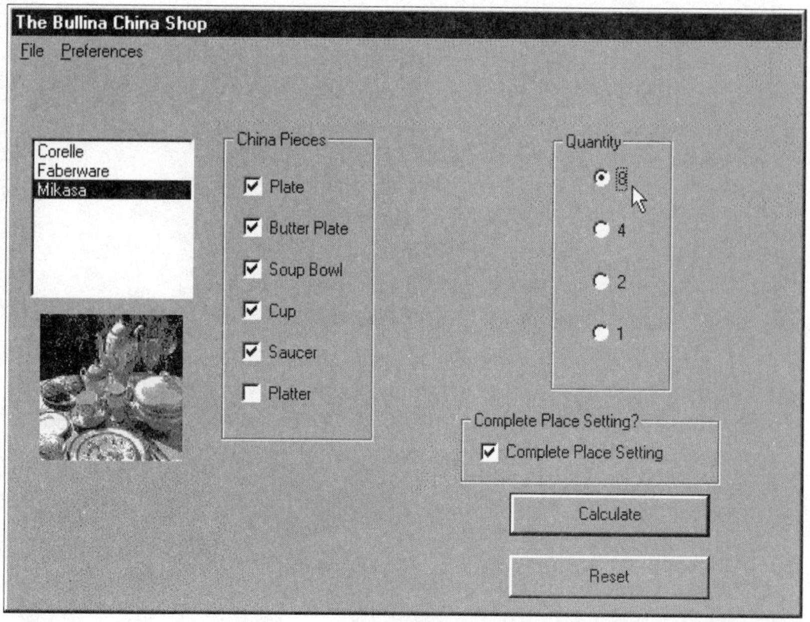

Having made his choice of china brands, china pieces, and quantities, the moment of truth arrives. Gil calculates his price quotation by clicking – logically enough – on the Calculate button:

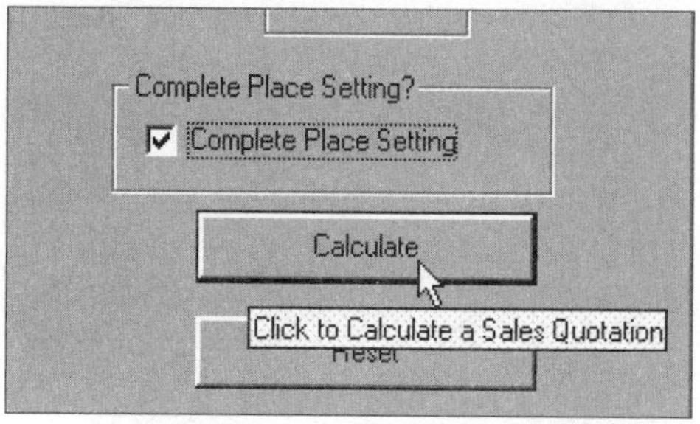

As he selected a complete place setting, Gil is rewarded with a message box telling him that he's entitled to a discount:

Gil dismisses the message box by clicking on the OK button, and the calculated price of his selected china is displayed – along with some descriptive text – using the caption of a label control in the lower left-hand corner of the form:

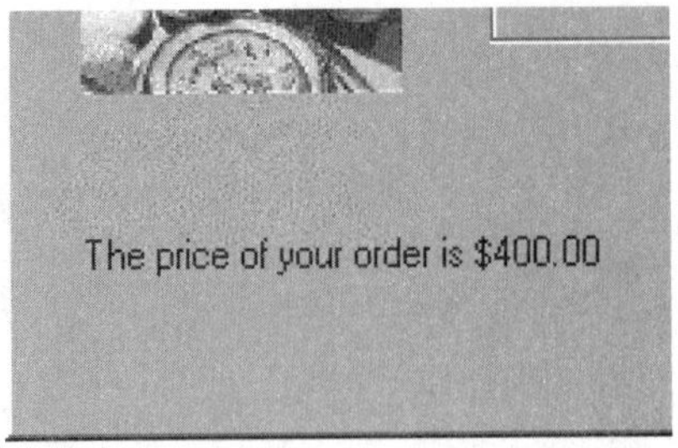

Now, it so happens that while Gil has been processing his quotation, his wife Rita has been waiting at his elbow, patiently watching him move through the steps on-screen. When she sees the price of the order, she decides to take over – after all, she *is* the accountant in their household, and *he* wouldn't know where to start cooking something that was worthy of being served up on Mikasa china.

Settling herself in front of the screen, Rita uses the mouse to click on the Reset command button. The form's controls – the price label, the check boxes, the option buttons, and the list box selection – are reset, leaving the form ready for a new quotation:

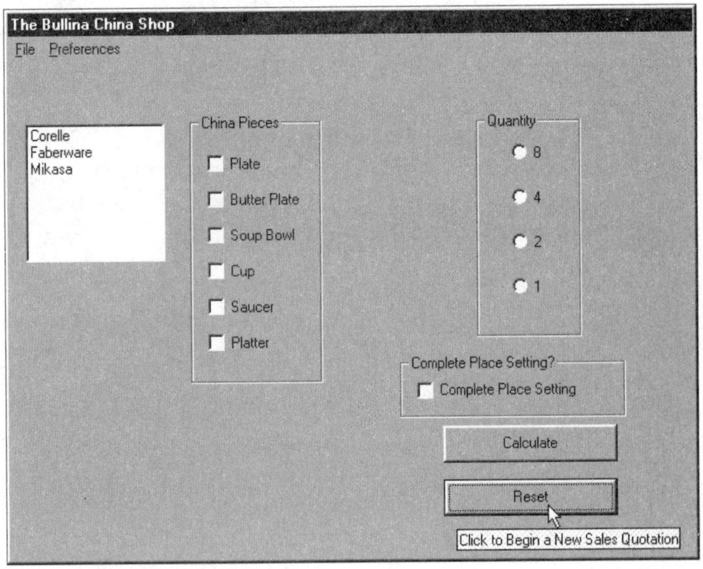

Before getting her fresh price quotation under way, Rita explores some of the menu items displayed at the top of the form. She finds that there's an option to Exit the program...

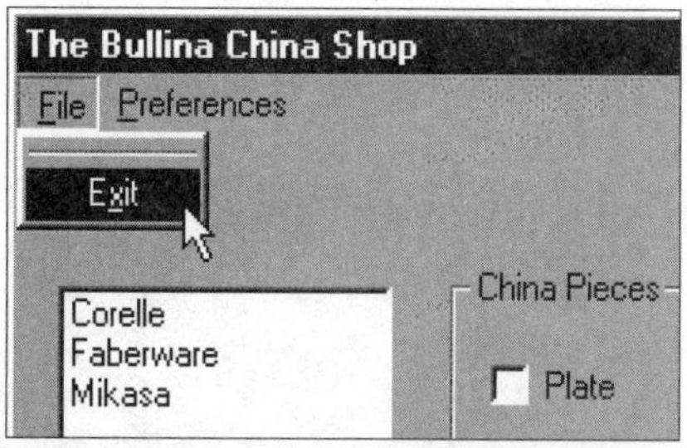

...and, as she's an adventurous type, she clicks on it. A message box appears:

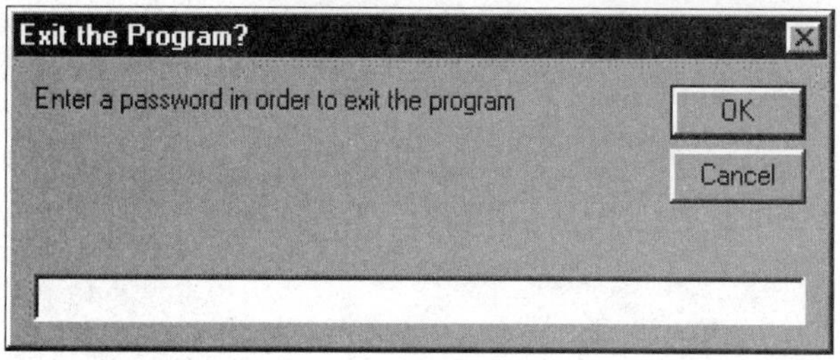

She doesn't know what the password is, and figures – rightly – that this menu item is password-protected so that only members of staff can close down the program.

To shut the program down, a staff member would have to enter the password 061883 into the text field in the message box.

Rita clicks on the OK button to get rid of the message box, and then she tries out the rest of the menu options. She finds that she can change the background colors of the form:

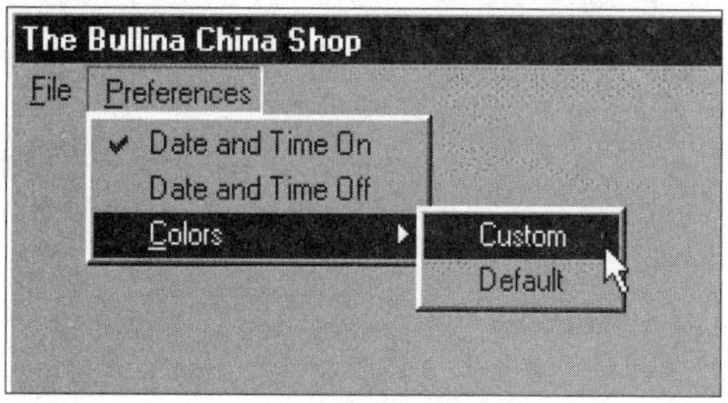

Choosing the Custom option will bring up a dialog box that lets her pick a background color from the Windows palette:

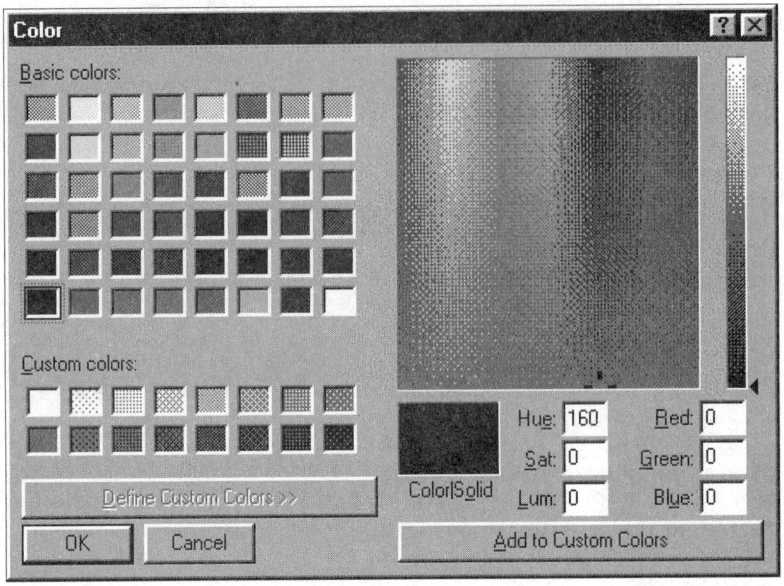

Rita doesn't know it, but if she changes the background color, the program stores this change in the Windows Registry and restores this background color the next time that the program is started.

There's also a menu option that lets Rita turn the program's Date and Time display on and off:

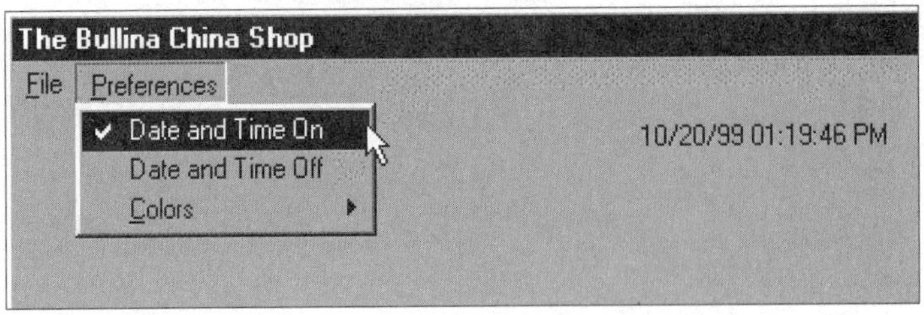

Having checked out the menu options, and deciding to try for a cheaper option than Gil chose, Rita selects the Faberware china brand in the list box:

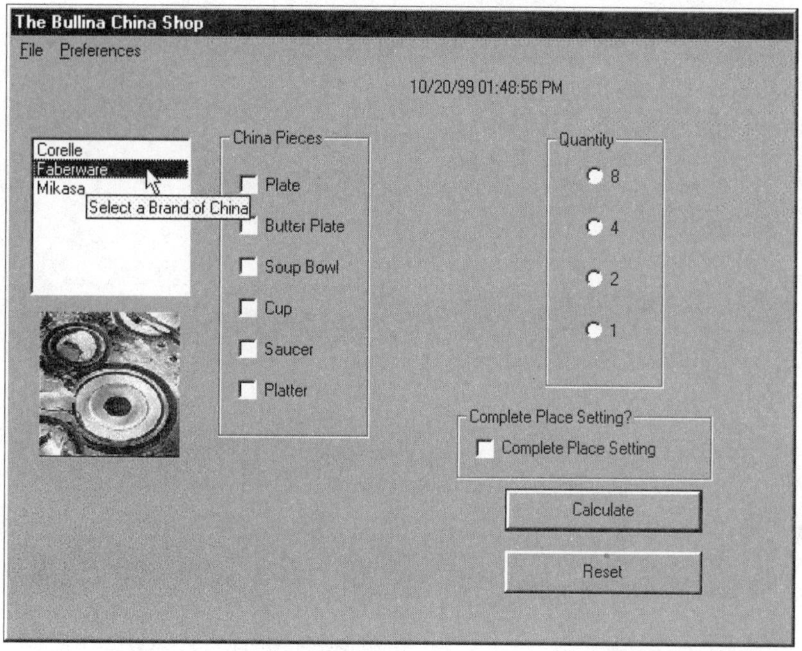

Unlike Gil, Rita only wants to buy a selection of a few china pieces – not a complete place setting. Accordingly, she selects the plate, cup, saucer, and platter items from the China Pieces frame:

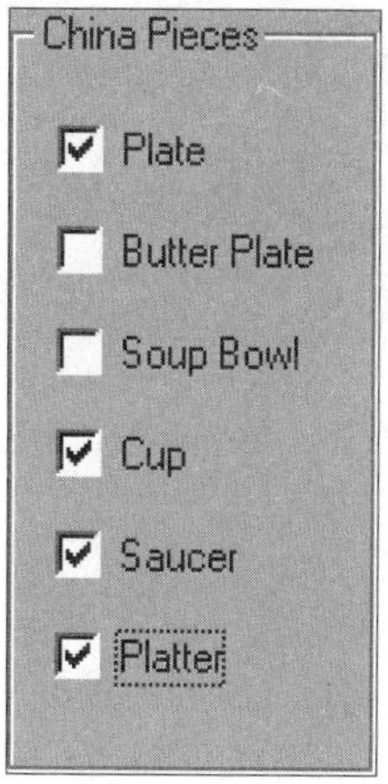

Thinking about the number of guests she's likely to want to entertain in real style, Rita decides to use the option button to choose a quantity of 4 of each item:

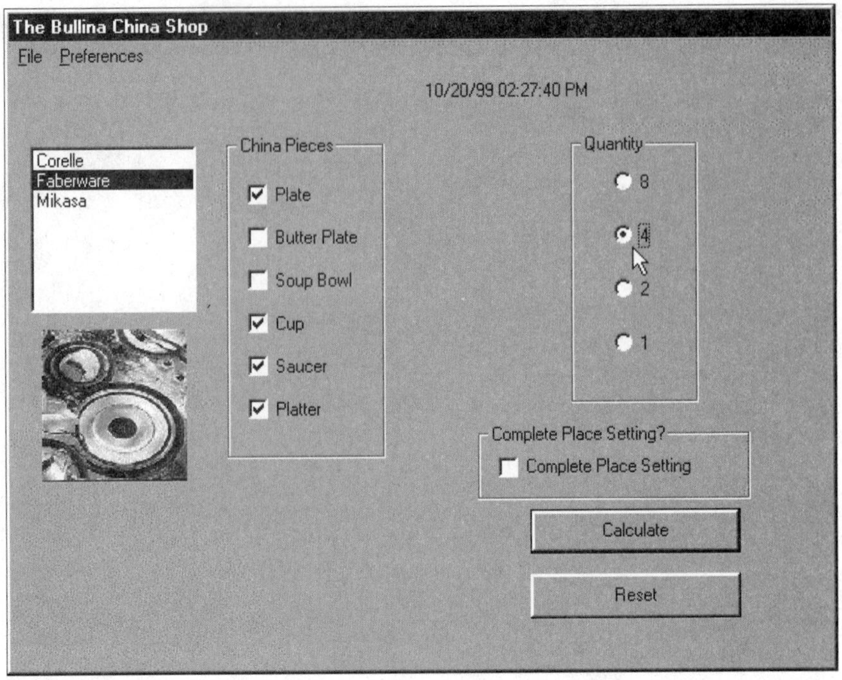

Rita reflects that a platter is a *big* piece of china, and that she only really needs one of them – otherwise her table would get mighty crowded. With this in mind, she looks to see if there's anywhere to specify quantities for individual types of china item. There isn't: Joe Bullina only sells fixed quantities – 8, 4, 2, or 1– of the smaller china pieces, and (again for business reasons) customers are limited to buying 1 platter per purchase. A little puzzled that she can't specify that she just wants a single platter, Rita decides to click on the Calculate button regardless. When she does this, the following message box appears:

The 'single platter per customer' rule is built into the program's logic, and the message box makes it clear to Rita that she'll only be charged for a single platter – which was what she wanted all along!

When Rita clicks on the message box's OK button, the price quotation appears on the form as before – just a little cheaper this time:

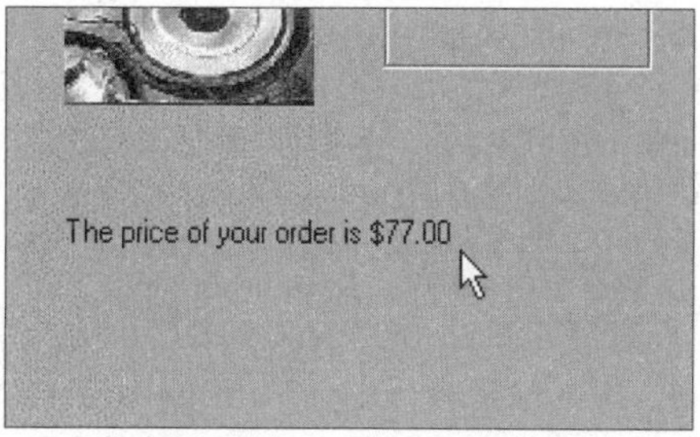

Apparently pleased with the price, Rita and Gil head towards the counter to buy their Faberware china pieces. The assistant boxes and wraps their china, and Rita and Gil make their way to the door. Another happy pair of customers; our typical purchase scenario is over.

So, that's what the China Shop program does, and that's the program we presented to Joe. In developing, building, and delivering the program for Joe Bullina, my class learned about the process of creating a program from start to finish in a real-world context, and gained their foundation knowledge in the Visual Basic programming language, too.

Those of you who were present on the day that we unveiled the completed program for Joe and his staff may recall the terrific party that he threw for us. After the party trash was all cleared away, we followed up on the delivery of our program: as part of the class's agreement with Joe, students from the class continued to check-in with him from time to time to see how the program was operating. All the reports that I got from the students indicated that the program was operating extremely well – and that Joe and the rest of the staff of the China Shop were very pleased with what we had provided for them.

On reflection, all seemed to be well in Bullinaland.

The Return of the China Shop...

It was a few months after we'd delivered the program to Joe and, in the first week of a cold, cold January, I was sitting in my home office. Fresh snow covered the lawn outside that afternoon, and the light reflecting through my window was cool, white, and calming. I needed some calming: I was leafing through some papers on my desk, doing some prep work for teaching my upcoming spring semester **Visual Basic Objects** course. Quite honestly, I wasn't looking forward to it with the same enthusiasm as the introductory course. Why? Well, I had taught the objects course several times before, and although it was always well-received and considered a success, I was worried that it might pale in comparison to the experience of developing a real-world project like the China Shop program. The fact that most of the students on the objects course would be veterans of that first class only added to my anxiety: no doubt they'd find the lack of a real-world programming project disappointing as well.

In the midst of my course preparation I decided to take a break, so I stepped out of my home office to grab a fresh cup of coffee from the kitchen. When I returned, I saw the light flashing on my Caller ID unit, indicating that I'd missed an incoming call while I was 'slacking' by the stove. Glancing to see who the call was from, I was startled to see the Bullina China Shop number displayed in glowing red characters! I wasted no time in returning the phone call.

Joe Bullina answered the phone himself and, after exchanging a few good-natured remarks with him, I asked – not without some apprehension, I might add – if anything was wrong.

"Wrong?" Joe echoed, "Oh no, quite the opposite, John! I've been meaning to give you a call over the holidays to tell you what a difference your program made during our Christmas rush.The program handled all of the routine price quotations – there must have been hundreds of them – and the sales staff could concentrate on serving customers who actually wanted to purchase something. This Christmas season was our best ever, and I'm delighted with the program. However, there is *one* thing..."

"What's that, Joe?" I asked, intrigued.

Joe's new Sideline

"Well, for some time now, I've been doing a little bit of small-scale selling by mail – nothing too extensive, you understand – and I've been thinking of expanding into this area in a more organized way."

"That makes sense, Joe," I said. "As a specialty shop, you could really expand your business like that. How about getting a website designed?"

"A website? Oh no, nothing like that!" Joe said. "I don't think I'm quite ready for my own website, yet!" he laughed. "But I'm getting more computer-literate all the time – so you never know!"

"What's on your mind, then, Joe?" I prompted.

"Well," he went on, "I do have this gentleman in Seattle whose custom I really value – a Mr. Gates..."

I raised my eyebrows (I don't think Joe heard me) but said nothing, and Joe continued with his train of thought:

"...and he orders Mikasa china from us on a fairly regular basis – there are very few shops that stock the Mikasa range, you see. Anyway, out of the blue, he just ordered a whole load of Faberware china for his company canteens, and he asked me if I could take his order over the telephone and ship the china to him directly. Now, I can do this as a one-off, but it really crystallized something I've been turning over and over in my mind for some time. I said to myself, '*Joe,*' I said '*why don't you make this process a permanent part of your business?*' "

"The mail order process, you mean?" I asked.

"That's right, John," Joe enthused, "I want my own mail-order catalogue, and a toll free number – the works! I've already done some quick checking, and found I can get a toll free number at low cost, and that I can advertise my inventory and price list nationally in a fine china magazine – at least until I get my catalogue printed. I figure that I can soon be doing some high-volume mail order business."

"Is that as far as you've got?" I asked, realizing that Joe must have had a very busy morning.

"No, there's some more," said Joe excitedly. "I've sketched out a deal with a local shipper who happens to be a friend of mine," he continued, "and the practical principles of the mail order business are all established."

"Wow, Joe" I said, "you don't mess around, do you? What time did you get up this morning?"

I heard Joe chuckle, and then he went on to describe how he saw the mail-order business working in practice.

"When a prospective customer calls on our new toll free number," Joe explained, "a dedicated telephone will ring at the front counter of the store. I envisage that the prospective customer will have my magazine ad in front of them listing the prices of all our china offerings. All they'll need to do is tell the sales clerk on the other end of the line what merchandise they want, and the sale can be finalized quickly, over the phone."

"OK, I'm with you so far," I said.

I could already picture Joe's scheme in my mind:

"What happens after the clerk has taken the customer's order?" I asked. "How does the information get processed after that?"

"My clerks will prepare the orders as they come in over the phone, and at the end of each business day my shipper friend will send a truck by the shop to pick up the packaged china and ship it to its final destination."

"Sounds like you've got this all worked out already, Joe," I said, laughing. "How can I help you here, exactly?"

"My one real problem," Joe said, "is actually working out the shipping charges 'in flight' – my staff need to be able to quote shipping charges to the customer at the time they take the call. Most customers want this information at the time they transact the sale – and anyway, my sales clerk needs it to process the customer's credit card information properly."

"OK," I said, "so why exactly is it difficult to work out the shipping charges?"

"I guess the real problem is that the shipping charges aren't uniform," Joe explained. "The shipper has identified several 'price zones' throughout the United States, each containing a number of states. This means in essence that the sales clerk will need to calculate the shipping charges based on the *state* that the china is being shipped to." Joe hesitated for a moment, then said, "My real question is: could you write a program that would do this for me?"

"Well...I don't really see that it's too difficult in principle," I said, "but I'll need a few more details. How many sales zones are we talking about?"

"At a guess, somewhere between fifteen and twenty, at this stage," Joe replied. "Of course, I know your prices, and would be willing to pay the going rate – I think I appreciate what computers can do for my business a bit more than I did when I first came to you!" he added.

"That sounds great!" I said.

There was a pause on the other end of the line, and I could tell that Joe had something else he wanted to say. "Is there anything else at all, Joe?" I prompted.

"Well, I've bought another computer and my nephew showed me how to install the price quotation program you designed for me on it. I reckon my sales clerks could use the program to calculate the price of any telephone orders they receive." Joe said.

"Yes?" I said. "Go on."

"Well, I was thinking..." Joe continued. "Wouldn't it be cheaper to just add the mail-order charges to the *existing* program?" Joe didn't give me time to answer, but instead went on himself: "It would make sense, too, if my sales clerks could use the same program to calculate the price of the china and the shipping costs all in one go..."

Now it was my turn to think. I could hear Joe's excitement on the other end of the phone, and I didn't want to disappoint him. However, I could already see that, while modifying the existing program was the most obvious choice from the user's – Joe's – point of view, it wasn't the easiest from the computer programmer's perspective.

Change can Be Painful

When my class and I had originally designed the price quotation program, we hadn't really designed it with future modifications of this type in mind. On the contrary, it was seen as a standalone, one-off program, and was written as such. I could already see a few problems with making the new code work with the old.

"I'm going to have to think about this one some more, Joe." I said. "As an answer to your first question, I can certainly give you a pretty firm 'yes' – I will be able to make a program that can calculate your shipping costs for you. As for your second question, I can't guarantee that I'll be able to incorporate that calculation process into the original program."

Joe sighed, and I could sense his disappointment. He'd clearly convinced himself that by modifying the original China Shop project he could keep his costs down. "OK, John," he said. "I trust you to make the right decision based on what's actually possible. I guess I still have a lot more to learn about computers than I'd thought!"

"Don't worry, Joe," I told him. "I'll get back to you as soon as I can, and together we'll hammer something out at a cost you can afford."

Joe seemed reasonably reassured by this. I said goodbye to him, made a few notes about our conversation, and went back to working on my upcoming course, vowing that I'd give as much thought to Joe's problem as I could.

My Dilemma

Later that evening, after my daily jog through the cold, slush-flecked streets of Philadelphia, I was eating dinner (meat loaf, my favorite!) with my wife, Linda, and pondering how to approach Joe's request for fresh functions in his program. Linda must have been able to read the indecision on my face, during the meal.

"What's up, Hon?" she asked as I put down my knife and fork, "you look worried about something."

"Oh, it's nothing too serious," I replied, "just a consulting problem that I keep turning over in my mind. I'm not really sure about the best way to approach it."

Linda nodded: "So...tell me about it. "

"OK."

I paused, wondering where to start. My wife has a fine analytical mind, but I wasn't sure how much she knew about the China Shop. I went on: "Do you remember the work I did with my class last year on Joe Bullina's China Shop?"

"Remember? I could hardly forget! You talked about the class and the project non-stop all through Fall!"

I chuckled, recalling how exciting and energizing the China Shop experience had been for the whole class.

"Well," I said, grinning sheepishly, "it *was* exciting."

"What's the problem, then? Is there something wrong with the program?"

"No, no," I assured her, and went on to tell her about Joe's call and the discussion that we'd had about adding a mail order component to the China Shop program, and about the potential problems of integrating the new functions with the old program.

When I'd finished, Linda still looked a little non-plussed, and she said: "I still can't see what's wrong. It's not technically difficult to add these processes to the program, is it?"

I couldn't do anything but agree with her, but I went on to say: "The real question in my mind is about the future, and about how many more enhancements Joe might ask for. The nature of his business will probably remain the same, but it's possible that he'll keep finding extra little bits of functionality that he wants to add to the China Shop program. That could be a real pain in the long run."

"Why is it such a pain? After all, you've said that the code to achieve Joe's aim isn't tricky."

I nodded. "Yes, but – there's always a 'but', isn't there – this is where we're getting to the real nitty-gritty. The way we built the China Shop program originally means that it might be difficult to keep adding extra bits and pieces to it."

"What are the difficulties?" Linda asked next.

"There are two main ones that I can think of: efficiency-levels and maintenance. If we keep adding more and more bits of code to the original program, the simplicity of the original China Shop code will start to disappear underneath all the modifications. It's as if the hull of sleek, ocean-going racing yacht was getting overgrown with a load of barnacles, and snagged with seaweed – it'll still float, but it'll be slow, and it'll look real ugly up close."

"What's more," Linda put in, "I guess that if you came to do any maintenance work on the yacht, you'd have to try and clear all the clutter out of the way before you could get to work on the structure."

"That's about right." I replied, laughing. "There'd be barked knuckles, and slime under your fingernails – very messy!"

"Now, I don't mean to be critical," said Linda, "but doesn't this mean that there was something wrong with the original program design?"

"No, not really. I understand what you're saying, but Joe never suggested he'd want future enhancements. What's more, building the China Shop program was a great way to teach the fundamentals of Visual Basic, and I chose a design that let the students learn the basics thoroughly. The kind of program that we built is similar to millions and millions of programs that have been built in recent years."

"How so?" queried Linda.

"Essentially," I explained, "it's a **procedural** program, which means that the structure of the program is broken up into separate chunks of code, called **procedures**. Each procedure is responsible for a particular process – for example, calculating a price based on the china selections that a customer has made on the China Shop form."

"That sounds sensible – you write code to undertake specific activities."

"I agree – it is pretty sensible. The complicating factor is the way that procedural programs treat the values that they operate on – the names and prices of the china pieces, for example. What happens is that these values get stored as variables, and these values get changed, or reset, as the program goes about its business and interacts with the user of the program."

"And the user, in Joe Bullina's store, is the customer, right?" said Linda.

"Indeed."

"So," Linda went on, "can you give me an example of an actual variable in the China Shop program, to help me visualize what you're talking about?"

"Sure," I replied. "For instance, a Mikasa butter plate costs $10. The price the customer pays for the butter plate is represented inside our program by storing it as a value of '10' in a variable of type 'currency'. We try to remember what this value actually *relates to* in the real world by giving the variable that stores it a meaningful name. In fact, we do that for all the variables that we declare and use in the China Shop program."

Linda nodded, indicating that she was more than familiar with my crusade in favor of Hungarian notation and the meaningful naming of all program components. I smiled understandingly, and got up to pour us both some coffee before continuing.

"The key thing," I resumed, as I settled back into my seat, "is this: at the end of the day, the values in the variables are still just numbers (or strings, or whatever), and all these values are stored separately, in isolation – just like all the other numbers and strings the program deals with. The bulk of the code in the program consists of procedures whose job it is to manipulate the values stored in the variables – and, of course, do the job that the program was designed to do! The really tricky thing is that it's up to the programmer to keep track of all these values and remember how they relate to each other, and what to do with them all. "

"Yes, I can see the difficulty with that," Linda sympathized, "but that's just what programming's like, isn't it? Surely it's the programmer's job to cope with these difficulties – it's what you get paid for, after all!"

"Yes," I said, "I can't deny that. But the problem with any computer program is that, as the task the application is asked to perform gets more and more elaborate, so the code gets longer and longer, and the relationships between the individual variables gets more and more complicated, and more difficult to track."

"Uh-huh," Linda said, nodding in understanding, "I guess that'd be especially difficult if I was someone coming along to add enhancements to an existing program that I hadn't written?"

"Absolutely right. Even if we're religious about our naming conventions, and we make sure that the name of each procedure describes exactly what it does, that still doesn't mean it's obvious *why* it does it. The overall logic of a procedural program – how it relates to the real-world problem that it's dealing with – is rarely self-evident, even if you put in plenty of comments, explaining what's going on. Splitting the programming problem up into lots of separate pieces of data – variables – makes the program pretty abstract compared to the apparently simple real-world task that we're performing."

"Why so?" Asked Linda.

"Well, partly because you can't touch or see what the variables represent as a single whole." I replied. "Splitting the real-world thing into a series of variables makes it tricky to keep a grip on what it is they all mean." I paused. "And there are many variables – loop variables, for instance – that exist solely for the purposes of the procedure: they don't represent anything in the real world. Sadly, that's how procedural programming tends to go: the more complex the problem, the bigger the code, and the greater the number of variables. When a system maintainer is faced with modifying the code, the first hurdle they face is even understanding what it *does* before they can make their changes."

"I see that – it does sound a messy business. But how often is that a problem, in reality?"

"Well," I answered, "a successful piece of software is one that lasts a long time: one that people still want to use long after it was written. I think we all aim to build programs like that."

"Uh-huh – I'd hope that was the case!"

"However," I went on, "it would be an exceptional program that could remain useful without needing some modifications from time to time. The ongoing implementation of any successful application almost by definition means constant modification and redesign."

"So..." Linda recapped, "the program's 'sponsor' – Joe Bullina, as far as we're concerned – comes back to you with some new business needs that they want incorporated into their program. And, every time they come back, the program gets bigger and more complex, and the task of updating and implementing the new changes gets more difficult?"

"That's it, in a nutshell," I agreed. Bottom line is that I don't want to have to face modifying the China Shop program time after time – it's already going to be a little tricky to integrate Joe's new mail order and shipping charge calculations smoothly into the existing project."

"Well," said Linda, looking serious, "you have to face the fact that that's the situation you're in now, and either take on the work, or turn it down."

"I certainly don't want to turn the work down: I like Joe, and I want to do a great job for him."

Linda didn't reply immediately, but sat silent for a while, pursing her lips. Then she said: "Let's step back from where we are at the moment and see if we can get some fresh perspective on this."

I nodded my agreement – Linda is great at getting back to first principles and finding a way through.

"OK," she went on, "how would you have gone about designing and building the China Shop project if you hadn't been constrained by your need to teach your class the fundamentals of Visual Basic, and if you hadn't needed to simplify the program design to let them learn more easily?"

"That's easy – I'd have designed and built an **object-oriented program**."

And the Winner is...Object-oriented Programming!

"Hmm..." said Linda, a little dubiously, "I've heard you use that phrase before, and it sounds a little intimidating. What exactly does it mean?"

"It's not so scary really," I reassured her. "In essence, it means that the programs we design are constructed using **objects** as their central components. In an object-oriented program, the objects work together, combining to perform the job that the program is designed to do. The objects are like members of a team with a common goal – they know their job, and they know how to work with the other team members to get the overall job done."

"OK..."said Linda, "now that begs the question – what *are* **objects**?"

"Well, fundamentally, an object is a **representation in code** of something in the real-world. For example, the China Shop might require us to represent a *customer* as an object, and a *complete order of China pieces in a box* as an object. These are both tangible things that we could see and touch in the real world, and we can understand their part in the processes that take place in the china shop."

"Just a minute," interrupted Linda. "You said earlier that in procedural programs, we represent the real-world things – like the Mikasa butter plate – as a collection of variables. What's the difference?"

"The essential difference," I explained, "is that an object collects all the information about the real-world thing in one place in the program: inside the programmatic object – the code that represents the real-world object – itself. So, instead of representing the real-world object using a series of variables that the programmer constantly has to keep track of, our programmatic object keeps all the relevant data together, ready for us to access at any time."

"Is that all there is to it?"

"No, our programmatic objects also embody the things that the real-world objects can *do*."

"What?" Linda asked, surprised. "What do you mean by that?"

"Let me explain. I'll take it step by step. First up, a programmatic object represents a real-world object, or thing – such as a customer, or a box of china. OK?"

"Yes, I'm with you so far. Carry on."

"OK. Now, the real-world customer will probably have a name, an address, and a telephone number – to name but a few attributes. And a box of china would have a size, a weight, a shipping destination, and a related shipping charge. These are the things that describe the customer and the box of china, and we'll mirror these things in our programmatic objects, maintaining and changing their values inside the program."

"Right," said Linda, "I understand that, I think. The values kept inside the program's objects effectively replace the scattering of variables that we had in a procedural program."

"Yes, that's right. Now, our customer isn't just a collection of bits of data. They can do things as well – walk, chew gum, and so on."

"Uh-huh – sometimes simultaneously!" She said, laughing.

"In the context of our program," I continued, "we might want to mimic some of the things that the customer does in the real-world. Maybe not chewing gum, but in Joe's China Shop, for example, customers in the store will want to select china pieces, get price quotations, and make purchases. All of these different activities are things that people *do*. And these actions – or **behaviors** – are things that we might consider representing in the code of our program."

"So..." queried Linda, "would we write procedures to represent those actions... er... behaviors?"

"Not quite. We do write procedures that execute in the body of the program, but in an object-oriented program, the detailed behaviors are associated with, and built into, particular objects."

"Why's that? What's the benefit of doing it that way?"

"Well, if you think about it, in the real-world all these actions are performed *by* someone, or *act upon* something, or are things that a real-world object can do." I said. "Things in the real-world have a repertoire of things that they can do, and they put these behaviors into action when they're asked to do so, or when something happens to trigger them. In an OO program, objects work with other objects, communicating with each other and asking each other to do things: so the best way to group such behaviors is to attach them to the most appropriate object – the one that will execute the behavior."

"And the advantage of this is?" Linda asked, listening intently.

"Well, each object has to be sure that the other objects will always do the same thing when called upon." I said. "Building behaviors into the objects that will actually perform them is one way of ensuring that this happens."

"OK..." said Linda, "I have to admit that I can't quite see that clearly yet."

"Well, this is just a sketch that I'm giving you here. " I reassured her, "To get the full picture on this, we'd need to talk some more about object-oriented theory and design, and see some code in action – getting a firm grip on these things is something that will come with time, and with practice. In fact, that's exactly the material that I'll be covering in detail on my upcoming Objects course."

"Maybe," said Linda, "I should sit in on that class myself, someday. I feel like I'm getting the general picture, but I need some more 'time and practice', as you put it, to make it a bit clearer. I want some more detail!"

Linda frowned, and then the light of inspiration came into her eyes. She said "Isn't there a simple solution here? Use your Objects class to re-engineer Joe's program? Get the students to do the work *and* learn object-oriented programming thoroughly on a real-world project, like they did before with their Visual Basic fundamental knowledge?"

I nodded: I could see what Linda was getting at. "Yeeees," I said slowly, "that would be great for the class, and it would really hammer home the advantages of the object-oriented approach."

Linda had noticed my slow '*Yeeees*', and she said: "You don't sound convinced. What's the problem?"

I frowned. "The issue there is that object-orienting the China Shop will mean a more substantial internal redesign of the project than I think Joe's bargaining for..."

"It's time we put the kids to bed!" I said, suddenly noticing the time. "Let's talk about this some more later."

Later that Evening...

After we'd cleared the TV room of its evening's-worth of toys and cracker wrappers, and our three little angels were safely tucked up in bed, Linda and I settled back gratefully into our armchairs. Outside, the snow was falling again, drifting thickly past the streetlamps. I felt privileged to be warm and safe indoors.

"Hon," Linda said, "I've been thinking about those China Shop amendments..."

"That's good. Got any answers?"

She laughed: "More questions, actually!"

"OK – what's on your mind?"

"Well, to be honest, it seems like all the advantages of the object-oriented approach benefit the programmer. If you were to re-engineer the China Shop project, isn't it going to disrupt Joe's business and upset him? Thing is, I can see the benefits for you and your class of using the China Shop program in your Objects class, but are there any benefits for *Joe* in having the China Shop project – have I got the phrase right – object-oriented?"

"I understand your concerns" I answered her, "but the truth is that object-orienting the China Shop is in Joe's best interest, too."

"How so? What are the advantages for Joe, then?" Linda pressed.

"The key thing is that an object-oriented programming solution is mapped directly to the business processes that go on in Joe's store."

"Say again?"

"Well, an object-oriented program will be made up of programmatic objects that mirror the objects in the real-world China Shop. What that means for Joe is that the program closely reflects the things that go on in his store every day, and that the program is more likely to be easily modified if any of his business needs change. The chances are that the essentials of Joe's business will stay the same, so that any changes we need to make can be more easily implemented. They should be easier to make in the program because we add them to the existing core of the program in the same way that Joe adds extra processes to the core of his business. Ultimately, for Joe, this means that his program is more flexible, and the bills for subsequent programming jobs on his applications will be smaller!"

"Well," said Linda, "I guess that's a good enough incentive for him! You seem to be saying that object-orientation makes for better programs for everybody."

"That's certainly the consensus in the computer industry." I replied. "There's a little more to learn, and a different approach to analysis and design, but the end result is well worth the effort – you're more likely to end up with a program that's fit for the purpose, and amenable to future extension and modification."

"Well then," Linda responded, setting off on a typically positive track, "sounds like you've made your mind up! Now it's your job to sell the idea to Joe!"

The Way Ahead

Having made my decision, I slept well. I spent the next day planning how to adapt my Objects course to include making the modifications to the China Shop program and build a realistic syllabus around them. When I was happy with my outline plan, I phoned Joe Bullina's store. Midge, one of Joe's most trusted employees, took the call. She explained that she was the last one in and was just locking up for the evening – Joe had already gone home.

I looked at my watch and realized that it was a lot later than I'd thought! I had been so engrossed in my work and the idea of how I could include the China Shop modifications into the syllabus that I'd completely lost track of time! I explained why I was phoning, and Midge immediately gave me Joe's home phone number. "He's very keen to hear from you, Mr. Smiley," she added.

I thanked her and dialed the new number. "Hi, Joe. It's John." I said, when Joe picked up.

"John! I'm just home – Midge must have given you my number, huh?"

"That's right," I replied. "Sorry I didn't call earlier, but I got wrapped up in what I was doing. The good news is that I think I've got a solution to our problem that will appeal to you!"

I could almost see him smiling at the other end of the phone line. "Let me guess, John, you've got a new programming class starting next Saturday, and you think the amendments I've asked for would make a great project for them to work on!"

"Well, actually, it's a *week* Saturday, but that's about the shape of it." I replied. "My new course deals with a method of programming that makes computer applications like yours much easier to maintain and change after they've been written."

"John, that's music to my ears!" Joe exclaimed. "Tell me more."

Selling the Idea to Joe

I paused, gathering my thoughts for what I had to say next: "The reason I hesitated the first time you asked me to change the existing price quotation program is that the application wouldn't be all that easy to modify it as it stands."

"And now you have a solution?" Joe enquired, cautiously.

"What I'd like to do with my class," I said, "is go through your program and more or less rebuild it from the inside as a teaching exercise – using the principles I'll be covering in the course. This'll not only make it much easier to introduce the changes you want at the moment, it'll also mean that any modifications you want in future will be much simpler to apply!"

I could sense Joe's hesitation at the other end of the line. "I don't know, John, I'm kinda happy with the program as it runs now – are you sure these changes are really necessary?"

"Don't worry, Joe," I said, "nothing about the current behavior of the program will change as far as the user is concerned – with the exception of the shipping charge calculation you are asking for, of course! The only real changes will be under the hood, so to speak. Outwardly, except for the addition of the shipping charges process, the program will appear to be identical."

"But on the inside, you'll have changed the program quite a bit, is that right?" Joe asked.

"Exactly Joe," I agreed. "We'll rewrite the program from what is known as an 'object-oriented' standpoint. By doing this, we'll make any future enhancements to the program much easier, for whomever makes them."

"I see. These changes are really necessary, are they?"

"Sooner or later, yes, they are, Joe." I said. "I guess in the long run, I should have built the project as an object-oriented package from the start, but as I said, I needed a project for my Introductory course, and introducing object-orientation on such a course just wouldn't be fair on the students – never mind fitting in such a move with my syllabus!"

"Hey, don't worry about that!" Joe assured me. "I got a bargain, I realize that, now! Anything you do is fine with me – I trust you, and we get along well. Just so long as you can give me the shipping charges enhancements, and the program still behaves the same in every other respect, I'll be more than content. How long will I have to wait for the new version of the program to arrive?"

"Ah…the course runs for ten weeks!" I told him, suddenly realizing that this might be a problem. "But by the end of it, I'll undertake to have got you new version of the China Shop project in a good condition for you to take delivery of it."

"Ten weeks?" Joe said. I could picture him thinking about how this would fit in with his plans. After a few moments, he said: "Hmm...actually, that might be for the best. It'll give me enough time to build up my mail order business more gradually! I obviously intend for this to be a major part of my sales in the future, but right now I have to admit that I don't expect we'll be taking so many orders my sales staff won't be able to cope until your software arrives. I must admit, I was originally intending to just dive straight in, but I can see now that I really ought to take things more slowly. Yes, ten weeks is fine!"

"And, of course, you'll be getting your new program at a discounted rate – just like the last one!" I said, as an added inducement.

"Hey! Now I know how much difference computers can make, I'd be happy to be a *lot* more generous this time!" Joe said.

"I'll discuss it with my class, Joe, but I'm sure that if you pay us $450, like you did last time, that'll be fine." I said. "It's more important to my students that they can say they've designed a real-world computer program for someone, than how much they actually got paid for it. By taking my object orientated programming course, they're investing in their futures – I'm sure they'll take the long term view."

"OK, John," said Joe. "I must say, I admire them for it. I wish I had the time to take one of your classes myself."

"One day, Joe, who knows...?" Seemed like everybody wanted to take this class!

With that, we wrapped the conversation up. I asked Joe if he would mind meeting with us on the first day of my class to explain his problem. I wanted my students to have a clear sight of the task Joe had set us while we were making the other changes to his application. I felt this would be easier if they got to meet him and hear him explain his needs to them. Joe agreed.

"Would 10 A.M. be OK?" He asked.

"10 A.M. would be ideal, Joe." I assured him.

I Meet my Objects Class

Two weeks later, on a sunny and pleasant wintry Saturday morning, I entered the computer lab to begin my Visual Basic Objects class, smiling and nodding to the students who had arrived early. I should tell you that my University classroom is about 40 feet by 20 feet, with a double set of three rows of long tables, each table supporting three PCs. Each student has the use of their own PC, and I have a computer of my own at the front of the class. My machine is cabled to a projector that lets me display the contents of my video display on a large screen in the front of the classroom.

I noticed immediately that some changes had been made since the end of the previous semester. There was new carpeting on the floor, and the old PCs had been upgraded with new 450Mhz computers. '*Good,*' I thought, '*that should help things run a little quicker!*'

The first day of a follow-on class like this one is almost like a reunion day. Having spent sixteen Saturday mornings together the previous semester, many of the waiting students were talking comfortably with one another as they entered the classroom. Just about all of the faces were familiar. I exchanged greetings with several of the students and asked how everyone was. They all seemed well, and told me how they were looking forward to the course. After my conversations with Joe Bullina, I'm glad to say that I was, too.

As nine o'clock rolled around, I began the lesson and formally welcomed everyone.

"Let me say this one thing before I get going on the administrative part of the class," I said. "Learning about Visual Basic Objects and object-oriented programming is a really important step to take in your programming lives. In this class, I won't blind you with science – I'll teach you what you really need to know at the foundation level: by the end of the course, you'll have a firm grasp of what objects are for, and how to use them.

That's our goal. For the moment, just forget about all the worries you have about objects, and remember three things: firstly, you can think of an **object** as a self-contained piece of code that performs a useful task for us in a program. Secondly, **object-oriented programming** is the art of making programs that use objects as their main components. And thirdly, object-oriented programs are the best way of **representing the real world in code** – that's why they're becoming the industry-standard, and that's why we're learning about them!"

I paused, letting that all sink in, before continuing: "OK – let's get the administration issues out of the way!"

My inspirational speech over, I opened up my roll book and asked each of my eighteen students to write a brief biography of themselves, explaining their motivations for being in the class. I'd been going through this ritual with my students for a number of years; the written biography gives me a chance to get to know the students a little bit, without the pressure of forcing them to 'open themselves up' in front of the class.

Introducing the Students

All in all, there were fourteen repeat students in the class, and four new students. **Steve, Kathy, Dave, Ward, Blaine, Kate, Mary, Chuck, Lou, Bob, Valerie, Peter, Linda** and **Rhonda** had all been members of the Introductory Visual Basic class. I was particularly glad to see Rhonda back: she always asked useful questions, and it was her version of the China Shop Program that we had eventually delivered to Joe Bullina. In the Introductory class, even though we basically developed the China Shop program as a team, each student had been encouraged to complete their own version of the program. Although I personally don't like the idea of competition in my classes, we really hadn't a choice but to hold a little 'election' on the last day to see whose program would be the one installed and run in the China Shop. The consensus had been for Rhonda's version of the program. She'd been thrilled!

Kevin, Tom, Melissa and **Dorothy** were new students. I did my best to make them feel at home. I didn't want them to feel 'left out' because they hadn't been present for the development of the original China Shop project.

I quickly skimmed through the biographies as I walked around the classroom collecting them, sometimes remarking on something a student had written. I then slipped the bios gently into my briefcase; I would read them in more detail at home.

You'll find the detailed student biographies documented in Appendix A.

Some of the students from the previous class wanted to know if I'd heard anything from their colleagues who *hadn't* returned for this class. Begging the indulgence of the new students, I told them what I knew about their missing comrades. Barbara had changed jobs – she'd been laid off from her post as a COBOL programmer, but had quickly found a new position as an entry-level Visual Basic programmer. Sadly, this meant that she was too busy to take this follow-on course. Another student, Joe – with the help of the Introductory course, he'd told me! – had taken and passed the Visual Basic Certification test, and he'd relocated to San Diego. And finally, there were Rose and Jack. They were, I happily announced, honeymooning in the South Pacific after getting married – romantically – on the bridge of an oil tanker that they had been stress-testing for the engineering company that employed them both. A happy set of outcomes and, I thought, a good omen for this new class.

Introducing Joe's New Problem to the Class

Going back to the business in hand, I distributed a catalog from the University bookstore listing the academic software titles in stock and then distributed the two-page class syllabus I had worked out. This semester I had also gone high-tech – using the classroom projector, I displayed an HTML version of the class syllabus that resided on my web site.

In the syllabus I had outlined the new China Shop project in the broadest terms, describing it simply as an existing sales quotation program which we would be redesigning from an object-oriented approach in order to replicate its existing behavior and incorporate some new features.

As the students read through the two page document I saw one or two looks of wonder coming over the previous members of the introductory class, as they realized that the new project bore a startling similarity to the program they'd written for Joe.

"I have a little announcement to make," I said.

"You've found another client willing to let us work on a real-world project!" Rhonda said, looking up from her syllabus.

"Better than that," I said, "I didn't just find someone – Joe Bullina found *us* again. Joe wants us to modify the program we wrote for him last semester – and while we're making the modifications, I thought we should also 'object-orient' the program – that is, remake it using Visual Basic objects as its core."

"Why?" asked Rhonda.

"Well, because I've got a feeling Joe has big plans, and that he'll be making extensive use of this program in the future," I explained. "One of the great benefits of object-oriented programming is that it makes it easier to design, build, and maintain effective programs that do the job for the client. Since Joe's delighted with the program we built for him, I think we should give it an object-oriented overhaul – that way, he can continue to use it productively, well into the future."

The four new members of the class appeared a little confused, so I explained that in last semester's Introductory class we'd developed a real-world application built around Joe's China Shop. We wrote the program in Visual Basic, using the **Systems Development Life Cycle (SDLC)** methodology as a guide. I also explained, for the benefit of the new students, that the SDLC was a series of steps that aided the development of a software program from its inception right through to implementation and maintenance, helping us to ensure we don't leave out any important stages in the development.

> **If you're unfamiliar with the SDLC, you'll find a summary of its stages in Appendix C of this book.**

"So there's already a program written – and we're going to take that program and do...what to it?" Melissa asked.

"Joe Bullina has requested a pretty simple enhancement to the existing program," I said. "The great news is that he has given us the go-ahead to rewrite it using object-oriented Visual Basic techniques. This means that we can learn about objects in a real-world programming context, and that Joe benefits in terms of the long-term 'maintainability' and 'updatability' of the application. I think you'll have a great time with it. I certainly *hope* you do."

"That sounds cool," Tom said. "By focusing on a real-world program we'll be able to see what we're doing in a realistic environment!"

"That sounds great to me too," Kevin said, "but for those of us who weren't here for the Introductory course, could you give us a run-through of the China Shop program?"

"I think that would be a good idea for everyone. I have the **Requirements Statement** for the original China Shop project right here," I said, "along with some other slides that illustrate the project. These slides also show snapshots of the Visual Basic controls that we added to the program's user interface to satisfy these requirements."

A Review of the China Shop Project

I displayed the slide showing the original China Shop project's requirements statement using the classroom projector:

Requirements Statement

Bullina China Shop

General Description

1. The program will consist of a main form, on which there will be:

a. A list box containing brands of china:

b. 6 check boxes for china piece components:

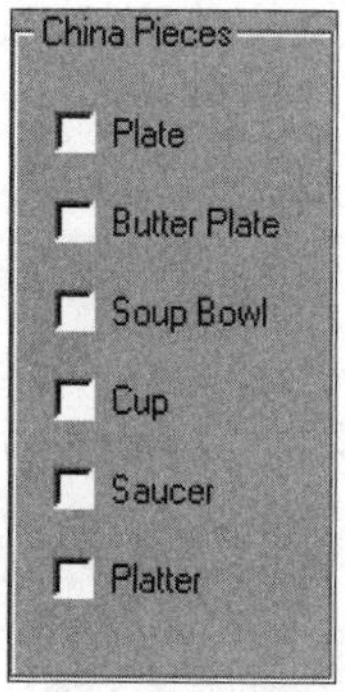

c. A single check box to let the customer select a "Complete Place Setting":

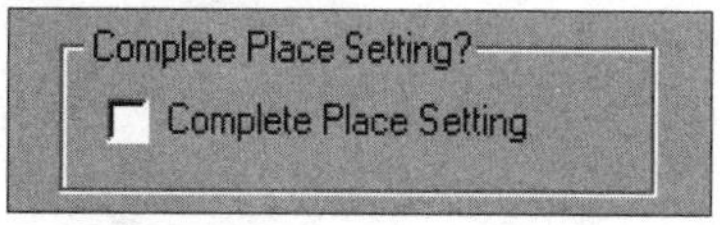

d. 4 option buttons representing quantities:

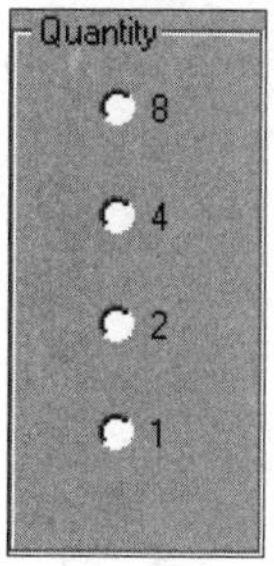

e. A button which, when clicked, performs the price calculation:

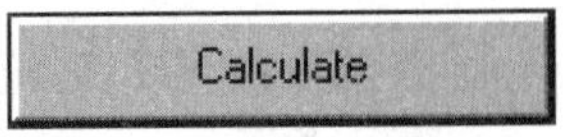

f. A button, captioned "Reset" which, when clicked, clears the selections in the list box, check boxes, and option buttons:

g. A menu with submenu items for File and Preferences:

"This next slide summarizes the result of translating these requirements into a usable interface for Joe's customers:"

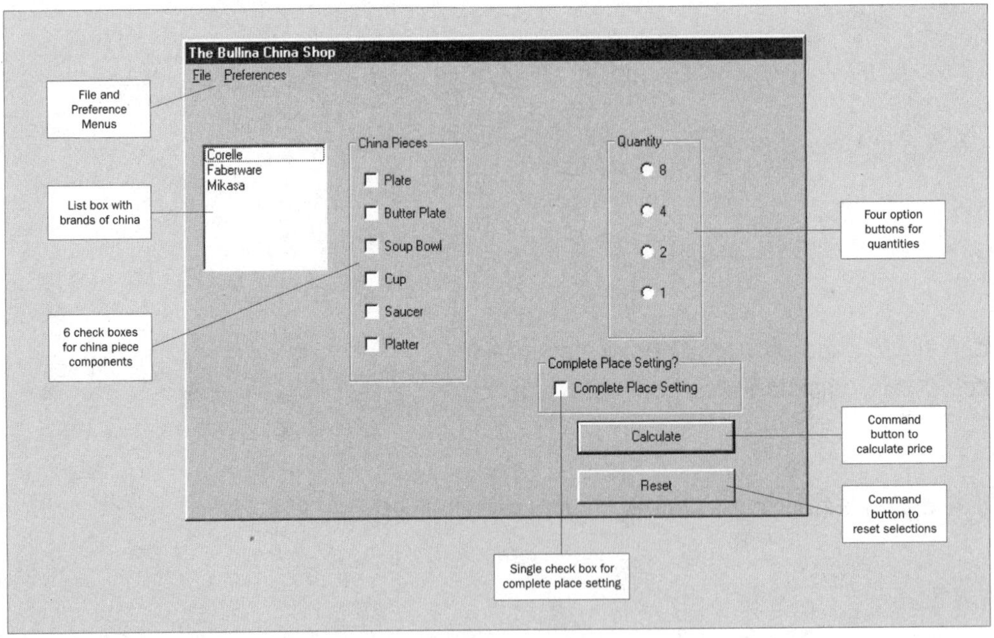

I let the class – and especially the new students – digest this slide for a while, and gave them the opportunity to ask any questions. Then I continued with the slides that showed the details of the original requirements statement:

2. The File submenu will display only an Exit command. The File menu will be alternatively accessible by pressing the *Alt+F* combination. The Exit command will be alternatively accessible by pressing the *Alt+X* combination.

3. The Preferences submenu will display a submenu called Colors and a command called Date and Time.

4. The Colors submenu will consist of two commands called "Customize" and "Default". The Customize command will permit the customer to set the color of the main form to any color they desire through the use of a color dialog box. The Default command will set the color of the main form back to a predetermined color.

5. The Date and Time command will permit the user to switch the displayed date and time off and on.

6. A password will be required to exit the system from the Exit command of the File submenu.

Output from the System

1. A price quotation contained in a label displayed on the main form.

2. Current Date and Time displayed prominently on the form.

Input to the System

The customer will specify :

1. A single china brand (to be selected from a list box).
2. One or more component pieces (to be selected using check boxes).
3. A quantity for the component pieces (to be selected using an option button).

The following is not customer input, but:

1. The program will read china brands and prices from a text file. The inventory and prices can be updated when necessary by the sales clerk using Microsoft Notepad.
2. Any changes made to the user's color preferences will be saved to the Windows Registry and read by the program at startup.

3. Any changes made to the user's preference for Date and Time display will be saved to the Windows Registry and read by the program at startup.

Business Rules

1. No more than one platter may be selected.
2. Quantities may not be mixed and matched in an order. Only one quantity selection per order.
3. Brands may not be mixed and matched in an order. Only one brand per order.

Definitions

1. Complete Place Setting: A user's selection composed of a plate, butter plate, soup bowl, cup and saucer of the same brand.

Other

1. The program will read china brands and prices from a text file, which can be updated when necessary by the sales force.

2. Any changes made to the user's preferences (colors, Date and Time display), will be saved, and read by the program at startup. Therefore, both colors and the Date and Time display will be the same they were when the program ended.

I could see from the looks on the faces of my new students that they had a bit of a learning curve to negotiate. From their biographies, I could see that the new students were already familiar with the fundamentals of Visual Basic – but they didn't know the China Shop, and they didn't know Joe Bullina.

"Do you think," said Rhonda, "that it might be useful for the new members of the class to see the China Shop program in action?"

"That's a great idea," I agreed, eagerly seizing on the opportunity to familiarize the whole class with the practical workings of the program. I started Visual Basic, found the China Shop program on my PCs hard drive, and loaded up the project. "Rhonda," I said, "would you mind doing the honors and running us through a typical purchase scenario?"

For the next ten minutes, Rhonda treated us to a virtuoso display of how the China Shop program is used in Joe's store. Her demonstration mirrored the scenarios that we walked through with Gil and Rita earlier in this chapter – this isn't surprising, as the way that Gil and Rita used the program is highly representative of the way that customers interact with the program.

After Rhonda had run through her demonstration of the China Shop program's typical use scenarios, there were a few questions from the new members of the class. For instance, Melissa had anticipated Rita's confusion about choosing a platter quantity that we saw earlier in the chapter. But, overall, the demonstration really seemed to solidify their understanding of the program.

If you haven't already loaded up the China Shop project on your PC, you really should do it now. See Appendix B for details on how to do this.

I thanked Rhonda for her excellent demonstration. After she had returned to her normal seat, she asked the million-dollar question: "What enhancements is Joe Bullina looking for in the program?"

"Excuse me, John," Dave interjected, "but before you answer Rhonda's question, am I right to assume that we'll be developing a new requirements statement for the *enhancements* to the China Shop program, just like we created a requirements statement for the original program in the Introductory course?"

"Yes, Dave." I said, "If we're doing things by the book, then, according to the principles of the SDLC, we'll need to develop a new requirements statement for the program modifications."

"So, what *are* the modifications?" Rhonda persisted.

I Reveal Joe's new Requirements

I smiled – Rhonda's enthusiasm is one of her most winning characteristics.

"Well," I explained, "I spoke to Joe about ten days ago, and he told me that in a few weeks the China Shop will be taking orders via telephone. Joe would like the program to calculate shipping charges."

"That's quite a simple change, isn't it?" Steve asked.

"You're right Steve," I answered, "this *is* a pretty minor change to the functionality of Joe's program. However, since we're tinkering with the program anyway, this is a great opportunity to re-work the China Shop program in an object-oriented way. Joe Bullina says he won't mind as long as the program continues to perform and work as it does now – with the added telephone mail order function as well, of course!"

"Telephone mail order?" Linda asked, sounding a little perplexed. "Why doesn't Joe just go for a web site that lets him engage in **electronic commerce**?"

"Well, I did ask Joe about developing a web site for him," I explained, "but he told me that he's not quite ready for that yet. Just as well, really, since my 'Visual Basic and the Web' course here at the University won't be offered until the summer semester anyway...maybe he'll be ready then, and give us another project to work on! It's my suspicion that he will, and that's why it's so important to pull the existing program into the 21st century before that!"

"I'd love to work on *that* project," Kate said.

"Sign up for my Web/VB course, and who knows, Kate?" I laughed.

"Can you tell us how you think we'll be using Visual Basic objects in this course?" Bob asked.

"Sure, Bob. You'll be pleased to hear that I've thought about this, and if you take a look at the syllabus, you'll see how I've broken down the jobs we'll be doing on Joe's program." I said.

I displayed my revised syllabus on the projection screen. I'd listed the following points:

Week 1	Course Introduction
Week 2	Introduction to objects
	Visual Basic Collections
Week 3	Visual Basic System Objects
Week 4	Objects in theory and practice
	Designing the objects for the China Shop program
Week 5	Building the China Shop's objects, part one
Week 6	Building the China Shop's objects, part two
Week 7	Incorporating Collection Objects into the China Shop
Week 8	Using our objects with other applications – ActiveX
Week 9	Creating our own ActiveX components
Week 10	Project completion and delivery

"Don't worry about any of the things on the list that you don't understand, yet," I reassured the class. "We're going to take everything stage by stage. The bottom line is that I'll introduce you to object concepts and programming practice gently: I'll start next week by talking about some objects that are built into Visual Basic, and which you've been using without realizing it! That discussion will continue in Week 3, and then in Week 4 we'll see how what we've learned about these objects fits in with the broader theory of objects and their use. After that, the rest of the course will be dedicated to applying all the theory and techniques we've learned so far to the enhanced China Shop project."

"So," said Kate, "this course is not solely about how to create objects and work with them?"

"That's correct, Kate," I said. "Creating and using objects in general is a big part of the course, but there're Joe's requirements to cater for as well. Working on Joe's enhancements will really hammer home what we're learning on the theory side."

"How much of the code from last semester will need to be converted?" asked Linda.

"I would guess that just about every procedure will change in some way," I said. "But I think you'll be pleasantly surprised: the code should shrink in size, and its complexity will also diminish. I should warn you that the **shipping charges** code will most likely require us to create another form for the project – something we didn't learn how to do in the Introductory course."

"How can we design the shipping charge code without Joe Bullina's input?" Melissa said, "if we're following the SDLC, shouldn't we really interview the user of the program to determine their needs?"

"For the original program, Melissa," Linda intervened, "Professor Smiley personally interviewed Joe Bullina to gather the preliminary requirements for the program. I then made a second trip to perform a more detailed systems analysis." Then, turning to me, Linda asked: "Have you already been to see Joe, Professor?"

"No, not yet," I confessed. "Aside from a couple of brief conversations with him on the telephone two weeks ago," I answered, "I haven't discussed the detailed changes to the program with him at all. But I can reveal that you'll be doing that with Joe yourself, right here, today!"

"Joe Bullina, here in the classroom?" exclaimed Dorothy.

Right on cue (he'd been listening outside the door while he waited!), Joe Bullina knocked on the door and entered the classroom.

"Am I on time, John?" Joe asked, as he nodded to the class and shook my hand. "I was thinking I might be late – you *did* say 10 A.M., didn't you?"

"Perfect timing Joe," I said, "you're here on the dot. We were just talking about you."

"Nice things, I hope," chuckled Joe.

We Agree to Do Business with Joe Bullina

"Hi everyone," Joe said, as he removed his winter coat. Looking around the class, he said: "Good to see you all. For those of you who don't know me, I'm Joe Bullina, owner of the Bullina China Shop, and *proud* owner of the Bullina China Shop program. John has said that he'd be pitching the idea to you of modifying the excellent program you wrote for me last semester – I hope you agree to take it on. The China Shop program saved me so much money over the Christmas holidays, I may even be able to double what I paid you for the original program!"

"Pay us?" Kevin asked.

"Last semester," Joe explained, "I paid the class $450 to develop the China Shop program. At the time I was really running the business on a shoestring – I may be able to double that this time!"

"That's right, Kevin," I confirmed, "Joe's payment of $450 gave everyone in the class the chance to become a paid professional programmer in their very first Visual Basic class. I'm sure the enhancement to the program can be done for the same price. And," I continued, turning to Joe, "as I said to you when we talked on the phone, it's more important for the class to say they've got a real, paying program to their name, than how much they got paid for it."

Everyone in the class agreed with that (at least, I think so!)

"OK," said Joe, "$450 it is – if you're sure?"

"We can't put a price tag on the opportunity you're giving us, Joe," I said, "writing the application is the important thing."

Joe Describes His Problem to the Class

"OK," Joe said, and I asked him to address the class.

"The reason I'm here today," he began, "is that John asked me to stop by and assist you in developing a requirements statement for the modifications to my program. I'm pretty new to all of this myself, but I do know from last semester's experience how important agreeing the requirements statement is to a successful project!"

"How right you are, Joe!" I said, approvingly. "We were just discussing the requirements statement when you came in."

At this point, Lou caught my eye and said: "I know you said earlier that we should use the SDLC for the enhancements, but as we're only *modifying* the program here, do we really still need to use it? What I'm getting at is this: as the program is already developed, can't we take a shortcut to do the modifications?"

"Shortcuts are a notoriously bad idea," I said, "you'd be surprised how easily something can fall through the cracks, even when you're making the smallest modifications. The SDLC is like a good angel sitting on our shoulder, encouraging us to do the right thing."

"While we're on the subject of how we go about working on the project, I have a related question," said Valerie.

"Go ahead, Valerie," I encouraged her.

"What about **UML**?" Valerie continued. "I've heard some different terms used when people are talking about how you set about developing object-oriented programs. One of the phrases I've heard a lot is UML – is UML a replacement for the SDLC?"

"UML? UML? What on earth is *that*?" Rhonda asked, furrowing her brows.

"Relax," I said. "UML stands for **Unified Modeling Language**, and it's just one of the many different tools that you can use to help you develop an object-oriented program."

"So is it like flowcharting? I remember discussing that last semester – that was a design technique, wasn't it?" Mary asked.

"Well, Mary, it's similar in that it's one of a number of possible techniques we can use," I replied. "For those of you who weren't here last semester, in the Introductory class I mentioned that there are a number of tools and conceptual models that systems analysts and designers use when they're designing new computer systems – flowcharting is just one of the possible techniques that can be employed. Similarly, in the world of designing object-oriented programs, UML is one tool among many – it just happens to be the most *popular* tool amongst computing professionals when they're designing object-oriented programs, because it's a universal, powerful and efficient way of modeling computer systems."

"Will you be teaching us UML in this class?" Kevin asked.

"No, Kevin," I answered, "teaching these techniques in detail won't be possible due to the limited time that we have available. For that same reason, I didn't teach flowcharting techniques in the Introductory class. It's really beyond the scope of this class, in any case. A full discussion and treatment of UML is appropriate for a complete course on systems analysis and design, and it would take us several class sessions to cover."

> ! **If you're interested in finding out some more about UML, I suggest that you visit this website –** `http://www.omg.com/` **– this is the home of the Object Management Group, the independent group that developed the UML approach to object-oriented design.**

"So," Dave asked, "how will we set about designing the object-oriented parts of the China Shop? If we won't be learning UML, what's the alternative?"

"Well, Dave," I replied, "we'll be using a general approach that's very common in the world of objects. That approach is called **modeling**."

"Modeling..." began Lou, questioningly, "you used that term before, and I wondered what it really meant in this context. What's the scoop?"

"Well, Lou," I answered, "modeling is pretty much what it sounds like – it's a way of constructing a 'smaller than life-size' version of the system that we want to build. The model of that we create of the computer system lets us think clearly about the program, and allows us to change things around and see what happens – all without us having written any code. Once we've created a model that works, we can set about translating that model into the code that satisfies its requirements."

Rhonda raised her hand. "Professor, can you run that by me again, please?"

"Sure thing, Rhonda. Look at it this way: when we're designing an object-oriented system, we need to build up a picture of what the system is going to do – a mental model, if you like. We build this picture by thinking about the ways that the system will be used in the real world, and this allows us to create our mental model of what the finished system should be able to do. Additionally, the model will give us strong clues about the components that we'll need to build into the program's code – that is, the components that will satisfy the functions that the program's users want."

"Let me get this straight," said Steve. "Are you saying that modeling means thinking about what the finished program has to do, and creating a model of that reality? Like a model 747 represents the real thing, but less complicatedly, and smaller?"

"That's about the size of it, Steve" I agreed, with an unintentional pun. "The model will show us – in simplified form – what the program will do, and it'll help us to decide on the objects that we need to create to make the program work. Remember, objects are essentially just pieces of code that represent real-world objects, and they work together to make our object-oriented program work as efficiently as possible. Our job as programmers is to analyze what those objects should be, to build them, and then to cement them together in the completed program using code as glue."

"And my next question," Steve went on, "is this: how will we actually set about building a model of the modified China Shop program?"

"When we model the objects in the China Shop," I explained, "we'll be using a methodology that's partially derived from UML. Using this methodology, we'll run through several **scenarios**, which mimic the way that the program is going to be used when it's complete.

"Can you tell me a little more about what a scenario is?" asked Linda.

"A scenario is much like the demonstration of the China Shop that Rhonda ran us through just a little earlier in the class," I answered. "In the design phase of the SDLC, where we're modeling the system we want to build, we try to run through as many different scenarios as possible, documenting each one on a piece of paper. What we end up with on those pieces of paper is the foundation for creating our model of the system."

"Does that mean we need to create a scenario for each and every type of possible china purchase?" Kate asked.

"Not necessarily, Kate," I said, "but we might want to run through different scenarios for a customer who selects individual pieces of china, and for a customer who selects a complete place setting. However, there's no need to consider each and every possible permutation of china selections – there are too many."

"But I don't quite understand that," said Rhonda. "*Why* don't we need to think of all the different scenarios in detail? Won't our model be inaccurate without them?"

"Well," I explained, "it wouldn't be useful to create a scenario for all the possible combinations of pieces and quantities. If we did do that, we'd end up with a scenario for a purchase of 1 Mikasa plate, one for 2 Mikasa plates, one for 4 Mikasa plates, and so on through every possible permutation of brands, pieces, and quantities. That would mean creating literally *hundreds* of scenarios."

"Wow, yes," said Rhonda, "I can see that. What do we do instead?"

"What we need to do," I explained, "is concentrate on what this multitude of possible scenarios have in common. That is, we focus on the things in each interaction that represent the 'typical' purchase scenarios. Essentially, all the purchase scenarios in the China Shop come down to the same thing: making a choice of brands, pieces, and quantities. The only significant thing that we'll need to allow for is where the customer wants a complete place setting – remember, that entitles them to a discount, so the program needs to cater for that."

"I can see that, now," said Rhonda, "and I'd hate to have to organize all those sheets of paper, anyway!"

"And with Joe's enhancements," Dave said, "I guess there will probably be a few more scenarios to consider, on top of the ones we saw when Rhonda demo'd the program earlier?"

"That's right Dave," I replied.

"What happens," Peter asked, "after we have all the scenarios written down on pieces of paper?"

"Then comes the fun part!" I said. "After we've developed every scenario we can think of, we take three different colored pens and circle all of the nouns, verbs and adjectives that we we've written down when describing the scenarios. These words refer to things that we imagine happening in the real-world China Shop. For example, the **nouns** equate to the *names* of things that are involved in the purchasing process – such as china pieces, or shipping cartons. The **verbs** equate to the *actions* that occur in the China Shop – like sending a package to a customer, or choosing china items. Finally, the **adjectives** model the *data*, or values, that we need to keep in our program, such as numbers of china pieces, or the value of a shipping charge. We'll see later – in Week 4's lesson, to be precise – that identifying these three types of words in our scenarios feeds directly into designing the objects that we need to create for our program to do its job."

I waited a moment before continuing: "So, using scenarios is doubly useful – they let us concentrate on what the system needs to do, *and* they help us move towards creating the core components of the system."

"It sounds deceptively simple in theory," Valerie said. "I can't wait to see how that technique works in practice."

"We're not quite ready to do that yet," I said. "As I said, we won't be ready to start creating our own China Shop objects until Week 4."

"Right now," I continued, "I think it's time to take a detailed look at the program modifications that Joe wants. In fact Joe, just before you walked in, Rhonda was asking what kinds of enhancements you are looking for in the program – can you tell us about the changes you think your program needs?"

"Sure thing, John," said Joe, who'd been listening intently.

Detailing the New Requirements

"In a nutshell," Joe explained, "the China Shop will soon be selling china by mail order, via a toll free telephone number – we'll be delivering to all fifty states in the US, plus the District of Columbia, of course. This is how I see it working: when the customer agrees to purchase the china over the phone, they'll give us their address for delivery purposes, and I want my sales clerk to then be able to tell the customer the shipping charge, right there and then on the phone. That would mean, I guess, that the sales clerk would somehow have to tell the program the state that the customer lives in – based on that, the program could then work out and display the shipping charges. That's really all I need."

"Those modifications don't seem all that difficult to me," Ward said. "Are they, Professor?"

"I don't think they'll pose much of a challenge for us," I said. "But you never know in programming – we must always be prepared for anything!"

Joe raised his hand, smiled, and said: "My only other requirement I have is that I'd prefer to have these modifications made to the existing program, if that's what John thinks we need, rather than risk having all sorts of problems with a brand new, additional one."

Now it was Kate's turn to raise her hand – Joe seemed to have set a trend. "You said earlier," she said, directing her comment excitedly to me, "that we might need a second form in the project, right? We only had a single form in the original China Shop project, and I'd love to learn how to add a second one!"

"It's certainly a possibility, Kate," I said. "Provided that it fits with our design, I'll certainly show you how to add and use a second form. At the moment, I can see that we might create a second form that prompts the user for the customer's state, and then displays the shipping charges."

"Instead of a second form," Chuck suggested, "we could do the same thing using a menu item, couldn't we? Much like we do in the existing program when the user wants to change the color of the form."

"Or we could even use a pop-up menu," Dave chimed in.

I could see Kate looking a bit dejected – she'd obviously set her heart on that second form. I registered this and held up my hands to stop the flow of ideas for a moment. "Those are all good suggestions," I said, and then, turning to Joe Bullina, asked him: "Joe, do you have a preference?"

"I was thinking," Joe replied carefully, "that we could put a button on the existing form. The button could read 'Calculate Shipping Charges' – or something like that."

"I like that," Rhonda said. "You're suggesting that when the program's user clicks on this button, they'll be prompted to enter the state that the china should be shipped to, right?"

"That's right, Rhonda," Joe affirmed.

"Wait a minute," Peter said. "Now I have a question. Rhonda just said that 'the program's user' would click on the new command button. Didn't you say, Joe, that your primary reason for wanting this change to the program is to accommodate telephone orders? It's the sales clerk who'll be using this facility, isn't it? Do you really want the customer to see this button in the existing program?"

"That's a good point," Joe conceded. "The thing is that, in the past, some of my 'in store' customers have asked us to ship their purchases either to their home or to friends and relatives out of state. So I think that incorporating this same functionality into the kiosk system on open use in the store would be a great idea, too – that way, the customer can calculate for themselves how much extra cost shipping would add to their order."

"But what about the sales clerks?" Melissa asked, "You don't want them to be sitting out in the middle of the store by the kiosk system, do you?"

"Aha!" exclaimed Joe, lightheartedly, "this is where I reveal my masterstroke! I've bought a second computer – a brand new machine, really zippy, too! I'd like to use that to run the 'behind the counter' sales quotations and shipping charges, and leave the old 486 machine out on the sales floor, for the customers' to use. Any of the sales clerks at the front counter will be able to take a telephone order, using the newer machine. I've already ordered a second telephone line to accommodate the toll free 'hot line'. The phone attached to this second line will sit beside the new computer. This means that whenever that telephone rings, the sales clerk will know that it's a mail order customer call, and they'll have the new computer ready to hand."

Ward furrowed his brow, saying: "If you're running more than one PC, won't there be a problem coordinating them?"

"I don't know," Joe admitted. "What do you mean, exactly?" I'd always noticed that Joe was the kind of guy who was very keen to hear about any problems that might arise, and in that respect he was a fairly typical software customer.

"In your case, Joe," I said, taking over from Ward, "you'll just need to ensure that the inventory information describing the china pieces' prices is identical on both PCs. For instance, if you update china prices on the PC in the middle of the sales floor, you also need to remember to update the PC behind the counter."

"I don't think that will be much of a problem," Joe said, "after all, the manufacturers don't change their prices too frequently."

"No, I think you'll be fine while there're only two PCs involved," I assured him.

"What about setting Joe up with a network?" Linda suggested. "Being a Network Administrator myself, I know that I could help out with that."

"I think a network of some kind would definitely be something we could pursue down the road a bit," I replied, "particularly if Joe determines that he needs to add more PCs. It's the possibility of that kind of development that makes me so keen to do the object-oriented overhaul right now. For that reason, I'd like to keep things as simple as possible, and just go with a stand-alone second PC for now – otherwise we might get sidetracked."

"So it looks like we'll display a second command button on the form," said Dave. "What happens in the program when this button get clicked?"

"A second form gets displayed?" suggested Kate, hopefully.

"Intuitively," I said quickly, before any alternatives could be put forward, "that sounds like the best way to go, Kate. How about this: when the new button is clicked, we display a second form with a list box containing all fifty states, plus the District of Columbia. When the user clicks on the name of the state in the list box, we display the applicable shipping charge in a message box."

"Sounds ideal," said Joe Bullina.

"Great," I said, "we're making progress."

"Mr. Bullina," Valerie ventured, "do you have a list of states and their relevant shipping charges yet?"

"Yes, I do," Joe confirmed. "In fact, I brought it with me today." Joe handed me a table that he'd had made up on a slide, and I displayed it on the classroom projector for everyone to see:

Shipping Zone	States Included in this Zone	Shipping Charge
1	Delaware, New Jersey, Pennsylvania	$6
2	District of Columbia	$7
3	Connecticut, New York, Rhode Island	$8
4	Massachusetts, New Hampshire, Vermont	$9
5	Maine	$10

Shipping Zone	States Included in this Zone	Shipping Charge
6	Maryland, Virginia, West Virginia	$8
7	Florida, Georgia, North Carolina	$10
8	Illinois, Indiana, Michigan, Ohio	$11
9	Kentucky, South Carolina, Tennessee	$12
10	Alabama, Arkansas, Louisiana, Mississippi	$13
11	Iowa, Minnesota, Missouri, Wisconsin	$14
12	Kansas, Nebraska, Oklahoma, Texas	$15
13	North Dakota, South Dakota	$16
14	Colorado, Montana, New Mexico, Wyoming	$17
15	Arizona, Idaho, Utah	$18
16	California, Nevada, Oregon, Washington	$19
17	Alaska, Hawaii	$20

"As you can see," Joe said, handing me another slide, which showed the various shipping zones on a map of the US, "there are seventeen 'price zones', with shipping charges ranging from $6 to $20."

I displayed his second slide for the class to see:

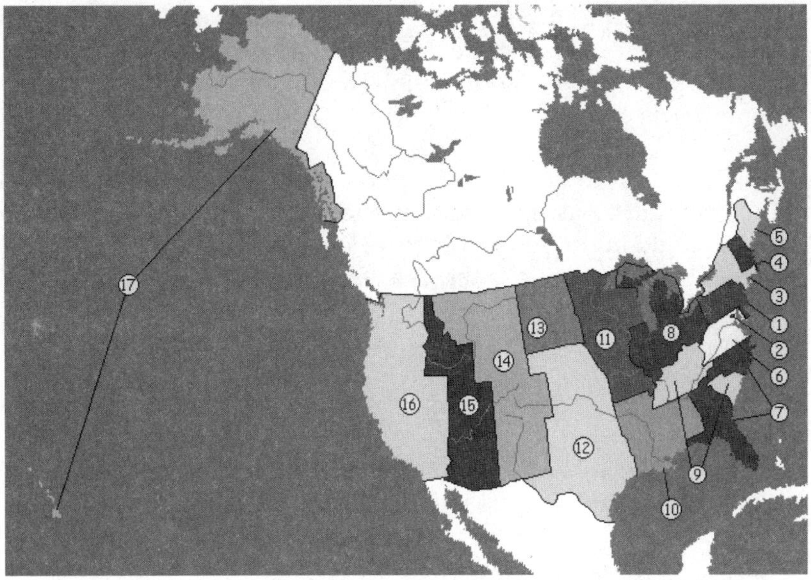

Joe went on: "I was wondering – will there be a way for me to update the charges in the program if my shipper changes them?"

"No problem, Joe," I said. "We already store the prices of your inventory in a text file called `Prices.txt`, and we can use the same approach for keeping a record of your shipping costs. One of your sales clerks – Midge I'd guess – can then update the file using Notepad whenever necessary."

We all then spent about ten minutes discussing in more detail the sales process that Joe had just outlined for us, and Dave volunteered to record our discussions in a Word document. When we'd reached a consensus on exactly what was required, I displayed the finished document on the classroom projector:

> The China Shop program will be modified to display a command button labeled 'Shipping Charges' on the main form of the program. If the user clicks on this button, a new form captioned 'Shipping Charges' will be displayed, showing a list box containing the fifty United States plus the District of Columbia. When the user clicks on a destination state of their choice, a Visual Basic message box will be displayed showing the appropriate shipping charge.

Then one of the students asked a question that I figure must have been on her mind for a while: "I don't mean to be a 'downer' here," Melissa said, "but how is the calculation of shipping charges actually related to object-oriented programming?"

"That's a valid question, Melissa," I said. "In fact, I thought the same thing myself when I first spoke to Joe about this enhancement. I was more than willing to do it for him, but I only wanted to do the modification in the context of this class if it furthered our object-oriented education."

"So, will it?" asked Dave. "I know you said that we're going to look at the existing China Shop program by using scenarios, and that doing this would help us identify any objects that we could build into an object-oriented version. But is there really an object hidden away in the modifications that we've discussed this morning?"

"I think so," I said. "How about a 'package' object?"

"A 'package'?" said Rhonda.

"I think so, Rhonda," I replied. "Consider: what is it that we've been talking about shipping to the customer for the last half hour or so? A package!"

Rhonda pressed on: "Do you mean the type of package that has wrapping, string, and a mailing label?"

"Exactly, Rhonda," I said. "That's a *real-world* description of a package. The beauty of object-oriented programming is that we can take that real-world object, analyze what goes to make it what it is, and then redefine it in Visual Basic – although I think you'll find we won't need to create programmatic equivalents for wrapping and string! Essentially, that's what we'll be doing in a few weeks when we add the new functionality to the China Shop – creating a package object. And I really think you'll be amazed at what we can do with this new object. For example, once we've created the package object within Visual Basic, other programs can use it too – such as Word and Excel."

"Does this imply," Ward said, "that we'll will be able to access the shipping charges in Joe's program from within an Excel spreadsheet?"

"That's right Ward," I said, "and from within Word, too. This is another advantage of using objects – if you want them to, they can share your information outside the Visual Basic program where they live." To reassure Joe, I added: "Of course, we as programmers decide what parts of the program will be accessible to other applications. This is another important feature of object-oriented programming that we'll be discussing during the course – how objects communicate with the rest of the program that they live in and how they can communicate with the outside world, too."

I then turned to Joe.

"Joe," I said, "I have a suggestion for a program modification that isn't something you said you wanted, but which will be great experience for the class, and useful for you, too. It'll let the class see how to use Visual Basic objects in conjunction with other applications, and it'll let *you* use your shipping charges data more flexibly – for instance, you could use them directly in a Word document, or in an Excel spreadsheet. To do this, we'll use a feature called **ActiveX Automation**."

"I'm not sure what ActiveX Automation is," Joe said, "but tell me about your suggestion."

"Well," I explained, "one thing the program *doesn't* have now, and that I think would be very worthwhile to add, is the ability to print the price quotation for the customer. I'd like to suggest that when the quotation is displayed, another command button labeled 'Print Quotation' be displayed on the form – and that this button, when clicked by the customer, uses Word to print out the price quotation."

"That's an excellent idea," Joe enthused. "Doing this would eliminate some of the problems that I've seen when customers approach one of my sales clerks after getting their price quotation on-screen. Some customers forget the exact combination of china they've received the quotation for, and others swear that the price charged them by the sales clerk differs from the quotation that they saw on the computer screen. And guess what? My nephew recently picked up a printer for me – so we're all set up in that respect as well!"

"I'm glad you like that idea, Joe," I said, relieved that he hadn't turned the idea down. "Printing using Word and the program's objects will be great experience for the class."

"What about the Printer object you told us about last semester?" Ward asked. "Couldn't we use that?"

"Yes, we *could*," I said. "In principle, the Printer object – which is pre-built into Visual Basic – is a great tool for routing simple reports to the PC's default printer. But for more elegant reports, Word is the way to

> **For more on using the built-in Printer object, see Chapter 11 of my original book: *Learn to Program with Visual Basic 6.***

"Does this mean that we'll need to have Microsoft Word installed on the China Shop's PC?" Dorothy asked.

"That's a good point Dorothy," I said, "and the answer is 'yes' – the PC in the middle of the sales floor *will* need to have Word running on it. As I recall, you already have Word installed, don't you, Joe?"

"Yes, we already have Word," Joe answered. "In fact, only this morning I was using Word to compose a letter to one of my suppliers – and I printed it this morning using that second-hand laser printer my nephew picked up for me over the holidays. The printer prints letters out very well – do you think it will do for the price quotation you're talking about?"

"I'm sure it will be fine, Joe," I said.

At this point I thought it would be a great idea to document a formal requirements statement based on the notes he'd taken so far.

Confirming the Formal Requirements

While the class was taking a fifteen-minute break, Dave and I worked on the amended requirements statement for the modified China Shop program. When the class reconvened after the break, Dave displayed the following requirements statement on the classroom projector:

Requirements Statement:
Bullina China Shop Modifications

The existing China Shop program will be modified in this way:

1. The China Shop program will be modified to display a command button labeled 'Shipping Charges' on the main form of the existing China Shop program. If the user clicks on this button, a new form captioned 'Shipping Charges' will be displayed with a list box containing the names of the fifty United States, plus the District of Columbia. When the user clicks on a destination state of their choice, a Visual Basic message box will display the appropriate shipping charges.

2. The program will also be modified to display a command button labeled 'Print Quotation' whenever a price quotation is displayed. If the user clicks on this button, a price quotation will be printed on a printer attached to the PC.

I gave everyone a few moments to review the modified requirements statement and ask questions.

"What about the object-oriented changes you said we'll make to the program?" Peter asked. "Should those changes be specified in the new requirements statement too – or don't we need to include those details?"

"The answer to that," I replied, "is that we don't really need to include these details in the requirements statement. Remember, the true purpose of the requirements statement is to clarify and agree with the customer – Joe Bullina – exactly what he'll be getting from us in terms of a finished system. From the point of view of Joe and the China Shop staff, this requirements statement is fine – it details exactly what new functionality we'll be delivering to them. How we set about making those changes, and the actual code modifications that we make inside the program, are all really irrelevant as far as the user is concerned – so long as we deliver the functionality they want, at the price they agreed, in the time scale that we committed to. I think Joe will agree with me that he's not really interested in knowing about the nuts and bolts inside the program..." – Joe nodded vigorously at this point – "...what he's really interested in is making sure that the program does what he wanted it to do."

I looked around the classroom. It had been a long first day of class, and I could see fatigue on the faces of several of the students. Joe Bullina looked happy though – and, for a systems developer, a happy customer is the most important thing in the world.

"I know that everyone is probably anxious to get started on these modifications," I said, "but we need to learn quite a bit about the theory and practice of objects before we begin working on the China Shop code in detail. In this course, much of what we do early on will involve familiarizing ourselves with how objects work, examining the existing China Shop program, and looking for ways to use Visual Basic objects to make our programming better and more efficient. That's the journey we'll be setting out on next week, when we start looking at objects in Visual Basic. And I reckon you'll be pleasantly surprised to find that you've been working with objects in Visual Basic already – even though you may not have realized it!"

I turned to Joe, thanked him for coming in, and told him that in nine weeks he would have his modified China Shop program, ready to roll. And with that, and a word of thanks for their attention and interest, I dismissed class for the day.

Chapter Summary

This chapter was the start of my class's journey through the world of objects. Part of this journey's first stage was concerned with providing some background on why the object-oriented approach is such a strong force in the programming world, but the bulk of my time was spent in laying the foundations for object-orienting the China Shop project itself. It's by modifying the China Shop program that my students will really make their learning about objects stick in their minds.

Here's a summary of what we learned about **object-oriented programming** (OOP) in this chapter:

- OOP is designed to help us build better programs
- OOP offers advantages over more traditional programming styles: it helps us create systems that closely match real-world needs, and it improves life for programmers *and* for the people who buy their programs
- At the heart of the object-oriented approach is the idea of a design approach that models the real-world activities that the finished system will need to perform. There are a number of different ways that this modeling can be done – we'll be using **scenarios** to model the China Shop's real-world usage
- OOP systems are built using objects. **Objects** are code-based representations of the real-world objects that the program aims to mimic

And here's a summary of the important things that we did in relation to the China Shop itself:

- We walked through the program's existing functionality with Rita and Gil – my class did exactly the same thing, this time with Rhonda at the controls!
- We heard about Joe Bullina's new requirements: firstly, enabling sales clerks to tell customers the shipping charges for their telephone order, depending on the state that they live in; and secondly, adding the facility to print a paper copy of a price quotation
- Joe helped us clarify the details of his requirements, and agreed to let us incorporate the modifications of his program into my Objects class. This will benefit Joe by giving him a leaner, fitter program that's easier to upgrade in future, and it will give my class the chance to work on a realistic program and apply their growing knowledge of objects

Next week, we'll start looking at objects themselves in more detail, and explore some of the programming techniques that we can use to get the most out of them. I think my class will be pleasantly surprised that they've already been working with objects in their Visual Basic programs – even though they might not have realized it at the time!

Join us for next week's class.

Learn to Program Objects with Visual Basic

Chapter 2

Visual Basic Objects in Action

In this week's class, my students and I will move on from Joe's new system requirements and our discussion of the benefits offered by the object-oriented approach to programming problems. This week's lesson will concentrate on bridging the gap between those discussions and the way that object-oriented programming is implemented in Visual Basic.

In this week's lesson, my class will be pleasantly surprised to find that they've been working with objects in their Visual Basic Programs all along – they just didn't know it! They'll discover that many of the common components that they've been building into their programs – such as command buttons and check boxes – are in fact treated as **objects** by Visual Basic. The class will also learn that every Visual Basic program has built-in features that help it – and us – keep track of all the objects in our programs, and they'll start learning about how we can use these features to make our programs more efficient and more fully object-oriented.

The Road Ahead

Both this week's and next week's classes will familiarize my students in using and manipulating objects in code. We'll be working with some extremely useful objects that are built into VB, and in doing so, we'll achieve two main objectives: firstly, we'll explore how we can usefully incorporate these built-in objects in our programs; secondly, all the theory and practice we cover will give us a great preparation for creating and using the objects of our own that we'll build for the China Shop.

Specifically, here's what we'll cover in this chapter:

- We'll see that there are objects built into Visual Basic that we can work with in our code, and which can interact with the objects that we create for ourselves
- We'll learn that these built-in objects are created from a pre-defined template, or **class**

- We'll look in detail at some of these built-in objects, and explore some of the coding techniques that let us use them in our code
- Finally, we'll see how we can put all of these principles to work in creating objects of our own

This second class is an important one: it gets us much closer to the coal-face of Visual Basic code, and sets us on our way to understanding how objects are used in our programs. It also covers how we can get the best out of them by using Visual Basic's built-in facilities (and how we can mirror these facilities in our own code).

My approach in this lesson is to take my students from the familiar territory of Visual Basic controls – text boxes, command buttons and so on – and show the class how these controls fit into the bigger context – how Visual Basic uses object-oriented techniques in practice, and what the benefits of this are for us as programmers. Let's join the class now.

The Class Reconvenes

On the second Saturday of the course, the weather was gloomy and overcast, with heavy gray skies threatening snow – it was so dark, in fact, that I had to drive all the way to the University with my headlights on. But inside the classroom, all the lights were shining brightly, and there was a warm atmosphere as the students shared the pleasure of being indoors on such a cold, miserable day.

"Today," I told the class, as I introduced the second lesson, "we're going to begin our hands-on exploration of object-oriented programming. By looking at some real live objects in Visual Basic, we'll be able to start getting a grip on how we can use objects in the code that we write ourselves."

"I think that'd be really valuable," said Ward. "Although I think I'm beginning to get an idea of how important object-oriented programming is, I can't really see what's wrong with what you might call the more 'traditional' methods. I feel like I already *know* how to program. I'm having to take it on trust that object-orientation is worth learning," he continued, with surprising fluency. "I feel like a guy that's standing on the shore looking into a boat and deciding whether to step into it!"

There were a few nods and smiles of agreement from around the room, and I felt the familiar vibe of anxiety that's usually apparent in the early stages of the Objects course: people feel that they should already understand about objects, whereas the truth is that you need to work with them in theory and practice for a little while before you're really comfortable with them. There's an inevitable period early on where you just have to trust the teacher – later, things fall into place.

"OK," I said, "I can understand how you feel. Taking the main ideas of object-oriented programming on board means thinking about your programs in a new way, and that always takes a little time. In fact, that's why this course takes a gradual, step-by-step approach to teaching you about using objects."

I paused a moment, and smiled, then struck out to sea positively: "The good news," I announced, "is that you've already been working with objects in just about all the Visual Basic programs that you've created in the past – including the original China Shop project!"

"How's that?" exclaimed Rhonda, "we didn't create any objects for the China Shop last semester, did we? Least ways, I certainly don't recall doing that!"

Again, there were nods of agreement from other students.

"OK," I said, smiling, "I won't keep you in suspense any longer. Let me explain what I mean when I say that you've been using objects all along."

Some Objects You already Know about...

"When Microsoft were developing and enhancing the Visual Basic application," I began, "they thought about how the end users of the application – that's us Visual Basic programmers! – would use the application. The bottom line here is that we use Visual Basic to create programs that we – or our clients – can use. Essentially, when we start up Visual Basic and code and test our programs in the design-time environment, we're running a program (Visual Basic) that lets us create Visual Basic programs of our own."

"OK," said Ward, " I understand that – Visual Basic is a development environment, for sure."

"That's right," I agreed, "and it's also one of the easiest program development environments to use. That's partly because it's very 'visual' in its approach, but it's also because Microsoft's developers thought about what we'd be trying to do with it."

"What exactly do you mean by that, Professor?" said Rhonda.

"I mean that the developers knew that we'd be using Visual Basic to create Windows programs that looked like other Windows programs, so that our program's users could interact with them intuitively. In essence, that means creating programs that consist of a form (or forms), each of which has a number of controls placed on it at design time – command buttons, image controls, option buttons etc. It's these controls that the end-user sees and interacts with when they run our program. One of the beauties of VB is that Microsoft's developers built all of the controls for us and made them available for us to use – saving us a heck of a lot of time and effort!"

"How about an example?" said Linda. "You keep saying that anyone who uses VB is already using objects – can you give me an example of what one of these objects looks like?"

"Sure," I replied. "Think of the command buttons we use when we're creating a Visual Basic program. When we've placed a command button on our form, we can change it around so that it has a different look, depending on what we want it to do. Here's a selection of command buttons from different programs to show you what I mean:"

I left this slide up on the projector screen and continued with my explanation.

"These command buttons have been taken at random from a variety of Windows applications. Can you see how similar they are to each other? They have a common shape, and each one has a highlight and a shadow on it, to make it look three-dimensional."

"Oh yes!" said Rhonda, "but...well, I'd always sort of taken that for granted."

"Yes, I think I take it for granted, too, most of the time, if I'm honest with you," I agreed. "The important thing to realize here is that we didn't have to code any of these essential characteristics for ourselves, did we? The rectangular shape, the highlighting, and the shading on the buttons are **features of command buttons in general**: all command buttons have these characteristics by default. Furthermore, if we click on a command button, it'll automatically perform a pre-set animation sequence that makes it look like it's been pushed inwards:"

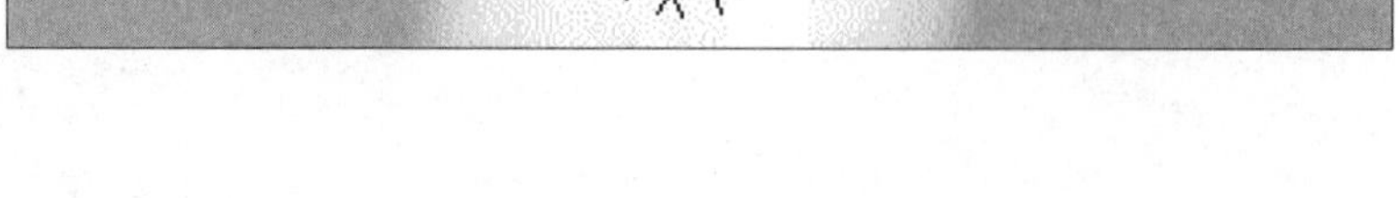

"This animation is one of what're known as the **default behaviors** of the button. Every command button that we place on a form in Visual Basic knows how to do this – the animation behavior is built-in. It's similar to the way that a baby 'knows' how to cry, sleep, and eat; these are default behaviors that don't have to be taught by the baby's parents – the behaviors are inherent, just because the baby is a baby. Imagine how much more wearisome parenting would be if we had to *explicitly teach* babies each and every aspect of their behavior..."

At this point, I noticed a few wry smiles on the faces of the parents among the students!

"Like the baby," I resumed, "the command button is 'born knowing' how to do the things that all command buttons do. This is because the people who created Visual Basic sat down and thought of the controls that we'd be likely to want to use in our programs. They decided what each of these controls should look like, and their behaviors – what they should be able to do."

"So you're talking about the making of Visual Basic itself, now?" Asked Rhonda.

"Yes," I replied. "In creating Visual Basic, the designers were distilling out the essence of what we VB programmers need to do in the real world – which is create Windows programs for other people to use. They determined the key things that Visual Basic programs must contain to let users interact with them. These 'key things' are the controls that we put on our forms, because VB programs are driven by how the user interacts with the forms and controls we present them with. Our job as programmers is to join up these controls using code – and the whole ensemble should do the job of work that the program's sponsor asked us to cater for."

"So the conclusion you're leading us to, is that the controls we use are actually objects as far as Visual Basic is concerned?" Ward suggested.

"Exactly," I replied. "They're pre-defined lumps of code that we simply assemble together to do a job in our program."

"I think I see what you're getting at..." began Rhonda. "The object-oriented programmers at Microsoft analyzed the requirements of VB's users (us programmers!) and created a set of objects that would help us to do our job!"

"That's about right," I nodded. "Imagine having to write the code for each and every different control you wanted to add to the form – I think you can see that VB's designers have saved us a lot of work."

The class seemed to take that on board, so I moved in for the coup de grace...

"So," I went on, "the controls that we add to our forms are actually objects with predefined characteristics and abilities, created for us by the people who designed Visual Basic. And the selection of default objects that we can use is held in the Visual Basic toolbox:"

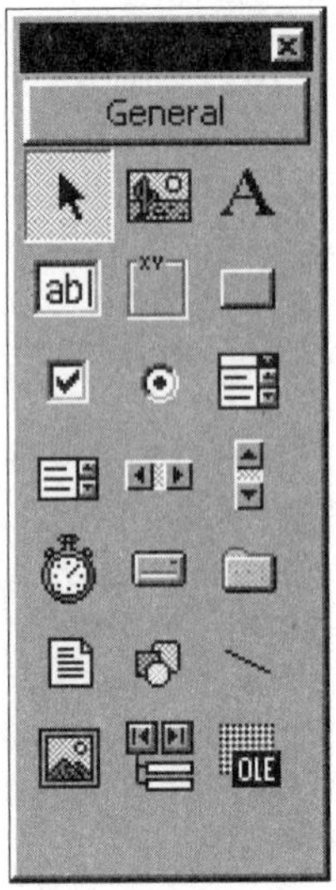

"The range of different objects you see in the toolbox," I went on, "depends on which version of VB you're running, and can be expanded by adding different components to our Visual Basic project. However, the controls shown here are the default controls that are *always* available for us to use. The different types of controls that are found in the toolbox are **templates** that we use to create individual control objects on our forms. When we place the individual controls on our form, Visual Basic treats them as **Control Objects** – that is, objects that happen to be controls, and VB knows what they are capable of, based on the predefined template."

I waited a moment before continuing: "Let's take a peek at some real-world control objects that are already in existence on the main form of the China Shop program."

An Example of Control Objects in the China Shop

"If you look on the China Shop form, you'll see we've got six China Pieces check boxes that the customer can use to indicate which china pieces they want to buy:"

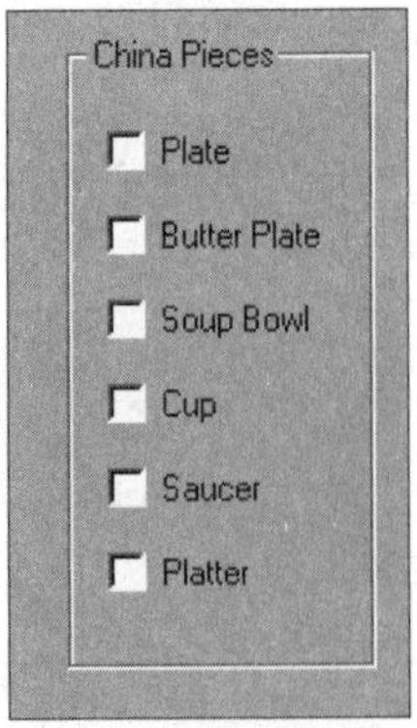

"They're all pretty similar to each other," I went on. This isn't surprising, since they're all based on the general control object of the `CheckBox` type – which is one of the essential control object types that are built into Visual Basic, courtesy of the designers of VB. Another way of looking at it is to say that they're all based on the same template that has been predefined for us by the Visual Basic designers."

I paused, to let that soak in before continuing: "However, each check box on the form is also unique," I went on. "It has its separate property settings that distinguish it from its fellow check boxes. These properties include such things as: whereabouts the check box is on the form; the check box's `Caption` property; it's `True/False` property, and, of course, the check box's individual name. Take a look at this next slide – it shows the Properties windows for two of the check boxes on the China Shop's main form:"

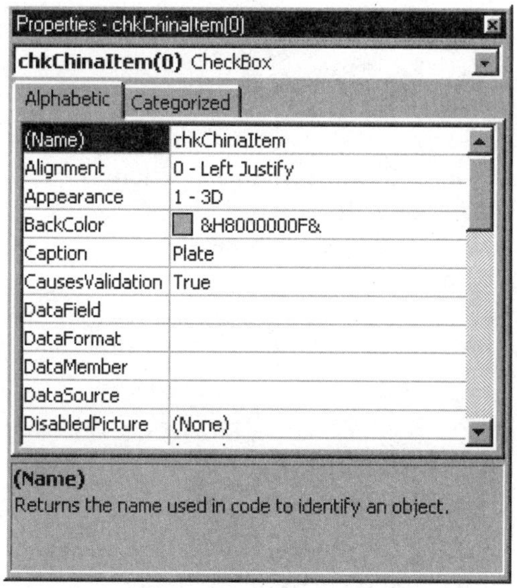

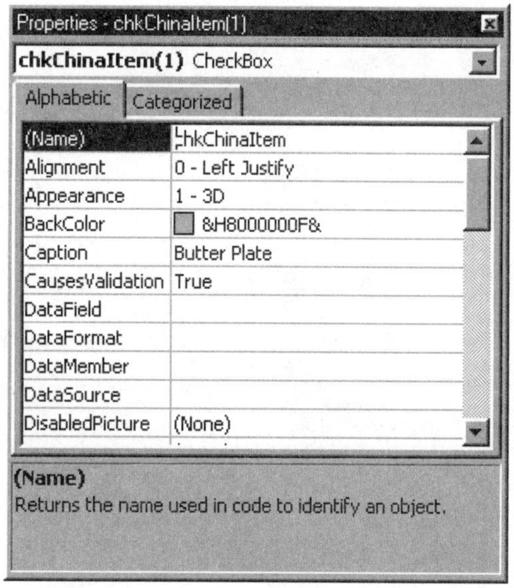

"As you can see, the lists of **properties** that each check box has available to it are identical – again, this isn't surprising, as each check box is based on the same object template from the toolbox. But the actual **settings** for these common properties are different, and it's these property values that make each individual copy of the template – each object – unique. For instance, each check box on the form has a unique name that the program uses to identify the check box object. This can be seen in the white box at the top of the Properties window:"

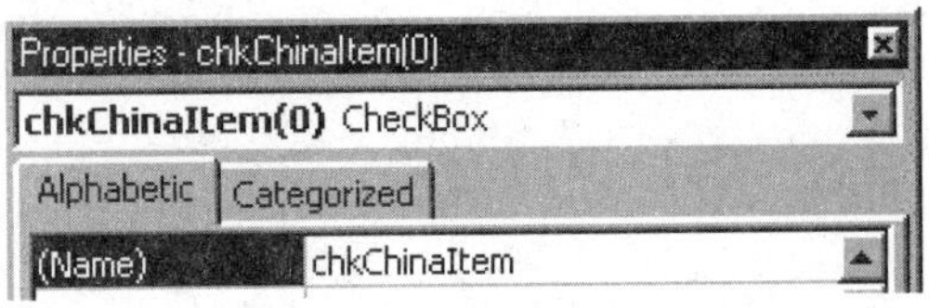

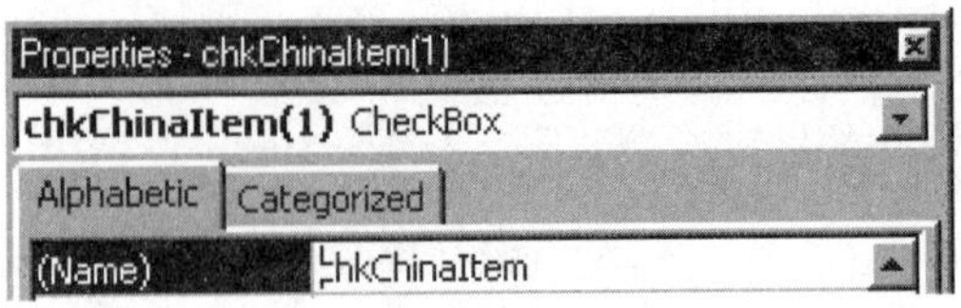

Note that these two check boxes have the same value in the **`Name`** property box – this is because these two check boxes are part of a control array. Individual objects in a control array share the same **`Name`** property, but are distinguished by the bracketed number in the name of the object itself.

I paused for questions, scrolling down through some of the other properties in the Properties window.

"These property values..." began Melissa. She hesitated.

"Yes?" I encouraged her, "go on."

"I can see that they store the same *kind* of information – the caption of a particular check box, or its width, for example – but I was wondering where these values are actually stored. Do they automatically get declared as variables and stored somewhere in the program when we create each individual check box on the form?"

"That's a great question! The answer is that the values for the properties are stored *within* each check box object."

"When you say 'within', what do you mean exactly?" asked Chuck.

"I mean as a part of the individual object's own code block," I replied. "Each object stores its properties in variables that only exist within that individual object's code. This is part of making sure that we minimize the complexity of storing and referring to data in our programs: since these properties describe this individual object, it makes sense – in object-oriented terms – to store these values inside the object itself. The object is like a distinct living entity that 'knows' about the properties that define it, and looks after them itself, pretty independently. Other objects, and other pieces of code in the program, can talk to the check box object and ask it questions: for example, our code can 'send a message' to the check box and ask it to reveal the value of its **`Value`** property. And since all check boxes are based on the same template, we know that we can always do the same thing *for any check box*."

"So each object has its properties?" Lou asked, speaking slowly, as he thought through what he was saying. "And the controls we put on our forms are just objects the same as any other... so that when we change things in the Properties window for a control, we're really just changing variables for that individual control object?"

"Yes," I replied. "Looking at it another way, the properties of the 'Butter Plate' check box on our form are the values that make it unique from the other five 'China Pieces' check box objects. As a result, they're stored within the 'Butter Plate' check box object's own code. This stops them getting confused with the properties of any of the other check boxes."

"OK," said Ward, "I can see that. But you also said that objects have their own behaviors built-in. Can you give us and example of that?"

"Yes," I said. "In objects, these built-in behaviors – also known as **methods** – are common to all objects of the same type. For example," I went on, "notice that, by changing the `Value` of each check box from one to zero – `True` to `False` – we automatically call a procedure *within* the object itself that either draws or erases that little tick-mark inside the box on the form."

I could see some looks of revelation around the room.

"We don't have to code any of that in for ourselves," I went on, "or worry about whether it may or may not happen correctly, each time we change `Value` from `True` to `False`, or vice versa. We *know* it will happen, because that behavior is built into every instance of any check box object that's created using the template from the toolbox."

"That's really neat," observed Bob.

"This is an example of an **object method** in action." I explained. "The whole process of changing the `Value` property and erasing or drawing the little tick-mark is already coded into the check box as part of its **click event**. We can see from this that each object can have its own **properties**, **methods** and **events**."

"It's own *events*?" asked Lou, a little startled.

"Yes," I confirmed. "Let me explain. When we write some code in the click event of, say, a command button, we're actually adding the custom code that makes that button's `Click` event unique from any other. An event is an interface that lets the object communicate with the outside world. But the button has it's own built-in, default behavior, which it displays when it's clicked."

"You mean it runs its animation code to look like it's being pressed inwards?" suggested Dorothy.

"Exactly," I replied. "This default behavior is part of the command button object's **event code**, whose execution is automatically triggered by the `Click` event. Then we add our own code to customize the `Click` event in further ways. So you can see that any individual control object is a combination of things: first, it embodies the shared characteristics – properties, methods, and events – that the control inherits from the template when it's created; and secondly, the control is made unique, and customized, based on the specific property values that we give it, plus any specialized event handling code that we write."

"Hmm..." said Linda, sounding dubious, "can you just run that template idea by me again? I want to have a clear picture in my head of exactly where the default behaviors of the built-in objects in VB come from."

"Of course," I replied. "You're right to want to understand this properly – it's an important part of learning about objects in Visual Basic. We've already discussed – a little – how the standard types of object we include on our program's forms are based on templates that we find in the Visual Basic toolbox. The key thing to understand is what that template consists of. To understand that, I'll introduce you to what may be a new term to you – **Classes**. Classes are what define the shared characteristics and behaviors of objects, and they're central to building and using objects in Visual Basic."

Classes are Templates

"Each 'control template' in the Visual Basic toolbox," I continued, "represents a **class**. A class is the distillation of all the important shared characteristics and behaviors that we want objects of the same type to have. Fortunately for us, the people who built Visual Basic have established how the different control objects should behave, and they've created the relevant templates – classes – for us. Similarly, each Visual Basic object of our own that we define requires that we first create a class that describes the essential features of all objects of that type."

"So," said Dave, "we need to design and create classes for the new objects that we'll put into the amended China Shop program?"

"Yes, that's right," I said, "and that's exactly what we'll be doing in Week 4 of this class. We have some more ground to cover before we can do that, but that's what we're aiming for."

"Just a moment," said Rhonda, "I can understand the idea of a template, I think, but what is a class, like, physically?"

"Well, Rhonda," I answered, "a class is basically a module of code that contains the template for the objects that we'll later **instantiate** from it."

"Instantiate?" Kevin asked, maybe wondering if he'd heard correctly.

"That's right," I said, writing the word on the wipeboard so that the students could see the spelling. "Instantiate means 'to create an instance of an object.' For example, when we add a new command button to a form, we create an **instance of a command button object**, based on the **command button class** that was created by the nice folks who wrote Visual Basic."

"So, is the command button icon in the Visual basic toolbox a command button's **class**?" Dorothy asked.

"That's excellent, Dorothy," I said, "that's exactly what that icon represents."

"So, will the classes that we create for Joe's program appear in the toolbox, too?" Mary asked.

"That's a good question, Mary," I said. " It's certainly possible to create similar objects that would appear in the toolbox – they're called ActiveX controls, and when they're properly designed they behave just like any other control. However, we won't be creating any objects like that here, since there's quite a bit of design work involved, which lies outside the scope of this course. I've talked about controls as examples of VB objects so much here because they're ready-made for us and we can visualize them easily in our mind's eye."

"Can we get back to that notion of an object template again?" Tom asked. "You called it a –" he checked his notes " – a '**class**'. Can you explain that idea of a template again for me? – I want to get this real clear!"

"Yes, Tom," I said, "If you check the Microsoft documentation, they compare a **class** to a **cookie cutter**, and an **object** to the cookie that is created from it."

I put up the following picture on the projection screen:

"I get it!" Ward said. "Cutting out the cookie shapes from the cookie mix and putting the cut mix onto the baking tray is kinda like putting our buttons and check boxes and stuff on the form, right?"

"Right," I said, "but the same process occurs whenever we instantiate an object of any given class – not just a control object. The class – the cookie cutter – defines the default behaviors and properties of the new cookie object – such as wiggly edge, five millimeters thick, and so on. It's then up to us to us to give each individual cookie object it's custom properties – such as sugared or non-sugared."

There were several smiles from around the room.

"I've come across that word 'cookies', from time to time in Microsoft literature," Linda said, "usually when I was just getting out of my depth. I must confess, I used to wonder just what kind of cookies they were eating over there in Seattle!"

Now we all laughed.

"So these special values – the properties – of each object," Melissa went on, "are they stored in variables?"

"Yes, we call the variables that store the individual properties of an object **instance variables**, because they define the features of that particular instance of the object."

"When do we declare them?" Asked Kate.

"Instance variables are declared in the class module that defines the class, and they get created with each instantiation of a new object based on that class," I said. "For each object, there's a single **class module** that describes the object – and many objects of the same type can then be created from it with copies of the instance variables built-in – just like an unlimited number of cookies can be created from a single cookie cutter – provided that you don't run out of cookie mix!"

"By defining our own classes to create objects from," Rhonda queried, "will writing programs be easier? It still sounds kinda complicated to me."

I hesitated a moment before answering.

"Ultimately, Rhonda," I said, "I think you're going to have to make up your own mind about that. The main thing is, it'll be a lot easier to maintain, modify and reuse the code you write using objects."

I glanced at Ward, who was nodding. "I'm excited by what you've shown me so far," he said. "I hadn't realized I was already using objects that other people had written for me! I can't wait 'til we start making some objects of our own. It'd be really neat."

"Sure," I said, "We're going to come to that in good time. Next though – after we've taken a coffee break – we need to look at some of the other objects that come ready-made with Visual Basic."

"More objects?" said Valerie. "Do you mean the other objects we create from the templates – sorry, **classes** – in the toolbox?"

"No, not quite," I explained. "All the standard control objects that we create from the classes represented in the toolbox act pretty similarly: that is, we create instances of the objects based on the underlying class, and we can then set each instance's properties, use their methods, and write code to handle their events. Doing these things ties these control objects together in our program, enabling it to perform the function we want it to. The objects that I want to talk about after the break are objects that Visual Basic automatically creates and uses each time our program runs. These are in addition to any control objects that we put on our forms, and Visual Basic uses these additional objects – called **System Objects** – to keep track of what our program consists of, and what it's doing."

Rhonda looked puzzled, and said: "So VB creates these...system objects without us asking for them?"

"That's right," I replied. "System objects are built into Visual Basic – they're part of the way that Visual Basic looks after our code 'behind the scenes', and they help Visual Basic operate more effectively. The good news is that, as programmers, we can step 'behind the curtain' and make use of these system objects ourselves. That's what I want to concentrate on next – what these system objects are for, how they work, and how we can usefully interact with them as programmers. So... let's take that break, and come back refreshed for some really important new material!"

Introducing Visual Basic System Objects

"Welcome back," I said, as the students resumed their seats after their coffee and candy. "Let me just recap the main things that we covered in that first session." So saying, I displayed the following slide that I'd prepared:

Visual Basic has a load of pre-defined objects that we can use. These objects come with their own built-in behaviors and characteristics

Among these built-in objects are the controls that we use on our forms. Our controls are actually control objects

The individual objects that we create – instantiate – on our forms are based on predefined templates called classes

"OK, let's move on, now." I said. "Before the break, I started talking about Visual Basic system objects. Just let me reiterate that when you run your program, Visual Basic is doing a lot of work behind the scenes to ensure that the control objects and code that you've assembled work properly. I also mentioned that we can make use of the system objects that VB creates automatically when the program is run. These system objects help us get the most out of our own objects, and help us to interact with them in code. What I want to do in this next session is start describing some of these important system objects, and work through some demonstrations of how to use them in code."

I knew from experience that the students would gain valuable insight from working through the code examples – the use of the system objects was an important set of concepts to learn, and it would stand the students in good stead for refashioning the China Shop into an object-oriented program.

"The first kind of system objects to talk about," I resumed, "are **collections**. As the name suggests, collections are where Visual Basic keeps information about groups of similar things. We can also create our *own* collections to store data about groups of things – we'll see how to do that near the end of today's lesson. When we create our modified China Shop program, I want to simplify the way the data about brands, china pieces and prices are stored by gathering it all together into a collection. For now, let's take a look at the general principles behind collections."

Collections

"A **collection**," I reiterated, "is a group of related **items** stored under a common name. Visual Basic automatically creates and maintains specific collections that keep track of different types of items that live in our programs, and we can also create our own collections."

"Would an *item* be roughly equivalent to an element in an array – that is, like a single variable in an array of variables?" Melissa asked.

"That's a good comparison," I said. "But one big difference between an array and a collection is that a collection can contain items of different data types – such as numbers, strings, dates and, indeed, objects. In a variable array, each element in the array must be of the same data type."

"I remember that from the Introductory course," Ward said. "When you declare an array, you need to specify the data type for the members of that array – the **array elements**."

"Just like with arrays," I resumed, "we can carry out quick, multiple changes to the members of a collection using a `For...Each` loop."

"Let me just get one thing straight," said Melissa. "Is a collection an object, or do you collect objects together?"

"A collection is an object in itself," I replied, "and it can also hold a collection of objects. That may seem illogical, but in fact, a collection simply holds is a series of memory-addresses referring to the items that make it up. When a program accesses a member of a collection, the collection gives the program the precise details of where in the computer's memory it can find the object referred to by that item."

"Like an index in a book?" Suggested Linda.

"Yes," I replied, "an index doesn't contain the information you want, only where to find it in the book. When a program needs to read from or modify an item in a collection, it first goes to the collection to find out where to find the item in memory, then it goes to the item itself, does what is needed and comes back."

"I've just thought of something," said Ward. "Our China Pieces check boxes are all members of a control array, aren't they? Does an array work the same way as a collection in how it stores its contents?"

"Yes, Ward," I replied. "In fact, this is a feature common to *most* modern computer languages. An array simply holds a **memory address** for any of its elements. You can have an array of objects, just like you could have a collection. The key difference, as I mentioned before, is that a collection can hold items of different kinds, rather than just a single type."

"So is an array of variables – like the arrays we created last semester – an *object*?" Rhonda enquired.

"No, Rhonda," I replied, "an array isn't an object in itself: it *is* a structure for storing and manipulating data, but it doesn't qualify as an object, because it doesn't have properties and methods," I replied.

"So... collections are objects," Kate said, "and what you've just said implies that they have properties and methods, just like other objects do. Precisely what properties and methods do collection objects have?"

Collection Characteristics

"Collections have just a single property, called **`Count`**," I replied, "and three methods, called **`Add`**, **`Item`** and **`Remove`**." I paused and let that settle in. "So, can anyone guess what that **`Count`** property represents?" I asked.

"I'm guessing," Dorothy said, "that since a collection is a group of related items, **`Count`** tells us how many of those items are in the collection. Is that right?"

"Great work, Dorothy," I said, "that's *exactly* what the **`Count`** property tells us."

"The **`Add`** and **`Remove`** methods," Rhonda said, "sound like they are used to add or remove items from the collection."

"You're absolutely right, Rhonda." I replied.

"Well, what about that **`Item`** method?" she prompted.

"The **`Item`** method permits you to refer to an *individual item* in a collection," I said. "We'll see how this works next, as we start dealing with two of the system collections which are built into Visual basic – the **`Controls`** and **`Forms`** collections."

System Collections in more Detail

"I want to start by studying the System Collections because they are already created for us in Visual Basic," I explained to the class. "Furthermore, we don't need to write any code for adding or removing items from these collections – Visual Basic does all that for us. In the last part of today's work, we'll create a collection of our own – learning how to declare it, and how to add and remove items from it."

The Controls Collection

"First, the **`Controls`** collection," I said. I put the following statement up on the screen, to highlight it:

> **The Controls collection is a group of items in which each item represents a control on a form. Each form in your project has its own dedicated Controls collection.**

"When you say that each item represents a control," Kevin asked, "are you saying that the actual control can be found in the collection?"

"No," I replied. "Let me reiterate this, because it's an important point: an item in any collection is merely a memory address that enables our program to find the thing the item points to. There's no sense for the **`Controls`** collection to actually contain a control and all of the properties and code that may be contained within it. Better to simply have the address for the area of memory that stores the control itself:"

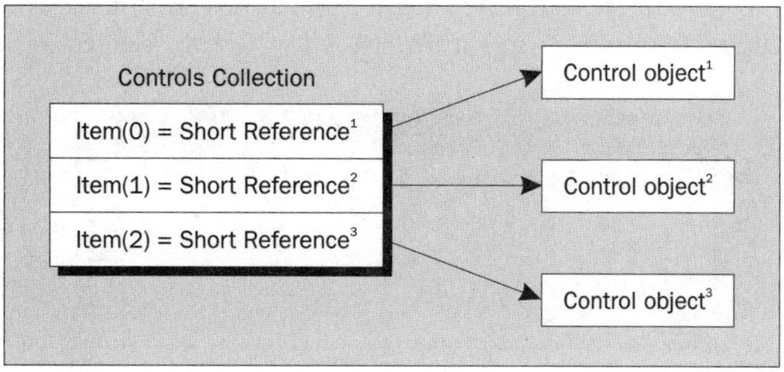

"By *'points to'* do you mean, *'tells the computer exactly where to go to in memory'*?" suggested Kate.

"Exactly," I replied. "The program uses the item reference in the collection to tell it exactly what part of memory to reach into. We call it a **pointer**."

"So a pointer is more memory-efficient, then, I guess?" suggested Linda.

"Yes, a pointer occupies just four bytes – 32-bits – of computer memory," I explained. "And all it contains is the bare minimum of information on where the program can find something more substantial – such as an object."

I waited to see if there were any questions.

"I think this would be a good time to show you a little demonstration," I said.

I started a new Visual Basic **Standard.EXE** project, resized the form and placed an option button, check box, command button and list box on it:

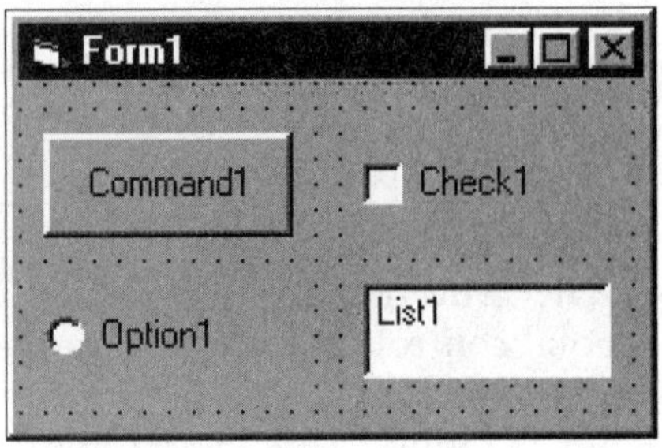

"We've got four controls on the form, as you can see," I said. "Let's run the project, pause it and then use the Immediate window to examine the **Controls** collection."

The Controls Collection's Count Property

I ran the program, paused it by clicking on the break button, (you can't do this in design mode!) and then typed the following statement into the Immediate window:

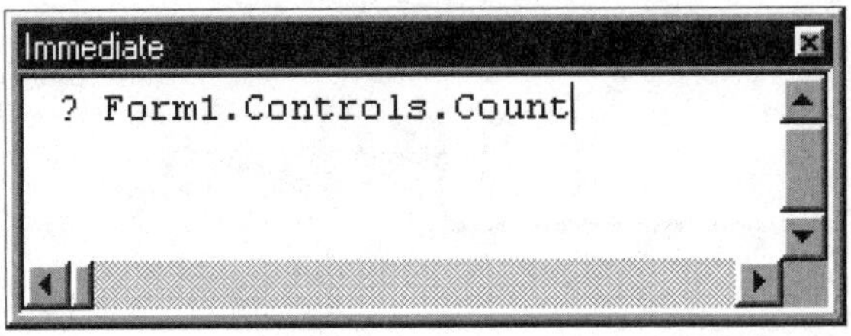

When I hit the *Enter* key, the answer to the question that I was asking Visual Basic – *tell me the value of the Count property for Form1's Controls collection* – was returned in the Immediate window:

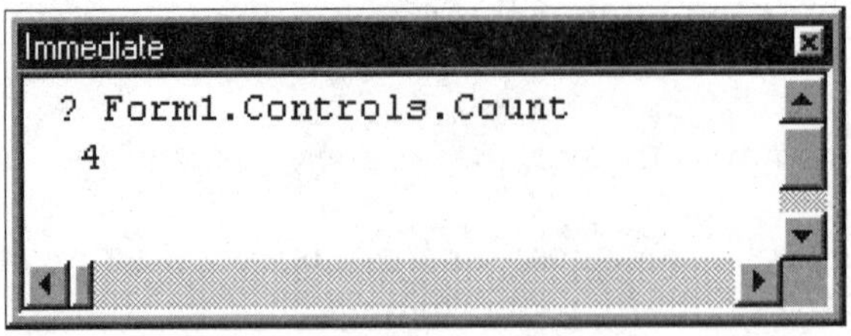

"The **Count** property, as I mentioned earlier, is the one and only property of a collection," I said, "and as you can see, the **Controls** collection for this form contains four items – one each for each control on the form."

"I notice you prefaced the name of the **Controls** collection with **Form1**," observed Ward.

"Yes," I replied. "**Form1** is the name of our one and only form in the project. Each form has its own set of controls, and thus Visual Basic automatically creates a **Controls** collection dedicated to each form."

"Is it really necessary to prefix the **Controls** collection with the name of the form?" Ward asked, "especially as there's only one form in the project?"

"It's good practice to always try and be specific," I said. "Although, you're right in a way. In this case, we *could* have entered this statement into the Immediate window..."

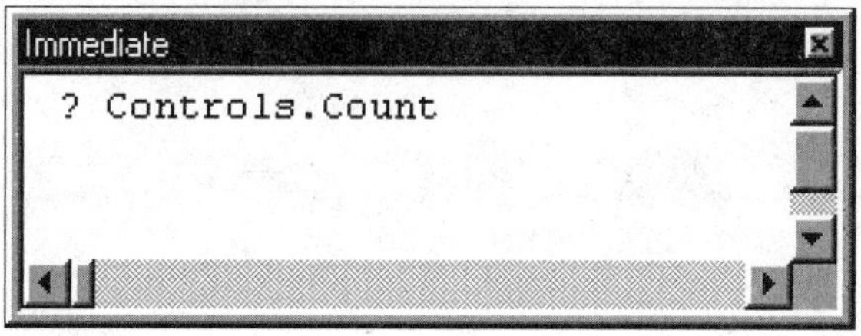

"...and the answer would still have been the same. However, a project with more than one form is a different story. When we're working in the Immediate window with a multiple-form project, Visual Basic will have no way of knowing which form you are referring to unless we specify its name. Unfortunately, however, not specifying a name won't stop VB from 'guessing' and returning a result from one of the forms anyway!"

"What about referring to the **Controls** collection in code?" Steve asked. "Should we be explicit there as well?"

"Yes, we should really – it's a good habit. If you refer to the **Controls** collection in your code without naming the specific form, Visual Basic will again take a guess." I explained. "Here we've only one form to guess from, but a rule of thumb is to always specify the form name. There's really no reason not to be explicit."

"Let's see what the effect of deleting a control from the form is," I went on.

I stopped the program and deleted the list box control from the form:

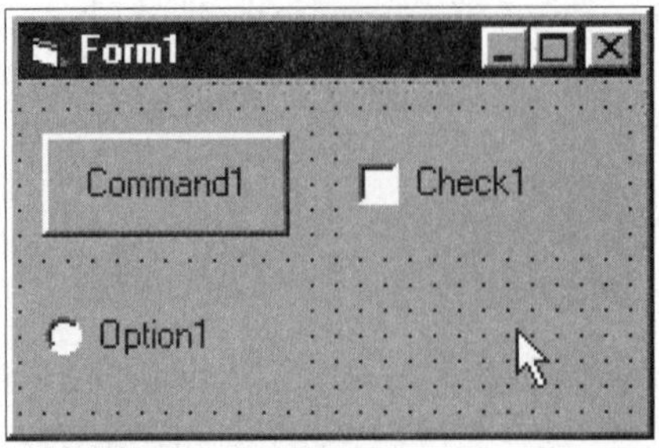

I then re-ran the program, paused it, and typed the following statement into the Immediate window: **`? Form1.Controls.Count`** – before hitting the *Enter* key:

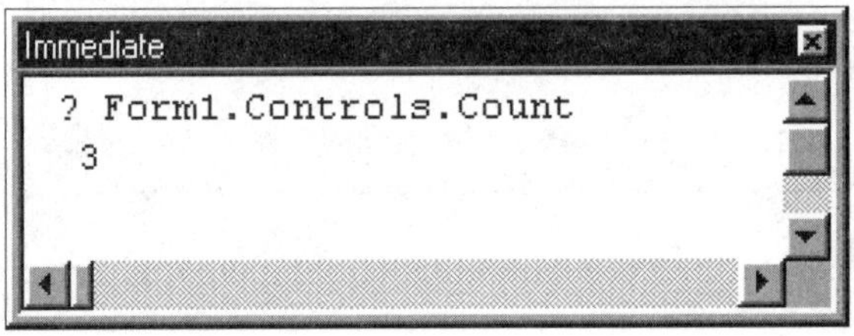

"Notice that the **`Count`** property of the **`Controls`** collection now reads three," I said, "we're down to just three controls on the form, and Visual Basic is keeping track of that for us in the **`Controls`** collection, which now has three items in it that reference our controls."

"That's cool," said Ward.

"Yes, that's impressive," said Rhonda, "but I have a question. I can see that it could be useful to be able to find out in code how many controls there are on a form, but can we learn anything more about the controls by interrogating the **`Controls`** collection?"

"I was wondering about that, too," said Mary. "For example, is there any way to know what each item in the collection represents? Like, could we find out which control is represented by item number one in the collection?"

"Yes, we can," I answered. "Let me show you how to do that."

Properties of individual Items in the Controls Collection

"OK," I continued, "each item in a collection has an item number – much like the subscript number of the control array elements we saw earlier when I showed you the two check boxes' Property windows side by side. The two system collections we'll look at today – the **`Controls`** and **`Forms`** collections – are **zero-based** – which means that the first item in the collection is item number **zero**. Getting back to your question, Mary, we can see the control that a particular item in the **`Controls`** collection represents by typing this statement in the Immediate window..."

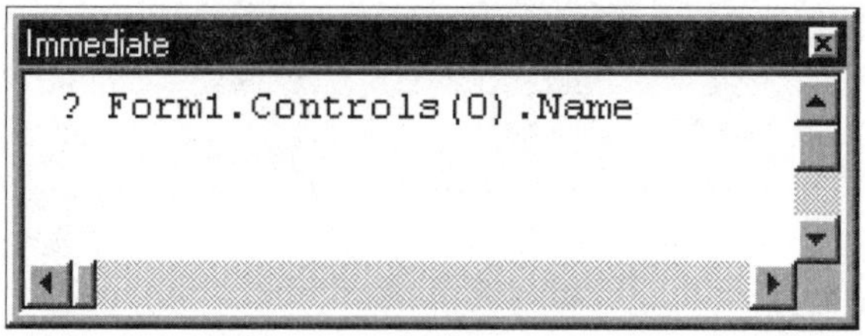

"...and then hitting the *Enter* key:"

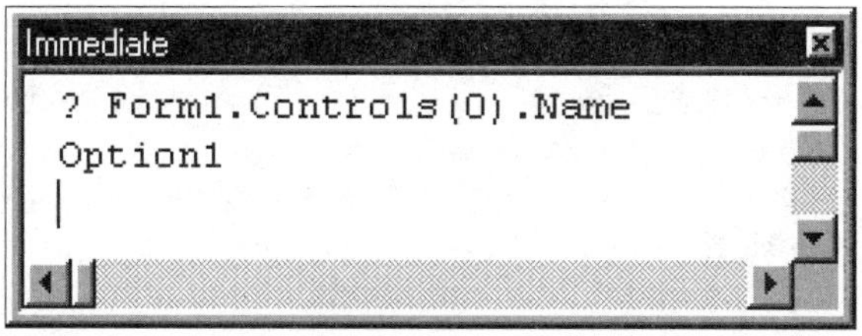

"If you read the statement I typed from right to left," I went on, "you can see that I've asked Visual Basic to tell me: the value of the **`Name`** property of the first item (item 0, remember) in the **`Controls`** collection that's dedicated to **`Form1`**. And, as you can see, Visual Basic tells me that the name of the control referenced by item **`(0)`** is **`Option1`**."

"Why do we need the full stop before **`Name`**?" Rhonda asked.

"Because the current value of the **`Name`** property for item 0 is the one we want to inspect," I explained. "Remember, the item doesn't store the actual object itself, just a reference to the place in memory where the object can be found. The statement on the screen above tells the program to go to the memory address of the first member of the **`Controls`** collection of **`Form1`** and read-off its **`Name`** property. Using the dots like this is called **dot notation**. Dot notation lets us refer to objects and their properties – in this case, we've used the dots, plus the object, item, and property names to tell VB what it is we're interested in finding out. We'll be talking about dot notation in more detail in next week's lesson."

"What would happen if you hadn't typed **Name**?" Steve asked. "What if you'd just referenced item zero of the **Controls** collection without specifying a property?"

"Visual Basic would have displayed the value of the **default property** of the control represented by **Controls(0)** – each control has a default property that Visual Basic will look at if we don't specify one."

To demonstrate this, I entered the following statement into the Immediate window and pressed the *Enter* key:

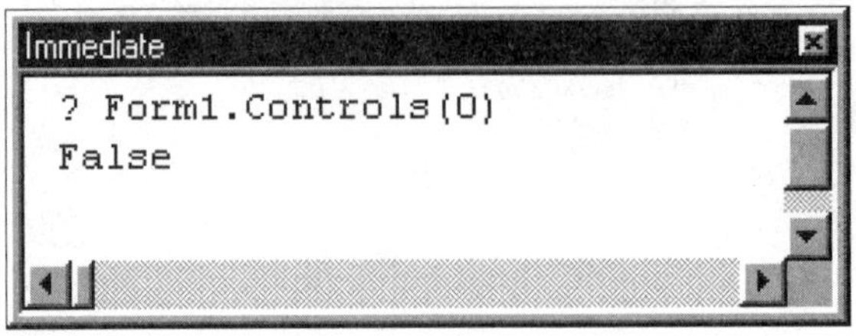

"**False**?" Kate said, looking at the answer that Visual Basic had returned. "What's that telling us?"

"The control represented by the item **Controls(0)** is the option button," I replied, "and the default property of this control is **Value** – that's the one selected if none other is specified. So, VB is telling us the current value of the **Value** property – which is **False**, indicating that the option button hasn't been clicked-on to select it. The key thing to remember here is that each control has a default property which is the one which Visual Basic will assume you are referring to if nothing else is specified. In the case of the option button, the default value is the **Value** property. For the text box control, it's the **Text** property."

"OK," said Bob, "let me ask a question about another aspect of this. Could we also ask Visual Basic to tell us the **Top** property of the second item in the collection?"

"The **Top** property?" asked Rhonda.

"Let me explain that," I said. "The **Top** property stores a value describing where the of the top of the control is located on the form. And in answer to Bob's question, yes, we can do that easily. Take a look at this..."

Returning to the Immediate window, I typed in and entered the following statement:

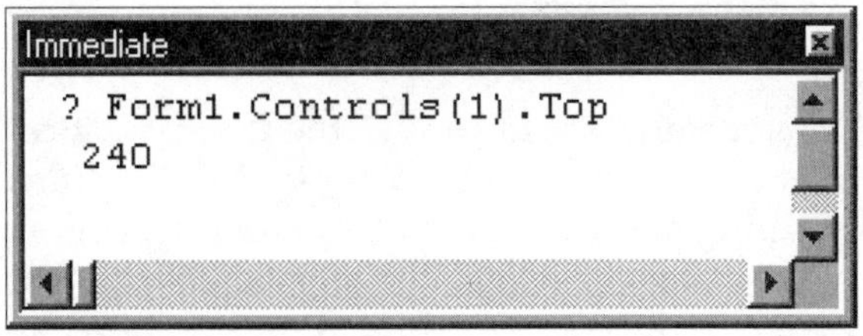

"Item one is the second item in the **Controls** collection, remember," I said. "All we needed to do was reference the item number, followed by a dot, followed by the name of the property whose value we wanted to know. This is a principle that we can apply widely in our use of objects, and it's part of the reason why dot notation and objects are so powerful. And there's more – in addition to *retrieving* our control objects property values this way, it's also possible to *change* them via the **Controls** collection. For instance, look at this..."

This time, I typed three statements into the Immediate window, hitting the *Enter* key at the end of each statement:

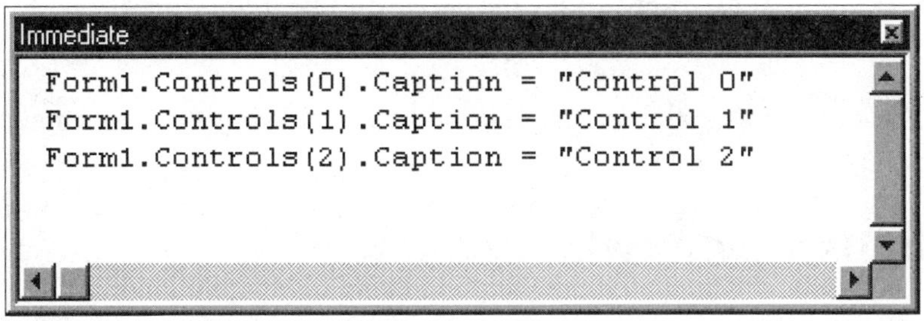

As I entered each statement in turn and hit return, the caption of each control was changed to the name that I'd specified in the statement's quotation marks. Finally, all three captions had been altered via the **Controls** collection:

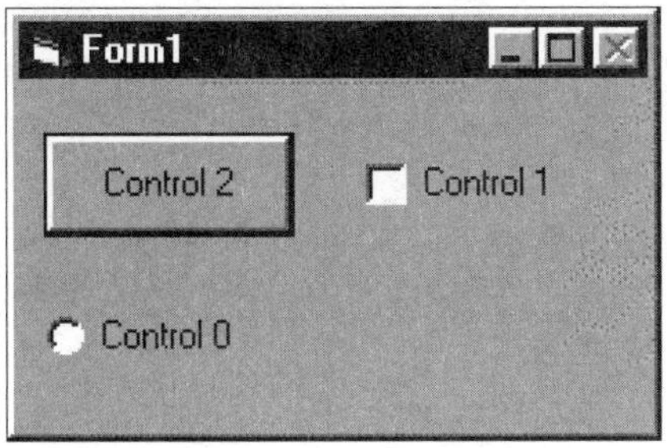

"Can you see what we've done?" I asked, turning to the class. "By interacting with the **Controls** collection I was able to change the **Caption** property of each one of the controls on the form."

"I was just wondering," Peter said, "could we use the **Controls** collection to change the **BackColor** property of each control on the main form of the China Shop project? Something that's been nagging at me about the China Shop program is the fact that when the user changes the color settings to set their preferred color, only the **BackColor** property of the form changes – the controls' appearance remains unchanged."

"Yes, we could do that," I agreed. "In fact, we could do it using a **For...Each** loop with the **Controls** collection, as I mentioned earlier. However, in practice, if you make every control the same color as the form, you could end up with a confusing and distracting color scheme. We won't be implementing this kind of modification here, but maybe it's one you could try on your own version of the project when we've learned some more about how to work with collections?"

Peter nodded – "Yes, maybe I will try that later on. Thanks."

"But, going back to the main point," Dave said, "with just a few lines of code we *could* have chosen to change the **BackColor** property of every control on the China Shop form?"

"That's right," I said. "Let me demonstrate how we can use the **For...Each** statement with a new project."

Preparing to Use Loops with Collections

"OK," I said, "now we're going to take a look at using a **For...Each** loop structure to manipulate all the controls referenced in the **Controls** collection. To do that, I need a simple demonstration project..."

I started a new Visual Basic project and added the following cosmopolitan selection of controls to the default form:

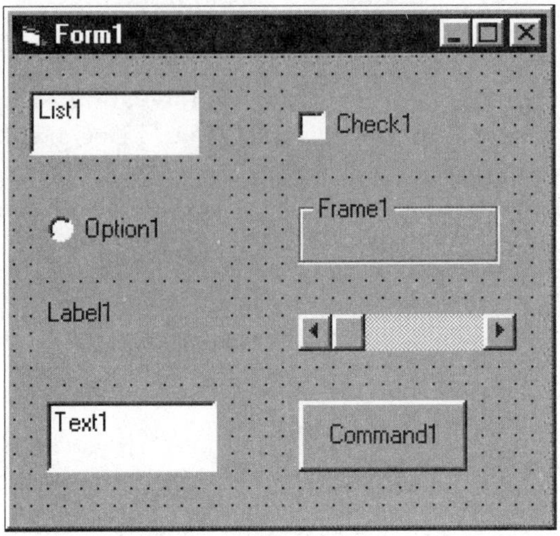

"All right," I said, "there's our example project."

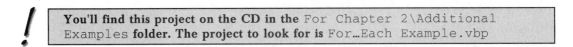

> **!** **You'll find this project on the CD in the** `For Chapter 2\Additional Examples` **folder. The project to look for is** `For…Each Example.vbp`

"As I mentioned earlier," I continued, "one of the great things about collections is the ability to loop through each item they contain, using a **`For…Each`** loop structure. However, in order to do so, we must first declare something called an **object variable**. Declaring the object variable gives our loop structure something to work with – I'll explain this in detail shortly when we code up our loop. First, let's talk about object variables themselves for a moment. "

Object Variables

"I think everyone here is comfortable with the notion that a standard variable contains a value of some kind. However, **object variables** are different. In a way, they're similar to items in a collection: an object variable doesn't actually contain an actual control, but rather a reference that points to the control. In a **`For…Each`** loop, we use the object variable's reference to 'point' to an item in a collection. So the object variable is needed to allow our loop to work with the items stored in a collection."

I noticed some slightly bemused looks, so...

"Let me make this by clearer by walking you through the process," I said. "Take a look at this..."

I double clicked on the form to open the Code window, and began to type the declaration statement for a variable called **Smiley** into the General Declarations section of the form. As soon as I finished typing the space after the word 'as' in the declaration, I paused so the class could see what happened:

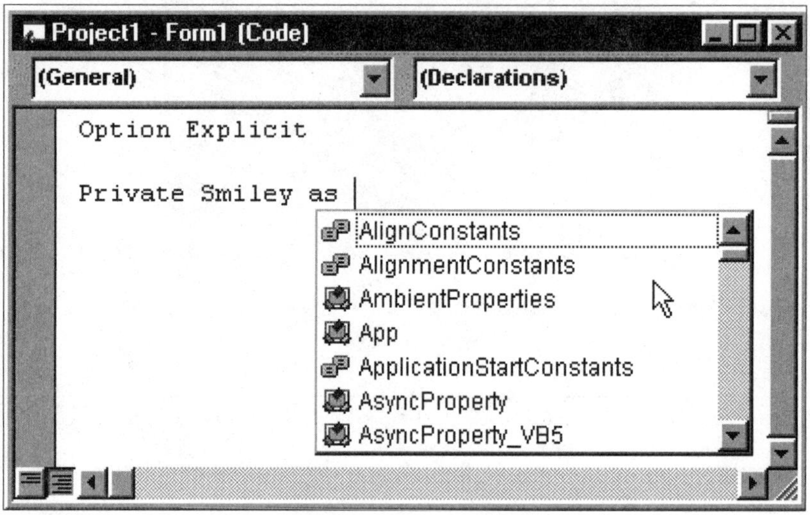

"I don't know whether you've ever noticed," I continued, "but as soon as you type the space after the word 'as' in a variable declaration, a window opens to display the valid declaration entries we can use. As you can see, there are a bunch of variable types available to us besides the common **Integer**, **String**, **Single** and **Double** data types that we learned about last semester."

> **!** **If you don't see this list of valid entries drop down when you type 'as' and press the space bar, go to Tools on the VB menu bar, select Options and, on the Editor tab, select the Autolist Members checkbox.**

"I've often wondered what those are," Rhonda said.

"These are all valid variable types," I said. "Some of them are beyond the scope of this course, but if we scroll through the list, you'll see that there are some interesting variable types that you may not have known existed. For instance..."

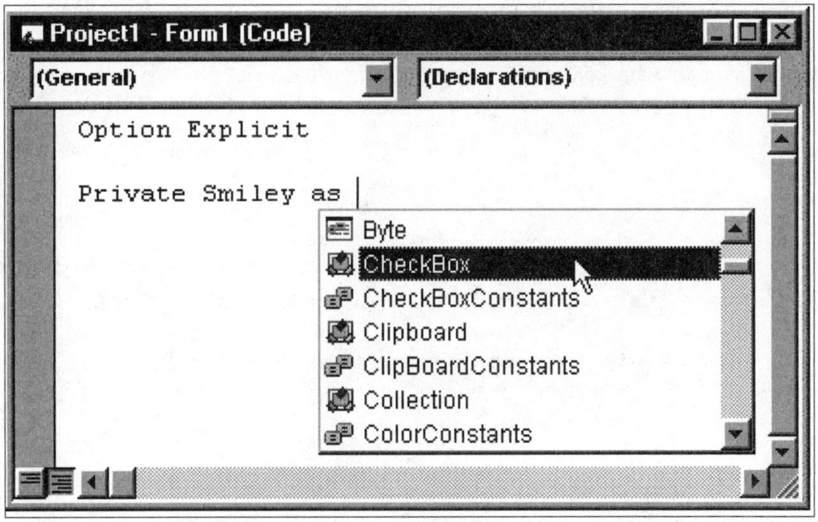

"CheckBox!" Rhonda exclaimed. "That's a variable type?"

"Yes, it is," I said. "It's surprising, I know, but just as it's possible to declare a variable of type `Integer`, it's also possible to declare a variable of type `CheckBox` – and as you might have guessed, this is an object variable that's specifically designed to point to a check box control."

I waited to see if I had lost anybody – I could certainly see they all were concentrating hard, but there were no obvious signs of distress as yet.

"I notice," Linda said, "that the symbol next to `CheckBox` is different from the symbol for the other data types we learned about last semester."

"That's correct," I affirmed. "If you take a close look..."

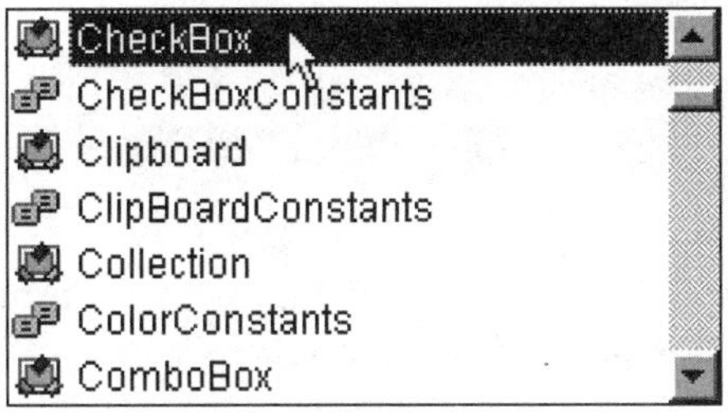

"You can see that there's a little box symbol, with red, yellow and blue flashes at the edge. This symbol indicates that the variable we're working with is actually an **object variable**. If we chose to declare our `Smiley` object variable as a `CheckBox` type object variable, we'd be indicating to our program that when we referenced this variable, it would ultimately be pointing to a check box object on our form."

"So is that what we'll choose to do here?" asked Lou.

"No, we need to choose a different object variable type when we declare the `Smiley` variable here. Let me explain why. First, take another look at our form:"

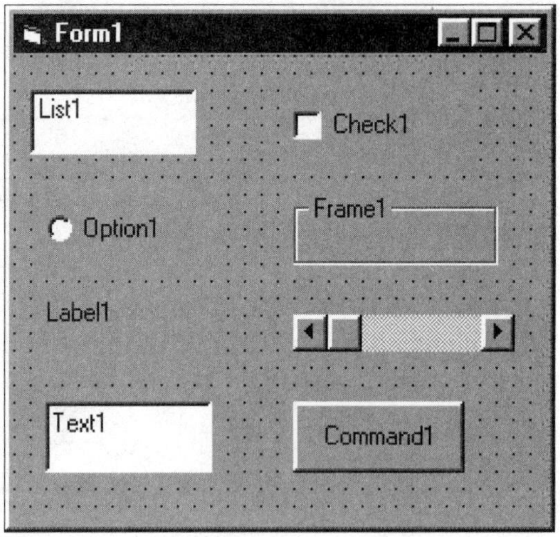

"Now," I asked the class, "are all of the controls on the form the same *type* of object?"

There was a moment of silence, then Rhonda said: "No, they're different types – we've got a text box, a command button, a list box – in fact, we've got a whole load of different types. Why does that matter here?"

"Think about this: if we declare an object variable for our loop to use, the program has to be sure that the variable we declare matches the type of object that the code will ultimately be manipulating in the loop. So..."

"If we declared the `Smiley` object variable as a `CheckBox` type, it wouldn't match the other types of controls that the Controls collection knows about?" hazarded Dave.

"That's spot on," I said. "Remember, the loop will use the object variable we declare to interact with the `Controls` collection and, ultimately, with the controls on the form that the collection holds references to. This means that the **Smiley** object variable needs to be able to able to reflect all of the different control types that we've got on our form."

I paused for a moment, letting this sink in, then continued:

"So, what we need is an object variable type that will let us encompass all of the control types on our from."

"How the heck do we do that?" said Rhonda, sounding exasperated.

"Bear with me," I replied. "Fortunately, there's an object variable type that lets us be less specific about the type of objects that the program is going to work with. We can choose to declare our **`Smiley`** variable as a **`Control`** type, rather than as a **`CheckBox`**. Look:"

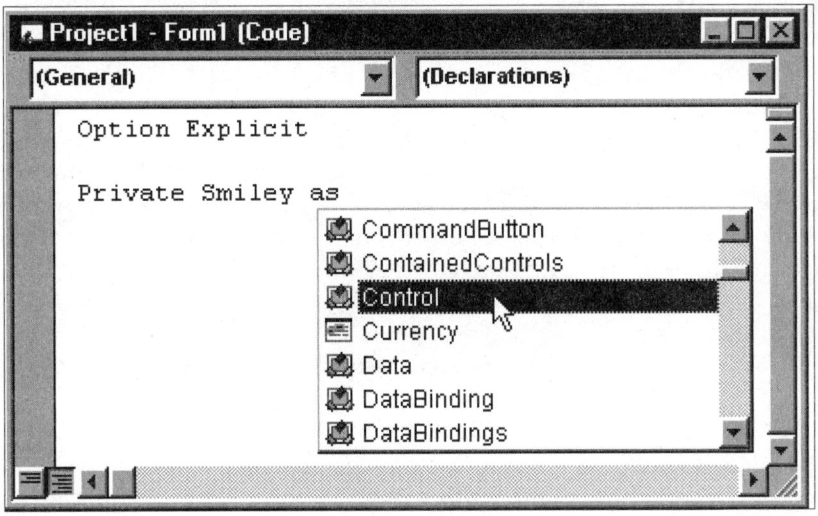

"The **`Control`** object variable type is more generic, and it can be used to point to, or reference, any kind of control. Declaring the **Smiley** variable as type **`Control`**," I continued, "allows our **`For...Each`** loop to work with any kind of control that's found in the **`Controls`** collection."

I then went on. "There's an *even more* generic data type called **`Object`**..."

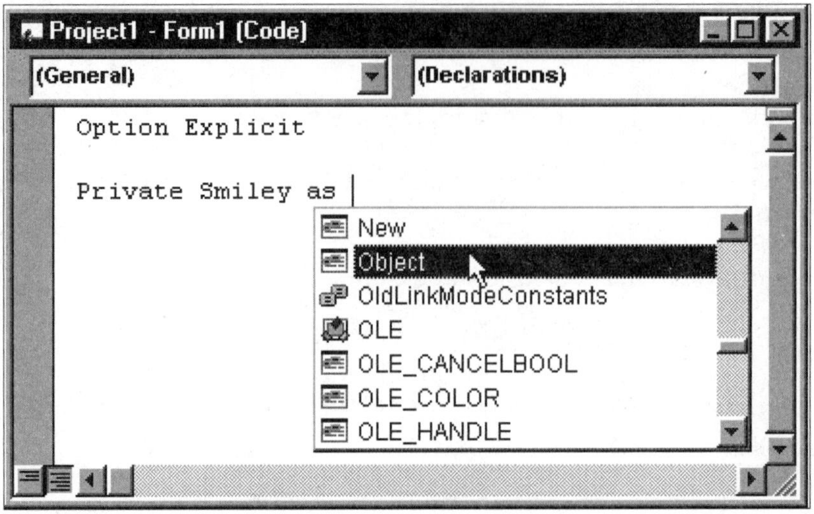

"Unlike the **`Checkbox`** variable," I said, "which can only be used to point to a check box, and the **`Control`** variable, which can only be used to point to any type of control object, the **`Object`** variable can be used to point to any kind of object at all. Remember, in this example we're just working with standard control objects. In real-world programs you'll have other types of built-in Visual Basic objects to work with, as well as the objects that you create specifically for your program – like the objects we'll be creating for the China Shop in a few weeks."

"Is there a rule about using one type of object variable instead of another?" Kathy asked.

"You should declare the **`Object`** variable **as specifically as possible**," I said. "For instance, if you know that the variable you are declaring will be used to point to – or reference – only a command button, declare it as a **`CommandButton`** variable type. If you know the variable will reference every control on a form, as it will if you are using a **`For...Each`** statement to loop through the items in the **`Controls`** collection, then you should declare the variable as the type **`Control`**. If you know it will reference not only controls but the forms in your application, you should declare the variable as an **`Object`** type."

"Is there anything more generic than the **`Object`** type?" Dave asked.

"Yes there is, Dave," I said. "If you choose, you can also declare the variable as a **`Variant`** – a **`Variant`** data type will accept anything."

Then Chuck asked a question: "Professor, does it really matter which type of object variable you declare? If all the potential objects in our program can be covered by always using the `Object` type in the declaration, why bother using anything else?"

"That really is a good question, Chuck," I acknowledged. "The main answer is that your decision about which object variable type to declare can influence the speed and efficiency of your program. This issue is related to an internal Visual Basic process called **binding**."

"Binding?" said a number of voices, almost in unison.

Binding

"That's right," I chuckled. "Essentially, binding is the process that lets Visual Basic finalize all the things that it needs to do and talk to when the program runs. If you like, it's VB's way of fully resolving all of your code and deciding on all of the objects, variables, and system resources that it needs to define for your program to work properly. The choices we make about the types of object variables we use partially determines how efficiently Visual Basic can resolve our code, and how it can best connect to the objects that we want it to use."

"Could you expand on that a little, please?" said Dave, "I don't understand why the object variable types make a difference to the way that Visual Basic works these things out."

"Sure," I told him. "As I suggested, binding is really about Visual Basic determining how and when to connect to our objects so that our program can function. There are two different types of binding, **early** and **late**. Which of these types occurs will depend on how we declare our object variables."

Early and Late Binding

"The binding process," I went on, "relates to how quickly Visual Basic is able to determine the actual type of object your variable is pointing to. For instance, if you declare an object variable as a `CheckBox` type, Visual Basic knows immediately – even before your program begins to run – that this variable will be pointing to an actual check box control that exists on a form somewhere. That's **early binding** – the fact that we'll be using a check box is made explicit to VB early on. If on the other hand, you declare an object variable as the more generic `Object` data type, Visual Basic will not know until run time which object the variable will actually point to. That's **late binding** – when we leave it vague exactly which type of object we'll be using when the program runs."

"Is early binding good?" Rhonda asked.

"Yes, it is," I replied. "The earlier that Visual Basic is able to finalize exactly which objects it will be using, the faster your program will execute. An analogy I use for early binding is this: you invite a couple of guests to your house for dinner. Dinner is on Saturday night, and on the preceding Tuesday, you ask them what they'd like to eat. Once you find out, you purchase the ingredients, and begin to cook dinner on Saturday afternoon – that way, when your guests arrive at your house Saturday evening, you can seat them immediately, and start serving dinner. That's early binding."

"What about late binding, then?" Peter said, "would that be like having yours guests arrive at your house Saturday night, and you having no idea what food they liked until they actually turned up on your doorstep? And while they're in your living room, you have to run down to the corner grocery store to buy ingredients, bring them home, pop them in the oven, and actually begin dining several hours later?"

"You hit the nail on the head Peter," I said. "That's not really the most efficient way to go about hosting a successful dinner, is it?"

"So the rule of thumb then," Dave said, "is always to bind early?"

"Yes, in general." I agreed. "However, there may be occasions when you have no choice but to declare your object variable generically and employ late binding. For instance, you might declare an object variable to point to both a control *and* a form. Just remember – there's early binding, and then various grades of late binding. The best approach is to pick the object variable type as close as possible to the actual object you'll be referring to, and you'll be doing fine."

I waited for a second or two, and then decided to get us back on track after our slight detour: "OK, folks, we started this discussion because we were going to use a `For...Each` structure to loop through the items in the `Controls` collection. Having established that declaring the right kind of object variable is significant, let's get back to our example project and look in detail at how we can work with collections – and the items that they reference – using code."

Working with System Collections in Code

"Let's resume our coverage of how to work with collections programmatically by returning to our example project..."

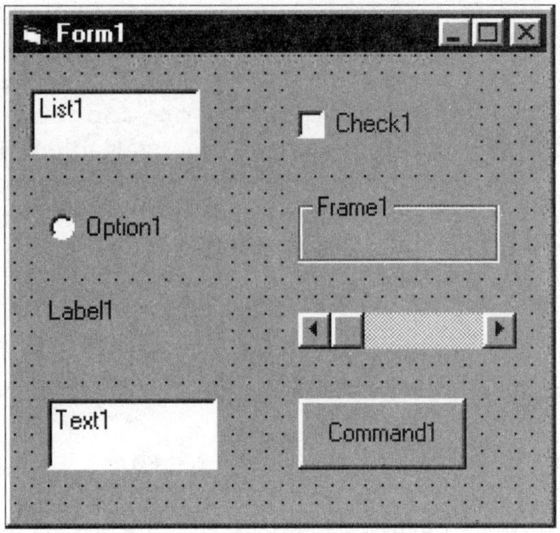

"...and looking in detail at how we can work with the controls on the form using the form's **`Controls`** collection, and a **`For...Each`** loop structure."

The For...Each Statement

"It's high time," I said, "that I showed you how to loop through the items of a collection using the **`For...Each`** statement. What we're doing here," I went on, "is using the **`For...Each`** statement to loop through each item of the **`Controls`** collection. In other words, this loop is going to use the references found in the **`Controls`** collection to 'look up' every actual control object that's on the form. In the code in the body of the loop, we're going to change the **`Caption`** properties so that the controls are captioned Control1, Control2, and so on. Take a look at this code..."

I then typed the following highlighted lines into the **`Click`** event procedure of the example project's command button:

```
Private Sub Command1_Click()

 Dim objControl As Control
 Dim intCounter As Integer
```

```
For Each objControl In Form1.Controls
   objControl.Caption = "Control" & intCounter
   intCounter = intCounter + 1
Next
```

```
End Sub
```

"Here's how the code works," I started to explain. "Prior to the execution of the **For...Each** statement, we first declare an object variable called **objControl**: this is an object variable of type **Control**. If you remember, this type of object variable will be able to work with any of the controls that we placed on the form. We need to declare the object variable so that our loop has a variable to work on. Here's the declaration of the object variable itself:"

```
Dim objControl As Control
```

"Once this object variable is declared, we can feed the variable into the **For...Each** loop. We'll see exactly how the **For...Each** statement uses the object variable in a moment."

"Is this an example of late or early binding?" Peter asked.

"It's actually a mixture of *both*," I said. "Declaring the object variable as **Control** is not as specific as something like **CheckBox** or **CommandButton** would be, but it's better than using the more generic **Object** or the extremely general **Variant**. In this example project, it can't really be helped – we have a mixture of control types that we want to modify as we loop through them. If we had declared the object variable as a specific type of object – say a **Checkbox** type – then as soon as the **For...Each** statement encountered an item of a **CommandButton** type in the **Controls** collection, our program would have bombed."

"So," Valerie said, "in choosing the **Control** object variable type, we've really chosen the lowest common denominator," "

"That's a good way of putting it," I said. "If you're declaring an object variable to loop through the **Controls** collection, you can't go wrong in declaring it as a **Control** type – after all, each item in the **Controls** collection will always reference an actual control."

"I suppose," Bob interjected, "that we *could* have declared the object variable as type **Object**? But I suppose that would be even 'later' binding, if there is such a thing?"

"We could have done that," I said, "and that code would have worked fine – but ultimately, it would make the program run slower than it does if we use the more specific **Control** object variable type declaration."

The students seemed fine with that, so I continued.

"Let's take a look at the rest of the code now," I said. "The second line of code is the declaration of an **`Integer`** variable called **`intCounter`**, which we'll use to generate a number that will give each control a unique **`Caption`** property:"

```
Dim intCounter As Integer
```

"The rest of the code," I continued, "shows us the magic of the **`For...Each`** statement. With just a few lines of code we're able to change the **`Caption`** property of every control on the form: each and every control will have a reference stored as an item in the **`Controls`** collection. This next line of code sets the ball rolling:"

```
For Each objControl In Form1.Controls
```

"This is a really important line of code, and a lot happens in the background when Visual Basic runs it. The first thing it does is set up the loop with a **`For...Each`** statement. Next comes the name of the object variable – **`objControl`** – that we've declared for the **`For...Each`** statement to use as it goes about its looping business. The next part of the line – **`In Form1.Controls`** – effectively tells Visual Basic to look in **`Form1`**'s **`Controls`** collection and see how many items are in it. Visual Basic will then assign the first item's reference to the **`objControl`** object variable. Essentially, when the loop starts, the **`objControl`** variable gets populated with the first item reference – **`Item(0)`** – in the **`Controls`** collection. This points the loop to the actual control object referenced by the first item in the **`Controls`** collection."

I saw the signs of dawning recognition on several faces as the link between the object variable and the control objects fell into place. I continued with my explanation of the code.

"Now that our object variable **`objControl`** is pointing to an actual control on the form, this next line of code is used to change the **`Caption`** property of that control, using the string **`"Control "`** concatenated with the current value of the **`intCounter`** variable:"

```
   objControl.Caption = "Control " & intCounter
```

"Having changed the **`Caption`** property of the first item in the Controls collection, we increment the value of our counter variable:"

```
   intCounter = intCounter + 1
```

"And finally, this line of code tells Visual Basic to continue the process until it has looped through each item in the `Controls` collection:"

```
Next
```

"After the first time through the loop, the loop will move on to the second item in the `Controls` collection, and then on to the third, and so on."

"That is impressive," Ward said, "I can see a lot of use for this. I can't wait to see this run."

"Let's do that," I said, "but I must warn you, there's going to be a slight problem with the code..."

I ran the program, clicked on the command button, with this result:

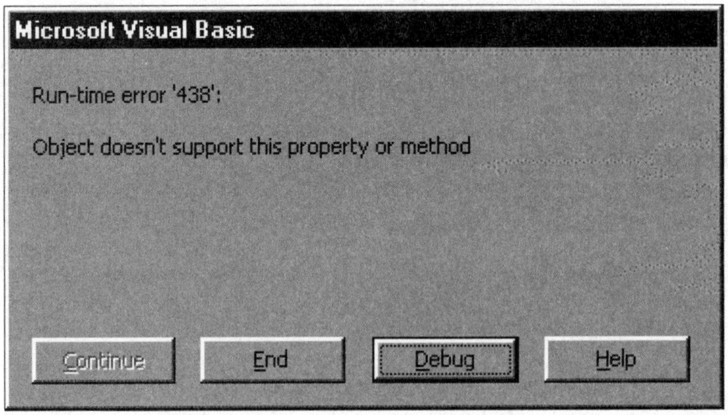

"Uh-oh," I heard Kevin say. "Something *is* wrong. I take it that this is the problem you said we would have with the code?"

"I'm afraid so," I said, and clicked on the Debug button. The following screenshot appeared:

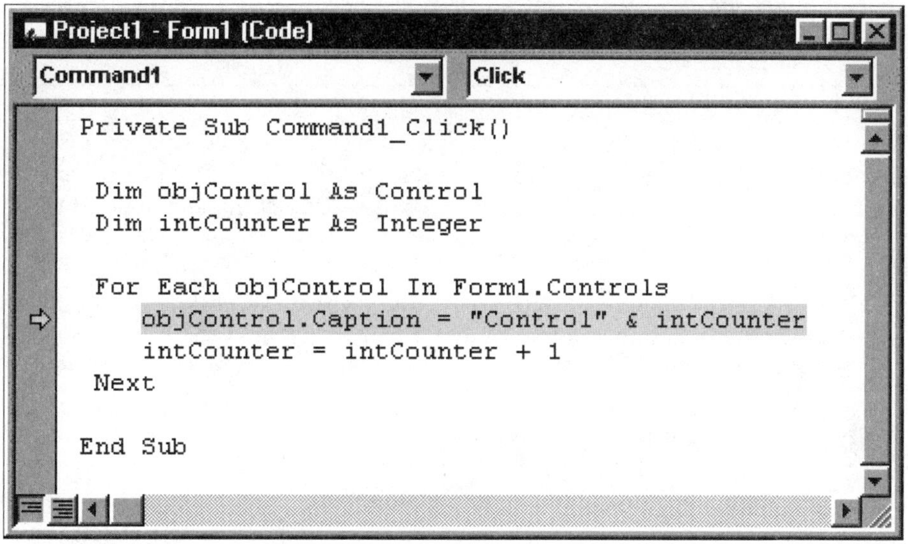

"There must be something wrong with this line of code" Rhonda said, "but off hand, I don't see any problems."

"It's not so much the line of code itself," I said. "Rather, the problem lies with the object that we're trying to execute the code against. Let me ask you this question: does every control on the form have a **`Caption`** property?"

While the class pondered that question, I brought up the Immediate window, typed the following statement into it, and hit return:

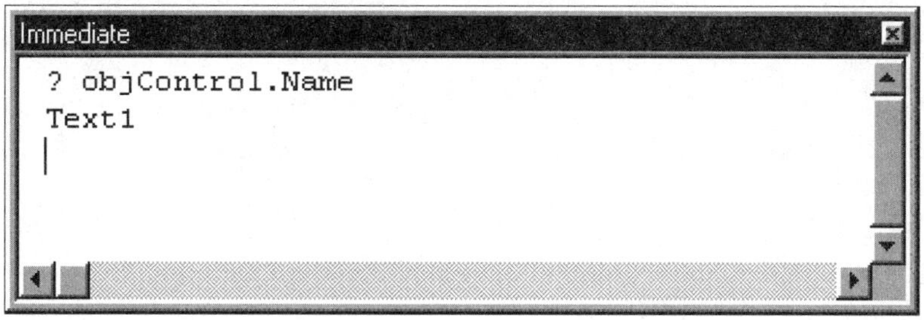

"Remember," I said, "as I clicked on the Debug button after the program bombed, our program is now paused. That means that we can use the Immediate window to determine the name of the control that we are currently working on within the **`For...Each`** loop. As you can see, it's the **`Text1`** text box control. Does this give anyone a clue as to why the program bombed?"

> **!** **Depending on the order that you put the controls on your form, your own version of this example program may come to a halt on a control other than the text box.**

"I think I know," Dave said. "The text box control doesn't have a **Caption** property, and when we tried to change that non-existent property within the body of the **For...Each** loop, the program fell over. That's what the error message – Object doesn't support this property or method – is telling us."

"Excellent, Dave," I said. "When you work with the **Controls** collection, you have to be careful about those magical operations you can perform against the object variable within the body of the **For...Each** loop. In this case, when the loop started to work with the item in collection representing the **Text1** control, the object variable **objControl** referenced the **Text1** text box control, and this line of code..."

```
objControl.Caption = "Control " & intCounter
```

"...attempted to change the **Caption** property of the text box – a property that doesn't exist! Hence the error message. The same thing would have happened if we'd tried to change the caption of a timer control, picture box, or any of the other controls that don't possess a **Caption** property."

"Is there anything we can do about this?" Mary asked. "I don't see much sense in using the **For...Each** statement if the program is going to crash or if we need to restrict what we do within the loop."

"Not to worry, Mary" I reassured her. "There are a number of things we can do to get around this problem. For instance, Visual Basic has a **TypeOf** operator that can be used to determine the type of control represented by the object variable. Look at this..."

I then added a couple of lines of code to the **Click** event procedure of the command button so that it looked like this next snippet (as ever, changed lines are highlighted)...

```
Private Sub Command1_Click()

 Dim objControl As Control
 Dim intCounter As Integer

 For Each objControl In Form1.Controls
    If TypeOf objControl Is CommandButton Then
    objControl.Caption = "Control " & intCounter
```

```
        intCounter = intCounter + 1
    End If
Next

End Sub
```

"What this will do," I explained, "is use the **TypeOf** operator to determine if the type of control represented by our object variable is a command button – and if it *is*, we'll change its caption."

I reran the program and clicked on the command button...

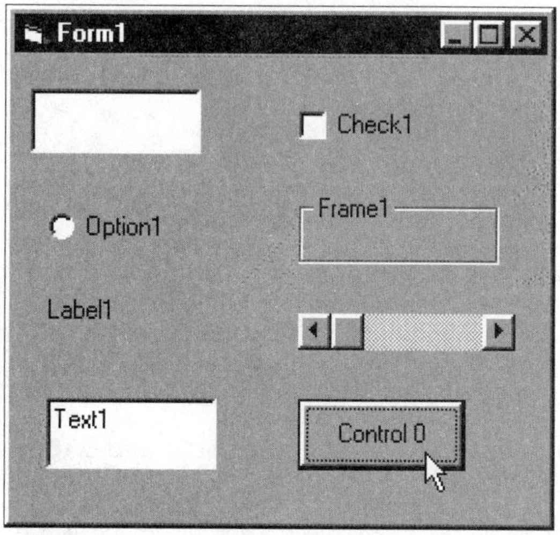

"Well," I said, "that's an improvement – the program didn't bomb this time – unfortunately, the only control whose **Caption** property we changed was the command button."

"I suppose," Valerie said, "that we could modify the code to use the **TypeOf** operator to check for other controls that support the **Caption** property, such as the check box, option button, label and frame...?"

"Yes, we can do that," I said, "it's a little bit tedious, but it *will* work."

I changed the code to look like this:

```
Private Sub Command1_Click()
```

```
Dim objControl As Control
Dim intCounter As Integer

For Each objControl In Form1.Controls
  If TypeOf objControl Is CommandButton Or
    ↳TypeOf objControl Is CheckBox Or
    ↳TypeOf objControl Is OptionButton Or
    ↳TypeOf objControl Is Label Or
    ↳TypeOf objControl Is Frame Then
        objControl.Caption = "Control " & intCounter
        intCounter = intCounter + 1
  End If
Next

End Sub
```

> Remember that where you see the ↳ character, this indicates that this line of code is a continuation of the previous line. You should either type the lines on a single line, *without* the ↳ character, or use the VB continuation character (a space and an underscore) to spread the code across multiple lines. The ↳ character is only used to make the code easier to read on the page – don't try and include it in your code!

… and then ran the program and clicked on the command button once more:

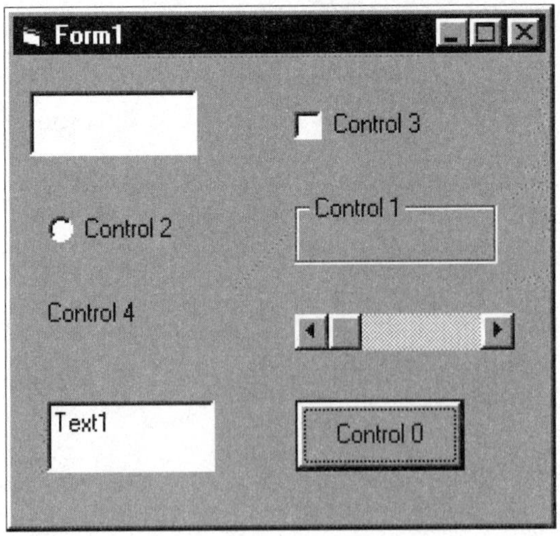

"That's even better," I said. "Once again, the program didn't crash, and now every control that possesses a **Caption** property has had its caption changed."

"Is there any rhyme or reason," Lou said, "to the order in which items are found in the **Controls** collection?"

"Microsoft cautions you not to read anything into the order of the items in the **Controls** collection." I replied. "Even adding a new control to the form can 'reshuffle' whatever the current arrangement of items is in the collection. The only thing you can be certain of is that every control on the form is represented by an item in the **Controls** collection."

"It's very tedious, though, this code, isn't it?" Ward said, "It requires that we use the **TypeOf** operator for every different type of control item. It seems you'd need a pretty good awareness of all of the controls in the Visual Basic environment, and of the properties they each have. Surely there's a better way than that?"

"There is," I said. "Let's think about this and see if you can work out what it is. Now, we received an error message when we first tried to change the non-existent **Caption** property of the text box. Think back to our Intro class: is there anything we learned there that might be useful as a way of *reacting* to that error message – rather than avoiding it, as we did here?"

"I think I know!" Linda said. "Error handling! Can't we 'trap' the error that is generated when we refer to a property that doesn't exist? What was the error we got again...?" – she checked her notes – "...error number 438?"

"Absolutely right, Linda!" I said, starting to modify the code once more.

Handling Errors

"We need to delete the **If...Then** loop and the **EndIf** statement from the example project..." – I did just that – "...and then add these highlighted lines to the code:"

```
Private Sub Command1_Click()

On Error Goto ICanHandleThis

 Dim objControl As Control
 Dim intCounter As Integer

 For Each objControl In Form1.Controls
    objControl.Caption = "Control " & intCounter
    intCounter = intCounter + 1
```

```
 Next

Exit Sub

IcanHandleThis:

Select Case Err.Number
      Case 438
            Resume Next
      Case Else
            MsgBox "Unanticipated Error Encountered"
      End Select

End Sub
```

"Note the use of the error handler," I said. "Everyone from the Intro class should be familiar with the use of an error handler. An error handler is simply a piece of code that we write to 'handle' errors that we know *could* occur when the program runs. We make our programs more robust, and less likely to fall in a heap at the user's feet, by anticipating errors and building error handlers that can deal with them. Here, we're creating an error handler called **IcanHandleThis** that's invoked if an error occurs. This line of code breaks out of the program's normal sequence and calls the error handler if Visual Basic detects an error..."

```
On Error Goto ICanHandleThis
```

"...and in the body of the error handler – which is defined at the bottom of the code listing – we use a **Select Case** statement to evaluate the number of the error that's been generated. If the error is the **438** error we've anticipated, we execute the **Resume Next** statement, which tells Visual Basic to go back to executing the next iteration of the **For...Each** loop, bypassing the control that generated the error. Incidentally, Visual Basic retrieves the actual error number from another built-in system object – the **Err** object, which is automatically created when an error occurs. In this line..."

```
Select Case Err.Number
```

"...we're telling the **Select Case** statement to work with the **Number** property of the **Err** object. That's where our program goes to look to find out the number of the error that we need to handle."

I then ran the program, clicked on the command button, and the following screen shot was displayed:

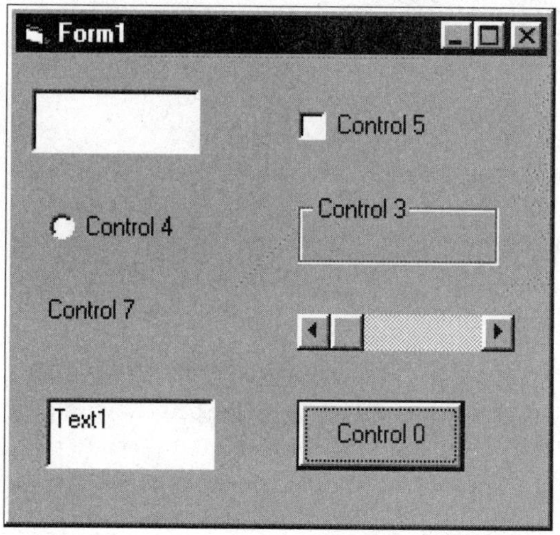

"That's great," Ward said. "Now I really am starting to see the benefits of the `Controls` collection. One thing, though – the `Captions` of the controls are showing different numbers from the last time we ran the code, aren't they?"

"Well spotted! That's because the number in the caption now properly reflects the control's actual location in the `Controls` collection," I explained. "When our previous versions of this code ran, they didn't increment the `intCounter` value if a control didn't support the `Caption` property. As a result, the controls were labeled Control 0 through Control 4. In *this* code, `intCounter` is incremented regardless of whether the control supported the `Caption` property or not. As a result, the controls are properly labeled, in accordance with their item number in the `Controls` collection."

"There's one more thing I want to show you," I continued, "before we move on from the `Controls` collection to look at the `Forms` collection, and that's **Inline Error Handling**."

Inline Error Handling

"With **inline error handling**, there's no need to write an error handler procedure as we did previously. Instead, a single statement can be used to handle *any* errors that might occur in the event procedure. Let's try that out in our example code."

I then deleted all of the error handling code from the example program and added the highlighted line shown here:

```
Private Sub Command1_Click()

On Error Resume Next

 Dim objControl As Control
 Dim intCounter As Integer

 For Each objControl In Form1.Controls
    objControl.Caption = "Control " & intCounter
    intCounter = intCounter + 1
 Next

End Sub
```

"As you can see," I said, "the code has been streamlined quite a bit. Instead of writing a specific error handler procedure, we simply tell Visual Basic that, whenever an error occurs, it should just move on to execute the next bit of code – in this case, the next iteration of the loop. That's what this line of code does:"

```
On Error Resume Next
```

"That does save some coding, doesn't it?" Tom said.

"It certainly does," I agreed. "Inline error handling is great if you want to handle every error that occurs in the same way – as we're doing here."

"Does `intCounter` increment when an error is encountered?" asked Dave, "like it did in the previous case?"

"Yes, it does," I replied. "The outcome of running this bit of code is exactly the same as the previous example."

To confirm this, I ran the amended code, and the class verified that the same numbers were showing on the controls' captions – Control 0, 3, 4, 5 and 7.

"Just to get this straight..." Rhonda said. "If we use an item in the `Controls` collection to point us to a control that doesn't support the `Caption` property, we generate an error, and that single line of code instructs Visual Basic to skip to the next line and resume execution of our program there?"

"That's right, Rhonda," I said. I looked around the classroom and saw that everyone was looking in good shape, but I decided to take another quick break just the same – the second class is always a long one, and invariably overruns!

A well-deserved Coffee Break, and a short Precis

"OK, folks," I said, "I'm going to take five now before we continue. Get yourselves a cup of coffee and stretch your legs."

After the break, I did a quick recap on what we'd covered in the lesson so far.

"Before we get going again," I said, "we've already seen that Visual Basic automatically maintains certain system objects that we can talk to and use in our programs – and we've looked at the `Controls` collection in particular, which stores references to all the controls on our form. We've also done some experiments in code that show how we can work with the contents of collections using a `For...Each` structure – remembering that we need to declare a suitable object variable for the loop to work with. What I'm going to do next is talk about another important collection object – the `Forms` collection – that'll prove useful to us. Once again, we'll be exploring it using some practical code that will help familiarize us with how to get the most out of the system objects. Everyone sitting comfortably? OK, I'll begin!"

The Forms Collection

"Like the `Controls` collection," I went on, "the `Forms` collection is a group of related items. In the same way that the `Controls` collection contains pointers to the controls on your forms, the `Forms` collection groups together references to all of the **forms** in your Visual Basic application."

"I know the China Shop Project has only one form," Melissa said, "but I also know that Visual Basic projects can have multiple forms. Is that the sort of situation where something like the `Forms` collection would come in handy?"

"Exactly, Melissa," I said. "Just as we saw that we could use the `Controls` collection – in conjunction with a `For...Each` statement – to perform an operation on every control on a form, you can use the `Forms` collection to do the same thing with multiple forms. Let me show you."

Adding Extra Forms to a Project

I started a new `Standard.EXE` project in Visual Basic to demonstrate the example code on.

"Now," I said, when the project had fired up, "adding a second form to a Visual Basic project is pretty easy. All we need to do is select the Project | Add Form option from the menu bar..."

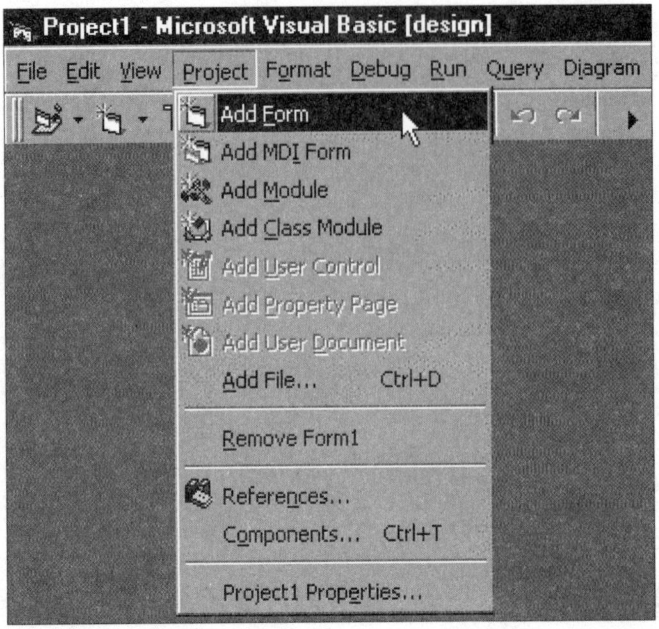

"...then, when this Add Form window appears..."

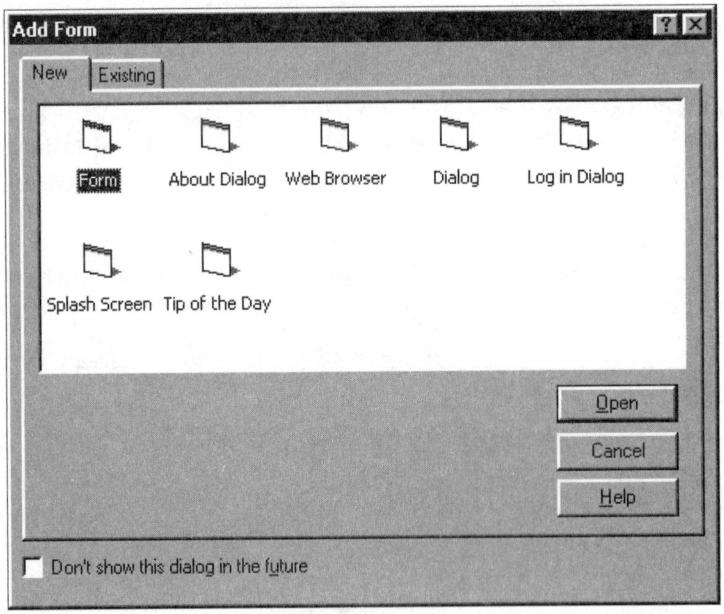

"...make sure the 'New' tab is selected, and then double-click on Form, or select 'Form', and then click on the Open button. Visual Basic will then display a new form in the IDE for us, with a caption of Form2."

> **If your menu options and New Form screen look different from those shown here, don't worry – different versions of Visual Basic have slightly different options available. What're shown here are the base options that you'd expect to see.**

"If we now bring up the Project Explorer window," I continued, "we should now see two forms – Form1 and Form2:"

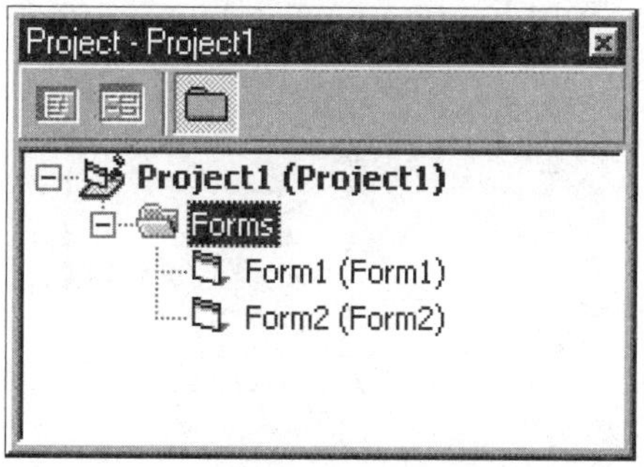

"To make our demonstration more meaningful," I said, "let's repeat this process to add a *third* form to the application." I did exactly that, once again selecting Project | Add Form from the menu bar.

"Once again," I said, "if we look in the Project Explorer window, we can verify the number of forms in our project – three:"

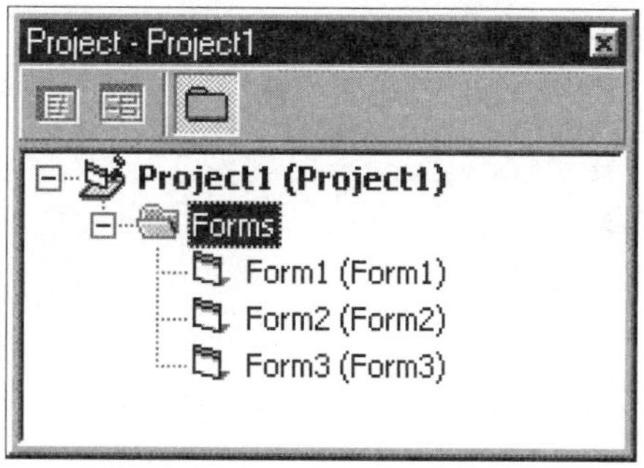

"Now that we have three forms in our project," I continued, "let's see what we can do with them. Does anyone have any idea what will happen if we just run the program right now?"

"Just guessing," Dave said, "but I think all we'll see is the first form – Form1. The other two, although present in the project, won't appear without some intervention on the part of the programmer."

"That's precisely what will happen," I said, "good description, Dave. A Visual Basic project with multiple forms will *automatically* load and display the first form – and that's it. To see the second and third forms in the application, we need to actively *do something* to make them visible – and we do that by placing code somewhere on the first form."

Making Extra Forms Visible

I double-clicked on Form1 in the Project Explorer window, and added a list box and three command buttons to the form, laid out as shown in the next screenshot. I then changed the captions of the command buttons to Load Form 2, Load Form 3, and Show me the loaded forms! respectively:

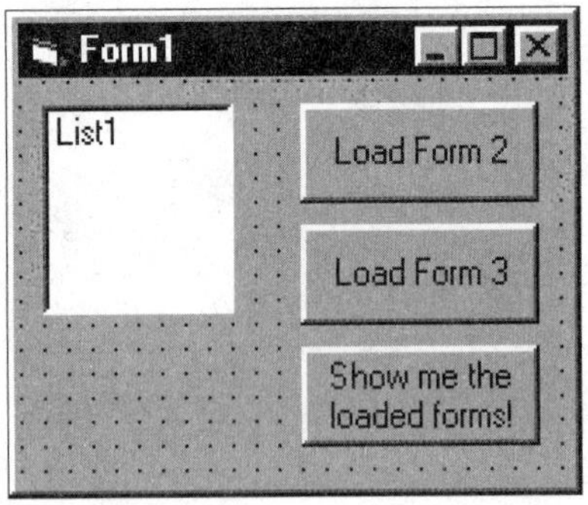

"Now let's place some code in the **Click** event procedure of that first command button," I said. "This code will display the second form when the first command button is clicked."

"Will you be using the **Load** statement?" Kate asked. "As you can probably guess, I've been reading up on multiple forms in Visual Basic projects!"

"I suspected as much, Kate," I said, "from your enthusiasm over using multiple forms in the China Shop project! And yes, you *could* code the **Load** statement in the **Click** event procedure of the first command button, like this:"

```
Load Form2
```

"That would load the second form, but unfortunately, you wouldn't see it – it would be loaded, but invisible! Loading a form isn't enough to make it visible."

"So what's the **Load** statement for?" asked Rhonda, miffed.

"It runs the **Form_Load** event, which opens the form in **memory**," I explained. "This puts all the default properties of a form's controls in place, so that these values can then be accessed and modified, even though the form isn't yet displayed."

"And why is it," Chuck asked, "that when the main form of the China Shop program is loaded, it immediately becomes visible? Why don't we need to do anything explicit in the code to let the user see *that* form?"

"There's a good reason for that," I replied. "In a Visual Basic project, the form identified as the **StartUp** object in the project's Project Properties window is automatically loaded and made visible when the program runs. But that's the default behavior of the **StartUp** form *only*. If you use the **Load** statement to load any other forms that you've added to the project, they won't become visible automatically."

"So how do we make the additional forms visible?" Kate asked.

"You have three choices, Kate," I said. "You can execute the **Load** statement, as we just did, and then either set the **Visible** property of the form to **True**, like this:"

```
Load Form2
Form2.Visible = True
```

"Alternatively, you can execute the **Load** statement, and then run the **Show** method of the form, like this:"

```
Load Form2
Form2.Show
```

"However, the easiest thing to do is to simply execute the **Show** method of the form on its own. A little-known behavior of Visual Basic is that executing any method of an unloaded form, or resetting any of its properties will automatically cause that form to load."

"Can you show us that, please?" asked Ward.

"Of course," I said. To demonstrate what I'd just described to the class, I typed the following code into the first command button's **Click** event procedure...

```
Private Sub Command1_Click()

Form2.Show

End Sub
```

...and this code into the **Click** event procedure of the second command button:

```
Private Sub Command2_Click()

Form3.Show

End Sub
```

"OK," I explained, "now that we've added this code, clicking on the first command button will display **Form2**, and clicking on the second command button will display **Form3**. Now for that third command button. What we want to do with the third button is use a **For...Each** statement to loop through the items in the **Forms** collection, and then display the names of the loaded forms – the forms that have been loaded into memory – in the list box."

"The **Forms** collection only works with loaded forms, then?" Mary asked.

"That's right, Mary," I replied, "Visual Basic only adds loaded forms to the **Forms** collection – unloaded forms are *not* added. Here's the code for the **Click** event procedure of the third command button – **Command3**:"

```
Private Sub Command3_Click()

Dim objForm as Form

List1.Clear

For Each objForm In Forms

      List1.AddItem objForm.Caption

Next

End Sub
```

"As you can see, " I said, "this code looks very similar to the code we used when working with the **Controls** collection. Once again, we're using an object variable, **objForm**, which we declare as a **Form** object type to make the binding process efficient. This is the object variable that we feed into the **For...Each** statement, which in turn loops through the items in the **Forms** collection. Within the body of the loop, we use this statement..."

```
      List1.AddItem objForm.Caption
```

"...to add the **Caption** of the loaded form to the list box. Remember, the loop has used the **objForm** object variable, and the item reference from the **Forms** collection, to retrieve the **Caption** property of the actual form object. The **List1.AddItem** part simply adds this retrieved **Caption** value to the list box. This process is carried out for as many iterations as it takes for the loop to go through all the items currently in the **Forms** collection. Let's see this in action."

I fired up the program and, without loading any additional forms, clicked straight away on the command button captioned Show me the loaded forms! This was the result:

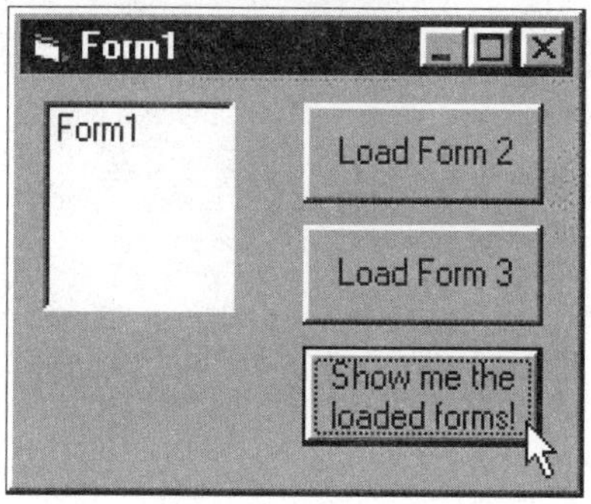

"As you can see," I said, "with just the startup form – **Form1** – loaded and displayed, and so just a single item in the **Forms** collection, we see just a single entry in the list box. Let's click on the first command button now to load and display **Form2**..."

I clicked on the Load form 2 button and, as planned, **Form2** appeared, floating above **Form1**.

"If I now move **Form2** out of the way..." I said, "...and click on the button captioned Show me the loaded forms!, the list box should now have two entries – Form1 and Form2." I clicked on Show me the loaded forms! button and, sure enough...

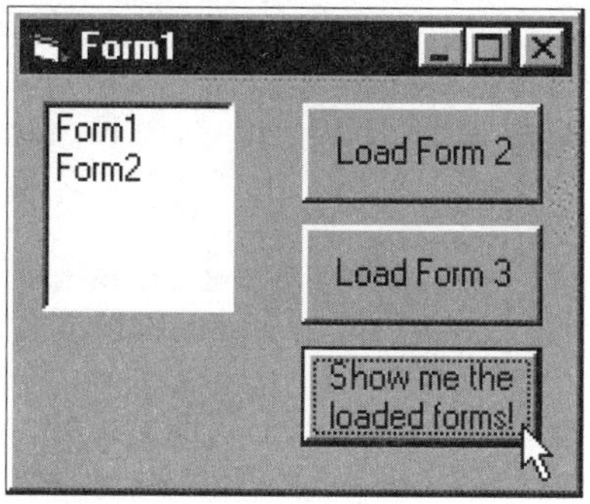

"This time," I said, "we have two items in the list box – since there are now two forms represented by items in the **Forms** collection."

Continuing with the demonstration, I clicked on the second command button to load and display **Form3**, and the third form – captioned **Form3** – appeared above the other two forms. Moving **Form3** out of the way, I clicked once more on the Show me the loaded forms! button, and this time the class saw the following result:

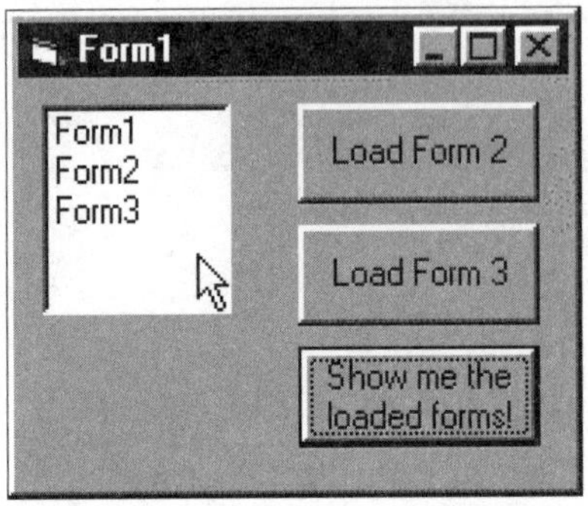

"With three forms loaded," I said, "there are now three items in the **Forms** collection, and our code has used these references to retrieve the **Caption** properties of the three forms and add them to the list box."

"I see how this all this is working," Ward said, "but I just don't see any practical use for it. Do you use the **Forms** collection in any of your commercial work?"

"Yes, I do," I answered. "I use the **Forms** collection to unload all of the loaded forms in my project. Otherwise, if the main form is unloaded, all of the others would be left 'orphaned' in memory, as I call it."

"That sounds sad," Valerie said. "What happens to an orphaned form?"

"That depends," I said, "on whether or not the form can be unloaded by clicking on its close button," I said. "If, for some reason, you've disabled the icons that normally let the user minimize, maximize, or close the form, the forms will remain loaded until you reboot the PC."

"Is that possible?" Rhonda said. "I would have thought that Visual Basic would automatically unload all of the other forms if the main form was unloaded."

"Visual Basic *will* do that in the case of a Multiple Document Interface – **MDI** – application," I said.

"Could you just remind me what an MDI application is, again?" asked Rhonda.

"MDI," I replied, "means an application like Word, which has a main form that acts as a window for displaying other forms inside of it."

"What about an single document interface application – such as the China Shop project?" Ward asked.

"Unloading the forms in an SDI application is the responsibility of the programmer," I replied, "and that means us! Let me show you how."

I then clicked on the close icon of **Form1** in the example project. The form closed, but **Form2** and **Form3** remained loaded and visible.

"The other two forms are still there," Linda said, obviously surprised. "That's not good – it looks really messy!"

"It's certainly not the behavior we want," I agreed. "Typically, the first form loaded in the application should be the last form *unloaded*. We can ensure that happens by implementing this next piece of code in **Form1**'s **Form_QueryUnload** procedure:"

```
Private Sub Form_QueryUnload(Cancel As Integer , UnloadMode As Integer)

Dim objForm As Form

For Each objForm In Forms
      Unload objForm
Next

End Sub
```

"In this code, we use the **Forms** collection again," I said. "Here, we make sure we don't accidentally leave one of your forms loaded after ending your program by closing **Form1**."

I ran the program one more time, loaded both **Form2** and **Form3**, and then closed **Form1** by clicking on its 'close' button. In the blink of an eye, all three forms unloaded and disappeared.

> **You can find the complete code for this example on the CD in the** `For Chapter 02\Additional Examples\Load Forms Example` **folder.**

"That *is* impressive," Tom said. "Will we be using either the **`Controls`** or **`Forms`** collections in the modified China Shop program?"

"I don't think we'll be using the **`Forms`** collection," I said. "Although we'll be adding a second form to the project in order to facilitate Joe's shipping charges calculation. I suspect we'll be loading the second form **modally**, which means the users won't be able to interact with the main form until they close that second form. For that reason, we probably won't need to use the **`Forms`** collection to unload the second form."

"What about the **`Controls`** collection?" Asked Dave.

"We've already discounted using the **`Controls`** collection to change the **`BackColor`** property of the controls on the main from, so I don't think we'll be using the **`Controls`** collection either. But don't worry, even if we don't use either of these collections in the China Shop program, looking at them and working with them in code is an important contribution to understanding how objects work and how we use them. I'm certain that we'll be creating and using collections of our own in the China Shop, and using the principles we've been discussing. In fact, we'll be creating an example collection of our own in a moment – just as soon as you come back from break!"

With that, I sent everyone off for a fifteen-minute break so that they could recharge their batteries and refresh themselves.

Creating and Working with Collections

"So far today," I said, after everyone returned, "we've spent time talking about Visual Basic's in-built system collections, which are collections that Visual Basic creates and maintains for us. In the second half of today's class, I want to show you how easy it is to create your own collections and add items to them."

"Why do programmers create their own collections?" Dorothy asked.

"Collections are frequently used to store data, replacing arrays." I said. "Let's begin our discussion of creating collections by looking at something we're already familiar with – arrays."

Starting with Arrays...

"Consider this," I went on. "Microsoft defines an array in this way:"

> An ordered collection of data contained in a variable and referenced by a single variable name. Each element of the array can be referenced by a numerical subscript.

"What does that definition sound like to you?" I asked the class.

"That sounds very much like a collection," Melissa said.

"That's right, Melissa," I said. "An array is very much like a collection. However, collections have two big advantages over arrays. First, in an array, each element must be of the same data type. Secondly – and this is probably the most important advantage – you can store an item in a collection using a **key value** of your own choosing. This key value can then be used later to directly locate the item, without having to hunt through each item in the collection to find it."

"Yes," Linda said, "I recall that to find an element in an array, you have to start with the first element and move through each element in the array until you find the one that you want."

"I'd love to use a collection for that direct access feature," Dave said. "Will you show us how to do that?"

"I'm going to do that right now," I said.

Creating and Working with an Array

"Let's pretend we're the owners of a company in Pennsylvania, and that our company has offices in thirteen states. We want to write a program that displays the number of employees who work in each state, and we also want to display the total number of employees in the company. We can solve this problem in many ways, but for my demo here, I'm going to do it using array processing first – later, we'll see another approach that uses a collection."

I paused for a second before continuing: "First, let's create a `String` array called `m_States` to store both the name of the state and the total number of employees for that state. Like this..."

I created a new Visual Basic project, and placed two command buttons on the blank form that presented itself to me:

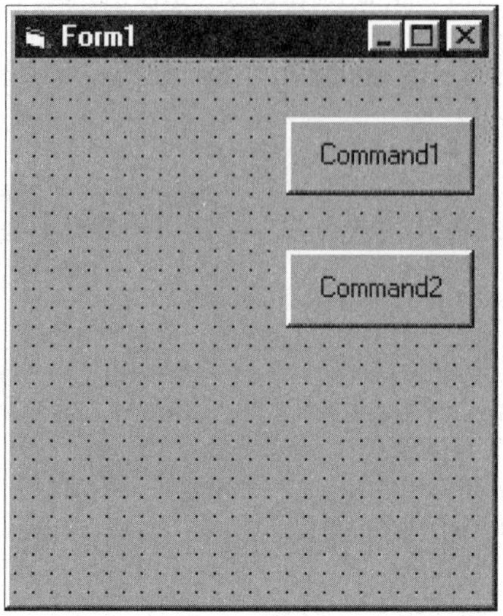

Next, I typed the following variable array declaration in to the General Declarations section of the form:

```
Private m_States(12) As String
```

"This declaration creates a one dimensional, fixed array of 13 elements called **m_States**," I explained. "Remember, the number in parentheses indicates the upper bound of the array, *not* the total number of elements. By default, arrays in Visual Basic are zero-based, which means that the first element is zero, in the same way that the ground floor of a building is marked 'G' on an elevator, the first floor is marked '1', and so on."

See Chapter 13 of *Learn to Program with Visual Basic 6* for an in-depth treatment of arrays.

"Why did you declare the array in the General Declarations section of the form?" Lou asked.

"Because," I answered, "we'll be referring to elements in this array from two different event procedures in the form – the **Click** event procedures of **Command1** and **Command2**. That means that we want the variable to be available to all parts of our program, not just within a single procedure."

"OK," I went on, "now we need some code to load the elements of the array. For the sake of this demonstration, we're loading both the name of the state and the number of employees working in that state as a single value in each array element, but you'd probably want to do something a bit more flexible in real life. Let's get back to our example. Here's the code that I need to key into the **Click** event procedure of the first command button – **Command1**:"

```
Private Sub Command1_Click()

m_States(0) = "123-Connecticut"
m_States(1) = "523-Delaware"
m_States(2) = "12-Georgia"
m_States(3) = "311-Maryland"
m_States(4) = "23-Massachusetts"
m_States(5) = "11-New Hampshire"
m_States(6) = "43-New Jersey"
m_States(7) = "410-New York"
m_States(8) = "56-North Carolina"
m_States(9) = "1012-Pennsylvania"
m_States(10) = "22-Rhode Island"
m_States(11) = "12-South Carolina"
m_States(12) = "83-Virginia"

End Sub
```

Having typed this code into the command button's **Click** event, I said: "This is a pretty straightforward assignment of values into the elements of a one dimensional array. All we're doing is populating the elements of the array with the 'Number of Employees–State' combination."

"I think it's a strange-looking arrangement, myself," Valerie observed. "Why didn't you place the name of the state first?"

"Placing the number of employees first," I explained, "will make it easier for us to sum the total number of employees in this array using the Visual Basic **Val** function. You'll see in a minute that we'll be using a little trick of the **Val** function to do that – the only drawback is that the number of employees must go first. This arrangement is just for convenience so that I can demonstrate these principles fairly quickly – otherwise the lesson might last all day!"

"Now that we've written the code to load the array," I continued, "we need to write the code to loop through the elements of the array, and then print the names of the states and their associated number of employees on the form. Finally, we also want to display the grand total number of employees on the form. Here's some code that can do that."

So saying, I keyed this next batch of code into the second command button's **Click** event procedure:

```
Private Sub Command2_Click()

Dim intCounter As Integer
Dim intTotal As Integer

For intCounter = LBound(m_States) To UBound(m_States)
  Form1.Print m_States(intCounter)
  intTotal = intTotal + Val(m_States(intCounter))
Next

Form1.Print
Form1.Print "Total Number of employees: " & intTotal " in
      ↳" & intCounter & " states"

End Sub
```

"You should be familiar with what we're doing here from the Intro course," I said. "We're executing a **For...Next** loop that moves us through the elements of the array, using the **LBound** and **UBound** functions to determine the lower and upper limits of the array. In essence, the lower and upper bound functions tell us the element number to start our loop from, and the element number at which to stop."

"What about that totaling going on here?" Ward said, "this is a new one on me. What exactly does the **Val** function do?"

"The **Val** function," I said, "takes a **String** argument and reads any numeric digits from it. Say our string reads '77' – **Val** would read this and return the numeric value 77. The interesting thing about **Val** is that it starts processing from the left-hand end of the string, and continues until it encounters the first non-numeric character. That produces an interesting effect when you have a string whose first characters are numbers – as soon as it encounters the first non-numeric character, it stops reading the string. We're making use of that characteristic here, which is why we arranged the data in the array the way we did."

"So *that's* why we placed the number of employees on the left side of the string," Kate said.

"That's it, Kate," I said. "This way, we can use the **Val** function to extract the numerical value for the number of employees from each string value held in the array elements. Once we have that number, we add it to the variable **intTotal**, which acts as an accumulator variable for the total number of employees in the company. Let's fire up the machine..."

I ran the program and clicked on the first command button – this populated the array. Next, I clicked on the second command button and triggered the body of the code, with this result:

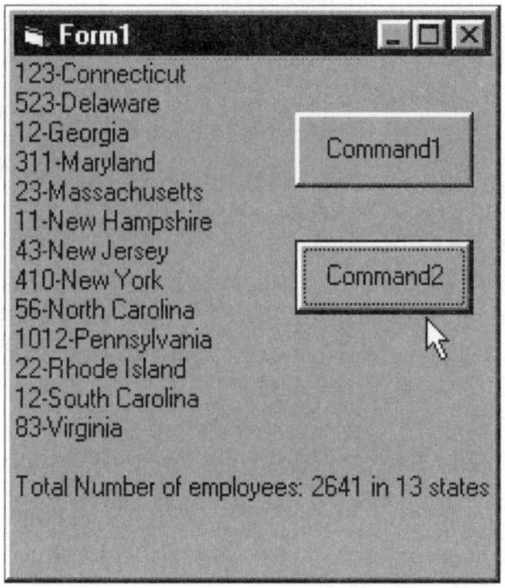

"That's pretty clever," Linda said, "I never would have thought of that myself."

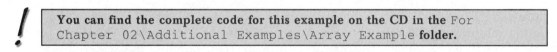

> **!** **You can find the complete code for this example on the CD in the** `For Chapter 02\Additional Examples\Array Example` **folder.**

"So how does a collection fit in here, then?" Ward asked. "Could we use a collection in place of an array to store the data about states and employees?"

"Yes, Ward," I said.

Using Collections instead of Arrays

"A collection can be used where you would use a one-dimensional array. In fact, because of the powerful direct-access feature that allows us to add an item to it using a key value, we'll be able take the seven one-dimensional arrays in the current China Shop program and use just a single collection object instead – this will greatly streamline our code."

I could see the interest of the class perk up.

"I know you mentioned key values a few minutes ago," Rhonda said, "what are they exactly?"

"**Key values**," I answered, "are used to explicitly reference an item that we create in our own, programmer-created collections. We didn't see this with the **`Forms`** or **`Controls`** collection, because Visual Basic added items to those collections for us. In contrast, items are added to a programmer-declared collection explicitly, using an **`Add`** method. The **`Add`** method has one required argument, **`Item`**, and three optional arguments, **`Key`**, **`Before`** and **`After`**. Programmer-declared collections are 'one-based', meaning that the first item added to the collection is added as item number 1 – in contrast to the system collections, which are zero-based. However, when you supply the optional **`Key`** argument, the item is not only kept track of using the item number – that is, the bracketed number we use after the name of the collection – we can also track it by referring to it via the **key value** that we specified using the **`Key`** argument. This means that you can later retrieve the item directly from the collection using that same key value."

"That will be quite useful in the China Shop project," Dave said, "because we'll be able to quickly retrieve a price for a particular item of china."

"That's a good thought, Dave," I said.

"I'm afraid you're losing me here," Rhonda said. "Can you explain what you just said?"

"Sure thing, Rhonda." I said. "In short, adding an item to a collection using the **`Key`** argument allows us to locate that item later. Let's think of it in terms of this demo program. Now, our fictitious company has offices in thirteen states: suppose the owner of the company wants to know how many employees work in the New York office? Using an array, we'd need to loop through each element of the array until we found the New York office. In an array containing just thirteen elements this isn't a big deal – but suppose there are thousands or even millions of elements in the array? Starting from the first element of the array and working toward the last element could be very time consuming indeed."

"And that's different with a collection?" Rhonda asked.

"Yes, it is," I said, nodding. "With a collection, provided you have added the items to it using the optional **`Key`** argument, you can quickly find any item – in this instance New York – in the collection, using a single statement that directly accesses the item you're interested in."

I could see that my explanation helped, but that a demonstration was still in order.

"Let me show you how our demo project would work using a collection instead of an array," I said.

Creating and Using a Collection of our own

The first thing to do was create a new program to act as a vehicle for the collection we were going to create. Once more, I started a new Visual Basic project. I added two command buttons to the new project's default form...

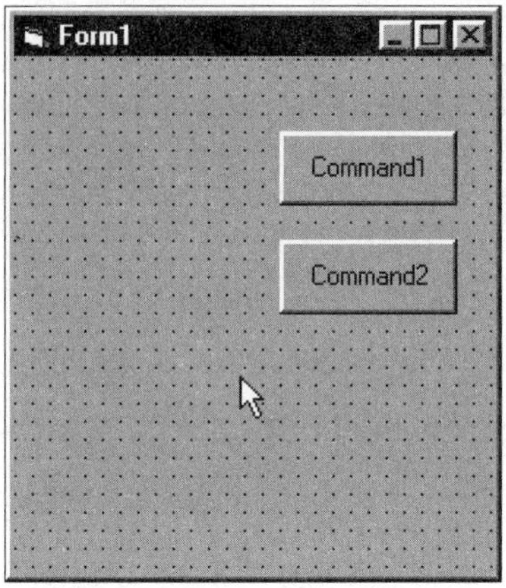

...and then typed this next piece of code into the form's General Declarations section:

```
Private m_colStates As New Collection
```

"Notice that this declaration is different from the array declaration in the previous example," I said. "What we're doing here is creating a collection called **`m_colStates`**. A collection is declared as a **collection object**. Like the control objects that we create by using the templates in the toolbox, Visual Basic has a predefined template – a class – that we use to create our own collections. So the **`As New Collection`** part of the declaration tells Visual Basic to create our **`m_colStates`** collection based on the characteristics of the pre-defined **`Collection`** class. Our specific **`m_colStates`** collection is a new instance of the **`Collection`** class. The cookie cutter is in action again!"

"I see," said Lou. "And we're declaring the collection in the General Declarations section again, I notice."

"That's right, Lou," I said. "We're declaring this collection here in the General Declarations section of the form because – again – the **`m_colStates`** collection will be accessed from several event procedures on the form."

"Don't you need to declare a data type for the collection?" Mary asked.

"No, you don't," I replied. "Unlike an array, where each element must be the same data type – like the strings in the previous demo project – a collection can contain data of any type, including objects, so there's no need to specify the data type of the members of the collection when we declare it. You simply declare the collection as type **Collection**."

I let this sink in for a moment, then continued.

"OK," I said, "that piece of code will create our very own collection object for us to use. As it's based on the pre-defined **Collection** class, our collection will inherit a lot of characteristics and abilities from that class. Next, we need to take a look at those characteristics and see how we can make use of them in our particular collection – **m_colStates**. Let's begin by looking at the method that we use to add items to our collection – the **Add** method."

The Add Method

"The **Add** method," I continued, "is the built-in collection method that we use to add items to a collection. Here's the syntax for the **Add** method:"

```
Add (Item As Variant [, Key As Variant] [, Before As Variant]
                      [, After As Variant] )
```

"Let me explain this," I said. "By default, items are added to a collection starting at item number 1, followed by item number 2, and so forth. It's possible to specify an optional **Before** or **After** argument if you want to position a new item in a particular location within the collection, either before or after an existing item. However, if you specify only the mandatory argument to the **Add** method – the Item argument itself – then the first item you add to the collection will be item number 1. For instance, this code..."

```
m_colStates.Add "123-Connecticut"
m_colStates.Add "523-Delaware"
m_colStates.Add "12-Georgia"
m_colStates.Add "311-Maryland"
m_colStates.Add "23-Massachusetts"
m_colStates.Add "11-New Hampshire"
m_colStates.Add "43-New Jersey"
m_colStates.Add "410-New York"
m_colStates.Add "56-North Carolina"
m_colStates.Add "1012-Pennsylvania"
m_colStates.Add "22-Rhode Island"
m_colStates.Add "12-South Carolina"
m_colStates.Add "83-Virginia"
```

"...will add 13 items to the **m_colStates** collection. To populate the collection, all we need to do is write the collection object's name – **m_colStates** – followed by a dot – the dot, remember, indicates here that we're going to use one of the collection object's methods – followed by the content of the item that we want to add. In this case, the item will consist of the string that we enclose in quotation marks. The first item will be stored as item number 1 and the last item will be stored as item number 13."

"Are you saying that a programmer-defined collection is **one-based** then?" Steve asked. "Weren't the system collections that we looked at earlier zero-based?"

"That's right, Steve," I said. "Both the **Forms** and **Controls** collection are zero-based, with the first item in those collections stored at position 0 – however, with a programmer declared collection, the first item is stored at position 1."

"Why?" asked Rhonda.

"Using one-based collections is a more intuitive way of operating," I replied. "The item members run from one to **Count**. Contrast that with a zero-based collection, where they go from zero to one-less-than-**Count**. The **Forms** and **Controls** collections are quite early aspects of the Visual Basic language, though, and thus use the older zero-based convention."

"Can you show us an example of how that **Key** argument works?" Rhonda asked.

"I sure can, Rhonda," I assured her. I added the following code to the **Click** event procedure of **Command1**:

```
Private Sub Command1_Click()

m_colStates.Add "123-Connecticut", "Connecticut"
m_colStates.Add "523-Delaware", "Delaware"
m_colStates.Add "12-Georgia", "Georgia"
m_colStates.Add "311-Maryland", "Maryland"
m_colStates.Add "23-Massachusetts", "Massachusetts"
m_colStates.Add "11-New Hampshire", "New Hampshire"
m_colStates.Add "43-New Jersey", "New Jersey"
m_colStates.Add "410-New York", "New York"
m_colStates.Add "56-North Carolina", "North Carolina"
m_colStates.Add "1012-Pennsylvania", "Pennsylvania"
m_colStates.Add "22-Rhode Island", "Rhode Island"
m_colStates.Add "12-South Carolina", "South Carolina"
m_colStates.Add "83-Virginia", "Virginia"

End Sub
```

"Do you see the difference between this and the previous code?" I asked. "This code contains the optional **Key** argument. This is included inside the second set of quotation marks after the comma in each line – and we're using the name of the state as the key value. That means that later on, we'll quickly be able to locate these items using the name of the state as the key that gives us direct access to the information we want, wherever it's located in the collection."

To demonstrate this, I ran the program and clicked on the first command button to load the items into the collection – **Command1**. Next, I paused the program, and entered the following statement in the Immediate window:

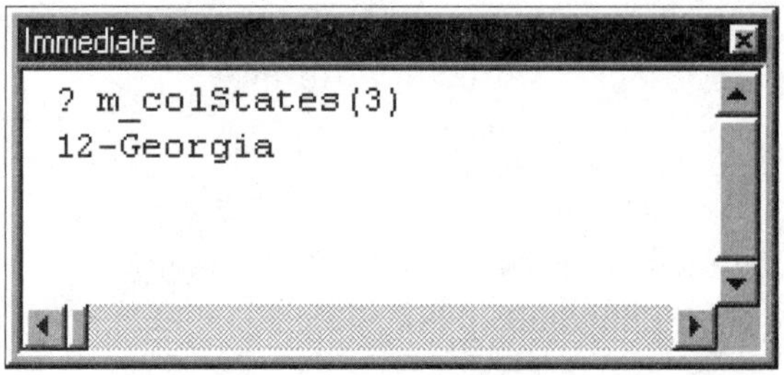

"With the program paused," I said, "we're able to refer to an individual item in the **m_colStates** collection, much as we would an array element, by referring to the item's number – in this case 3. As you can see, item **(3)** is Georgia, which has 12 employees."

"OK," Ward persisted, "but that's just using the item's numeric position in the collection to retrieve that item's values. How about using the key value itself to retrieve information?"

"Watch this," I said.

Using the Optional Key Value

"Because we added these items to the collection with the optional key argument," I continued, "we can also retrieve the items from the collection by referring to the item by the key value that we specified. Like this..." Again, I keyed a statement into the Immediate window:

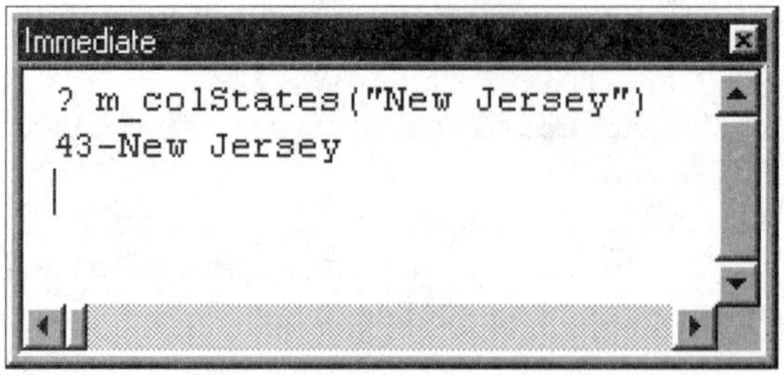

"Notice that all I did was to replace the item number with the key value 'New Jersey'," I said. "Either of these techniques will retrieve the value of the item in the collection – but this second method is very powerful, because it really gives us the ability to directly access any item in the collection – something we just can't do with an array."

"Does the key value need to have quotes around it?" asked Rhonda.

"Yes, because it's a **String** argument," I replied.

"Can we use a **For...Each** statement to loop through the items in a programmer-declared collection, like we did with the system collections earlier?" Ward enquired.

"Yes, we certainly can," I confirmed. "For instance, this code will do exactly that..."

I keyed the following highlighted lines of code into the **Click** event procedure of the **Command2** command button:

```
Private Sub Command2_Click()

Dim objItem As Variant
Dim intTotal As Integer

For Each objItem In m_colStates
  intTotal = intTotal + Val(objItem)
  Form1.Print objItem
Next

Form1.Print
Form1.Print "Total Number of employees: " & intTotal & " in " &
      ↳m_colStates.Count & " states"

End Sub
```

"Here," I said, "we're using the **For...Each** statement to loop through each item in the collection. First, we declare our object variable as the highly generic **Variant** variable type:"

```
Dim objItem as Variant
```

"...this variable then is used within the **For...Each** structure to loop through each item in the collection:"

```
For Each objItem In m_colStates
  intTotal = intTotal + Val(objItem)
  Form1.Print objItem
Next
```

"Now look at the final line of code:"

```
Form1.Print "Total Number of employees: " & intTotal & " in " &
      ♥m_colStates.Count & " states"
```

"Here, we use the one and only property of a collection – the **Count** property – to display the number of elements in the collection."

I ran the program, clicked on the first command button (this populates the collection, remember) and then clicked on the second command button, with this result:

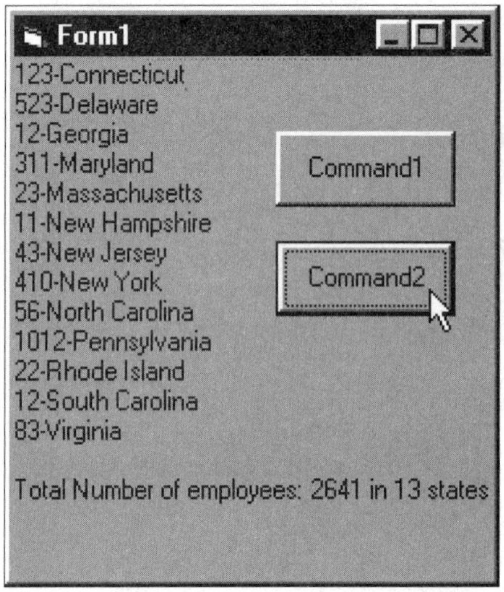

You can find the complete code for this version of the example on the CD in the `For Chapter 02\Additional Examples\Collection Example` **folder.**

"All in all," I said, "this version of the program, which uses a collection, is pretty similar to the version we saw that used an array. The main difference is that using a collection is much more 'object-oriented' – items are added to the collection by executing the **Add** method, and the count of the number of items in the collection can be obtained by interrogating the **Count** property. We're using the built-in properties of the collection object to manipulate the data it stores. The consistency that we get from always using an object's own properties, methods and events when we work with it is an important object-oriented principle that we'll be seeing much more of later. This all contributes to objects being self-contained blocks of code that other parts of the program can always rely on to behave in the same way."

"Can I just go back a little?" asked Linda, and I nodded to her to carry on with her question. "Suppose you attempt to add an item to the collection," Linda continued, "and you specify a key value that already exists. Will that generate an error?"

"Excellent question, Linda," I said. "It's perfectly OK to have an item in a collection with the same *value* as another item – but you may *not* specify a key value that already exists. Take a look at this..."

I then added the following line to the end of the code in the **Click** event procedure of **Command1**:

```
m_colStates.Add "Testing1-2-3", "New York"
```

"This line tries to add another item to the collection," I said, "but it has a key value of **"New York"** – the same as the eighth item in the existing list. Watch what happens when I run the program this time..."

When I ran the program and clicked on the first command button, we saw this:

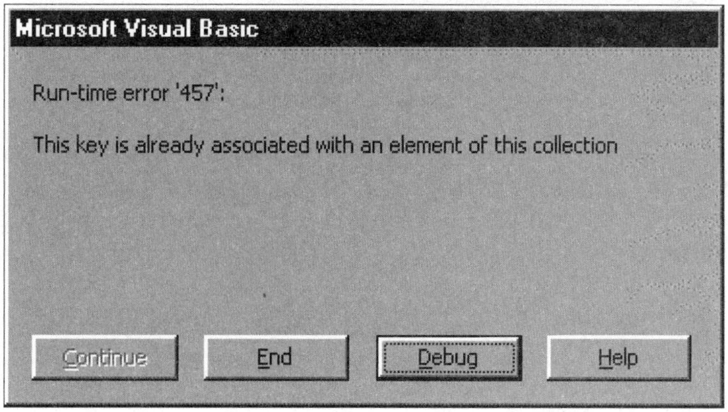

"This error message," I said, "is telling us that the key value we've specified for this item already exists."

"What about those other optional arguments that can be used with the **Add** method," Peter asked, "**Before** and **After**. How do they work?"

Using the Before and After Arguments

"The **Before** and **After** arguments allow you to specify the **location** of a new item in the collection," I said. "For instance, suppose you decide to add another item to your collection – and you want to position it before or after an item that's already in the collection. You can do that by specifying either the **Before** or **After** argument – but not both – with the collection's **Add** method. Take a peek at this code..."

I amended the code in the **Click** event procedure of the **Command1** button to look like this...

```
Private Sub Command1_Click()

m_colStates.Add "123-Connecticut", "Connecticut"
m_colStates.Add "523-Delaware", "Delaware"
m_colStates.Add "12-Georgia", "Georgia"
m_colStates.Add "311-Maryland", "Maryland"
m_colStates.Add "23-Massachusetts", "Massachusetts"
m_colStates.Add "11-New Hampshire", "New Hampshire"
m_colStates.Add "43-New Jersey", "New Jersey"
m_colStates.Add "410-New York", "New York"
m_colStates.Add "56-North Carolina", "North Carolina"
m_colStates.Add "1012-Pennsylvania", "Pennsylvania"
m_colStates.Add "22-Rhode Island", "Rhode Island"
m_colStates.Add "12-South Carolina", "South Carolina"
m_colStates.Add "83-Virginia", "Virginia"
m_colStates.Add "1-SMILEY", "Smiley", "MARYLAND"

End Sub
```

"That last line of code," I said, "is telling Visual Basic to add an item to the collection with a value of **1-SMILEY** and a key of **Smiley**, and to place it **before** the item in the collection that contains the key value **MARYLAND**. Now watch what happens when I run the program."

I went through the usual routine of clicking on the two command buttons in sequence. This time...

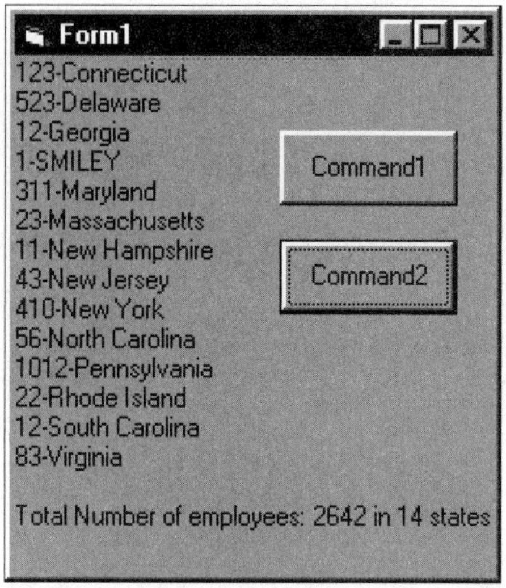

"The item **`1-SMILEY`**," I said, "has been added *before* Maryland. Likewise, if we wanted to place an item in the collection *after* an existing item in the collection, all we need to do is specify a value for the **`After`** argument."

To demonstrate this, I amended the **`Click`** event procedure of the first command button with this highlighted line:

```
Private Sub Command1_Click()

m_colStates.Add "123-Connecticut", "Connecticut"
m_colStates.Add "523-Delaware", "Delaware"
m_colStates.Add "12-Georgia", "Georgia"
m_colStates.Add "311-Maryland", "Maryland"
m_colStates.Add "23-Massachusetts", "Massachusetts"
m_colStates.Add "11-New Hampshire", "New Hampshire"
m_colStates.Add "43-New Jersey", "New Jersey"
m_colStates.Add "410-New York", "New York"
m_colStates.Add "56-North Carolina", "North Carolina"
m_colStates.Add "1012-Pennsylvania", "Pennsylvania"
m_colStates.Add "22-Rhode Island", "Rhode Island"
m_colStates.Add "12-South Carolina", "South Carolina"
m_colStates.Add "83-Virginia", "Virginia"
m_colStates.Add "1-SMILEY", "Smiley", , 1

End Sub
```

"That last line of code," I said, "is telling Visual Basic to add an item to the collection with a value of **'1-SMILEY'** and to place it after the first item in the collection. Notice that this time we didn't specify a key value for the after argument – but an actual item number, which comes after the two commas in the argument list. Watch what happens when I run the program."

I ran the program again, clicked on the first command button to load the collection, and then clicked on the second command button to display it, with this result:

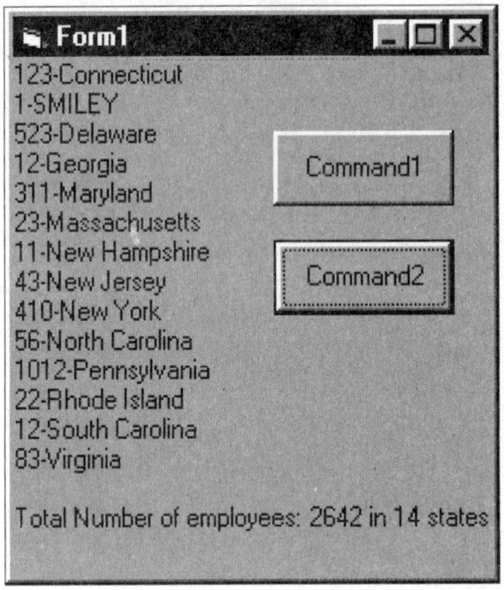

"As promised," I said, "the value **1-SMILEY** has been added *after* the first item in the collection."

"I'm puzzled by the format for the **Add** method," Rhonda said. "What's confusing me is the extra comma in that line of code when we passed the **After** argument to the **Add** method."

"I understand your confusion," I said. "Remember that Visual Basic always expects to receive the arguments for a given method in the same strict sequence. Since we're passing only one optional argument here –the **After** argument – and since it comes *last* in the sequence of argument list, we needed to specify a comma placeholder for the optional **Before** argument:"

```
m_colStates.Add "1-SMILEY", "Smiley", , 1
```

"The comma just tells Visual Basic that the **Before** argument isn't being supplied on this occasion, and VB moves on to the next argument in the list – which is the **After** argument, for which we've specified the value 1," I explained.

"Didn't we mention in the Intro class that there's an easier way to pass optional arguments?" Ward queried.

"That's right – thanks for reminding me!" I told him. "Rather than use the comma placeholder that we used here, there *is* an easier way of passing optional arguments: we can pass **named arguments** instead. To implement this, we *could* have written the code to look like this:"

```
Private Sub Command1_Click()

m_colStates.Add Item:="123-Connecticut", Key:="Connecticut"
m_colStates.Add Item:="523-Delaware", Key:="Delaware"
m_colStates.Add Item:="12-Georgia", Key:="Georgia"
m_colStates.Add Item:="311-Maryland", Key:="Maryland"
m_colStates.Add Item:="23-Massachusetts", Key:="Massachusetts"
m_colStates.Add Item:="11-New Hampshire", Key:="New Hampshire"
m_colStates.Add Item:="43-New Jersey", Key:="New Jersey"
m_colStates.Add Item:="410-New York", Key:="New York"
m_colStates.Add Item:="56-North Carolina", Key:="North Carolina"
m_colStates.Add Item:="1012-Pennsylvania", Key:="Pennsylvania"
m_colStates.Add Item:="22-Rhode Island", Key:="Rhode Island"
m_colStates.Add Item:="12-South Carolina", Key:="South Carolina"
m_colStates.Add Item:="83-Virginia", Key:="Virginia"
m_colStates.Add Item:="1-SMILEY", Key:="Smiley", After:=1

End Sub
```

"That's better," I said. "As you can see, what we do here is use the argument name, followed immediately by a colon, followed by the argument's value. Then we have another comma, the next argument name, and so on. This way, you don't have to remember the argument sequence every time, or worry about how many placeholder commas to use. In fact, using named arguments is a far easier practice to follow."

"You did say it's possible to remove an item from a collection as well, didn't you, a while back?" Chuck asked.

"That's right, Chuck," I said. "Let's talk about that for a moment."

Removing Items from a Collection

"Items," I resumed, "can be removed from a collection by using the aptly-named **`Remove`** method. Here's the syntax for using the **`Remove`** method:"

```
object.Remove index
```

"So, to remove an item from a collection," I said, "all you need to do is supply that item's index number or key value. Like this..."

I altered the **Click** event procedure of the **Command1** command button to look like the next code listing:

```
Private Sub Command1_Click()

m_colStates.Add Item:="123-Connecticut", Key:="Connecticut"
m_colStates.Add Item:="523-Delaware", Key:="Delaware"
m_colStates.Add Item:="12-Georgia", Key:="Georgia"
m_colStates.Add Item:="311-Maryland", Key:="Maryland"
m_colStates.Add Item:="23-Massachusetts", Key:="Massachusetts"
m_colStates.Add Item:="11-New Hampshire", Key:="New Hampshire"
m_colStates.Add Item:="43-New Jersey", Key:="New Jersey"
m_colStates.Add Item:="410-New York", Key:="New York"
m_colStates.Add Item:="56-North Carolina", Key:="North Carolina"
m_colStates.Add Item:="1012-Pennsylvania", Key:="Pennsylvania"
m_colStates.Add Item:="22-Rhode Island", Key:="Rhode Island"
m_colStates.Add Item:="12-South Carolina", Key:="South Carolina"
m_colStates.Add Item:="83-Virginia", Key:="Virginia"
m_colStates.Remove 3

End Sub
```

"In this code," I said, "we add the usual thirteen items to our collection, but then give things an exciting twist by removing the third item from the collection. That's what the highlighted line does, using the syntax that I sketched just now."

I ran the program and clicked on the first command button. This time, it should have deleted an item from the collection after populating it. Then I clicked on the second command button, and...

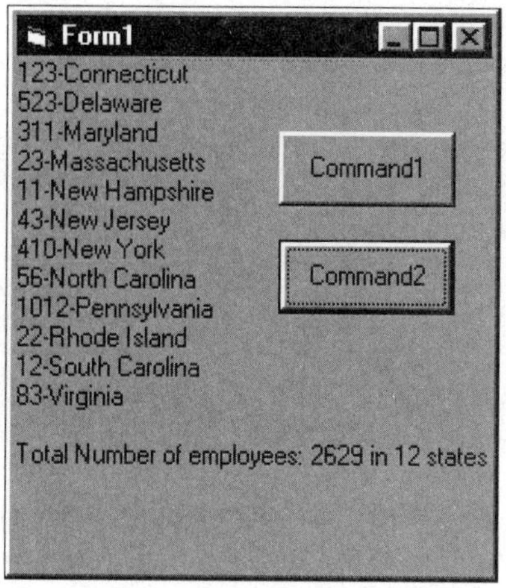

"As you can see," I continued, "the third item in the collection, **Georgia**, has been removed from the collection. Notice also that the total number of employees and total number of states has changed."

"I have a question," Mary asked. "When we removed that third item – **Georgia** – what happened to the third position in the collection? Is it empty, or did everything move up?"

"That's a good question, Mary," I said, "and you're instinct is correct – everything moved up. The item that was fourth in the collection – **Maryland** – is now third."

To prove this, I typed this statement into the Immediate window and hit the *Enter* key:

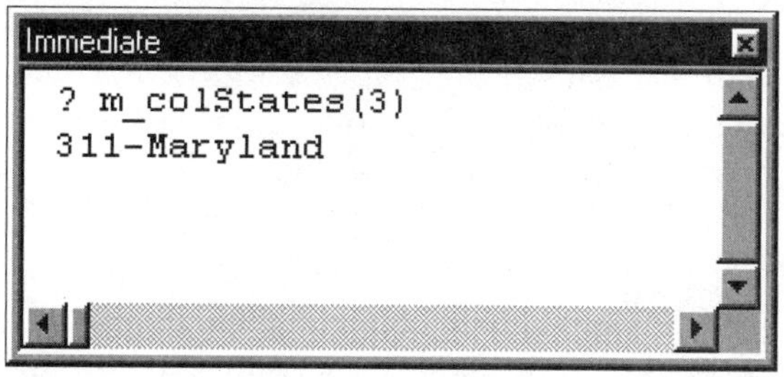

"D'you see what I mean?" I said. "**Maryland**, which *had* been in the fourth position, is now third."

"So, what you're implying," Dave said slowly, "is that with a collection that has a fair amount of additions and deletions, we shouldn't count on finding an item in the same position that it originally occupied when we added it?"

"That's right," I said. "You should never count on an item in a collection remaining in a particular location. This is another good reason to add the item to the collection using a key value. The key value *never* changes and it can't be duplicated – so you'll always be able to find it, and thereby, the item that you want. Of course, you can always find an item by searching through each element of the collection one by one, in the same way you can with an array – it will just take longer to find."

"Speaking of keys," Ward said, "once you have added an item to a collection, is there any way to display the key value of a particular item, or the key value of *every* item in the collection? For instance, if you forget that the key value of `123 Connecticut` is `Connecticut`, is there any way to display it?"

"Unfortunately not!" I replied. "Try as you might, there is no way to display the key value of an item in the collection. That means that if you forget the key value, you're basically out of luck."

"Does that also mean," Dave put in, "that once an item is added to a collection, that item's value can't be changed – I guess you would first need to remove the item from the collection and then add it back with a different value?"

"Exactly right, Dave," I replied, "once you add an item to the collection – `123-Connecticut` for instance – there's no way to change the value of that item to something else, such as `456-Connecticut`. You would need to remove it first, using the **`Remove`** method, and then add it back with its new value, using the **`Add`** method."

"As the questions are coming thick and fast," Valerie said, "I might as well ask mine, too. During the Intro class last semester, I accidentally referred to one of the China shop program's check box controls – which of course are members of a control array – without specifying a subscript number. When I did that, a window in the **`ListMembers`** popped up showing me the properties and methods for a particular control – I believe I saw a **`Count`** property and an **`Item`** method. Is that the same **`Count`** property and **`Item`** method that we've been discussing today?"

Control Arrays as Collections

"Good question, Valerie," I began, but I could see some puzzled looks on the faces of some of the students in the class, so I decided to do a quick demonstration. I created a new Visual Basic project, placed a command button on the form, and created a control array of four check boxes.

To create a control array, remember that you need to add the first check box control, then copy it to the clipboard. Then you should paste it back onto the form, and you'll be prompted with this message box:

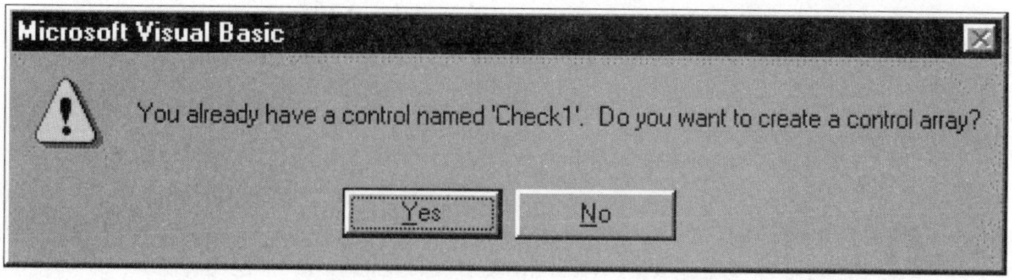

Click on the Yes button, and then keep pasting controls until you have the number you require in your control array. Here's the control array of check boxes I created in my example project, plus the command button I put on the form:

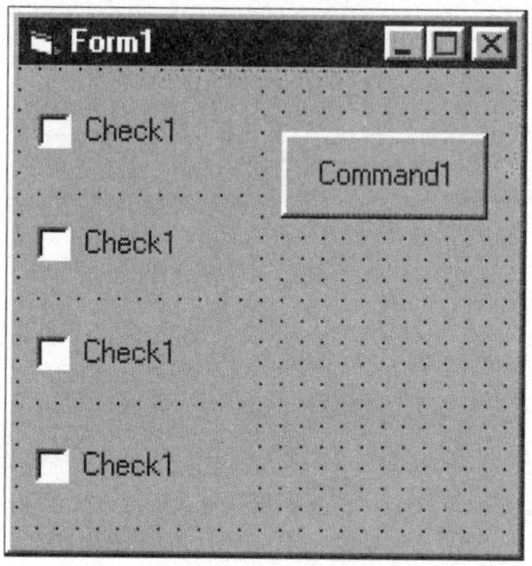

"I've created a control array called **Check1**," I explained to the class, "and once you create a control array, you should thereafter refer to any members of the control array by typing the name of the control, followed by its **Index** property within parentheses. Like this..."

I ran the program, paused it, and then entered this next statement in the Immediate window. When I typed the dot after the parentheses...

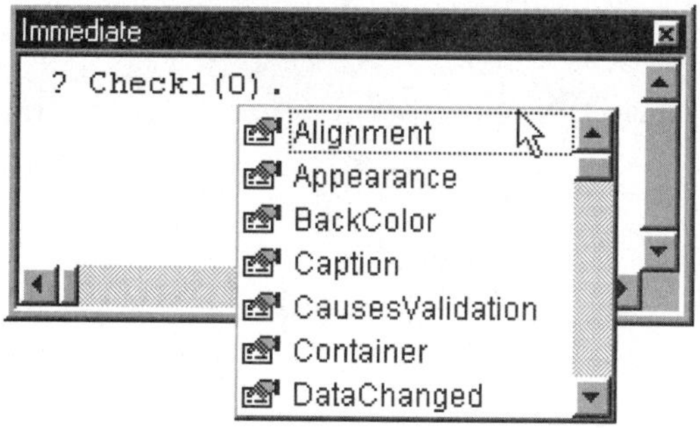

"As you can see," I said, "**`ListMembers`** displays the full list of properties and methods associated with the check box control."

"So what was Valerie's problem, again?" Chuck asked.

"Valerie was saying that she accidentally forgot to include the index value," I replied, "and when she followed the name of the control with a dot, she saw something that I didn't get, because I *did* use the index value in parentheses. Here's what Valerie saw:"

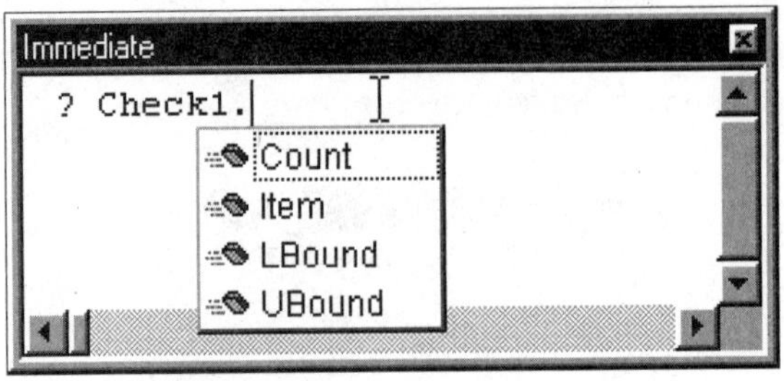

"OK," Chuck said, "I see what she's talking about now. Yes, that's happened to me also – I finally figured out that I was dealing with a control array."

"A control array," I said, "is a kind of collection. It's really another kind of system collection, and as was the case with the **`Forms`** and **`Controls`** collections, it's a collection that's created and maintained by Visual Basic."

"Well, now I'm curious," Chuck went on. "Are **`Count`** and **`Item`** that we see here the equivalent to what we've been talking about today in regard to collections?"

"All four methods you see here – **`Count`**, **`Item`**, **`LBound`** and **`UBound`** – are methods of the control array itself. So they *are* like the properties and methods of a collection."

"I remember **`LBound`** and **`UBound`** from our Intro class," Rhonda said. "As I recall, **`LBound`** returns a value equal to the lowest index value in a control array, and **`UBound`** returns a value equal to the highest index value. Is that right?"

"That's perfect, Rhonda," I said. "Let's experiment with both of those for a moment."

I proceeded by entering these next statements into the Immediate window:

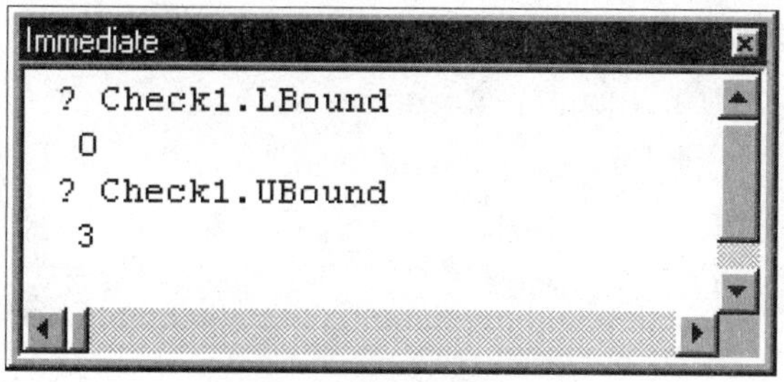

"As Rhonda has said," I continued, "**LBound** returns the lowest index property – **0**, and **UBound** returns the highest – **3**."

"Would I be correct in assuming," Ward said, "that the **Count** method returns the number of elements in a control array?"

"Yes, you're right there, Ward." I said, and I entered another statement into the Immediate window:

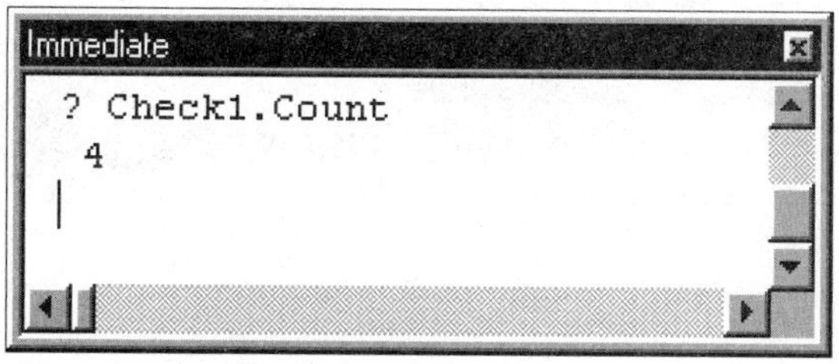

"What about the **Item** method?" Mary asked.

"First off," I replied, "the **Item** method isn't essential for getting at an individual member of a control array – all you need to do is type the name of the control, and then the index number within parentheses, followed by a property or method name. If you want, you can use the item method like this..."

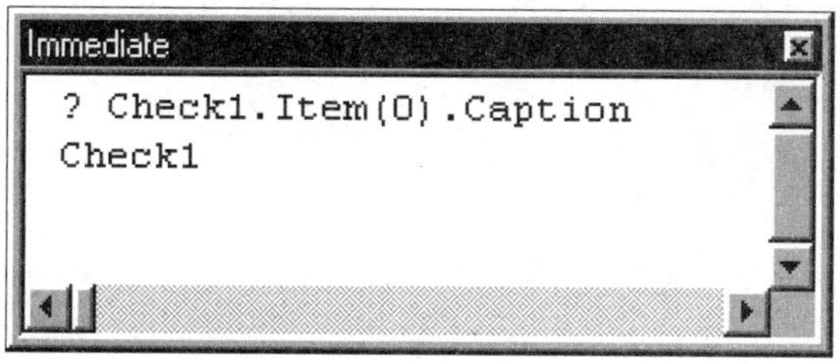

"...but as I say, it's not really necessary. You're better off using this notation instead:"

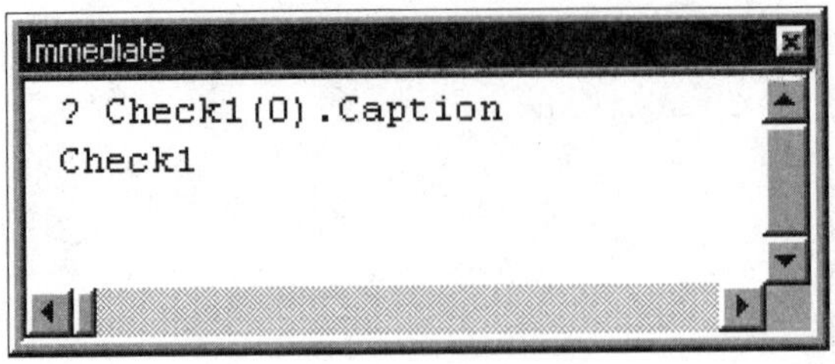

"Can we use a **For...Each** statement to loop through the members of a control array in the same way we can with a collection and a variable array?" Lou asked.

"Yes, we can, Lou." I answered. "Look at this code..."

I then placed this code in the **Click** event procedure of the command button...

```
Private Sub Command1_Click()

Dim chkObject As CheckBox

     For Each chkObject In Check1
          chkObject.Caption = chkObject.Index
     Next

End Sub
```

"As you can see," I said, "what we're doing here is using the **For...Each** statement to loop through each member of the control array. Within the body of the loop, we're then setting the **Caption** property of the member equal to its **Index** property. Notice how we declared **chkObject** as a check box type object variable:"

```
Dim chkObject As CheckBox
```

"That's most definitely early binding!"

I ran the program, and clicked on the command button, with this result:

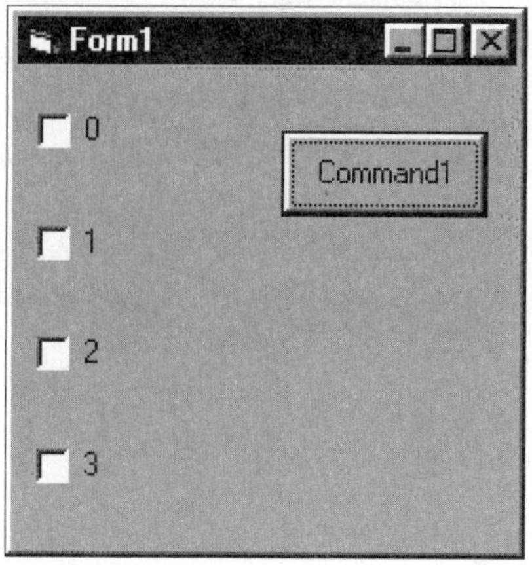

"The **For...Each** loop," I said, "has let us change the **Caption** property of every member of the control array, very quickly."

"I can see some practical applications for this already," Dorothy said. "I had no idea you could do this."

"I hope you've all seen how very valuable collections can be in a Visual Basic program," I said. "We'll be putting this new-found knowledge of collections to good use in the China Shop program in just a few moments. Before we do that, let me just summarize what we've seen in this session."

I displayed this next slide on the projector:

The Forms collection is another of the built-in objects created and maintained by Visual Basic. We can use it to help make sure that our program runs smoothly and effectively

We can create collection objects of our own to use instead of arrays. Collections can store different types of data – not just data of one type, as is the case with arrays

Collections have built-in methods and properties that we can work with in our code

We worked in detail with a collection that we created, and saw how to use its Add method and its arguments – Item, Key, Before and After

We saw how to use named arguments with a collection

Importantly, we saw that we can use a key value to uniquely identify and retrieve an item in a collection

We saw how a control array is an object, and how we can work with it

"At this point," I said, "it's time to turn our attention to the China Shop program, and work our way through some exercises that will set us off on the modification trail. That's how we'll finish off today's class, so stick with it – we're nearly there!"

Collections in the China Shop Program

"There are a number of modifications we can make to the China Shop program that use collections, and in the second exercise I've prepared, you're going to take the seven one-dimensional arrays we currently have in the program and replace them with a single collection. Before we can do that, however, we need to modify the structure of the China Shop's **`Prices.txt`** disk file. Remember, this file contains the China Shop's inventory prices – the prices of all the China Pieces that Joe's store sells."

Having set the scene, I distributed the first exercise for the students to complete. This is where you start to really get your hands dirty, too, as you modify the existing China Shop project that you should have installed on your own machine by now!

Exercise - Modifying the China Shop's Prices.txt file

In this exercise, you'll change the format of the **`Prices.txt`** file to accommodate the collection that you'll create in the exercise that follows this one. Let's begin!

1. Locate and open the **`Prices.txt`** file in your `[`*`drive letter`*`]` **`\VBFiles\China`** folder. Open the file in Notepad, or your preferred text editor.

2. Currently, the file looks like this:

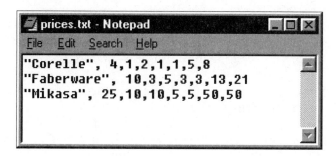

```
"Corelle", 4,1,2,1,1,5,8
"Faberware", 10,3,5,3,3,13,21
"Mikasa", 25,10,10,5,5,50,50
```

3. In order to make it easier to read the prices into a collection, modify the file so that it looks like this next screenshot. Type very carefully!

```
"Corelle","Plate", 4
"Corelle", "Butter Plate",1
"Corelle", "Soup Bowl",2
"Corelle", "Cup",1
"Corelle", "Saucer",1
"Corelle", "Platter",5
"Corelle", "Complete Place Setting",8
"Faberware", "Plate", 10
"Faberware", "Butter Plate",3
"Faberware", "Soup Bowl",5
"Faberware", "Cup",3
"Faberware", "Saucer",3
"Faberware", "Platter",13
"Faberware", "Complete Place Setting",21
"Mikasa", "Plate", 25
"Mikasa", "Butter Plate",10
"Mikasa", "Soup Bowl",10
"Mikasa", "Cup",5
"Mikasa", "Saucer",5
"Mikasa", "Platter",50
"Mikasa", "Complete Place Setting",50
```

4. Don't forget to save the file!

Discussion

"Why are we changing the format of the **Prices.txt** file?" Peter asked.

"This format," I said, "will make it easier for us to read the China Shop inventory prices into a collection of our own. Each line in the file fully represents a separate piece of inventory – it describes each china piece's brand, name, and price in dollars."

"Just a second," said Rhonda. "Won't this new file structure mean that the China Shop staff will need to update inventory prices differently?"

"No, Rhonda," I said. "Essentially, they'll still be able to update the inventory prices in the same way, using good old Notepad. In fact, I think this layout is less confusing than the old file. But we should ensure that we make sure that Joe's staff are made fully aware of the new file layout when we deliver the modified project."

"OK, I'll make a note of that," said Rhonda.

With that, I moved on to the next exercise.

Exercise - Loading Inventory Prices into a Collection Object instead of into Arrays

Here, you'll modify the China Shop project to load the inventory prices found in the **Prices.txt** file into a collection object. This collection object replaces the arrays that were used in the original project.

1. Load up the China Shop project.
2. Modify the code in the General Declarations section of the form so that it looks like the next listing. The additional line – adding a declaration for your own collection object – is highlighted, but ensure that you carefully delete the existing references to seven dynamic variable arrays. Your General Declarations section must look exactly like the code shown here:

```
Option Explicit

Private m_intQuantity As Integer
Private m_lngBackColor As Long
Private m_blnDateDisplay As Boolean
Private m_colDishPrice As New Collection
```

3. Locate the **ReadPrices** subprocedure in the General section, and carefully modify the code so that it looks like the code below. As usual, new lines, and lines that replace deleted code, are highlighted, but take great care to ensure that your modified code exactly matches what you see here. We'll talk the code changes through after you've made the amendments.

   Here's the code:

```
Public Sub ReadPrices()

On Error GoTo ICanHandleThis

Dim strTest As String
Dim strBrand As String
Dim strItem As String
Dim curPrice As Currency

Open "C:\VBFiles\China\Prices.txt" For Input As #1
   Do While Not EOF(1)
      Input #1, strBrand, strItem, curPrice
         m_colDishPrice.Add Item:=curPrice, Key:=strBrand & strItem
            If strBrand <> strTest Then
               lstBrands.AddItem strBrand
               strTest = strBrand
            End If
   Loop
Close #1

Exit Sub

ICanHandleThis:
Select Case Err.Number
  Case 53       'File not found
   MsgBox "A file required by the " &
      ➥"China Shop program " & vbCrLf &
      ➥"is missing. Please ensure that " & vbCrLf &
      ➥"Prices.txt is in " & vbCrLf &
      ➥"the China Shop directory " & vbCrLf &
      ➥"on the computer's hard drive"
   Unload frmMain
   Exit Sub
```

```
  Case Else
   MsgBox "Unexpected error has occurred" & vbCrLf &
       ↳"Contact John Smiley"
   Unload frmMain
   Exit Sub
 End Select

End Sub
```

4. Now modify the code in the `Click` event procedure of `cmdCalculate` to look like this:

```
Private Sub cmdCalculate_Click()

'Declare our variables
Dim curTotalPrice As Currency
Dim curBowlPrice As Currency
Dim curButterPlatePrice As Currency
Dim curCupPrice As Currency
Dim curPlatePrice As Currency
Dim curPlatterPrice As Currency
Dim curSaucerPrice As Currency
Dim curCompletePrice As Currency

'Has the customer selected a brand of china?
If lstBrands.Text = "" Then
  MsgBox "You must select a China brand"
  Exit Sub
End If

'Has the customer selected one or more china items?
If chkChinaItem(0).Value = 0 And
   ↳chkChinaItem(1).Value = 0 And
   ↳chkChinaItem(2).Value = 0 And
   ↳chkChinaItem(3).Value = 0 And
   ↳chkChinaItem(4).Value = 0 And
   ↳chkChinaItem(5).Value = 0 Then
 MsgBox "You must select one or more china items"
 Exit Sub
End If
```

```
'Has the customer selected a quantity?
If optQuantity(8).Value = False And
   ↪optQuantity(4).Value = False And
   ↪optQuantity(2).Value = False And
   ↪optQuantity(1).Value = False Then
  MsgBox "You must select a quantity"
  Exit Sub
End If

'If the customer has selected a platter
'warn them that there is only 1 permitted per sales
'quotation
If chkChinaItem(5).Value = 1 And m_intQuantity > 1 Then
  MsgBox "Customer is limited to 1 Platter per order" &
     ↪vbCrLf & "Adjusting price accordingly"
End If

'All the pieces are here, let's calculate a price
'Calculate subtotal prices by item
```

```
Dim strBrand As String

strBrand = lstBrands.Text

curBowlPrice = m_colDishPrice(lstBrands.Text & "Soup Bowl") *
  ↪chkChinaItem(2).Value

curButterPlatePrice = m_colDishPrice(lstBrands.Text & "Butter Plate") *
  ↪chkChinaItem(1).Value

curCompletePrice = m_colDishPrice(lstBrands.Text & "Complete Place
Setting")

curCupPrice = m_colDishPrice(lstBrands.Text & "Cup") *
  ↪chkChinaItem(3).Value

curPlatePrice = m_colDishPrice(lstBrands.Text & "Plate") *
  ↪chkChinaItem(0).Value

curPlatterPrice = m_colDishPrice(lstBrands.Text & "Platter") *
  ↪chkChinaItem(5).Value

curSaucerPrice = m_colDishPrice(lstBrands.Text & "Saucer") *
  ↪chkChinaItem(4).Value
```

```
If chkChinaItem(0).Value = 1 And
   ↳chkChinaItem(1).Value = 1 And
   ↳chkChinaItem(2).Value = 1 And
   ↳chkChinaItem(3).Value = 1 And
   ↳chkChinaItem(4).Value = 1 Then
  MsgBox "Price includes a Complete Place Setting Discount"
   curTotalPrice = (curCompletePrice * m_intQuantity) +
      ↳curPlatterPrice
Else
 curTotalPrice = (((curBowlPrice + curButterPlatePrice
    ↳+
     ↳curCupPrice + curPlatePrice + curSaucerPrice) *
        ↳m_intQuantity) + curPlatterPrice)
End If

'If the price is greater than 0, display the price and
'make the label visible
If curTotalPrice > 0 Then
  lblPrice.Caption = "The price of your order is " &
     ↳Format(curTotalPrice, "$##,###.00")
  lblPrice.Visible = True
End If

End Sub
```

5. Save the China Shop project by clicking on the save icon or using the menu options. Phew!

6. Run the program. Select Mikasa as your choice of china brand, select 2 for quantity and select Plate, Butter Plate and Soup Bowl as your china items. Then click on the Calculate command button. A calculated price of $90 should be displayed.

Discussion

"Let's take a good look at all this code," I said. "Firstly, let's go back to the change we made in the General Declarations section. I don't think anyone will have had any trouble with the declaration of the collection object in the General Declarations section of the form:"

```
Private m_colDishPrice As New Collection
```

"This collection will store all of the inventory prices," I said. "We declared the collection in the General Declarations section, because it needs to be accessed from multiple places within our project. Next, let's take a look at the modifications we made to the form's **ReadPrices** subprocedure. Remember that this subprocedure is called when the form loads, and that it's designed to read the inventory prices from the text file and use them to populate the 'brands' list box, and make the price information available to us in other places in the program. Now, because of the changes to the format of the file **Prices.txt**, the subprocedure's input statement has changed. We're no longer reading three records with eight fields of data each: instead, we're reading 21 records, one for each item of inventory in the China Shop, with three fields each. The first field represents the china brand, the second field the china piece (butter plate, soup bowl, cup, etc.), and the third field the price of that piece. In the code itself, after opening the **Prices.txt** file for input, we read these fields from **Prices.txt** and assign them to three variables that we can use in our program, using this next line of code:"

```
Input #1, strBrand, strItem, curPrice
```

"Note that the commas that separate the fields in the **Prices.txt** file allow the values there to be read into these three variables. The next line of code within the **Do** loop," I continued, "executes the **Add** method of the collection:"

```
m_colDishPrice.Add Item:=curprice, Key:=strBrand & strItem
```

"Notice how we're using named arguments here (I saw Rhonda smile at this point), and adding the price of each china piece from **Prices.txt** as an item of the **m_colDishPrice** collection. We're also specifying the combination of brand and china-piece name as the key argument."

"That's pretty clever," Kate said. "So the actual **Item** in the collection is the price of a china piece – the third field in **Prices.txt**, while the **Key** is the combined first and second fields – the brand and description of the china-piece?"

"That's right, Kate," I said, "we **concatenate** the two strings – brand and description – to obtain the key. Using this key value, we'll be able to locate the price of any item in the inventory quickly – just by using its brand and china-piece name. Look..."

I started the China Shop project, then paused it, and entered a statement in the Immediate window:

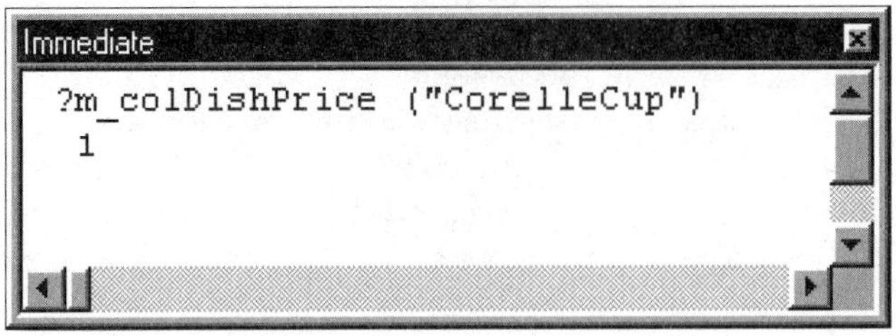

"What I've done here is interrogate the **colDishPrice** collection. I've asked it to access the item whose **Key** value is CorelleCup – remember, this is the concatenation of the two fields from **Prices.txt** – and it's telling me that item 1 refers to this piece of inventory."

"Cool," said Dave, "that's really cool."

"What's going on with that next section of code?" Linda asked. "I'm afraid that lost me entirely!"

"You must mean this part," I said, as I displayed this next code snippet on the classroom projector:

```
If strBrand <> strTest Then
    lstBrands.AddItem strBrand
    strTest = strBrand
  End If
```

"That's it," Linda confirmed, "what the heck is this doing?"

"This confuses everyone at first," I reassured her. "What I'm doing here is using an old programming trick – an **algorithm**, for those of you who remember that term from our Intro class – that I use whenever you have duplicate values in an input file."

"Duplicate values?" Chuck asked. "Where are the duplicate values?"

"Take a look at the **Prices.txt** input file again," I said. "The previous version of the file had just a single record representing each brand. This time, because of the way we want to read the data into our collection, we have seven records for each brand."

"I see," Ward said, "the brand name is repeated seven times!"

"That's right," I said, "and if we're not careful, we'll wind up with duplicated brand names in the list box on our form, since we're using the brand name in the input file – **`Prices.txt`** – to load them."

"Right!" Mary said, nodding. "Seven Corelles, seven Faberwares, seven Mikasas! And this code will prevent that, will it?" she asked.

"That's correct, Mary," I said. "What we've done is declare a variable called **`strTest`** that's used to determine if the brand name in the record just read is one which the program hasn't read before. We compare the current value of **`strBrand`** – the brand name of the record just obtained from **`Prices.txt`** – to the current value of **`strTest`**:"

```
If strBrand <> strTest Then
```

"If they're different, that means that **`strBrand`** is a new brand name, and we add it to the list box using the list box's **`AddItem`** method:"

```
lstBrands.AddItem strBrand
```

"Otherwise, we ignore it. More importantly, we then assign the value of **`strBrand`** to **`strTest`**, so that the next time through the loop, we'll know the last brand name added to the list box..."

```
strTest = strBrand
```

"...That way, if the next record read contains the same brand name, **`strBrand`** and **`strTest`** will be equal, and that brand name will not be added to the list box."

"And it won't be, until a record with a different brand name comes along," Valerie said.

"That's right, Valerie," I said. "By the way, vitally important to the effectiveness of this algorithm is the fact that the file we are reading is sorted by brand name – that's another bit of information we need to ensure we make clear to Joe's staff."

"But what about the first time you read a record in the file?" Peter said, "There's no value in the variable **`strTest`** at that stage. What happens then?"

"A **`String`** variable is initialized to an empty string," I explained. "An *empty* string is just as much a string as any other, and can be compared with other strings without the program bombing. The first time the comparison of **`strBrand`** and **`strTest`** is made, the two values are unequal – and the brand name is added to the list box, as we want."

"That's a pretty neat algorithm," Rhonda said, "it seems really clever."

"The rest of the code in that section is the same error handler that the project has always used," I said. "Let's take a look at the **cmdCalculate** command button's code now."

"I love that code in the **Click** event procedure of the command button," Valerie said. "It looks like we've dropped all references to the arrays we had in the original code and replaced it with collection references – that sure streamlined the code, didn't it?"

"You're right about that, Valerie," I said "we're no longer using the variable arrays we coded in the Intro course – but using collections instead. The ability to retrieve a collection item using the key value makes collections a great tool. For instance, with this line of code, using the combination of the **Text** property of the list box and the literal value **SoupBowl** – which matches the key value that we used when we populated the collection from the **Prices.txt** file – we can retrieve the price of the specific brand's soup bowl item from our collection:"

```
curBowlPrice = m_colDishPrice(lstBrands.Text & "SoupBowl") *
  ↳chkChinaItem(2).Value
```

"We then multiply that by the value of the check box for that item – which, because it is either **True** or **False**, one or zero, either preserves or eliminates that value for the purposes of our calculation." I explained. "We then continue that process for all of the other component pieces:"

```
curButterPlatePrice = m_colDishPrice(lstBrands.Text & "ButterPlate") *
  ↳chkChinaItem(1).Value

curCompletePrice = m_colDishPrice(lstBrands.Text & "Complete")

curCupPrice = m_colDishPrice(lstBrands.Text & "Cup") *
  ↳chkChinaItem(3).Value

curPlatePrice = m_colDishPrice(lstBrands.Text & "Plate") *
  ↳chkChinaItem(0).Value

curPlatterPrice = m_colDishPrice(lstBrands.Text & "Platter") *
  ↳chkChinaItem(5).Value

curSaucerPrice = m_colDishPrice(lstBrands.Text & "Saucer") *
  ↳chkChinaItem(4).Value
```

"The rest of the code," I said, "is identical to what we had before."

Again I waited to see if there were any other questions. No one seemed to be having any problems understanding what was going on, as they busily put their own versions of the China Shop project through their paces.

"I don't know about anyone else," Ward said, "but I find this code a great deal easier to follow than the previous version. I think I prefer using a collection to using an array."

"A lot of people feel that way about collections," I said, "once they find out about them."

"What about that technique you showed us a few minutes ago," Kate said, "where we were able to change the **Caption** property of every check box in a control array? I think you said we might be able to put that to practical use in the China Shop project."

"That's right, Kate" I said. "In fact, our final exercise of the day is to do exactly that."

Here's the exercise:

Exercise - Modifying the cmdReset Button to use an Object Variable

In this exercise, you'll modify the **cmdReset** button to use an object variable to reset the controls on the main China Shop form.

1. If it's not already loaded, open up the China Shop project.
2. Modify the code in the **cmdReset** button's **Click** event procedure so that it matches the following code (you'll be deleting a lot of lines that reset the check boxes and option buttons and replacing them with a **For...Each** structure). Again, make your changes carefully:

```
Private Sub cmdReset_Click()

Dim chkObject As CheckBox
Dim optObject As OptionButton

lstBrands.ListIndex = -1

For Each chkObject In chkChinaItem
  chkObject.Value = 0
Next
```

```
For Each optObject In optQuantity
  optObject.Value = False
Next

chkCompletePlaceSetting.Value = 0
lblPrice.Visible = False
imgChina.Picture = LoadPicture()

End Sub
```

3. Save the China Shop project.

4. Run the program. Select Mikasa as your choice of china brand, select 2 for quantity and select Plate, Butter Plate and Soup Bowl as your china items. Then click on the Calculate command button. A calculated price of $90 should be displayed. Now click on the Reset command button. The list box will be unselected; the check boxes will be unchecked; the option buttons will be unselected; the Price label will become invisible; and the image control will be cleared.

Discussion

I set about explaining this exercise's code: "All we've done here is create some control object variables..."

```
Dim chkObject As CheckBox
Dim optObject As OptionButton
```

"...and we've simplified the resetting process by using the **For...Each** statement to loop through the members of the check box and option button control arrays:"

```
For Each chkObject In chkChinaItem
  chkObject.Value = 0
Next

For Each optObject In optQuantity
  optObject.Value = False
Next
```

"That's very neat." Ward observed.

"Thanks Ward," I said, gratefully. "I think you can see that the work we've done in this lesson has already contributed to slimming down the China Shop's code, as well as giving us some really important background knowledge on objects, classes, collections, and a host of other things. I'm sorry we overran by so much – there really is a lot to pack into this lesson. But don't worry, next week's lesson is a shorter one, so you'll be able to get your breath back!"

"OK, folks," I went on, "let's close down the China Shop program and wrap up for the day."

Since we were working in Design mode, we didn't have to go through the Exit menu, as we would have done in the working model of the application.

"Just before we finish up, Professor," said Tom, "could you give us a quick summary of all that we've done today? We've covered so much ground that I'd like to try and pull it all together before I leave."

I saw a lot of heads nodding in agreement, so I kept the class for just a few moments longer while I summarized our busy day.

Chapter Summary

In this chapter we saw how Visual Basic collections – both the system collections that Visual Basic creates and maintains, and the programmer-created collections that we make ourselves – can make our programming tasks much easier. Here are the main points of the lesson that I summarized for the class on the projector screen:

- We saw that Visual Basic programs have a number of objects built into them. Specifically, we looked at **control objects**, and at the **system objects** that can help us in our programming
- We learned that objects are based on special templates called **classes**. These classes define the built-in **properties**, **methods**, and **events** for objects of the same type
- We learned about **collections**, which are objects that Visual Basic uses to store references to a group of **items**. These references **point** the program towards the actual objects that the collection stores information about
- We looked at the `Controls` and `Forms` collections in detail. We saw that collections come with their own built-in **methods** and **properties** that we can use to interrogate and manipulate the items in the collection

- We also learned about using **object variables** in code, and how they can be used with loop structures and collections to perform multiple operations on a group of controls or other objects
- We created a collection of our own, and saw how to add items to it using the built-in `Add` method and a range of arguments

Then I summarized the changes that we'd started to make to the China Shop program:

- We modified the `Prices.txt` inventory prices file so that it could be used with a programmer-defined collection
- We created a programmer-defined collection to load the inventory price information into. This collection object will make the inventory price information available to our program so that it can be used in a consistent, object-oriented way. We also wrote the code that reads the `Prices.txt` file and loads it into the collection
- We started modifying the code in the `cmdCalculate` and `cmdReset` buttons

"Next week," I said, "we'll be discussing some more Visual Basic system objects, and explore how we can work with them in more depth. This will expand our knowledge of objects and give us some more important background on using them in the modified China Shop program. Thank you for your patience and attention this week, and I'll see you all next week!"

With that, I dismissed the class, and we all pulled on our coats and hats and made our way out into the parking lot.

Learn to Program Objects with Visual Basic
Bullina's
China

Chapter 3

Visual Basic System Objects

This week's class is concerned with helping my students build up their understanding of the objects that are built into every Visual Basic program by default. We describe them, and see them in action. These **system objects** can give your Visual Basic program a lot of pizzazz and power, and I think you'll find them quite useful.

I'll start this week's lesson by introducing the concept of how to make a Visual basic program more aware of its location within the Windows operating system, and we'll go on to show how we can utilize tools within that operating system to perform some expert-looking effects.

With regard to the China shop program, we'll be introducing a few small changes which, while simple to implement in themselves, are actually not just the minor alterations they may first appear to be: they'll give the application a far greater degree of portability and give it a much more professional feel.

Here's a preview of what we'll cover in this week's lesson:

- The **`Global`** object. This is the most 'universal' object in a Visual Basic program, and it acts as a container for a number of other objects that give our program the ability to interact with the Windows Clipboard, with printers, and with the monitor screen
- We'll also look at the other system objects that are contained within the **`Global`** object: including the **`App`** object, the **`Printer`** object, and the **`Screen`** object. Working with these adds flexibility and consistency of operation to our programs
- Employing the Clipboard object to cut, copy and paste within our application and between our application and other Windows programs
- We'll also put what we learn about these objects to work in the China Shop program – this will make the China Shop more robust and user-friendly

Let's join my class for the third lesson.

The Visual Basic System Objects

The third week of the Objects class fell on a bright, chill February morning: the kind of Saturday that's so quiet it feels like a Sunday. The ornamental ponds in the University grounds had frozen over, and on my way up from the car park I threw some crusts of bread to the cluster of forlorn ducks that were squatting under the bare trees by the gate.

Some of the students were already in the classroom when I arrived, shaking the frost out of their bones. They greeted me cheerily as I set down my briefcase and threw off my overcoat. I didn't start the lesson straight away, as I was anticipating a few late arrivals due to the cold weather. Sure enough, one or two people struggled in a few minutes after time. Ward was last in, and he apologized: his car had broken down and he'd had to catch the bus. I told him not to worry – I was pleased at the effort that all of the students had made to get here on such an inauspicious morning.

"Today," I began, as Ward settled into his seat, "I want to discuss the Visual Basic **system objects** – although technically speaking, they're all really properties of what we call the `Global` object."

"You're saying that the system objects are themselves properties of another object – this `Global` object?" Dave enquired.

"Yes," I replied, "the system objects are the built-in components that handle communication between your Visual Basic program and the various objects that make up the Windows operating system itself. Windows operating system objects like the Clipboard and the Printer Object contain functionality which can be really useful in a Visual Basic application, and the Visual Basic system objects that we'll discuss today allow our program to communicate with those Windows objects and use their functionality."

"I don't quite follow that," admitted Rhonda. "Are the Visual basic system objects the same things as the Windows operating system objects?"

"No, and this is quite a subtle point, so I'll emphasize it," I said. "Remember how I said that objects in you program represent things in the outside world? Well, as far as Visual Basic is concerned, the Windows operating system is part of that outside world. The Visual Basic system objects are what Visual Basic uses to let our programs communicate with the operating system. So the VB system objects act as an interface – a channel of communication between our program's self-written code and the world outside."

I displayed this summary graphic for the class to look at:

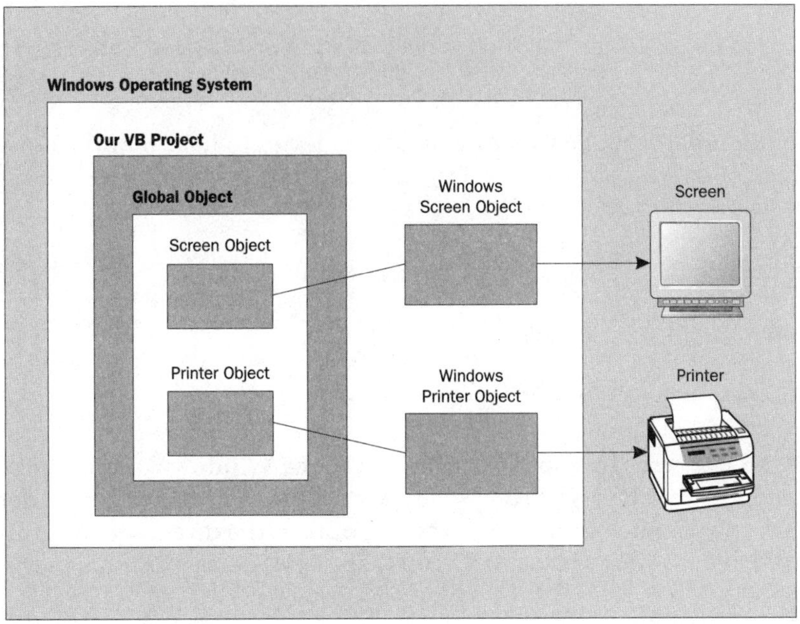

"So," I explained, "there are several layers between our program and the outside world. But the bottom line is that we talk to the system objects inside our program, and they take care of communicating with the operating system for us. And it's the Windows operating system that talks direct to the outside world. Fortunately, this interface functionality is all embedded in the Visual Basic system objects – all we need to do is reference them, and their built-in behavior takes over, insulating us from all the hazards that lie between our program and the outside world."

I paused, and then said: "And the premier Visual Basic system object is the **`Global`** object."

The Global Object

"So what does the **`Global`** object actually do?" Rhonda asked.

"Not a lot, in itself," I replied. "The **`Global`** object assembles all of the Visual Basic system objects in one logical place. In fact, we tend not to actually refer to the **`Global`** object explicitly. In many ways, it acts simply as a container for the system objects – rather like the way a form presents our controls to the user in a neat, easy-to-use format."

"So can the Visual Basic system objects can be regarded as system *properties*?" Ward suggested. "That is, as properties of the **`Global`** object?"

"Good, Ward," I replied. "You've hit the nail on the head. You can think of them either way – as objects in themselves, or as properties of the **Global** object."

"So, are we going to be creating a **Global** object this lesson?" asked Rhonda, slightly worried.

"Good question, Rhonda," I replied, "and you'll be relieved to hear that the answer is 'no'. The **Global** object is *automatically* created for us when our program runs – it's a 'given' in every Visual Basic program we write."

"And its properties are the system objects?" prompted Rhonda.

"Exactly," I replied.

"What can the system objects tell us?" Blaine enquired.

"Apart from giving us access to some neat features of the Windows operating system, like the Clipboard and Printer objects," I said, "they also allow our application to determine things about itself at run-time: things like whereabouts in the directory structure of your computer's hard drive it's files are located. You'll see how we can use this in the China Shop project shortly."

"So what exactly are the system objects?" Asked Mary.

"Well, I don't suppose it'll surprise you if I tell you you've been using some of them already!" I replied, with a smile. "The **Forms** collection which we saw last week was one of them." I revealed.

No one seemed overly surprised by this, but I could see they were interested.

"We can use the Visual Basic Object Browser to view the properties of the **Global** object," I said. "Let me show you."

I created a new Visual Basic project and selected View | Object Browser from the Visual Basic menu bar to display the Object Browser on the classroom projector. The following screenshot was displayed:

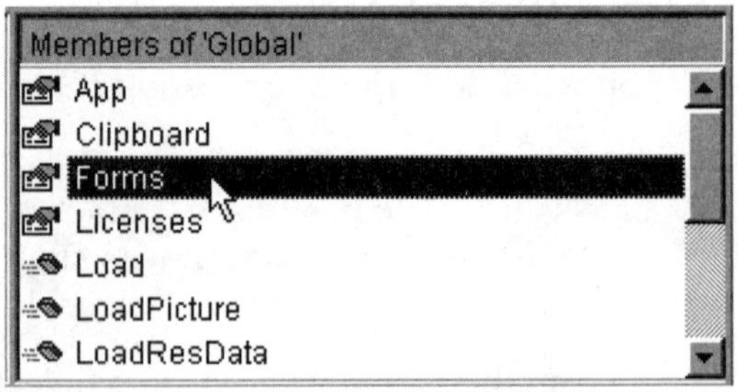

"The Object Browser," I said, "enables us to see the objects held in the object libraries that our Visual Basic program is using."

"By 'libraries', what are you referring to?" Kate asked.

"The Visual Basic **libraries** contain pre-written code for the objects that you're likely to need," I explained. "The libraries contain the underlying class-templates for these objects, and this saves having to create them for yourself."

"By 'class', do you mean that thing you likened to a cookie cutter last week?" Rhonda asked.

"Exactly, Rhonda," I said. "A class is a blueprint or template for an object. Every object in Visual Basic has a template or class defined for it someplace. All of the control objects – such as the check box and command button – are contained in the VB library."

I selected the VB library from the libraries list box, to show that this was indeed so:

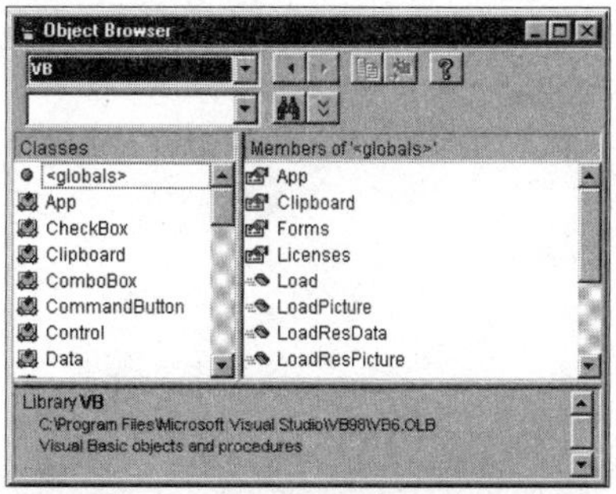

"Every Visual Basic project we create uses at the very least the **stdole**, **VB**, **VBA** and **VBRUN** libraries." I went on. "Those are the four libraries that appear in the drop-down list box. To see the properties and methods of the Visual Basic `Global` object, all we need to do is type the word 'global' into the Objects Browser's search box, and then click on the binoculars. When we do, a list of the members of the `Global` object will be displayed:"

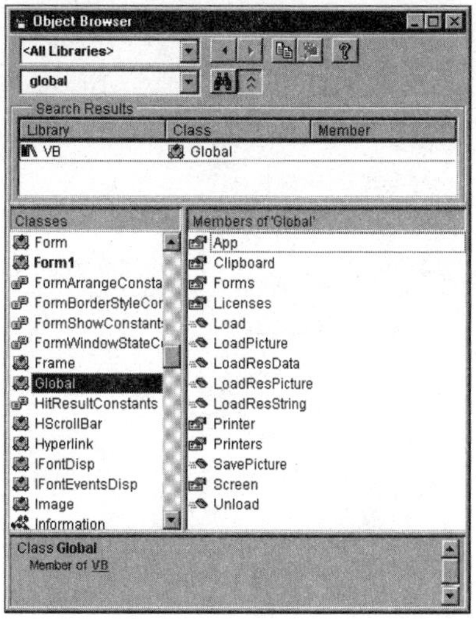

"As you can see," I said, "the `Global` object – or rather, its class – is defined in the VB library."

"You mentioned the word 'members' a minute or so ago?" Kevin said. "What do you mean by that?"

"**Members**," I said, "refers to the properties, methods and events of an object. Let's take a closer look at the `Global` object in the Object Browser. As you can see, there are 14 members of the class – seven properties and seven methods. In the Object Browser, **properties** are represented by the – let's call it the 'pointing hand' icon..."

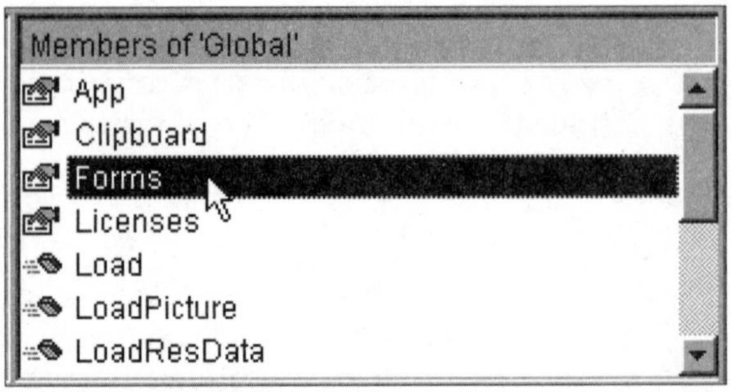

"...and methods are represented by the 'green brick' icon:"

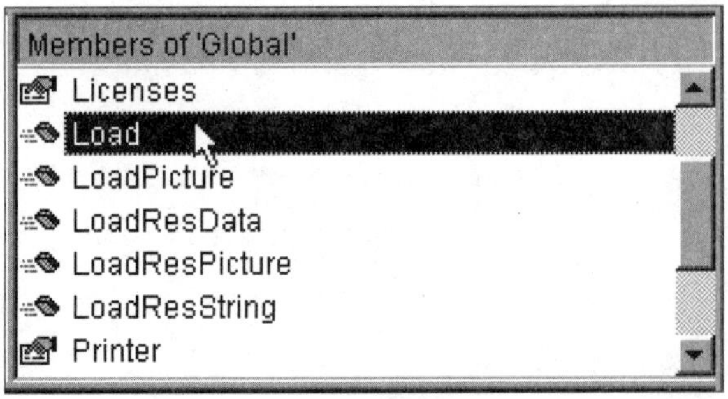

"In today's class we'll be interested solely in the properties of the **`Global`** object – **`App`**, **`Clipboard`**, **`Forms`**, **`Licenses`**, **`Printer`**, **`Printers`** and **`Screen`**:"

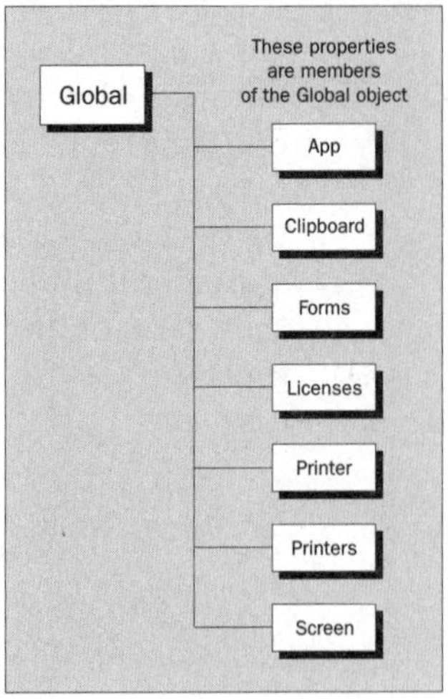

"Is there ever a need to refer to the `Global` object in our code?" Bob asked.

"Not specifically," I said, "but if we wanted to, we could. Let's see how it could actually be done in a project that we're already familiar with."

I loaded up the demo project from the previous week's class and displayed the form to remind the class of what it looked like:

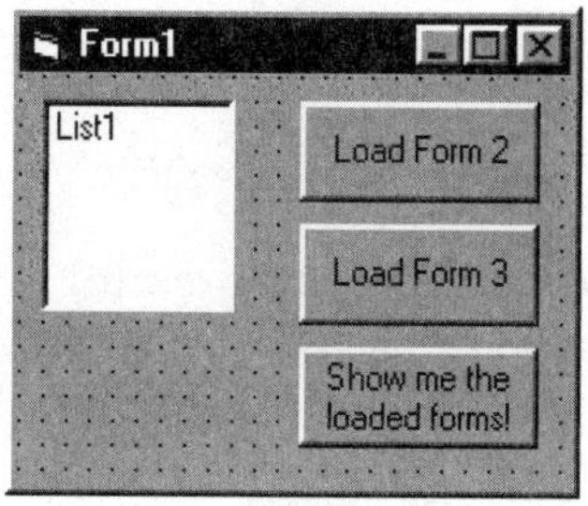

"Let's recap," I said, "this demo shows how we can load and unload different forms into and out of the **Forms** collection in a multi-form project."

"Yeah, I remember," said Ward. "You wanted to show how we could use the **Forms** collection to loop through the loaded forms and unload them, to ensure we didn't leave any 'orphaned' forms lying around!"

"Well, now I'll show you how to use the **Global** object to do the same thing," I explained, and I modified the code for the **Click** event of **Command3** to look like this next code snippet, replacing the existing **For Each** statement with the one highlighted here:

```
Private Sub Command3_Click()

Dim objForm As Form

List1.Clear

For Each objForm in VB.Global.Forms
      List1.AddItem objForm.Caption
Next

End Sub
```

"Notice that we're now using **dot notation** to reference the **Forms** collection as a member of the **Global** object, which is, itself, contained within the **VB** Library," I said:

```
For Each objForm in VB.Global.Forms
```

"Previously we just referred directly to the **Forms** collection..." I added, showing the previous code for comparison:

```
For Each objForm in Forms
```

"Those two bits of code don't actually look that different," Observed Rhonda.

"You're right, they're not," I told her. "It's just that in the first case, we're referring to the **Global** object explicitly by name; in the second, the **Global** object is accessed implicitly. It isn't necessary to reference the **Global** object explicitly when referencing any of its properties. What I'm trying to show you here is that the **Global** object really *is there*, behind the scenes."

I ran the program and clicked on the command button captioned Show me the loaded forms!:

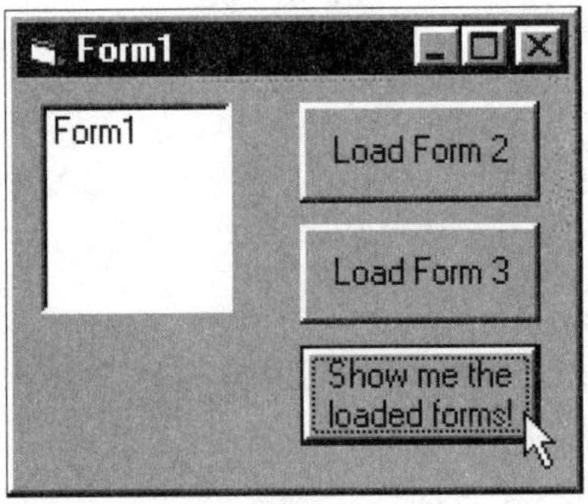

"The program runs just as it did before," I pointed out.

To prove that this, I clicked on the buttons captioned Load Form 2 and Load Form 3, moved both forms out of the way of Form1, and then clicked again on the button captioned Show me the loaded forms!:

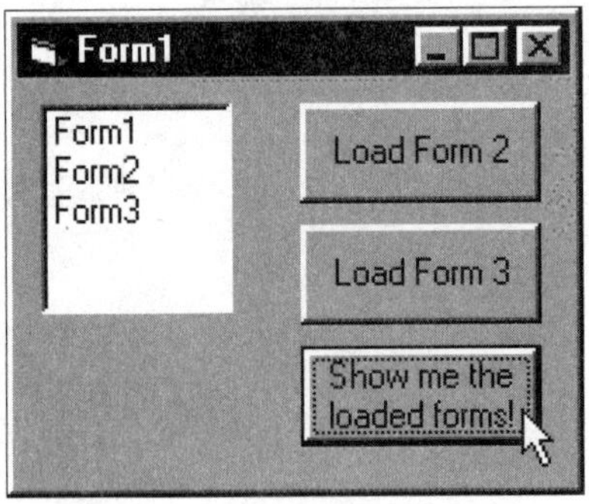

"As was the case last week," I said, "by clicking on the Show me the loaded forms! command button, the captions of all the loaded forms in our application are displayed in the list box. The results are identical – despite the fact that in this code we explicitly used the **Global** object to refer to the **Forms** collection."

"So, the **Forms** collection is both an object in itself – as we saw last week – and a property of the **Global** object?" Dave offered, tentatively.

"Bang on, Dave!" I replied. "I'm glad you're following this."

"I have a question," Melissa said. "You said that a property of an object can itself be an object. Can that second object then have properties which are *also* objects?"

"Absolutely!" I answered. "The **Forms** collection is a property of the **Global** object, but it has it's own properties – such as the controls that sit on the form – which are, in themselves, objects. We call this an **object hierarchy**, and the **Global** object sits at the top of this hierarchy and is thus referred to as a **top-level object**. You'll find that object hierarchies can go pretty deep. Later on in the course, when we look at manipulating Microsoft Word and Excel objects from within our Visual Basic programs, you'll see an object hierarchy that is many levels deep."

"Can we go back to the Object Browser for a minute?" Kathy said. " Some of those methods for the **Global** object ring a bell – like the **Load** statement and the **LoadPicture** statement: I'm sure we've seen those before. I always thought **Load** and **LoadPicture** were Visual Basic statements. Are you telling us they're actually methods of the **Global** object?"

"That's right, Kathy," I said. "The **LoadPicture** statement – or what you thought was the **LoadPicture** statement – is actually a method of the **Global** object. As was the case just now, when we worked with the **Forms** control in code, there's no need to preface **LoadPicture** with the name of the **Global** object – Visual Basic assumes by default that this is where to find it."

"So, if we'd wanted to," Steve suggested, "we could fully reference the name of the **Global** object when we used the **LoadPicture** method to load the china inventory brand icon into our image control?"

"That's right, Steve," I answered. "We *could* have – but again, it isn't necessary."

"So it's the properties of the Visual Basic **Global** object that we'll be discussing today, is that right?" Dorothy said.

"That's right, Dorothy," I said. "There are seven properties of the **`Global`** object. Last week, when we talked about the **`Forms`** collection, we were actually discussing the **`Forms`** property of the **`Global`** object. In the Intro course we covered the **`Printer`** property – as the '**`Printer`** object'. Now, we just don't have that much use for the **`Licenses`** property in this course, so we'll just be discussing the other four in detail today: the **`App`**, **`Clipboard`**, **`Printers`** and **`Screen`** properties. For good measure, we're going to discuss one other property – the **`Fonts`** property – which is a property of both the **`Printer`** and **`Screen`** object."

"Sounds like we have our work cut out," Mary said. "Where do we start?"

The App Object

"Let's start with the **`App`** object," I said, "This stands for **Application** object. As you might expect from its name, the **`App`** object provides information about our complete Visual Basic application – our program – itself: such as its **Title**, information about which **Version** it is, the **Path** and **Name** of its executable file, and whether or not there are any other instances of the application running already."

"In other words," Tom said, "the **`App`** object is telling the Visual Basic project information about itself."

"That's one way of looking at it, Tom," I said. "A lot of the information that the **`App`** object provides are attributes of the project, and are supplied at run-time. There are two properties of the **`App`** object that I find especially useful – the **`PrevInstance`** property and the **`Path`** property."

The App Object's PrevInstance Property

"**`PrevInstance`** property?" Steve asked. "Does that let our program know there's another instance of the program running?"

"That's a good guess, Steve," I said, "and you're correct. This can come in quite handy if you want to actually *prevent* more than one instance of your program from being run at the same time."

"How could that happen?" Rhonda asked. "I certainly can't imagine anyone in the China Shop doing that."

"I don't think that anyone in the China Shop would intentionally run two instances of the program simultaneously," I said, "but it could happen accidentally. We've taken measures in the China Shop program to prevent the main form being minimized, but suppose one member of the China Shop staff were to start up the China Shop program and then start Microsoft Word – the China Shop program would automatically be minimized to an icon on the Windows taskbar at the bottom of the screen. Since it's no longer obvious that the China Shop program has already been started, another instance might be started up by the user."

"I see what you mean," Peter said. "But is it bad to have two instances of the same program running?"

"Not necessarily," I said. "It really depends on what the program is doing. Some programs – the kind that update files or databases – could be severely impacted by having the same program running twice. A good example is Microsoft Word. If two copies of Word were allowed to open at once, they would each be able to make changes to the same document simultaneously. This could be disastrous, and Microsoft has taken steps to prevent it from ever happening."

"But Windows seems to have let *me* open up two copies of Word!" Said Ward. "I just tried it while you were talking."

"*Seems* to, yes," I replied, glancing at his monitor and recognizing his mistake. "You double-clicked on the Word icon and got two documents on your Windows taskbar that you can now flip between. However, only one version of the Word program itself has been opened. The second instance you opened was of a second *document*, which opens within the same copy of Word. Remember, Word is an MDI – a Multi Document Interface. Fresh documents open up, which exist as sub-forms within the main application's form."

"Oh, yeah. I'd forgotten that," Ward conceded.

"So, we can use the `App` object to do the same thing – to prevent more than one instance of the China Shop program from running?" Kate asked.

"That's right, Kate," I answered. "You'll see in a minute that it's a simple operation to use the `App` object to determine if another instance of the program is already running – and if it is, to terminate the second instance of the program."

Now Dave had his hand raised.

"You say we haven't got this functionality built into the China Shop project, yet," he said, "but I just tried running two copies of the China Shop program here on my PC in the computer lab, and Visual Basic wouldn't let me – it said the project file was already opened. How come?"

"That's because you're trying to open the China Shop program from within two different instances of the Visual Basic IDE," I explained, after taking a look at his machine. "Visual Basic won't permit you to open a project file twice like that. In order to test the **App** object's **PrevInstance** property, we're first going to have to compile the China Shop program and produce an executable file. Then we'll try to run two instances of the executable."

Rhonda and several other students immediately had a puzzled look on their face.

"I know we didn't do that last Semester," Kathy said, "compile the China Shop program into an executable, that is. Don't the China Shop staff run the program from within the Visual Basic IDE?"

"That's true," I said, "the China Shop staff do just that. Does anyone remember why?"

"I believe," Ward suggested, "that it's because last semester we were using the **Visual Basic Working Model Edition**. That version of Visual Basic doesn't have the functionality to let you create an executable – isn't that right?"

"That's exactly right, Ward," I said. "That's why, at the end of last semester, we installed a copy of the Visual Basic Working Model Edition on the China Shop PC, and that's how the program is run – from within the Visual Basic IDE."

"Are we still using the Working Model here in the lab?" Dorothy asked.

"Yes and no," I said. "My PC up here at my Instructor's station has a copy of **Visual Basic Enterprise Edition** loaded, but all of the student PCs are still loaded with the Working Model Edition. Although this means you won't be able to test the **PrevInstance** property of the **App** object, I'll be able to demonstrate how it works for you. Let me load up the China Shop project now, and compile it into an executable..."

I started up Visual Basic, opened the China Shop project, and selected File | Make China Shop.Exe from the Visual Basic menu bar:

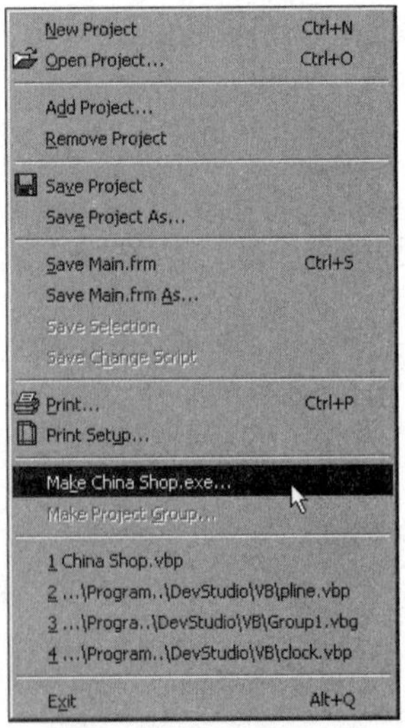

I then specified that the executable should be saved in the `\VBFiles\China` subdirectory.

"If we now bring up the Windows Explorer," I said, "and double-click on the China Shop executable, we'll start up an instance of the China Shop project..."

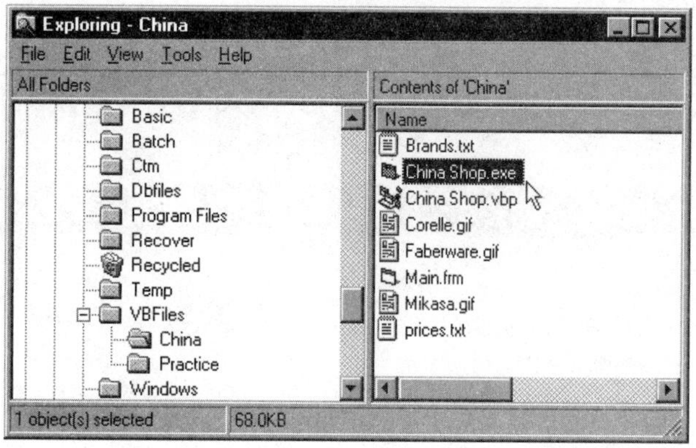

I did just that. The China Shop program started up, with the main form displayed.

"So, what's happened here exactly?" Dorothy asked.

"When I compiled the program, I made a machine-code version of the China Shop," I explained. "This machine-code version has all the material it needs from the Visual Basic libraries built-in to it, so that it can run within the Windows operating system without the support of the Visual Basic IDE."

"So, if you start two instances of the China Shop program on your machine now, what'll happen?" asked Dave.

"Well, let's find out!" I said.

I double-clicked on the executable again in Windows Explorer. A second instance of the China Shop program immediately started up. I spent a few minutes interacting with both programs (doing my best not to get confused, I should add!), made two distinct selections of china pieces, and received two distinct price quotations.

"I see what you mean," Kate said. "If the China Shop executable were represented by an icon on the desktop, it would be pretty easy to have two or more instances of the program running simultaneously."

"Yes, Kate," I said, "I don't think it's too far-fetched to imagine a user doing this. But there's a quick fix..."

Using PrevInstance in the China Shop's Code

"In fact, I have an exercise here that everyone in the class can complete to prevent more than one instance of the China Shop program from running at the same time." So saying, I distributed this exercise for the class to complete:

Exercise - Check for Existing Instances of the China Shop Program

1. Load up the China Shop project.

2. Modify the code in the **Load** event procedure of **frmMain** so that it looks like this:

```
Private Sub Form_Load()

If App.PrevInstance = True Then
  MsgBox "The China Shop program is already running..."
  Unload Me
  Exit Sub
End If

Call ReadTheRegistry
Call ReadPrices

If m_blnDateDisplay Then
 Call mnuPreferencesDateandTimeOn_Click
Else
 Call mnuPreferencesDateandTimeOff_Click
End If

frmMain.BackColor = m_lngBackColor

End Sub
```

3. Save the China Shop project.

4. If the version of Visual Basic that you are running supports compilation, select File | Make China Shop.Exe from the Visual Basic menu bar, and compile the program into an executable.

> **Even if your version of Visual Basic doesn't support the creation of executables, you can test this by trying to start up two versions of the China Shop using the executable we've supplied on the CD. The China Shop executable file can be found in the `For Chapter 03\China Shop Code\China Shop` EXE folder. The executable file is called `China Shop EXE.exe`.**

5. Then use Windows Explorer to run the executable. After the first instance of the China Shop program starts up, use Windows Explorer again to try to start another instance of the program – you should receive a warning message telling you that the China Shop program is already running.

> **Remember that you can shut down this executable version of the China Shop by using the File | Exit menu options, then keying the password 061883 into the dialog box.**

Discussion

As I mentioned earlier, the PCs in the computer lab were still running the Visual Basic Working Model Edition, and so the students couldn't compile the China Shop program into an executable. Fortunately, my PC had Visual Basic Enterprise Edition loaded, and I *could* do so. When prompted by Visual Basic I gave the compiled program the title **`China Shop EXE.exe`**.

"I've just had a brainwave," I exclaimed, gazing at the compiled executable of the China Shop program I'd just made. "Why don't I just e-mail this program to all of you over the classroom's local area network?"

"Hey, that's a terrific idea," Ward declared. "We could all experiment with it, then."

I opened up my mail server, started a new mail message and put the China Shop executable I'd just built into it as an attachment. I then copied all of the classroom machines into the address list and posted the mail message out to the class.

"Be very careful," I cautioned them, as they opened up my mail message. "Be sure to move the attached file into the **`C:\VBFiles\China`** directory before you try running it: if you don't, the program won't be able to find the **`Prices.txt`** or image files – and because this is an executable version of the program, it will lock-up and you won't be able to escape from it."

"Boy, thanks for reminding me about that!" Ward declared. "I was just about to double-click on the executable straight from the e-mail attachment you just sent! That could have been messy!" He laughed.

I gave them all a few moments to move the executable file into the **`VBFiles\China`** directory on their own machines, and make sure that the new **`Prices.txt`** we made last lesson, plus all the image files for the pictures of the china brands, were in there as well.

"Let's use Windows Explorer to execute the program," I said, as soon as everyone had the executable in place.

I double-clicked on my copy of the executable to start up a first instance of the China Shop program. Everything worked fine. I then attempted to start a second instance by repeating the process. This message box was displayed:

"Just the behavior we wanted," I said, as I clicked the OK button to close the message box. "The second instance of the program has ended gracefully – you should have seen the same thing happen on your own machines. Now let's take a look at the section of code we changed in the **`Load`** event procedure of the form, to see how we did this..."

```
If App.PrevInstance = True Then
  MsgBox "The China Shop Program is already running
  Unload Me
  Exit Sub
End If
```

"What we're doing here," I said, "is calling the **`PrevInstance`** property of the **`App`** object to see if it's **`True`**. If it is, another instance of our program must be running. If that's the case, we display a user-friendly message to inform the user of this fact and, after the user clicks the OK button to say they've understood this, we unload our form using the **`Unload Me`** statement."

"Why did you put in an **`Exit Sub`** statement there?" Mary asked.

"Because I wanted to avoid executing the rest of the code," I answered.

"Do you mean that the rest of the code following the **`End If`** statement would have executed?" Blaine asked. "Why would that happen if we unloaded the form?"

"Thanks for raising that point, both of you," I said to them. "Something that a lot of programmers don't realize is that even if a form is unloaded, any code in the **`Event`** procedure following the **`Unload`** statement will still be executed."

"Wow," Steve said, "I didn't realize that. What would be the impact here? Would it be significant?"

"Yes," I replied. "If we were to allow the rest of the code in the **`Load`** event procedure to execute, the impact would be damaging – the form would wind up being loaded again!"

"Why is that?" Ward asked.

"One of the statements following the **`End If`** statement," I replied, "sets a property of the form. One of the behaviors of Visual Basic objects is that if you set a property of an unloaded object, that object is automatically loaded. As a result, when we set the **`BackColor`** property of the form later on in the **`Load`** event procedure – even though the form may have been unloaded – it is immediately loaded by Visual Basic. Worse still, this in turn re-triggers the **`Load`** event procedure, and reiterates the code we've just written. We wind up with what is known as a **Cascading Event** – which is the event-equivalent of an endless loop!"

"So if I understand this properly," Valerie said, "we would have an unending cycle – the message box being displayed, the form being unloaded, the **`BackColor`** property being set, and the form being re-loaded, etc."

"That's right Valerie," I said, "all because the code in the event procedure continues to be executed – even when the form is unloaded. That's the reason for the **`Exit Sub`** statement."

"Wow! That's quite a good reason!" Mary said. "I'll be sure to remember that one!"

"Let's take a look at another very valuable property of the **`App`** object," I said, " – the **`Path`** property."

The App Object's Path Property

"This property tells you the path that your program is being run from. By **`Path`**, we mean the drive and directory or folder from which the program is being executed," I said. "In other words, if the program is being run from the **`\VBFiles\China`** directory of your hard drive, the **`Path`** property of the **`App`** object will read **`C:\VBFiles\China`**"

"I see," Rhonda said, "but what's the practical application for the **`Path`** property? Is it useful to know the drive and directory from which a program is being run?"

"You'll see in a minute that it can be extremely useful," I said, as I stopped the China Shop program. "It can help make the China Shop program a lot more bomb-proof. I'll show you just how. Let's move the China Shop program – project and form – and all of the other files to another directory."

I was about to do this, when Chuck cut in with: "Hang on, John, won't that be a problem? Isn't the China Shop program looking for the **Prices.txt** file in a particular location?"

"And the graphics files we load into the image control are also expected to be found in that same spot," Blaine pointed out. "You were very careful to warn us about this earlier, when we were about to run the executable you sent us."

"Exactly right," I replied. "Moving these files will confuse our program. However, I want to generate exactly that problem, in order to show how the **Path** property of the **App** object can be used to overcome it."

I then used Windows Explorer to create a directory called **\Smiley** and moved all of the files in the China Shop directory – **\VBFiles\China** – to my new **\Smiley** directory.

"What do you think will happen if we now try to run the China Shop program out of the **\Smiley** directory?" I asked.

"I can tell you exactly what will happen," Steve said, "since I did something like this accidentally last semester! As soon as the program runs, it will come back and tell you that it can't find the **Prices.txt** file."

"Absolutely right, Steve," I said, as I loaded up the China Shop project from the **\Smiley** directory and ran the program. Sure enough, the following screenshot was displayed on the classroom projector:

"It's not that the file is missing," I said: "it just isn't where we told the program to look. Fortunately, this isn't an executable, so I can escape from this situation using the `Ctrl+Break` keys, which will take me back to the Visual Basic IDE."

"I'm a bit mystified," said Melissa. "Since I wasn't here last semester, can you show us where exactly in the program we have instructions to look for this file?"

"Yes, sure," I replied. "We open this file in the **ReadPrices** subprocedure we wrote last semester. Here's the code for the **Open** statement in that subprocedure:"

```
Open "C:\VBFiles\China\Prices.txt" For Input As #1
```

"Let me explain." I said. "This line of code is telling our application to open the data file called **Prices.txt** in the directory with the path **C:\VBFiles\China**. By **Open**, I mean, 'use its contents to read data values from'."

"Is this a big issue when writing and installing programs?" Rhonda enquired.

"It can be," I said. "In general, it's a bad idea to 'hard code' the location of a file into your program like this. After the program is installed in the location of your choice on the user's machine, the user may themselves either move the program files to a new directory, or rename the directory itself. The program will then bomb."

"And the **Path** property of the **App** object can help?" Kevin asked.

"Yes it can, Kevin," I said. "As long as all the files the program needs – data and graphics files – are located in the *same* directory as the Visual Basic program, we can use the **Path** property of the **App** object to find out what this directory is and how to find it, without having to hard-code it into our application. Let me show you."

Using the Path Property in the China Shop Code

With that, I distributed this exercise for the class to complete.

Exercise - Using the App Object's Path Property

1. Load up the China Shop project.

2. Modify the code in the **ReadPrices** subprocedure (it's in the General section) so that it looks like this next code listing. The highlighted code below replaces the existing line that starts with an **Open** statement. Note that I haven't shown the whole of the code for the **ReadPrices** subprocedure, only the first section, where we're actually changing something at the moment. The omitted sections are indicated by the ellipsis (...):

```
Public Sub ReadPrices()

On Error GoTo ICanHandleThis
```

```
Dim strTest As String
Dim strbrand As String
Dim strItem As String
Dim curprice As Currency

If App.Path = "\" Then
  Open App.Path & "Prices.txt" For Input As #1
Else
  Open App.Path & "\Prices.txt" For Input As #1
End If

Do While Not EOF(1)
  Input #1, strbrand, strItem, curprice
  m_colDishPrice.Add Item:=curprice, Key:=strbrand & strItem
  If strbrand <> strTest Then
    lstBrands.AddItem strbrand
    strTest = strbrand
  End If
Loop
Close #1

Exit Sub
...
```

3. Modify the code in the `Click` event procedure of `lstBrands` so that it looks like the next code snippet. The first line of the existing procedure stays in place, but the rest of the code is replaced with the highlighted lines below:

```
Private Sub lstBrands_Click()

If lstBrands.ListIndex = -1 Then Exit Sub

If App.Path = "\" Then
  imgChina.Picture = LoadPicture(App.Path & lstBrands.Text & ".gif")
Else
  imgChina.Picture = LoadPicture(App.Path & "\" & lstBrands.Text &
    ↳".gif")
End If

End Sub
```

4. Save the China Shop project.

5. Create a folder or directory with your last name, and **move** (not copy) all of the files in the China Shop directory – `\VBFiles\China` – to that folder. Load the China Shop project from that directory and run the program. The program should run normally. Ensure that the China Shop graphics appear in the image control and that the prices are calculated normally.

6. When you're satisfied that the program is running properly, end the program and move your program and files back to their location in `\VBFiles\China`.

Discussion

"Let me explain what's going on here," I said. " In the old version of the code, we were looking for `Prices.txt` in a particular location that we hard-coded into our program. This caused problems whenever we moved the China Shop files to a new directory. Now we're using the `Path` property to give our program the ability to automatically determine its location in the directory tree. Let's take a look at the `Load` procedure of the form – once you understand that, I don't think you'll have any problems understanding the code in the `Click` event procedure of the list box:"

```
If App.Path = "\" Then
  Open App.Path & "Prices.txt" For Input As #1
Else
  Open App.Path & "\Prices.txt" For Input As #1
End If
```

"This next section of code reads the `Path` property of the `App` object and concatenates the name of the file `Prices.txt` onto it," I explained. "It then opens the file."

"The `If` statement seems to check first whether the path consists simply of a backslash – what's that checking for?" Dorothy asked.

"Good question, Dorothy," I said. "With one exception, the `Path` of every directory on the user's PC *won't* end in a backslash. The exception, is the root directory of the hard drive."

"I'm confused," Rhonda admitted.

"Well," I continued, "we saw earlier – before moving the China Shop program out of the `\VBFiles\China` directory – that the `Path` property of the `App` object was..."

```
\VBFiles\China
```

"Notice that there's no backslash at the end of this path. Right now, as I am running the China Shop program out of the `\Smiley` directory, the `Path` property of the `App` object is ..."

```
\Smiley
```

"...Again, notice that there's no backslash at the end of the path. This means that, in order to open the file called **Prices.txt**, we need to concatenate a backslash and the name of the file **Prices.txt** onto the **Path** property. Visual Basic will then look to open this file..."

```
\Smiley\Prices.txt
```

"That makes sense," Bob said. "But what about that exception – the root directory?"

"What **Path** returns, when asked for the path of the root directory, is simply a backslash." I replied. "The **Path** property of the **App** object will look just like this..."

```
\
```

"Isn't the root directory the one where the **Autoexec.bat** and **Config.sys** files are located?" Blaine interjected.

"I thought I read somewhere," Tom added, "that you shouldn't put files of your own in the root directory – certainly I wouldn't think to put an entire program in that directory."

"It's not a great idea to put files of your own there," I agreed. "And you're absolutely right: I wouldn't place the China Shop Program in the root directory, either. But remember – once you install your program on the user's PC, and leave them to work with it, anything can happen – and you should prepare your program as best you can for any eventuality. And that means dealing with a program whose files have been moved to the root directory!"

"In which case," Dave said, "the **Path** property of the **App** object will be a single backslash..."

"Correct," I said.

"So that's why you checked for a **Path** property of a single backslash," Valerie said. "If the **Path** property is a backslash the files must be in the root directory, and you don't want to concatenate another backslash to it, or we'll end up with a false path name."

"That's right," I said. "We just concatenate the name of the file to the backslash, so that it looks like this:"

```
\Prices.txt
```

"I understand now what you meant when you said using the **Path** property of the **App** object will make your code much more flexible," Rhonda said.

"There is one case where this use of the **Path** property won't help you, however, " I said, "and that's if the user moves the **Prices.txt** file to a location separate from the program itself. Remember, the **Path** property returns the location of the program. If files are in separate directories, using the **App** object won't help – in fact, nothing will. The program will just fail to find the file – and that's a good reason to always include error handling in any code that needs to find a file of any kind. I should also add that techniques like this are the kind of thing that prospective employers look for in your coding."

Having seen some of the extremely useful features of the App object, it was now time to take a look at another powerful system object – the Clipboard object.

The Clipboard Object

"Let's take a look at the Clipboard object now," I said. "Even though you'll see that we don't have a direct use for the Clipboard object in the China Shop project, I think you'll still find it interesting to work with. The Clipboard object has six methods – but no properties."

"When you say the Clipboard object, are you talking about the Windows Clipboard?" Lou asked.

"That's right, Lou," I said. "Anyone who has used a Windows program is probably familiar with the Windows Clipboard. It's the Clipboard that allows Windows programs to implement cut, copy and paste operations and also to share data with other programs. You can implement these same features in your own programs by using that same Windows Clipboard – and it's the Visual Basic Clipboard object that permits you to do so."

"Is there more than one Clipboard in Windows?" Rhonda asked.

"No, Rhonda," I said, "there's just a single Clipboard in the standard Windows operating system, and most people believe that whatever is placed on the Clipboard will overwrite whatever happens to be already there. However, that's not entirely true. As you'll see a little later, there are two broad categories of data that you can place on the Clipboard – text and graphics – and you can actually have both types of data on the Clipboard at the same time."

> **The Office 2000 clipboard allows for multiple items to be on the clipboard, but we won't be dealing with that innovation here.**

"Is there a way to determine if something is already on the Windows Clipboard?" Ward asked.

"Yes, there is," I said. "To see how we can do that, and the other facilities that the Clipboard gives us, let's begin by examining the Clipboard object's methods."

Clipboard Methods

"Although the Clipboard object has no properties, it does have six methods that enable us to manipulate it: `GetFormat`, `Clear`, `GetData`, `GetText`, `SetData` and `SetText`. Let's sketch these before we get into the practicalities of using the Clipboard in code."

The GetFormat Method

"It's the `GetFormat` method," I continued, "that enables us to determine if something is on the Clipboard. From its name, you might gather that it can also be used to determine the type of data that is on the Clipboard. I mentioned earlier that there are two categories of data that can be placed on the Clipboard, text and graphics. However, within that broad categorization, there are actually many types of data."

"Such as?" interjected Ward.

"Well," I explained, "for example, text data can be saved as either plain text – without any information about formatting or styles built into it – or rich text, with all of that information included. Similarly, a graphic can either be what's known as a **raster graphic** – like a bitmap, which is drawn as an assemblage of little colored pixels – or a **vector graphic** – typically metafiles, which use lines and polygons to create the image. I'll not go into this here, since it's outside the scope of this course, but here're the nine basic data types the clipboard can hold..."

I put the following list of data types up on the screen:

DDE conversation information

Plain Text

Rich Text

Bitmap (.bmp files)

Device-independent bitmap (DIB)

Metafile (.wmf files)

Enhanced Metafile

Color palette

Filename List (for Microsoft Windows Explorer)

"I'll be listing the relevant formats for each of the Clipboard methods as we come to them," I said, "but, as I said, the only two that we'll be discussing today are text and bitmap data. Here's the syntax for the **GetFormat** method."

I put the following line of text on the screen:

GetFormat(format)

"Let me guess," said Ward, "**GetFormat** tells us what kind of data is currently stored on the Clipboard?"

"Not quite," I replied. "However, many beginners assume that's what it does, so you're not alone! Since the Clipboard can contain multiple types of data simultaneously, you actually have to supply the **GetFormat** method with an argument called **format**, which is used to specify the type of data you are looking for on the Clipboard. **GetFormat** then returns a **True** or **False** value, depending on whether that data type is present on the Clipboard or not. Here are the types we can supply for the **format** argument..."

Constant	Value	Description
vbCFLink	&HBFOO	DDE conversation information
vbCFText	1	Text
vbCFBitmap	2	Bitmap (.bmp files)
vbCFMetafile	3	Metafile (.wmf files)
vbCFDIB	8	Device-independent bitmap (DIB)
vbCFPalette	9	Color palette
vbCFEMetafile	14	Enhanced Metafile
vbCFFiles	15	Filename List (Microsoft Windows Explorer)

"You can use either the numeric value or the named constant for the **format** argument," I said. "Visual Basic Help provides this example of how to use the **GetFormat** function to determine the type of data currently on the Clipboard. Using this code, you can determine the type of data, if any, on the Clipboard."

I then created a new Visual Basic project, and placed this code, taken directly from Visual Basic Help, in the `Click` event procedure of the form...

```
Private Sub Form_Click ()

Dim ClpFmt, Msg

On Error Resume Next

If Clipboard.GetFormat(vbCFText) Then ClpFmt = ClpFmt + 1
If Clipboard.GetFormat(vbCFBitmap) Then ClpFmt = ClpFmt + 2
If Clipboard.GetFormat(vbCFDIB) Then ClpFmt = ClpFmt + 4
If Clipboard.GetFormat(vbCFRTF) Then ClpFmt = ClpFmt + 8
Select Case ClpFmt
  Case 1
    Msg = "The Clipboard contains only text."
  Case 2, 4, 6
    Msg = "The Clipboard contains only a bitmap."
  Case 3, 5, 7
    Msg = "The Clipboard contains text and a bitmap."
  Case 8, 9
    Msg = "The Clipboard contains only rich text."
  Case Else
    Msg = "There is nothing on the Clipboard."
End Select

MsgBox Msg

End Sub
```

"Let's see how this works," I said. "If we now start up Microsoft Word, type some text into a document, then select it and copy it to the Windows Clipboard..." – I did just that – "...and then run our new VB program..."

I ran the program and clicked on the form. This message box then appeared on the classroom projector:

"As you can see," I said, "this code is reporting not only that the Clipboard contains data, but specifically that it contains text data and nothing else... and it was this line of code that did the trick:"

```
If Clipboard.GetFormat(vbCFText) Then ClpFmt = ClpFmt + 1
```

"When Visual Basic performed this code," I said, "the return value of the **GetFormat** function was **True**, so we added 1 to the value of the variable **ClpFmt**. The result of the next three **If** statements were **False**, since data of the requested type weren't found on the Clipboard..."

```
If Clipboard.GetFormat(vbCFBitmap) Then ClpFmt = ClpFmt + 2
If Clipboard.GetFormat(vbCFDIB) Then ClpFmt = ClpFmt + 4
If Clipboard.GetFormat(vbCFRTF) Then ClpFmt = ClpFmt + 8
```

"...and so, when the **Select...Case** statement was finally executed, the value of the variable **ClpFmt** was **1**..."

```
Case 1
    Msg = "The Clipboard contains only text."
```

"Notice that the values we assign for each data type allow us to distinguish the exact combination of data types on the Clipboard." I added. "This works because we know that only a maximum of two cases can return a **True** value at any one time.

"Can we see this program run with bitmap data on the Clipboard?" Dorothy asked.

"Sure thing," I said. I then started up Microsoft Paint, wrote the name of one of my favorite entrepreneurs, and saved the file as **Bill.bmp**.

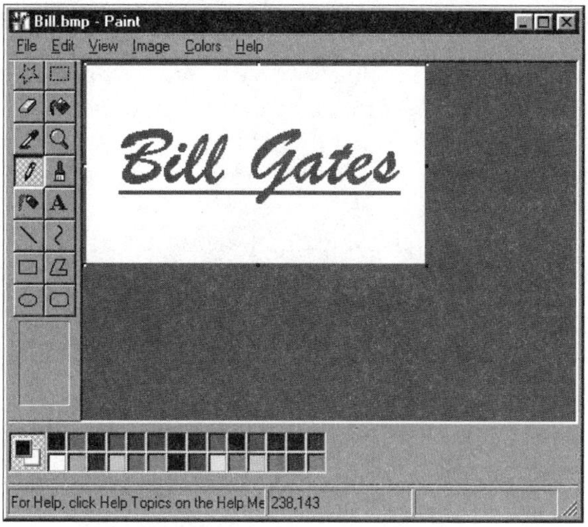

I then selected Edit | Copy from Paint's menu bar to copy the image to the Clipboard.

"Let's run the program again," I said. I did so and clicked on the form. This message box was then displayed on the classroom projector:

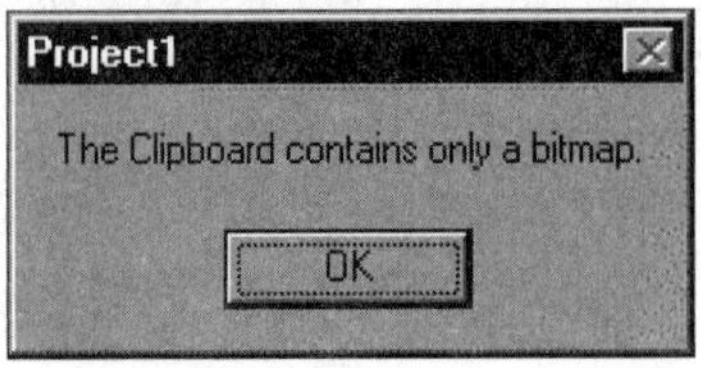

"As you can see," I said, "our code is now reporting that the Clipboard contains only bitmap data."

"I thought that the Clipboard could contain more than one type of data simultaneously." Ward said. "We didn't erase the text we'd already placed on the Clipboard – why's the program reporting that only bitmap data is on the Clipboard?"

"That's a good question, Ward," I said. "You're right – theoretically, the Clipboard can contain more than one type of data simultaneously. In practice, however, most software programs follow Microsoft's own recommendation by first clearing the contents of the Clipboard before writing any data to it."

"So Microsoft Paint first cleared the Clipboard?" Melissa asked.

"That's right, Melissa," I answered.

"Are we able to clear the Clipboard in our own programs?" Valerie asked.

"Yes we can," I said, "to do that we need to execute the `Clear` method of the Clipboard object."

I then suggested that we learn more about the Clipboard object by creating a Visual Basic project and implementing cut, copy and paste features via a Visual Basic menu.

"We'll create a single form with two text box controls and a picture box control," I said. "We'll use the text box controls to demonstrate cut, copy and paste operations on text data, and we'll be using the picture box to demonstrate cut, copy and paste operations on bitmap data."

So saying, I quickly created a demonstration Visual Basic project containing two text box controls and an image control:

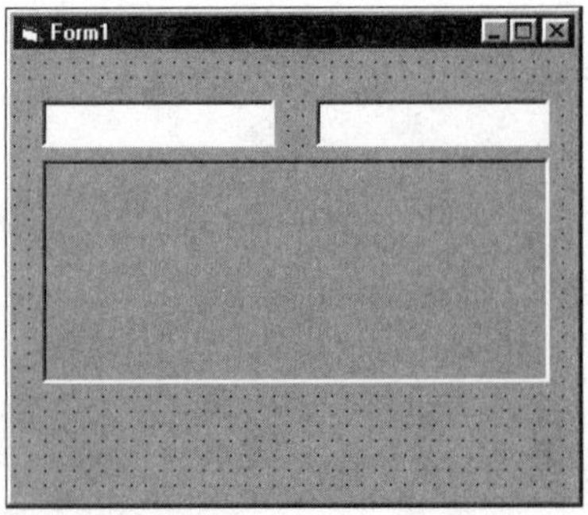

! **This project can be found on the CD in the For** `Chapter 03\Additional Examples\Clipboard Example` **folder as** `Clipboard App.vbp`

I then added a Visual Basic menu consisting of an Edit menu, with three submenu items captioned Cut, Copy and Paste...

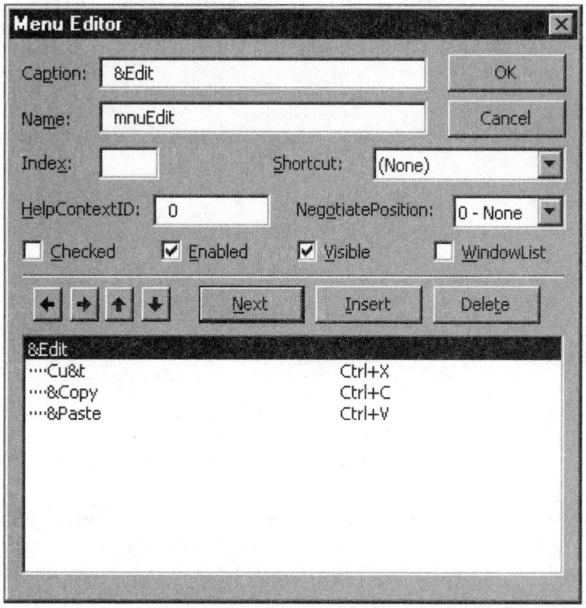

"Notice," I said, "that I have taken care to follow the Windows design standards for naming the captions of the Edit menu items, and also in the assignment of access keys and shortcut keys for each menu item – `Ctrl+X` for cut, `Ctrl+C` for copy, and `Ctrl+V` for paste. Finally, we'll place three command buttons on the form, and name them **`cmdCut`**, **`cmdCopy`** and **`cmdPaste`** respectively. These command buttons will be used to cut, copy and paste to and from the picture box control, and the menu items will be used to cut, copy and paste to and from the text box controls:"

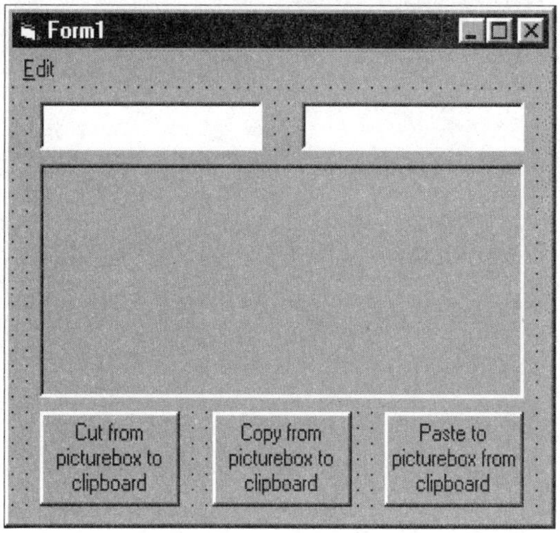

"Now that we have the visual portion of this demonstration project in place," I said, "I want to briefly discuss the remaining methods of the Clipboard object – **`Clear`**, **`GetData`**, **`SetData`**, **`GetText`** and **`SetText`**."

The Clear Method

"The **`Clear`** method of the Clipboard," I continued, "as I mentioned just a moment ago, clears the contents of the Clipboard."

"Does that mean **everything**?" Kevin asked. "Since the Clipboard can contain multiple types of data simultaneously, do you need to execute multiple **`Clear`** methods for each data type?"

"That's a good question, Kevin," I said. "Even though you may have multiple types of data on the Clipboard at the same time, executing the **`Clear`** method *will* clear everything from the Clipboard – regardless of data type. As I mentioned earlier, Microsoft recommends that you first clear the contents of the Clipboard before placing any data – text or bitmap – on it. Here's the syntax for the **`Clear`** method..."

```
Clipboard.Clear
```

"Clearing data from the Clipboard is simple enough," I said, "and I'll be demonstrating it in action in just a little while. Let's take a look at the Clipboard method which allows us to retrieve bitmap data from the Clipboard – the **`GetData`** method."

The GetData method

"The **`GetData`** method," I continued, "is used to retrieve **graphical** data from the Clipboard."

"What do we do with the graphic once it's retrieved?" Mary asked.

"Most times," I said, "you'll assign it to a Visual Basic property that is expecting a graphics file, such as the **`Picture`** property of the form or picture box. The **`GetData`** method has one optional argument, **`Format`**, which you may use to specify the type of graphic data that you wish to retrieve from the Clipboard. If you omit the optional **`Format`** argument, Visual Basic assumes the default type of bitmap. Here's the syntax for the **`GetData`** method..."

```
Clipboard.GetData(Format)
```

"...where **Format** is a constant or value that specifies the graphics format, as described below:"

Constant	Value	Description
vbCFBitmap	2	Bitmap (.bmp files)
vbCFMetafile	3	Metafile (.wmf files)
vbCFDIB	8	Device-independent bitmap (DIB)
vbCFPalette	9	Color palette

"These arguments are basically the same values that we saw for the **GetFormat** method," Mary said, "except that they are graphic-specific, rather than text-specific. Will you be demonstrating this method too?"

"You're absolutely correct, Mary," I said. "These are the graphic specific formats that we saw earlier with the **GetFormat** method. And yes, I will be showing you this method in action in just a few minutes. Before I do that, however, I want to discuss the method used to write graphical data to the Clipboard. That's the **SetData** method."

The SetData Method

"The **SetData** method," I continued, "is just the opposite of the **GetData** method in that it places graphical data on the Clipboard. Like the **GetData** method, it has one optional argument, **Format**, which can be used to specify the type of data to be placed on the Clipboard. If **Format** is not supplied, then Visual Basic automatically determines the graphic format itself. Here's the syntax..."

```
Clipboard.SetData(Format)
```

"...where **Format** is a constant or value that specifies the format of the graphic. If format is omitted, **SetData** automatically determines the graphic format. The settings for format are:"

Constant	Value	Description
vbCFBitmap	2	Bitmap (.bmp files)
vbCFMetafile	3	Metafile (.wmf files)
vbCFDIB	8	Device-independent bitmap (DIB)
vbCFPalette	9	Color palette

"Before we see the **GetData** and **SetData** methods in operation," I said, "let's first take a look at the two Clipboard methods designed to work specifically with text data."

The GetText Method

"As the name implies," I said, "the **GetText** method retrieves text data from the Clipboard. Like the **GetData** method, **GetText** has one optional **Format** argument. If **Format** is omitted, Visual Basic assumes that the data type is text. Here's the syntax for the **GetText** method:"

```
Clipboard.GetText(format)
```

"...where **Format** is a constant or value that specifies the text format, as described below:"

Constant	Value	Description
vbCFLink	&HBF00	DDE conversation information
vbCFText	1	(Default) Text
vbCFRTF	&HBF01	Rich Text Format (.rtf file)

"Notice," I continued, "how the values for the **Format** argument are the text file types we first encountered with the **GetFormat** method. Now, just before I begin our demonstration," I said, "the final Clipboard method I want to examine is the **SetText** method."

The SetText Method

"The **SetText** method is just the opposite of the **GetText** method in that it places text on the Clipboard using a specified text format. As was the case with the other methods, the **SetText** method has one optional argument, **Format**. If it's omitted, Visual Basic assumes that you are placing plain old text on the Clipboard. Here's the syntax for the **SetText** method:"

```
Clipboard.SetText(Format)
```

"...where format is a constant or value that specifies the format of the text. The settings for **Format** are:"

Constant	Value	Description
vbCFLink	&HBF00	DDE conversation information
vbCFRTF	&HBF01	RichText Format
vbCFText	1	(Default) Text

"With these six Clipboard methods," I said, "we'll now be able to implement robust cut, copy and paste features in our demonstration project. Let me show you..."

Working with Text and the Clipboard

"The first thing I want to demonstrate," I said, "is how to 'cut' text data to the Windows Clipboard from a text box on our form."

Cutting Text to the Clipboard

"Let's put some code in the **Click** event procedure of the menu item **mnuCut** to do exactly that. We *could* write this code to cut text from a specific text box. Even better, though, we can use the Screen object's **ActiveControl** property to identify the control which currently has focus and, in conjunction with the **SelText** Property of that text box, cut whatever text is currently selected to the Windows Clipboard. Like this:"

```
Private Sub mnuCut_Click()

Clipboard.Clear
Clipboard.SetText Screen.ActiveControl.SelText
Screen.ActiveControl.SelText = ""

End Sub
```

"Isn't the **Screen** object on our discussion list for later today?" Ward asked, looking at his syllabus.

"Yes, it is," I said. "We'll be talking about some other properties of the **Screen** object later on. For now, though, just notice how the **ActiveControl** property of the **Screen** object can add a lot of flexibility to our project. If we had multiple text box controls on our form, this code would still work. **ActiveControl** allows us to identify which text box has focus, no matter how many there are, and cut the data from it. As you can see, cutting text from the currently selected control to the Clipboard is a three-step operation. First, the Clipboard is cleared using the **Clear** method..."

```
Clipboard.Clear
```

"...then we use the **Screen** object's **ActiveControl** property to identify the control on the form that currently has focus. Once identified, we place its selected text on the Windows Clipboard using the **SetText** method of the Clipboard:"

```
Clipboard.SetText Screen.ActiveControl.SelText
```

"What's the **SelText** property?" Valerie asked.

"That's the text in the text box that the user has selected with their mouse," I answered. "If the user has entered 'I love Visual Basic' in the text box, and has selected the 'Visual Basic' part of it, that's what the **SelText** property will contain."

"Makes sense," Valerie agreed.

"Finally," I continued, "because this is a cut operation, we want to erase the selected text in the control that has focus by setting its **SelText** property to **""** – an empty string:"

```
Screen.ActiveControl.SelText = ""
```

"So let me make sure I understand this," Peter said. "The Screen object's **ActiveControl** property points to the control that has the focus in our application, is that right?"

"That's right, Peter," I said.

"I can't wait to see this work," Ward said, "when will you be doing the demo?"

Copying Text to the Clipboard

"Just let me finish talking about the copy and paste code for text," I said, "and then we'll fire up the demo. Copying text to the Clipboard is nearly identical to cutting text, except that in a copy operation we don't erase the currently selected text from the control that has focus – it stays right there. Here's the code for the **Click** event procedure of **mnuCopy**..."

```
Private Sub mnuCopy_Click()

Clipboard.Clear
Clipboard.SetText Screen.ActiveControl.SelText

End Sub
```

"This code," I said, "is nearly identical to the code in **mnuCut** – minus the line of code that erases the selected contents of the active control."

Pasting Text from the Clipboard

"And finally," I said, "there's the paste functionality. For the paste operation, we execute the **GetText** method of the Clipboard, which returns the text contents of the Windows Clipboard and, in this case, assigns that text to the **SelText** property of the **ActiveControl**:"

```
Private Sub mnuPaste_Click()

Screen.ActiveControl.SelText = Clipboard.GetText()

End Sub
```

"What's this code doing again?" Rhonda asked. "I guess I'm still confused about the **SelText** property."

"**SelText**," I said, "is a property of the text box that tells us what text is currently selected in the text box. If something is selected in the text box, the new text will overwrite the selected text. If nothing is selected in the text box, then the paste operation will place the text from the Clipboard into the text box immediately after wherever the cursor happens to be. Make sense?"

"I think so," Rhonda said. "Of course, as you always say, a picture is worth a thousand words..."

"Exactly, Rhonda" I said, "let's run our demo program and see how all of these Clipboard text methods fit together."

Text and the Clipboard – Putting it all together

I ran the program. "Initially, let's key some text into the first text box," I said, typing in these magic words:

I love Visual Basic

"Then we'll use our mouse to select part of that text...." I went on, selecting the words Visual Basic from the line of text:

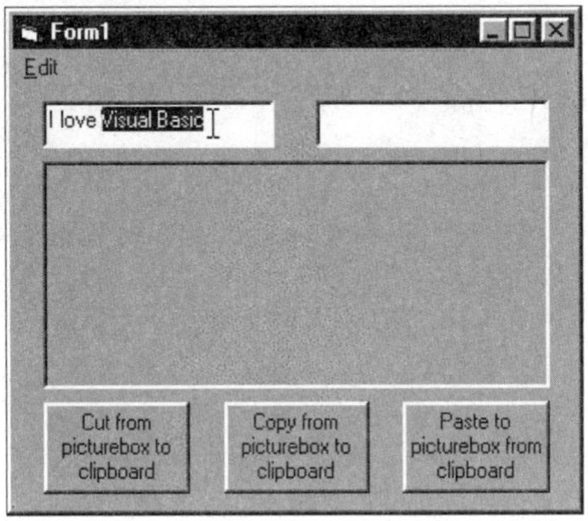

"If we now select Edit | Cut from the menu bar, the selected text in the first text box will disappear..."

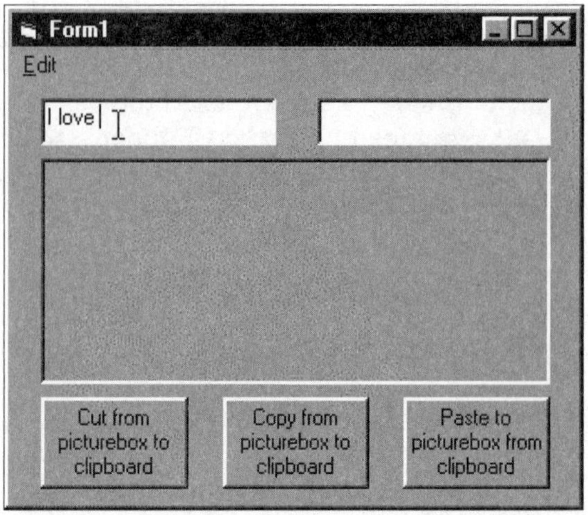

"Right now, the words Visual Basic are sitting in the Windows Clipboard," I explained. "If we now click or tab to the second text box to give it focus, and then select Edit | Paste from the menu bar, the cut text will then appear in that second text box..."

I did this, and the class saw the following effect:

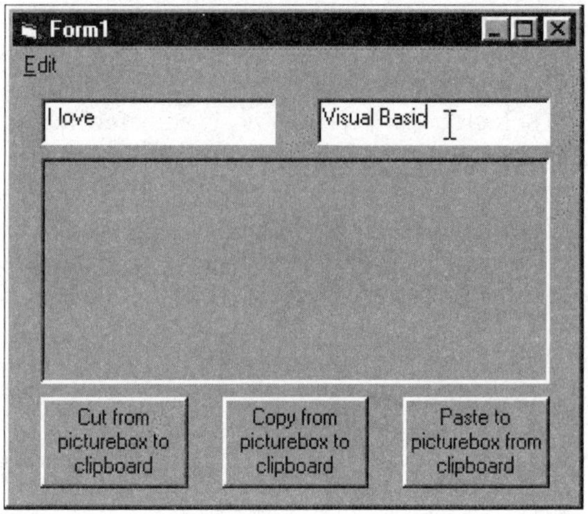

"I must say I'm impressed," Linda said. "Of all of the things I thought a Windows program might want to do, I really dreaded cut, copy and paste processing. Now I see that they may not be so bad after all. Can we see the copy operation now?"

"Sure thing, Linda," I said. "As I mentioned just a minute ago, copy operations work in a similar manner to cut operations, except that the selected text is not erased. This time, instead of copying the selected text to another text box, let's copy it to another application – Notepad."

I then started up Notepad, and proceeded as I had done before – by selecting text in the first text box of our VB application:

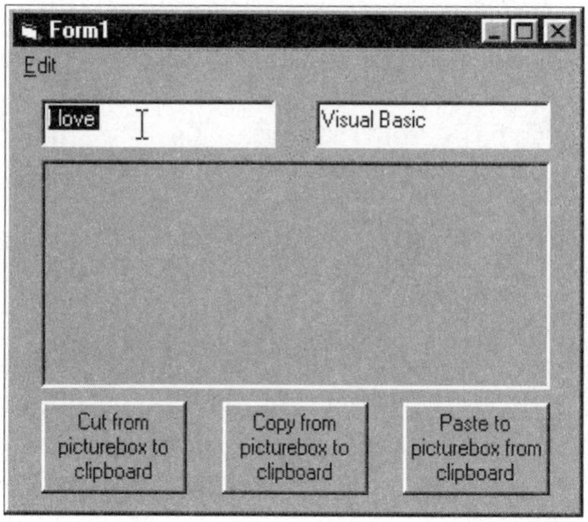

"Now let's select Edit | Copy from the menu bar of our program, and switch to Notepad, where we'll select Edit | Paste from its menu bar," I said.

I did this: the copied text appeared in Notepad...

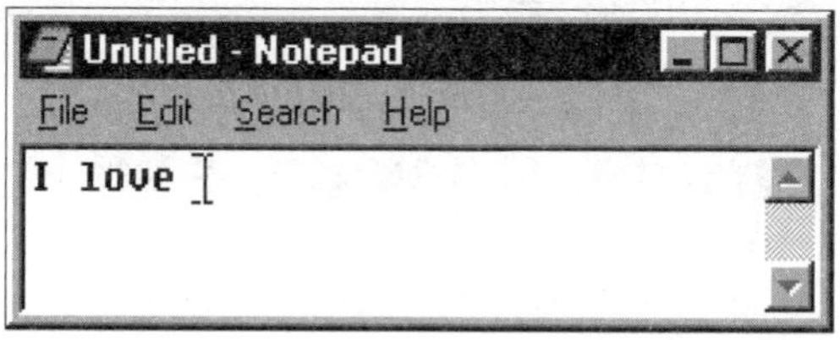

"That's really great," Blaine said, "This is really a lot easier than I thought it would be."

"All in all," I said, "working with the Visual Basic Clipboard object to gain access to the Windows Clipboard isn't difficult at all. I'm sure you all agree that using the Clipboard object makes dealing with the complexities of the Windows Clipboard simple – and by the way, that's the beauty of objects – they simplify complex operations – at least for the programmer using them."

"I just noticed," Dorothy said, "that when I accidentally right-clicked in the first text box, a shortcut menu appeared that has cut, copy and paste menu items."

"That's right, Dorothy," I said. "The text box control has cut, copy and paste functionality built into it via a pop-up menu that appears when you right-click your mouse in the text box:"

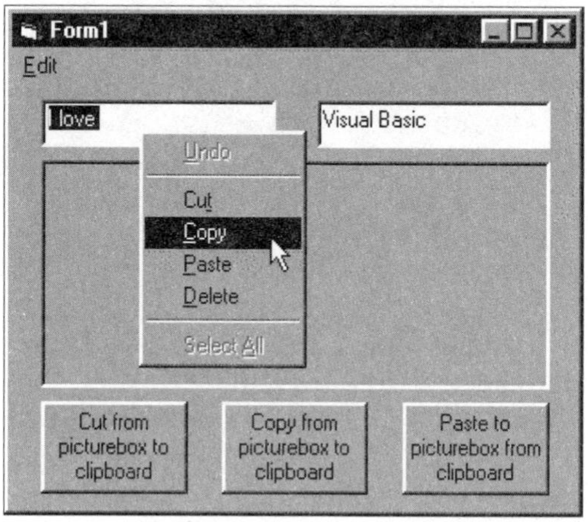

"I never knew that was there," Rhonda said. "So, cut, copy, and paste functionality is automatically built into text box controls?"

"That's right, Rhonda," I said. "This was a brainwave of whoever designed the text box object – and it's a very good idea."

"Kinda makes a nonsense of our carefully-constructed menu, though, doesn't it?" observed Dave, with a wry smile. "I guess this is just a demo, though – huh?"

"Well, Dave," I laughed, "this is still all great practice for working with Visual Basic objects." I knew that, however simple the example was, merely going through the exercise was valuable in itself, helping my students to internalize the principles and practice of object-oriented programming.

At this point I suggested that the class take a ten-minute break before continuing with our discussion of cut, copy, and paste operations on graphic data.

Cutting, Copying, and Pasting Graphic Data

"Cut, copy, and paste operations on graphic data," I said, after our break, "follow the same basic processes as the operations on text data."

Cutting Graphic Data to the Clipboard

"Cutting graphic data is also a three-step operation," I said, "just like cutting text data from a control and placing it on the Windows Clipboard. Here's the code that we'll place in the `Click` event procedure of `cmdCut` to cut our graphic data from our picture box:"

```
Private Sub cmdCut_Click()

Clipboard.Clear
Clipboard.SetData Picture1.Picture
Picture1.Picture = LoadPicture()

End Sub
```

"What we're going to be doing here," I said, "is cutting graphic data from a picture box and placing it on the Windows Clipboard. The first step is to clear the Windows Clipboard using the `Clear` method, just as we did when working with text data..."

```
Clipboard.Clear
```

"Copying graphic data to the Clipboard," I continued, "requires that we execute the **SetData** method. What we're going to do is copy the graphic from the picture box, so we use the picture box's **Picture** property as an argument to the **SetData** method:"

```
Clipboard.SetData Picture1.Picture
```

"Because this is a cut operation," I continued, "our final step is to cut the graphic from the picture box by executing the **LoadPicture** function with a null argument – that is, we don't put anything in the parentheses that come after the function name. This clears the graphic from the picture box:"

```
Picture1.Picture = LoadPicture()
```

"Isn't that the same technique," Kate asked, "as we use on the image control in the China Shop project when the user clicks on the Reset button?"

"Yes, you're right," I said. "For the benefit of our new colleagues, that's what we did last semester to erase the **Picture** property in the **cmdReset_Click** event procedure of the china Shop program: we executed the **LoadPicture** function with a null argument."

Copying Graphic Data to the Clipboard

"Copying graphic data to the Clipboard," I continued, "is nearly identical to cutting graphic data – but again with the exception that we don't erase the graphic from the picture box control. Here's the code to copy graphics data to the Windows Clipboard – we'll place this code in the **Click** event procedure of **cmdCopy**:"

```
Private Sub cmdCopy_Click()

Clipboard.Clear
Clipboard.SetData Picture1.Picture

End Sub
```

Pasting Graphic Data from the Clipboard

"Finally," I said, "let's take a look at the code for the paste operation. For the paste operation, we'll be copying graphic data from the Clipboard to the picture box. To do that, we'll execute the **GetData** method of the Clipboard, which returns the graphics contents of the Windows Clipboard – we'll then assign that graphic to the **Picture** property of the picture box:"

```
Private Sub cmdPaste_Click()

Picture1.Picture = Clipboard.GetData()

End Sub
```

Graphic Data and the Clipboard – Putting it all together

"Let's run this demo program now and see how it all fits together," I said. "First, let's switch back to Microsoft Paint and work with that bitmap we created earlier:"

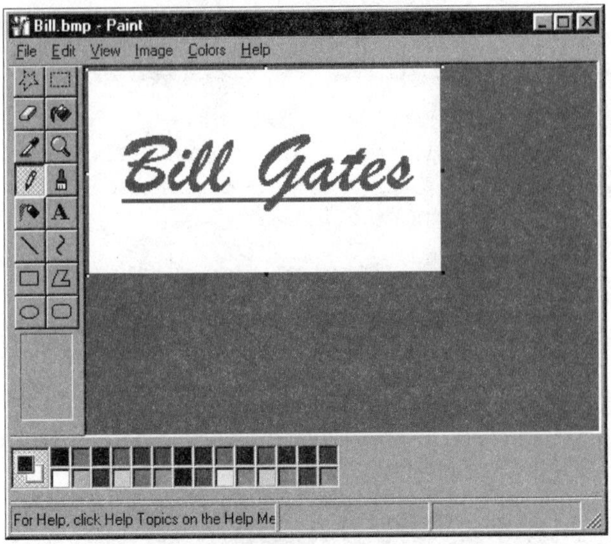

"Now let's set the **Picture** property of our picture box control to point to this file:"

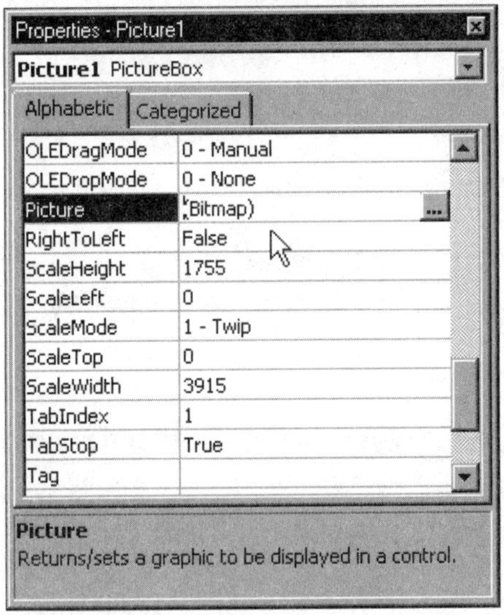

I clicked on the **Picture** property's ellipses and navigated to the **Bill.bmp** file.

"Now when we run this program, we'll see this graphic in the picture box:"

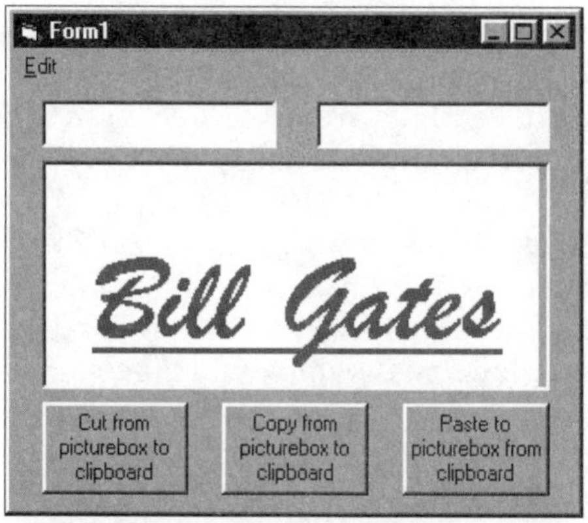

"...and if we now click on the Cut from PictureBox to Clipboard command button, the graphic will disappear from the picture box..."

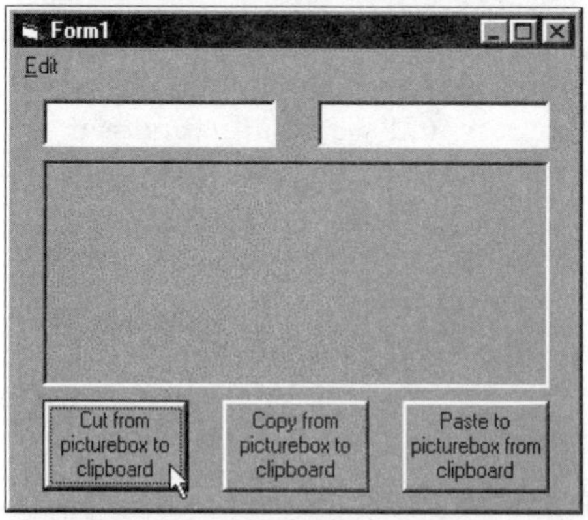

"The picture has gone to the Windows Clipboard." I said. "Let's click on the Paste to PictureBox from Clipboard command button: the image will reappear."

Sure enough, that's what happened:

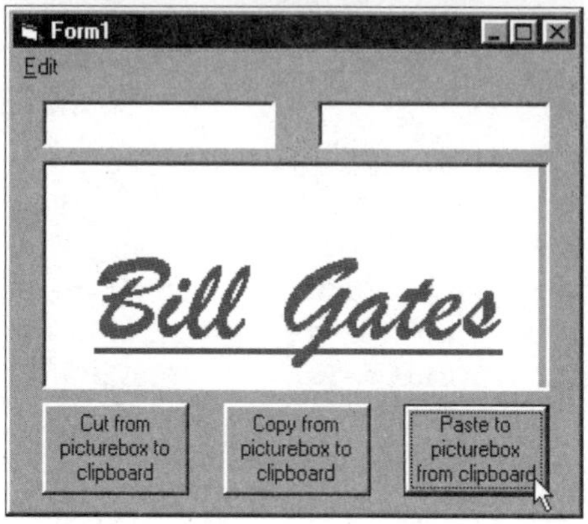

"The Copy from PictureBox to Clipboard button works in a similar manner," I said, "except that the image won't be cleared from the picture box – just copied to the Clipboard."

After a moment's pause, I continued. "There are some potential pitfalls that you might encounter when working with the Clipboard object and its methods," I warned the class.

Problems You might Encounter

"What pitfalls are those?" Melissa asked. "Do they involve the different types of data that you might find on the Clipboard?"

"Exactly, Melissa," I said, "Problems occur when we try to cut and paste incompatible data formats. As you've seen, since there are separate Clipboard methods for working with text and graphic formats, you need to be careful to use the correct method for the data – text or graphic – with which you'll be working."

"How so?" Rhonda asked.

"For instance," I said, "you can't use the **GetText** method on a graphic in a picture box, nor can you use the **GetData** method on the text in a text box – the formats are just not compatible with the kind of data in those controls. Let's go back to our demonstration program and see what happens if we click on the picture box, thereby making it the **ActiveControl** – and then select Edit | Cut from the menu bar..."

I did that, and the following error message flashed up:

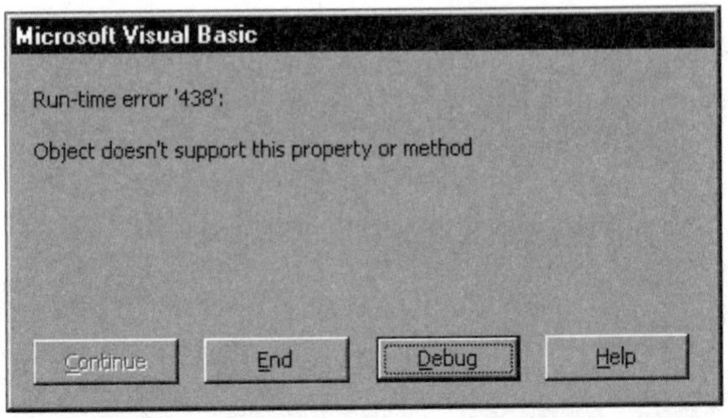

"What's wrong?" Rhonda asked.

"The reason for this error," I said, "is that we're asking Visual Basic to return the value of the **SelText** property of the **ActiveControl** – something that is impossible because **SelText** is not a property of the picture box control:"

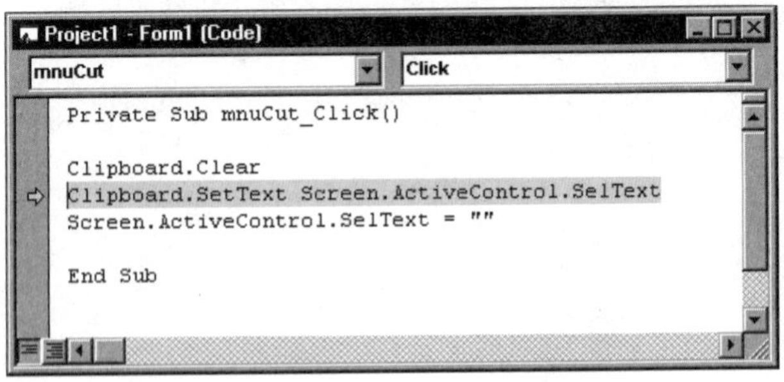

"I see," Peter said. "How can we avoid this type of error?"

Curing the Faults

"One thing we can do," I said, "is use an **If** statement to make sure that we only execute that line of code if the active control supports the **SelText** property."

"In this case, if it's a text box," Dave pointed out.

"Exactly, Dave," I agreed. "We can check if the type of control that the **ActiveControl** property is pointing to is a text box by using the **TypeOf** keyword, like this..."

```
Private Sub mnuCut_Click()

If TypeOf Screen.ActiveControl Is TextBox Then
  Clipboard.Clear
  Clipboard.SetText Screen.ActiveControl.SelText
  Screen.ActiveControl.SelText = ""
End If

End Sub
```

"That tidies things up," I said. "Now the cut operation will only execute if the **ActiveControl** is a text box. Likewise, we should change the code in **mnuCopy** to look like this..."

```
Private Sub mnuCopy_Click()

If TypeOf Screen.ActiveControl Is TextBox Then
  Clipboard.Clear
  Clipboard.SetText Screen.ActiveControl.SelText
End If

End Sub
```

"If we now run the program," I said, "both the menu cut and copy operations are 'bomb proof', even if the user has not first set focus to one of the text boxes."

"But what about the paste operation?" Lou asked. "Won't that be a problem?"

"Let's see," I said. "Suppose we attempt to paste a graphic from the Clipboard into a text box. What will happen?"

We still had a graphic in the picture box, so I clicked on the 'Copy from PictureBox to Clipboard' command button.

"At this point," I said, "the graphic from the picture box control is on the Windows Clipboard. Now let's type a few characters into the first text box and select them using the mouse..."

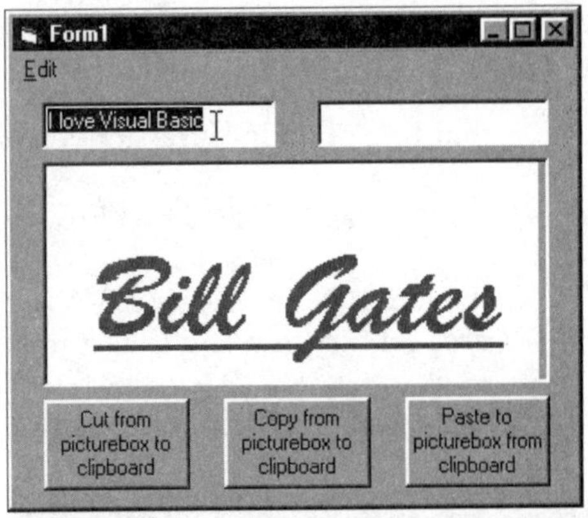

"Now let's select Edit | Paste from the menu bar."

I did that, and the following screenshot was displayed:

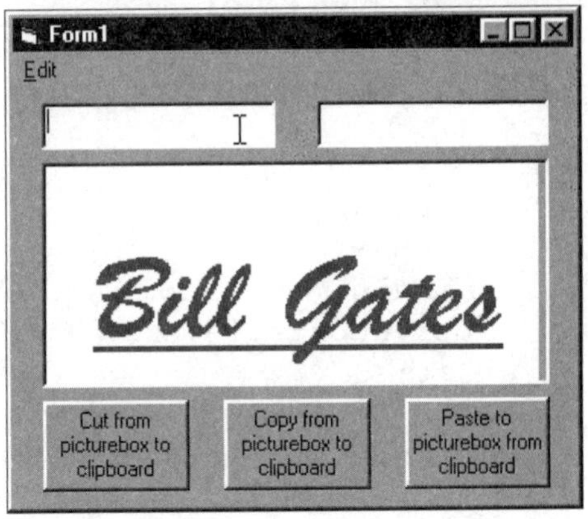

"Nothing happened," Mary said. "I half expected the program to bomb, since you were trying to paste a graphic into a text box. "

"Not quite, Mary," I said. "The program didn't bomb, but did you notice that the text we selected in the text box has been erased?"

"You're right," Mary said, "I didn't notice that. That's not exactly ideal behavior."

"I agree," I said, displaying the code from the `Click` event procedure of `mnuPaste` on the classroom projector:

```
Private Sub mnuPaste_Click()

Screen.ActiveControl.SelText = Clipboard.GetText()

End Sub
```

"What we're trying to do with this code," I said, "is assign the return value of the **GetText** method of the Clipboard to the **SelText** property of the text box. As it turns out, when the **GetText** Clipboard method is executed, if data of the specified type – in this case text data – is not found on the Clipboard, the **GetText** method returns a zero-length string, which is really just an empty string. What that means is that any text currently selected in the text box control will be replaced with a zero-length string – that's why the selected text in the text box was cleared – and replaced with nothing. As you can see, even though this code didn't bomb, this isn't the outcome we really want."

"So what can we do in this case?" Steve asked.

"We can first use the **GetFormat** method to determine if text data is present on the Clipboard," I replied. "If there is, then we can set the **SelText** property of the text box with the text found on the Clipboard:"

```
Private Sub mnuPaste_Click()

If Clipboard.GetFormat(vbCFText) Then
  Screen.ActiveControl.SelText = Clipboard.GetText()
End If

End Sub
```

"However, if we try to paste graphic data into a text box, we won't be able to do so."

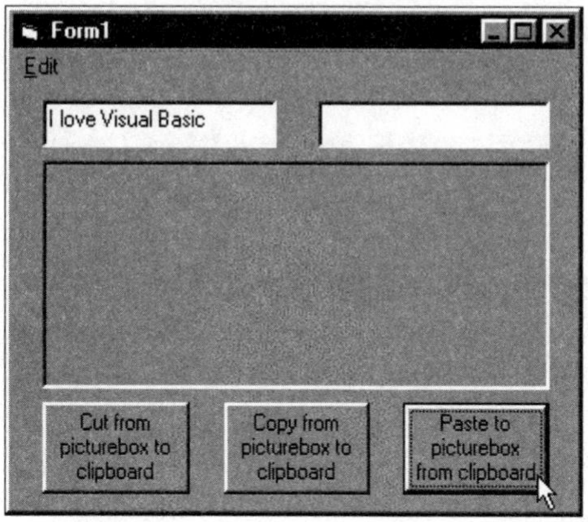

I let the class play around with the demo program for a few moments, just to prove to themselves that this was true.

"That's great," Blaine said, "but what about trying to paste text into a picture box? Can we do that?"

"Let's see," I said. "Let's put some text into the first text box, and then copy it by selecting Edit | Copy, and then clicking the Paste to PictureBox from Clipboard command button..."

"The contents of the picture box have been erased, but no text has taken its place," Dave said. "Of course, the picture box doesn't support a text property, so that's not surprising."

"You're correct, Dave," I said. "We should modify the code in the **Click** event procedure of **cmdPaste** to see if graphic data is present on the Clipboard first, before proceeding with the paste operation..."

```
Private Sub cmdPaste_Click()

If Clipboard.GetFormat(vbCFBitmap) Then
  Picture1.Picture = Clipboard.GetData()
End If

End Sub
```

"Now, if graphic data is not present on the Clipboard, we simply won't attempt to set the **Picture** property of the picture box – the result is that the graphic in the picture box will remain."

I saw just about everyone busily experimenting with the cut, copy, and paste processes. This was a long session that we'd just gone through, but I knew that all this work with the Clipboard object would pay off as the students' familiarity and comfort grew with using objects in code. At this point I still had a few more objects to discuss and, knowing that some students wanted to take some more time with their experiments, I suggested that we take another short break.

After our return, I told the students that I'd just a few more topics to discuss before calling it a day.

"For the rest of today's class," I explained, "we're going to be looking at some of the other global system objects." I knew that discussing these objects would help embed object-oriented programming principles in the students' minds, as well as giving them insight into how we can use these objects in our own programs.

More System Objects

"The next property of the **Global** object I want to discuss," I went on, "is the **Forms** property."

The Forms Collection

"The **Forms** property of the **Global** object points to the **Forms** collection."

"We discussed the **Forms** collection last week," Ward said, "Are they really one and the same thing?"

"Yes, they are," I said. "The **`Forms`** property of the **`Global`** object is the same thing as the **`Forms`** collection we discussed last time."

I could see Rhonda smilingly nervously.

"Yes, I know Rhonda," I said, "it *is* a bit confusing at first. I think all of this will make a lot more sense to you when you start to create your own objects."

"Easy for you to say," she said, laughing.

"And it's true!" I reassured her, before moving along to the next system object – the **`Licenses`** collection.

The Licenses Collection

"The **`License`** property of the **`Global`** object," I said, "points to something called the **`Licenses`** collection. The **`Licenses`** collection is something that you are not very likely to use until you are pretty well advanced in the art of Visual Basic programming."

"What sort of information does the **`Licenses`** collection contain?" Blain asked.

"The **`Licenses`** collection," I said, "allows the programmer to add **License Keys** for ActiveX controls that they may be adding to the **`Controls`** collection at runtime. Licensing essentially allows someone else to use any ActiveX controls you make for your application in projects of their own. The license keys are what locks or unlocks this ability. Failure to add the license keys for your ActiveX controls to the **`Licenses`** collection would prevent the controls from working. However, since we won't be covering ActiveX controls in this course, the **`Licenses`** collection is beyond the scope of the course, as well. The next property of the **`Global`** object I want to cover is the **`Printer`** property," I said.

The Printer Object

"The **`Printer`** property represents the system default printer. For those of you who took the Intro course with me last semester, you're already familiar with the **`Printer`** object, and so we won't be covering it any further here today. For the others, let me just say that you can use the **`Printer`** object to print to the default system printer, which is something we'll be doing with the China Shop program later on in the course."

The Printers Collection

"Next up is the **Printers** property of the **Global** object," I said. "This points to the **Printers** collection."

"The **Printers** collection is different from the **Printer** object?" Kate asked.

"Yes, Kate," I answered her. "The **Printer** object represents the system default printer, and is used to facilitate printing operations in a VB program. The **Printers** property is a collection which contains items representing *all* of the available printers installed on the user's PC."

"You mentioned that the **Printer** object represents the system default printer," Peter said. "Suppose you want to print to a printer other than the default. Is there a way to change the selected printer from within Visual Basic?"

"There are two ways to change the selected printer," I said. "Within your program, you can display the common dialog control Printer Dialog box, and let the user to change the printer selection there – much as you would see in any Windows program. Another way is to interrogate the **Printers** collection and select a printer installed on the user's PC through the use of the **Set** statement. Let me show you."

I then created a new Visual Basic project, and placed the following code into the **Click** event procedure of the command button:

```
Private Sub Command1_Click()

Dim objPrinter As Printer

For Each objPrinter In Printers
  Form1.Print objPrinter.DeviceName
Next

End Sub
```

"Not surprisingly," I said, "we can use the **For...Each** statement to loop through the items of the **Printers** collection. Each item in the **Printers** collection represents an installed printer. If we now run this program, every printer installed on PC will be printed on the form."

I did exactly that, and the following screenshot was displayed on the classroom projector:

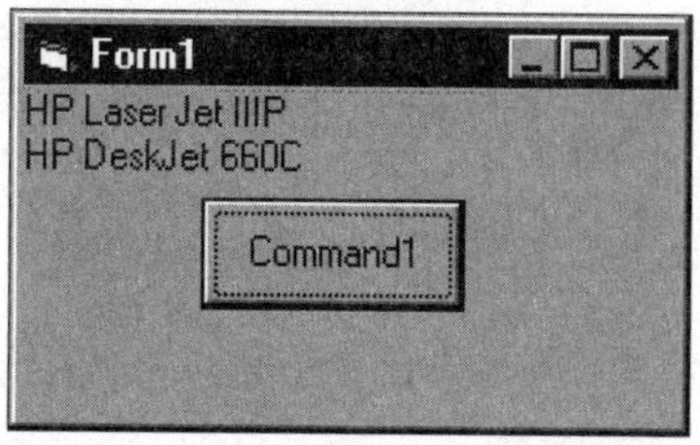

"This tells us that there are two installed printers on the Instructor's PC here in the classroom," I said. "This could come in very handy if I was to write an application with a fancy report that I wanted to print in color. Using the **Printers** collection, I could determine if a color printer was installed on the user's PC and, if so, I could then change the default printer from within the program. Like this..."

```
Private Sub Command1_Click()

Dim objPrinter As Printer
Dim blnFoundColor As Boolean

For Each objPrinter In Printers
  If objPrinter.DeviceName = "HP DeskJet 660C" Then
    Set Printer = objPrinter
    blnFoundColor = True
    Exit For
  End If
Next

If blnFoundColor = False Then
  MsgBox "Sorry, printer not found..."
End If

End Sub
```

"What's going on here?" Chuck asked.

"What I've done," I said, "is to add a variable declaration for a **Boolean** variable called **blnFoundColor**, which we will set to **True** if we find a specific printer among the installed printers on the PC..."

```
Dim blnFoundColor As Boolean
```

"The **For...Each** loop," I explained, "will enable us to loop through each item in the **Printers** collection. Each item represents a different printer, installed on the user's PC. In the **For...Each** loop, we use an **If** statement to hunt for our desired color printer we are looking for..."

```
If objPrinter.DeviceName = "HP DeskJet 660C" Then
```

"As soon as we find it," I continued, "we set the default printer of the user's PC equal to the color printer using the **Set** statement with this line of code:"

```
Set Printer = objPrinter
```

"That's it?" Linda said. "That wasn't so bad. Somehow I thought it would be harder."

"Working with objects makes everything easier," I said. "If we'd had to deal directly with a printer without benefit of either the **Printers** collection or the **Printer** object, things would be very hard indeed."

I waited, to let them absorb this information before continuing.

"These last few lines of code," I said, "are used to set the **Boolean** variable **blnFoundColor** to **True** if we find our desired printer. Then we exit the **For...Each** loop prematurely by executing the **Exit For** statement, because we don't want to bother looping through the remaining items in the **Printers** collection after we've found the printer we're looking for:"

```
blnFoundColor = True
Exit For
```

"Once we've finished looping through the items in the **Printers** collection," I said, "we then use an **If** statement to check the value of **blnFoundColor**..."

```
If blnFoundColor = False Then
  MsgBox "Sorry, no color printer found..."
End If
```

"If **blnFoundColor** is **False**, that means that none of the printers in the **Printers** collection is the one we're looking for, and we display a message to the user informing them of this fact."

"Wow, using the **Printers** collection can make our programs very sophisticated!" observed Ward.

"Absolutely," I replied. "Indeed, everything we can use through the **`Global`** object can be used like this to give our program what I call **application level awareness** – a kind of self-awareness, that lets our program examine the environment in which it exists and find out about things like this, and then use them."

"We have just one more property of the **`Global`** object to discuss," I went on, "and that's the **`Screen`** property. However, before we do that, let's take look at the **`Fonts`** collection."

The Fonts Collection

"This collection may seem a little unusual in that, as a property, it is shared by both the **`Screen`** object we'll be looking at next, and the **`Printer`** object we've just covered."

"How's that possible?" asked Dorothy.

"Well, even though an object may be a property of an other object, this doesn't mean it is necessarily *contained* by that object." I explained. "In fact, do you remember when I described that business about pointers last week? I said that a pointer is just a four-byte memory reference that allows our system to gain access to a particular location in memory."

"Yes, you also called it a reference, didn't you?" Ward said.

"That's correct," I told him. "For our purposes we can use the phrase almost interchangeably. A pointer references a particular memory location."

"So, let me guess," Ward said, "when an object acts as a property of another object, what we're actually doing is *referencing* the second object in memory, using a pointer from the first object."

"I'm glad you said it, Ward, because I've a graphic here that I hope explains exactly that concept," I replied, putting the following picture up on the screen:

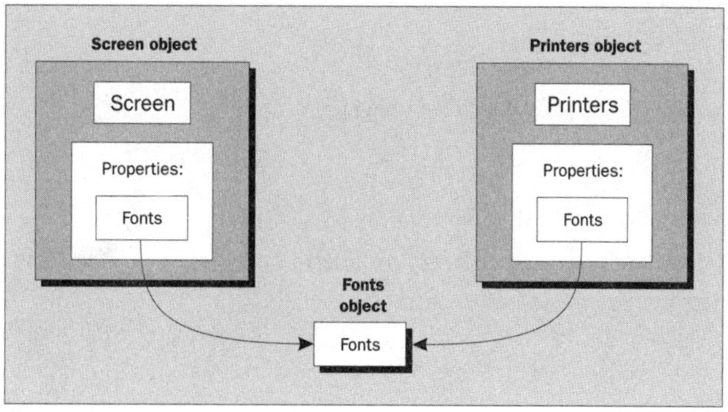

"**Fonts** exists as an object in itself – but by using pointers, both the **Screen** and the **Printer** objects can gain access to it and use it as one of their properties," I told the class. "Indeed, this is how the **Global** object uses the system objects as its properties. Just about every object that has other objects as its properties operates in exactly this way."

I saw some startled looks around the room, and one or two delighted faces.

"Wow, you sneaked that one past us!" declared Dorothy.

"All this objects-as-collections-as-properties-of-other-objects stuff is pretty dazzling," exclaimed Rhonda, "but I think I'm getting the hang of it."

"Great," I replied. "If we're ready, then, let's move on to the **Screen** object."

The Screen Object

"The **Screen** object is the property of the **Global** object which represents the entire windows desktop," I said. "It has several properties of its own. Let's take a look at them now."

The ActiveControl Property

"The **ActiveControl** property of the **Screen** object," I said, "returns the control that currently has the focus. We saw this earlier when we were discussing Clipboard methods. Just to refresh your memory, let me do a small demonstration for you..."

I started a new project, resized the default form, and placed a command button and a text box control on it, like this:

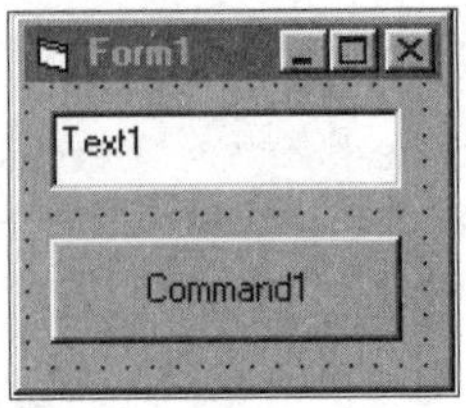

I then keyed this line of code into the form's **Click** event procedure:

```
Private Sub Form_Click()

    MsgBox Screen.ActiveControl.Name

End Sub
```

I ran the program, set focus to the text box, and clicked on the form. The following message box was displayed:

"Visual Basic is telling me that the control with focus is the text box," I said. "By the way, did you notice how I appended the **Name** property to the end of the **ActiveControl** reference? A lot of beginners make the mistake of coding references to the **ActiveControl** like this:"

```
MsgBox Screen.ActiveControl
```

"If you code the statement like that," I said, "you'll see nothing but an empty message box when you click on the form. Remember, when you are working with properties that point to other objects, you also need to append the name of the object's property or method you want to access."

The ActiveForm Property

"The **ActiveForm** property," I said, "is a property of the **Screen** object that returns the form which is the active window in your Visual Basic project. As we just saw with the **ActiveControl** property, you need to append a property or method to the **ActiveForm** property to do anything of significance with it. For instance, this code..."

```
Debug.Print Screen.ActiveForm.Name
```

"... will print the name of the active form in the Immediate window."

"You mentioned a term I'm not familiar with, there," Chuck said. "What's the **active window**?"

"In Windows," I said "only one form can be the active window, and that's the window that appears in the foreground with a highlighted title bar or border."

The FontCount Property

"The **FontCount** property," I went on, "is a property of the **Screen** object that tells us how many screen fonts are installed on the PC. In conjunction with the **Fonts** property of the **Screen** object, which we'll discuss in just a moment, it can be used to determine if a particular screen font exists on the user's PC."

"Is there a difference between the term 'font' and 'screen font'?" Ward asked.

"That's a good question, Ward," I said. "There are actually two types of fonts available for our use on the user's PC – screen fonts, which display characters on the PC's monitor, and printer fonts, which appear on the printed page. If you print out a document on a high-quality printer and compare the paper document with the one on the screen, you'll probably notice that the paper version is actually a lot nicer-looking. In just a moment, we'll discuss the **FontCount** and **Fonts** properties as they pertain to the **Screen** object – but the **Printer** object also supports the **FontCount** and **Fonts** properties."

I then started up another fresh Visual Basic project and entered the following code into the form's **Click** event procedure:

```
Private Sub Form_Click()

Form1.Print "Screen Fonts: " & Screen.FontCount
Form1.Print "Printer Fonts: " & Printer.FontCount

End Sub
```

...and ran the program, with this result:

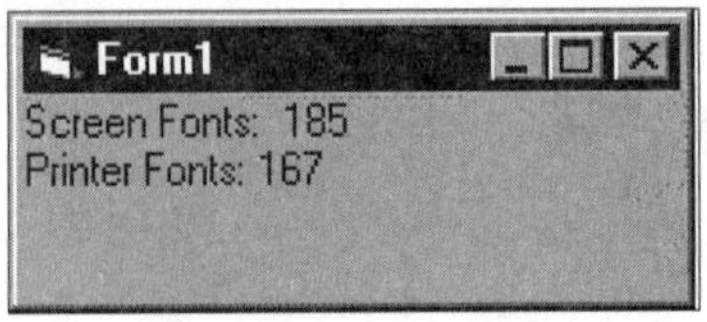

"As you can see," I said, "the PC at my desk has 185 Screen Fonts installed, and 167 Printer Fonts available for use on the default system printer."

The Fonts Property

"The **Fonts** property," I said, "returns the names of all of the **Screen** fonts installed on the user's PC. As I mentioned a moment ago, there's also a **Fonts** property of the **Printer** object. Let's write some code to display all of the installed **Screen** fonts on my PC in a list box..."

I then created a new Visual Basic project, placed a command button and a list box on the form...

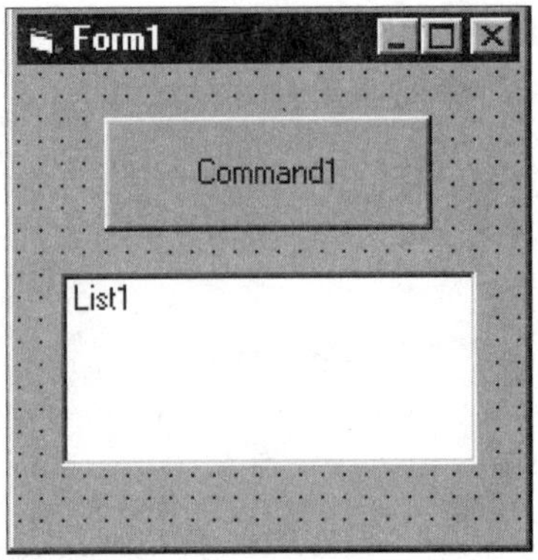

...and added this code to the command button's **Click** event procedure:

```
Private Sub Command1_Click()

Dim intCounter As Integer

For intCounter = 0 To Screen.FontCount - 1
  List1.AddItem Screen.Fonts(intCounter)
Next intCounter

End Sub
```

Next, I ran the program, clicked on the command button, and the following screenshot was displayed:

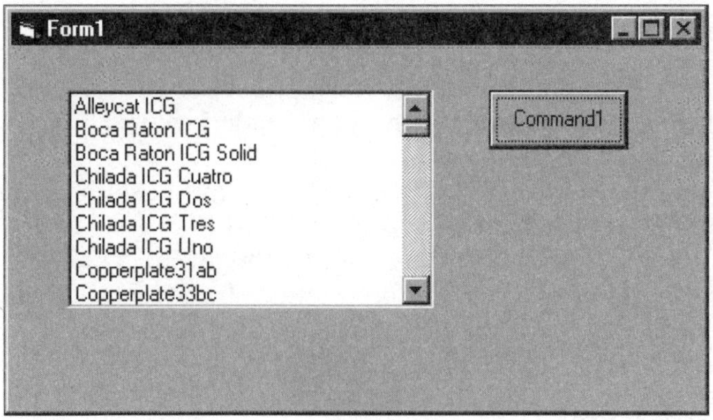

"The `For...Next` loop," I explained, "goes through all the items in the `Fonts` list – notice that, since the list is zero-based, we have to subtract one from the `FontCount` property to obtain the upper limit. Within the body of the loop we have a statement that adds the fonts, one by one, to the `List1` list box."

```
List1.AddItem Screen.Fonts(intCounter)
```

"I can see a lot of practical uses for this," Melissa said. "For instance, in determining if a particular font exists on the user's PC before setting the `Font` property of a control. I only have one question – why didn't you use the `For...Each` statement to loop through all of the fonts?"

"Because the `Fonts` property is not a Visual Basic collection," I said. "We can use the `For...Each` statement to loop through a collection object – as we did with the `Forms` and `Controls` collection – or an array, as we also did last week, but we can't use the `For...Each` statement on the `Fonts` property – we need to use the `For...Next` statement in conjunction with the `FontCount` property."

The Height and Width Properties

"The `Height` and `Width` properties," I said, "return the dimensions of the screen measured in **twips**."

"Twips..." said Melissa, "I wasn't here for the Intro course, but I take it everyone knows what a twip is – a **TW**ent**I**eth of a **P**oint?"

"Yes, I brought this term in early on in my Intro course, when I was discussing screen resolutions." I replied. "But just as a reminder, a twip is 1/1440th of an inch, or **1/20th of a printer's point**. That means there are 1440 twips to an inch, or about 567 twips to a centimeter."

"I think you gave us an example of using the **Screen** object with its **Height** and **Width** properties in our Intro course, as well, didn't you?" Valerie asked.

"Yes, I did, Valerie," I replied. "I showed you how you could use the screen's **Height** and **Width** properties to center a Visual Basic form within the screen. Here's an example out of Visual Basic Help, where the **Width** and **Height** of the form is altered so as it occupies 75% of the screen's dimensions, and is centered within the screen..."

```
Private Sub Form_Load()

Width = Screen.Width * .75
Height = Screen.Height * .75
Left = (Screen.Width - Width) / 2
Top = (Screen.Height - Height) / 2

End Sub
```

I went back to the program I'd just created and added the same code to the **Form_Load** event procedure. Then I ran the program: sure enough, the form was perfectly centered, with its **Height** and **Width** properties set so that the form occupied three quarters of the screen:

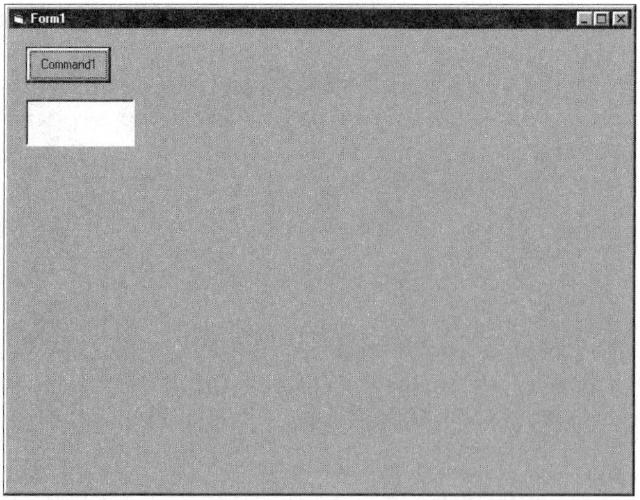

I noticed that Rhonda was looking at form on the classroom projector intently.

"What's wrong Rhonda?" I asked.

She hesitated a minute before answering.

"The form has gotten much larger," Rhonda said, "but since the location and size of the list box and command buttons didn't change, they really look funny sitting all by themselves in the upper left hand corner of the form. It's a shame that Visual Basic doesn't automatically readjust them for us."

"That's certainly true, it does look funny," I said. "Unfortunately, Visual Basic doesn't help us much with things like this. That was one reason we didn't let the user change the size of the China Shop form – if they did, the form would look pretty awkward."

"Is there a way to write code to dynamically change the size and locations of your controls if the form size changes?" Dave asked.

"Yes there is, Dave," I said, "but writing that code can be pretty complicated. You could purchase a third party control: there are several vendors who have designed ActiveX controls that when placed on a form, will automatically adjust the size and locations of other controls on the form when a form is resized."

"Speaking of the size and location of forms," Ward said, "suppose you write a program and design a form for it using a monitor with a particular screen resolution – what happens if you move the program to a computer with a different screen resolution?"

"That's a good point, Ward," I said. "As a professional programmer, you need to consider the impact of different screen resolutions on your program."

Chuck put his hand up. "I'm not sure I'm following you," he confessed.

"Well, for instance," I said, "suppose you create a form for your application that just about covers the monitor screen of your computer. The screen resolution is, say, 1024 by 768. If you run that same program on a monitor whose resolution is set to 640 by 480, the form will be bigger than the user's screen and so any controls situated towards the 'edges' of the form will be off the side of the monitor's field of view."

"What exactly do you mean by 1024 by 768 and 640 by 480?" Rhonda asked.

"1024 by 768 and 640 by 480 represent two popular screen resolutions," I said. "It's a simple x/y relationship: the first number is the number of pixels, horizontally; the second number is the number of pixels vertically."

"So a monitor whose resolution is 640 by 480," Steve asked, "has 640 dots horizontally and 480 vertically?"

"That's right, Steve," I said. "Microsoft's recommendation for avoiding this problem is very simple: design your programs on a monitor whose resolution is set to 640 by 480. If a user has a higher-resolution monitor, the form will still fit on it, even though it will appear smaller."

"Is there anything more elegant we can do?" Kate asked. "I know from experience that 640 by 480 is very 'grainy'. If there's a way of knowing the screen resolution of the user's monitor, couldn't we do something smarter?"

"Well," I said, "there is a way of determining the resolution of the user's monitor at run time through the use of the **TwipsPerPixelX** and **TwipsPerPixelY** properties of the **Screen** object."

The TwipsPerPixelX and TwipsPerPixelY Properties

I placed the following code in the **Click** event procedure of the form...

```
Private Sub Form_Click()

Dim lngPixelsWide As Long
Dim lngPixelsHigh As Long

lngpixelswide = Screen.Width / Screen.TwipsPerPixelX
lngpixelshigh = Screen.Height / Screen.TwipsPerPixelY

MsgBox "Your screen resolution is " & lngPixelsWide &
    ↳" x " & lngPixelsHigh

End Sub
```

I then ran the program and clicked on the form. The following screenshot was displayed:

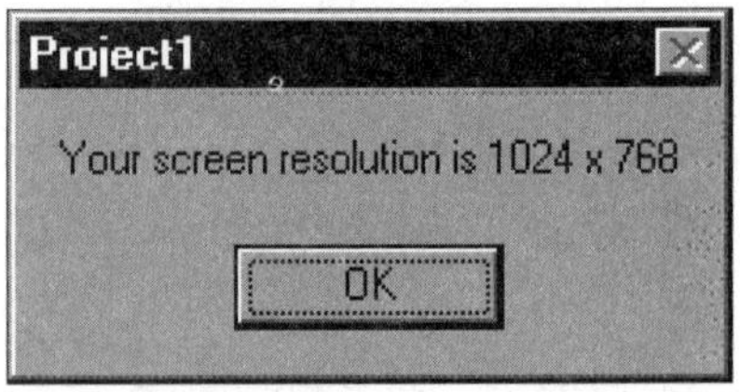

"Dividing both the **Height** and **Width** properties of the **Screen** object," I said, "by the number of twips per pixel, gives us the figures for the screen resolution. Once we know the screen resolution, there are a number of different things that we could do."

"What would those be?" Steve asked.

"In the case of the China Shop Project," I said, "probably the easiest solution would be to design different forms to accommodate the four most popular monitor resolutions – 640 by 480, 800 by 600, 1024 by 768 and 1600 by 1200."

"What else?" Mary asked.

"We could do what Dave alluded to earlier," I said: "write code that dynamically resizes and relocates every control on the form, based on the screen resolution – not an easy undertaking!"

"What about those third party controls you mentioned earlier?" Ward asked.

"That's the final alternative," I said. "There are several good ones on the market, and I know several of my associates are using them quite successfully. On the whole, though, it's better to just avoid this kind of problem, if you can."

The MouseIcon and MousePointer Properties

"We have just two more properties of the **Screen** object to discuss," I said. "The **MouseIcon** and **MousePointer** properties. **MousePointer** allows you to select the mouse icon you want. There are 16 standard icons. Here's the list:"

Constant	Value	Description
vbDefault	0	(Default) Shape determined by the object.
VbArrow	1	Arrow.
VbCrosshair	2	Cross (crosshair pointer).
VbIbeam	3	I beam.
VbIconPointe	4	Icon (small square within a square).
VbSizePointer	5	Size (four-pointed arrow pointing north, south,east and west).
VbSizeNESW	6	Size NE SW (double arrow pointing northeastand southwest)
vbSizeNS	7	Size NS (double arrow pointing north and south).

Continued on Following Page

VbSizeNWSE	8	Size NW SE (double arrow pointing northwest and southeast)
vbSizeWE	9	Size W E (double arrow pointing west and east).
VbUpArrow	10	Up Arrow.
VbHourglass	11	Hourglass (wait).
VbNoDrop	12	No Drop.
VbArrowHourlgass	13	Arrow and hourglass.
VbArrowQuestion	14	Arrow and question mark.
VbSizeall	15	Size all.
vbCustom	99	Custom icon specified by the MouseIcon property

"Notice that the last option is for a custom icon." I continued. "In other words, if you set the **MousePointer** property to 99, you can specify your own a custom mouse pointer graphic in the **MouseIcon** property. The syntax is:"

```
MouseIcon = LoadPicture(pathname)
```

"Does *pathname* tell the computer which directory to find the graphic for the new icon in?" Dorothy asked.

"Yes, Dorothy, that's exactly what is does," I replied.

"Don't some of the Visual Basic controls have these **MouseIcon** and **MousePointer** properties, as well?" Ward asked. "For instance, the command button and the text box controls?"

"That's true," I said, showing the relevant properties of the command button we used in the last example project on the screen:

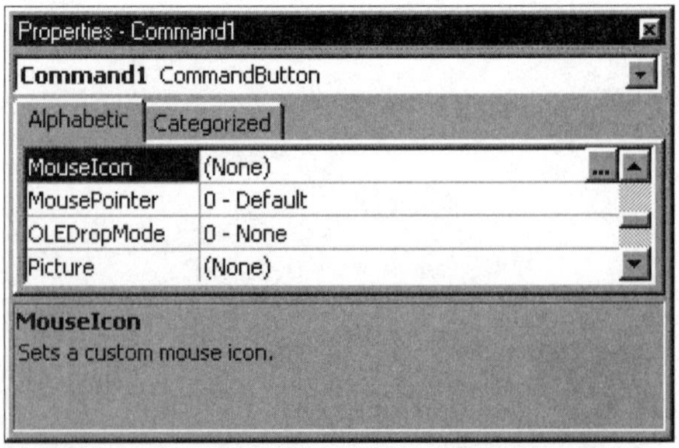

"How are those different than the **MouseIcon** and **MousePointer** properties of the **Screen** object?" Ward asked.

"They're not," I replied. "They're just specific to that particular object. Every Visual Basic form and just about every control has its own **MouseIcon** and **MousePointer** properties, which you can set independently. They specify the mouse pointer to be displayed when the user moves the mouse *over* that particular form or that control. However, the control or form's own **MousePointer** setting is overridden by the **Screen** object's setting."

"Can you clarify that?" Rhonda asked. "I'm afraid I don't quite understand what you mean by 'overridden'."

"Sure thing, Rhonda," I said. "For instance, suppose you specify a **MousePointer** property of 2 – a **vbCrossHair** – for a form, and 3 – a **vbIbeam** – for a text box control on that form. If the user moves the mouse over the form, a cross-hair icon appears: if the user moves the mouse over the text box on the same form, the icon changes to an I-beam. Now suppose in your code you then assign the screen's **MousePointer** property a value of **vbHourGlass** – an Hourglass Icon will now appear, regardless of its location – even over the text box. That's what I mean by overriding."

"It looks to me," Chuck said, "like setting the **Screen** object's **MousePointer** property to an hourglass temporarily, would be a good way to let the user know that they need to wait for something."

"That's right, Chuck," I said. "Using the **MouseIcon** property like this can create some clever effects in your program – just don't overdo it. Inappropriate use of mouse icons can confuse users, especially if you stray too far from the accepted Windows standards."

I glanced up at the clock before switching off the classroom projector and shutting down my computer.

"That's it for today," I said. "We've covered a lot of ground, and I hope you've found it interesting and useful – even if a lot of it may not be directly applicable to the China Shop program. I wanted to go over this material because it'll give you a much better grounding in Visual Basic objects. Next week, we'll start looking at making our own objects for the China Shop program, which will involve us looking into how objects operate internally. Let me just summarize quickly what we've covered in this lesson before we wrap it up."

Chapter Summary

In this chapter we learned about the existence of the Visual Basic **`Global`** object, and used some of the system objects, which constitute its properties.

- We discussed the Visual Basic **`Global`** object
- We saw that the **`Global`** object has seven properties, which are themselves objects
- We learned how to implement cut, copy, and paste functionality by using the Clipboard object
- We briefly examined the **`License`** collection and learned its importance to programmers who're creating their own ActiveX controls
- We saw that the **`Printers`** object can be used to determine the installed printers on a User's PC and search for a specific printer
- We saw how to find out the number of different fonts on a user's PC
- We saw how to find out the names of all the fonts using the **`Fonts`** property
- Through the **`Fonts`** property, we introduced the idea of objects referencing other objects using pointers
- We learned about the **`Screen`** object and its many properties

More specifically, with the China Shop project:

- We used the **`PrevInstance`** property of the **`App`** object to prevent two copies of the application being run at once
- We used the **`Path`** property of the **`App`** object to let the application find out its location on the user's drive system, and infer from that, the location of the **`Prices.txt`** and **`.gif`**-image files

In next week's lesson, we really delve inside objects and practice using them some more. We'll also identify and document the objects for the China Shop project, and make some more amendments to the China shop program. See you there!

Learn to Program Objects with Visual Basic
Bullina's China

Chapter 4
Objects – the Inside Story

In this chapter, you'll sit alongside my class as they really start to get inside the world of object-oriented programming.

We start out by exploring the core components that individual objects all share – properties, methods, and events – and then we see why these are important and how we can interact with them effectively in code. In the course of doing this, my students will be delighted to discover that they can create their own customized properties and methods, and that they can even add them to standard Visual Basic objects – such as a project's default form.

Learning these things will prepare my students for implementing these vital object-oriented programming practices in their own objects when they come to create them. Specifically, the topics that we cover in this lesson will feed into the creation of the China Shop program's objects, which we'll start building in the second half of this chapter.

Here's a summary of the important ground that we'll cover today:

- Defining what an object is in detail
- Discussing object properties, methods and events in theory and practice
- Adding custom properties and methods to standard forms
- Utilizing properties, methods and events in code
- Determining the objects that we need in the China Shop program
- Starting to create the China Shop's objects

Now let's join my students as they flock in for the fourth lesson of the class...

Welcome Back

"Good morning," I said as I welcomed the students into the warm classroom. "I think you'll find today's session very exciting. In the latter part of today's class, we'll be designing the objects for the China Shop project. What I'd like to do first, however, is take you on a 'behind the scenes' tour of some aspects of Visual Basic objects you may not be familiar with yet. We're going to take our understanding of exactly how objects operate up another level by looking at the workings of some common objects. Doing this will allow us to see how we can apply these principles to the objects that we'll create for Joe Bullina's China Shop program – a process that we'll set in train today. I'll begin by asking that classic rhetorical question – *'What is an object?'*

"I must tell you," Mary said, "that object theory really scares me. I hope I can follow along with this. I took a course called *Object-Oriented Theory* last year, and I found it pretty tough going."

"I know what you mean, Mary," Rhonda said. "I took a similar course last summer and, quite honestly, I was completely lost most of the time."

"I think the basic problem that you probably both had," I said, "was the fact that you did not have any Visual Basic programming experience under your belts at the time. As I've said before, You may not have realized it, but you've been using objects for the last few months as you developed the China Shop program – standard Visual Basic objects like check boxes and command buttons, forms and text boxes, and so on. That would have been clear to you on those courses if you'd done some more programming in VB."

"I understand that," said Steve, "but we didn't create any objects of our own in the China Shop program, did we?"

"That's true, Steve," I said, "but as we discussed Lessons 2 and 3, what we've been doing is using the standard objects that Visual Basic has supplied for our use – ready-made and primed for action. As we saw, the standard controls that we find in the Toolbox are all objects – and the difference between using those predefined objects and designing and creating your own is not that great a leap to make. We'll do the run-up to that leap today."

What is an Object?

"I know we've talked about objects as discrete units of code that perform a job in our programs," said Rhonda, "but can you give us a *formal* definition of an object? Just so that it's all clear and above board?" Rhonda asked.

"Yes indeed, Rhonda," I replied. "Let's get those definitions straight before we go anywhere else."

Definitions

"In fact," I went on, "I've even got a slide with the definition on it to help remind us."

I put the following slide up on the screen and read the words aloud to the class:

> **An object is a programmatic representation of a real world thing, created from a class module or template, which contains properties, reacts to methods, and raises events.**

"Can you give us that one more time, but *slowly* this time," Rhonda said, smiling.

"OK," I said, "how about this slide:"

An object is the representation of a real world thing, created from a class module or template. Also:

> **An object contains Properties – these describe attributes or characteristics of the object. For example, an Automobile object might have a Color property, which could be set to a value of Green, Red, Blue etc., depending on what color we painted the bodywork.**

> **An object has Methods – these are the predefined repertoire of things that an object can *do*, and they're built into the object. Programmers can use these methods to perform actions on the object and the properties that describe it. For example, an Automobile object could have an Accelerate method – we could call this method and execute it if we wanted the automobile to speed up.**

> **An object raises (or produces) Events – these are signals that the object can put out to let the program know that something has happened. For example, if our Automobile object's Fuel Level property drops below a certain level, the Automobile could raise a FillMeUp! event that signaled a visit to a gas station was called for.**

"The properties, methods, and events of an object are what ties it into the fabric of the surrounding program," I went on. "It's through them that other objects and code can communicate with the object: our program can look at an object's properties, interact with the object through the methods built into the object, and respond to the events that the object raises. The rest of this course is about how we can take advantage of objects and their properties, methods, and events in our programs."

I paused to take a breath before going on:

"Now, it's critical that you remember that an object's properties, methods and events are defined in the **class** – the template – that the individual object is created from."

Objects and Classes

"As we discussed in Lesson 2, an object's class is a template for objects of that particular type, and it's from the class that the individual object is created or **instantiated**. Remember that I said you can think of an object's class as a cookie cutter, and the objects that are instantiated (created) from it as the cookies that are created when the cookie cutter is pressed on a sheet of cookie dough. Each object that's created from a given class will have the same properties, methods, and events – these are all defined in the class template. Each object created from the class is identical – initially at least."

"One of the reasons I've enjoyed taking courses with you so much," Rhonda said, "is that you tend not to overwhelm us with computer nerd-type terms. But what exactly does **instantiate** mean again?"

"Instantiate means 'to create from', or 'to be born'," I said. "So when you hear that an object has been instantiated, that means that an individual copy of an object – an instance – has been created from its class or template. As a reminder example, think of the command button icon in the Visual Basic Toolbox. When we double-click on the command button in the Toolbox, an object representing the underlying `CommandButton` class is instantiated on our form. If we double click on the command button icon in the Toolbox again, a second identical instance of the command button is created on the form. That's instantiation – and if you want, you can use the terms 'born' or 'created' interchangeably. Just remember, the official term is instantiation."

"So more than one object of the same type," Chuck said, "can be instantiated from the same cookie cutter or class – is that right?"

"That's right, Chuck," I replied. "There's no limit to the number of objects that can be instantiated from a single class module. The class module, remember, is where Visual Basic actually stores the class definition."

"I understand that the designers of Visual Basic created classes for command buttons, check boxes, and all the other common control objects that we use," said Chuck. "But how will we get the objects that we create ourselves to appear in the Toolbox?" Chuck asked.

"The objects that we create during this semester's course," I answered, "will *not* have a visual interface, and that means that they won't appear in the Toolbox. The objects that we create for Joe's China Shop won't actually need to be in the toolbox: they'll only need to exist inside the China Shop program itself as distinct pieces of code that can work together. But even though the objects that we create only appear as code in our program, and not as icons in the Toolbox, they still have lots in common with the control objects that we've already looked at. They still have properties, react to methods, and raise events, just like the Visual Basic objects we've been using all along."

> **The pre-defined objects that appear in the Toolbox are actually of a special type of object called ActiveX Controls – we'll talk about this type of control in detail later in this book.**

"So, although our China Shop objects won't have a visual interface that will appear in the Toolbox, they're still implementing exactly the same object-oriented programming principles that we've been looking at so far. To help make this clearer, let's take an even closer look at these common features that Visual Basic objects all have in common – properties, methods and events."

Inside the Object

"Let's start by examining object **properties**," I suggested.

Properties

"Do you have a formal definition of a property?" Rhonda asked.

"Try this," I replied. "A **property** is a characteristic or attribute of an object that affects its appearance or behavior," I went on. "Properties are something that you all probably take for granted – after all, you've been working with properties a lot in the last few months. Let's take a look at the Visual Basic Properties window now..."

I then displayed this graphic on the classroom projector:

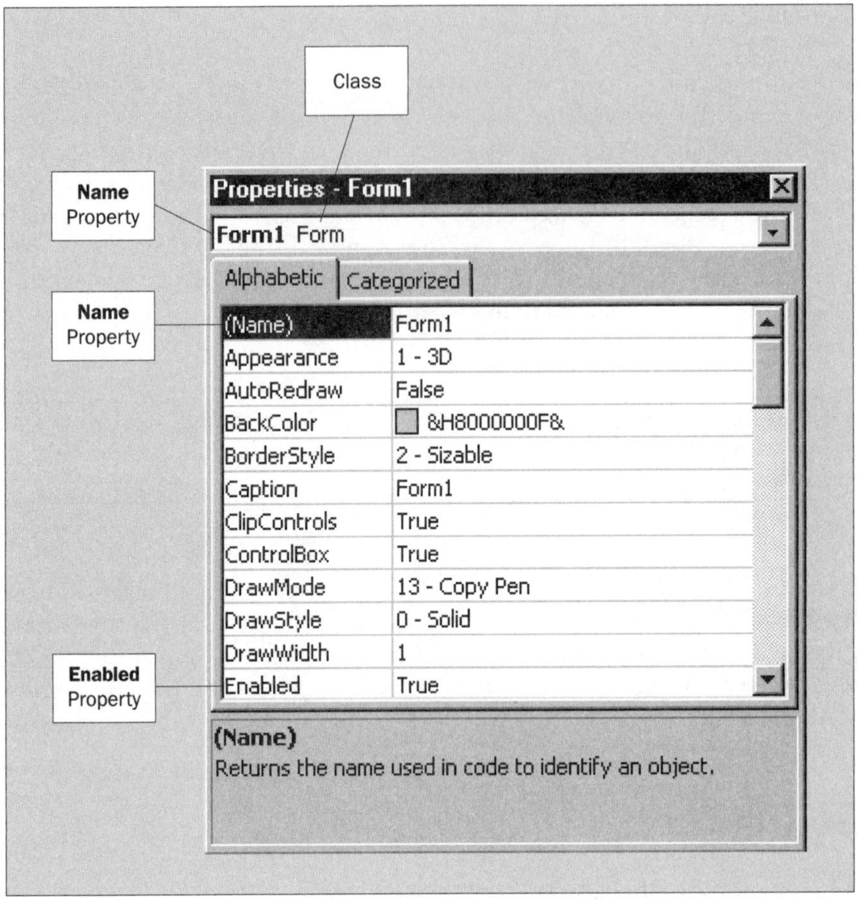

"As you can see," I explained, "there's a drop-down list box at the top of the Properties window containing the name of the form – in this case **`Form1`**:"

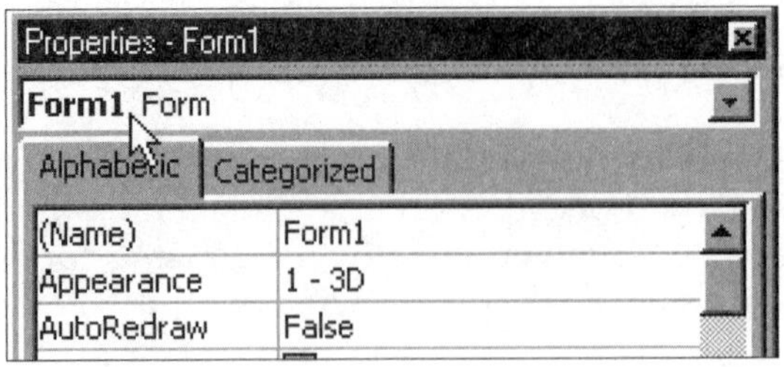

"...and **Form1** is also the specific **Name** property of this particular form object:"

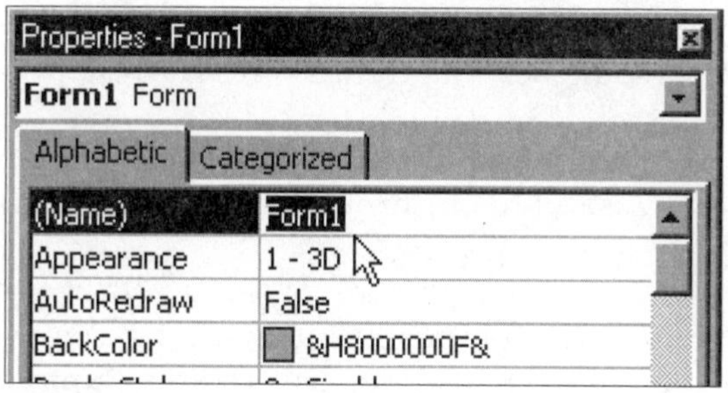

"But what I think you may not have realized is that the word Form right next to the name of **Form1** in the drop-down object list box box..."

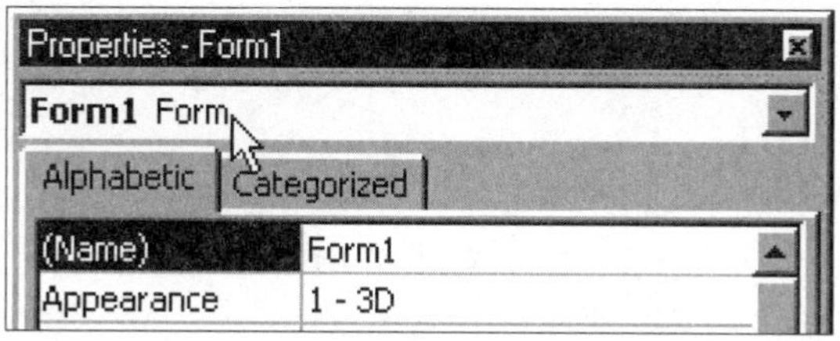

"...is the name of the class from which the form was instantiated. So you can see in the Properties window that the **Form1** object was instantiated based on the class called Form."

"Within the body of the Properties window, as you should already be aware, the left-hand column holds the names of the various properties, and the right-hand column holds those properties' values:"

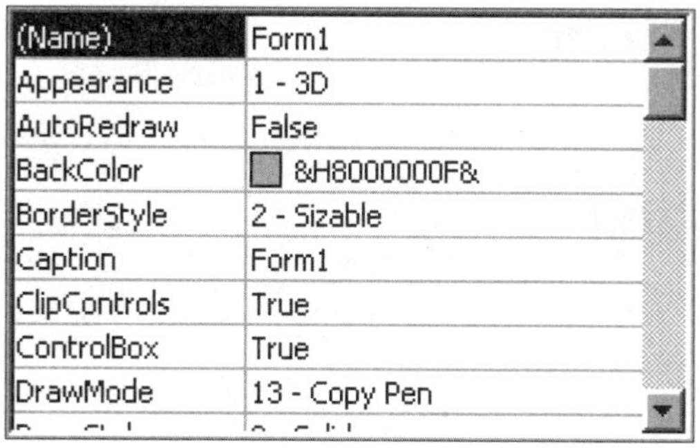
(Name)
Form1
Appearance
1 - 3D
AutoRedraw
False
BackColor
&H8000000F&
BorderStyle
2 - Sizable
Caption
Form1
ClipControls
True
ControlBox
True
DrawMode
13 - Copy Pen

"Take note also that each of the properties of the object is instantiated with initial values preset – these values are also derived from the class that the object was created from."

"This is so cool," said Rhonda. "I've always wondered what the word Form was doing after the form's name – it's the class name for the object!"

"Exactly, Rhonda," I said. I could see that things were starting to fall into place for Rhonda.

"If there's a `Form` class, does that mean that each and every default form, and each and every additional form that we add to our project, are identical?" Melissa asked.

"That's absolutely right, Melissa," I confirmed. "When we first start a new Visual Basic project, the properties of the form are identical to every other form that we would create in the IDE – with the exception of the `Name` property and the `Caption` property. Of course, once the form appears in the IDE, the programmer then has the freedom to change the properties of the form as he or she see fit – but initially, the property values come from the original class template."

"Is the same principle true for every other control in the Visual Basic Toolbox?" enquired Ward.

"Yes," I confirmed. "For instance, if we place a command button on the form, that command button is created from the underlying `CommandButton` class."

"I remember you saying that Microsoft themselves created these classes you've been talking about," Peter said, "but can we see what the definitions of these classes actually look like?"

"Yes," I said, "Microsoft did indeed create the `Form` class, along with the classes for all the other controls in the Toolbox. But I'm afraid those class modules are hidden from view inside the Visual Basic code itself, so unfortunately we can't look at them."

I then suggested that we continue by taking a look at the command button icon in the Visual Basic Toolbox. This would let us start using some of the default properties of the standard controls 'in anger'.

Properties in Action

"When we double-click on the command button icon," I said, "a command button is placed on the form. Like this..."

I double-clicked on the command button icon in the Toolbox, and a fresh command button appeared right in the middle of my form:

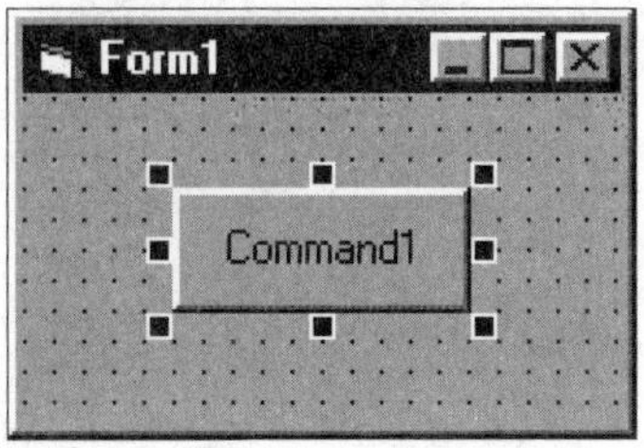

"Now, if we bring up the Properties window for this command button," I said...

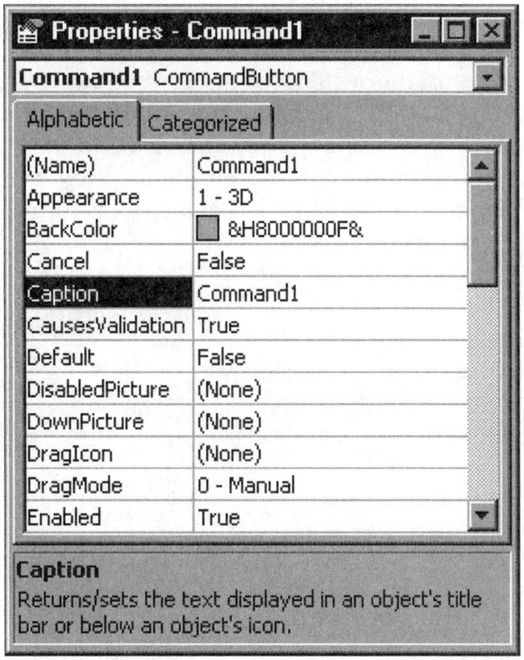

"...you'll see that it looks very similar to the Properties window we saw for the form a moment ago. The name of the command button, Command1, appears in the object drop-down list box, and it's immediately followed by the class name for the command button – CommandButton. Now let's see what happens if I double-click on the command button icon in the Visual Basic toolbox and create a second instance of the command button class on the form..."

True to my word, I double-clicked on the Toolbox's command button icon, with this result:

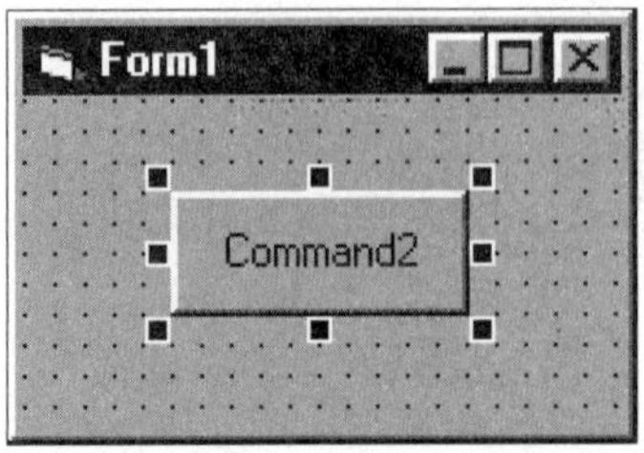

"Look," I said, "the second command button has been placed directly on top of the first command button."

"Why does that happen?" Blaine asked.

"I bet I can answer that," Kevin interjected. "Since both command buttons were created from the same cookie cutter – that is, the same **`CommandButton`** class – they both have identical properties – including the **`Left`**, **`Top`**, **`Height`** and **`Width`** properties. Therefore, when the second command button was placed on the form by double-clicking the command button in the toolbox, it inherited the same default property settings from the class, and landed right on top of the first one. Wham!"

"I couldn't have said that better myself, Kevin," I replied. "You're absolutely right: every property of the second command button is *identical* to the first – with the exception of the **`Name`** and **`Caption`** properties. That's because of the cookie cutter-type behavior of the class module. Let's take a look at the Properties window of the second command button:

"Why was it," Tom asked, "that the **`Name`** and **`Caption`** property changed when the second command button was placed on the form?"

"That's a characteristic of ActiveX controls," I said. "Remember – the control objects that we create from the Toolbox icons are actually ActiveX controls. When an ActiveX control object is placed on the form, it's smart enough to increment both the **`Name`** property (and in the case of the command button, the **`Caption`** property) by 1, when placed on the form."

I let them take this in for a second or two before continuing.

"OK," I went on, "so much for the default properties that an object inherits from the class that it's based on. These default properties are clearly vital, but there's more: with many objects, we can also add properties of our own to supplement the core ones defined in the class."

"Can we really?" exclaimed Kathy. "How do we do that?"

"I'll show you in a moment," I said. "The most striking example is where we add properties and methods of our own to a form. We call properties that we add to a form like this **Custom Form Properties**."

Custom Form Properties

"Did I hear you right?" Rhonda asked, "Did you say you can create form properties of your own? As in: created from scratch?"

"Absolutely, Rhonda," I said. "It's possible to create a property of the form that can be accessed just as any existing form property can be – by using **object dot notation**."

"Object dot notation..." Chuck said. "Is that when we refer to a property of an object by specifying its object name, then a period, then the property name?"

"Right you are, Chuck," I said. "And here's an example from the sample project that I just added the command buttons to."

So saying, I started up my two-command button project, paused it, and then started typing a statement into the Immediate window:

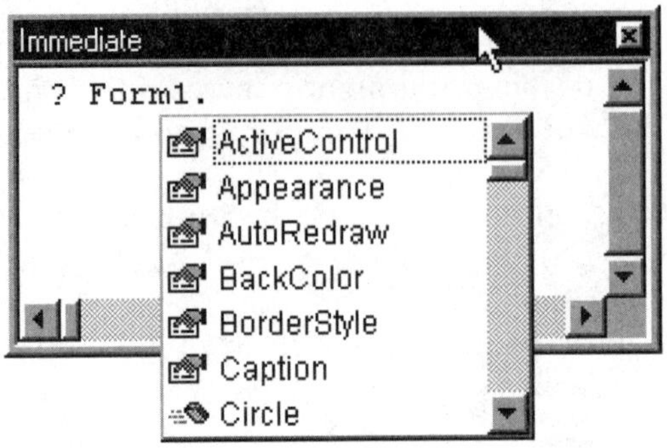

"As you can see," I said, "when I type the period after the name of the **Form1** form object, Visual Basic gives me a list of all the properties, methods, and events that are attached to – or are members of – the form object. These are all shown in the List Members box that drops down in front of the Immediate window when I type the period. Visual Basic keeps track of all of these members as soon as a new object is created, allowing us to access them in code. So, a big advantage of defining your own custom form properties is that they can be referred to by using object dot notation, just like this."

"How do we create a form property of our own?" Kathy asked.

"All we need to do," I said, "is to declare a **Public** variable in the General Declarations section of the form."

Public Variables

"For instance," I explained, "suppose I have a form called **Form1**, and I want to create a custom property for that form called **Smiley**. All I have to do is to declare a variable in **Form1**'s General Declarations section, like this..."

I went back to my example project and added this statement to the General Declarations section:

```
Public Smiley As Integer
```

Then I began adding a new line of code to the first command button's **Click** event, referring to the **Smiley** property that I'd just defined. This is what I began to type:

```
Form1.Smiley = 22
```

However, I never got that far. As soon as I typed in the period after the word Form1 in the code window, the List Members box appeared and, when I scrolled down through it, there was my newly-defined **Smiley** custom form property, ready for me to select:

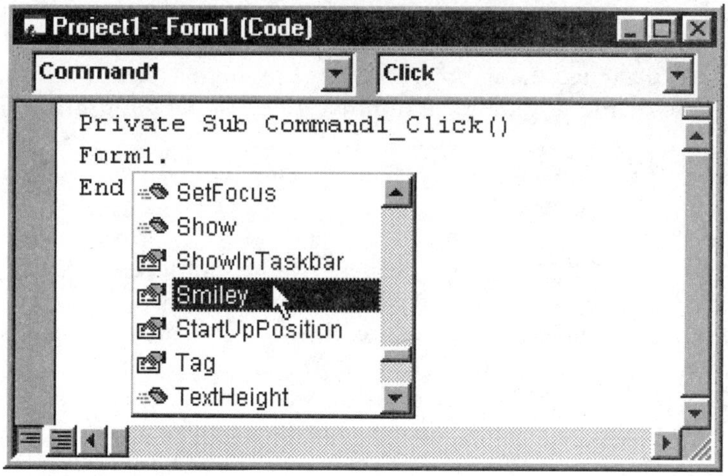

"Now *that*, I like," declared Linda.

"But why would we want to do that?" Ward asked. "Why not just create a variable that you can refer to by name in your program? I guess I just don't see the point of creating a custom property to store a data value."

"That's a valid question, Ward," I said. "The answer is two-fold. Firstly, creating a custom property lets us implement object-oriented program principles more rigorously by storing data inside the object that it relates to – in this case, by storing it as a property of a from object. This also lets us get at the value using object dot notation. Secondly, as you'll probably hear me say over and over again in this course, much of the work that goes into creating objects in Visual Basic programs is not just for the benefit of the programmer creating the objects."

"Who else is getting the benefit here, then?" Valerie asked. "If it's not the programmer coding the objects or creating the custom form property, then whom?"

"In the corporate world," I replied, "the majority of the time that a program needs to be modified – and that can be pretty often – it's done by someone other than the programmer who did the original programming. In fact, most times, the modifications are done by the most junior members of the programming team. Sad, but true – we all have to pay our dues!"

"So," Dave ventured, "all of the work that goes into creating Visual Basic objects – in this case custom form properties – is done for the benefit of some junior programmer somewhere?"

"It's not the whole story," I said, "but it's certainly a big part of it. One of the biggest payoffs in Programming with objects is in modifying the program once it's finished. A program that's been designed using objects is just that bit easier to maintain – whether that maintenance is done by the original programmer, or by some poor junior!"

"And how does creating a custom form property make that easier?" Mary asked.

"Well, for one thing," I said, "there's this: if another programmer needs to do some work with this form, then rather than look in the General Declarations section of the form and scan through for a list of all the variables that the form's using, all they need to do is type the name of the form, followed by a dot. Here, they're implicitly taking advantage of the fact that the form is an object, and that our custom property is a property of the form object. There's an established relationship – a dependency – between the custom property and the form that contains it. When the programmer types the name of the form, followed by a dot, the List Members window will automatically appear, showing them all of the properties and methods of the form – including any custom form properties that we've created ourselves. Here, let me show you..."

Demonstrating Custom Form Properties

I started up a new Visual Basic project, and entered this code into the General Declarations section of the form:

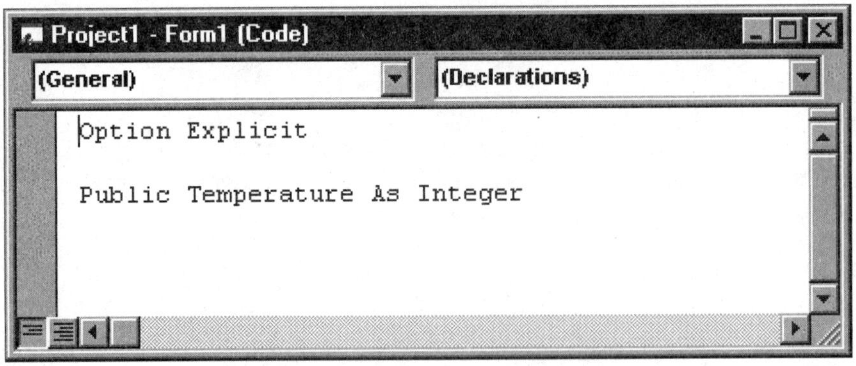

"What I've done here," I said, "is declare a **`Public`** variable called **`Temperature`** in the General Declarations section of the form – in effect creating a custom property of the form. By declaring this variable as **`Public`**, we're telling Visual Basic that it will live inside the **`Form1`** object: this means that it will be a property of the form. The **`Public`** declaration also means that this property will be directly available for other forms and code in our project to interact with. Now watch what happens when I enter code into the Code window that refers to that property..."

I brought up the **`Load`** event procedure of the form and typed the word **`Form1`** followed by a period, and the letters **`Te`** for **`Temperature`** in the Visual Basic Code Window:

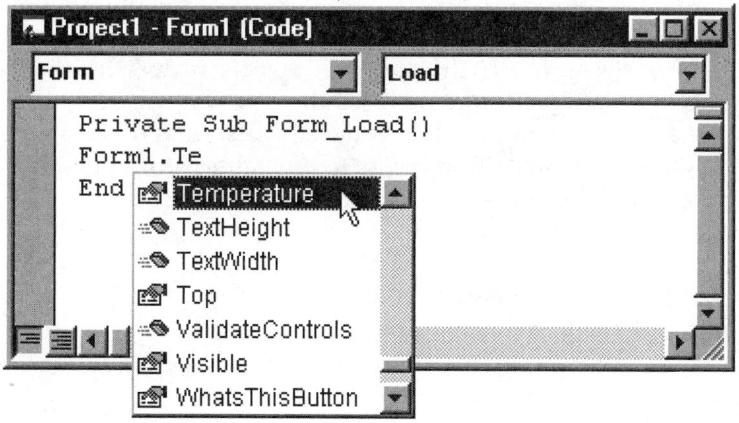

"Notice how the custom form property, **`Temperature`**, shows up in the List Members window?" I said.

"Does this mean," Valerie asked, "that we could have coded the China Shop's module level variable **`m_intQuantity`** as a public custom form property and referred to it using object dot notation throughout the program?"

"I'm not familiar with that code from the China Shop project," Dorothy said. "What's **`m_intQuantity`**?"

"**`m_intQuantity`**," I explained, "is a form-level, integer-type variable, and it represents the quantity of china items that the customer has selected using the Quantity option button on the China Shop's main form. The variable's **`m_`** prefix is the convention used for module-level variables – the 'module', in this case, effectively being the form. Our **`Public`** property declaration makes our property available from anywhere in the program."

"But getting back to Valerie's question," Blaine said, "should we change the declaration of `m_intQuantity` to a public custom form property in the China Shop?"

"That's not a bad idea," I said. "That would allow us to use object dot notation."

"Is this something we should look to do in every program that we write?" Rhonda asked.

"Again," I said, "it's not a bad idea to consider the use of custom form properties, especially if your organization is full of junior programmers!"

"Is this how we'll create properties in our own classes?" Tom asked.

"No, not quite, Tom," I said. "Unlike custom form properties – which are declared as `Public` variables – we'll see shortly that our own objects' properties should be declared as `Private` variables in a class module. You'll see that the way we declare these custom properties – as `Public` or `Private` – determines the way that other objects and code in our program can use them. Controlling access to the values stored inside a property is part of making our object-oriented programs robust and reliable – but, as I say, more on that later!"

"Next," I continued, "I'd like to move on from this discussion of object properties, and look at the next object component on our list – **methods**."

Methods

"You mentioned a little earlier," Chuck said, "that objects have their own methods, implying that they *react* to actions done on them by changing something internally. I've always thought of a method as something that a programmer *does to an object*."

"Both perspectives are correct," I said. "For example, if we execute a form's `Hide` method, you can look at the result from two different perspectives. First, you could say that the form reacts to the execution of the `Hide` method by making itself invisible. Alternatively, you could say that the programmer *hides* the form. Either way, the result is the same: the form becomes invisible. Strangely enough, an object's methods are essentially just procedures that are executed by a programmer. In the case of the form and the controls in the Toolbox, the methods are hidden deep within the object – this is sometimes referred to as **encapsulation** – and executed using the same object dot notation we saw in action when we referred to a property just a little while ago."

"Is it possible to create a custom form method, in the same way that we created a custom form property?" Bob asked.

"It sure is, Bob," I said. "If a custom form *property* is created by declaring a `Public` variable in the General Declarations section of a form, do you have any idea as to how we can create a custom form *method*?"

"Just guessing here," Dorothy said, "but considering the hint you gave us earlier when you said that a method is really just a procedure inside an object... can we create a custom form method by creating a `Public` procedure in the General Declarations section of the form?"

"Spot on," I said. "All we need to do is create a `Public` procedure, and we have ourselves a custom form method. The method can consist of either a function – which returns a value – or a subprocedure – which doesn't automatically return a value. Once again, as was the case with the custom form property, the big advantage is that we can use object dot notation to refer to any custom method that we create – in exactly the same way as we refer to an object's built-in methods."

"I'm still a little uncertain over the mechanics of creating a custom form property or method," Rhonda added. "Is there anything you can do to help me out with that?"

"It just so happens that I have an exercise for everyone to complete that I think will help clear up whatever confusion you may have," I said. I then distributed the following exercise for the class to complete.

Exercise - Creating your very first Custom Form Property and Method

In this exercise, you'll create your own custom form property and method, illustrating how they work, and what you can do with them.

1. Start a new `Standard.EXE` Visual Basic project.
2. Add two command buttons to the form, accepting the default names that Visual Basic assigns (`Command1` and `Command2`):

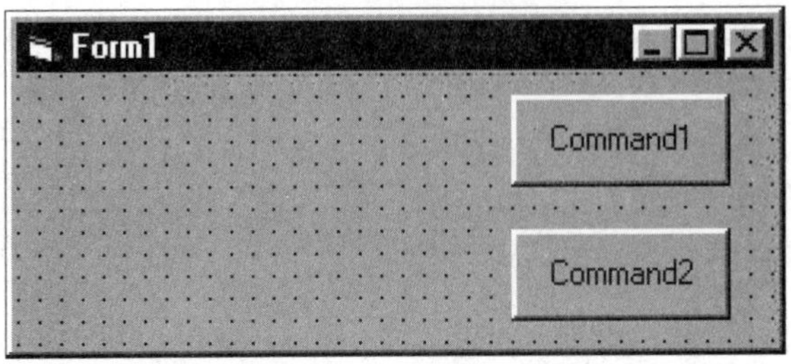

3. Now key the following code into the General Declarations section of the form. This will create a custom form property called **Temperature**:

```
Option Explicit
Public Temperature As Integer
```

4. Now create a custom form method called **WhatsTheTemp** by creating a sub procedure using the code below. This method will permit you to display the custom form property – **Temperature** – that you just created. For those of you who may have forgotten how to do this from our Intro course, the easiest way create your own sub procedure in your form is to type the code directly in the General Declarations section of the form.

```
Public Sub WhatsTheTemp()

Select Case Temperature
Case Is < 32
    MsgBox "Wow, it's very cold at " & Temperature
Case Is > 85
    MsgBox "Wow, it's very hot at " & Temperature
Case Else
    MsgBox "I can live with this temperature at " & Temperature
End Select

End Sub
```

5. Place the following code in the **Click** event procedure of **Command1** – this code will prompt you to assign a value to the form's **Temperature** property:

```
Private Sub Command1_Click()

Dim varRetval As Variant

varRetval = InputBox("What's the temperature?")
Form1.Temperature = varRetval

End Sub
```

6. Now type the next line of code into **Command2**'s **Click** event procedure. This code will execute the form's **WhatsTheTemp** custom method and display the value of the form's **Temperature** property in a message box:

```
Private Sub Command2_Click()

Form1.WhatsTheTemp

End Sub
```

7. Run the program. Click on **Command1** and enter a value for a temperature. Then click on **Command2** to execute the **WhatsTheTemp** custom method.

Discussion

Virtually no-one had any trouble completing this exercise, but there was one little 'issue'.

"I noticed," Chuck said, "that when I was writing the code for the **Click** event procedure of **Command2**, the **WhatsTheTemp** method didn't show up in the List Members window. I kept typing anyway, but when I ran the program and clicked on the command button, I received an error message..."

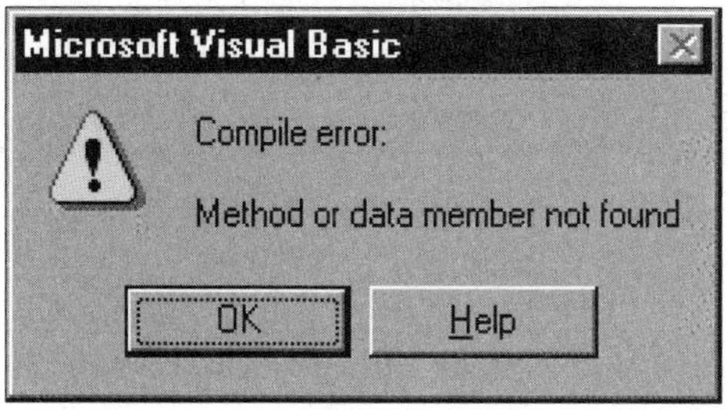

"...indicating that the method or data member wasn't found. Can you tell me what I may have done wrong?"

"I have a pretty good idea," I said. "Check the declaration of your `WhatsTheTemp` sub procedure. I bet that you accidentally declared the sub procedure as `Private` – only a `Public` sub procedure becomes a custom form method, with its name appearing in the List Members window."

I gave Chuck a minute to check that out.

"Ah…that's exactly what I did," he said. "It's running fine now. Thanks."

While Chuck was checking out his problem, I noticed a number of students spending quite a bit of time experimenting with their custom form property and method.

"This is great," Blaine said. "I can't believe that this is all there is to creating your own objects, properties and methods! "

"Be careful, Blaine," I said, "we haven't done anything with an object of our own yet. All we've done so far is to add a custom form property and a custom form method to an existing form. It won't be until next week that we actually start creating object classes of our own – but the experience you've had working with form methods and properties will make that transition easier."

"I, for one, appreciate what you've done here for us," Valerie said. "Almost from the first day I started learning Visual Basic I had this great uncertainty about properties and methods. Seeing that a property is in effect just a variable, and that a method is really just a sub procedure has gone a long way towards easing that uncertainty."

"Thanks, Valerie," I said. "That's a good way to think about things." So saying, I placed another slide on the projector:

Remember:

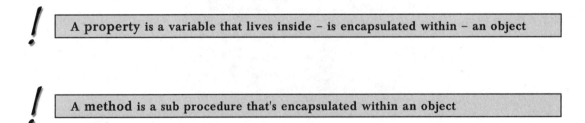

! **A property is a variable that lives inside – is encapsulated within – an object**

! **A method is a sub procedure that's encapsulated within an object**

> **We can access these encapsulated properties and methods using object dot notation.**

"So," I continued, " I hope that you can see that the ability to add custom properties and methods to our forms helps us program in a more object-oriented way. Other parts of the program can access our object's properties and methods, and having them contained as **members** – parts of – an object means that they're easily accessible via object dot notation."

"Members?" queried Rhonda. "Can you run that bit by me again, please?"

"Sure, Rhonda. When we use dot notation in the Code window, the List Members window appears when we type the name of an object followed by a period:"

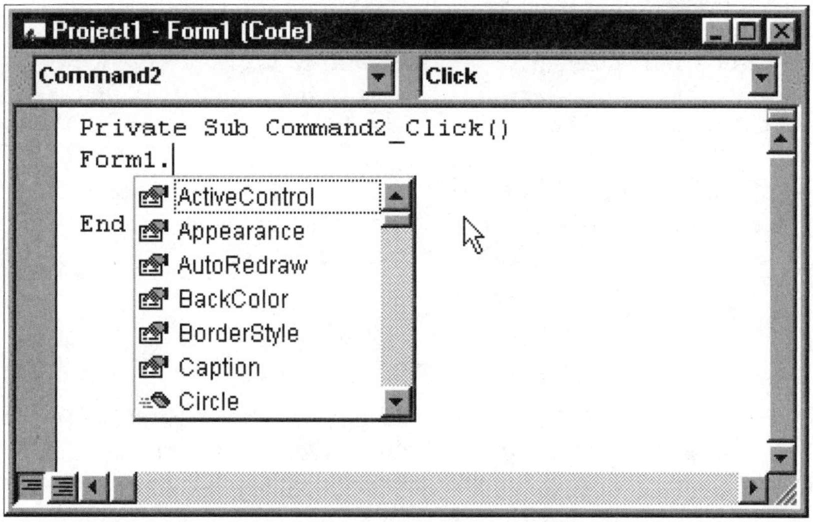

"What this window is showing us is all of the properties and methods that live inside the object, and which are there for us to use. These are the **members** of the object – they're part of the object, and they belong to it. They're encapsulated within the object itself."

"OK," said Rhonda, "I think I got that now!"

"Can we do the same thing with events?" asked Valerie.

"I'm afraid I can't quite work that same magic with events, Valerie," I said. "It's not possible to create new events that the form can react to."

"Somehow that doesn't surprise me," Dave said. "Aren't the events that the form and other objects react to actually standardized Windows system events that are being passed to those objects from the operating system?"

Events

"That's true, Dave," I replied. "Events like a **`KeyPress`** or **`MouseDown`** are perfect examples of what you're talking about."

"Considering that fact," Dave said, "I'm surprised that you can define and raise events from within your own objects. How is that possible?"

"Unlike the built-in Windows events that forms and controls automatically respond to," I replied, "the events that we define and then raise in the objects that we create ourselves are not actually Windows events like the **`KeyPress`** or **`MouseDown`** events. The events that we build into our own objects are more like the return value from a function – they're meant to signal to the program code using our object that something has happened within the object. For example, we might want one of our objects to raise an event signaling to the rest of the program that one of its property values has changed."

"I'm a little unsure of this term 'raise'," Rhonda said. "Is that what triggers the object's event?"

"That's right, Rhonda," I said. "It's then up to the programmer using the object to respond to the event – provided he or she wants to do that. Just as with Visual Basic's form and control event procedures, the programmer using the object will have an **Event Procedure stub** – that is, the subprocedure head and tail, like this..."

```
Private Sub Form_Load()

End Sub
```

"...into which they can insert code. But it's up to the programmer to place the detailed code there there, and to react accordingly. We'll see more about this later."

"OK," said Ward, "I have a question I'd like to ask. Why do we want to create events for our objects anyway?"

"Well," I explained, "this is all part of the object-oriented approach. We want to make our objects as self-contained as possible, and give them a repertoire of behaviors that other programmers and objects can make use of. Building the capacity to raise events into our objects is part of this. What we're doing, essentially, is thinking about the things that our object does in the overall program, and assessing the kinds of signals that it's likely to need to send to other parts of that program. Giving our objects the ability to raise certain types of event when the conditions arise contributes to them doing their job as part of the team of objects in the overall program."

Having discussed properties, methods and events for some while, I thought that it was time for the class to refresh themselves with some more practical work.

"OK, folks," I began, "let's take some time now to get our hands dirty with some code – some China Shop code, to be precise."

A Little Light Work in the China Shop

"What I'd like to ask you to do now," I said, "is to code a custom form property for the China Shop project that will replace the variable `m_intQuantity` – you'll remember that we talked earlier about replacing this with a custom form property."

I then distributed this exercise to the class:

Exercise - Creating a Custom Form Property for the China Shop Project

In this exercise, you'll create a custom form property for the **`Main`** form of the China Shop project. This will help us work towards encapsulating the China Shop's data inside the program's objects. In this case, the data will be stored as a property – a member of the program's **`Main`** form object.

1. Open up the China Shop project.
2. Modify the General Declarations section of the form so that it looks like this following block of code. As usual, modified code is highlighted:

```
Option Explicit

Private m_lngBackColor As Long
Private m_blnDateDisplay As Boolean
Private m_colDishPrice As New Collection
Public Quantity As Integer
```

3. Now amend **optQuantity**'s **Click** event procedure so that it matches the next code listing:

```
Private Sub optQuantity_Click(index As Integer)
    frmMain.Quantity = Index
End Sub
```

4. Modify the `Click` event procedure of `cmdCalculate` so that it looks like the code below (remember that we've only shown the section that are changing – code we're omitting for clarity is indicated by the ... markers):

```
Private Sub cmdCalculate_Click()

...

'Has the customer selected a quantity?
If optQuantity(8).Value = False And
      ↳optQuantity(4).Value = False And
      ↳optQuantity(2).Value = False And
      ↳optQuantity(1).Value = False Then
   MsgBox "You must select a quantity"
   Exit Sub
End If

'If the customer has selected a platter
'warn them that there is only 1 permitted per sales
'quotation
If chkChinaItem(5).Value = 1 And frmMain.Quantity > 1 Then
   MsgBox "Customer is limited to 1 Platter per order" &
         ↳vbCrLf & "Adjusting price accordingly"
End If


'All the pieces are here, let's calculate a price
'Calculate subtotal prices by item

...

If chkChinaItem(0).Value = 1 And
      ↳chkChinaItem(1).Value = 1 And
      ↳chkChinaItem(2).Value = 1 And
```

```
        ↳chkChinaItem(3).Value = 1 And
        ↳chkChinaItem(4).Value = 1 Then
    MsgBox "Price includes a Complete Place Setting Discount"
    curTotalPrice = (curCompletePrice * frmMain.Quantity) +
            ↳curPlatterPrice
Else
  curTotalPrice = (((curBowlPrice + curButterPlatePrice
       ↳+
         ↳curCupPrice + curPlatePrice + curSaucerPrice) *
         ↳frmMain.Quantity) + curPlatterPrice)
End If

...
```

5. Run the program, select the Mikasa brand of china, select the Plate, Butter Plate and Soup Bowl items, and a quantity of 2. Click on the Calculate button. The price displayed should be $90.

6. Make sure that you save the program!

Discussion

The changes to the program were few – but it did give everyone the chance to code their own custom form property.

Essentially, what we did here was declare **`Quantity`** as a custom form property and change the China Shop code so that it referenced this form property rather than the **`m_intQuantity`** variable that we were using before. Perhaps the most interesting code is this part:

```
Private Sub optQuantity_Click(index As Integer)
    frmMain.Quantity = Index
End Sub
```

Here, we use the **`Index`** property from the **`optQuantity`** option button control array. The value of the **`Quantity`** custom form variable is based on the quantity selection that the customer has made using the option buttons: the Index values for the different option buttons match the china quantities that the option buttons represent (one of 1, 2, 4, or 8). When the option button is clicked, the relevant value is passed as an argument in the event procedure, and used by the line...

```
frmMain.Quantity = Index
```

...to set the value of the **Quantity** custom form property – this is then available for use throughout the program.

"Is that really all there is to creating your own form property?" Rhonda asked, when we'd discussed the code. "You just declare a **Public** variable in the General Declarations section of the form?"

"That's all Rhonda," I said. "But remember – we'll also be creating properties for our own objects later on in the course, and that will be a little more involved. We'll be ready, though!"

After that short practical interlude, we returned to talking about Visual Basic objects. In particular, I wanted to show the class how we could use objects dynamically, when a program was running. Again, this would extend their knowledge of the variety of ways in which we can use object programming principles.

Using Objects Dynamically

"So far this morning," I said, "we've looked at ways of adding custom properties and methods to form objects. What I'd like to do now is show you how you can create new instances of Visual Basic objects at runtime – something I doubt that anyone in here has ever done."

"What we'll see in the next few minutes," I continued, "will provide you with good experience for creating objects of your own next week. To date, every object that we've created in the Intro class and in this one has been achieved by selecting a control in the Visual Basic Toolbox. Now I want to show you how to create forms and controls without having to select Project | Add Form from the Visual Basic menu bar or select a control icon from the Toolbox."

Creating Forms at Runtime

I started a new Visual Basic demonstration project and placed a single command button on the form.

"A little later today," I said, "we'll be creating a second form for the China Shop Application – one that will permit the customer to view Joe's new shipping charges for his mail-order business. We'll create that second form at design time, by selecting Project |Add Form from the Visual Basic menu bar. However, I want to show you next is that you can also create additional forms while the program is running – by utilizing the template of an existing form."

"There's that word template again," Rhonda said wryly.

To start the demonstration, I keyed the following code into the new demonstration project's `Click` event procedure:

```
Private Sub Command1_Click()

Dim frmObj As Form1
Set frmObj = New Form1
frmObj.Show
frmObj.Caption = "New Copy of Form1"

End Sub
```

I then ran the program...

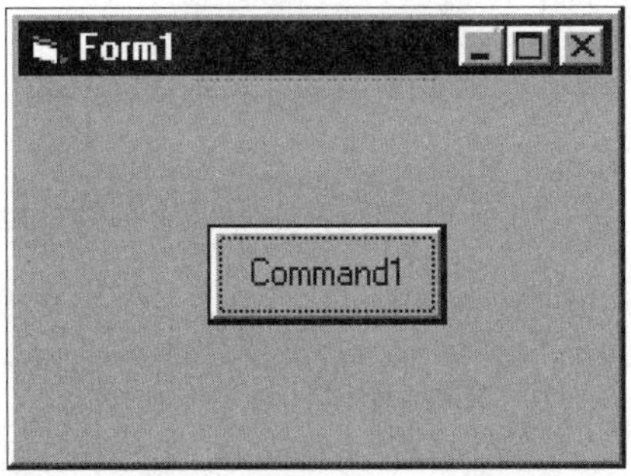

...and clicked on the command button, with this result:

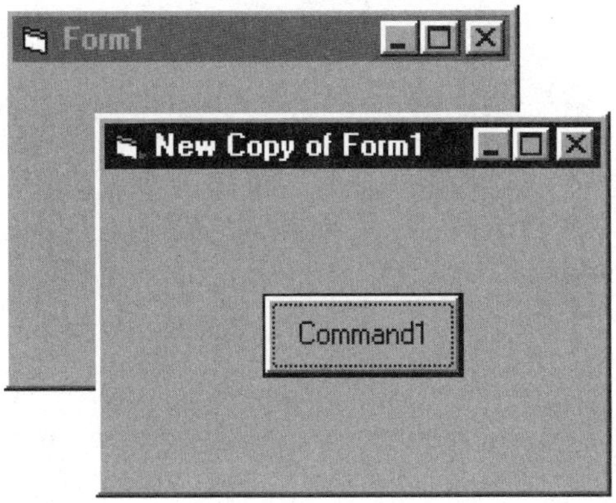

"OK," I said, "but we now have two forms in our program. This is the second form, complete with a command button of its own, and a custom caption."

"That's really amazing," Rhonda said. "Are you saying that the second form was created using the first form as the cookie cutter? And hey, the second form even has the command button from the first form on it."

"That's right Rhonda," I said. "We've made an exact copy of the first form, right down to the command button – in fact, even the code within the **Click** event procedure of the command button has been duplicated. Watch this..."

To prove my point, I clicked on the command button of the second form, and a third form appeared:

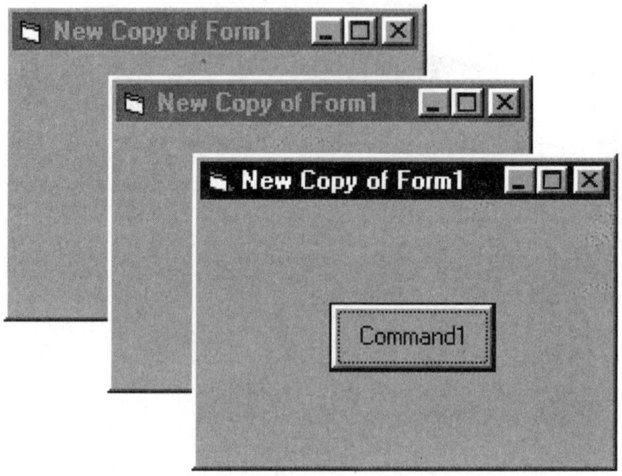

"Wow," Kate said, "this is great. Can you explain what's going on in the code now?"

"I'd be glad to Kate," I said. "You're probably somewhat familiar with this first line of code. It's the declaration of an object variable, much like we saw a couple of weeks ago when we used the **For...Each** statement to loop through the items in the **Forms** collection:"

```
Dim frmObj As Form1
```

"...On that occasion, however, the object variable type was **Form**. Here, the object variable type is **Form1**, so what we're doing is telling Visual Basic that we intend to refer to a new instance of **Form1**."

"What is the line of code that actually creates the new copy of **Form1**," Tom asked. "Is it the **Set** statement?"

```
Set frmObj = New Form1
```

"That's right, Tom," I said. "Merely declaring the object variable doesn't create a new copy of **Form1** – it just prepares Visual Basic by giving it a place to put the new form. It isn't until we execute the **Set** statement that we declare our intention to copy **Form1** – and it's the **New** keyword that tells Visual Basic to create a new instance of **Form1** for us, filling up the **frmObj** object variable with the new instance of the form. Remember, what we're doing here is using **Form1** as a template for the subsequent forms we instantiate. These other forms inherit the basic characteristics that **Form1** automatically derived from the **Form** class when it was created. In addition, the forms that we create based on the template of **Form1** *also* inherit any changes that we made to the default form – like the command button we added."

"This is powerful stuff!" I heard Ward murmur, as he gazed into his computer screen.

"In the other examples we looked at," I continued, "we used object variables to point to or refer to an existing object – such as a form in the **Forms** collection or a control in the **Controls** collection. I believe this is the first time we declared an object variable to refer to an object that does not yet exist – a new copy of **Form1**. But this is notation that you'll need to get used to – this is how we'll create objects from the class modules we design and code for ourselves later."

"What's the purpose of that next line of code?" Linda asked, "the one executing the form's **Show** method?"

"Well," I said, "as we'll see in just a few minutes when we create the Shipping Charges form, merely creating an instance of the form doesn't make it visible to the user. We have to actively do something make it visible. By far the easiest thing to do is execute the **Show** method of the form – in this case using the object variable **frmObj**, which contains a reference that points to the new instance of the form – plus some dot notation:"

```
frmObj.Show
```

"I know this will sound like a silly question," Rhonda said, "but how do we know the name of the new form?"

"We don't need to name the form in any way, as we created a reference to it using the object variable **frmObj**. We declared the object variable **frmObj** to refer to the new **Form1** – and that's how we need to refer to the new form, and its properties and methods, for the duration of our program."

"Finally in our code," I continued, "to differentiate the new **Form1** from the original, we change the **Caption** property of the form:"

```
frmObj.Caption = "New Copy of Form1"
```

"I must say," Rhonda said, "that I was a little surprised to find that when I closed the first copy of **Form1**, the others that I'd created using this code still remained loaded and visible. Somehow I thought that those replica forms would disappear when the original **Form1** was closed."

"I love to see students experimenting," I said. "What you've discovered is that there's no lasting relationship between **Form1** and its descendants. The new forms are independent of the 'parent' from that they're replicated from, just as there's no link maintained between the command buttons you put on a form, and the command button icon in the Visual Basic Toolbox."

I took this opportunity to point out that there was an alternative form of code that we could have used in the **Click** event procedure of the command button.

"This code," I said, "combines the declaration of the object variable **frmObj** and the **Set** statement into one statement..."

```
Private Sub Command1_Click()

Dim frmObj As New Form1
frmObj.Show
frmObj.Caption = "New Copy of Form1"

End Sub
```

"I see," said Melissa. "Is there an advantage of one technique over the other?"

"It depends," I replied. "The single statement version is more efficient from a coding point of view. Generally, any time you can combine two statements into one you've achieved coding efficiency. The only difference is in when the resources for the object variable are actually used by Windows."

Rhonda prompted: "By resources, you mean what?"

"The area of memory that is set aside for our new instance," I explained. "With the first version of code, the object variable, though declared, is empty until the new `Form1` is actually created by executing the `Set` statement. With the second version of code, resources for the object variable are set aside earlier on in the execution of the code – with the declaration of the object variable. We're splitting hairs in this program even discussing the differences, but in general it's best to 'put off' using object variable resources until you actually need them. It's possible, for instance, that you might declare an object variable for a new form, but never create a new instance of the form."

"In which case, it would be best to use the declaration statement followed by a separate `Set` statement, as in the first example?" Dave suggested.

"Yes," I replied, "But in this program the advantage is tiny."

"I must say that what I've seen here is impressive," Ward said. "But again, I've got to ask the question: is there a practical use for creating forms like this at run time?"

"Certainly there is, Ward," I said, "The technique we've used here to create a form at run-time is the technique used in the Multiple Document Interface applications – like Word – that we spoke about in Lesson 2." As you probably all know, if you're working in a Word document and you want to work on another document in addition to the current one, it's not necessary to start up another instance of Word. Instead, you can just click on File | New from the Word menu bar and open up a brand new document. The technique we've used here in this code – where we create a new instance of an existing form at run-time – is exactly how that's done in Word."

"I just tried to use similar code to create a second command button at runtime," Blaine said. "but it didn't work. I got an error message:"

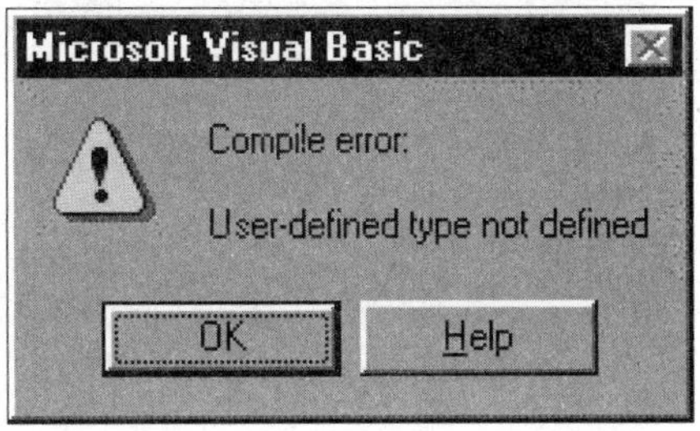

"What went wrong?" he asked.

Creating Controls At Runtime

"Unfortunately Blaine," I said, "we can't create controls at runtime the same way that we can create copies of a form. The rules are different. I'm not saying we can't do it: we just need to create a control array first."

"Do you mean like the check boxes and option buttons we have on the China Shop program's **Main** form?" Kate asked. "

"That's right Kate," I said. "For the members of the class who weren't here for our Intro course, let me remind you that a control array is one or more controls of the same type which share the same name, but which have unique values for their **Index** properties. For instance, in the China Shop program we have four option buttons, each of which is named **optQuantity**, and each of which has a unique **Index** property value. One of the great things about a control array is that each member of the control array shares a single event procedure with all the other members of the control array. Another great thing about them is the ability to create new members of the control array at run time. Watch this..."

I created a new Standard.EXE project, and placed a command button and a check box control on the form:

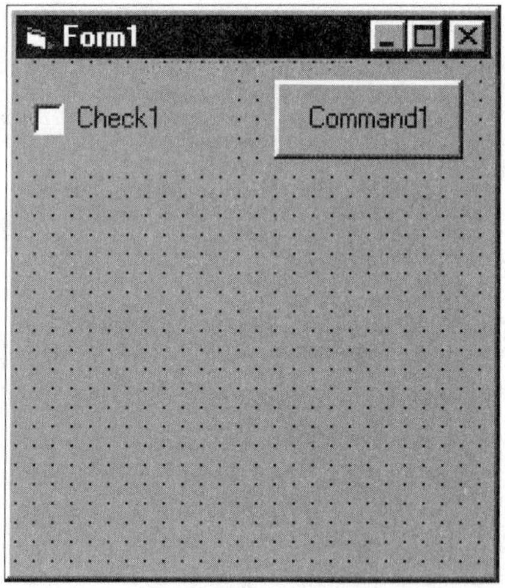

"When we create this lone check box, its **`Index`** property is set to the default value – null:"

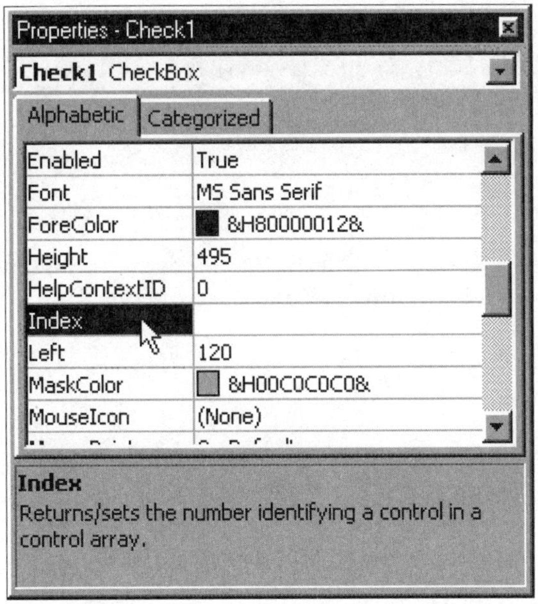

"We'll now set the **`Index`** property of the check box to a value of 0..."

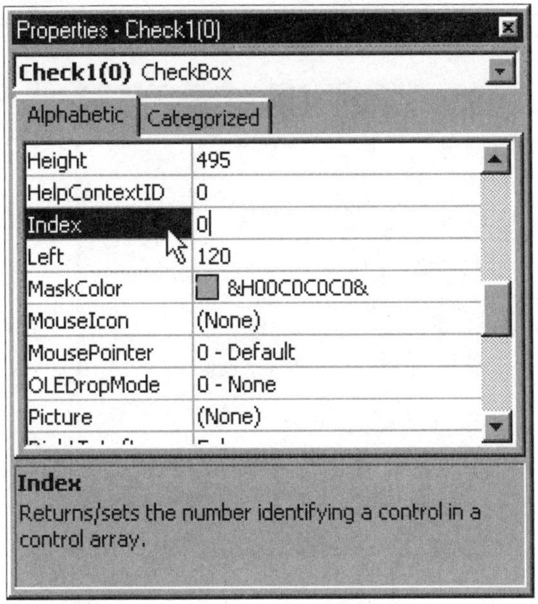

"...you can see that this check box has been transformed into the first – and currently the only – member of a control array called **Check1**:"

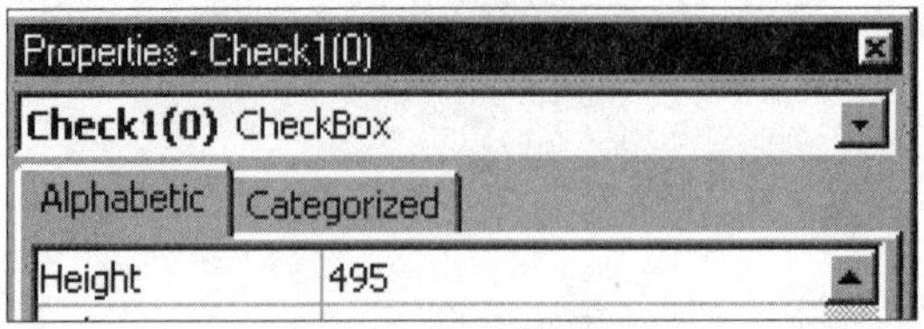

"Now we can code in the command button's **Click** event to instantiate a new instance of the check box on the form – using this simple piece of code:"

```
Private Sub Command1_Click()

Load Check1(1)

End Sub
```

"What I'm doing here," I said, "is telling Visual Basic, via the **Load** statement, to create a new instance of **Check1** – and to create it with an **Index** property of **1**. When it sees this statement, Visual Basic is smart enough to determine the current highest **Index** property value in the control array and to increment that value by 1."

When I ran the program and clicked on the command button, this is what we saw:

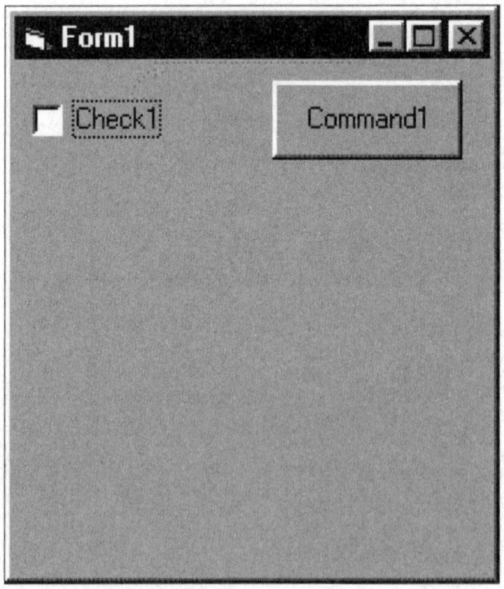

"Did this work?" Lou asked. "I only see the original check box. I thought you said the **Load** statement would create a second check box?"

"The **Load** statement *did* create a second check box," I answered, "What's happening here is that the new check box is sitting on top of the first one!"

"Aha!" said Lou.

"That's right, Lou," I said. "The **Load** statement created a new instance of the check box, based on the template of the first check box, which was already on the form. Because of that, the new check box inherited most of the properties of the first check box – including the **Left**, **Top**, **Height** and **Width** properties. Remember, objects always inherit the characteristics of the template that they were instantiated from – whether that template is a class, or an existing object that's been created from a class and then modified. **Inheritance** is a vital feature of object-oriented programming. As a result of inheritance, the second check box is sitting right on top of the first one. But that's not the only problem. The default behavior of VB is to instantiate the second check box with its **Visible** property set to **False**! We can take care of the positional problem by changing the **Left** property of the newly instantiated check box so that it is no longer sitting on top of the first one, and by changing its **Visible** property to **True**. Like this..."

I then changed the code in the **Click** event procedure of the command button to look like this:

```
Private Sub Command1_Click()

Load Check1(1)
Check1(1).Top = Check1(0).Top + Check1(0).Height
Check1(1).Caption = "New one"
Check1(1).Visible = True

End Sub
```

And ran the program again...

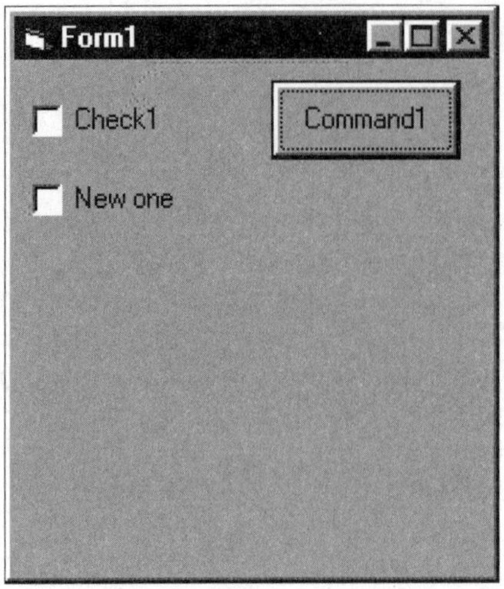

"That's much better," I said, "now we can actually see the newly-created check box."

"Suppose there were two or more members of the check box control array on the form?" Dave asked. "Which one of them would the **Load** statement use as the template for the new control?"

"It would use the member with the lowest value for its **Index** property," I answered.

"I just clicked on the command button twice," Dorothy said, "and the program bombed with a message telling me that the object is already loaded:"

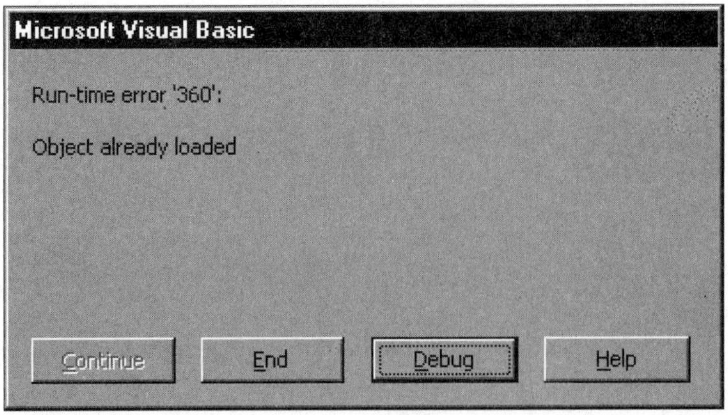

"What happened?" asked Rhonda.

"The code in the **Click** event procedure of the command button isn't very sophisticated," I answered. "If you click it twice, the second click will attempt to instantiate a new member of the control array, with the same **Index** property of 1, which is hard-coded into the program:"

```
Load Check1(1)
```

"This member of the control array has already been created by the first click of the command button – hence the error. If we really want to get fancy, we can modify the code so that the command button can be clicked over and over again. All we need are a few variables and a small algorithm. Here's the code:"

```
Private Sub Command1_Click()

Dim intOld As Integer
Dim intNew As Integer
Static intCounter As Integer

intOld = Check1.UBound
intNew = Check1.UBound + 1
intCounter = intCounter + 1

Load Check1(intNew)
Check1(intNew).Top = Check1(intOld).Top
      ↳+ Check1(intNew).Height
Check1(intNew).Caption = "New one # " & intCounter
Check1(intNew).Visible = True

End Sub
```

I ran the program and clicked on the command button five times in succession. This time...

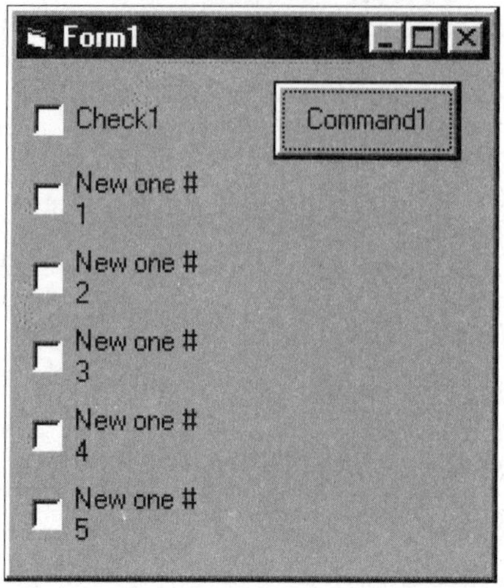

"This code," I said, "has a little more intelligence built into it. For one thing, it won't bomb if you click on the command button more than once, and it also places the new controls on the form in such a way that we can see them. The first thing we do is to declare two integer variables to keep track of two things: the **`Index`** value of the last control placed on the form, and the **`Index`** value of the next control that'll be placed on the form:"

```
Dim intOld As Integer
Dim intNew As Integer
```

"The next bit of code uses the **`Check1`** control array's **`UBound`** method to determine the member of the control array with the highest **`Index`** value and assign it to the **`intOld`** variable:"

```
intOld = Check1.UBound
```

"Here, executing the control array's **`UBound`** method retrieves the upper bound of the control array's **`Index`** values. Now, this next line of code assigns the **`Index`** value for the new control to the **`intNew`** variable:"

```
intNew = Check1.UBound + 1
```

"This is the interesting bit," I said. "The **UBound** method of the control array returns the highest current index value, and we can just increment that using the plus sign and a number. The **UBound** method comes in handy here in helping us to decide what the **Index** value of the next copy of the existing control on the form should be. While we're here, let me tell you that the control array itself has four methods of its own..."

I typed the following statement into the Visual Basic Immediate window:

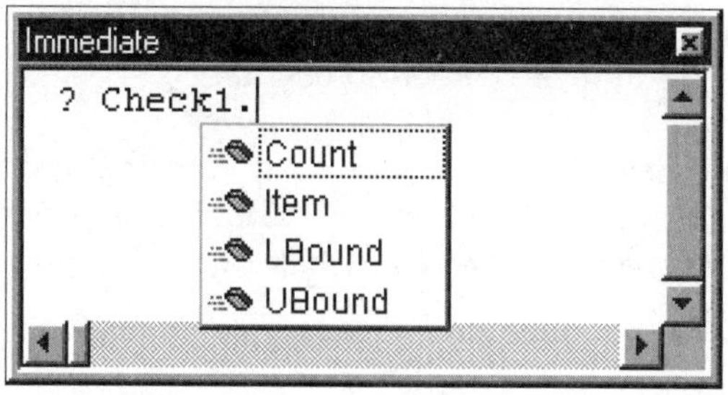

"I know that a lot of students discover this by accident," I said, "but if you type the name of a control array by itself in the Code window, leaving out the **Index** value, Visual Basic assumes that you want to work with the control array object as a whole, and displays its four methods for you!"

"Those look familiar," Rhonda said, "aren't those the same four methods that we looked at two weeks ago when we examined collections?"

"Almost, Rhonda," I answered. "The methods and properties of a collection are actually **Add**, **Count**, **Item** and **Remove**. But you're on the right track! If you think about it, a control array is very much like a collection, with each control that's a member of the control array being like an item in a collection."

I continued with our discussion of the code.

"Next," I said, "we have a line of code that instantiates the new check box control with the next available **Index** value, which we previously stored in **intNew**:"

```
Load Check1(intNew)
```

"Finally," I concluded, "the last three lines of code adjust the **Top**, **Caption** and **Visible** properties so that we can see the new control:"

```
Check1(intNew).Top = Check1(intOld).Top
      ↳+ Check1(intNew).Height
```

```
Check1(intNew).Caption = "New one # " & intNew
Check1(intNew).Visible = True
```

It was clear that my students were intrigued by this code: I could see them trying out their own variations. After a few minutes letting them play, I said:

"OK, folks, we need to turn our attention back to the China Shop for a while."

"Are we at the point where we can begin to design the objects in the China Shop project yet?" Chuck asked. "I'm getting pretty keen to do that."

"I agree with you, Chuck," I said, "I think now's a great time to do that. Why don't we take a fifteen-minute break and, when we return, we'll begin the process of identifying the objects in the China Shop project – then next week, we'll begin to actually code them. Sound OK?"

The class nodded that this was indeed OK.

Designing the China Shop Objects

After the break, I resumed our discussion on identifying the China Shop's objects.

"A great thing about object-oriented programming," I said, "and beginning the process of identifying objects in your application, is that for the most part you're working with things that you can see and touch – customers, sales clerks, china pieces and packages."

"Sounds like you already have this mapped out," Steve said. "Is it really that simple – just identify the objects you can see?"

"It *can* be, Steve," I said. "Of course, those of you who took the Intro course with me know how much emphasis I placed on the Systems Development Life Cycle as a means of avoiding disastrous development projects. I wouldn't want to stand up here and suggest that you take a cursory glance at your application and start to identify objects – but on the other hand, I don't think there's a need to make a big deal out of it for smaller-scale projects."

"So what will we do here?" asked Steve.

"Well, I've decided to compromise by adopting a hybrid analysis and design methodology – this methodology will let us identify and design our objects for the China Shop project."

Our Design Methodology

"Just as the SDLC is a methodology to assist us in systems design and development, there are several methodologies in use today that can help us discover and identify objects within the scope of an application. One of the most popular is the **Use-Case** methodology, which is a **scenario-based** methodology used to identify and verify the objects in an application."

"What exactly do you mean by a scenario-based methodology?" Dorothy asked.

"A **scenario** is a story," I said. "With the Use-Case methodology, the designer develops typical scenarios – scenes or stories – based on the current system, and analyses the scenario to identify the objects that are found in it. The scenarios look at what goes on in the business or process that you're modeling, and at how the requirements of the business are currently met."

"Would an example of a scenario be the run-through of the China Shop program that Rhonda did for us in Week 1?" Steve asked.

"That's an excellent example, Steve," I said. "Use-Case scenarios are really a great way of discovering or verifying the objects in your application. In fact, the objects in your application will just about hit you in the face. You'll see when you develop scenarios of your own that objects are typically the nouns that you find in the scenarios that you analyze."

"Nouns?" Kevin asked.

"Yes, Kevin," I said. "**Nouns** – the names of things that emerge when you document a scenario – usually turn out to represent the **objects** that you need to create. Similarly, the **adjectives** – words that describe things, such as blue, large, hot – usually match up to the **properties** of an object. Remember, the properties of an object usually describe or qualify the object in some way – so any word that describes or qualifies a noun in the scenario is usually a property. And since **methods** are actions that are performed on an object, then **verbs** – words that describe doing something, like walking, or hitting, are frequently identified as methods of an object in the scenario."

I summarized this with another slide:

Nouns (names of things) = Objects

Adjectives (descriptive words) = Properties

Verbs (actions) = Methods

"I think I'm still a little unclear about this scenario process," Rhonda said. "Should we be developing scenarios around the *current* China Shop program, or scenarios based on the China Shop *before* the kiosk-based PC was installed?"

"That's really an excellent question, Rhonda," I said, "well done. The answer is that we should be developing scenarios based on a China Shop as it was without the kiosk-based PC: we need to pretend that the China Shop program does not exist at all in order to do a proper Use-Case methodology. That's because we want to focus on the real-world needs of a business or process, unencumbered by the logic of any existing computer system that's already been put in place. What we're trying to do is free ourselves of any preconceptions and focus on the things that the business actually does in the real world with real people and real things."

"Is there a limiting factor in the scenarios?" Valerie asked. "You mentioned a few minutes ago something about 'scope'. How wide and how far should these scenarios go?"

"Another excellent question," I said. "As with any development effort, including the original development for the China Shop program last semester, a statement of **scope** is very important. It's vital to note that, ordinarily, the identification of objects for the China Shop program would have taken place last semester at the time of the original development of the program. At that point, a statement of scope would have been made, limiting the study of the system in some way. For instance, we know that Joe Bullina is only interested in having us write a program to present a sales quotation to the customer – he's not interested in having the program track china inventory or generate payroll for the employees of the shop. That's an example of a statement of scope, and that statement should limit the development of the Use-Case scenarios as well."

"So what you're implying, then," Ward said, "is that in the case of the China Shop we shouldn't develop scenarios based on anything but a customer obtaining a sales quotation?

"Exactly, Ward," I agreed, "anything else would be a waste of our time."

"I can think of a pretty simple scenario," Kate said. "A customer enters the store, approaches a sales clerk, and requests a quotation on one or more pieces of china. I see three objects there – the customer, the sales clerk, and the inventory – that is, the stock that Joe keeps, and its prices."

"That's good, Kate," I said. "But let's extend that scenario a little bit."

Walking through a Customer Purchase Scenario

"Do you remember the scenario that Rhonda ran through for us the first day of class, where Rita and Gil come into the store to buy some china? Let's use that same scenario, but modify it so that it's just as if Rita and Gil are entering the China Shop a year before the kiosk PC was installed."

Over the next twenty minutes, we developed a basic 'Customer Purchase' scenario for the China Shop, based on the original Rita and Gil scenario.

When we'd finished, I then displayed the documented scenario on the classroom projector:

> Rita and Gil enter the Bullina China Shop and approach the front counter.
>
> Gil tells the sales clerk at the counter that they want some dishes – Rita immediately corrects him by saying that she wants some fine china – not dishes.
>
> The sales clerk tells Rita that the China Shop offers 3 brands of china – Corelle, Faberware and Mikasa.
>
> Rita answers that she is interested in the Mikasa brand, and asks what items of china are available in that brand.
>
> The sales clerk informs her that the China Shop sells plates, butter plates, soup bowls, cups, saucers and platters in each brand. The China Shop also offers a price discount for a complete place setting which consists of one each of a plate, butter plate, soup bowl, cup and saucer.
>
> Rita indicates that she would like a Mikasa complete place setting.
>
> The sales Clerk asks what quantity of place settings Rita wants.

Rita tells the sales clerk that she would like 8 complete place settings of Mikasa china.

The sales clerk calculates the order and tells Rita that the total price of the order will be $400 – pointing out that the price includes a discount for a complete place setting.

Gil looks at Rita, then glance at his watch and remarks to her that they will probably be late for their movie.

Gil tells Rita that he thinks the price of the Mikasa Brand is too expensive, and that he would prefer to purchase the Faberware Brand.

Gil doesn't think they need a complete place setting. Instead, he tells the sales clerk to calculate the total price of an order for just a plate, cup, saucer and a platter – 4 each of the plates, cups and saucers, but just one platter.

The sales clerk calculates the total price of the order and tells Gil that the price will be $77.

Gil and Rita both seem happy with the total price of the order and decide to purchase the china.

The sales clerk asks if they would like to take the china with them, or have it wrapped as a package and shipped somewhere.

Rita and Gil think that's a wonderful idea, and decide to have the china packaged and shipped to their son's home in Orlando, Florida.

Gil inquires about the shipping charges to send the package to the state of Florida.

The sales clerk looks down at a chart on the counter, and informs Gil that the shipping charges to the state of Florida are $10.

Gil and Rita happily agree, and purchase the china.

Everyone agreed that this scenario painted a picture of a typical transaction at the China Shop. I pointed out that, ordinarily, we would have worked through additional scenarios to cover every eventuality. However, I had already done a thorough scenario analysis on my own at home, and I knew that any additional scenarios developed in class would not result in the discovery of any new objects for the project: all of the objects we would need to design and code were there to be found in this scenario. And so, in the interest of saving time, I suggested that we move forward in our process of identifying the objects in the China Shop project.

"Now that we have a scenario," I said, "the next thing we need to do is thoroughly analyze it and identify all of the nouns – the names of things – in it."

Analyzing the Scenario

"Before we start going through the scenario, let me just repeat the key points here, so that they're absolutely clear. **Nouns** usually become **objects** in our program. **Verbs** that perform actions on those nouns usually become **methods** of the object, and any **adjectives** in the scenario that further define or qualify a noun usually become properties of the object. A word of caution, though – sometimes the words in the scenario turn out to be *instances* of the object instead – such as Rita and Gil. Rita and Gil may both appear to be objects – but they are actually instances of a more general 'customer' object."

I reminded the class that some of the objects identified in this process would be out of the scope of program. "For instance," I said, "one object that is obviously out of the scope of our program is the customer object. At this point Joe Bullina has no requirement to maintain information about customers. The same is true of the sales clerk object – although both the potential customer and sales clerk objects are identified as nouns in the scenario, they're actually beyond the scope of our program."

"Darn," Rhonda said, "I had both of those already chalked up as objects. I guess I'll have to cross them out."

"There's nothing wrong with identifying objects that are out of the scope of the project," I said. "In fact, excluding potential objects at this point in the process *can* be a mistake. I advise you to identify all of your potential objects – it certainly can't hurt. You can always exclude them later if you verify that they are definitely beyond the scope of the program. That's better than missing them altogether."

"What do we do now?" Mary asked.

"At this point," I said, "what I'd do is go through the scenario and identify the nouns, verbs and adjectives. I capitalize every noun, underline every verb, and double-underline every adjective. That helps me to pick out the objects, methods and properties in the scenario."

I then asked everyone in the class to analyze the scenario, and to go through it in an effort to identify nouns, verbs and adjectives.

Identifying our Objects, Properties and Methods

"You can use my method of marking up the scenario, or one of your own," I said. "Do whatever you're comfortable with. After you've done that, take a sheet of paper and write the objects that you've discovered in the scenario across the top line of it. Underneath each object, write the methods and properties for each one on subsequent lines."

I then asked the class to take the next twenty minutes on their own, working on identifying objects, methods and properties in the scenarios.

At the end of those twenty minutes, I displayed my own list of objects, properties and methods on the classroom projector, and I asked everyone to compare their versions with mine:

OBJECTS	Customer+	Dish	Order*	Package	Sales Clerk+
PROPERTIES	First Name	Brand Item (type of China piece) Quantity Price**		Charges ** State	
METHODS	Buys	Calculate	Add Count Item Modify Remove TotalPrice		Sells

* Collection object
\+ Beyond scope
** Read-only property

I noticed that most of the students seemed pleased – apparently they were on the same track, and had identified pretty much the same sort of list. I moved on to discussing what we'd discovered.

Thinking about the China shop Objects

"Armed with the documented and analyzed scenario," I continued, "we can now look at mapping the objects, methods, and properties that we've identified to the China Shop program. I've been able to identify five objects in this scenario – **Customer**, **Dish**, **Order**, **Package** and **Sales Clerk**. You may have identified more – some of the ones I initially identified, such as Store and Counter, I quickly discounted. Of the five remaining objects, I think it's safe to say that Customer and Sales Clerk are beyond the scope of the China Shop program – as there's no requirement to maintain information about the customer or the sales clerk in the program."

I then displayed this modified list of objects on the classroom projector:

OBJECTS	**Dish**	**Order***	**Package**
PROPERTIES	Brand Item Quantity Price**		Charges** State
METHODS		Add Count Item Modify Remove TotalPrice	

* Collection object
** Read-only property

"So...it looks as though we'll have three objects in the China Shop project," I said. "**Dish**, **Order** and **Package**. The **Dish** object will have four properties – **Brand**, **Item**, **Quantity** and **Price** – and **Price** will be read-only. The **Order** object will have six methods – **Add**, **Count**, **Item**, **Modify**, **Remove** and **TotalPrice**. And finally, **Package** will have two properties – **Charges**, which is read-only, and **State**."

"What's a **Dish**?" Rhonda asked.

I explained to everyone that last year, shortly after my first phone call with Joe Bullina, I told my wife that I would be visiting a potential client who owned a dish store. My wife told me in no uncertain terms that if I referred to Joe's Fine China Shop as a 'Dish Store' that she didn't think I had much chance of getting the business!

"When we delivered the program to the China Shop last semester," I said, "after I was certain that Joe Bullina really liked the program, I told him the dish story and he couldn't stop laughing. Since then the term 'dish' has been a private joke of ours. But I think there's more than a kernel of truth in calling it a 'dish'. I don't know about you, but when I pick up a plate, I see a dish – a dish object – possessing characteristics and properties that differentiate it from another dish. After all, a plastic dish and a dish of fine china are really the same kind of object – something to eat off – but it's the characteristics and properties of each one that makes the plastic dish inexpensive and the fine china dish expensive."

"Why is it that the **Dish** object in your final table has no methods?" Chuck asked. "When I went through this scenario, I identified a Calculate method for the **Dish** object – this method would work out the price of the dish."

"That's a good point, Chuck," I said, "There's certainly no harm in you designing and coding the **Dish** object with a Calculate method – I've just elected to build that functionality into a **Price** property instead."

"Will that make a big difference?" Valerie asked., "I mean using a property, rather than using a method? Can they both achieve the same result?"

"The bottom line," I said, "is that we need a way to calculate the subtotal price of each selected item of china – whether we do that via a method, via a property, or even both doesn't matter – just so long as we do it right. In fact, when you begin to design your own objects, you'll see that properties and methods are both stored internally as procedures in a class module anyway – much more on this later in the course!"

"I don't think this question is unique to this issue," said Kate, "there are other parallels. After all, there are two ways to make a form invisible aren't there? You can either set the **Visible** property of the form to **False**, or execute its **Hide** method."

"You're right Kate," I agreed. "Either technique will do the trick. I'm sure the same sorts of discussions were held at Microsoft about the properties and methods of the form and all of the controls in the Visual Basic Toolbox. Ultimately, it's the end result that's important – these different approaches just give us more flexibility."

"I guess we could have a `Calculate` method for both the `Dish` and `Order` objects if we wanted to, couldn't we?" Steve asked. "Is it OK to have two objects with the same method name?"

"It's not a problem to have two objects with the same method name," I answered.

"I was just reviewing my own object list," Peter said, "and I've included an object for Plate, Platter, Cup, Butter Plate, Saucer, and Platter. Is that wrong?"

"Those objects you've identified," I said, "are really the six possible values of the `Item` property of the `Dish` object. Remember, I mentioned earlier that it's easy to confuse values of instances of an object for separate objects, so don't worry. A lot of this will come with practice and experience."

"Calling the Plate an object would be the like calling John Smiley an object in a Use-Case scenario for this class," Dave said. "In reality, John Smiley can be seen as a value for the Name property of the Teacher object – just as, in the China Shop, `Plate` is a value for the `Item` property of the `Dish` object."

"That's right Dave," I agreed. "Another example is where Gil and Rita would be values for the Name property of a Customer object – we wouldn't identify them as types of object that occur universally in every sales transaction. The universal object is the Customer, of which Rita and Gil are two specific instances, uniquely identified by their name properties."

"On a different tack," said Melissa, "what do you mean when you say that a property is read-only?"

"Read-only properties," I said, "are properties of an object that cannot be changed by the programmer using our object. That is, after we've built the program and the objects, we want these properties to be maintained by the object itself, and not by any code in the surrounding program that will interact with the object – for example, by using code that uses object dot notation. We want to seal these properties off so that the outside world can't change them. We'll have two read-only properties in the China Shop project – the `Price` property of the `Dish` object and the `Charges` property of the `Package` object."

"If the programmer can't change the `Price` property of the `Dish` object," Rhonda asked, "how will the `Price` be updated?"

"The **Price** property of the **Dish** object," I said, "will be updated by the **Dish** object itself."

"Where will the **Dish** object get the data necessary to perform the price calculation?" Lou asked. "Will it have access to the **m_colDishPrice** collection that we coded two weeks ago?"

"Better than that Lou," I said. "The **Dish** object will read the **Prices.txt** file directly into a collection of its own."

I waited a moment for this to sink in before explaining why we'd do it like this.

Encapsulation

"In object theory," I said, "there's a term called **encapsulation**, which means that as much as possible about the object should be contained – **encapsulated** – within the object itself. In the case of the **Dish** object, that means that every time the **Dish** object is created – instantiated – it will open the **Prices.txt** file and read the inventory prices into a collection defined within the object. Remember – the objects that we design should be as self-contained as possible."

"Why is that?" Kathy asked.

"Self-containment, or encapsulation," I continued, "are terms that describe an object that can be used, as far as possible, without depending upon other objects and data outside of it. For instance, if we don't read the **Prices.txt** file within the **Dish** object, then we would have no access to inventory prices for the china items selected by the user of the program. That means we would to rely on the programmer who comes after us to open the file on behalf of our **Dish** object, and to read the inventory prices into an array or a collection accessible by our object – that's hardly ideal: it's preferable to encapsulate all of an object's associated processing inside the object itself – that way, we rely less on the world outside, and we're less likely to be impacted when something changes elsewhere in the program."

"I see what you're saying now," Ward said, "but isn't there going to be a certain amount of interaction outside of the object anyway? Your object is always going to have to talk to other parts of the program, isn't it? How can you avoid it?"

"Next week," I said, "when we begin to code the objects in the China Shop project, all the interaction between our objects and the environment outside of it will be through the objects' properties and methods, and through any arguments that are passed when the method is called. Essentially, what we're doing is creating a self-contained object that has built-in ways of maintaining its internal data. The methods and properties that we build into our objects act as an **interface**, through which the rest of the program can communicate. The interface provides a consistent and robust set of communication channels that the rest of the program can use to talk to our object. Again, these things are encapsulated inside the object itself."

With that, we got back to the specific objects that we'd identified.

"I have a question about the **`Order`** object," Dave said. "When I was reviewing the scenario, I wasn't sure that **`Order`** was really an object that we would be coding – to me it seems like a collection of **`Dish`** objects."

"Correct, Dave" I confirmed. "The customer order described in the Rita and Gil scenario can be described as a *collection* of individual dishes – **`Dish`** objects, each with their own **`Brand`** and **`Item`** properties and so on. So it's not all that surprising that we'll implement the **`Order`** object in the China Shop using a collection object. Our own collection objects are coded to behave much like the Visual Basic collections we examined a few weeks ago."

"If the **`Order`** object is a collection object," Kevin said, "what are the **`Items`** that it will contain?"

"As you know," I explained, "collection objects contain references to other objects. These short references are the collection's Items. The **`Order`** object that we create will contain items that are references to individual **`Dish`** objects. There'll be an individual **`Dish`** object for each piece of china that the customer chooses."

I displayed the following slide to clarify how this would work:

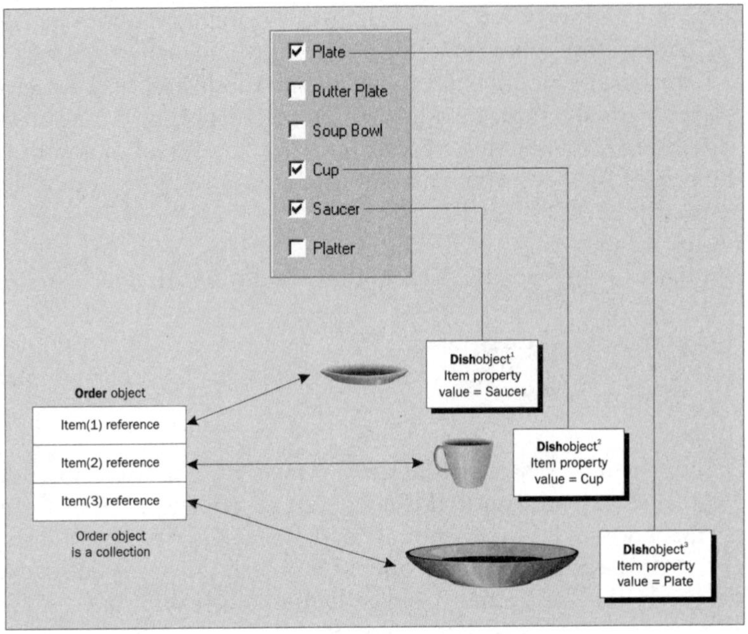

"Is that why the **Order** object's properties and methods include the **Count** property and the **Add**, **Item** and **Remove** methods?" Linda asked. "Aren't those the same collection properties and methods we learned about two weeks ago?"

"That's right Linda," I said. "I think you'll see that creating a collection object will make the coding in the China Shop project very efficient."

"The new collection object sounds pretty complex to me," Ward said, "do you think we'll be able to handle it?"

"I think so," I answered. "We'll tackle the **Order** collection object after we've had a chance to work with the **Dish** object."

Back to the China Shop Project

I told everyone that we would be spending the remainder of today's class creating and writing code for the China shop program's **`Shipping Charges`** form.

The Shipping Charges Form

"OK, folks," I continued, "what we're going to do first, is create the basis for the **`Shipping Charges`** form. This second form, remember, is the one that will let Joe's staff check out the shipping costs for a customer's order, based on the state that they want their package sent to."

I noticed Kate smile – she'd been waiting to add a second form to the China Shop Program for a long time. I distributed the following exercise for the class to complete.

Exercise - Creating the Shipping Charges Form

In this exercise, you'll add a second form to the China Shop project, and immediately save it in your **`\VBFiles\China`** directory.

1. Continue working with the China Shop project.

2. Select Project | Add Form from the Visual Basic menu bar:

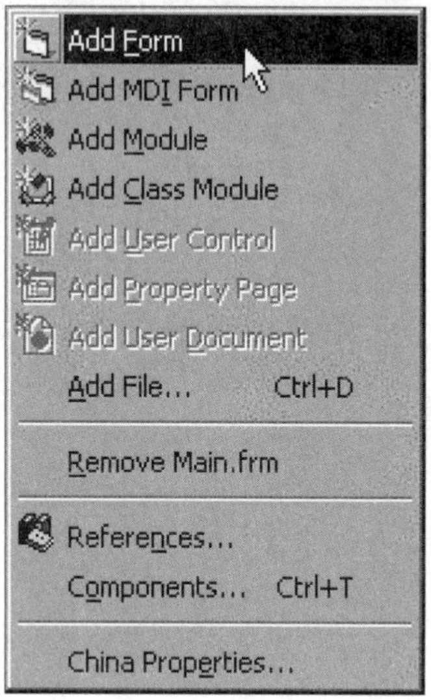

3. When the Add Form screen appears...

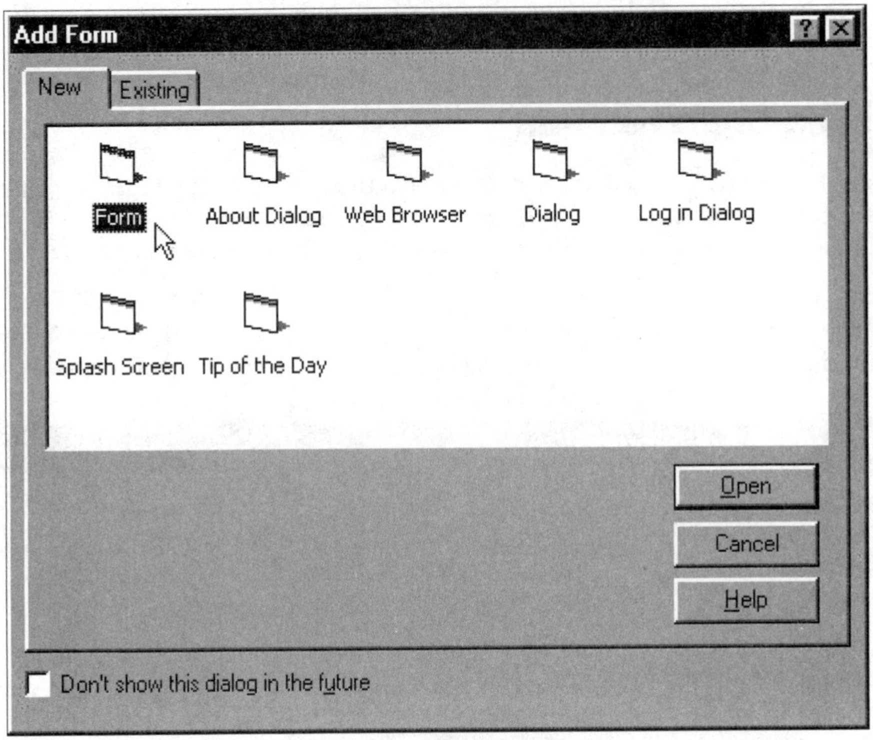

4. ...make sure the New tab is selected, and then either double-click on Form or select Form and click on the Open button. Visual Basic will then display a new form for you in the IDE, with a caption reading **`Form1`**.

5. Select the new form in the IDE and bring up its Properties window. Find the **`Name`** property, and change it from **`Form1`** to **`frmShipping`**:

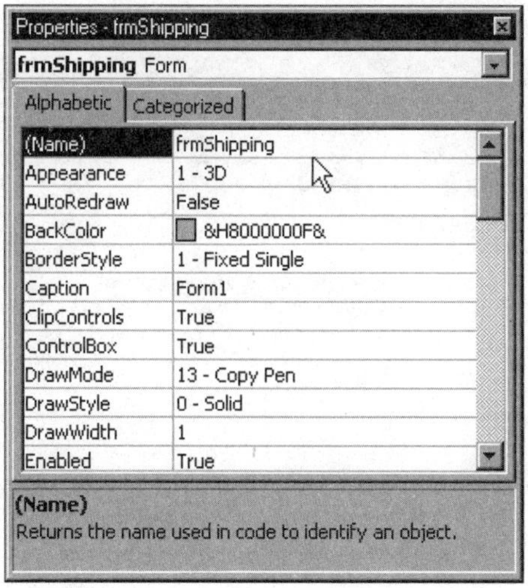

6. Click on the Save button on the Toolbar. Visual Basic will immediately prompt you to save the new form with a disk filename of **`frmShipping`**. **DON'T** save the form with that name. Instead, after ensuring that the form will be saved in the correct folder or directory (**`\VBFiles\China`**), change the file name to **`Shipping`**:

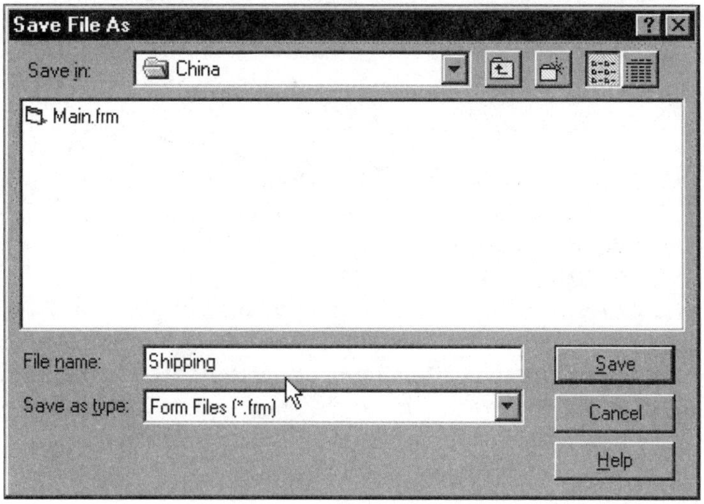

... and click on the Save button.

7. Bring up the Project Explorer window, and you should now see two forms – Main (with a **Name** property of **frmMain**) and Shipping (with a **Name** property of **frmShipping**):

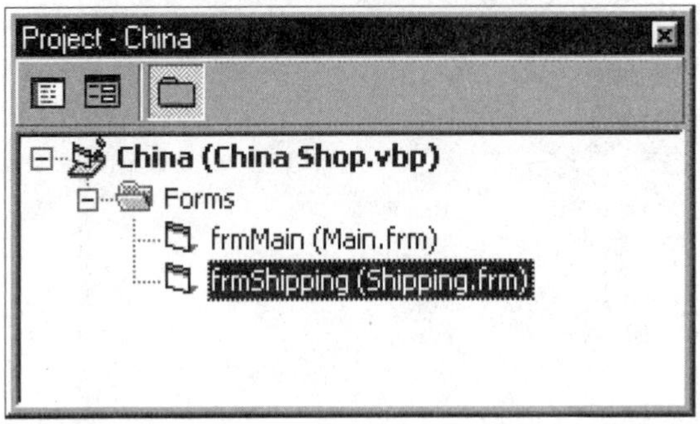

Discussion

Adding a second form to a Visual Basic project was something that most members of the class had never done before, and that inexperience showed up in small ways. Saving projects and forms in Visual Basic can be an adventure – and it's important to do it right the first time.

For instance, despite my warnings, several students clicked too quickly on the Save button before changing the disk file name of the form from **frmShipping** to **Shipping**. This mistake meant that I had to assist the students in using Windows Explorer to find and rename the form's disk file name. One student inadvertently saved the new form in the wrong folder. Another student accidentally selected New MDI form from the Visual Basic menu bar instead of New Form. As a result, the exercise that I had thought would take us about five minutes to complete took well over fifteen minutes – but in the end everything was fine.

"I'm sure you covered this in the Introductory course," Dorothy said, "but I wasn't a member of that course. Why's the **Name** property of the form different from the file name that we specified when we saved the form?"

"The **Name** property," I replied, "is an 'internal' name used by Visual Basic to identify the form when referring to it in code. By convention, the **Name** property for a form should begin with the letters **frm**. The disk file name is different – that's the name that we specify in the Save File As dialog box, and it's the name of the form file that's physically saved to your hard drive. You'll never refer to your form by that name within your program, however."

"I have a question," Valerie put in. "When we clicked on the 'save' button on the Visual Basic Toolbar, why weren't we prompted to save both the project and our other form – **`Main`**?"

"You'll only see the Save File As dialog box the first time you save a project or a form," I said. "The reason is that Visual Basic needs to know both their names and location the first time it saves them. After you've saved a form or project the first time, Visual Basic assumes that you want to save them with the same disk file name and in the same location, and won't prompt you again with the Save File As dialog box unless you choose one of the Save As menu options on the Menu Bar."

"Will we be completing the **`Shipping Charges`** form today?" Ward asked.

"Yes, we will," I answered. "In fact, here's an exercise to do exactly that."

Exercise - Adding Controls to the Shipping Charges Form

In this exercise, you'll add the controls to the new **`Shipping Charges`** form so that Joe's staff can interact with it.

1. Continue working with the China Shop project.

2. Display the Project Explorer window and select the Shipping form...

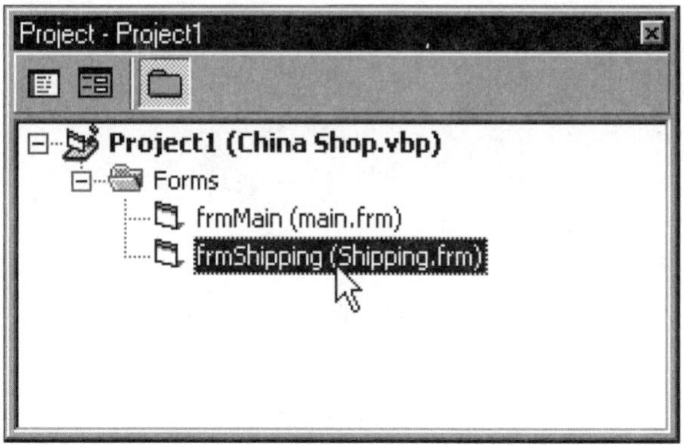

3. ...and open it up in design view.

4. Place a frame, a list box, a label and a command button on the form, located roughly according to the next screenshot. Ensure that the list box control is contained within the frame by selecting the frame control, then clicking once on the list box control icon in the Toolbox, moving the mouse pointer until you see the crosshairs, then using the left mouse button to explicitly draw the list box control *within* the frame. You can check that the list box is contained within the frame by moving the frame – if the list box moves with it, it's properly contained in the frame. Here's how your form should look:

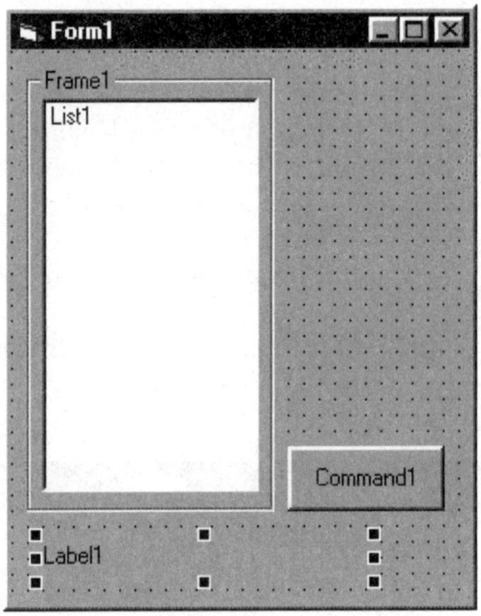

5. Use the following table to make changes to the properties of **`frmShipping`**:

Property	Value
Name	frmShipping
BorderStyle	1-Fixed Single
Caption	Shipping Charges
ControlBox	False
Height	4590
MaxButton	False
MinButton	False
Moveable	False
StartUpPostion	CenterScreen
Width	4815

6. Next, make these changes to the frame currently called **`Frame1`**:

Property	Value
Name	fraStates
Caption	Select a State

7. Now use this next table to alter the list box currently named `List1`:

Property	Value
Name	lstStates

8. Now make these changes to the `Command1`command button:

Property	Value	Comment
Name	cmdReturn	
Caption	Return to main form...	
Default	True	Makes the command button the Default command button on the form. Its Click event procedure will be triggered if the user presses the Enter key, regardless of which control on the form has focus.

9. Finally, amend the `Label1`label using this last table:

Property	Value	Comment
Name	lblCharges	
Caption	(blank)	Clear the property by selecting it and pressing the BackSpace or Delete keys
AutoSize	True	To accommodate a caption of varying size

10. Your form should now look similar to this screenshot:

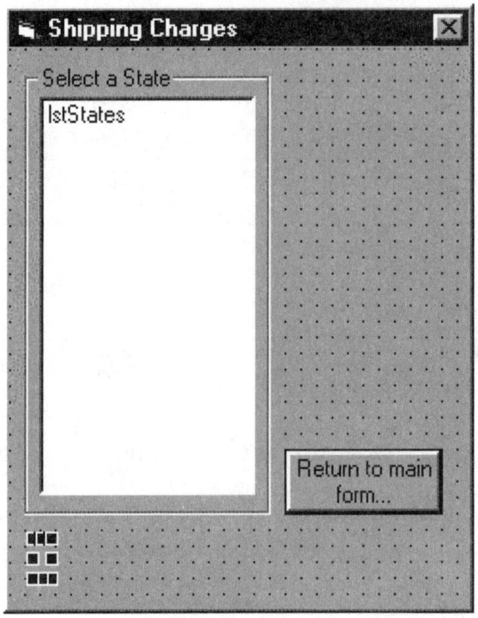

11. Save the China Shop Project.

12. At the moment, there's no way to test the behavior of the new **`Shipping`** form. Right now, the China Shop's **`Main`** form is the only form that is displayed in the program, and we don't yet have a way to make the **`Shipping Charges`** form visible. However, we'll be doing that in a few minutes – so hang on!

Discussion

Unlike the previous exercise, no one seemed to have any trouble with this one – there was just a single question:

"I ran the program," Melissa said, "and, as you indicated in the exercise instructions, at the moment there's no way to make the **`Shipping Charges`** form visible. How will we do that?"

"We'll be adding a new command button to the China Shop's **`Main`** form soon," I said. "When this new command button is clicked, it will display the new **`Shipping Charges`** form. However, before we do that, we still have some other work to complete. First, we need to create a text file containing shipping information, with a line for each of the fifty United States plus the District of Columbia, along with the respective shipping charges for each. After that, we need to add some code to the new **`Shipping Charges`** form."

The Shipping.txt file

"First thing's first, though. Here's an exercise to create the `Shipping.txt` file."

Exercise - Creating the Shipping.txt File

In this exercise, you'll create the `Shipping.txt` file. This file will supply the program's objects – and, through them, Joe's sales clerks – with all the information that they need about shipping charges for customer orders.

1. Use Notepad to create a file called `Shipping.txt` using the table shown below in **step 3**.

2. Make sure that the name of the state is enclosed within quotation marks, as this screenshot shows:

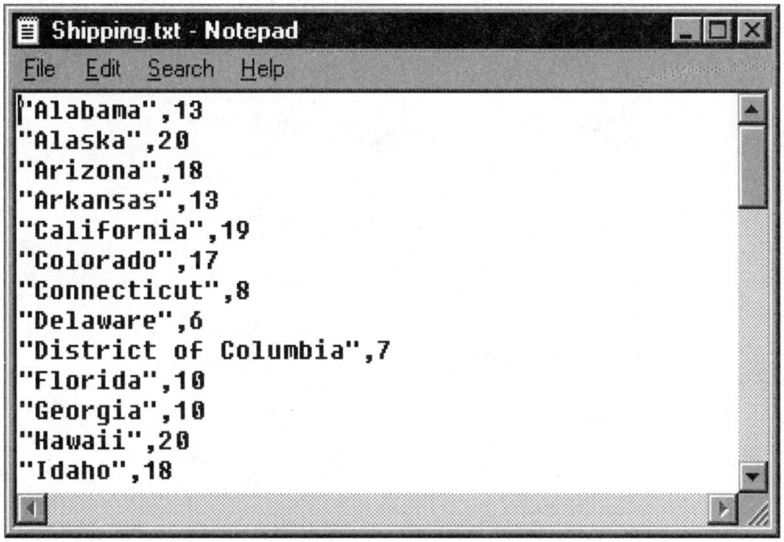

3. These are the 51 records to add to the file **in alphabetical order**:

State	Charge	State	Charge
Alabama	13	Montana	17
Alaska	20	Nebraska	15
Arizona	18	Nevada	19
Arkansas	13	New Hampshire	9
California	19	New Jersey	6
Colorado	17	New Mexico	17
Connecticut	8	New York	8
Delaware	6	North Carolina	10
District of Columbia	7	North Dakota	16
Florida	10	Ohio	11
Georgia	10	Oklahoma	15
Hawaii	20	Oregon	19
Idaho	18	Pennsylvania	6
Illinois	11	Rhode Island	8
Indiana	11	South Carolina	12
Iowa	14	South Dakota	16
Kansas	15	Tennessee	12
Kentucky	12	Texas	15
Louisiana	13	Utah	18
Maine	10	Vermont	9
Maryland	8	Virginia	8
Massachusetts	9	Washington	19
Michigan	11	West Virginia	8
Minnesota	14	Wisconsin	14
Mississippi	13	Wyoming	17
Missouri	14		

4. Save this file as **Shipping.txt** in your **\VBFiles\China** folder.

Discussion

"Our next step," I said, "is to add some code to the new **Shipping Charges** form. This code will load the contents of the **Shipping.txt** file into a Visual Basic collection when the form is displayed by the user. This'll enable the user to look up the shipping charges for a destination state of their choice. We'll look at the detail of that next."

Coding the Shipping Charges Form

"Remember," I went on, "we're using collections to store data in the China Shop program because they allow us to keep that information inside the object to which it relates – in this case, that means the collection object that's created when the user opens up the **Shipping Charges** form. The collection object is a member of the **Shipping Charges** form object. This is a much more object-oriented way of doing things: we don't have to use and maintain a whole load of variables, and we get the benefits of being able to use the data in our code using object dot notation."

That said, I distributed the next exercise to the class.

Exercise - Adding Code to the Shipping Charges Form

In this exercise, you'll add code to the **Shipping Charges** form. This code will create the collection object that stores the data from the **Shipping.txt** file, and let the user display the shipping charges that they're interested in. we'll discuss the code after we've keyed it in.

1. Continue working with the new **Shipping** form of the China Shop program.
2. Add the following line of code to the General Declarations section of the form.

```
Option Explicit

Private m_colShippingCharges As New Collection
```

3. Now key the following code into the **Shipping Charges** form's **Load** event procedure:

```
Private Sub Form_Load()

On Error GoTo ICanHandleThis

Dim strState As String
Dim curPrice As Currency

If App.Path = "\" Then
    Open App.Path & "Shipping.txt" For Input As #1
Else
    Open App.Path & "\Shipping.txt" For Input As #1
End If

Do While Not EOF(1)
    Input #1, strState, curPrice
      m_colShippingCharges.Add item:=curPrice, Key:=strState
      lstStates.AddItem strState
Loop
Close #1

Exit Sub

ICanHandleThis:
Select Case Err.Number
   Case 53               'File not found
      MsgBox "A file required by the " &
            ↳"China Shop program " & vbCrLf &
            ↳"is missing. Please ensure that " & vbCrLf &
            ↳"Shipping.txt is in " & vbCrLf &
            ↳"the China Shop directory " & vbCrLf &
            ↳"on the computer's hard drive"
       Unload Me
       Exit Sub
    Case Else
       MsgBox "An unexpected error has occurred." & vbCrLf &
             ↳"Please inform a member of staff."
       Unload Me
      Exit Sub
End Select

End Sub
```

4. Add the following code to the **Click** event procedure of the **lstStates** list box:

```
Private Sub lstStates_Click()

lblCharges.Caption = "Shipping charges for the State of " &
            ↳lstStates.Text &
            ↳" are: $" & m_colShippingCharges.Item(lstStates.Text)

End Sub
```

5. Now type this single line into the form's **Query_Unload** event procedure:

```
Private Sub Form_QueryUnload(Cancel As Integer, UnloadMode As Integer)

Set m_colShippingCharges = Nothing

End Sub
```

6. Finally, key this line into the **cmdReturn** button's **Click** event procedure:

```
Private Sub cmdReturn_Click()

Unload Me

End Sub
```

7. Save the China Shop program.

8. As was the case with the last exercise, there's still no way to test the behavior of the new **Shipping Charges** form. But stay tuned – we'll be doing that in the next exercise.

Discussion

"Professor," Kate asked, "can you give us the big picture of what's happening in this code, please?"

"Sure thing, Kate," I answered. "I'll do that quickly before I take you through the important parts of the code line by line, OK? When the **Shipping Charges** form is first displayed, we're loading the names of each state into the **lstStates** list box. At the same time, we're adding the shipping charges for each state into the **m_colShippingCharges** collection, using the state's name as the unique key to each item in that collection. When the user selects a state from the list box, the **Click** event procedure will look up the charges for the selected state in the **m_colShippingCharges** collection, and we'll display the charge using the **Caption** property of **lblCharges**."

"Now to the detail. First, let's take a look at the collection declaration that we placed in the General Declarations section of the form:"

```
Private m_colShippingCharges As New Collection
```

"This declaration," I continued, "is similar to the declaration we made for the **m_colDishPrice** collection in the **Main** form two weeks ago. As with that collection, we're declaring this collection in the General Declarations section of the form since it needs to be accessed from several event procedures on the Shipping Charges form. Likewise, the code in the **Load** event procedure of the Shipping Charges form is also similar to the code in the **ReadPrices** subprocedure of the China Shop's **Main** form, which we also modified two weeks ago. This first line declares an error handler in the event that the **Shipping.txt** file is missing:"

```
On Error GoTo ICanHandleThis
```

"Now we declare two variables to store the values for the state and shipping charges that we're going to read from the **Shipping.txt** file:"

```
Dim strState As String
Dim curPrice As Currency
```

"This next section of code uses the **Path** property of the **App** object – which we talked about in depth last week – to locate and open the **Shipping.txt** file from the same folder that the China shop program is being run from:"

```
If App.Path = "\" Then
    Open App.Path & "Shipping.txt" For Input As #1
Else
    Open App.Path & "\Shipping.txt" For Input As #1
End If
```

"The next chunk of code executes a **Do...While...Loop** structure to read each record (all 51 of them) in the **Shipping.txt** file, and then adds the shipping charge, which comes from the current value of the **curPrice** – as a new item in the **m_colShippingCharges** collection. The code also gives each new item in the collection a key, which is equal to the name of the state currently in the **strState** variable:"

```
Do While Not EOF(1)
    Input #1, strState, curPrice
    m_colShippingCharges.Add item:=curPrice, Key:=strState
    lstStates.AddItem strState
Loop
Close #1
```

"This loop will run for each of the 51 records in the **Shipping.txt** file, and add an item for each to the collection. It's similar to the code we saw for the **m_colDishPrice** collection that we coded in Lesson 2."

"Notice," I added, "that we also add the state to the list box **lstStates**:"

```
lstStates.AddItem strState
```

"Incidentally, now that the list box has some items of data in it, we can refer to the currently selected list box item in our code by using the list box's **Text** property. The list box's **Text** property is a runtime-only property, so don't try and find it in the Properties window!"

"Our work in the **Load** event procedure is basically all done now," I said, "so we code an **Exit Sub** statement here to bypass the code in the error handler – which should only be executed if we have a problem locating the **Shipping.txt** file:"

```
Exit Sub

ICanHandleThis:
Select Case Err.Number
   Case 53          'File not found
      MsgBox "A file required by the " &
            ↳"China Shop program " & vbCrLf &
            ↳"is missing. Please ensure that " & vbCrLf &
            ↳"Shipping.txt is in " & vbCrLf &
            ↳"the China Shop directory " & vbCrLf &
            ↳"on the computer's hard drive"
       Unload Me
       Exit Sub
```

```
    Case Else
      MsgBox "An unexpected error has occurred." & vbCrLf &
             ↳"Please inform a member of staff."

         Unload Me
      Exit Sub
End Select
```

"Let's look at the code in **Click** event procedure of the **lstStates** list box," I said. "The code's fairly straightforward: when a state in the list box is clicked, we pass the value in the **Text** property of the list box as an argument to the **Item** method of the **m_colShippingCharges** collection. This method locates the shipping charge item in the collection whose value matches the state that's been selected in the list box: it does this by finding the collection item with a key value that matches the state's unique name. When the item is located in the collection, the shipping charge value is concatenated with some text strings into the **Caption** property of the **lblCharges** label:"

```
lblCharges.Caption = "Shipping charges for the State of " &
lstStates.Text &
lstStates.Text &
            ↳" are: $" & m_colShippingCharges.Item(lstStates.Text)
```

"I'm OK with that," Valerie said, "but what's going on with that line of code in the **Query_Unload** event of the form?"

"Good question, Valerie," I said. "This line of code..."

```
Set m_colShippingCharges = Nothing
```

"...destroys the **m_colShippingCharges** collection, and all of its data."

"Why do we need to do that?" Chuck asked.

"The code in the **Query_Unload** event procedure is executed when the **Shipping Charges** form is unloaded," I said. "If we didn't destroy the collection at this point, and the user opened this form again, the program would crash."

"Why?" Ward wondered.

"If we didn't destroy the collection," I said, "when the **Shipping Charges** form was unloaded, the collection and all of the data within it would still be alive in the computer's memory. If the form was reloaded by the user trying to look up another shipping charge, the code in the **Load** event procedure of the form would execute again and attempt to add the data from **Shipping.txt** to the collection. We would be trying to add items to the collection with key values that already existed. Remember, Visual Basic won't allow a collection to have duplicate key values – if it did, it wouldn't be able to choose between the different items that shared the same keys. Destroying the collection by setting its object variable to **Nothing** takes care of the problem: the collection is created afresh each time the form is loaded."

"That's a surprise to me," Tom said. "I always thought that variables declared within a form die when the form is unloaded."

"You're learning more about objects all the time, Tom" I said. "That's only true of ordinary variables. A user defined collection is different – the object variable used to refer to it is still alive and well – even when the form it was declared within is unloaded – and so we need to explicitly destroy it by setting it to **Nothing** before unloading the **Shipping Charges** form."

I waited to see if there were any other questions.

"The last code we have to discuss," I said, "is the code in the **Click** event procedure of **cmdReturn**. All we're doing here is unloading the form using the **Unload Me** statement:"

```
Unload Me
```

"**Unload Me** unloads the form," I said, "triggering the **Query_Unload** event procedure of the form, which in turn destroys our collection object."

"I can't wait to see this work," Ward said. "What's next?"

"Next," I said, "let's add the code that will let us display the **Shipping Charges** form as an option on the China Shop's **Main** form."

Integrating the Shipping Charges Form into the China Shop

"All we need to do is add a command button to the **Main** form of the China Shop program," I said, "and place a single line of code in its **Click** event procedure."

With that, I distributed the final exercise of the day:

Exercise - Bringing up the Shipping Charges Form from the Main Form

In this exercise, you'll place a command button on the **`Main`** form of the China Shop program which, when clicked, will display the **`Shipping Charges`** form.

1. Open up the China Shop's **`Main`** form in design view.
2. Add a command button to the bottom right of the **`Main`** form, in a similar location to the one shown in the next screenshot:

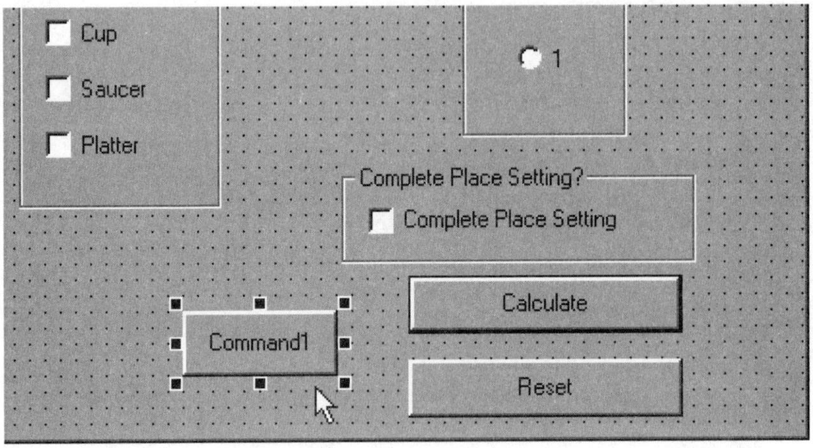

3. Change the command button's **`Name`** property to **`cmdShipping`**, and its **`Caption`** property to **`Shipping Charges`**:

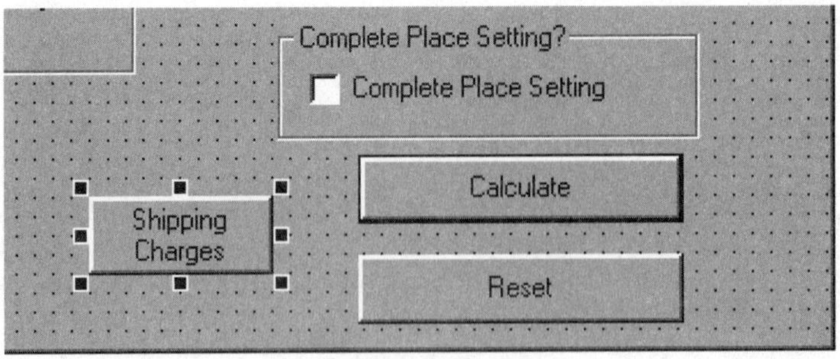

4. Add the following code to the **Click** event procedure of **cmdShipping**:

```
Private Sub cmdShipping_Click()

frmShipping.Show vbModal

End Sub
```

5. Save the China Shop program.

6. Now run the China Shop program and click on the Shipping Charges button. The **Shipping Charges** form should appear. Click on the state of New Jersey in the list box – you should see shipping charges of $6 displayed in the **Caption** of **lblCharges**.

Discussion

I ran the program myself, immediately clicked on the Shipping Charges button, and selected the state of New Jersey, with this result:

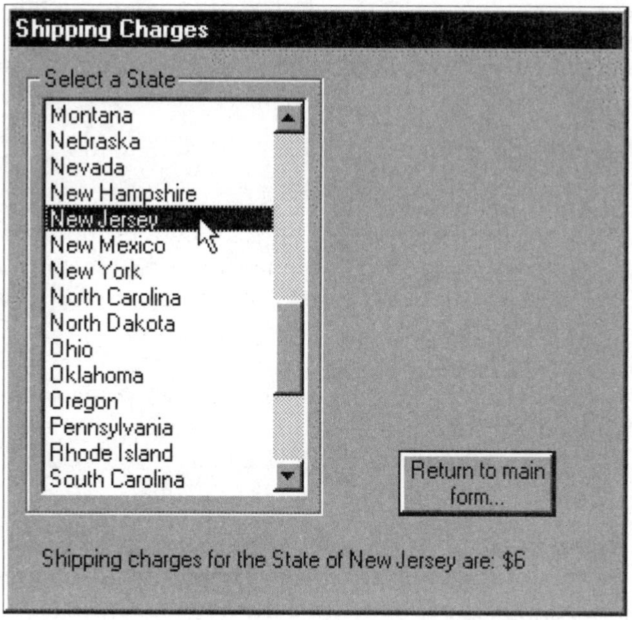

"I love this," Kate said, "I've been waiting a long time to add another form to a project. I have only one question: I've seen code used where a second form is loaded using the Visual Basic **Load** statement. Here, you used the **Show** method instead."

"That's right Kate," I said, "you sometimes see the **Load** statement used to load a second form, as in:"

```
Load frmShipping
```

"This would load the **Shipping Charges** form into memory. Unfortunately, using the **Load** statement by itself would **not** result in the user being able to see the **Shipping Charges** form."

"What?" Rhonda asked. "We wouldn't be able to see the form?"

"That's right," I said. "As we saw earlier in this course, all the **Load** statement does is load the form into memory: it doesn't make the form visible. To do that, you need to explicitly make the form visible. You can do that by setting the form's **Visible** property to **True**, like this:"

```
Load frmShipping
frmShipping.Visible = True
```

"But getting back to the code we wrote for the China Shop," Valerie said, "are you saying that by executing only the **Show** method of the form you're both loading the form *and* making it visible at the same time?"

"Perfectly correct, Valerie," I said. "One line of code is doing the work of two here."

"Oh yes, I remember," she responded. "Changing a form's property – any property – automatically loads the form! You told us that a few weeks ago – sorry."

"Can you explain the meaning of **vbModal**," Tom asked. "Is that an argument of the **Show** method?"

"Good question, Tom," I replied. "**vbModal** is an argument of the **Show** method. It tells Visual Basic to display the **Shipping** form as a **modal** form, which means that no other form in the China Shop project can be accessed until the **Shipping** form is closed. This is like when you get an important message box in a Windows program – you have to answer the message box by clicking on OK or Cancel before the program will let you do anything else. However much you try and click on another window, you can't get out of the message box until you've answered it. The message box runs modally because it wants your attention and doesn't want you to do anything else before you've dealt with what it has to tell you."

There were no more questions. It had been a long class, and so I briefly told the students that, next week, we'd start the creation of the China Shop's core objects. I light-heartedly warned everyone to be full of energy for next Saturday's class.

With that, I summarized the material that we'd covered during the lesson:

Lesson Summary

In this lesson, we learned more about the internals of Visual Basic objects, and saw how we could set about starting to build our own objects. Specifically, we extended our knowledge of objects and how to use them by seeing that:

- An **object** is a programmatic representation of a real world thing, created from a class module or template
- An object contains **properties** – these describe attributes or characteristics of the object
- An object has **methods** – these are the predefined repertoire of things that an object can *do*, and they're built into the object. Programmers can use these methods to perform actions on the object and the properties that describe it
- An object raises **events** – these are signals that the object can put out to let the program know that something has happened
- We can refer to objects in code, and to their properties, methods, and events, using **object dot notation**. This gives our programs higher levels of clarity, flexibility, and maintainability
- We can add our own **custom properties and methods** to some of Visual Basic's standard objects – such as a form
- We can create objects – such as forms and controls – in code, at program runtime

We also did some important work on the China Shop project, implementing some of the features that we've learned about in the course so far:

- We walked through a customer purchase scenario and used it to identify the China Shop's objects, and those objects' properties and methods
- We created the new `Shipping Charges` form, created a collection object to store the shipping charges, and integrated the new form with the China Shop's `Main` form

In the next Lesson, we'll begin creating the China Shop's core objects – the objects that will embody the China Shop's old and new functionality in an object-oriented fashion. Creating these objects will pull together and reinforce all that we've learned so far.

Learn to Program Objects with Visual Basic

Chapter 5
Creating Your Own Objects

In this chapter, you'll follow my Visual Basic objects class as we begin to create our own objects. This creation process essentially consists of building the template that we'll use to instantiate individual objects from.

To begin with, we'll create a demonstration program, which we'll be using to 'test-bed' the new concepts we'll be dealing with before implementing them in the China Shop program. We'll continue using this program to try out new ideas over the coming weeks as we progress. After we've practiced on the demo project, we'll apply the new concepts to the China Shop project itself.

The main things we'll cover in this week's lesson are:

- Creating the basis of a class template by building a **class module**
- Adding the **properties** that describe the attributes of the class (and the objects instantiated from it) to the class module foundation
- Using the class module to instantiate individual objects in a program
- Giving the rest of the program access to our objects' properties so that they can be read and updated. We'll look at the special procedures (called `Property Let` and `Property Get` procedures) that allow the program to interrogate and change property values
- Putting all this knowledge to work in a demo program

For the China Shop program, we'll be covering the following very important ground:

- We'll make a `Dish` class module, which we'll use to instantiate objects that represent the China Pieces selected in a sales quotation
- We'll define the properties of the **Dish** class within this module
- We'll code the **Property Let** and **Property Get** procedures for the **Dish** class
- We'll integrate the **Dish** objects constructed from our new **Dish** class with the rest of the China Shop program by making some changes to the project's `Main` form

Let's join my students for their fifth lesson in object-oriented programming.

The Heart of the Matter

For the fifth week of my Visual Basic course, I made sure I got into the University good and early: I had a lot of graphics that I'd put together to reinforce the more difficult concepts I'd be putting across in today's lesson, and I wanted to make sure they were going to show up properly on the classroom projector. The coverage of creating class modules and properties that we'd work through today would provide my students with really solid experience of creating their own objects. Normally I'd use slides, but I hadn't had time to put these together, so I was going to use the art package on the PC in the classroom to display the images one by one. However, I had a slightly different version of the same art package on my laptop, which was where I'd tested my presentation out, and I wanted to make sure the classroom machine was going to behave as expected.

I was still playing around with the graphics when the first members of the class filed in. I greeted them and told them to go grab themselves a cup of coffee while the others turned up. Ward offered to get me a drink from the lobby while he was out there – which I gratefully accepted, giving him the necessary change. He brought it through to me and I sat sipping it as I reassured myself that everything was going to run smoothly.

Then, when everyone had arrived, I focused their attention on what we were going to do today.

"I think you're really going to enjoy today's session," I said. "Today you'll create your very first China Shop object, based on the object design we made last week. By the end of today's class, you'll have created the class template for the China Shop's `Dish` object, defined its properties, and seen how the objects instantiated from this class work in the China Shop program. Next week, we'll conclude the creation of the `Dish` object by adding methods and events to it as well."

Creating Your Own Objects

"Is this going to be a painful process?" Rhonda asked. "I mean, is it difficult to create objects of our own? Is there some kind of Visual Basic menu item that starts the ball rolling for us?"

"I may be biased," I said, smiling, "but I think creating your own objects is a lot of fun. Do you remember last week when I said that the template for an object is something called a class? Well, in Visual Basic, the first step in creating objects of our own is to add a class module to a Visual Basic project."

"The class module is the template or cookie cutter that you mentioned last week, isn't it?" Kate asked.

"That's exactly right, Kate," I said. "In Visual Basic, the class module is indeed the cookie cutter that we use to create specific instances of the object when the program runs. We'll follow the process right through from creation to use in code. In fact, we're going to do this for two different projects today: later on, we'll be creating and using the `Dish` class and its objects in the China Shop program itself. Before that, though, we're going to work on a demonstration project that will make it easier for us to create our first objects, and to see how they work."

I paused for a moment before continuing:

"We'll be starting that demo project in today's lesson, and we'll carry on working with the demo project throughout the next few lessons as well, as we introduce new concepts and coding techniques. This will let us test out our new-found knowledge before we implement it in the China Shop program."

I knew that working on this demo project would ease the students more gently through the learning curve: once they'd had some practice at creating objects in the demo project, applying this knowledge to the China Shop would be much easier. As I never tire of telling people – there's no substitute for practice! Next, I moved on to introducing the demo project that we'd be looking at in the next few lessons. This demo project focuses on a class-full of students and on calculating their term grades.

Introducing the Student Grades Demo Project

"What I'd like to do today," I resumed, "is go through the process of writing a program to compute the grades of the students taking a course with a professor here at the University. As we create that demo program over the next few weeks, we'll create a `Student` object, complete with its own properties, methods and events, and incorporate that object in the program. First, though, lets' talk about what the program needs to do in a little detail."

The Student Grades Program's Requirements

"Let's assume," I continued, "that a professor at the University is teaching a course in which each student is required to take a **mid-term examination** and a **final examination**, and that they also have to write a **term paper**. Let's say that the **mid-term** grade accounts for 40% of the student's grade, the **final exam** another 40%, and the **term paper** the remaining 20%."

"That seems a simple-enough calculation," Ward observed.

"OK," I continued, "suppose the professor hears about this class's programming prowess. She contacts me and asks us to write a program that lets her enter a student's information – **name**, **mid-term**, **final exam** and **term paper** grades – onto a form, and to display the student's overall numeric grade on the form. Additionally, the Professor wants to write a record of the student's information and final grade to a file on her PC. At the end of the process, she also wants to be able to display the **overall class average** for the whole course. I think everyone in here could probably do that without a great deal of trouble:"

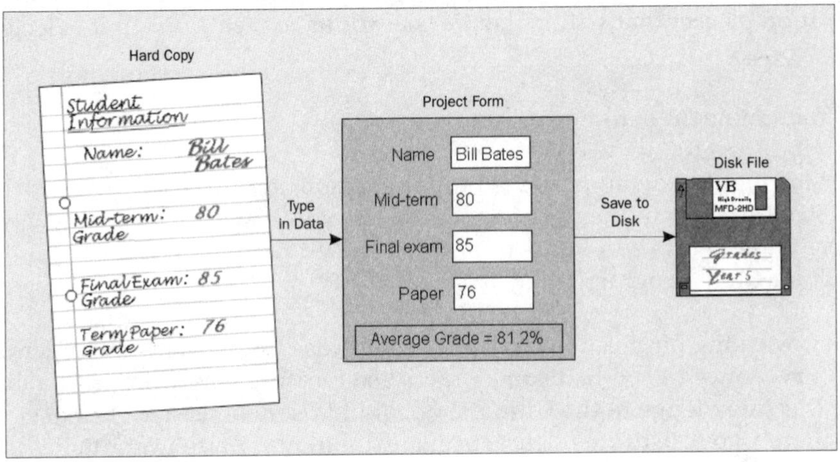

"I wouldn't think that would take us more than a half hour or so to do," Dave said. "Those are pretty much the skills we picked up in the Intro course."

"I agree, Dave," I said.

"Would creating a `Student` object enable us to develop the program faster than if we used those Intro course techniques?" Rhonda asked.

"Actually Rhonda," I said, "the program would take longer to develop initially if we took the time to create a `Student` object first. We'll create the basic demo project first, and then object-orient it."

"Why bother creating an object-oriented version if the basic version works OK?" Rhonda countered.

"A number of reasons," I answered. "First, you'll see that for yourself that once we've done the up-front work and created a `Student` object, the rest of the program will be much easier to write. Secondly, a program that uses objects is much easier to maintain than a program that doesn't. Thirdly, once we have the `Student` object defined in a class module, we'll be able to incorporate that object into any other programs we might write – and the development of those programs will be quicker."

> **There was another reason, too – this simple, non-mysterious application was a great example to illustrate basic object creation. We could really perform this simple process in a few minutes in an Excel spreadsheet, but I knew that working through the theory and practice in this demo project would do the class a power of good.**

"So the payback's further down the line," Valerie said, " but it *is* there."

"Most definitely," I said. "When it comes to object-oriented programming, you need to realize that you are now wearing two hats. One hat is that of the programmer who is developing the template for the object in a class module. The second hat is that of the person using the object. In many large organizations, these roles are filled by separate people."

"In other words," Chuck said, "the programmer designing and coding the object is not necessarily the person who later uses it?"

"That's right, Chuck," I said. "Although it's also the case that in some smaller organizations, the programmer who designs the object may turn right around and use it in his or her own program."

The students seemed happy with that – they'd already seen for themselves how using object-oriented programming principles could simplify their coding tasks.

"At any rate," I resumed, "why don't we get on with writing this grade computation program? That way, we'll all have a chance to see exactly what creating our own objects is all about. First, we'll achieve the solution to the professor's problem by conventional coding, then we'll convert the program to make use of some objects – we'll create these later. The end result will be the same functionality as the conventional code, but making use of our self-created objects. Let's begin the conventional approach by creating the visual part of the program – the form."

Building the Student Grades Form

I began by opening up Visual Basic and creating a new `Standard.EXE` program. Then I added some controls to the from, as shown in the screenshot – five label controls, four text boxes, and three command buttons:

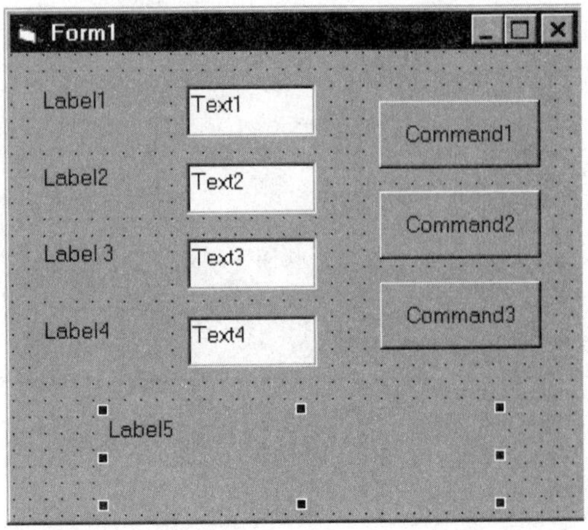

Next, I changed the `Name` properties of the **text boxes** to match this table:

Old Name	New Name
Text1	txtName
Text2	txtMidTerm
Text3	txtFinalExam
Text4	txtTermPaper

I altered the `Name` and `Caption` properties of the **label controls** to accord with the next table:

Old Name	New Name	New Caption
Label1	lblName	Name
Label2	lblMidTerm	Mid-term
Label3	lblFinalExam	Final Exam
Label4	lblTermPaper	Term Paper
Label5	lblFinalGrade	(leave blank)

The next task was to modify the **Name** and **Caption** properties of the command buttons:

Old Name	New Name	New Caption
Command1	cmdCalculate	Calculate Grade
Command2	cmdAddRecord	Add Record
Command3	cmdClassAverage	Class Average

I also cleared the **Text** properties of all of the text boxes, and changed the form's **Caption** property to **Calculate Student Grades**. By now, my form looked like this next screenshot – and so should yours (you are working through this exercise with me, aren't you?):

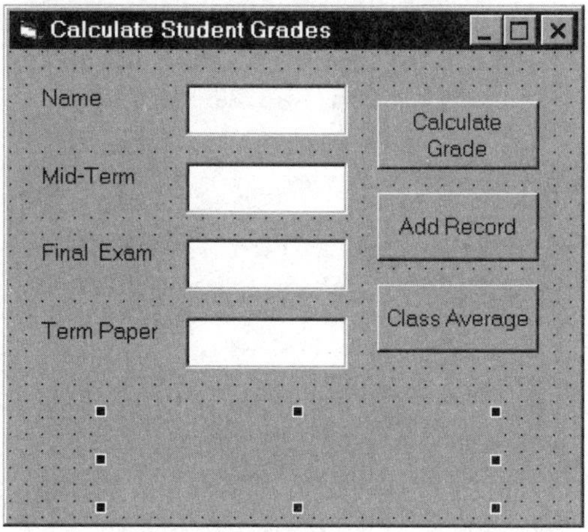

"Now," I continued, "let's create the code for the Student Grades demo."

Conventional Code for the Demo Project

"Here's the code," I said, "to calculate a student's final grade."

First, I added the following variable declarations in the General Declarations section of the form:

```
Option Explicit

Private m_intRunningTotal As Integer
Private m_intRunningCount As Integer
Private m_sngFinalGrade As Single
```

"As you can see from the **Private m_** prefix, I'm declaring these variables as module-level variables," I said, "which means they can be 'seen' from any procedure on the form. You'll see how we use them in just a moment."

I then placed the following code in the `Click` event procedure of `cmdCalculate`:

```
Private Sub cmdCalculate_Click()

If txtName.Text = "" Then
    MsgBox "Enter the student's Name"
    txtName.SetFocus
    Exit Sub
End If

If txtMidTerm.Text = "" Then
    MsgBox "Enter the student's Mid-term Grade"
    txtMidterm.SetFocus
    Exit Sub
End If

If txtFinalExam.Text = "" Then
    MsgBox "Enter the student's Final Exam Grade"
    txtFinalExam.SetFocus
    Exit Sub
End If

If txtTermPaper.Text = "" Then
    MsgBox "Enter the student's Term Paper Grade"
    txtTermPaper.SetFocus
    Exit Sub
End If
m_sngFinalGrade =
        ⇘(Val(txtMidTerm.Text) * 0.4) +
        ⇘(Val(txtFinalExam.Text) * 0.4) +
        ⇘(Val(txtTermPaper.Text) * 0.2)

lblFinalGrade.Caption =
    ⇘"The grade for " & txtName.Text & " is " &
      ⇘m_sngFinalGrade &
      ⇘". Click on the 'Add Record' button to save the record."

End Sub
```

"I think you'll probably all understand what's going on here," I said. "The first section of code – the `If...End If` structures – just ensures that the user of the program has given us all of the information we require – the student's name, their mid-term grade, their final examination grade, and their term paper grade. If not, we display a message, set focus to the text box with the missing value, and exit the `Click` event procedure."

"The next part is the code that calculates the final numeric grade," I explained. "What we do is multiply the user's entry in **txtMidTerm** by 40%, multiply the user's entry in **txtFinalExam** by 40%, and multiply the user's entry in **txtPaper** by 20%. We then sum the results of the three multiplications together to produce the final grade, and assign that result to the **m_sngFinalGrade** module-level variable:"

```
m_sngFinalGrade =
        ↳(Val(txtMidTerm.Text) * 0.4) +
        ↳(Val(txtFinalExam.Text) * 0.4) +
        ↳(Val(txtTermPaper.Text) * 0.2)
```

"The value of this module-level variable is then concatenated with some explanatory text to the **Caption** property of **lblFinalGrade**..."

```
lblFinalGrade.Caption =
    ↳"The grade for " & txtName.Text & " is " &
    ↳m_sngFinalGrade &
    ↳". Click on the 'Add Record' button to save the record."
```

"...along with a prompt to the user to click on the Add Record button. We'll be writing code for the **Click** event procedure of that command button shortly. I should also mention that if this were a full-fledged application, and not a demonstration program for our class, we would write some code to ensure that the text boxes accepted only valid numeric entries."

"Why did you declare the variable **m_sngFinalGrade** as a module-level variable?" Kate asked. "Are we going to be using it again?"

"Yes, we are, Kate," I confirmed. "We'll use the value in that variable to write a record of the student's grade to a text file. Eventually, the calculations that we just put in the **Click** event procedure of **cmdCalculate** will be encapsulated inside the **Student** object – we'll code that object in a few minutes. Before we get to that, however, we still have some more work to do. Let me show you how the program works so far..."

Running the Student Grades Program

I ran the program, entered the name and grades of a fictitious student into the four text boxes, and clicked the Calculate Grade button – with this result:

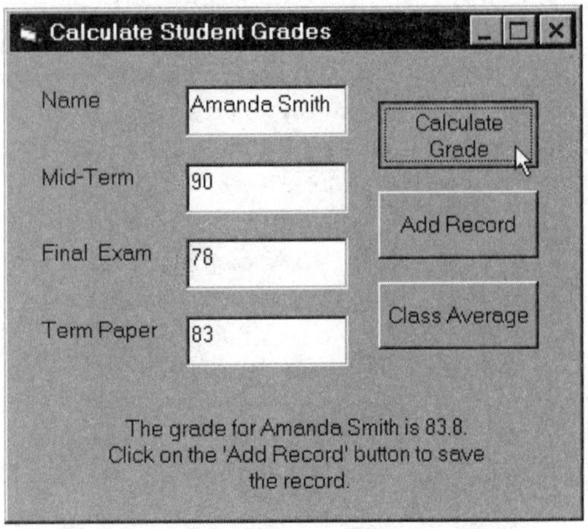

"As you can see, the final grade for our fictitious student works out to 83.8," I said. "Any questions?"

"What will the Add Record command button do?" Linda asked.

"Once the user of the program verifies that the student's information is correct," I said, "they can click on this button, and a record of the student's information will be written away to a disk file."

"How exactly will we do that?" asked Dave.

"We'll open the file, write the student's information, and then close the file each time the user clicks on the Add Record button," I explained. "The number of records in the file will continue to grow by one each time this button is clicked. Here's the code for that..."

I stopped the program and added this next section of code to the **`Click`** event procedure of **`cmdAddRecord`** (we'll discuss the code shortly):

```
Private Sub cmdAddRecord _Click()

Open App.Path & "\Grades.txt" For Append As #1

Write #1, txtName.Text,
        ↳Val(txtMidterm.Text),
        ↳Val(txtFinalExam.Text),
        ↳Val(txtTermPaper.Text),
        ↳m_sngFinalGrade
Close #1
```

```
m_intRunningTotal = m_intRunningTotal +
        ↳m_sngFinalGrade
m_intRunningCount = m_intRunningCount + 1
txtName.Text = ""
txtMidterm.Text = ""
txtFinalExam.Text = ""
txtTermPaper.Text = ""
txtName.SetFocus
lblFinalGrade.Caption = ""

End Sub
```

"Let's take a look at the code now," I said. "This code is designed to open up an external disk file to add a record to. It also keeps track of the total of all the grades entered and the number of records that have been created – this is so that we can work out the average Course Grade later. We begin by opening a file called **`Grades.txt`** in **`Append`** mode:"

```
Open App.Path & "\Grades.txt" For Append As #1
```

"You may remember from our Intro class that opening a file in **`Append`** mode tells Visual Basic to look for the file and, if it finds it, to add records *to the end of the existing file*. If however, the file *cannot* be found, our use of **`Append`** mode tells Visual Basic to *create* the file and then to write the records. Note that we use this notation..."

```
As #1
```

"...so that we can refer to the disk file in code by that short reference – **`#1`**."

"This next section of code uses the **`Text`** properties of the four text boxes, plus the **`Caption`** property of the **`lblFinalGrade`** label control, as arguments to the Visual Basic **`Write`** statement. This results in the student's information being written to the **`Grades.txt`** file:"

```
Write #1, txtName.Text,
        ↳Val(txtMidTerm.Text),
        ↳Val(txtFinalExam.Text),
        ↳Val(txtTermPaper.Text),
        ↳m_sngFinalGrade
```

"Once we've written a record containing the student's information," I continued, "it's time to close the file:"

```
Close #1
```

"What's going on in this next section of code?" Rhonda asked.

"This is the code," I said, "that we use to produce the overall **class average** that our Professor wants. We want to add each student's grade to a variable to maintain a running total, so that when the user of the program clicks on the Class Average button, we can display a result equal to the 'running total divided by the total number of students' that have been entered in the program. That's why we declared those two module level variables **`m_intRunningTotal`** and **`m_intRunningCount`** earlier. The individual student's grade, stored in the **`m_sngFinalGrade`** variable, is added to the current value of the **`m_intRunningTotal`** variable:"

```
m_intRunningTotal = m_intRunningTotal +
        ↳m_sngFinalGrade
```

"Next, the current value of **`m_intRunningCount`** is incremented by 1 to keep track of the number of students whose grades have been entered:"

```
m_intRunningCount = m_intRunningCount + 1
```

"Finally," I concluded, "we prepare for the entry of the next student's scores by clearing all four text boxes and the **`Caption`** of the **`lblFinalGrade`** label, and set focus to the **`txtName`** text box:"

```
txtName.Text = ""
txtMidTerm.Text = ""
txtFinalExam.Text = ""
txtPaper.Text = ""
txtName.SetFocus
lblFinalGrade.Caption = ""
```

The code explanation over, I ran the program once again and entered the same scores for the mid-term, final exam and term paper grades of our fictitious student. Then I clicked on the Calculate Grade button. Content that I had not made any typos with my data entry, I clicked on the Add Record command button. The form's text boxes were cleared...

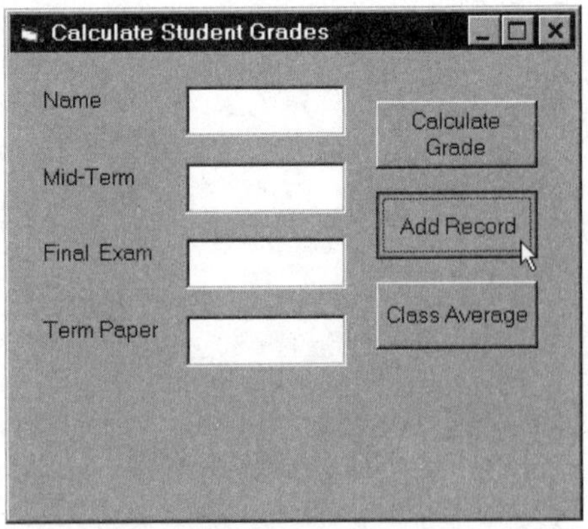

...and the absence of any error messages indicated to me that the code had been successful, and that we'd written records to the **Grades.txt** disk file. Using Notepad, I located and opened **Grades.txt**, and verified that a record of Amanda Smith's grades had indeed been written to the file:

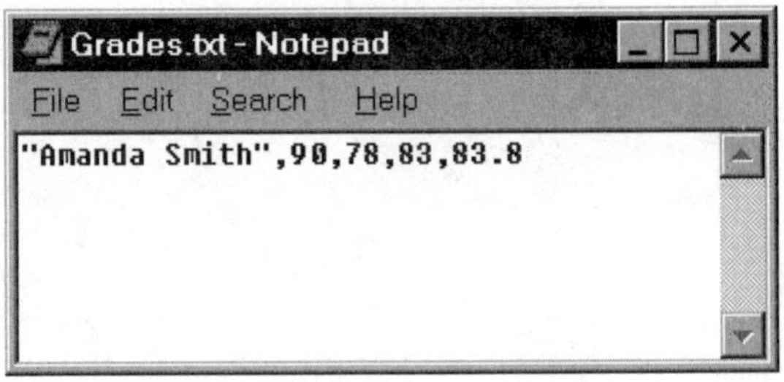

"There's the record," I said. "It contains one field each for the student's name, mid-term, final exam, term paper, and final numeric grade. Now let's add some code to the Class Average command button now..."

So saying, I keyed following line of code into the **cmdClassAverage** button's **Click** event procedure:

```
Private Sub cmdClassAverage_Click()

MsgBox "The Final Class Average is " &
        ↳m_intRunningTotal / m_intRunningCount

End Sub
```

"All we're doing here," I said, "is taking the value of the global variable **m_intRunningTotal** and dividing it by the global variable **m_intRunningCount**. In the final object-oriented version of this demonstration project, we'll encapsulate this processing as well."

I went through the cycle of entering and calculating grades, and clicking on the Add Record command button for two more imaginary students (with very good grades), thus adding their results to the file. Then I displayed the **Grades.txt** file for the class to view again:

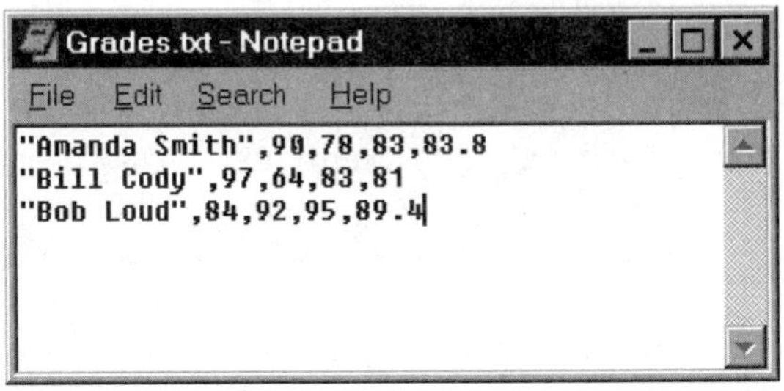

" Now let's click on the Class Average Button," I said.

I did so, and the following message box appeared:

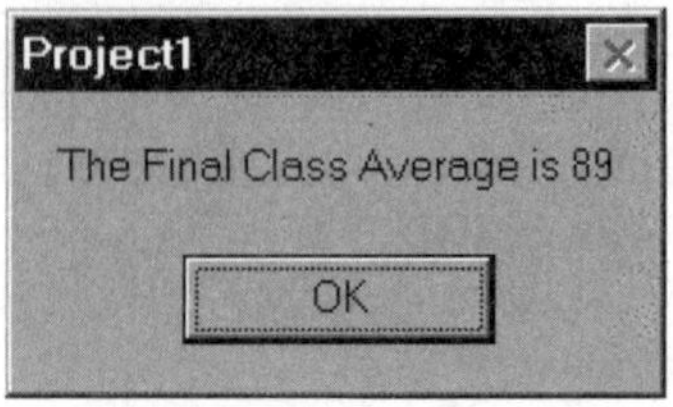
Project1
The Final Class Average is 89
OK

"So...the class average is 89 – or thereabouts," said Bob, precisely.

"That's about right, Bob," I said. "I think everyone would agree that, at this point, we've fully met the Professor's requirements. The program works, in the sense that it properly calculates a student's grade and summarizes the class average. Over the next two weeks, as we progress in our knowledge of how to create our own Visual Basic objects, I think you'll be amazed at the changes we make in this program, and how much more streamlined the code will become. We'll eventually encapsulate all of the grade calculation logic into a `Student` object and, two weeks from now, we'll create a `Course` collection object whose items will be the actual `Student` objects. But first thing's first – let's start by creating the `Student` object."

Object-orienting the Student Grades Program

"OK," I continued, "the first thing we're going to do is create the cookie cutter template – the class – that the `Student` objects in the demo program will be instantiated from. In a Visual Basic program, we create a cookie cutter template by defining a **class module** in our program. Let's start on that now."

Class Modules

"As I've already mentioned," I said, "a Visual Basic object starts with a **class module** – a module full of code that describes the characteristics of our object, and defines what the object can do, and how it should behave."

"Well," Rhonda said, "that sounds like an objects properties, methods, and events. Is that what goes into the class module."

"Essentially, yes," I confirmed. "That's what we'll be doing over the next few weeks: creating the objects for the Student Grades program – and for the China Shop, of course – and building up the properties, methods and events that embody the processing that these objects need to perform. We'll begin with the class module that defines the `Student` object in the Student Grades program."

Creating the Student Class Module

I stopped the Student Grades program, saved both the project and form to the `\VBFiles\Practice` directory on my hard drive, and then selected Project | Add Class Module from the Visual Basic menu bar:

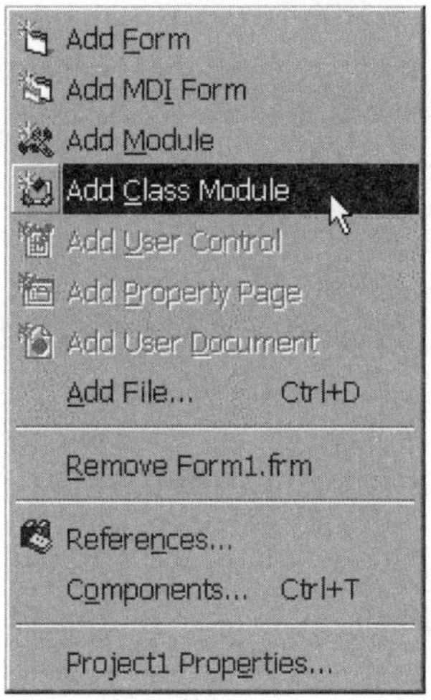

> **Remember that your menu options may look slightly different from mine, depending on which version of Visual Basic you're running. Don't worry – every version of Visual Basic has the essential tools that we need here.**

The following window appeared:

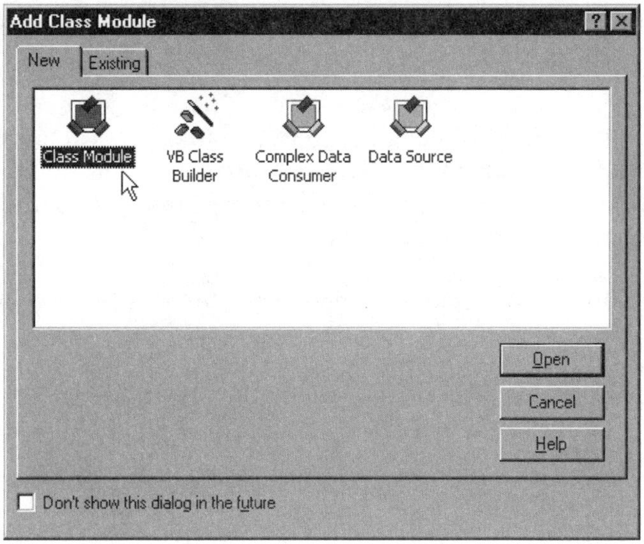

"This is the Add Class Module window," I said. "It looks very similar to the Add Form window we saw last week when we added a second form to the China Shop project – but this time we're telling Visual Basic that we wish to add a new **class module** – which describes a new type of object that we want to add to our program. There are two tabs – New and Existing. The New tab tells Visual Basic that – not surprisingly – we want to add a *new* class module to our project. Notice also that Visual Basic provides us with some pre-built class module templates that we can use."

Again, your Add Class Module may look different from mine – that's OK!

"We can also select the Existing tab to find and add to our project a class module that already exists – perhaps one that we've coded for ourselves, perhaps one built by another programmer. In this case, we want to double-click on the Class Module icon displayed on the New tab, and a brand new – empty – class module will appear in the IDE."

I did this, and a window for the new class module appeared in the Visual Basic IDE, ready to be worked on:

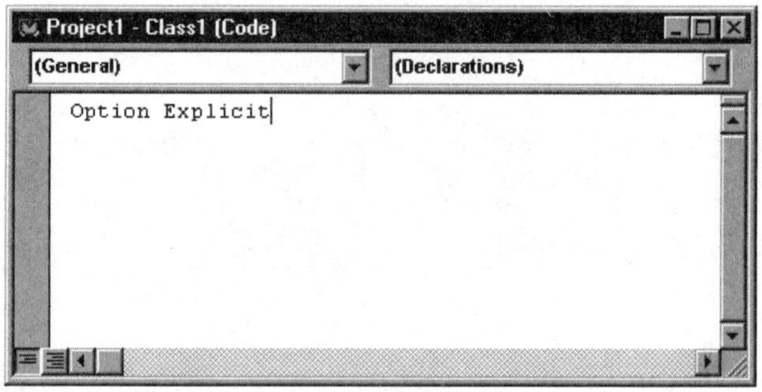

"Where's the form?" Rhonda asked.

"Well, Rhonda," I replied, "there isn't actually a form to display – class modules have no visual part that they can display. Unlike the forms that we've worked with before, class modules only consist of code. Remember, the objects that we'll be creating for ourselves here have no visual aspect to them."

"Actually," Blaine said, "the class module looks just like the Code window in a form module,".

"That's a pretty accurate description, Blaine," I agreed. "Since a class module has no visual part to it, it's made up entirely of code – so all you'll ever really see is this **code** portion of the class."

"Do class modules have a Properties window, like the form?" Kathy asked.

"Yes, they do," I said, "and you can view the Properties window for a class in the same way you can for a form."

Class Properties

"Probably the easiest way to view a class's Properties window is to select the class module with your mouse, and then press the `F4` function key. You'll then see this window:"

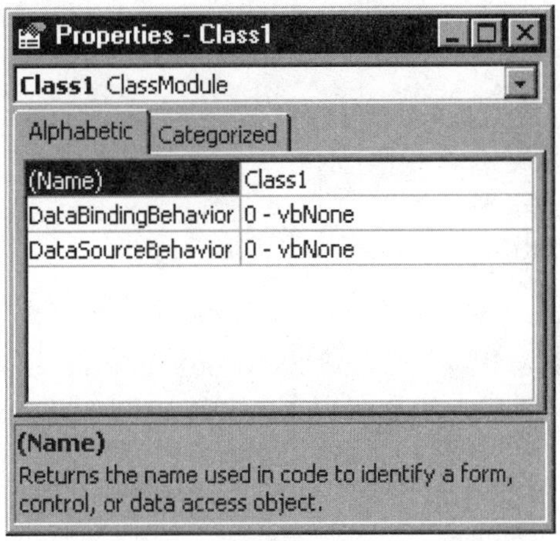

Once more, relax if you don't see all three of these properties – we only need the Name property here.

"The class module only has three default properties," I said, "and the only one we're interested in is the **`Name`** property. Like the **`Name`** property of the form and other Visual Basic controls, the class's **`Name`** property allows us to refer to our object in code using a meaningful name."

I waited a second before starting to modify the default class module that had been created for us. Then I said:

"Let's change the **`Name`** of this class from **`Class1`** to **`Student`**..."

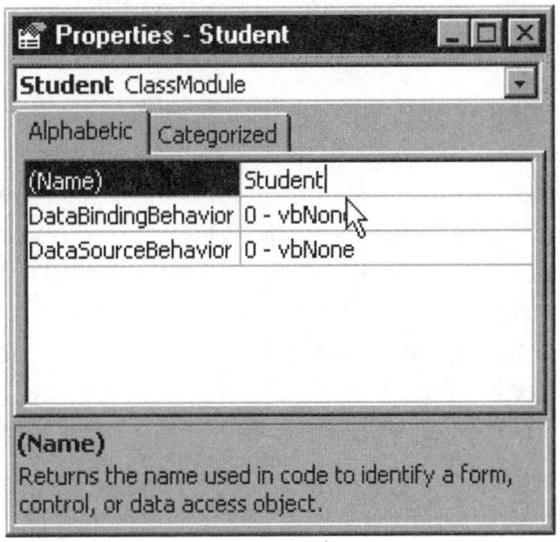

When I'd done this, Lou had a question:

"What about those other properties?" said Lou. "What are they for?"

"Those properties are really beyond the scope of what we're doing in this course," I said, "but I can tell you that they're used in more advanced object-oriented programs: in some programs, we can create objects that act as data sources for other objects, and these other two properties define how other objects can use the data sources that we're providing them with. As I say, that's all a little way beyond what we can cover in this course, but in a future course – who knows?"

It was time to get back to the property that we would be using in our Student Grades demo project.

"If we now take a look at our demo project using the Project Explorer window," I said, "we'll see that Visual Basic has assigned the class an internal name of **`Student`**:"

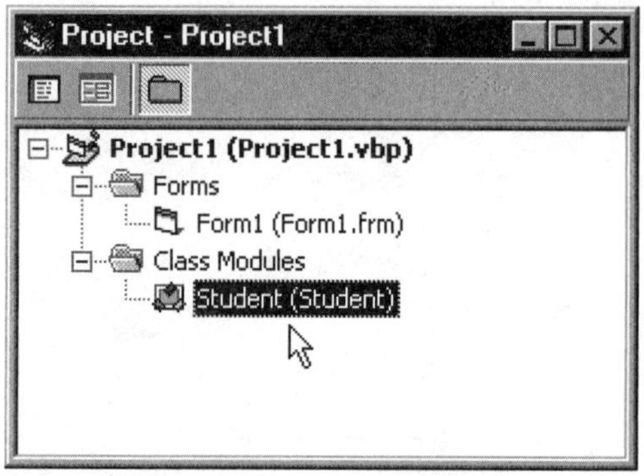

"Notice that Project Explorer is now separating the components of our project according to file type," I said. "Forms appear in a separate folder from class modules."

"I have a question concerning the **`Name`** property of the class module," Dave said. "I've read in some books that classes should be named beginning with a prefix of '**`cls`**', like a form is named with a prefix of '**`frm`**.' Then again, I've seen some other documentation – specifically, Microsoft documentation – that seems to be vague about this. What's your view on the subject?"

"I know what you mean, Dave," I replied, "I've seen the same contradictions. In terms of naming conventions for forms and Visual Basic controls, there seems to be a pretty clear-cut consensus. However, when it comes to naming classes, I know some programmers who prefix their names with '**`cls`**', and some who don't. My personal preference is to omit the '**`cls`**' prefix. By the way, you'll run into the same sorts of contradictions when it comes to naming collection objects. Some programmers construct their collection object name as the plural form of the object the collection holds: for example, if a collection object stores **`Widget`** objects as its items, then the collection object name would be **`'Widgets'`**. Other programmers construct the collection object name by prefixing the object name with '**`col`**'."

"So...which approach will we be taking here?" asked Melissa.

"We'll be taking a different tack in naming this demo project's collection object – whose items refer to **`Student`** objects. We'll be calling our collection object **`Course`**. One reason I do that is that it avoids any confusion with the **`Student`** object. And we'll do the same thing in the China Shop project: the collection object whose items refer to individual **`Dish`** objects will be named **`Order`**. Again, this is to avoid confusion here in the classroom. When you take your new found object skills back to your workplace, you should check your company's standards for naming classes, and be sure to adhere to those."

"So, programmers can have whatever preferences they like," Ward said, "but when they work for a company that has defined standards, then those are the standards that the programmer must stick to."

"Exactly," I said. "The main point, is that sticking to an accepted standard that's shared across an organization means that when other people have to maintain your code, compliance with the standard makes life easier for them – and the same applies when *we're* maintaining *their* code."

"Can you have more than one class module in your project?" Melissa asked.

"Yes, you can," I answered. "There's no limit to the number of classes you can have in your project – either classes you design yourself or classes that have been created by another programmer."

"I suppose," Ward said, "that a class module also has an external disk file name, just like a form?"

"That's right, Ward," I said. "To save a class module, all you need to do is click on the 'save' icon on the Visual Basic Toolbar, and Visual Basic will prompt you to save the class module, just as we're prompted to give our project or form a name the first time we save it."

To demonstrate this, I clicked on the Visual Basic Toolbar's 'save' icon, with this result:

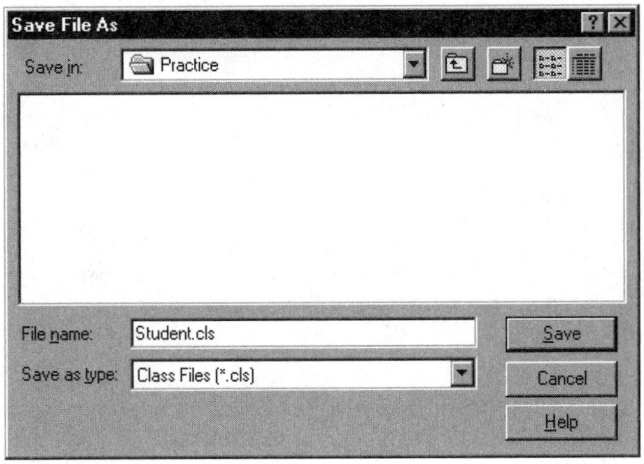

"Because we've already changed the class's **Name** property to **Student**," I said, "Visual Basic assumes that we want to save the class with the same external file name – and that will be fine on this occasion. Notice that the file extension for a class module file is '**cls**'.

I saved the class module as **Student.cls** in the **\VBFiles\Practice** directory on my PC.

"Notice that there is a slight change in the Project Explorer window," I said:

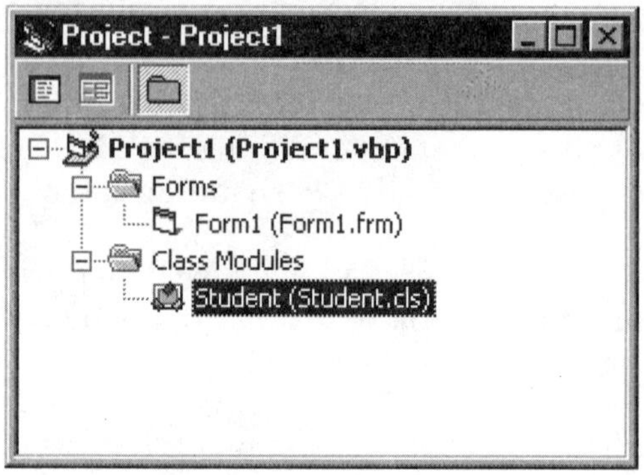

"It now reflects the external file name of the **Student** class – **Student.cls** – as well as the internal name that Visual Basic will use to refer to the class inside a program – **Student**," I continued. "At this point, what we have is an *empty* class module. We haven't actually added any of the code that will act as the template for any instances we create of the class. Let's start building the detailed template by creating the **properties** for the **Student** object."

The Student Class's Properties

"During the week," I said, "I did some object analysis on our grade computation scenario, and I identified the following **Student** attributes that our demonstration project is working with."

I then displayed this chart on the classroom projector:

Attribute	**Property Name**	**Variable Name**
Name	Name	m_strName
Mid-term Grade	MidTerm	m_intMidterm
Final Examination Grade	FinalExam	m_intFinalExam
Term Paper Grade	TermPaper	m_intTermPaper
Average	Average	m_sngAverage

"OK," I explained, "the left-hand column shows the real-world characteristics of the things – students – that we're going to use the object to represent. The middle column shows the property name of the **Student** object that I've identified to use for each of those characteristics. And the right-hand column shows the member name that we'll use to create each of those properties: remember, each property we create is defined as a variable that is a member – i.e. lives inside – the object that encapsulates it. So when we refer to the **Student** object's **Name** property, we're implicitly referring to the **m_strName** variable that lives inside the object and actually stores data values when the object is instantiated. Here's a graphic to summarize that:"

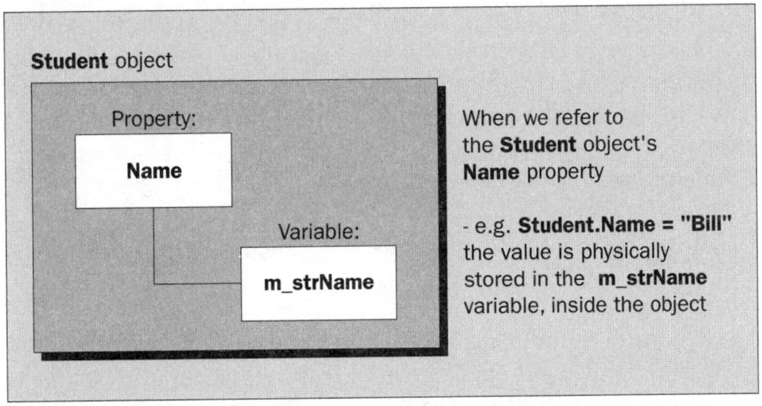

I gave everyone a minute to look the chart and the graphic over and familiarize themselves with what was going on.

"What about the class average?" Kate asked. "I don't see that on your chart. At the moment, the demo program is computing the average and displaying it on the form. Isn't that a property of the **Student** object?"

"Well, Kate, we *are* working with 'class average' as an attribute in the program," I replied, "but the class average is not really a property of the **Student** object – remember, a student object will represent an individual instance of a student. So, instead, the class average is an attribute derived from all the students – all the **Student** objects – together. This means that class average will be better represented in a collection object that we'll create in a couple of weeks – a collection called **Course**."

"I think I see what you mean," Kate agreed. "The course average doesn't really relate to an individual student, does it? It's actually an attribute of the course **as a whole**."

"That's right, Kate," I confirmed. "That means that it's not appropriate to use that attribute as part of the **Student** object – it belongs inside another object, one that reflects the global attributes that apply to all the students – the **Course** object."

"So, will class average be a *property* of the **Course** collection object?" asked Rhonda.

"Either a property, or a method," I answered, "I haven't quite made up my mind yet! As we discussed last week, sometimes the distinction can be hazy."

"I'm a little confused with the headings in your chart," Steve said. "I understand that the **Attribute** column is the real-world characteristic of the object, and **Property Name** is the name we'll use to refer to that attribute of the **Student** object within our programs...but what does the **Variable Name** column refer to?"

"Creating a property in a class module," I answered, "is a two-step process.First, the property is declared as a **Private** variable in the General Declarations section of the class module, using the name you see in the **Variable Name** column. However, that's not the name by which the property will be referred to by programmers using our object – that name will be established as the second step of the process, using something called **Property Let** and **Property Get** procedures."

"**Property Let** and **Property Get** procedures?" Valerie asked. "What on earth are they? I've never heard of those!"

"These procedures are unique to class modules," I answered. "But don't worry – they're not difficult to get to used to, and we'll explain them fully when the time comes to create them. For the moment, just remember that they're part of ensuring that the variable values stored inside an object can be accessed by the outside world, and manipulated in a consistent and robust way:"

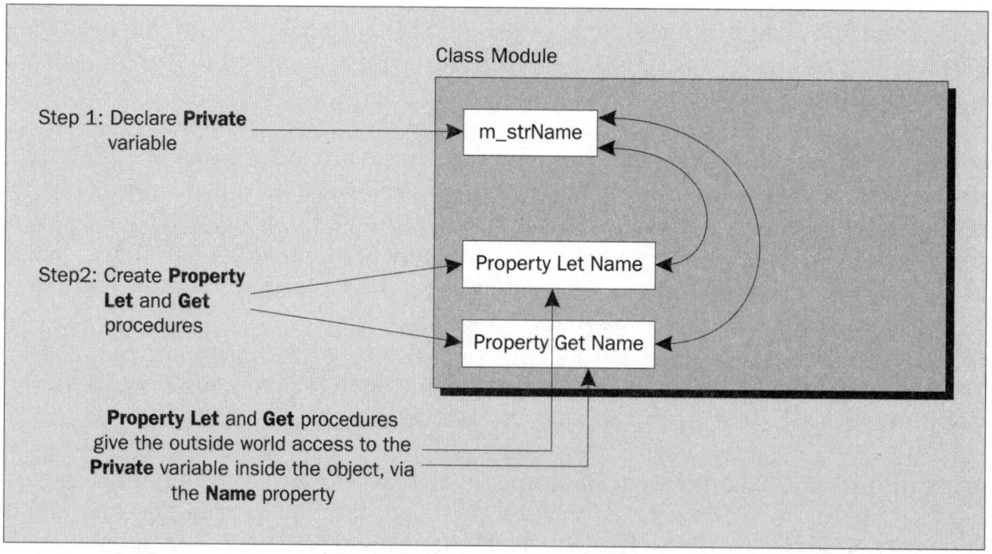

"We'll talk about these issues in a lot more detail shortly when we actually code up the properties. For now, just remember that the **Private** variable declaration defines the variable that we want to be encapsulated inside the object, and the **Property Let** and **Get** procedures give the rest of our program controlled access to these variables."

I paused for a few seconds before getting back to the nuts and bolts of our demo project.

"Now," I continued, "let's get on with creating the properties of the **Student** object, starting with the **Private** variable declarations."

Creating the Student Class's Properties

To set the creation process rolling, I added the following Variable declarations to the General Declarations section of the **Student** class module:

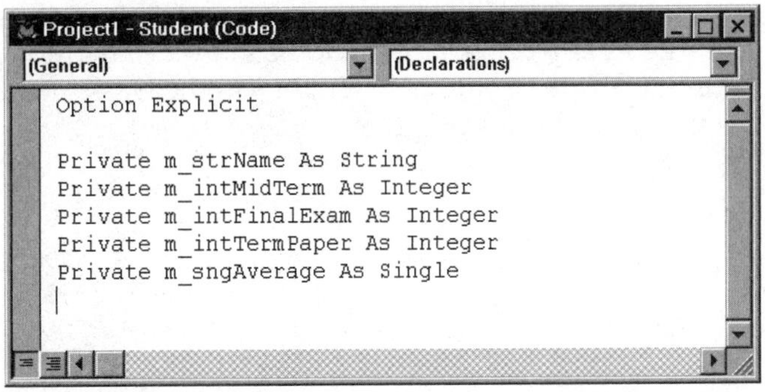
Project1 - Student (Code)
(General)
(Declarations)
Option Explicit
Private m_strName As String
Private m_intMidTerm As Integer
Private m_intFinalExam As Integer
Private m_intTermPaper As Integer
Private m_sngAverage As Single

"I must say I'm surprised to see **Option Explicit** coded here," Steve said. "The Code window for the class module really does remind me of a form's Code window!"

"You're right about that, Steve," I said. "In fact, **Option Explicit** serves the same purpose here in the General Declarations section of a class module as it does in the General Declarations section of a form – **Option Explicit** tells Visual Basic that any variable used in the class module must be explicitly declared up-front."

"I have a question," Ward said. "It's about the **Private** declaration of these variables. Correct me if I'm wrong, but **Private** in this context means that the variable can only be 'seen' by code that's within the class module – is that correct?"

"That's right, Ward," I replied. "Each one of these variables can only be accessed by any code written inside the rest of the class module."

"Well, if that's the case," Ward continued, "how will the person using the program – the programmer – be able to get at the values in the variables that live inside the **Student** object? How can they update them?"

"They won't be able to alter the variables *directly*," I answered, "and that's exactly the behavior we want. Since these variables are declared **`Private`** to the class, no code outside of the class itself will be able to directly access or update the value of any of these variables."

"Now *I'm* starting to get confused," Dave said. "If the programmer who uses this class module in his or her program can't write code that can access these variables, how will they be able to either retrieve or update these properties?"

"I see what's troubling you, Dave," I sympathized. "The answer is that there's actually a distinction between these **variables** and the **properties** stored inside the **`Student`** object itself. The programmer using the **`Student`** class module will be able to retrieve the value of the class's properties, and they'll also be able to update the value of those properties. What they won't be able to do is *directly* access these **`Private`** variables. Retrieval of values in the **`Private`** variables will be via the class module's **`Property Get`** procedure, and any update of these variables will be via the class module's **`Property Let`** procedure. Here, take a look at this diagram:"

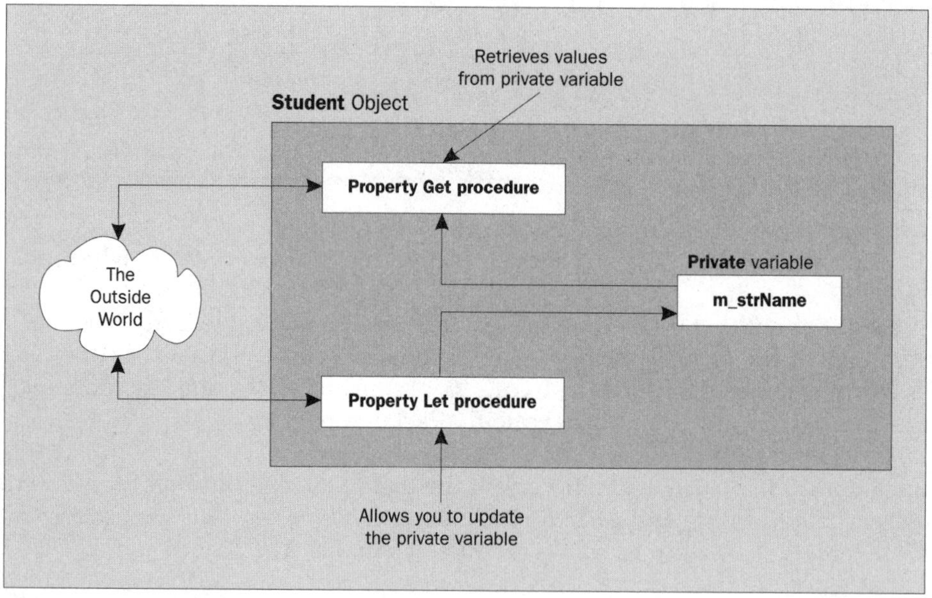

"So," I explained, "each property that we create for an object has it's values stored in an underlying **`Private`** variable, and each **`Private`** variable has its own dedicated **`Property Let`** and **`Property Get`** procedures that allow the rest of the world to communicate with these encapsulated variables."

"But why is that?" asked Rhonda. "Why do we have this extra layer? It sounds like unnecessary complication to me."

Property Let and Property Get procedures

"Well, Rhonda," I replied, "this is all tied up with the object-oriented principles that we've been talking about all through this course. We want to make sure that the objects we create are as independent as possible, so that altering one part of the program that they're components of doesn't have serious knock-on effects elsewhere. Furthermore, we want to ensure that any interactions that a programmer has are always carried out in a predictable and stable way; remember, the rest of the program depends on the fact that our objects will always behave in the same way every time that they're used – and that in turn means that they need to be sure that what's inside the object has always been manipulated in the way that the designer of the object meant it to be. That's where the `Property Get` and `Property Let` procedures come in – they're the procedures that our object makes available to the outside world. They have the update and access functionality for the object's internal variables – its properties – built into them, and they control how the outside world can change the properties that are encapsulated within the object. When we create the `Property Get` and `Let` procedures, we associate them with a property name, which itself refers to the underlying `Private` variable."

"It sounds to me as if the `Property Get` and `Property Let` procedures are like guard dogs," Kate said. "Is that their function?"

"That's a good analogy, Kate," I chuckled. "`Property Get` and `Property Let` procedures allow you to insulate the object's internal variable – which contains the values that we refer to by a property name – from direct update or retrieval from outside the object. It also allows you to have **read-only** properties, which you can create if you code a `Property Get` but not a `Property Let` procedure. You can also make **hidden** properties – which are properties of the class that are only accessible from within the class itself – you do that by coding neither a `Let` nor a `Get` procedure."

How Property Let Procedures Work

"Here's a schematic," I said, "that will shed some light on the role of the `Private` variable that stores the value of the property, and the `Property Let` procedure, which is what the object uses to allow the outside world to update the property's value:"

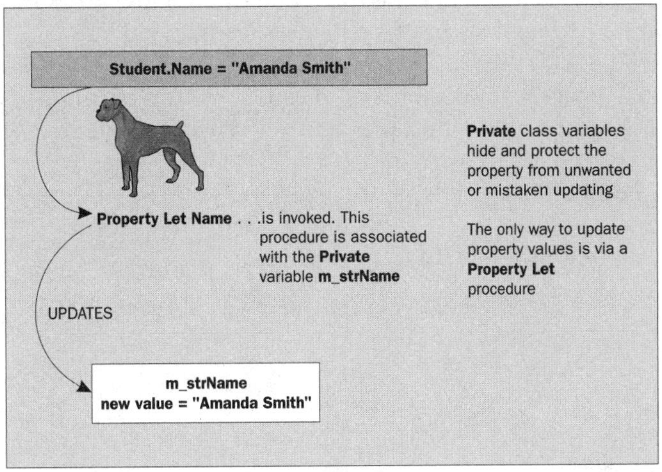

"Let me talk you through this, from the top of the diagram to the bottom," I said.

"First, we use some code to tell Visual Basic to change the **`Student`** object's **`Name`** property to a new value:

```
Student.Name = "Amanda Smith"
```

"This code syntax automatically invokes the **`Property Let`** procedure (inside the **`Student`** object) that's associated with the **`Name`** property – that's indicated by the line in the diagram that reads **`Property Let Name`**: we're implicitly using the **`Property Let`** procedure for the **`Name`** property, which operates on a **`Private`** variable that physically stores the property's value. The **`Property Let`** procedure takes the value that we've specified in our code – **`"Amanda Smith"`** and uses it to update the underlying **`m_strName`** variable.

"For instance," I said, "we have a **`Student`** object, which has a **`Name`** property. This property is called **`Name`**, but the **`Private`** variable that we declare to hold the property's value is called **`m_strName`**. Any program using the **`Student`** object will be able to retrieve the value of the **`Name`** property – but the **only** way to do it is by accessing the value of **`m_strName`** via the **`Property Let`** procedure. The **`Property Let`** procedure is the **interface** that exposes the property value to the world outside."

"Does the programmer using the **`Student`** object need to execute this **`Property Let`** procedure directly?" Rhonda asked.

"The **`Property Let`** and **`Property Get`** procedures are **not** explicitly executed by the programmer using the object," I said. "Instead, they're triggered automatically when the programmer refers to one of an object's properties by name using object dot notation."

"You mean when you type the name of an object in your code, followed by a period, and either a property or method name?" Melissa asked.

"That's exactly right, Melissa," I said. "For instance, this code would trigger the **`Student`** object's **`Property Let`** procedure that was associated with the **`Name`** property:"

```
Student.Name = "Amanda Smith"
```

"So that's all there is to it?" Ward said.

"That's all," I answered. "When you code the name of an object, followed by a dot, and then by a property name and then the equal sign, Visual Basic triggers that object's **`Property Let`** procedure – provided it has one. The **`Property Let`** procedure then assigns the value you've specified after the equal sign to the **`Private`** variable designated by the class to hold it. When we create the object, we create the **`Property Lets`** and **`Gets`**, and they're associated with the properties that they're designated to update and retrieve values from, and thereby with the underlying variables that hold that property's values. We'll see this for ourselves when we build up the **`Student`** class shortly."

"That's a bit circuitous, isn't it?" Linda commented.

"That's the guard dog approach to updating properties in an object," I said. "It's by design – to prevent the property from being updated in a way that the designer of the object did not intend – and it makes sure that the object's behavior is stable and predictable. **`Property Let`** procedures can also have code in them that restricts the type of updates that can be made to the property – and even limit the users who can make updates. One thing is for certain though – there's no way to update the value of the property without first going through the **`Property Let`** procedure. This is one of the features of object-oriented programming that makes sure our independent objects are used consistently, and that they remain reliable and trustworthy."

"I presume the **`Property Get`** procedure works in a similar way then?" Dorothy asked.

How Property Get Procedures Work

"That's right, Dorothy," I replied as I displayed another schematic on the classroom projector:

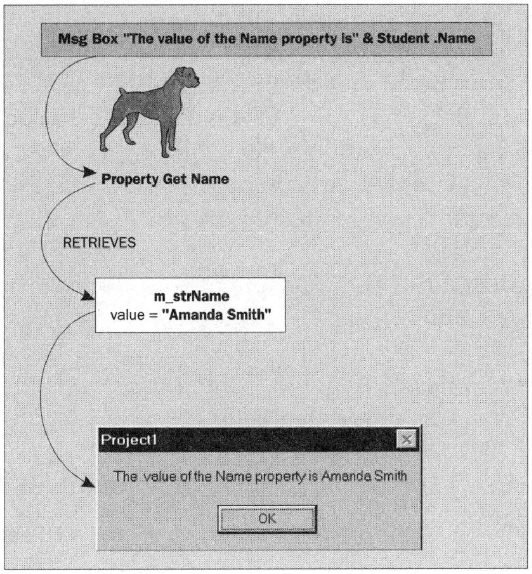

"Again," I explained, "the top line of the diagram is the line of code that we're using to access the property we're interested in – and again, that's the **Name** property of the **Student** object. This time, though, we're trying to display the value of the **Name** property in a message box:"

```
Msgbox "The value of the Name property is " & Student.Name
```

"As with updating one of an object's properties," I said, "since the variable **m_strName** is **Private** to the class module, the only way to retrieve the value of the **Student** object's **Name** property is by triggering its **Property Get** procedure – which is what happens in the diagram where you see the **Property Get Name** line: this represents the automatic invocation of the **Property Get** procedure for the **Name** property. And once again, Visual Basic recognizes that **Name** is a property of the **Student** object. And, as we've created a **Property Get** procedure that's associated with the **Name** property, the **Get** procedure executes and retrieves the value of the **Name** property from the underlying **m_strName** private variable. Then it displays it in the message box."

"You've mentioned this several times already," Rhonda said, "that the object's **Property Get** or **Let** procedures would be triggered 'if the class module has one'. I guess I'm just having a hard time understanding why you wouldn't code one of each for each property in your class. But apparently they aren't mandatory – is that right?"

"Yes, that's right, Rhonda," I confirmed. "There's no requirement to have **Property Let** and **Get** procedures coded for each **Private** variable you declare in the General Declarations section of your class module. As I mentioned a little while ago, if you code **neither** a **Property Get** nor a **Let** procedure, you in effect have an object property which can only be accessed internally – that is, from inside of the object itself. And, believe me, Visual Basic has some of these. If you do code a **Property Get** but no **Property Let**, you have a situation where the property can be **retrieved** from outside the class module but can't be **updated** outside of it – that's what's known as a **read-only** property. Again, there are instances of read-only properties in Visual Basic forms and controls."

"I guess a notable example of this is the **Name** property of the form or control at run-time," Dave said.

"Dave's right," I agreed. "The **Name** properties of both the form and of any Visual Basic control, while updateable at design time, are read-only at run-time."

I paused, then said: "OK, it's time to put all this into action in our Student Grades demo program."

Back to the Demo

"In fact, I continued, we'll start to see these principles in action when we make the **`Average`** property of our **`Student`** object read-only. We'll do that by coding a **`Property Get`** procedure for it, but we won't add a corresponding **`Property Let`**."

"How will the value of the **`Average`** property be updated then?" Tom said. "Won't we need a value in that property to display on the form?"

"That's an excellent point, Tom," I said. "We will be displaying the value of the **`Student`** object's **`Average`** property on the form. However, the computation of the **`Average`** property is based entirely on the values of other properties of the **`Student`** object – for that reason, there's no need to make the **`Average`** property updateable **outside** of the class module."

"I see," Valerie said, "the **`Average`** property will be computed internally within the **`Student`** object itself."

"You've got the idea," I said. "Preventing a property like this from being updated is a great concept – you don't want to rely on the programmer using the **`Student`** object knowing that they shouldn't be updating this property – better to *prevent* them from doing so."

"I think more of this will make sense to us," Dave said, "if we can see these **`Property Get`** and **`Property Let`** procedures in action."

"I agree, Dave," I said. "Let's code the first pair of **`Property Get`** and **`Property Let`** procedures – and let's start with the **`Name`** property of the **`Student`** class. In individual instances of the **`Student`** object, this is the property that will store – in the underlying **`Private`** variable – the name of the student."

Coding the Name Property's Property Let Procedure

I started by keying all of the following code for **`Student`** class's **`Name`** property's **`Property Let`** procedure into the General section of the **`Student`** class module:

```
Property Let Name(ByVal strNew As String)

m_strName = strNew

End Property
```

"To create the **`Property Get`** and **`Property Let`** procedures," I said, "all we need to do is start typing in the class module's code window."

I then displayed this summary chart on the classroom projector to clarify what the different parts of the class module's Code window referred to:

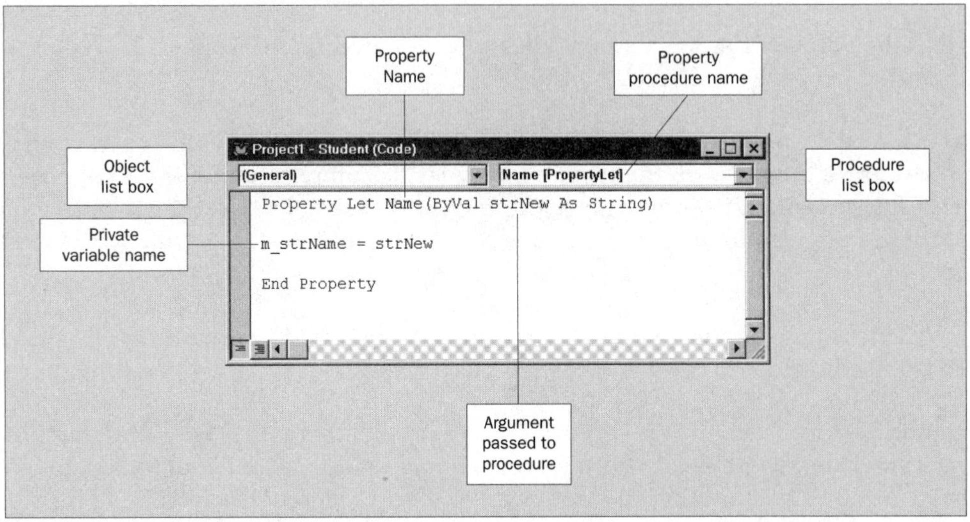

"The look and feel of the class module's Code window," I said, "is similar to the form's Code window. As you can see, at the top of the Code window are two drop-down list boxes. The one on the left is the **Object** list box, just as with the form's Code window, and the one on the right is called the **Procedure** list box – again, just like the form's Code window. **`Property Let`** and **`Property Get`** procedures appear in the General section of the class module, and if you look in the procedure list box, you'll see the name of the **`Property Let`** procedure for the **`Name`** property listed. Later on, you'll see that any methods that we code in the class will also appear in the General section."

"Can you discuss the objects list box a little more, please?" Mary said. "I just clicked on it, and I noticed there's only one object listed there – the **`Class`** object."

"That's right," Rhonda agreed. "I don't see any event procedures listed either. Why is that?"

"The only object that you'll see in the Objects list box is the **`Class`** object," I said, "and you won't see any event procedures listed in the Procedures list box for the General section. That's because the class module doesn't contain any controls. Remember, the procedures that go in the General section of a form are things like its form or controls. The class module is really just one big Code window – there are no controls to manage, so you won't see any other objects besides the one for the class itself."

I then clicked on the object list box:

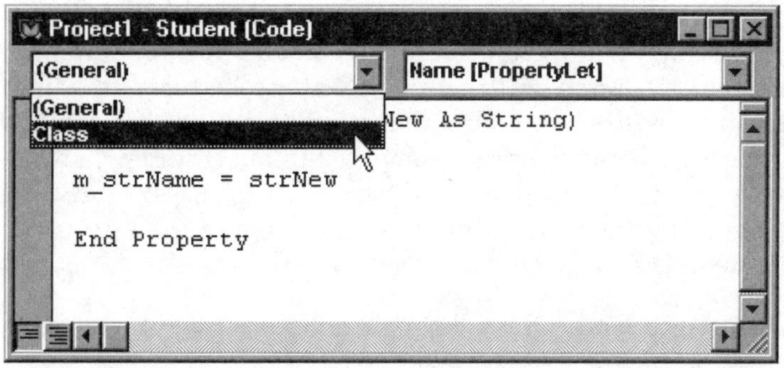

"If we then go down and select the **Class** object, under the General section, we can see that it reacts to two events of its own, " I said, "the Initialize and Terminate events – they're listed in the Procedures list box:"

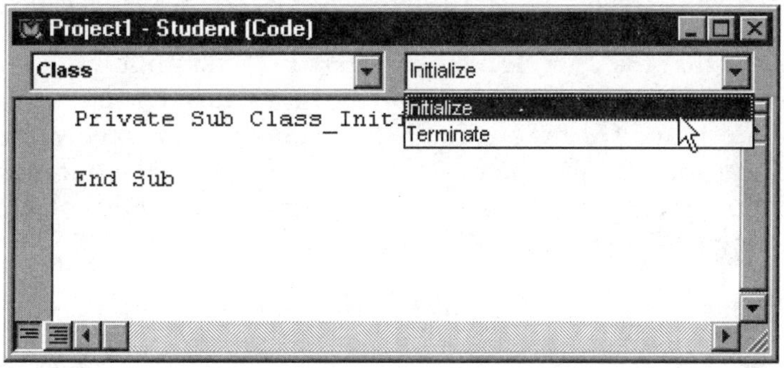

"We'll discuss both of these in more detail a little later," I said. "But I can tell you now that the class's Initialize event procedure is triggered when an object based on this class is instantiated – which, as we all know by now, is the fancy term meaning that the object has been born. The **Terminate** event procedure takes place either when an object has been set to **Nothing**, or when all references to the object fall out of scope – meaning that there's no code using the object any longer. The **Initialize** event procedure is a convenient place to put any code that you want executed when the object is first created. When we code the **Dish** object of the China Shop, the **Initialize** event procedure is where we'll put the code to read the **Prices.txt** file for current inventory prices."

"Can you explain the **Property Let** procedure header, please?" Chuck asked. "I've never seen that format before."

I displayed the **Property Let** procedure header on the classroom projector again:

```
Property Let Name(By Val strNew As String)
```

"You're probably all used to seeing the **`Private Sub`** statement in the many event procedures you've come across so far in your programming careers," I said. "However, the **`Property Let`** and **`Property Get`** procedures are slightly different. With the **`Property Let`** procedure, remember that what's going to happen is that a programmer will trigger this procedure via an assignment statement somewhere in their code. The value to be assigned to the property will be passed to the **`Property Let`** procedure, and the **`Property Let`** procedure will then update the **`Private`** variable which actually holds the value of the property."

I waited to let the class absorb this before I went on.

"Instead of beginning with the **`Private Sub`** statement," I continued, "**`Property Let`** procedures begin with the words '**`Property Let`**' followed by the name of the property itself that the **`Property Let`** refers to. What follows in the parentheses is vitally important – it's the argument that the **`Property Let`** procedure uses to update the underlying **`Private`** variable that actually stores the value of the property. It's this argument, in this case **`strNew`**,that's passed to the **`Property Let`** procedure. This argument is passed when the programmer using our object assigns a value to the property using an equals sign – like this..."

```
Student.Name = "Amanda Smith"
```

"The value to the right of the equals sign is passed to the **`Property Let`** when this code's dot notation automatically invokes the **`Property Let`** procedure."

"So you're saying that, in this example," Dave said, "the value of the argument **`strNew`** will be **`Amanda Smith`**?"

"Exactly," I said. "Because of the way that we coded the **`Property Let`** procedure, Visual Basic expects us to pass it an argument – remember that we included the argument in the procedure definition:"

```
Property Let Name(ByVal strNew As String)
```

"Here, the code in the parentheses defines the argument. The key thing is that the **`Property Let`** expects to be passed a value that it can assign to **`strNew`**, which is the argument name we've defined here. The procedure's expectation of receiving an argument to populate **`strNew`** is satisfied by the value that we key to the right of the equals sign in our code. This is where the **`Property Let`** procedure expects it to be. And once the value of **`strNew`** is passed to the **`Property Let`** procedure, the procedure uses it to update the value of the **`Private`** **`m_strName`** variable with this line of code:"

```
m_strName = strNew
```

"That makes more sense to me, now" Rhonda said. "And did you say that it's impossible for the programmer who's using this class module in their program to *directly* update the value of **m_strName**?"

"That's right, Rhonda," I said. "Because the variable **m_strName** was declared as a **Private** variable, only code from within the class module itself can access this variable. The other face of the **Property Let** – which allows us to update the **Private** variable – is the **Property Get** procedure. Let's take a look at the **Property Get** procedure, which is used to return the value of a property – stored as **Private** variable inside the object, remember – back to the code using the object."

Coding the Name Property's Property Get Procedure

I then keyed this code into the **Student** class's General section and displayed it on the classroom projector:

```
Property Get Name() As String

Name = m_strName

End Property
```

"This is the code for the **Property Get** procedure of the **Name** property," I went on. "Notice that it's similar to the **Name** property's **Property Let** procedure – the main difference here is that there's no argument passed to the procedure. Remember, when the **Property Get** procedure is triggered, the value of the **Private** variable storing the property value inside the object is passed back to the part of the program that called the **Property Get** procedure."

"That almost sounds like what a Visual Basic function does," Dave said, "it returns a value to the program that calls it."

"Very similar, Dave," I agreed. "In fact, take a look at this line of code:"

```
Property Get Name() As String

Name = m_strName

End Property
```

"Notice," I said, "that the name of the object's property – in this case, **Name** – is being assigned the contents of the underlying **Private** variable that holds its value. This is the same as the format for a Visual Basic function, in which the return value of the function is assigned to the name of the Function. Here, we're assigning the value of the **Private** variable to the name of the **Property** itself."

"Excuse me," Kevin said, "can you go over how the **Property Get** procedure would be triggered again, please?"

"Sure thing, Kevin," I said. "This code would do it:"

```
MsgBox Student.Name
```

"As soon as Visual Basic sees the object dot notation after the name of the **Student** object," I said, "it determines whether or not the **Student** object has a **Property Get** procedure for the **Name** property – that is, whether we've coded one or not, as this was an object that we created ourselves! And, if there is one, Visual Basic triggers it, returning the value of the **Name** property back to the program calling it."

"This is weird stuff," Rhonda said, "but so far, I think I'm getting it. Are methods and events just as easy?"

"They're easier, if anything," I said. "Objects aren't really that difficult to work with – you just need to have a solid foundation first, which is what we've spent the last few weeks giving you. Let's reinforce what we've done today by coding the **Property Let** and **Get** procedures for the rest of the **Student** object's properties."

First though, I let the students take a coffee break – they'd had a lot to take in today so far, and there was some more to come!

Creating the Rest of the Student Class's Get and Let Procedures

We resumed after the break, refreshed and full of coffee.

"As I say," I began, "what we need to do next is finish coding the rest of the **Property Let** and **Property Get** procedures for the other properties now."

I then spent about ten minutes entering the remainder of these **Property Get** and **Property Let** procedures into the **Student** class module. Remember that there will be no **Property Let** procedure for the **Average** property, as it's a read-only property.

The Property Get Procedures in Full

First, I got everybody to ensure that they had coded the **Property Get** procedure for the **Name** property:

```
Property Get Name() As String

Name = m_strName

End Property
```

"Remember," I said, "the word that you type after the **Property Get** statement – **Name**, in this case – is the word that defines the name of the property. It's this name that you use to refer to the property in code, so it's important to get it right and use it consistently across in your corresponding **Get** and **Let** procedures. The next line..."

```
Name = m_strName
```

"...is very important." I explained to the class that:

> **This is the line that associates the name of the property – Name – with the underlying Private variable that we declared in the General Declarations section of the class. This is where the link is made between the name of the property and the Private variable that stores its value.**

Next, we coded the **Property Get** procedures for the **MidTerm**, **FinalExam**, and **TermPaper** properties. Again, all of these are keyed into the class's General section:

```
Property Get MidTerm() As Integer

Midterm = m_intMidterm

End Property
```

```
Property Get FinalExam() As Integer

FinalExam = m_intFinalExam

End Property
```

```
Property Get TermPaper() As Integer

TermPaper = m_intTermPaper

End Property
```

"The **Property Get** procedure for the **Average** property," I continued, "is a little more complex than the other properties. When the **Property Get** procedure for this property is triggered, that's when we calculate the **Average** property based on the values of the mid-term, final exam, and term paper grades. Here's the code to key for this property's **Property Get** routine:"

```
Property Get Average() As Single

m_sngAverage = (m_intMidterm * 0.4) +
               ↳(m_intFinalExam * 0.4) +
               ↳(m_intTermPaper * 0.2)
Average = m_sngAverage

End Property
```

"OK," I said, "so much for the **`Property Get`** procedures. We now have the procedure in place to let other parts of our program access the values that are stored in each of the properties in the student object. Next, we need to turn our attention to the **`Property Let`** procedures, so that our properties are updateable."

The Property Let Procedures in Full

This is the code to key into the General section for the **`Property Let`** procedures for the **`Student`** object's properties:

Again, I first made sure that everybody had correctly coded the **`Name`** property's **`Property Let`** procedure:

```
Property Let Name(ByVal strNew As String)

m_strName = strNew

End Property
```

I reminded the students that the second word in the parentheses was the name of the argument that any code invoking this procedure would pass its values into. I also pointed out that this line...

```
m_strName = strNew
```

...was the active and critical part of the **`Let`** procedure.

> **This line takes the value that's been passed to the strNew argument by the calling program, and assigns this passed value to the Private variable that underlies the Property. This is how the property value is updated.**

Then we moved on to code the **`Property Let`** procedures for the **`MidTerm`**, **`FinalExam`**, and **`TermPaper`** properties:

```
Property Let MidTerm(ByVal intNew As Integer)

m_intMidterm = intNew

End Property
```

```
Property Let FinalExam(ByVal intNew As Integer)

m_intFinalExam = intNew

End Property
```

```
Property Let TermPaper(ByVal intNew As Integer)

m_intTermPaper = intNew

End Property
```

"Just to make sure we don't forget any property procedures," I said, "it's a good idea to click on the procedure drop-down list box. We should have a **`Property Get`** and **`Property Let`** procedure coded for each and every property except **`Average`** – which only has a **`Property Get`** procedure:"

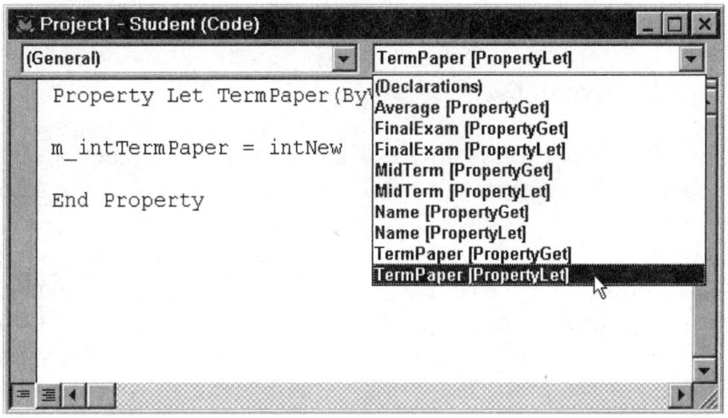

"There you are," I said, "we've now created the interface procedures that will let the outside world interact with our **`Student`** object's properties: the **`Property Get`** procedures allow programmers to **read** the properties, and the **`Property Let`** procedures allow the programmer to **update** the properties."

"I know you've mentioned this before," Rhonda said, "but why is it that we don't have a **Property Let** procedure for the **Average** property?"

"The **Average** property," I said, "is a read-only property of the **Student** object, and its value will be calculated within the **Student** object itself – we don't want the programmer who used the **Student** object to be able to update the **Average** property – although we don't mind if they view it. Incidentally," I went on, "the calculation is executed when the **Average** property's **Property Get** procedure is invoked."

"I just noticed," Blaine said, "that the **Property Get** procedure for the **Average** property isn't like the others. Is that because the calculation of the student's average is taking place with it?"

"Exactly, Blaine," I answered. "The **Property Get** procedure for the **Average** property is a perfect place to put that code:"

```
Property Get Average() As Single

m_sngAverage = (m_intMidterm * 0.4) +
               ↳(m_intFinalExam * 0.4) +
               ↳(m_intTermPaper * 0.2)
Average = m_sngAverage

End Property
```

"The calculation is encapsulated inside the object, and is done whenever the **Average** property is accessed – which will always be via the **Property Get** procedure that acts as the property's guard dog."

"I know what we're doing here is encapsulating the logic for the calculation of the student's grade into the **Student** object," Dave said, "but isn't there a down-side to this? Suppose the Professor comes back to us and tells us that she wants to change the percentages allotted to each of the grade components. For instance, suppose the mid-term examination percentage is changed to 35% and the final exam percentage is raised to 45%."

"In that case, Dave," I said, "we have two choices. First, we can easily modify the code in the **Property Get** procedure of the **Average** property to accommodate the change. Then we should notify the programmers using our **Student** object that a change has been made to the object's underlying **Student** class, and that if they have compiled programs using it, they need to recompile the program."

"How's that?" Steve said.

"Well, Steve," I said, "when an object changes its behavior, any programmer using the object in a compiled program needs to recompile the program with the updated version of the object in order to incorporate its new behavior. But believe me, this is a much better scenario than we would have if the programmer wasn't using the object."

"Why?" Rhonda asked.

"Suppose the Professor's grade calculation logic was explicitly coded in the `Click` event procedures of hundreds of programs," I said. "If her logic changed, then she would have to notify each one of those programmers to change their code to reflect the new logic – and human nature being what it is, mistakes would be made, not everyone would make the changes, etc. I think you'd have to admit that having the designer of the object change the code in a single class module is much cleaner than having individual programmers modify each of their programs individually."

"I'm beginning to love this idea of objects," Bob said. "Something like this could have saved me a whole load of work in the past. What you're saying is that if an object changes in the way that Dave suggested with the grade calculation logic, all that needs to be done is to change the object, and then have everyone using the object recompile the program with the updated class module?"

"That's right, Bob," I confirmed.

"You implied that there's another solution to the problem of the Professor changing her grade calculation logic?" Valerie said.

"Yes. Another alternative," I went on, "particularly if we believed that the Professor would be changing the grade components quite often, would be to create properties to represent the percentages of each component in the final numeric grade. For instance, we could create properties called **`MidTermPercentage`**, **`FinalExamPercentage`**, and **`TermPaperPercentage`**. As part of the **`Student`** object's **`Initialize`** event procedure, we could assign initial values, and still give the programmer using the **`Student`** object the ability to change the percentages if necessary."

"What's that?" Kate asked. "How do you assign an initial value to a property?"

"In the **`Initialize`** event procedure of the class," I said. "The **`Initialize`** event procedure is an ideal place for housekeeping like that."

"It would be great," Steve said, "if there was some way to change the object that didn't require that every program using the object be recompiled."

"Actually, there *is* a way, Steve," I said, "and that's to compile your object into something called a **Visual Basic Component**."

"Will you be showing us how to do that?" Dorothy asked.

"I'll do that in our penultimate class," I said, "but I must warn you, compiling objects into components is a feature that's only available in the Professional and Enterprise Editions of Visual Basic. Neither the Learning Edition or Working Model Edition supports this feature – but I think it's important enough to show you how to do it. It provides the most flexibility in terms of objects, since programs accessing your object do so at run time – so any programs using your object see the latest features that you've coded into it."

"That sounds great," Ward said. "By the way, I noticed that you used `ByVal` in the `Property Let` procedures..."

```
Property Let Name(ByVal strNew As String)
```

"...is that required?"

"Using `ByVal` in the `Property Let` procedures," I said, "is not actually *formally* required, but Microsoft does recommend passing arguments to `Property Let` procedures **By Value** (`ByVal`) instead of **By Reference** (`ByRef`), which is the default. For those of you who aren't familiar with `ByVal` and `ByRef`, I'll summarize: when you pass an argument to a procedure **By Reference**, an address is passed to the procedure – not the actual value. Passing an argument `ByVal`, on the other hand, passes the actual value of the variable to the procedure – and that's the Microsoft recommendation."

"OK," I resumed, "let's put this into practice, by actually using the class module that we've created."

Using the Student Class in the Demo Program

"What I'd like to do now," I said, "is modify the code in our grade calculation demonstration project to use the `Student` object for calculating a student's numeric class average. I think you'll find that using the `Student` object in a program, while not as easy as using a control in the Toolbox, is not bad at all."

"Won't we be coding any methods or events for the `Student` object?" Valerie asked.

"I'm glad you asked that, Valerie," I replied. "I won't be showing you how to write methods or how to raise events in our objects until next week. For today, we'll be concentrating on working with the properties of the `Student` object we just created – and later today, we'll create the `Dish` object of the China Shop project, and its properties."

"Do we need to do anything to include the **Student** object in our project?" Melissa asked.

"All you need to do, Melissa, is ensure that the **Student** class module appears in the Project Explorer window," I said. "If you see it there, that means that you can refer to the **Student** object from within your program."

I then brought up the code window for the **Student** demo project's form and modified the **Click** event procedure of the **cmdCalculate** command button to look like this next code listing. As usual, changed code is highlighted, but notice that we're losing the chunk of code that calculates **m_sngFinalGrade** – that functionality has been taken over by the **Student** object:

```
Private Sub cmdCalculate_Click()

Dim stuNew As New Student

If txtName.Text = "" Then
    MsgBox "Enter the student's Name"
    txtName.SetFocus
    Exit Sub
End If

If txtMidTerm.Text = "" Then
    MsgBox "Enter the student's Midterm Grade"
    txtMidterm.SetFocus
    Exit Sub
End If

If txtFinalExam.Text = "" Then
    MsgBox "Enter the student's Final Exam Grade"
    txtFinalExam.SetFocus
    Exit Sub
End If

If txtTermPaper.Text = "" Then
    MsgBox "Enter the student's Term paper Grade"
    txtTermPaper.SetFocus
    Exit Sub
End If
```

```
stuNew.Name = txtName.Text
stuNew.MidTerm = Val(txtMidTerm.Text)
stuNew.FinalExam = Val(txtFinalExam.Text)
stuNew.TermPaper = Val(txtTermPaper.Text)

lblFinalGrade.Caption =
    ↳"The grade for " & txtName.Text & " is " &
    ↳stuNew.Average &
    ↳". Click on the 'Add Record' button to save the record."

Set stuNew = Nothing

End Sub
```

As I was entering the code into the **`Click`** event procedure, I typed the period following the name of the object variable **`stuName`**, and this happened:

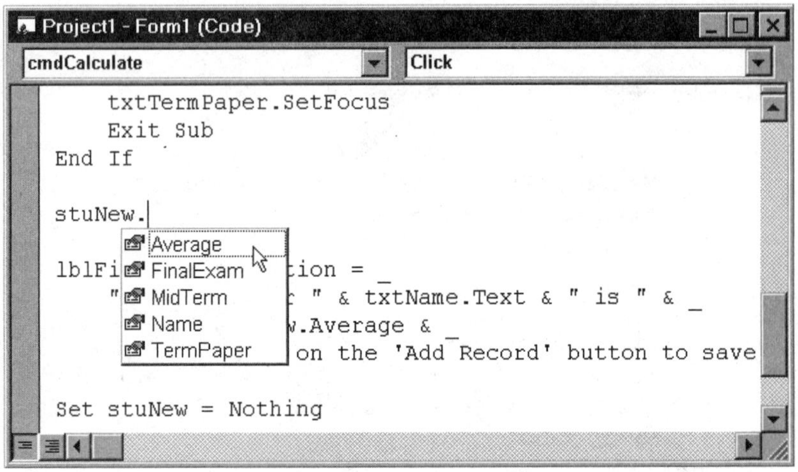

"Wow," Kate said, "the properties of the **`Student`** object show up in the List Members window. That's great!"

"That's one of the benefits of object-oriented programming," I said. "Properties and methods of our own object show up in the List Members window, just like the properties and methods of the standard pre-defined Visual Basic objects do."

I continued to enter the rest of the code into the **`Click`** event procedure.

"I'll explain this code in a minute," I said, "but first I want to run the program, and click on the Calculate Grade button to show you that the program's behavior hasn't changed."

I ran the program, entered grades for the same fictitious student into the text boxes on the form, and clicked on the Calculate Grade button:

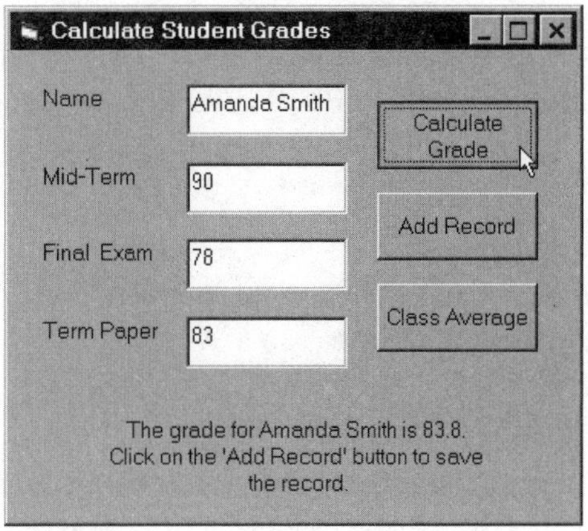

"As you can see," I said, "the program behaves identically to the way it did before. However, in this version of the code the **cmdCalculate** event procedure is now using the **Student** object, whose 'cookie cutter' template is coded in the **Student** class module. Let's take a look at that code now. I'm betting that you pretty much know what's going on in there already, because of all of the work we've done with Visual Basic objects over the last few weeks. Let's start with the most important line of code – this one:"

```
Dim stuNew As New Student
```

"This is the declaration of the object variable **stuNew**, which will be used to refer to the instance of the **Student** object that is instantiated when this code runs. You should all be comfortable with object variable declarations by now. Did you notice, by the way, that when I typed the object name **Student** into the Code window, the List Members window displayed the **Student** object as an available object type: "

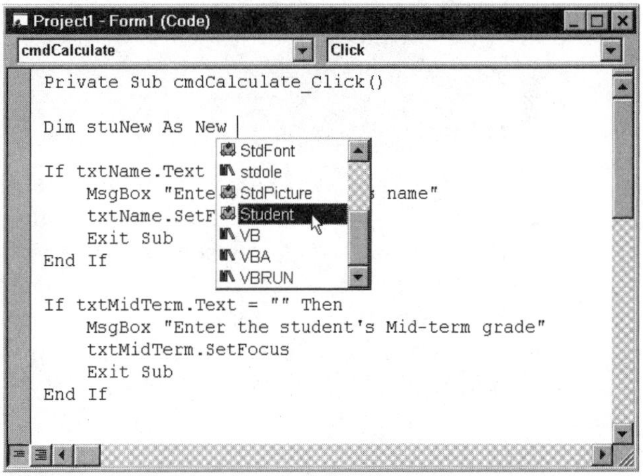

"Actually, I didn't notice that the first time around," Ward said. "Where does Visual Basic get the name **Student** in the List Members window? Is that the **Name** property of the class?"

"That's right, Ward," I said. "That's where the name of the object that will be displayed in the List Members window comes from. The rest of this code is pretty straightforward. We still have the section of code devoted to ensuring that the user enters all of the required information for the student. These next four lines take the values found in the four text boxes on the form and assign them to the respective properties of the **Student** object using object dot notation:"

```
stuNew.Name = txtName.Text
stuNew.MidTerm = Val(txtMidTerm.Text)
stuNew.FinalExam = Val(txtFinalExam.Text)
stuNew.TermPaper = Val(txtTermPaper.Text)
```

"As you know from our previous discussion," I said, "those assignment statements will trigger the **Property Let** procedures of the respective properties found in the **Student** object. Here's the line of code that displays the student's average in the **Caption** property of **lblFinalGrade**:"

```
lblFinalGrade.Caption =
    ↳"The grade for " & txtName.Text & " is " &
    ↳stuNew.Average &
    ↳". Click on the 'Add Record' button to save the record."
```

"Notice how we've modified the code by concatenating the **Average** property of the **stuNew** object to the label's caption..."

"Finally," I continued, "we follow the Microsoft recommendation by explicitly setting our object variable to nothing:"

```
Set stuNew = Nothing
```

"I'm sure you all realize," I said, "how much simpler this code is than the previous version. Using object dot notation is second nature for Visual Basic programmers, plus we've encapsulated the grade calculation into the **Student** object itself. In our role as the designer of the **Student** object, we know that there's quite a bit going on behind the scenes. However, in our other role, as the programmer using the **Student** object in our program, what could be easier than assigning three properties of the **Student** object values, and then displaying a fourth property – **Average** – in the **Caption** property of a label?"

"You're right," Ward said. "This is easy. I can't wait to get to work on Monday and start creating objects!"

I told everyone that I thought it would be a great idea if we now ran the program in **Step Mode**.

Inside the Demo Program

"Running the program in Step Mode will give us a chance to see the execution of our code line by line," I said. "It will also give us a chance to see the operation of the `Student` object in action – in particular I think you'll be interested in seeing when the `Student` object is born, how the `Property Let` and `Property Get` procedures are executed, and finally when the `Student` object dies."

"Before you do that," Steve said, "I have a problem. I've been coding the `Student` object along with you, and when I typed the line of code to declare an object variable into the `Click` event procedure of the command button, I didn't see `Student` as an available object in the List Members window. I didn't think too much of it, but then when I ran the program, and clicked on the command button, my program bombed at the line of code where I tried to assign a value to the `MidTerm` property of the `Student` object. What did I do wrong?"

I had a strong suspicion that I knew what was wrong, so I took a quick walk to Steve's PC to check out his problem. It didn't take me long to discover what was up.

"The reason you didn't see `Student` in the List Members window," I said, "is because you don't have the `Student` class included in your project. You must have coded the class module first, saved it, then started a new `Standard.EXE` project. Unlike Visual Basic objects, which for the most part are automatically included in your project, you need to ensure that the class module for any object you've created of your own is included in your project. At this point, all you need to do to include the `Student` object is to select Project | Add Class from the Visual Basic menu bar and, instead of specifying a New class, specify an Existing class, then find and add the `Student` class to the project that way."

I waited for Steve to go through those steps and, in less than a minute, he had added the `Student` class module to his project, and his version of the demo project was running fine.

"Now I have a question," Melissa said. "I know that it's unlikely, but suppose the programmer using the `Student` object in his or her program is not familiar with properties, methods and events that the `Student` object contains – is there any way, other than contacting the designer of the object, to discover what they are?"

"Good question, Melissa," I answered. "Yes there is – the programmer, once they've included the class module in their project, can always use the Object Browser to learn more about the `Student` object."

Viewing the Student Class with the Object Browser

To demonstrate, I opened the Object Browser (by selecting View | Object Browser from the Visual Basic menu bar), typed the word **`Student`** into the search box, and pressed the *Enter* key:

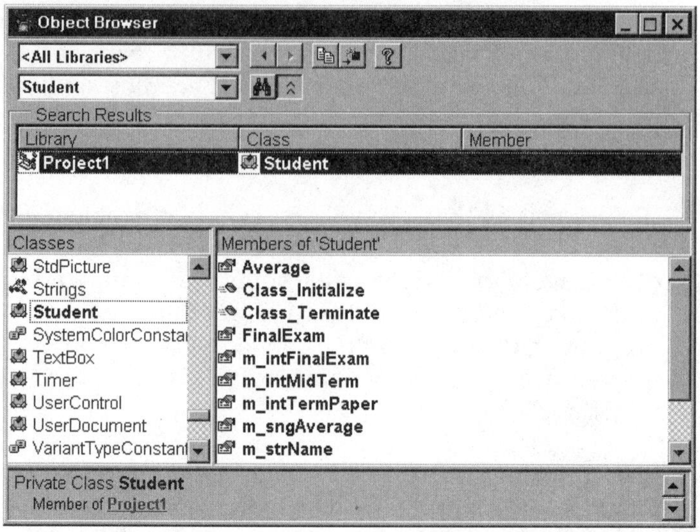

"If you use the Object Browser," I said, "make sure that <All Libraries> is selected in the Project/Library list box at the very top. Otherwise you won't see the objects contained in any of the class modules you've included in your project."

"Now," I continued, "as you can see, to the left in the lower half of the Object Browser is a window containing the classes available to our project."

"Notice that the **`Student`** class is highlighted..."

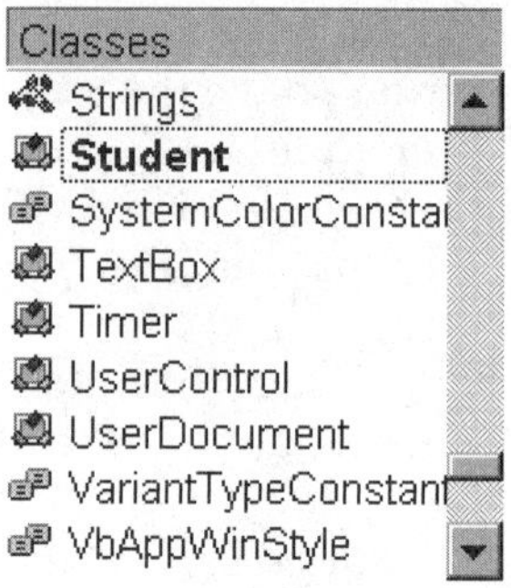

"...and that, if you look to the right, there's a Window containing the members of the **`Student`** class – **members** just means the properties, methods and events of a class. Let's click on the **`Average`** property in the right-hand window."

I did, and the display of the object Browser changed:

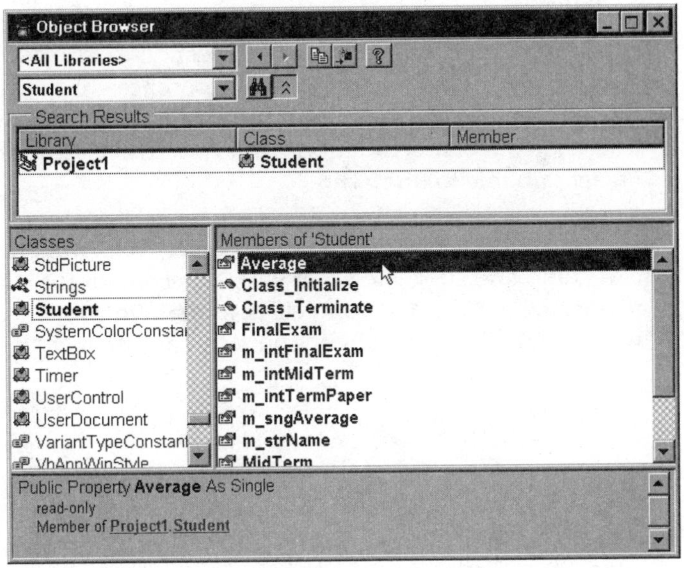

"Look at the bottom pane of the Object Browser," I said. "You'll notice that Visual Basic is telling us that the **`Average`** property is a Single data type, and that it's a read-only property."

"That *is* interesting," Tom said. "So, we can gather some information about the class by using the Object Browser."

"You mentioned a little earlier," Valerie said, "that an object's **`Initialize`** event procedure is triggered when the object is born, and that its **`Terminate`** event procedure is triggered when the object dies. When exactly do those events occur? When exactly is an object born? When exactly does it die?"

"Those are good questions, Valerie," I said, "and I hope to be able to show you those event procedures when we run this program in Step mode. In general, though, the span of an object's lifetime follows the same rules as for the lifetime of an ordinary variable. For instance, an object declared within an event procedure dies when the event procedure ends. An object declared in the General Declarations section of a form dies when the form is unloaded."

"If an object dies eventually anyway," Ward asked, "then why do we set the object variable to **`Nothing`**?"

"It's good coding practice," I said. "This program is a pretty simple one in which we have a single reference to the **Student** object. However, you may write programs in the future that have multiple object variable references to the same object – in which case each one of those object variables is consuming valuable Windows resources. It's a good idea – and Microsoft's recommendation – to explicitly destroy the reference to the object by setting the object variable to **Nothing**."

I sensed that the lifetime issue of objects was still a concern for several members of the class, and so I suggested that we place code in the **Initialize** and **Terminate** event procedures of the **Student** class so that we could see exactly when the **Student** object was born and when it died. I typed this code into the class's **Initialize** event procedure...

```
Private Sub Class_Initialize()

MsgBox "The Student object has been born..."

End Sub
```

...and this code into the class's **Terminate** event procedure:

```
Private Sub Class_Terminate()

MsgBox "The Student object has died..."

End Sub
```

"Now let's run the program in Step mode," I said. I started the program in Step mode by pressing *F8* function key. Then I entered information for our fictitious student into the four text boxes on the form and clicked on the Calculate Grade button, before repeatedly pressing the *F8* function key to advance the execution of the code step by step. When we executed the line of code to declare the **stuNew** object variable, no message box appeared to indicate that the **Initialize** event procedure of the **Student** object had been executed:

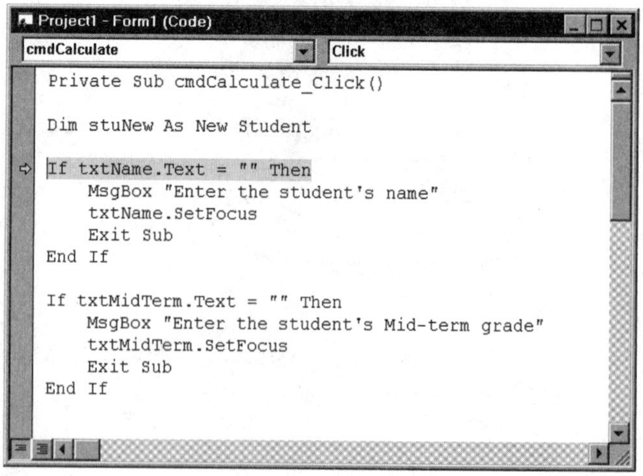
Project1 - Form1 (Code)
cmdCalculate
Click
Private Sub cmdCalculate_Click()
Dim stuNew As New Student
If txtName.Text = "" Then
MsgBox "Enter the student's name"
txtName.SetFocus
Exit Sub
End If
If txtMidTerm.Text = "" Then
MsgBox "Enter the student's Mid-term grade"
txtMidTerm.SetFocus
Exit Sub
End If

"That's significant," I said, "I bet some of you expected the **Student** object would be instantiated when the **Dim** statement was executed. But it's not the declaration of the object variable **stuNew** that instantiates the **Student** object. It's a later line of code – the one that sets the **Name** property of the object variable..."

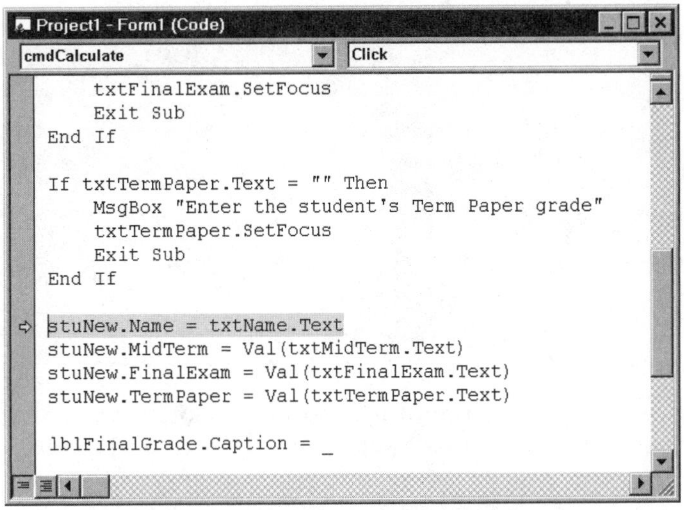

Project1 - Form1 (Code)
cmdCalculate
Click
txtFinalExam.SetFocus
Exit Sub
End If
If txtTermPaper.Text = "" Then
MsgBox "Enter the student's Term Paper grade"
txtTermPaper.SetFocus
Exit Sub
End If
stuNew.Name = txtName.Text
stuNew.MidTerm = Val(txtMidTerm.Text)
stuNew.FinalExam = Val(txtFinalExam.Text)
stuNew.TermPaper = Val(txtTermPaper.Text)
lblFinalGrade.Caption = _

"...that triggers the **Property Let** procedure of the **Name** property, and induces the birth of the **Student** object."

I then pressed the *F8* function key again, and when the line of coding assigning a value to the **Name** property of the **stuNew** object variable was executed, we saw the **Initialize** event procedure of the program execute. As I stepped through its execution, this screen shot was displayed:

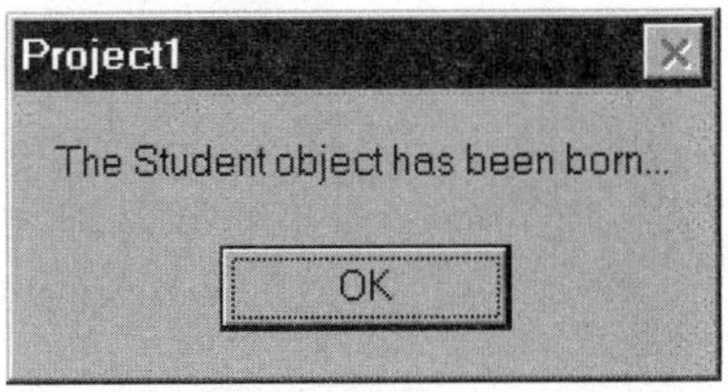

"So it was the first reference to the **Student** object," Dave said, "that actually created it. That's pretty interesting."

After clicking on the OK button of the message box, we continued to step through the code, a line at a time. We saw the **Property Let** procedure of the **Name** property execute, followed by the **Property Let** procedures for **MidTerm**, **FinalExam** and **TermPaper**. When the line of code to modify the **Caption** property of the **lblFinalGrade** label control was executed, we saw the **Property Get** procedure of the **Average** property run. Then, after the student's average was displayed in the caption of the label control on the form, the line of code to set the object variable to **Nothing** was poised to execute:

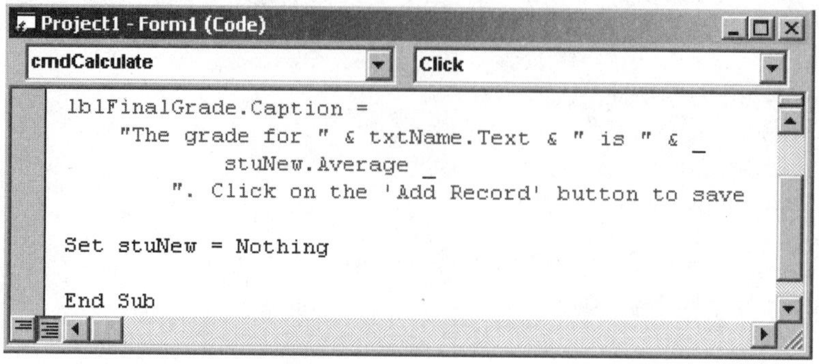
Project1 - Form1 (Code)
cmdCalculate
Click
lblFinalGrade.Caption =
"The grade for " & txtName.Text & " is " & _
stuNew.Average _
". Click on the 'Add Record' button to save
Set stuNew = Nothing
End Sub

"When the line of code setting the object variable to **Nothing** is executed," I said, "the **Terminate** event procedure of the **Student** object will run, and the object, sadly, will die."

I pressed *F8* again, and that's exactly what happened:

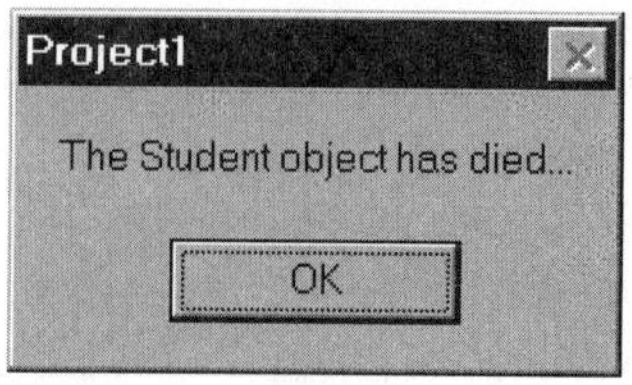
Project1
The Student object has died...
OK

"I know we've gone over this," Chuck said, "but I'm still a little shaky about it. Suppose we don't set the object variable to **Nothing** – will our instance of the **Student** object still die?"

"Yes, the **Student** object will still die," I said, "because when the **Click** event procedure ends, there's no other reference to the **Student** object anywhere in our program. As a rule, the **Terminate** event procedure of an object executes – and the object dies – when there are no longer any references to the object in the program. Even if we fail to set the object variable to **Nothing**, since its a variable declared in the **Click** event procedure of the command button, the object variable itself dies when the event procedure ends anyway. However, it's still a good idea to explicitly set your object variables to **Nothing** when you are done using them – this way, anyone who looks at your program can see its explicit behavior: that means that your program will have fewer surprises for them!"

To prove my point, I stopped the program and placed a comment character in front of the line that sets the object variable to **Nothing**. I ran the program one more time in step mode, repeated the steps of adding student information to the form, and clicked on the command button. The **Student** object was instantiated again and, finally, after the student's average was displayed on the form, the **End Sub** statement of the **Click** event procedure was executed. Then the **Student** object's **Terminate** event procedure was triggered, and the message box appeared notifying us that the **Student** object had died.At the moment, we haven't built the code to work out the class average in an object-oriented way, but we'll be doing that next week.

I urged everyone to save their versions of the Student Grades project – we'd be coming back to it over the next couple of weeks.

> **!** **Make sure you save your version of the Student Grades project, too – we'll be coming back to it over the next couple of chapters. The version of the Student Grades project that we've built so far can be found on the CD in the For Chapter 06\Additional Examples\Student Grades Demo folder.**

"I think we've had a pretty productive morning so far," I said, and displayed this summary slide:

<u>Summary</u>

So far, we have:

Analyzed the requirements of the Student Grades demo

Used conventional coding techniques to meet these requirements

Added the Student class module to the project

Incorporated the properties into the class

Written property Let and Property Get procedures for the properties of the Student class

Implemented the Student object in the demo program

Seen how properties automatically become visible in the Object Browser as soon as they're included in the code module of the class

"What I'd like to do is take a break now and, when we return, you're going to create your very first Visual Basic class module for the China Shop – this is the class template that the China Shop project's `Dish` object will be created from."

Back to the China Shop Project

Fifteen minutes later, when everyone returned from break, I explained what we were going to do next.

"Our next task," I said, "is to start incorporating some of this theory and practice into the China Shop project. And we'll start that process by creating the `Dish` class module."

Building the Dish Class Module

"Remember, this is the class that we'll instantiate the program's **Dish** objects from: these will be used to represent the china pieces that a customer chooses in a sales price quotation. There'll be one object instantiated for each separate piece of china that the customer chooses – like this:"

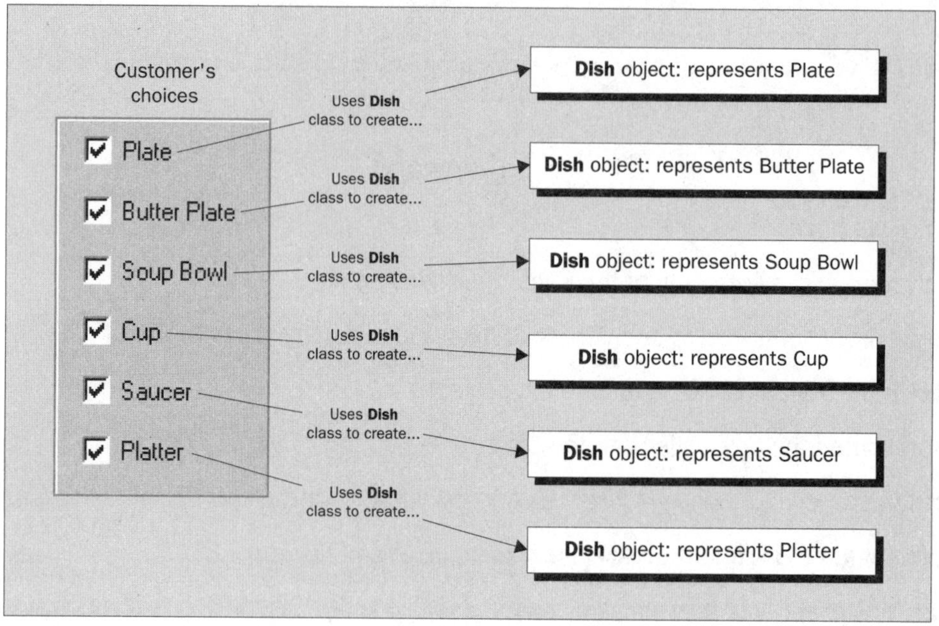

"We'll create the code, and discuss it as we go along. Let's begin!"

To get us under way, I handed out the following exercise for the class to complete:

Exercise - Creating the Dish Class

In this exercise, you'll create your first class module for the China Shop project, and save it in the **\VBFiles\China** directory.

1. Load up the China Shop project.

2. Select Project | Add Class Module from the Visual Basic menu bar.

3. When the Add Class Module dialog box appears, double-click Class Module on the New tab...

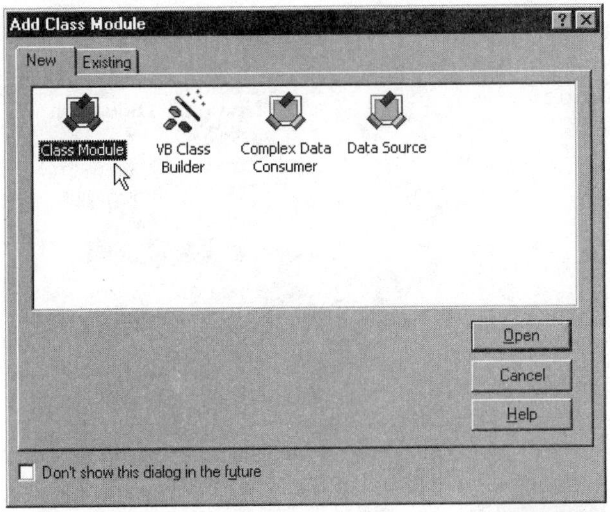

...and the new class module's Code window will appear in the IDE.

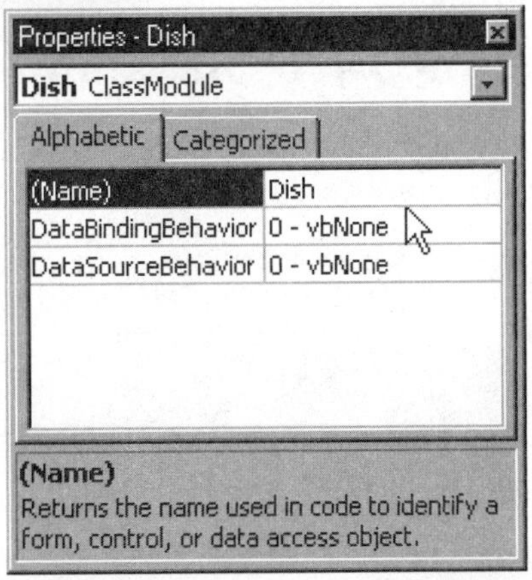

4. Bring up the Properties window for the class by pressing *F4*. Change the **`Name`** property of the class from **`Class1`** to **`Dish`**:

5. Click on the 'save' icon on the Toolbar and save this class, with the name **`Dish`**, to your **`\VBFiles\China`** folder:

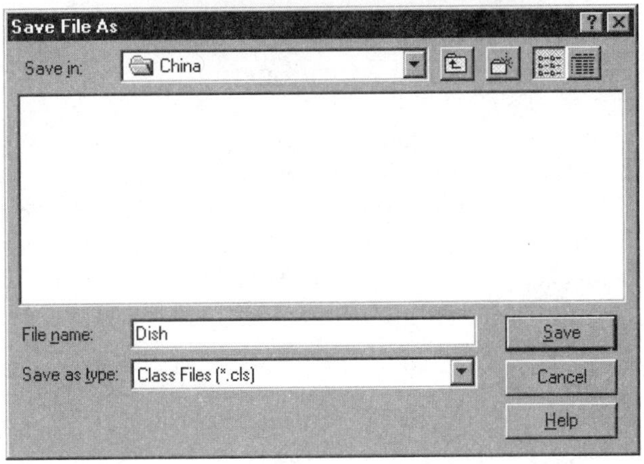

6. Now bring up the Project Explorer window. It should now be showing two forms and one class module:

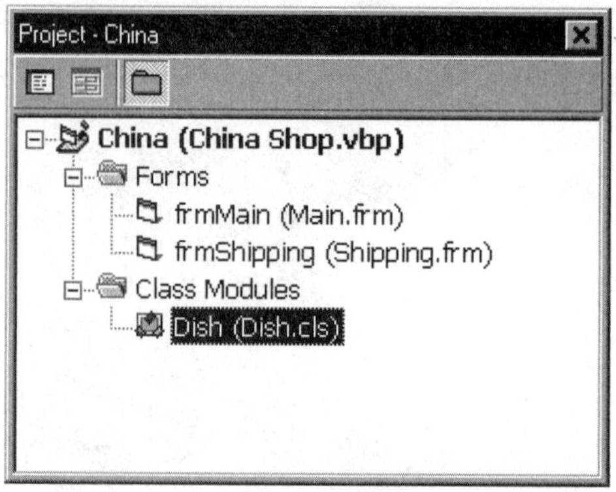

Discussion

"All we've done to this point," I said, "is to create a new class module and name it `Dish`. Our next step is to create the properties of the `Dish` object."

Building the Dish Class's Properties

"Let me display on the classroom projector the objects diagram we developed last week. You can look at this as you code the properties of the `Dish` class:"

OBJECTS	China/Dish	Order*	Package
PROPERTIES	Brand Item Quantity Price**		Charges** State

* Collection object
** Read-only property

"OK," I told the class, "in this next exercise, you'll continue working with the `Dish` class module you created in the previous exercise, as you declare `Private` module level variables to represent the properties of the `Dish` object we identified last week. You'll also be declaring a collection object in the General Declarations section of the class module into which you'll read the records from the `Prices.txt` file. This collection will store the inventory information that we'll need to use with the `Dish` objects.I then distributed the second exercise for the class to complete:

Exercise - Creating Private Variables in the Dish Class Module

1. Continue working with the **Dish** class module of the China Shop project.

2. Add the following code to the General Declarations section of the class module:

```
Option Explicit

Private m_strBrand As String
Private m_strItem As String
Private m_intQuantity As Integer
Private m_curPrice As Currency

Private m_colDishPrice As New Collection
```

3. Save the China Shop project.

Discussion

The first four variable declarations here were now becoming familiar to everyone – they were simply the declarations to create the **Private** variables that would store the **Dish** class's property values. The only problem we had with this exercise was a little confusion over the declaration of the **m_colDishPrice** collection in the class module:

"Why are we declaring the **m_colDishPrice** collection in the class module?" Rhonda said. "I thought that only variables representing properties go in the General Declaration section?"

"You're right, Rhonda, in that our **Student** demo class module only had variables related to the **Student** object's properties," I said. "However, the General Declarations section of a class module is no different from the General Declarations section of a form: you can declare variables of any kind in it, and in this instance we're declaring a collection into which we will load the inventory prices from the **Prices.txt** file – like this:"

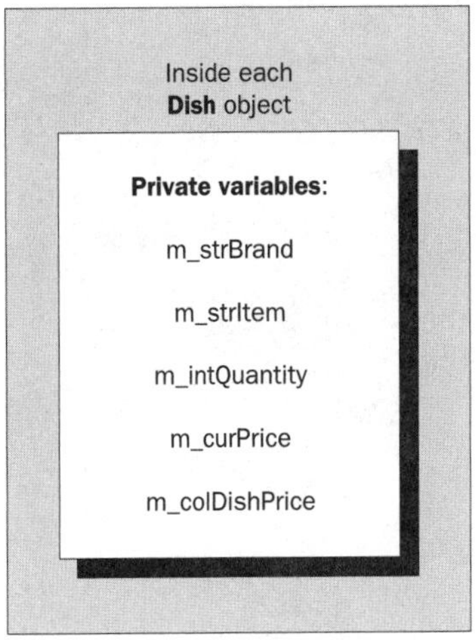

"That's right," Linda said. "You did say we would be reading the **Prices.txt** file in the **Initialize** event procedure of the **Dish** object. I suppose you need to declare the collection in the General Declarations section of the form so that it can be accessed from anywhere within the class module. Is that right?"

"That's exactly right, Linda," I answered. "The rules for variable scope are the same in a class module as they are in a form. If a variable needs to be seen from more than one procedure in a class module, it needs to be declared in the General Declarations section. By the way, notice how the names of the variables declared in the General Declarations section of the class module are prefixed with the letter **m** followed by an underscore – to indicate that they are module level variables."

The Dish Class's Initialize Event Procedure

"At this point," I said, "we've declared all the variables we'll need in the class module. We still have two major activities to perform. Firstly, we need to write some code in the **Initialize** event procedure, and we also need to code up the various **Property Let** and **Property Get** procedures for the **Dish** object's properties."

"What code will we place in the **Initialize** event procedure?" Mary asked.

"The **Initialize** event procedure of a class module," I said, "is the perfect place to put any code that needs to be executed when an object is instantiated. For the **Dish** object, we'll need to access to inventory information in order to calculate the **Price** property – for that reason we'll also want to read the inventory-price data contained in the file **Prices.txt** into the **m_colDishPrice** collection we declared in the General Declarations section of the class module:"

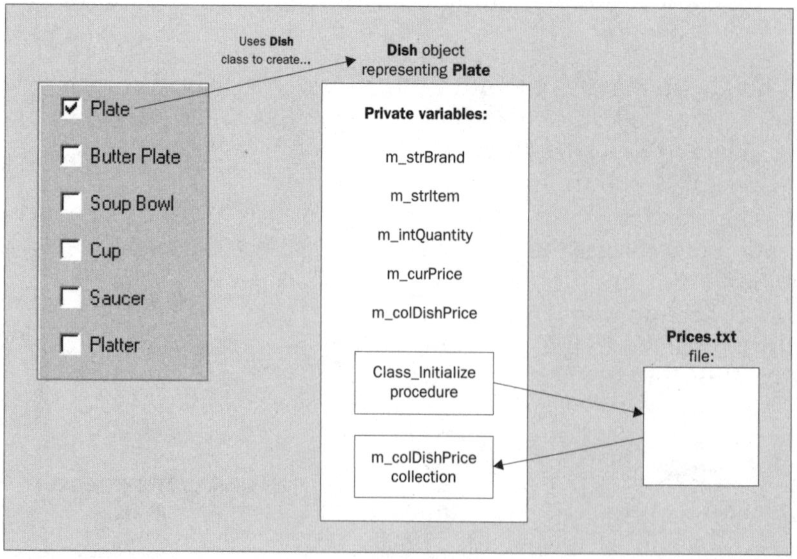

"In the China Shop program," Ward asked, "when will a **Dish** object be created? And will we have only one **Dish** object?"

"Actually, Ward," I said, "at any given time in the China Shop program, we may have from zero to six **Dish** objects alive – one for each item of china that the user selects. What will happen is that when the user selects an item of china in a check box, a **Dish** object will be created. When they uncheck the item, that **Dish** object will be destroyed."

"Does that mean," Melissa asked, "that every **Dish** object that is instantiated will have its own separate copy of the inventory prices?"

"That's right," I answered. "Each **Dish** object has its own **m_colDishPrices** collection to work with:"

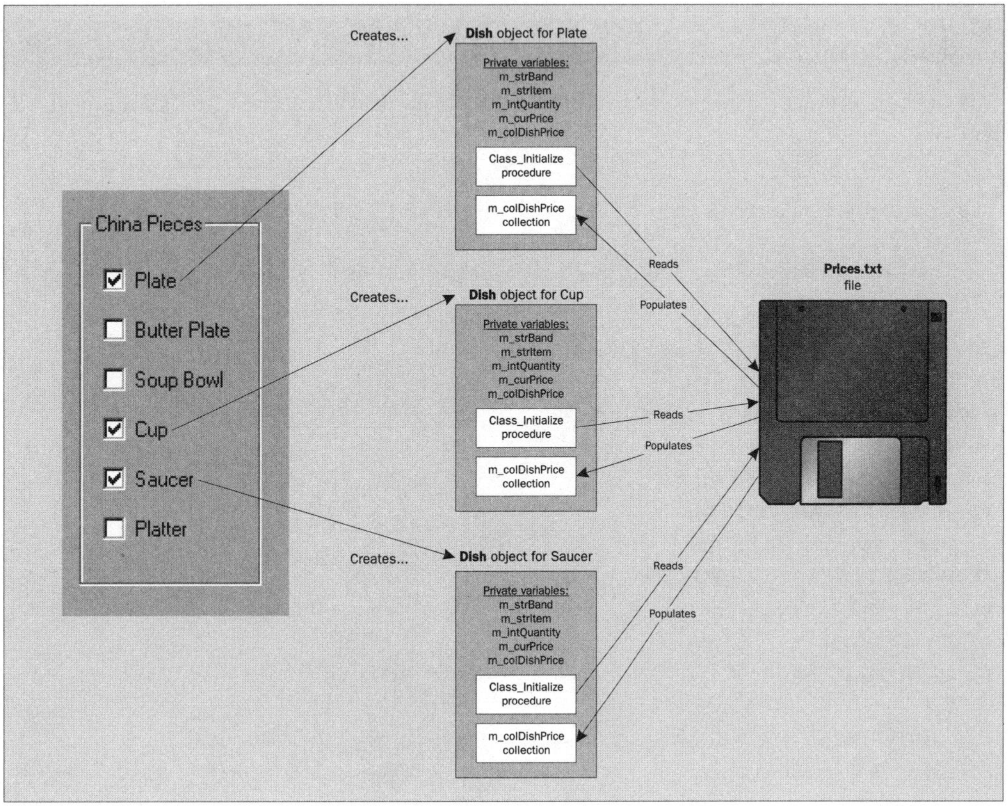

"That's what the encapsulation principle, that we discussed earlier, means – the object has access to the data that it needs, without having to rely on it being provided to it somehow from outside the object."

"Is it a problem that we're reading the **Prices.txt** multiple times?" Valerie asked. "Isn't that a waste of processing time? Why can't we load the inventory prices into a collection declared at the form level, and have the **Dish** object access that data?"

"Again, the answer is encapsulation," I answered. "It's better to have each instance of the **Dish** object read the **Prices.txt** file, than to have the **Dish** object rely on a programmer writing code to make the prices in **Prices.txt** available to the **Dish** object. We want to eliminate, as much as possible, the object's dependence on anything found elsewhere in the program that's using the object."

"I can hardly wait to get going with this," Rhonda said. "What do we do next?"

"Let's code the **Initialize** event procedure of the **Dish** object," I said, and I distributed another exercise for the class to complete:

Exercise - Coding the Dish Class's Initialize Event Procedure

In this exercise, you'll write code for the **Dish** class module's **Initialize** event procedure.

1. Continue working with the China Shop project's **Dish** class.

2. Add the following code to the class's **Initialize** procedure:

```
Private Sub Class_Initialize()
```

```
On Error GoTo ICanHandleThis

Dim strTest As String
Dim strBrand As String
Dim strItem As String
Dim curPrice As Currency

If App.Path = "\" Then
    Open App.Path & "Prices.txt" For Input As #1
Else
    Open App.Path & "\Prices.txt" For Input As #1
End If

Do While Not EOF(1)
    Input #1, strBrand, strItem, curPrice
    m_colDishPrice.Add item:= curPrice, Key:=strBrand & strItem
Loop
```

```
Close #1

Exit Sub
ICanHandleThis:
Select Case Err.Number
   Case 53
      MsgBox "A file required by the " &
            ↳"China Shop program " & vbCrLf &
            ↳"is missing. Please ensure that " & vbCrLf &
            ↳"Prices.txt is in " & vbCrLf &
            ↳"the China Shop directory " & vbCrLf &
            ↳"on the computer's hard drive"
      Unload frmMain
      Exit Sub
   Case Else
      MsgBox "Unexpected error has occurred" & vbCrLf &
             ↳"Contact John Smiley"
      Exit Sub
End Select

End Sub
```

3. Save the China Shop Project.

Discussion

"This code looks almost identical to the code that we have in the **ReadPrices** subprocedure of the **Main** form of the China Shop program," Blaine said.

"That shouldn't really be surprising," I said. "This code reads the china prices found in the file **Prices.txt** into the **m_colDishPrices** collection, which because it is declared in the General Declarations section of the **Dish** class module, is then available to every procedure in the class module."

"Does the fact that we're reading the prices directly into the **Dish** object mean that we won't need to access these prices from within the code of the **Main** form anymore?" Valerie asked.

"I see what you're getting at, Valerie," I said. "you're hoping to eliminate reading the **Prices.txt** file from outside of the **Dish** object. Unfortunately, that isn't possible – we still need to access inventory prices in **Prices.txt** from the code within the **Main** form of the China Shop Program in order to load the brand names of the china items into the **Main** form's **lstBrands** list box."

"Oh, right, I forgot about that," she admitted.

"Can't we load the items in the list box from within the **`Initialize`** event procedure of the **`Dish`** object?" Rhonda asked.

"In theory we could," I said, "but remember, you want to avoid directly interacting like that with controls outside of the object you design. There's an object-oriented term called **Coupling** used to describe the dependence of an object on other factors – data, controls, forms or applications – that are outside of the object itself. Objects are either **loosely-coupled**, **tightly- coupled**, or something in-between. Loosely-coupled objects have very little or no dependence at all on anything outside of themselves. Tightly-coupled objects are *highly* dependent on factors outside of themselves."

"How would you describe the **`Dish`** object?" Valerie asked.

"I think it's pretty much in the middle," I said. "The **`Dish`** object is dependent upon the **`Prices.txt`** file existing, and containing price data. If we were to enhance the **`Dish`** object so that it added items to the **`lstBrands`** list box, we would be increasing its coupling-level – since the object would need to add items to a list box control named specifically on a form somewhere. If the programmer using the object failed to add the list box to the form, or added it but named it improperly, the code in the object would bomb. That's why we want our objects to be as loosely-coupled as possible."

I waited a moment before moving on to the next stage of the **`Dish`** class creation process.

Coding the Dish Class's Property Get and Let Procedures

"Let's code the **`Property Get`** and **`Property Let`** procedures of the **`Dish`** object now," I said. "I think you'll have a lot of fun with this exercise."

I then distributed the following exercise for the class to complete:

Exercise - Creating the Dish Class Property's Get and Let Procedures

In this exercise, you'll code the **`Property Get`** and **`Property Let`** procedures of the Dish object.

1. Continue working with the **`Dish`** class module of the China Shop project.

2. Create the property procedures for the **`Brand`** property by coding its **`Property Let`** and **`Property Get`** procedures, as shown here, in the General section of the class:

```
Property Get Brand() As String

Brand = m_strBrand

End Property
```

```
Property Let Brand(ByVal strNew As String)

m_strBrand = strNew

End Property
```

3. Now create the property procedures for the `Item` property by coding a `Property Let` and `Property Get`:

```
Property Get Item() As String

Item = m_strItem

End Property
```

```
Property Let Item(ByVal strNew As String)

m_strItem = strNew

End Property
```

4. Now the property procedures for the `Quantity` property. Be careful with the `Property Let` procedure – we have some extra code in there, which I'll explain shortly.

```
Property Get Quantity() As Integer

Quantity = m_intQuantity

End Property
```

```
Property Let Quantity(ByVal intNew As Integer)

If m_strItem = "Platter" Then
    m_intQuantity = 1
Else
    m_intQuantity = intNew
End If

End Property
```

5. Create the property procedure for the read-only **Price** property. Remember that we do this by only coding a **Property Get** procedure:

```
Property Get Price() As Currency

m_curPrice = m_colDishPrice(m_strBrand & m_strItem)
Price = m_curPrice

End Property
```

6. Save the China Shop project.

Discussion

One or two people accidentally coded a **Property Let** procedure for the **Price** property. That was no big deal – I just told them they could delete it again in the Code window.

"I think you should all pretty much understand what's going on with the **Property Get** procedures," I said, as I displayed the **Property Get** procedure for the **Brand** property on the classroom projector:

```
Property Get Brand() As String

Brand = m_strBrand

End Property
```

"Remember that a **Property Get** procedure," I said, "is triggered when the code using the object refers to the property of the object in some way. Since the variable containing the value of the property – in this case **m_strBrand** for the **Brand** property – is declared **Private** to the class module, the only way to retrieve its value is via the **Property Get** procedure. As I mentioned earlier in today's session, the value of the property is returned to the program that's accessing our object using this statement..."

```
Brand = m_strBrand
```

"...which assigns the value of the **Private** variable – **m_strBrand** – to the **Brand** property."

"I'm OK with the **Property Get** procedure for brand," Rhonda said, "as well as the **Property Get** and **Property Let** procedures for all of the other properties of the **Dish** object – but can you please explain what's going on with the **Property Let** procedure for the **Quantity** property?"

"Well," I said, "the **Property Let** procedure for the **Quantity** property is a perfect illustration of the power of property procedures. Within a property procedure, we can perform validation and manipulation operations – like the one you see here. In this code, we're checking to see whether the current value of the **Item** property of the **Dish** object – stored in the variable **m_strItem** – is equal to **Platter**:"

```
Property Let Quantity(ByVal intNew As Integer)

If m_strItem = "Platter" Then
```

"If it *is*, then the **Quantity** property of the **Dish** object *must* be 1, as the customer is only allowed 1 platter per order:"

```
    m_intQuantity = 1
```

"If the **Item** property of the **Dish** object is not equal to a platter, then we set the value of the variable **m_intQuantity**, which represents the **Quantity** property of the **Dish** object, to whatever was passed to us in the **Property Let** procedure..."

```
Else
    m_intQuantity = intNew
End If

End Property
```

"I must have missed this somewhere," Lou said, "but what is the argument **intNew**?"

"**intNew** is the name of the argument that is passed to the **Quantity** property's **Property Let** procedure," I answered. "Back in the program code that triggered this **Property Let** procedure, the value of **intNew** was passed via some kind of assignment statement, like this..."

Dish.Quantity = 13

"What about the **Property Get** procedure for the **Price** property?" Linda asked.

"The **Price** property of the **Dish** object is a **read-only** property," I said, "and therefore has no **Property Let** procedure. Since the **Price** property of the **Dish** object is not updateable by the program that's using the **Dish** object, its value will be determined by other properties of the **Dish** object itself. That's what's going on here, as we're using the value of the **Dish** object's **Brand** and **Item** properties to look up the inventory price in the **m_colDishPrice** collection (remember that we created and populated this collection when the **Dish** object was instantiated). Here's the piece of code that works out the price inside the object:"

```
Property Get Price() As Currency

m_curPrice = m_colDishPrice(m_strBrand & m_strItem)
Price = m_curPrice

End Property
```

"That's pretty clever," Rhonda said. "So the **Price** of the particular china piece that this instantiation of the **Dish** object represents is calculated internally, by the **Dish** object itself."

"Exactly, Rhonda," I answered. "Each instantiation of the **Dish** object represents a piece of china that the customer has chosen, and each **Dish** object has all the information it needs to know about itself stored internally."

"I would think," Ward said, "that the code in the **Click** event procedure of **cmdCalculate** will be greatly reduced as a result of using the **Dish** object. Is that right?"

"That's spot on, Ward," I said, "and it will be reduced even more when we create the **Order** collection object two weeks from today. But before we modify the code in the **Click** event procedure of **cmdCalculate**, there are some changes we need to make to the General Declarations section of the China Shop's **Main** form."

"Does this mean we're done with the **Dish** object?" Steve asked. "That was pretty painless!"

"That's right, Steve," I said. "We've created the **Dish** class module, and we've coded the four properties of the **Dish** object. Next week we'll enhance the **Dish** object a bit by adding an event to it, but what we have now is enough for us to work with in the China Shop program."

"I'm relieved," Dorothy said. "Everyone at work had told me how hard creating objects in Visual Basic was. Now, with just a few variable declarations, and some **`Property Get`** and **`Property Let`** procedures, we're ready to go! Excellent!"

"Let's make those changes I mentioned to the **`Main`** Form of the China Shop program," I said. "What we're going to do next is modify the program so that it can use the **`Dish`** objects that we just created the class for."

Pointing the China Shop Project at the Dish Object

"In this next exercise," I explained, "you'll add code to the General Declarations section of the China Shop's **`Main`** form. We need to declare six object variables to point to the six distinct **`Dish`** objects that can be instantiated when our program runs – one for each china piece that the customer can choose on the form:"

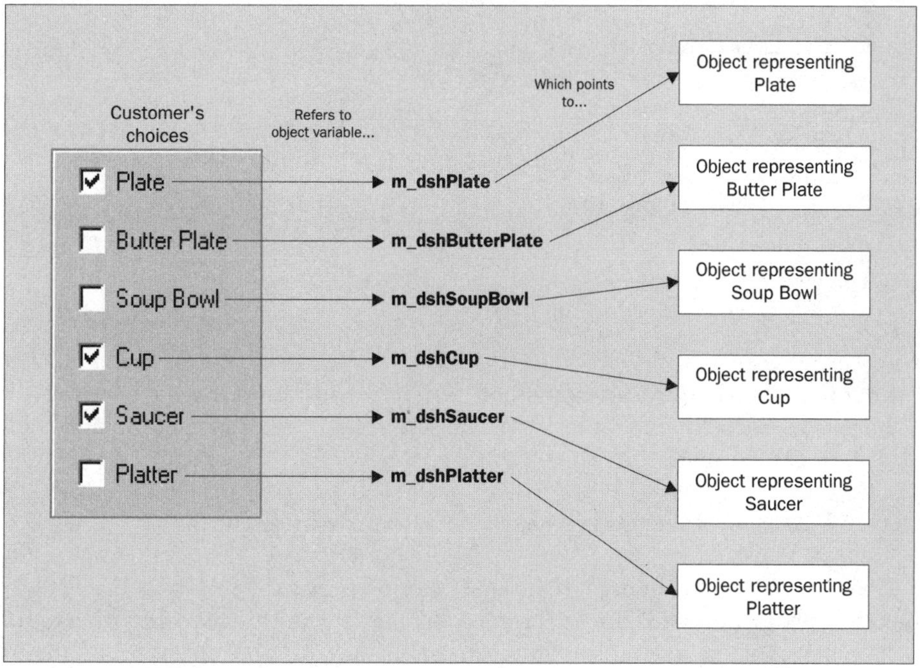

"If you think this is inefficient and that there should be a better way, you're right, but you'll have to wait until we learn more about collection objects to rectify that. For now, don't worry too much – you'll change this code in two weeks, and I think you'll be amazed at the differences. What we're doing is still good practice, and it'll teach you more about programming with objects."

I then distributed the exercise for the class to complete:

Exercise - Modifying the Main Form to Use Dish Objects

1. Continue working with the China Shop program.

2. Select **frmMain** in the Project Explorer window and modify the code in the General Declarations section so that it looks like the next code listing. Changed code is highlighted as usual:

```
Option Explicit

Private m_lngBackColor As Long
Private m_blnDateDisplay As Boolean
Private m_colDishPrice As New Collection
Public Quantity As Integer

Private m_dshPlate As Dish
Private m_dshButterPlate As Dish
Private m_dshSoupBowl As Dish
Private m_dshCup As Dish
Private m_dshSaucer As Dish
Private m_dshPlatter As Dish
```

3. Save the China Shop project.

Discussion

"Notice," I explained, when the students had finished coding their own versions of the project, "that we're declaring six object variables to refer to six distinct instances of the **Dish** object that can be instantiated in the program."

"As you said," Ward observed, "there has to be a better way than this."

"Exactly, Ward," I said. "But being a little inefficient for our first go-round with objects in the China Shop program won't hurt us any – particularly in this learning phase. Just remember – whenever the user selects an item of china, a **Dish** object will be instantiated, pointed to by one of these object variables. When an item of china is unchecked, one of the **Dish** objects pointed by one of these object variables will be destroyed."

"Now that we've written the code to declare our six **Dish** object variables," I said, "it's time to write the code that will actually instantiate them."

Instantiating the Dish Object in the China Shop

"OK," I continued, "the **Dish** object has now been declared in the General Declarations section of the form – but it's through the **Click** event procedures of the **chkChinaItem** check boxes that the **Dish** object actually comes to life – and dies!

To get this done, I distributed another exercise for the class to work through:

Exercise - Instantiating and Destroying Dish Objects in the China Shop

1. Continue working with the China Shop project's **Main** form.

2. Add the following code to the **Click** event procedure of **chkChinaItem**. All of the code in this event procedure is new:

```
Private Sub chkChinaItem_Click(Index As Integer)

Select Case Index
    Case 0:
        If chkChinaItem(Index).Value = 1 Then
           Set m_dshPlate = New Dish
           m_dshPlate.Brand = lstBrands.Text
           m_dshPlate.Item = "Plate"
           m_dshPlate.Quantity = frmMain.Quantity
        Else
           Set m_dshPlate = Nothing
        End If

    Case 1:
        If chkChinaItem(Index).Value = 1 Then
           Set m_dshButterPlate = New Dish
           m_dshButterPlate.Brand = lstBrands.Text
           m_dshButterPlate.Item = "Butter Plate"
           m_dshButterPlate.Quantity = frmMain.Quantity
        Else
           Set m_dshButterPlate = Nothing
        End If
```

```
    Case 2:
        If chkChinaItem(Index).Value = 1 Then
           Set m_dshSoupBowl = New Dish
           m_dshSoupBowl.Brand = lstBrands.Text
           m_dshSoupBowl.Item = "Soup Bowl"
           m_dshSoupBowl.Quantity = frmMain.Quantity
        Else
           Set m_dshSoupBowl = Nothing
        End If

    Case 3:
        If chkChinaItem(Index).Value = 1 Then
           Set m_dshCup = New Dish
           m_dshCup.Brand = lstBrands.Text
           m_dshCup.Item = "Cup"
           m_dshCup.Quantity = frmMain.Quantity
        Else
           Set m_dshCup = Nothing
        End If

    Case 4:
        If chkChinaItem(Index).Value = 1 Then
           Set m_dshSaucer = New Dish
           m_dshSaucer.Brand = lstBrands.Text
           m_dshSaucer.Item = "Saucer"
           m_dshSaucer.Quantity = frmMain.Quantity
        Else
           Set m_dshSaucer = Nothing
        End If

    Case 5:
        If chkChinaItem(Index).Value = 1 Then
           Set m_dshPlatter = New Dish
           m_dshPlatter.Brand = lstBrands.Text
           m_dshPlatter.Item = "Platter"
           m_dshPlatter.Quantity = frmMain.Quantity
        Else
           Set m_dshPlatter = Nothing
        End If
End Select

End Sub
```

3. Save the China Shop project.

4. If you run the program now and select one of the china items in one of the six check boxes, you'll actually be creating and destroying **Dish** objects. This would be a good time to either run the program in Step mode, or to place breakpoints in your code to see the wonder of objects in action.

Discussion

I sensed quite a bit of excitement as the students completed this exercise. Unfortunately, I think some students were in a hurry to see how everything would work as several of them made minor errors in an effort to rush to completion and run the program. I gave everyone about fifteen minutes to experiment with the program, during which time I noticed many of them running their own versions of the program in Step mode.

"The code in this **Click** event procedure," I explained, when everyone was happy with their program, "is executed whenever the user clicks on *any* one of the six check box controls in the **chkChinaItem** control array. Using the **Click** event procedure's **Index** property, we can determine which one of the six check boxes has been clicked. We use a **Select Case** statement with the **Index** argument of the **Click** event procedure:

```
Select Case Index
    Case 0:
```

"This determines which of the six check boxes has been clicked. Remember, each one of the six check box controls has a unique value for its **Index** property. Once we know which check box has been clicked, we need to make the decision to either instantiate a **Dish** object for that check box item, or destroy a **Dish** object for that check box item. If the **Value** property of the check box is 1, we know that the user has decided they want that item of china in their sales quotation:"

```
If chkChinaItem(Index).Value = 1 Then
```

"Therefore we should create a **Dish** object for that item of china. We do that by using the **Set** statement, in conjunction with the object variable name for that particular item of china:"

```
Set m_dshPlate = New Dish
```

"Then we assign values to the three properties of the **Dish** object that are updateable. The **Brand** property is assigned the value from the **lstBrands** list box's **Text** property..."

```
m_dshPlate.Brand = lstBrands.Text
```

"...the **Item** property is assigned the literal **"Plate"** ..."

```
m_dshPlate.Item = "Plate"
```

"...and the **Quantity** property is assigned the value of our **frmMain.Quantity** custom form property:"

```
m_dshPlate.Quantity = frmMain.Quantity
```

"If the **Value** property of the check box is not 1," I continued, "that means that the user has unchecked the check box, indicating that he or she no longer wants that item of china included in their sales quotation. So we destroy the object variable for that item by setting it equal to **Nothing**:"

```
Else
   Set m_dshPlate = Nothing
End If
```

"We have a **Case** statement for each one of the six check boxes within the **chkChinaItems** control array," I said. "Each check box is evaluated in the same way, and the code to instantiate the **Dish** object and set its properties is very similar throughout. What is different is the object variable name, and the string literal assignment to the **Item** property of the respective **Dish** objects. And in case you are wondering, we could have gotten clever and used the value of the **Caption** property of the check box that was clicked as part of the assignment statement for the **Item** property – but I decided this version of the code is more readable. When I'm teaching, I prefer to go for readability over elegance. Sometimes programmers get so wrapped up with the search for 'elegance' that their code becomes obscure and maintenance becomes a nightmare. I'm all for elegance, but not at the expense of maintainability. If you're going to write elegant, clever, but very obscure code, it must be well-commented. Always try to remember the programmers who comes along after you!"

"I really like that custom form property now," Ward said. "I must confess I really wasn't that convinced about its use until I saw it here in this code – I knew right away what it represented, and I'm not sure I would have immediately recognized the name of the module level variable **m_intQuantity** here."

Peter had a question:

"Let me make sure I understand this right," Peter said. "At any given point in the program, we may have zero to six **Dish** objects created, dependent upon the number of check boxes that are checked – is that right?"

"That's perfect, Peter," I said. "In a few minutes we'll be modifying the **Click** event procedure of **cmdCalculate** to use those **Dish** objects in its calculation of a sales price quotation. But first, we need to write some code to deal with actions that the user of the China Shop program may take which would change properties of these instantiated **Dish** objects"

Catering for the Customer Changing their Selections

"Changes?" Mary asked. "What kinds of changes?"

"At any given point in the program," I answered, "the customer may change their selection of either brand or quantity. Suppose the customer initially chose a single Mikasa plate. When they click on the plate check box, we instantiate a **`Dish`** object with a **`Brand`** property of **`Mikasa`**, an **`Item`** property of **`Plate`**, and a **`Quantity`** property of **`1`**. Now, suppose the customer then clicks on **`Faberware`** in the **`lstBrands`** list box. What do we do then?"

"I suppose we can just change the **`Brand`** property of all of the **`Dish`** objects," Dave said. "Is that right?"

"Precisely, Dave," I answered. "And we'll need to do the same thing if the customer changes their selected **`Quantity`**."

"How will we know which – if any – of the six **`Dish`** objects exists?" Kathy asked.

"That's where the **`For...Each`** statement that we learned about several weeks ago will come in handy," I said. "We'll be able to use it to loop through the **`chkChinaItems`** control array looking for check boxes have been selected – checked – if they are, we'll modify the **`Dish`** object associated with that item of China."

"Sounds complicated," Rhonda said.

"I don't think you'll have any problems with this," I said, as I distributed an exercise for the class to complete.

Changing the Brand Selection

In this exercise, you'll modify the **`Click`** event procedure of the **`lstBrands`** list box so that when clicked, the **`Brand`** property of every instantiated **`Dish`** object in the program is modified.

Exercise - Modifying Dish Objects when Customers Select a different Brand

1. Continue working with the **`Main`** form of the China Shop project.
2. Modify the code in the **`Click`** event procedure of **`lstBrands`** so that it looks like this. Changed code is highlighted as ever:

```
Private Sub lstBrands_Click()

If lstBrands.ListIndex = -1 Then Exit Sub
```

```
If App.Path = "\" Then
    imgChina.Picture = LoadPicture(App.Path & lstBrands.Text & ".gif")
Else
    imgChina.Picture = LoadPicture(App.Path & "\" & lstBrands.Text
     ↳& ".gif")
End If

Dim chkobject As CheckBox

For Each chkobject In chkChinaItem

Select Case chkobject.Value
    Case 1
        If chkobject.Caption = "Plate" Then
           m_dshPlate.Brand = lstBrands.Text
        End If
        If chkobject.Caption = "Butter Plate" Then
           m_dshButterPlate.Brand = lstBrands.Text
        End If
        If chkobject.Caption = "Soup Bowl" Then
           m_dshSoupBowl.Brand = lstBrands.Text
        End If
        If chkobject.Caption = "Cup" Then
           m_dshCup.Brand = lstBrands.Text
        End If
        If chkobject.Caption = "Saucer" Then
           m_dshSaucer.Brand = lstBrands.Text
        End If
        If chkobject.Name = "Platter" Then
           m_dshPlatter.Brand = lstBrands.Text
        End If
End Select
Next

End Sub
```

3. Save the China Shop project.

4. Run the program, select a brand of china, some items of china, and a quantity. Each time you click on the list box to select a new brand of china, the **`Brand`** property of each instantiated **`Dish`** object is changed. You may want to run this program in Step Mode to see this process in action for yourself.

Discussion

"This code should look very familiar to you," I said. "This code is triggered whenever the user clicks on an item in the **lstBrands** list box. We use a **For...Each** statement to loop through each item of the **chkChinaItem** control array:"

```
Dim chkobject As CheckBox

For Each chkobject In chkChinaItem
```

"Within the body of the loop," I said, "we use a **Select Case** statement to test the **Value** property of the check box:"

```
Select Case chkobject.Value
```

"If the **Value** property of the checkbox is 1..."

```
Case 1
```

"...that means that this check box is selected, implying that a **Dish** object already exists, and that we must update the **Brand** property of the appropriate **Dish** object with the value of the **Text** property of the list box:"

```
If chkobject.Caption = "Plate" Then
   m_dshPlate.Brand = lstBrands.Text
End If
```

"We have an **If** statement in place for each one of the six check boxes in the check box control array," I said.

"That's really something!" Ward said. "I think I'm starting to get the hang of this. But running this code in Step Mode is starting to get a little burdensome. I wish there was another way we could see the events of the **Dish** object taking place."

"There is, Ward," I said, "but we won't be able to implement it until next week. Next week we'll add an event to the **Dish** object: whenever any of the properties of the **Dish** object change, we'll raise a **DataChanged** event. This event procedure will be available to us on the China Shop's **Main** form, and what we'll do is write a message to the Immediate window whenever a **Dish** object's property changes."

"Now for the next exercise."

Changing the Quantity Selection

"In this exercise, you'll modify the **Click** event procedure of the **optQuantity** option button. This will mean that when it's clicked, the **Quantity** property of every instantiated **Dish** object in the program is modified."

Exercise - Modifying Dish Objects when a different Quantity is Selected

1. Continue working with the **Main** form.
2. Modify the code in the **optQuantity** control's **Click** event procedure so that it matches the following listing – you're replacing the single line of code in the event procedure with what follows here.:

```
Private Sub optQuantity_Click(Index As Integer)

frmMain.Quantity = Index
Dim chkobject As CheckBox

For Each chkobject In chkChinaItem
Select Case chkobject.Value
    Case 1
        If chkobject.Caption = "Plate" Then
           m_dshPlate.Quantity = Index
        End If
        If chkobject.Caption = "Butter Plate" Then
           m_dshButterPlate.Quantity = Index
        End If
        If chkobject.Caption = "Soup Bowl" Then
           m_dshSoupBowl.Quantity = Index
        End If
        If chkobject.Caption = "Cup" Then
           m_dshCup.Quantity = Index
        End If
        If chkobject.Caption = "Saucer" Then
           m_dshSaucer.Quantity = Index
        End If
        If chkobject.Caption = "Platter" Then
           m_dshPlatter.Quantity = Index
        End If
End Select
Next

End Sub
```

3. Save the China Shop project.
4. Run the program, select a china brand, some china items, and a quantity. Now change the quantity selection. Each time you click on a new Quantity option button, each instantiated **Dish** object's **Quantity** property of is being changed. You may want to run this program in Step mode to see this process in action for yourself.

Discussion

The code here was very similar to the code in the **Click** event procedure of the list box, so no- one had any trouble completing this exercise.

"Here," I said, "instead of updating the **Brand** property of each instantiated **Dish** object, we're updating the **Quantity** property."

"Just one more event procedure to code," I said, "and then the China Shop project will be truly object-oriented."

Using the Dish Objects in the Sales Quotation Calculation

In this next exercise, you'll modify the code in the **Click** event procedure of **cmdCalculate** to use the six **Dish** objects in its calculation of a customer's sales quotation.

Exercise - Modifying cmdCalculate to Use the Dish Objects

1. Continue working with the **Main** form.
2. Modify the code for the **cmdCalculate** button as shown by the highlighted lines in the listing below. Again, for clarity, we've used ellipses to represent where unchanged code has been omitted from the listing :

```
Private Sub cmdCalculate_Click()

On Error GoTo ICanHandleThis

...

'If the customer has selected a platter
'warn them that there is only 1 permitted per sales
'quotation
If chkChinaItem(5).Value = 1 And frmMain.Quantity > 1 Then
   MsgBox "Customer is limited to 1 Platter per order" &
         ↳vbCrLf & "Adjusting price accordingly"
End If
```

```
'All the pieces are here, let's calculate a price
'Calculate subtotal prices by item

curPlatePrice = m_dshPlate.Price
curButterPlatePrice = m_dshButterPlate.Price
curBowlPrice = m_dshSoupBowl.Price
curCupPrice = m_dshCup.Price
curSaucerPrice = m_dshSaucer.Price
curPlatterPrice = m_dshPlatter.Price

curCompletePrice = m_colDishPrice(lstBrands.Text &
      ↳"Complete Place Setting")

If chkChinaItem(0).Value = 1 And
      ↳chkChinaItem(1).Value = 1 And
      ↳chkChinaItem(2).Value = 1 And
      ↳chkChinaItem(3).Value = 1 And
      ↳chkChinaItem(4).Value = 1 Then
    MsgBox "Price includes a Complete Place Setting Discount"
     curTotalPrice = (curCompletePrice * frmMain.Quantity) +
            ↳curPlatterPrice
Else
  curTotalPrice = (((curBowlPrice + curButterPlatePrice
       ↳+
         ↳curCupPrice + curPlatePrice + curSaucerPrice) *
         ↳frmMain.Quantity) + curPlatterPrice)
End If

'If the price is greater than 0, display the price and
'make the label visible
If curTotalPrice > 0 Then
   lblPrice.Caption = "The price of your order is " &
         ↳Format(curTotalPrice, "$##,###.00")
   lblPrice.Visible = True
End If

Exit Sub
```

```
ICanHandleThis:

Select Case Err.Number
    Case 91          'object Reference Not Set
        Resume Next
    Case Else
        MsgBox Err.Number, Err.Description
        Resume Next
End Select

End Sub
```

3. Save the China Shop project.

4. Run the program, select the Mikasa brand of china, select the Plate, Butter Plate and Soup Bowl items, and a quantity of 2. Click on the Calculate Button. The price displayed should be $90. Well done! You've just created an object-oriented program.

Discussion

Not too much had actually changed in this event procedure, and virtually no one had a problem with the exercise. However, it was all I could do to get anyone's attention – they were really taken with their new object-oriented program.

"The first change to this procedure," I said, "is the introduction of an error handler, which we implement with this line of code at the top of the procedure..."

```
On Error GoTo ICanHandleThis
```

"... and these lines of code at the end:"

```
ICanHandleThis:

Select Case Err.Number
    Case 91          'object Reference Not Set
        Resume Next
    Case Else
        MsgBox Err.Number, Err.Description
        Resume Next
End Select
```

"We didn't have an error handler in the original version of this code," Ward said. "Why do we have one now?"

"Because of the technique we're using to retrieve the value of the **Price** properties of each of the six **Dish** object variables," I said. "Specifically, this code:"

```
curPlatePrice = m_dshPlate.Price
curButterPlatePrice = m_dshButterPlate.Price
curBowlPrice = m_dshSoupBowl.Price
curCupPrice = m_dshCup.Price
curSaucerPrice = m_dshSaucer.Price
curPlatterPrice = m_dshPlatter.Price
```

"These six lines of code," I said, "retrieve the value of the **Price** properties for each one of the six potential **Dish** objects in the program, and assign those values to the variables we declared in this event procedure, thus storing the subtotal prices for each item."

"So might these lines of code generate an error?" Kate asked. "I mean, because all of these objects may not really exist. For instance, if you try to retrieve the **Price** property of the object variable **m_dshCup** – what happens if the customer never selected the Cup check box?"

"That's exactly right, Kate," I said. "Referring to a property of a **Dish** object that doesn't exist will generate an Error 91 – object Reference Not Set. That's why, in our error handler, we tell Visual Basic to resume execution with the next line of code if that particular error is encountered."

"Isn't there another way to do this?" Blaine asked. "I would think there's a way to determine if an object variable points to an instantiated **Dish** object."

"Unfortunately not, Blaine," I said. "I'm afraid this is the best that we can do."

"I'm impressed with what we've done," Rhonda said.

"I think you'll be even more impressed when we implement the **Order** collection object in two weeks," I said. "Then the size of the code in this event procedure will be drastically reduced."

"I notice that you're still using the form's **m_colDishPrice** collection to calculate the price for a complete place setting," Ward said:

```
curCompletePrice = m_colDishPrice(lstBrands.Text &
      ↳"Complete Place Setting")
```

"That's right," I said. "For now, it can't be helped. Again, this is something that will go away when we implement the **Order** collection object – then we'll be able to move the calculation for a complete place setting discount to the **Order** collection."

"We have just one more exercise to compete," I said, "and then we'll call it a day. In this exercise, you'll add code to the **QueryUnload** event procedure of the form to destroy all of the **Dish** object variables when we're finished with them.

Destroying the Dish Objects when we're Done with them

I then handed out the following exercise:

Exercise - Destroying the Dish Object Variables

1. One more time, work with the China Shop's **Main** form.
2. Modify **frmMain**'s **QueryUnload** event procedure of so that it looks like this:

```
Private Sub Form_QueryUnload(Cancel As Integer, UnloadMode As Integer)

Set m_dshPlate = Nothing
Set m_dshButterPlate = Nothing
Set m_dshSoupBowl = Nothing
Set m_dshCup = Nothing
Set m_dshSaucer = Nothing
Set m_dshPlatter = Nothing

End Sub
```

3. Save the China Shop program away as usual.

Discussion

"This is really just housekeeping," I said. "We want to be sure that when the China Shop program ends, all of the references to the object variables – which point to the various **Dish** objects – are destroyed."

No one had any questions – perhaps they were tired. At any rate, everyone seemed very pleased with the work they had done in creating their very first object for the China Shop program – the **`Dish`** object, and with the code that we'd added to the China Shop to make use of these objects when they were instantiated from the **`Dish`** class.

"Next week," I said, "we'll continue working with objects as we learn how to create our own methods and events. If you had fun today, next week you'll have even more!"

Chapter Summary

Through the use of the Student Grades demonstration program, we've seen how to go about creating our own objects. Specifically we've seen how to:

- Create a **class module** and work inside its code window to define the characteristics of the objects that will be created from the class template
- Define and create the class's **properties**
- Use **`Property Let`** and **`Property Get`** procedures to retrieve and modify the property values of our objects

We've also done the following work on object-orienting the China Shop program:

- We made a **class module** for the **`Dish`** object
- We defined the properties of the **`Dish`** object within this module
- We coded the **`Property Let`** and **`Property Get`** procedures for the **`Dish`** class
- We implemented the **`Dish`** objects constructed from our new **`Dish`** class in the code of the main form of the China Shop program

Next week, we'll build on what we've covered here. We'll take what we've learned about creating class modules and defining their properties, and look at how to add **methods** and **events** to our own objects.

See you there!

Learn to Program Objects with Visual Basic
Bullina's China

Chapter 6
Adding Methods and Events

This week's class picks up where we left off last week – learning about creating objects in more detail. This week, we see how to create **methods** and code **events** for our objects, a topic that becomes clearer once you understand the difference between user-generated and object-generated events – something I'll be making clear in the next few pages. By the end of the chapter you'll have a much firmer understanding of the interrelationships between the objects trio you've already heard so much about – properties, methods, and events.

Here's a quick preview of the topics we'll discuss today:

- More on working inside the class module
- Creating methods in your class templates
- Understanding and creating events for your objects
- Reacting to object-generated events in your program

We'll be using the Student Grades demo from last lesson to examine a lot of these aspects, but we'll also be changing the China Shop program in the following ways:

- We'll be creating an event in the **Dish** object. This will let us know when the object's properties are modified by changes that the customer makes to their selections on the `Main` form
- We'll create a new **Package** class, used for calculating our shipping charges

By the end of today's lesson, you'll have done much of the important work on object-orienting the China Shop program, and will be the proud owner of an object-oriented China Shop application. In the remainder of the course, I hope to show you how having this object-oriented program in place will make further enhancements and modifications very much easier.

More On Objects

As I made my way into the college for the sixth Saturday lesson, my eyes were greeted by a world that was slowly awakening from the deep slumber of winter in readiness for the coming spring. Despite the fitful flurries of snow, the air seemed brighter, and the sunlight had more warmth in it.

Although I knew it was irrational, I couldn't help letting this spirit of optimism mingle with my positive feelings about how the course was going. Six weeks in, and I could see that the students were enjoying themselves, and that they were fascinated by the fact that, although the code for the China Shop project itself was changing quite radically *internally*, its outward behavior remained unaltered.

I was feeling pretty upbeat when I met my students in the classroom. I had a clear idea in my mind of how the rest of the course was going to shape up, and I felt it was time to reinforce their confidence.

The Way Ahead

"I want you all to know how much progress you've all made," I said, by way of introduction. "At the end of today's class, we'll have created the two main objects of the China Shop project – the `Dish` and the `Package`."

"Does that mean we'll have object-oriented the China Shop?" asked Kevin.

"Yes, Kevin, basically that'll be the case," I replied. "In today's class, you'll create a `Package` object that we'll use to calculate the China Shop's shipping charges. I'll also be showing you how to create methods and events in your own objects. Next lesson, we'll enhance the China Shop project even more by creating the `Order` collection, and the following week will see us using Microsoft Word to print a sales quotation for the customer from within the China Shop program. Then, in week nine, we'll reverse that process and make the `Package` object into an ActiveX component, which will enable us to use it in other Windows programs, such as Word or Excel. Then finally, in our last week, we'll tie up any loose ends and deliver the object-oriented China Shop program to Joe Bullina."

"Wow! I can see the light at the end of the tunnel when you talk like that!" Rhonda declared.

I smiled at her and continued: "To summarize what we did last lesson," I said, "You'll remember I spent some time demonstrating how to create an object – the **`Student`** object from our demonstration project – by creating a class module, declaring **`Private`** variables to store property values, and then creating the **`Property Get`** and **`Let`** procedures that would give the world outside access to those property values. Then we spent the remainder of last week's class creating the **`Dish`** object, and incorporating it into the China Shop."

"Will we be continuing to work with the Student Demo program?" Rhonda asked. "I found that watching you work with the **`Student`** object before coding the China Shop objects really helped me understand what was going on."

"I agree," Ward said, "I thought last week was a great week for us. Seeing you create the **`Student`** object in that demo really helped me concentrate on what I was doing when it came to creating the **`Dish`** object. I'm itching to start building methods and events of my own."

"Well, that's exactly what I was planning on doing today," I said. "Let's bring the Student Demo project up on the classroom projector to remind ourselves what it looks like..."

A Big Hand for the Student Grades Demo Program

I displayed the form from the demonstration project on the classroom Projector:

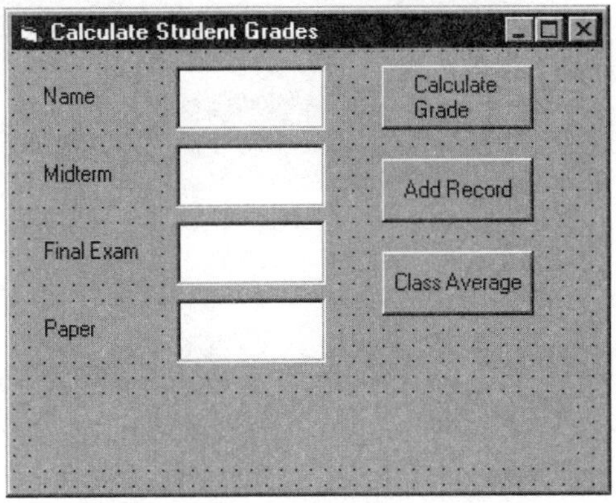

A quick Recap

"Last week," I said, "we placed code in the **Click** event procedure of the **cmdCalculate** command button to create a **Student** object, based on the **Student** class module that we'd built:"

```
Private Sub cmdCalculate_Click()
```

```
Dim stuNew As New Student
```

"We also set the **stuNew** object's **Name**, **Midterm**, **FinalExam**, and **TermPaper** properties to the values in the four text boxes on the form, respectively..."

```
stuNew.Name = txtName.Text
stuNew.Midterm = Val(txtMidterm.Text)
stuNew.FinalExam = Val(txtFinalExam.Text)
stuNew.TermPaper = Val(txtTermPaper.Text)
```

"...and we displayed the read-only **Average** property – calculated within the object itself – as part of the **Caption** property of the **lblFinalGrade** label:"

```
lblFinalGrade.Caption =
    ↳"The grade for " & txtName.Text & " is " &
    ↳stuNew.Average &
    ↳". Click on the 'Add Record' button to save the record."
```

"Our first task today," I went on, "will be to create a method for the **Student** object, called **AddRecord**."

Adding a Method to the Demo Project

"The method that we'll create here will add a record of the student's grades and average to the **Grades.txt** file. We'll be executing this method in the **Click** event procedure of **cmdAddRecord**. Let's take a look at the code currently in the **Click** event procedure for that command button:"

```
Private Sub cmdAddRecord_Click()
```

```
Open App.Path & "\Grades.txt" For Append As #1

Write #1, txtName.Text,
 ↳Val(txtMidterm.Text),
```

```
 ↳Val(txtFinalExam.Text),
 ↳Val(txtTermPaper.Text),
 ↳m_sngFinalGrade
Close #1

m_intRunningTotal = m_intRunningTotal +
 ↳m_sngFinalGrade
m_intRunningCount = m_intRunningCount + 1

txtName.Text = ""
txtMidterm.Text = ""
txtFinalExam.Text = ""
txtTermPaper.Text = ""
txtName.SetFocus
lblFinalGrade.Caption = ""
```

```
End Sub
```

"As you can see, it's pretty involved," I said. "We open the **`Grades.txt`** file and write a record to it containing the values from the form's four text boxes, plus the module level variable that holds the calculated value of the student's average mark – **`m_sngFinalGrade`**. Then we close the file:"

```
Write #1, txtName.Text,
 ↳Val(txtMidterm.Text),
 ↳Val(txtFinalExam.Text),
 ↳Val(txtTermPaper.Text),
 ↳m_sngFinalGrade
Close #1
```

"After we've closed the file, we add the student's average to the value of **`m_intRunningTotal`**, and increment **`m_intRunningCount`** by one:

```
m_intRunningTotal = m_intRunningTotal +
 ↳m_sngFinalGrade
m_intRunningCount = m_intRunningCount + 1
```

"Finally, we clear the four text boxes on the form:"

```
txtName.Text = ""
txtMidterm.Text = ""
txtFinalExam.Text = ""
txtTermPaper.Text = ""
txtName.SetFocus
lblFinalGrade.Caption = ""
```

"And you're saying the `AddRecord` method of the `Student` object we're about to code will streamline this event procedure?" Dave enquired.

"Considerably," I assured him. "Using the `Student` object's `AddRecord` method in this event procedure will abbreviate all this beautifully – I promise. And not to labor the point – but it does bear repeating – objects don't necessarily serve the programmer who writes the application, but rather those who come to the code at a later date, and are unfamiliar with it. Executing the `AddRecord` method from within a `Student` object is a lot neater, and easier to comprehend, than opening a file, writing a record, and then closing the file."

"Instead of coding an `AddRecord` method for the `Student` object," Chuck said, "couldn't we modify the code in this `Click` event procedure to write the five properties of the `Student` object *directly* to the text file?"

I paused before answering. "Ultimately, this kind of decision's up to you, as the programmer of your application," I said. "We've even seen instances in Visual Basic where Microsoft have coded both a property and a method to achieve the same result."

"That's right," Kate said. "You gave us an example of that last week. If you want to make a form invisible, you have two choices: set the form's `Visible` property to `False`, or execute its `Hide` method. It seems to me that the designers of the Visual Basic knew they'd coded a property and method that both achieved the same result – they deliberately provided us with either option."

"I've wondered about that," Tom said. "Is one technique more efficient than the other?"

"That's a good question, Tom," I said, "It has long been rumored in the Visual Basic world that the execution of a method is faster than setting or retrieving a property value. However, in the tests I've run, I've never noticed any difference. In the final analysis, when you design objects, you should be aware that most people are more comfortable retrieving and updating **values** by working with **properties**, and with performing **actions** by executing **methods**: it just seems more intuitive. I think you should try to adhere to that convention."

"So, because we're performing an action – adding a record to the `Grades.txt` file – we'll be writing a method for the `Student` object to do this?" Mary ventured.

"Absolutely," I assured her. "I can also tell you that, from long experience, I know that in this case writing an `AddRecord` method will lead to the neatest outcome, in terms of code-length."

I paused before going on.

Creating our first Method

"So, let's create the **AddRecord** method of the **Student** object," I said. "As I mentioned a few weeks ago, a method is just a public procedure in the class module of our object. To create a method called **AddRecord** for our **Student** object, therefore, all we need to do is open up the Code window for the **Student** class module, and code-in a procedure called **AddRecord**."

"It can't be that easy!" Valerie cried. "Can it?"

"It really is, Valerie," I confirmed. "Watch this..."

I opened the Student Grades demo project that we'd worked on the previous week and located the **Student** class module using Project Explorer:

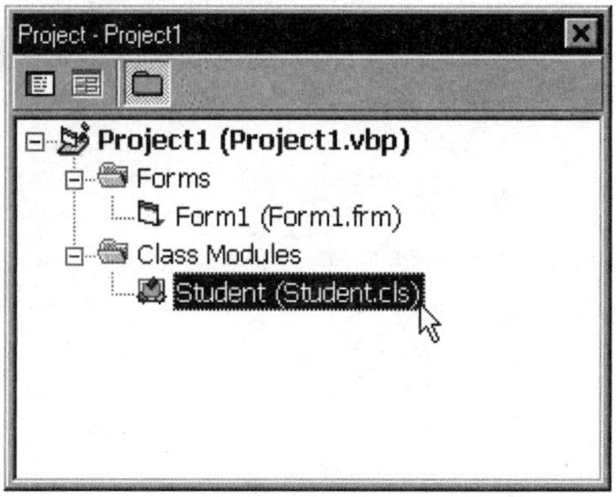

I opened up its Code window, and added the following code, including the event procedure's header and footer. You should do the same, and work through this example:

```
Public Sub AddRecord()

Open App.Path & "\Grades.txt" For Append As #1

Write #1, m_strName,
      ↳m_intMidTerm,
      ↳m_intFinalExam,
      ↳m_intTermPaper,
      ↳m_sngAverage
Close #1

End Sub
```

"You'll see that this code does essentially the same thing as the first seven lines of the **Click** event procedure of **cmdAddRecord**, on our form," I said. "It adds a record containing the student's information into the **Grades.txt** file. Shortly, we'll be remove all the equivalent code from the **Click** event procedure of **cmdAddRecord**, and replacing it with a line of code that will simply execute this method."

"So this is the method then?" Chuck said.

"Yes, Chuck," I said, "this **Public** procedure is the **Student** object's **AddRecord** method. Let's take a look in the Object Browser and see what Visual Basic makes of it."

I opened the Object Browser by selecting View | Object Browser from the Visual Basic menu bar, typed the word AddRecord into the Search box, and pressed *Enter*. The following screen shot was displayed:

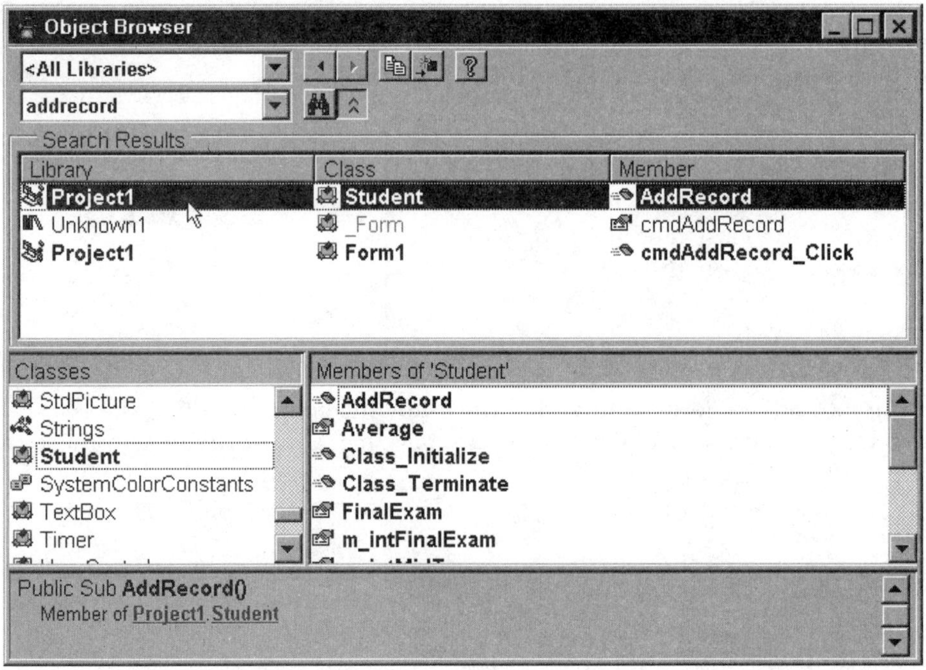

"Bingo!" I declared. "The Search Results box contains the name Student under the Classes heading and AddRecord under the Member heading – indicating that **AddRecord** has been found as a member of the **Student** class. You'll see in a moment how easy it is to execute this method from within an event procedure on the **Student** form. However, before we modify the code in the **cmdAddRecord** command button, we need to move the declaration of the **Student** object from the **Click** event procedure of the **cmdCalculate** command button and into the General Declarations section of the form."

"Why's that?" Dorothy asked.

"We need to ensure that the code in the **Click** event procedure of **cmdCalculate** and **cmdAddRecord** both refer to the same instance of **Student** object," I said. "Remember what we learned about the lifetime of objects last week? If we only declare the **Student** object in the **Click** event procedure of **cmdCalculate**, then, when that event procedure stops executing, the **Student** object will die, and we won't have access to it when the user clicks on the Add Record command button."

"I see," Dave said. "We need to declare the **Student** object in the General Declarations section of the form to give it **module-level scope**."

Declaring a new Instance of the Student Object

"Exactly, Dave," I said. I then added this line of code to the General Declarations section of the form:

```
Option Explicit

Private m_intRunningTotal As Integer
Private m_intRunningCount As Integer
Private m_sngFinalGrade As Single
Private m_stuNew As Student
```

"Didn't we use the syntax **As New Student** when we declared this object variable in the **Click** event procedure of **cmdCalculate**?" Linda asked. "How come we're not using it again here?"

"Yes, we did use the **New** keyword in the **Click** event procedure of **cmdCalculate**, Linda," I said, "and we could have written the declaration like this..."

```
Private m_stuNew As New Student
```

"Is there a difference?" Kevin asked.

"From a coding point of view," I said, "using the declaration with the **New** keyword is more elegant. If we don't use the **New** keyword in the declaration, we need to add a separate **Set** statement later on, to set aside some memory for the new **Student** object before referring to any of its properties or methods. Using the **New** keyword really combines the declaration and setting of the memory reference into one line of code."

The Life and Death of Objects

"So why are we declaring the object variable here without it?' Ward asked.

"I don't want to allocate the memory for our object variable until we press the **cmdCalculate** button," I explained. "Although we want this object to be available in the **Click** event procedures of both our **cmdCalculate** and our **cmdAddRecord** command buttons, we don't want it hanging around, occupying computer memory, at any other time."

"So what exactly will we do?" asked Rhonda.

"We'll use a **Set** statement to create a new instance of our **Student** object in the **Click** event procedure of **cmdCalculate**, then we'll use another **Set** statement – like this:"

```
Set m_stuNew = Nothing
```

"...to kill-off our object variable at the end of the **cmdAddRecord_Click** event procedure. Our object will have done its job, by then, and we won't need it. As we saw in Lesson Four, efficient use of memory like this is the flip-side of coding efficiency."

Modifying the Code

I then modified the code in the **Click** event procedure of the form's **cmdCalculate** button to look like this next code listing (for clarity, we haven't shown the four **If...Then** statements that we use to check for empty text boxes in this code listing. They're represented by an ellipsis here):

```
Private Sub cmdCalculate_Click()
```

```
Set m_stuNew = New Student
```

(This line replaces the existing `Dim stuNew As New Student` **line.)**

```
...
```

```
m_stuNew.Name = txtName.Text
m_stuNew.Midterm = Val(txtMidTerm.Text)
m_stuNew.FinalExam = Val(txtFinalExam.Text)
m_stuNew.TermPaper = Val(txtTermPaper.Text)
```

```
lblFinalGrade.Caption =
 ⤷"The grade for " & txtName.Text & " is " &
 ⤷m_stuNew.Average &
 ⤷". Click on the 'Add Record' button to save the record."

End Sub
```

Discussion

"Notice," I said, "that the first line of code uses the **Set** statement I was talking about a moment ago. The **Set** statement is used to assign the module-level object variable **m_stuNew** with a pointer to the new **Student** object. Notice that we've also removed the line of code declaring the old **Student** object variable, **stuNew**, and replaced all mention of it with **m_stuNew**. What we have to do now is add some code to the **cmdAddRecord** button so that it refers to the newly- instantiated **Student** object when we calculate the student's average. And, **very importantly**, we've removed the **Set stuNew = Nothing** line from the end of this event procedure – that's because we want the **Student** object that **m_stuNew** points at to stay alive so that we can add it's property values to the disk file."

Telling cmdAddRecord to Use the stuNew Object

I then modified the code in the **Click** event procedure of **cmdAddRecord** to look like this next code listing. As ever, modified code is highlighted...

```
Private Sub cmdAddRecord_Click()

m_stuNew.AddRecord
```

> **!** **This first line of code replaces the existing chunk that begins with** `Open App.Path...` **and ends with** `Close #1` **– this functionality is now encapsulated in the Student object's AddRecord method.**

```
m_intRunningTotal = m_intRunningTotal +
      ⤷m_stuNew.Average
m_intRunningCount = m_intRunningCount + 1
txtName.Text = ""
txtMidterm.Text = ""
txtFinalExam.Text = ""
txtTermPaper.Text = ""
txtName.SetFocus
lblFinalGrade.Caption = ""
Set m_stuNew = Nothing

End Sub
```

Discussion

"There's that line that sets **m_stuNew** to **Nothing**," observed Ward, pleased with himself.

"That's correct," I told him, with a smile. "Now, as you can see, we've removed the lines of code that opened, wrote to, and closed the **Grades.txt** file, and replaced them with a single line:"

```
m_stuNew.AddRecord
```

"This streamlines the code by six lines or so," I added.

"Wow, it sure did," Rhonda said. "That line of code is so compact, I almost missed it. It's just saying, *with this object, use this method*, right?"

"Correct," I replied. "With the object referenced by the **m_stuNew** variable, we use its **AddRecord** method. Not only is the code compact, it's a lot friendlier, too, because of its use of object dot notation. There aren't a lot of programmers, these days, who know in detail how to open and write to disk files. If a junior-level programmer is hired to work with this program – and I no longer consider any of you as falling under such a description – they could do so without concerning themselves with **Open**, **Close** and **Write** statements, because we've shielded them from all that – all they'd need do is execute the **AddRecord** method we've written for them in the **Student** object."

"That's neat," said Blaine.

"Another benefit that I can see of encapsulating the file access functionality into the **Student** object," Dave added, "is that if tomorrow we decide to add these records to a *database* instead of to our **Grades.txt** disk file, then none of the code in the actual program would have to be changed – only the **AddRecord** method of the **Student** class module."

"That's an excellent point, Dave," I replied.

"I see you're still maintaining a running total of the student's averages and a count of the student grades entered," Ward said. "Will you be changing that later?"

"That's a good point, Ward," I said. "Next week, we'll create a **Course** collection object to maintain that information. But for now, this bit of the code needs to remain the same."

Using The Modified program

"Now the important bit: let's see if the **AddRecord** method works," I said.

Before running the program, I deleted the version of the **Grades.txt** file we had created the previous week (remember, this file is created dynamically at run-time), and then ran the program. Once again I entered a fictitious student's name and grades and clicked on the Calculate Grade command button...

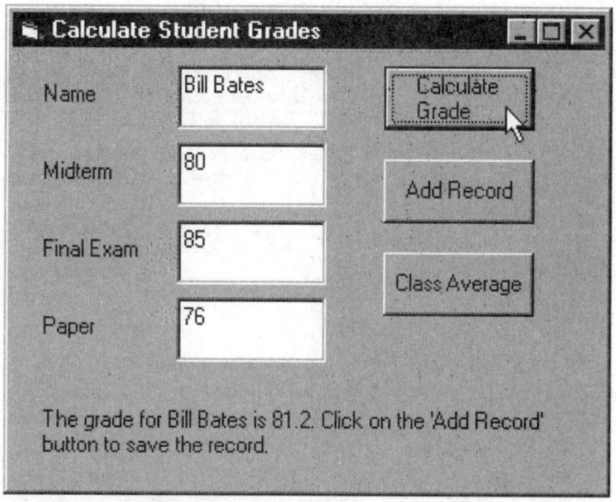

...then I clicked on the Add Record button, and everyone in the class seemed to hold their breath and hope that the **Student** object's **AddRecord** method would write a record to the **Grades.txt** file. The program seemed to work – it didn't bomb, and the text boxes were cleared. Just to be sure, I used Notepad to open the **Grades.txt** file:

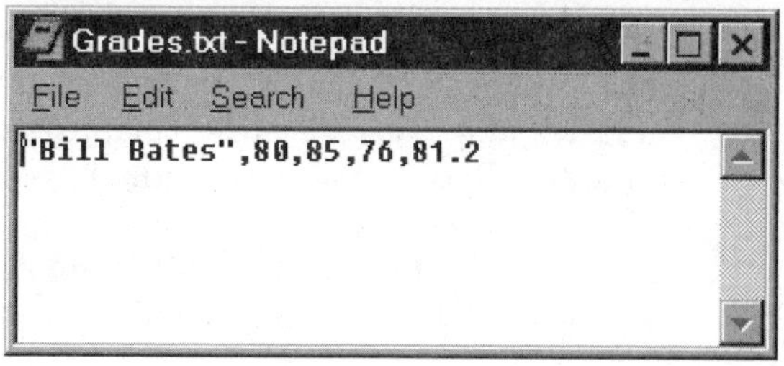

"There's Bill Bates," I said. The file had been created and the record added to it all in one go, just as was the case last week, except that now we were using the **AddRecord** method to do the work. At this point, Kate suggested that I set a breakpoint on the line of code in the **Click** event procedure of **cmdAddRecord**, so that we could see the **AddRecord** method in action. Adding the breakpoint would mean that when the program got to that point, it would automatically go into Step Mode – and we could see the detailed running of the program from that point on.

For those of you who have my first book, *Learn to Program with Visual Basic 6*, I deal with setting and using breakpoints in detail on pages 328-330.

"That's a great idea, Kate," I said, as I stopped the program, brought up the Code window, and set a breakpoint by clicking my mouse in the left hand margin of the Code Window:

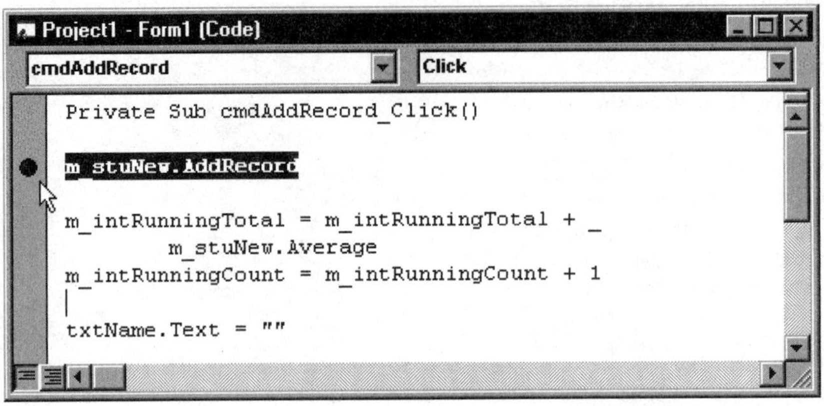
Project1 - Form1 (Code)
cmdAddRecord
Click
Private Sub cmdAddRecord_Click()
m_stuNew.AddRecord
m_intRunningTotal = m_intRunningTotal + _
m_stuNew.Average
m_intRunningCount = m_intRunningCount + 1
txtName.Text = ""

Once again, I deleted the **`Grades.txt`** file and ran the program. Again I entered Bill Bates' name and grades, clicked on the Calculate Grade command button, and then clicked on the Add Record button. Because Visual Basic then met my breakpoint, the program was immediately put into Step mode. I pressed the *F8* key to step through the code line by line.

"That's great – I'd forgotten all about setting breakpoints," Tom said, as we watched the code in the **`AddRecord`** method execute.

"That's all there is to it?" Lou said.

"That's all, Lou," I promised him. "Now it's time to learn how to create our own events."

Creating Your Own Events

"What I'd like to show you now," I said "is how to create events in your class module or object. When I say your own 'events', I'm not talking about creating a typical, standard, in-built Windows event. Windows events are generated as a response to user input – the system sits and waits for the user to do something, then raises the event we've told it to raise when that particular thing happens."

What kind of Event are we Creating?

"Then what type of events are you talking about?" Blaine asked.

"The events that we create and raise in the objects we design," I said, "are raised by the object itself, and they signal that a specific changes has been executed by the object." I put this little slide on the screen:

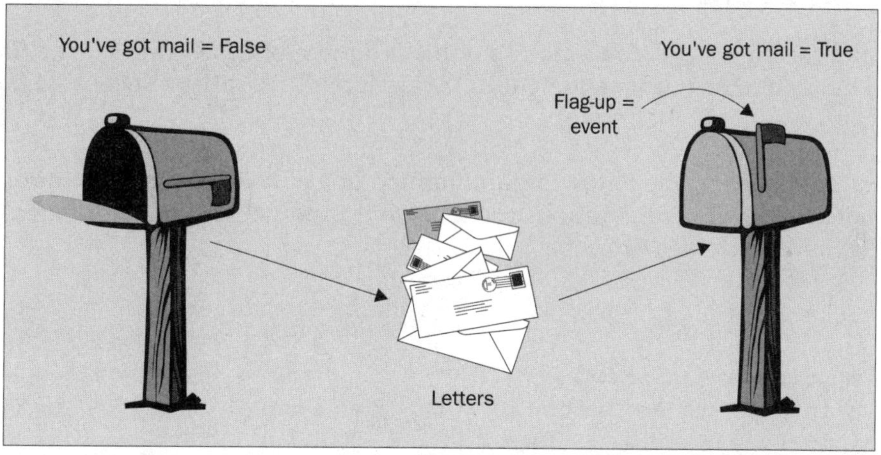

"Imagine you've got an old-fashioned mailbox at the end of your drive," I told the class. "When the mail delivery person delivers your letters, they put them in the box and lifts the little flag to tell you there's some mail for you. An event in our class module is a bit like the flag – telling the program using our object that a specific change has taken place – in this case, that the value of our imaginary variable – '`You've got mail`' – has gone from `False` to `True`."

"So, in some ways, then, they're like a return value from a function?" Ward suggested.

"How so?" Mary interrupted. "Functions return a value to the program that called them."

"That's right, Mary," I said, "but Ward's analogy isn't a bad one. In the same way that a function sends a message – the result of running the function – back to the program that called it, raising an event in a class module is a way of sending a message back to the program to say 'hey, something's happened'. The great thing about creating and raising events in your class module is that each event we define for our objects will have its own event procedure. The programmers who use our objects (including us) can place code in these event procedures, just like they can in the standard event procedures Visual Basic creates for us. We specify the event *as* an event – the programmer decides what to do about it in the code that they put in the event procedure.

This is another way of designing an object to do a job, and providing it with the tools to do that job. Events are one of those tools – tools that other programmers can interact with, and use flexibly with the properties and methods that we've also encapsulated inside the object."

"This I have to see," Rhonda said.

Declaring an Event

"Creating and raising an event in a class module is a piece of cake," I said. "The first thing we need to do is code an event statement in the General Declarations section of the **Student** class module."

I did just that by entering the following highlighted line of code into the **Student** class module's existing General Declarations section. Do this now if you're following along and building the Student Grades project:

```
Option Explicit

Private m_strName As String
Private m_intMidTerm As Integer
Private m_intFinalExam As Integer
Private m_intTermPaper As Integer
Private m_sngAverage As Single

Public Event AddSuccessful()
```

"This tells Visual Basic to include an event called **AddSuccessful** in the **Student** object. As you might imagine from its name, we'll raise this event from within the **Student** object to let the program using the **Student** object know that the record has been successfully added to **Grades.txt**."

"The empty set of parentheses seems to indicate that an event can pass arguments back to the object using our program," Steve observed. "Is that so?"

"That's right, Steve," I said. "Events that we code in our objects can have arguments, just like some of the other event procedures we've used. I think we should look into this a little further, in fact..."

Passing Arguments to Events

"Here's a neat little example you might find useful in your own projects," I told the students, showing them the following **Form_Unload** event code:

```
Private Sub Form_Unload(Cancel As Integer)

Dim intResponse As Integer

intResponse = MsgBox("Exit the Program?", vbOKCancel + vbQuestion,
"Exit")

If intResponse = 1 Then
    Cancel = 0
Else
    Cancel = 1
End If

End Sub
```

"It's a **Form_Unload** event," I explained. "**Form_Unload** is an event of the form class, which is raised whenever we click on the × button which is found at the top-right on the menu bar of most forms," I told them. "**Unload** is thus an event that is common to all forms."

"It seems to be taking an argument called **Cancel**," observed Ward.

Melissa spoke up: "I've actually used **Form_Unload** in exactly the way the Professor's showing us here, Ward. The **Unload** event can take an integer argument, which in this case we've called **Cancel**," she explained. "The argument has to equal zero for the form to go ahead and unload. As long as **Cancel** is **not** zero, the form won't unload."

"That's correct," I said. "When we click the × button on the title bar of our form, the **Form_Unload** event of the form is raised. In this case, it generates a message box that asks us if we really want to shut down the form."

I started a new Visual Basic project with a single blank form. I copied the **Form_Unload** event procedure into its code – nothing else – and ran the program. The blank form opened up and then sat there, waiting for me to close it down. I clicked the × button, and our message box appeared:

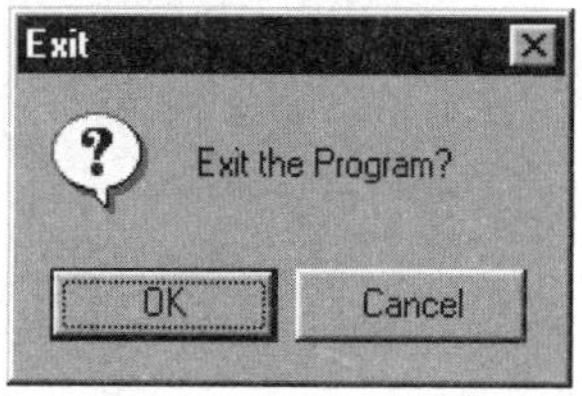

I clicked OK. The message box disappeared, the form vanished, and the program ended.

"We actually decide the value of **Cancel** from within the code block, and send it to the form object for evaluation," I explained. "We defined **intResponse** as the variable that stores our choice from the message box. If we select the OK button on the message box, the argument..."

```
MsgBox("Exit the Program?", vbOKCancel + vbQuestion, "Exit")
```

"...will evaluate as **True**, and **intResponse** takes the corresponding integer value, which is 1."

> **For more on using intrinsic constants as a shorthand way of structuring Visual Basic's message boxes, you can refer to my first book, *Learn to Program with Visual Basic 6*, pages 600-608.**

"**intResponse** is then used to set the value of **Cancel**:"

```
If intResponse = 1 Then
    Cancel = 0
Else
    Cancel = 1
End If
```

"That's a very efficient piece of coding," Dave observed.

"I wish I could take the credit for it," I told him, "but it's actually one of the commonest routines in Windows programming."

"So, let me get this straight," Ward said, "**Form_Unload** is an event, which is raised by us clicking on the × button on our form. Normally, it automatically shuts the form down, but here we're putting a message box in the way, asking us if that's really what we want to do?"

"Yes, Ward," I told him.

"As I understand it, Ward," Melissa said, "the variable we've called **Cancel** in this example, is an optional argument of the **Unload** event. If we don't provide an argument, Visual Basic uses its default value, which is zero, and shuts down the form. Here, however, we're using the message box to intervene and decide whether or not to use a non-zero value. If a non-zero value is passed back to the form object, it countermands the order to shut down the form."

"Exactly right, Melissa," I told her. "We can intercept the default behavior of the event by adding code in the event procedure that's triggered when the event is raised. That's the beauty of events: you define when they'll happen, and the programmer can decide what action to take when they do. Later on today," I explained to the class, "we're going to add an event to the **`Dish`** object of the China Shop project. For the moment, though, let's go back to our Student Grades demo and look at that line we've just added to General Declarations section of the **`Student`** class module..."

```
Public Event AddSuccessful()
```

"All we've done here is declare the event," I went on. "To raise the event – in other words to trigger the **`AddSuccessful`** event procedure back on the form that's using the **`Student`** object – we need to use the **`RaiseEvent`** statement within one of the **`Student`** class module's procedures."

Coding an Event for the Student Class

"Where should we raise the event?" Peter asked.

"That's entirely up to you," I said. "Events can be raised anywhere in a class module except for the General Declarations section. **Where** you raise the event depends on the reason you are raising it in the first place. In our case here, we want to let the user of the **`Student`** object know that the student record has been added successfully to **`Grades.txt`** – so it makes sense to raise the event **`AddSuccessful`** within the **`AddRecord`** method..."

I then modified the code in the **`AddRecord`** method of the **`Student`** class to look like this:

```
Public Sub AddRecord()

Open App.Path & "\Grades.txt" For Append As #1

Write #1, m_strName,
 ↳m_intMidterm,
 ↳m_intFinalExam,
 ↳m_intTermPaper,
 ↳m_sngAverage
Close #1

RaiseEvent AddSuccessful

End Sub
```

"Are you saying that just by executing the **RaiseEvent** statement within the class module of the **Student** object, the corresponding event procedure will be triggered?" Ward asked.

"That's right, Ward," I said. "Raising events from within an object of your own is a way of sending messages to the program using your object – and as you've seen, it's amazingly easy."

"What do we need to do to react to this event now?" Linda asked.

The WithEvents Statement

"Two things," I said. "First, we need to change the declaration of the object variable **m_stuNew** slightly in the General Declarations section of the form to use the keyword **WithEvents**."

So saying, I amended the existing line of code in the Student Grades program's **Form1** form so that it looked like this:

```
Private WithEvents m_stuNew As Student
```

"The object variable **m_stuNew** points to our current instance of the **Student** object," I said. "The **WithEvents** keyword tells Visual Basic that the object **m_stuNew** points to will be capable of sending events to our program."

"You said there were two things that needed to be done," Bob said. "That's the first. What's the second?"

"We need to find the **AddSuccessful** event procedure in the form's Code window and key up the event procedure itself," I said.

Adding Code that Responds to an Event

"Watch what happens," I said, "when I click on the object list box of the Code window, now that we're declaring the object variable using the **WithEvents** keyword."

I clicked on the object list box in the Code window, and found **m_stuNew**...

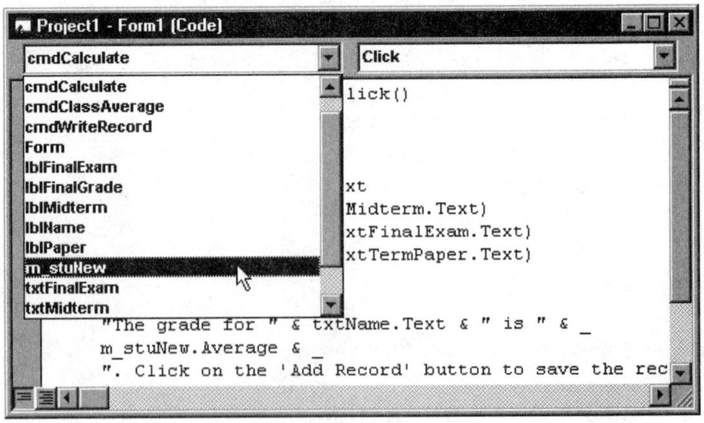

"Where did that reference to **m_stuNew** come from?" Rhonda asked. "I'm sure that wasn't there before."

"You're right, Rhonda," I answered, "it *wasn't* there before. Our object variable, **m_stuNew**, is now appearing in the object list box because we declared it with the keyword **WithEvents**."

I clicked on **m_stuNew** in the object list box:

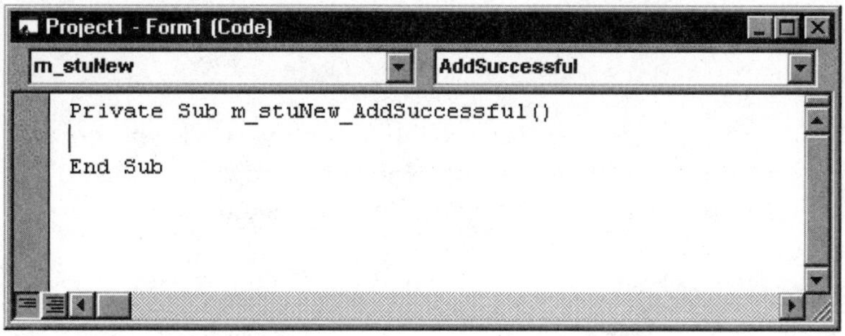

"There's the **AddSucessful** event procedure," I said.

"Eh? Wow! It just popped-up by itself!" exclaimed Rhonda. "That's magic!"

"If we had declared more than one event in the class module, would all of them have appeared in the procedures list box?" Valerie asked.

"We could have declared as many events as we wanted in a class module," I said, "and they would all appear in the procedures list box for us to choose from."

"Can we place code in this event procedure now?" Melissa asked. "I suppose that's the idea?"

"Exactly," I answered. "That way, whenever the **Student** object raises the **AddSuccessful** event within our form, whatever code is in its event procedure will be executed – just like any other event procedure."

I then added the following code to the **AddSuccessful** event procedure of the **m_stuNew** object variable:

```
Private Sub m_stuNew_AddSuccessful()

MsgBox "Student record successfully added"

End Sub
```

"Now let's run the program again," I said, "add some student information, click the Add Record button, and see what happens."

I ran the program, once again entered a "Bill Bates" and his grades, clicked the Calculate command button to calculate a grade, and then clicked on the Add Record command button:

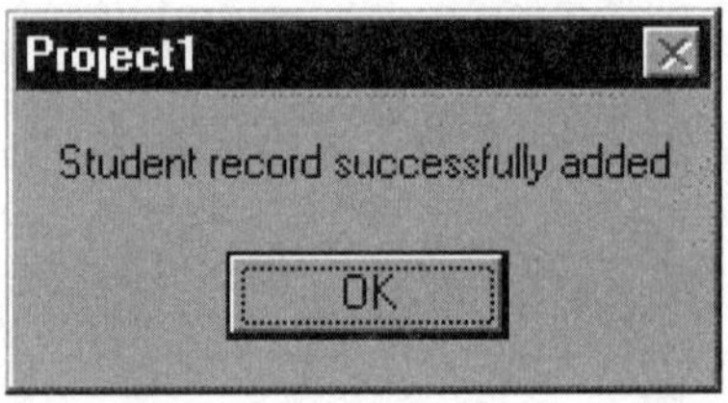

"So this message box was actually generated when the `AddSuccessful` event was raised from within the `Student` object, causing the `AddSuccessful` event procedure to be triggered – is that correct?" Rhonda asked.

"That's exactly right," I replied.

"I'm impressed," Ward said, smiling.

"What about the Class Average command button," Tom asked. "Are we going to modify that in any way to use the `Student` object?"

"I'm glad you mentioned that, Tom," I answered. "Yes, we'll be modifying that code next week – except we'll be modifying it to use the a *collection* of `Student` objects, instead, so that it can work with multiple instances of the `Student` object: one for each student in the class. The rest of today's session will be devoted to the China Shop."

Extending the China Shop Program

"First," I continued, "we'll be adding and raising an event in the `Dish` object, and then we'll create the `Package` object to be used to calculate shipping charges Joe wants so badly." I paused and looked at the clock. There was plenty of time.

Our next task was to set up some of the code that will let us incorporate event processing into the China Shop project. The first thing we'll do is create a `DataChanged` event that will allow us to let the program that's using our `Dish` object know when any changes occur to the values stored inside the object.

"You're probably in need of a rest," I observed. "We'll begin all that when we've had a break – how does that sound?"

The students rose and made their way out to the coffee machine. I could hear a lot of them talking about what they'd already learnt that morning.

Adding an Event to the China Shop Project

After the break, I distributed this exercise to set the class on the way to building events into their versions of the China Shop program:

Exercise - Creating the DataChanged Event in the Dish Class

In this exercise, you'll continue working with the **Dish** object of the China Shop by declaring and raising an event from within it.

1. Load up the China Shop project.
2. Using the Project Explorer, select and open up the **Dish** class module.
3. Modify the General Declarations section of the **Dish** class module so that it looks like this (modified code is highlighted in the usual way):

```
Option Explicit

Public Event DataChanged(Item As String, Value As Variant)

Private m_strBrand As String
Private m_strItem As String
Private m_intQuantity As Integer
Private m_curPrice As Currency
Private m_colDishPrice As New Collection
```

4. Modify the code in the **Property Let** procedure of the **Brand** property to look like this:

```
Property Let Brand(ByVal strNew As String)

m_strBrand = strNew
RaiseEvent DataChanged("Brand", m_strBrand)

End Property
```

5. Modify the code in the **Property Let** procedure of the **Item** property to look like this:

```
Property Let Item(ByVal strNew As String)

m_strItem = strNew
RaiseEvent DataChanged("Item", m_strItem)

End Property
```

6. Modify the code in the **Property Let** procedure of the **Quantity** property to look like this:

```
Property Let Quantity(ByVal intNew As Integer)

If m_strItem = "Platter" Then
 m_intQuantity = 1
Else
 m_intQuantity = intNew
End If

RaiseEvent DataChanged("Quantity", m_intQuantity)

End Property
```

7. Add the following line of code to the beginning of the **Initialize** event procedure of the **Dish** class module:

```
Private Sub Class_Initialize()

      Debug.Print "Dish object has been born..."

On Error GoTo ICanHandleThis

Dim strTest As String

...
```

8. Now add this next line of code to the **Dish** class module's **Terminate** event procedure:

```
Debug.Print "Dish object has died..."
```

9. Save the China Shop project.

Discussion

"The event that we're declaring, **DataChanged**," I said, "will be used to notify the program using the **Dish** object that one of the properties of the **Dish** object has changed – i.e. through the selection of another china item or a different quantity."

"Is that a fairly typical use for an event?" Valerie asked. "I noticed that quite a few of the controls in the Toolbox have some kind of 'changed' or 'clicked-on' type event."

"It's not a bad idea to code and raise an event in your object," I answered, "to let the user of the object know that something about it has changed. You can then leave it up to the user of the object to decide if they want to react to this event or not."

"What do you mean?" Steve asked.

"Well, for instance, all forms have a **Form_Click** event," I told him. "We've used it in a few of our demo programs, right here in this course. It represents what we want to happen when the user clicks on the form, and as such it's there – ready to accept code – in every form we create. However, I think it's fair to say that in the majority of Visual Basic projects we never put any code into it for any of our forms. Responding to the user clicking on the form is a strictly optional activity."

"So it's the same with the events we code into the objects we create?" Valerie said.

"Yes, Valerie," I said. "In fact, it'll only be today, while we're testing the code we write to interact with the **Dish** object, that we'll see the **DataChanged** event procedure of the **Dish** object in action. **DataChanged** is really only a useful debugging tool, so next week, when we code the **Order** collection object, we won't utilize the **DataChanged** event procedure."

"I have a question about the syntax of the event declaration," Mary said. "This syntax is different from the one we saw in the **Student** demonstration. I don't recall seeing anything within the parentheses of the **AddSuccessful** event declaration."

"You're right, Mary," I said, "the **AddSuccessful** event that we declared and raised in the **Student** object was pretty straightforward – it simply triggered the event, passing no arguments back to the program using it. However, with the **DataChanged** event, we're passing a **String** argument with the name of the property that's changed, and a **Variant** argument with the value the property's been changed to:"

```
Public Event DataChanged(Item As String, Value As Variant)
```

"The act of selecting a new brand, a different china piece, or changing the number of pieces in our order will change one of the properties of our **Dish** object and raise the event," I went on.

"I'm OK with the declaration for the **DataChanged** event," Tom said, "I can see what this event is supposed to do. However, can you review the syntax for raising the event and then passing the arguments back to the program from within the **Property Let** procedures of the class module?"

"Sure thing, Tom, let's take a look at the **Property Let** procedure for the **Brand** property," I said, as I displayed it on the classroom projector:

```
Property Let Brand(ByVal strNew As String)

m_strBrand = strNew
RaiseEvent DataChanged("Brand", m_strBrand)

End Property
```

"Our first step was to declare the event **DataChanged**," I said, "which we did using the event statement in the General Declarations section of the class module. Our second step, then is to raise the event – and that we do from any procedure of our choice within the class module. In the case of the **Dish** object, we want to raise the **DataChanged** event whenever a property of the **Dish** object changes – so we want to place that code within each one of the **Property Let** procedures. To raise the event, we use the **RaiseEvent** statement..."

```
RaiseEvent DataChanged("Brand", m_strBrand)
```

"...followed by the name of the event, and then, in the parentheses, the value of the two arguments we'll be passing back to the program: the name of the property which is being changed – which in this case is the string literal 'Brand' – and the value that the property has been changed to – which we include as the variable **m_strBrand**. Remember, the actual event accepts this second argument into a **Variant** data-type – which can accept either a string-value, as in this case, or a numeric value, as is the case when we select a different quantity of china pieces."

"That's not too bad at all," Rhonda said. "Can we run the China Shop program now to see how this event works?"

Integrating the DataChanged Event in the China Shop Code

"Not quite, Rhonda," I said. "We need to make some changes to the code in the main form of the China Shop program before our program can react to the **`DataChanged`** event. First, we need to change the declaration of the **`Dish`** object slightly to tell Visual Basic that the object we are using triggers an event."

"And that's by using the **`WithEvents`** statement, as we did before with the **`Student`** object?" Dorothy enquired.

"Yes, exactly, Dorothy," I replied. "Then, most importantly, we have to get our program to react to our event by placing code in the **`DataChanged`** event procedures of each of the **`Dish`** objects we declare."

"Why did we add code to the **`Initialize`** and **`Terminate`** event procedures of the class module?" Kate asked.

"That code will be triggered when the **`Dish`** object is born and when it dies," I said. "It will come in quite handy later in visualizing what's going on behind the scenes of our object."

There were no more questions, so I prepared to circulate the next exercise to the class.

Responding to Events

What we needed to do next was ensure that all of the **`Private`** variables that store the object's property values can trigger events when those values change.

"In this exercise," I told the class, "you'll modify the General Declarations Section of the main form of the China Shop program to tell Visual Basic that the **`Dish`** object is triggering events, and that you want to be able to react to them."

Here's the exercise:

Exercise - Letting the Program Respond to the Dish Object's Events

1. If the China Shop project isn't open on your PC, open it now.

2. Select **frmMain** in the Project Explorer window and replace the existing variable declarations for the six possible **Dish** objects in the General Declarations section with the modified declarations shown below:

```
Option Explicit

Private m_lngBackColor As Long
Private m_blnDateDisplay As Boolean
Private m_colDishPrice As New Collection
Public Quantity as Integer

Private WithEvents m_dshPlate As Dish
Private WithEvents m_dshButterPlate As Dish
Private WithEvents m_dshSoupBowl As Dish
Private WithEvents m_dshCup As Dish
Private WithEvents m_dshSaucer As Dish
Private WithEvents m_dshPlatter As Dish
```

3. Save the China Shop project.

4. You can run the program at this point – but you won't notice a difference in its behavior. The fact that we have told Visual Basic that the **Dish** object is raising the **DataChanged** event doesn't impact our program yet – at least, not until we place code in the **Dish** object's **DataChanged** event procedures.

Discussion

"All we've done here," I said, "is to change the declaration of each one of our six **Dish** object variable declarations to include the keyword **WithEvents**. As was the case with the **Student** object, **WithEvents** tells Visual Basic that the **Dish** object triggers events, and that we wish to react to those events within our program."

"Are you saying that if we choose to, we can ignore the events that the **Dish** object is triggering?" Valerie asked.

"That's right," I said. "The programmer using the **Dish** object can always choose to ignore the events emanating from an object, and they can do that in one of two ways: first, not code the declaration of the **Dish** object with the keyword **WithEvents**; secondly, not add any 'reactive' code to the event procedures of the object variables pointing to the **Dish** object."

"I still want to see this in action!" Rhonda said.

"We're just one step away, Rhonda," I said.

The DataChanged Event Code in Detail

"What we have to do now is add some code to the **DataChanged** event procedures of the six **Dish** objects that we've declared in the China Shop program."

Here's the exercise to accomplish this:

Exercise - Coding the Dish Object's DataChanged Events

In this exercise, you'll place code in the **DataChanged** event procedures of each of the six **Dish** objects. This code will print a message in the Immediate window whenever any of the property values of the **Dish** object changes.

1. If the China Shop project's **Main** form isn't open in your Visual basic IDE, open it.
2. Add this highlighted line to the **m_dshButterPlate_DataChanged** event procedure:

```
Private Sub m_dshButterPlate_DataChanged(Item As String, Value as
Variant)

Debug.Print "Butter Plate " & Item & " has changed: " & Value

End Sub
```

3. Add this code to the **m_dshCup_DataChanged** event procedure:

```
Private Sub m_dshCup_DataChanged(Item As String, Value As Variant)

Debug.Print "Cup " & Item & " has changed: " & Value

End Sub
```

4. Add this code to the **m_dshPlate_DataChanged** event procedure:

```
Private Sub m_dshPlate_DataChanged(Item As String, Value As Variant)

Debug.Print "Plate " & Item & " has changed to:" & Value

End Sub
```

5. Add this code to the **m_dshPlatter_DataChanged** event procedure:

```
Private Sub m_dshPlatter_DataChanged(Item As String, Value As Variant)

Debug.Print "Platter " & Item & " has changed to: " & Value

End Sub
```

6. Add this code to the **m_dshSaucer_DataChanged** event procedure:

```
Private Sub m_dshSaucer_DataChanged(Item As String, Value As Variant)

Debug.Print "Saucer " & Item & " has changed to:" & Value

End Sub
```

7. Add this code to the **m_dshSoupBowl_DataChanged** event procedure:

```
Private Sub m_dshSoupBowl_DataChanged(Item As String, Value As Variant)

Debug.Print "Soup Bowl " & Item & " has changed to:" & Value

End Sub
```

8. Save the China Shop project.

9. Run the program, select the Mikasa brand of china, choose the Plate, Butter Plate and Soup Bowl china pieces, and a quantity of 2. Click on the Calculate Button. $90 should be displayed. Now change the quantity from 2 to 4 and recalculate. The price should change to $180. As you interact with the program, the **DataChanged** Event of the **Dish** object will trigger, causing the code you placed in the **Dish** object's event procedures to print the statements we coded in the Immediate window.

Discussion

To say that everyone was pretty excited with what was going on in the China Shop program would be an understatement. No-one had any trouble at all with the exercise, and it was all that I could do to get everyone's attention as I began to run the program myself.

"Let's take a look more closely at what the program is doing now," I said. "The combination of the code that we have placed in the **`DataChanged`** event procedures, plus the code we placed in the **`Initialize`** and **`Terminate`** event procedures of the **`Dish`** object itself will give us a chance to really see what's happening, and when."

The DataChanged Event in Action

I then ran the program myself, clicked on the Mikasa brand of china in the list box, and then clicked on the check box captioned Plate. These lines appeared in the Immediate window:

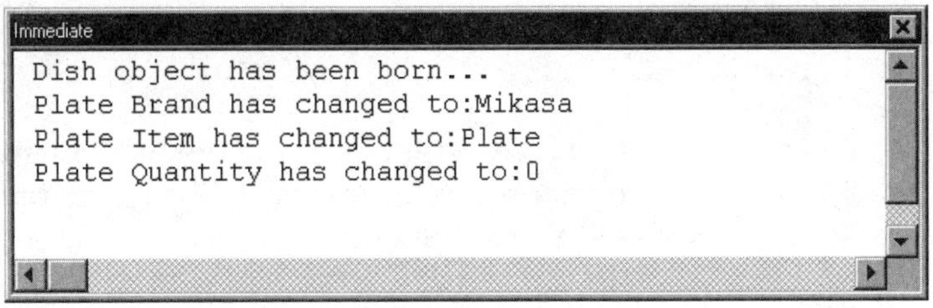

"Let me explain what's happened here," I said. "When we first click on one of the six check boxes representing an item of china – in this case the Plate item – a **`Dish`** object is created, and its three properties are set: the **`Brand`**, **`Item`** and **`Quantity`** properties."

"Why wasn't the **`Dish`** object born when you selected a brand in the list box?" Valerie asked.

"There's really only one section of code where **`Dish`** objects are created," I said, "and that's in the **`Click`** event procedure of **`chkChinaItems`**. The **`Click`** event procedures of **`lstBrands`** and **`optQuantity`** will modify the properties of any existing **`Dish`** objects, but not **create** them."

"I'm a little confused about why the properties are being changed when we first select an item of china," Chuck asked. "Aren't we just creating the **`Dish`** object then?"

"That's right, Chuck, we are," I answered. "But remember, the **`DataChanged`** event is being raised *whenever* the **`Property Let`** procedures of the **`Dish`** object are executed – and that happens not only when one of the properties of the **`Dish`** object are changed, but also whenever the **`Dish`** object is first created. Let me show you."

I then displayed the code from the **Click** event procedure of **chkChinaItem** on the classroom projector:

```
Private Sub chkChinaItem_Click(Index As Integer)

Select Case Index
 Case 0:
 If chkChinaItem(Index).Value = 1 Then
 Set m_dshPlate = New Dish
 m_dshPlate.Brand = lstBrands
 m_dshPlate.Item = "Plate"
 m_dshPlate.Quantity = frmMain.Quantity
 Else
 Set m_dshPlate = Nothing
 End If
```

"As you can see," I said, "right after the **Set** statement that points the object variable **m_dshPlate** to an instance of the **Dish** object, we immediately assign the initial values to the properties of the **Dish** object."

"So that's why the Immediate window tells us that three properties have changed," Rhonda said, "even though, at this point, we've only selected a **Brand** and an **Item**, but not a quantity."

"That's right, Rhonda," I said. "The **m_dshPlate** object was created with a **Brand** property of **Mikasa**, an **Item** property of **Plate**, and a **Quantity** property of zero."

"Is that a problem?" Blaine asked. "Shouldn't we wait until we have a valid value for **Quantity** before creating the **Dish** object?"

"Not at all, Blaine," I said. "As soon as the customer selects a quantity, we'll modify the **Quantity** properties of every **Dish** object that we've created. We have code in the **Click** event procedure of **optQuantity** to do exactly that."

I then checked the Butter Plate and Soup Bowl china pieces. These new lines appeared in the Immediate window:

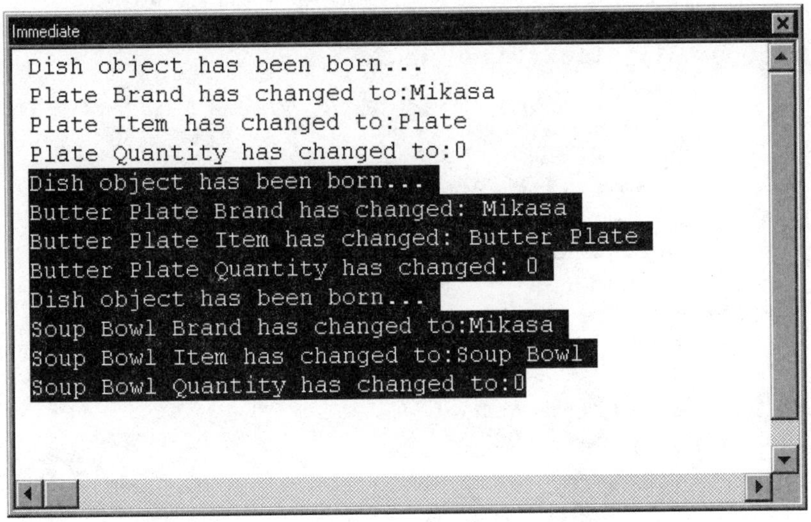

Immediate
Dish object has been born...
Plate Brand has changed to:Mikasa
Plate Item has changed to:Plate
Plate Quantity has changed to:0
Dish object has been born...
Butter Plate Brand has changed: Mikasa
Butter Plate Item has changed: Butter Plate
Butter Plate Quantity has changed: 0
Dish object has been born...
Soup Bowl Brand has changed to:Mikasa
Soup Bowl Item has changed to:Soup Bowl
Soup Bowl Quantity has changed to:0

"Selecting the Butter Plate and Soup Bowl china pieces," I said, "has triggered the creation of two more **Dish** objects."

"So at this point," Ward said, "We now have three **Dish** objects in existence, each one referenced by its own dedicated object variable – and all three objects have their **Quantity** properties set to zero?"

"Exactly, Ward," I said. "Now let's change the **Quantity** of our selected items to 2 using the Quantity option buttons."

I did that, and another three lines were added to the Immediate window:

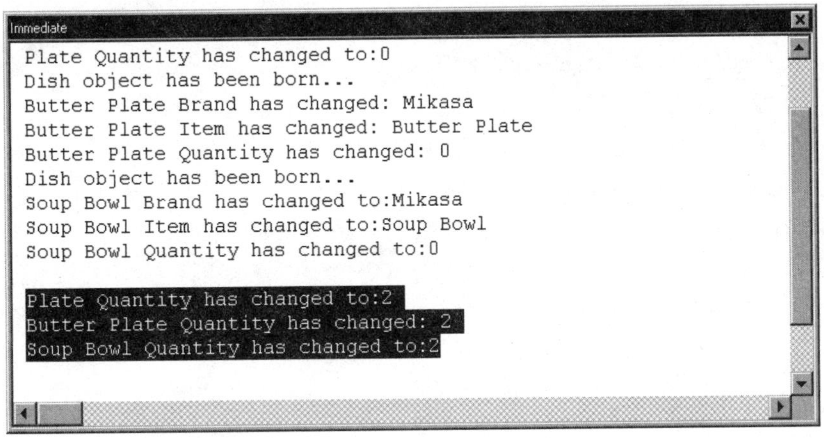

Immediate
Plate Quantity has changed to:0
Dish object has been born...
Butter Plate Brand has changed: Mikasa
Butter Plate Item has changed: Butter Plate
Butter Plate Quantity has changed: 0
Dish object has been born...
Soup Bowl Brand has changed to:Mikasa
Soup Bowl Item has changed to:Soup Bowl
Soup Bowl Quantity has changed to:0
Plate Quantity has changed to:2
Butter Plate Quantity has changed: 2
Soup Bowl Quantity has changed to:2

"Selecting a quantity of 2," I said, "has triggered the **Property Let** procedures for the **Quantity** properties of all three instantiated objects. To refresh your memory, let me display the code in the **Click** event procedure of **optQuantity** now..."

```
Private Sub optQuantity_Click(Index As Integer)

frmMain.Quantity = Index

Dim chkObject As CheckBox

For Each chkObject In chkChinaItem

Select Case chkObject.Value
 Case 1

 If chkObject.Caption = "Plate" Then
 m_dshPlate.Quantity = Index
 End If

 If chkObject.Caption = "Butter Plate" Then
 m_dshButterPlate.Quantity = Index
 End If

 If chkObject.Caption = "Soup Bowl" Then
 m_dshSoupBowl.Quantity = Index
 End If

 If chkObject.Caption = "Cup" Then
 m_dshCup.Quantity = Index
 End If

 If chkObject.Caption = "Saucer" Then
 m_dshSaucer.Quantity = Index
 End If

 If chkObject.Caption = "Platter" Then
 m_dshPlatter.Quantity = Index
 End If

End Select
Next

End Sub
```

"As you can see," I continued, "what we do is use a **For...Each** statement to loop through each item in the **chkChinaItem** control array. If it's selected, we change the **Quantity** property of the appropriate **Dish** object variable – which in turn triggers that object's **Property Let** procedure which raises the **DataChanged** event procedure, passing back to the China Shop program the name of the property that has been changed, along with its value."

"This is great," Rhonda said, "it's like having an x-ray of the internals of the object."

"That's right, Rhonda," I said, "it's a great teaching and debugging tool. Now watch this..."

I then unchecked the check box representing the plate item, with this result:

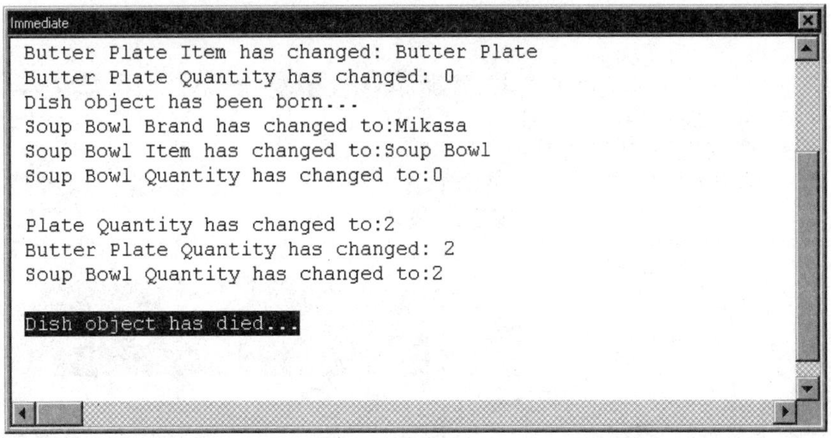

"Unchecking the check box representing the plate," I said, "has caused this highlighted line of code in the **Click** event procedure of **chkChinaItems** to execute:"

```
Select Case Index
 Case 0:
 If chkChinaItem(Index).Value = 1 Then
 Set m_dshPlate = New Dish
 m_dshPlate.Brand = lstBrands.Text
 m_dshPlate.Item = "Plate"
 m_dshPlate.Quantity = frmMain.Quantity
 Else
 Set m_dshPlate = Nothing
 End If
```

"When the code in the **Click** event procedure of **chkChinaItems** executed," I said, "it saw that the **Value** property of **chkChinaItem(0)** – the plate item – was **False**, meaning the check box was unchecked. It interpreted that to mean that the customer no longer wanted the plate. It then set the reference to the object variable for the Plate **Dish** object to **Nothing**, causing the death of the **Dish** object representing the plate. The plate's **Dish** object's **Terminate** event procedure was executed, and we received a message about its death in the Immediate window."

"Suppose the customer changes his or her mind again?" Dorothy asked.

"In that case," I said, "a new **Dish** object representing the plate will be created. Watch this..."

I then selected the check box representing a plate once more, and another four lines were added to the Immediate window:

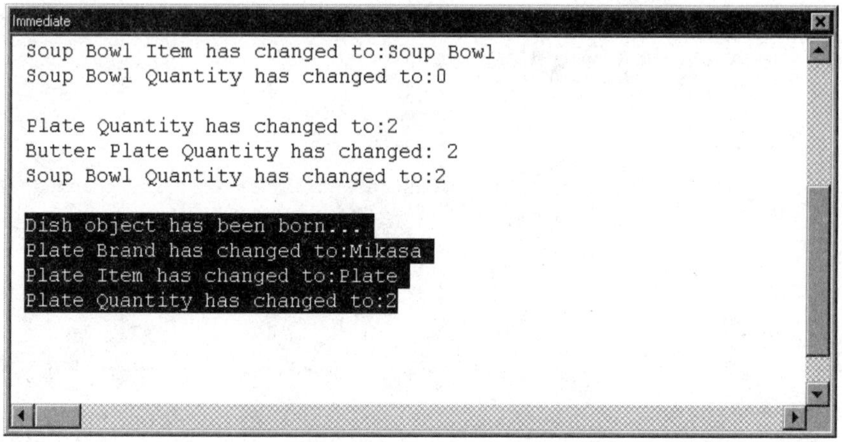
Immediate
Soup Bowl Item has changed to:Soup Bowl
Soup Bowl Quantity has changed to:0
Plate Quantity has changed to:2
Butter Plate Quantity has changed: 2
Soup Bowl Quantity has changed to:2
Dish object has been born...
Plate Brand has changed to:Mikasa
Plate Item has changed to:Plate
Plate Quantity has changed to:2

"Selecting the Plate," I said, "has created a **Dish** object with a **Brand** property of **"Mikasa"**, an **Item** property of **"Plate"**, and a **Quantity** property of 2."

"So this time," Steve added, "the **Dish** object was created with the user's currently selected **Quantity**."

"That's right, Steve," I said. "Now let's change the selected brand from Mikasa to Corelle – we should receive a message in the Immediate window that the three instantiated **Dish** objects have had their **Brand** property changed..."

I did that, and another three lines were added to the Immediate window:

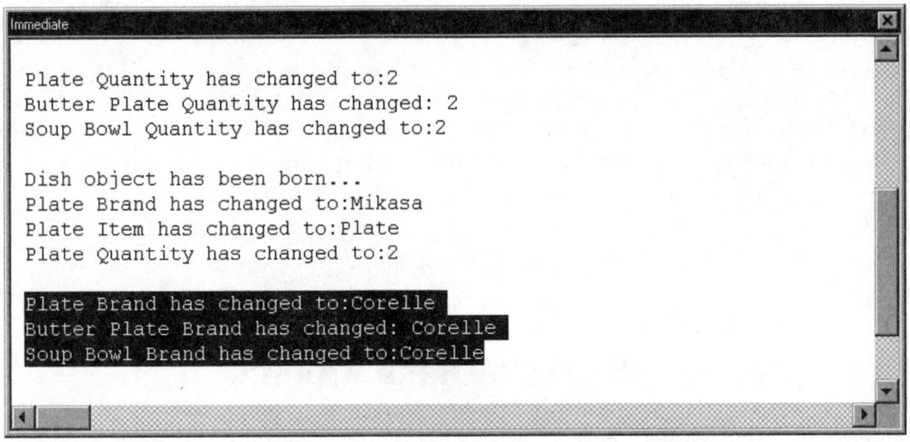
Immediate
Plate Quantity has changed to:2
Butter Plate Quantity has changed: 2
Soup Bowl Quantity has changed to:2
Dish object has been born...
Plate Brand has changed to:Mikasa
Plate Item has changed to:Plate
Plate Quantity has changed to:2
Plate Brand has changed to:Corelle
Butter Plate Brand has changed: Corelle
Soup Bowl Brand has changed to:Corelle

"As you can see," I said, "the **`Brand`** properties of all three **`Dish`** objects has been changed."

"This is pretty neat," Kate said, "using the **`DataChanged`** event procedure to write status messages to the Immediate window is helping me quite a bit."

"Writing to the Immediate window is a great thing to do while developing your program," I said. "When you're all finished, and content that your program is working properly, you can just remove the code from the **`DataChanged`** event procedure, or comment it out. Another alternative is to leave the code in there, because if you compile your program into an executable, the Visual Basic compiler ignores all **`Debug`** statements anyway – in the Visual Basic runtime environment, there is no Immediate window."

> **The final version of the China Shop program from our Intro class was delivered to Joe Bullina to be run from within the Visual Basic IDE. In the real business world, we'd usually generate an executable program and install it, plus some supporting Visual Basic runtime programs, on the user's PC. However, the Working Model Edition of Visual Basic supplied with my first book, *Learn to Program with Visual Basic*, doesn't have the Compile feature. Rather than confuse the readers of the first book, we chose to deliver the China Shop program to be run within the IDE. Compiling a Visual Basic program is easy – installing it not so easy. This is something I address in *Question 69* of my second book, *Learn to Program with Visual Basic Examples.***

"We still have one major task to complete today," I said, "and that's to code the **`Package`** object."

Building the China Shop's Package Object

I reminded the class that the **Package** object will be used to store information relating to which state a customer's order is being sent to, and what the shipping charges are for that state. A package object will be instantiated in the program each time the user clicks on a destination state in the list box on the **Shipping Charges** form. The package object will read the relevant state and shipping charge information from the **Shipping.txt** file and make that information available inside the object.

The first step, again, was to create a class module containing the code template for the **Package** class.

Creating the Package Object's Class Module

Here's the exercise I distributed to get the class started on implementing the **Package** class in the China Shop:

Exercise - Creating the Package Class

In this exercise, you'll create the **Package** class module for the China Shop project. Remember, the **Package** object is the object that ties up the state we're going to be delivering to with the charges associated with shipping china to that state.

1. If the China Shop project isn't open in your Visual basic IDE, open it.
2. Select Project | Add Class Module from the Visual Basic menu bar.
3. When the Add Class Module dialog box appears, double-click the Class Module option on the New tab:

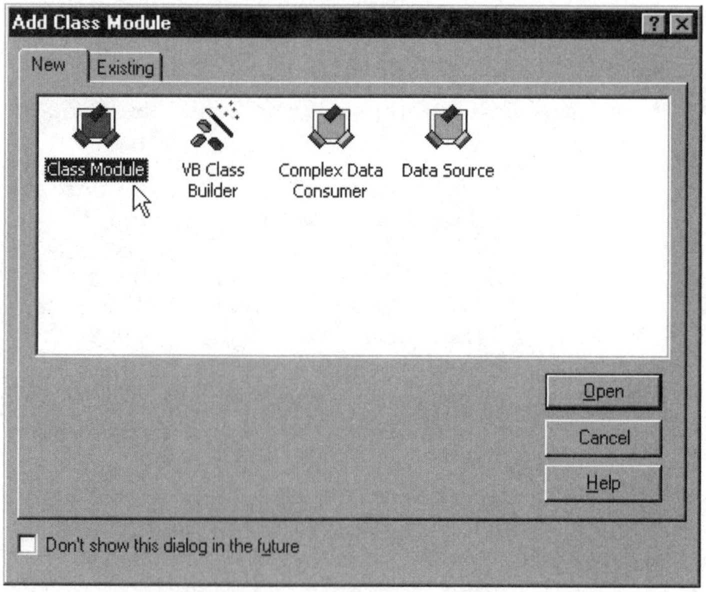

...and a new class module will appear in the IDE.

4. Bring up the Properties window for the class by pressing *F4*. Change the **`Name`** property of the class from **`Class1`** to **`Package`**:

5. Click on the save icon on the Toolbar and save this class, with the name **`Package`**, to your **`\VBFiles\China`** folder:

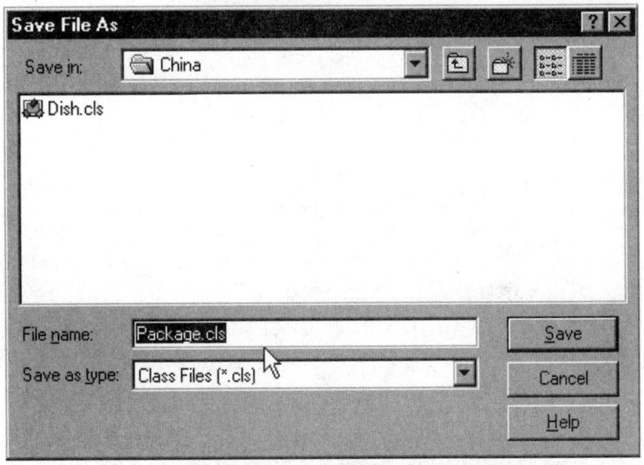

6. Bring up the Project Explorer window. You should now have two forms and two class modules:

Discussion

This was the second class module the students had created and saved, and they seemed a lot more comfortable with it now.

"All we've done to this point," I said, "is to create the class module and name it **Package**. Now it's time to create the properties that define the characteristics of the **Package** object."

Building the Package Object's Properties

"As a reminder of the properties that we need to add to the **Package** object, here's the properties chart we developed on the board in previous lessons. You can refer to this as you code the two properties of the **Package** class:"

OBJECTS	China/Dish	Order	Package
PROPERTIES	Brand Item Quantity Price		Charges State

I then distributed an exercise for the class to complete. In this exercise, you'll continue working with the **Package** class module you created in the previous exercise, as you declare **Private** module level variables to represent the two properties of the **Package** object we identified in Lesson Four. You'll also be declaring a collection variable into which you will read the contents of the file **Shipping.txt**.

Exercise - Creating the Package Class's Private Variables

1. Continue working with the **Package** class of the China Shop project.

2. Add the following code to the class's General Declarations section:

```
Option Explicit

Private m_strState As String
Private m_curCharges As Currency
Private m_colShippingCharges As New Collection
```

3. Save the China Shop project.

Discussion

"Remember, `m_colShippingCharges` is the collection into which we'll be reading the data from the `Shipping.txt` file," I said.

"As was the case when we created the `Dish` object," I said, "we still have some more work to do with the `Package` object. We need to write code in the `Initialize` event procedure to open, read, and close the file `Shipping.txt`. Then we need to code the `Property Let` and `Property Get` procedures to make the object's properties accessible."

"Will the `Package` object have methods or events?" Rhonda asked.

"No, it won't," I said, "just the two properties. One of these – `Charges` – is a read-only property, because we don't want the value of shipping charges for a given state to be changed at runtime."

"OK," I continued, "let's proceed by coding up the class's `Initialize` event."

I then distributed the next exercise to achieve this:

Exercise - Coding the Package Class's Initialize Event Procedure

In this exercise, you'll place code in the `Initialize` event procedure of the `Package` class.

1. Continue working with the `Package` class of the China Shop project.
2. Add the following code to the class's `Initialize` procedure:

```
Private Sub Class_Initialize()

On Error GoTo ICanHandleThis

Dim strState As String
Dim curPrice As Currency

If App.Path = "\" Then
 Open App.Path & "Shipping.txt" For Input As #1
Else
 Open App.Path & "\Shipping.txt" For Input As #1
End If
```

```
Do While Not EOF(1)
 Input #1, strState, curPrice
  m_colShippingCharges.Add Item:=curPrice, Key:=strState
Loop
Close #1

Exit Sub

ICanHandleThis:

Select Case Err.Number
 Case 53 'File not found
 MsgBox "A file required by the " &
 ↳"China Shop program " & vbCrLf &
 ↳"is missing. Please ensure that " & vbCrLf &
 ↳"Shipping.txt is in " & vbCrLf &
 ↳"the China Shop directory " & vbCrLf &
 ↳"on the computer's hard drive"
 Unload Me
 Exit Sub

 Case Else
 MsgBox "Unexpected error has occurred" & vbCrLf &
 ↳"Please contact a member of staff. "
 Unload frmMain
 Exit Sub

End Select

End Sub
```

3. Save the China Shop project.

Discussion

"You may recognize this as the code currently found in the `Load` event procedure of the `Shipping Charges` form," I said. "Its primary job is to build the `m_colShippingCharges` collection using the data in the `Shipping.txt` file."

"Will we be removing the code from the `Load` event procedure?" Blaine asked.

"No, we won't," I answered. "As was the case with the **Dish** object, we'll leave the code in the **Load** event procedure, in order to load the fifty states, and District of Columbia, into the list box of the **Shipping Charges** form. However, whenever the user clicks on an item in the list box, we'll create an instance of the **Package** object, set a value for its **States** property, and return the **Charges** property to be displayed in a label caption on the form."

There were no other questions.

"Now let's code the **Property Let** and **Property Get** procedures of the **Package** object," I said, distributing this exercise for the students to complete:

Exercise - Creating the Package Class Properties

In this exercise, you'll code the **Property Get** and **Property Let** procedures of the **Package** object.

1. Continue working with the **Package** class module.

2. Create the property procedures for the **State** property by coding (in the class's General Declarations section) a **Property Get**...

```
Property Get State () As String

State = m_strState

End Property
```

...and a **Property Let** procedure:

```
Property Let State(ByVal strNew As String)

m_strState = strNew

End Property
```

3. Create the property procedures for the read-only **Charges** property by coding a **Property Get** procedure:

```
Property Get Charges() As Currency

m_curCharges = m_colShippingCharges(m_strState)
Charges = m_curCharges

End Property
```

4. Save the China Shop project.

Discussion

The exercise ran smoothly, although Rhonda did seek a clarification as to what was happening in the **Property Get** procedure of the **Charges** property.

"The **Charges** property of the **Package** object is a read-only property," I said, "and has no **Property Let** procedure. We determine its value by using the value of the **State** property of the **Package** object to look up the shipping charges in the **m_colShippingCharges** collection, which we created and populated when the **Package** object was instantiated."

Integrating the Package Object into the China Shop

"It's time to work with the **Shipping Charges** form now," I said. "We'll modify the code in the **Click** event procedure of the list box to use our newly created **Package** object."

I then distributed the following exercise to the class:

Exercise - Telling the China Shop Program to Use the Package Object

In this exercise, you'll modify the **Click** event procedure of **lstStates**. This modification means that the program will use the **Package** object to calculate the shipping charges.

1. Continue working with the China Shop project.

2. Select **frmShipping** in the Project Explorer window and replace the existing code in the **Click** event procedure of **lstStates** with this code:

```
Private Sub lstStates_Click()

Dim pkgNew As New Package
pkgNew.State = lstStates.Text

lblCharges.Caption = "Shipping charges for the state of " &
      ↳lstStates.Text &
      ↳" are: $" & pkgNew.Charges

Set pkgNew = Nothing

End Sub
```

3. Save the China Shop project.

4. Run the program and click on the Shipping Charges button. When the Shipping Charges form appears, click on New Jersey in the list box – you should see shipping charges of $6 displayed.

Discussion

I ran the program myself, clicked on the Shipping Charges button, and selected New Jersey:

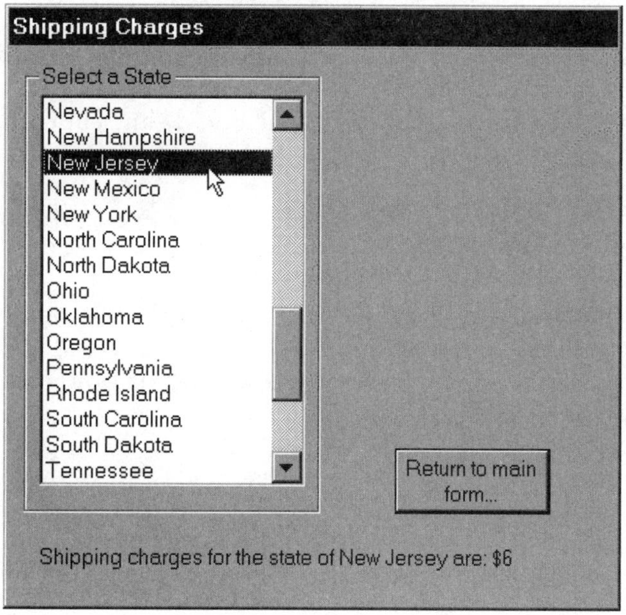

"That's beautiful," I heard Tom say.

"The **Shipping Charges** form is now using the **Package** object to calculate shipping charges," I said. "To the user of the program, nothing has changed, just as was the case when we used the **Dish** object on the main form – but to the programmer, coding is immensely easier. We've taken the tedium out of the **Click** event procedure of the list box. All we're doing now is declaring an instance of the **Package** object..."

```
Dim pkgNew As New Package
```

"...setting the **State** property of the **Package** object to the **Text** property of the list box..."

```
pkgNew.State = lstStates.Text
```

"...and then concatenating the value of the **Charges** property of the **Package** object to the **Caption** of the **lblCharges** label:"

```
lblCharges.Caption = "Shipping charges for the state of " &
      ↳lstStates.Text &
      ↳" are: $" & pkgNew.Charges
```

"I'm not seeing any messages in the Immediate window," Steve said.

"That's because we haven't coded any," I said, "but you can feel free to do that yourself if you wish."

"That's a good idea," Ward said. "I'd love to experiment a bit with this **Package** object – perhaps even add an event to it. Would that be OK?"

"That's fine, Ward," I said. "Feel free to enhance the China Shop project in whatever way you want in your own time. Make sure you're still using something that resembles our classroom version whenever you're working on the project in class, though, or you'll get yourself in a tangle!"

Just to ensure that everyone understood what we had done with the **Package** object, I used the remaining fifteen minutes of class time to run the program in Step mode. As had been the case when the students saw the **Dish** object in action, I could see that the class was impressed as we watched the **Package** object work behind the scenes.

"Be sure to be well-rested before next week's class," I cautioned. "Next week we learn more about **Collection** objects."

Chapter Summary

In this chapter we added to our knowledge of object-oriented programming by seeing how to create **methods** and **events** for our classes, and how to instantiate individual objects that use these events and methods.

Specifically, we saw that:

- Adding a **method** to a class **encapsulates** an **action** that's associated with that class's objects. We saw this with the `AddRecord` method of the `Student` object in the `Student Grades` demo project
- Encapsulating methods inside objects helps streamline our code and make it more efficient
- Adding **events** to our classes allows objects instantiated from them to signal to the outside world when something happens inside an object
- We, and the other programmers who make use of our objects, can add code that responds to these events when they occur

In the China Shop project, we finished coding the `Dish` class, and created the new `Package` object. Specifically:

- We created the `DataChanged` event for the `Dish` class and integrated this with the rest of the program. We also saw how this event, once defined, could help us see what was happening inside an object: we did this by displaying messages triggered by the `DataChanged` event in the Immediate window. We could, if we wanted, use the event to trigger any other action that we cared to code into the event procedure that responds to this event
- We created the `Package` class: the `Package` object will store the state and shipping charge data that the program uses
- We created properties of the `Package` class that store this data inside the `Package` object
- We created the `Property Get` and `Let` procedures that access these properties
- We modified the China Shop program to utilize the `Package` object in its shipping charges calculations

In next week's lesson, we take a much more detailed look at collection objects. Doing this will help us keep track of the different `Dish` objects as they're created and used in the China Shop program.

Until then, au revoir!

Learn to Program Objects with Visual Basic

Chapter 7
Collection Objects

This chapter will complete the core object-orientation of the China Shop project. We'll achieve this by building a **collection** object that will pull together all of the object-oriented programming that we've built into the China Shop already. Collection objects give us the ability to manage and manipulate the other objects that we have in our program. For example, the China Shop project can instantiate up to six **`Dish`** objects at any one time – not too tricky to keep a handle on. But how about a program that could be using a hundred **`Dish`** objects simultaneously, or a thousand? A bit more of a headache, I'm sure you'll agree. We can use collections to manage and manipulate large numbers of similar objects much more easily than we would otherwise be able to do. You'll see for yourself just how useful that can be in this chapter.

We'll start the chapter by discussing collection objects in the context of our Student Grades demo program – once again, we'll be putting the theory into practice there before we apply it to the China Shop program. In the China Shop, the collection that we build will act as a manager for the various **`Dish`** objects that get created when the customer makes their choices of china pieces. You'll see how this makes our code even more streamlined.

Here's a summary of the topics we'll cover this week:

- What **collection objects** are
- How collection objects can help us manage groups of other objects – such as the multiple **`Dish`** objects in the China Shop, or the **`Student`** objects in the Student Grades program
- Creating a **class module** that defines a collection object
- Coding the methods and properties that embody the collection object's functionality and let it look after our multiple objects
- Using collection objects in practice in the Student Grades demo
- Creating a **`Order`** collection object in the China Shop program

Now let's join the class.

Here Comes the Weekend

"Welcome to our seventh class," I said. "I'm convinced you'll find today's session enjoyable. Today we'll be talking about **collection objects**, which we can use to help us control and change the other objects in our programs. This can make life for the programmer much easier in the long run, and reduce the amount of code that we need in our programs. We can use the facilities of the collection object to create other objects, change those objects' properties, and destroy them when we're finished with them."

Today's Lesson

"Like the other objects we've built in recent chapters, collection objects are instantiated from an underlying template – a collection class, which we create in code in a similar way to how we build a class module. We'll see all this in action in the Student Grades project that we've already worked with. By the end of today's class, we'll also have built a collection class in the China Shop project and used the collection object instantiated from it."

"Are collection objects difficult to work with?" Bob asked.

"Not at all," I said, "collection objects can simplify the code you have to write when dealing with groups of objects of the same type – such as the `Student` objects in our demo program, or the `Dish` objects in the China Shop."

Linda said: "That sounds like a description of the Visual Basic collections we looked at a few weeks back – the `Forms` and `Controls` collections. Are collection objects similar to Visual Basic collections?"

"Yes, they are," I said.

Collection Objects are like System Collections

"If you keep in mind two of the more familiar Visual Basic collections that we looked at in Lesson Two – the `Forms` collection and the `Controls` collection – then you're thinking about the essence of a Visual Basic collection object: it's used to store references to other objects that exist elsewhere in memory, and it makes it easier for us to work with groups of objects in code:"

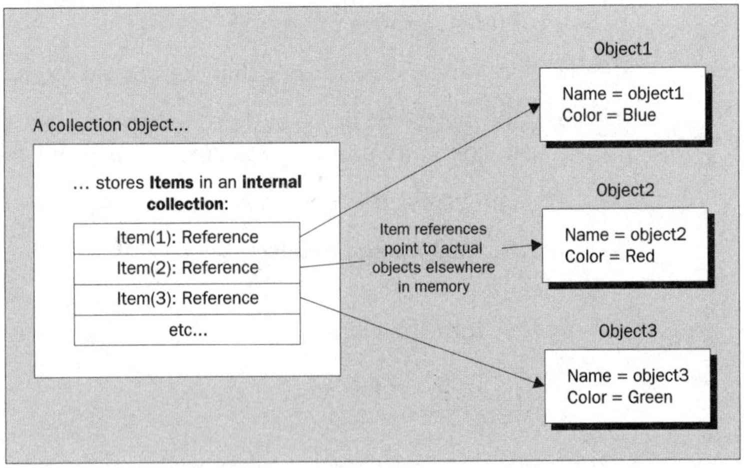

"Remember this: the **`Forms`** collection is a collection whose **items** – the things that it refers to – are **form** objects. The **`Controls`** collection is a collection whose **items** are **controls**. Today we'll create the **`Order`** object of the China Shop project – this collection will contain items that reference the China Shop's **`Dish`** objects:"

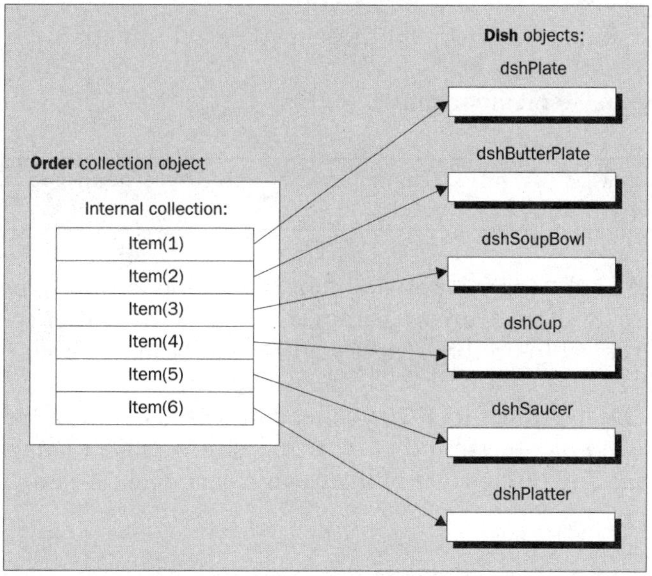

"And we can get access to the objects that a collection refers to just by specifying the **`Item`** that we want to use. The collection points our code to the object that we want to work with via the short **`Item`** reference. We saw in Lesson Two that we can use a loop to work our way through the **`Items`** in a collection and make changes to all of the actual objects that they refer to:"

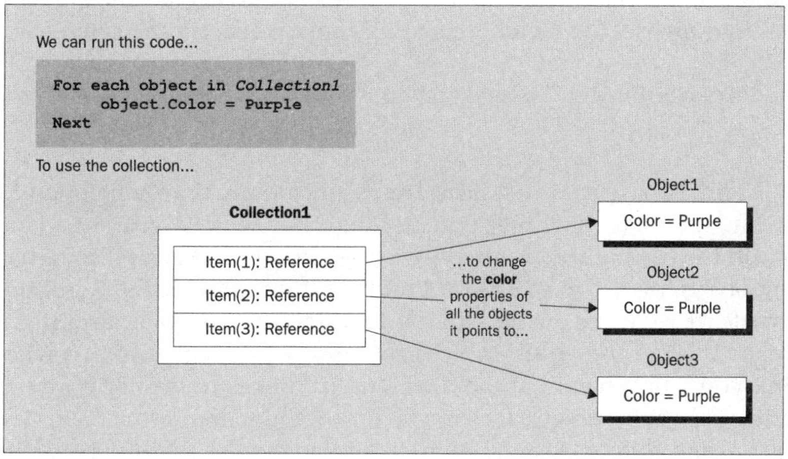

"Do the collection objects that we build have the **`Add`**, **`Count`**, **`Item`** and **`Remove`** methods that system collections have, already built-in?" Steve asked.

"They do," I said, carefully, "provided we create the code for the object that way."

"What do you mean?" Kate asked. "Aren't those methods automatic?"

"Not at all, Kate," I said. "Remember this:"

> **A collection object is just an ordinary class module that's been coded to imitate the behavior of a Visual Basic collection.**

"If we want it to have **`Add`**, **`Count`**, **`Item`** and **`Remove`** methods, and to be able to support the **`For...Each`** statement that we are accustomed to using with other collections, we need to explicitly code the object to do that. There's nothing automatic about it."

"I see," Valerie said. "Despite the fact that a collection object sounds a bit more complicated than an ordinary object, I like the sound of what it can do – make managing objects easier. Will we have to change any of the code in the **`Dish`** object when we create the **`Order`** object?"

Collection Objects in the China Shop

"No, Valerie, we won't," I said. "That's the beauty of a collection object – it's really just a way of referring to and communicating with a collection of other objects: when you create a collection object, you don't need to make any changes to the actual objects that are referenced as items within the collection. All you need to do is concentrate on creating the collection object. In our case, the **`Dish`** object will remain exactly the same."

"What about the **`Package`** object?" Chuck asked. "Will we be creating a collection object for packages?"

"No, we won't," I said. "There's no real need for it, since there'll only be one **`Package`** in existence at any one time – we can keep track of that quite easily without an associated collection object. In the case of the **`Dish`** object, however, it makes perfect sense to create an **`Order`** collection object, made up of **`Items`** that refer to **`Dish`** objects. Right now in the China Shop project, we're declaring six unique **`Dish`** object variables, and instantiating up to six **`Dish`** objects. We can use an **`Order`** collection object to simplify this whole process, and I really think you'll be amazed at the difference it makes to the code we have to write. By using an **`Order`** collection object, we can declare a single instance of the **`Order`** object within our program and then use the **`Order`** collection object's methods – such as **`Add`** and **`Remove`** – to make our job simpler."

I displayed this diagram, showing the **Order** object, on the classroom projector:

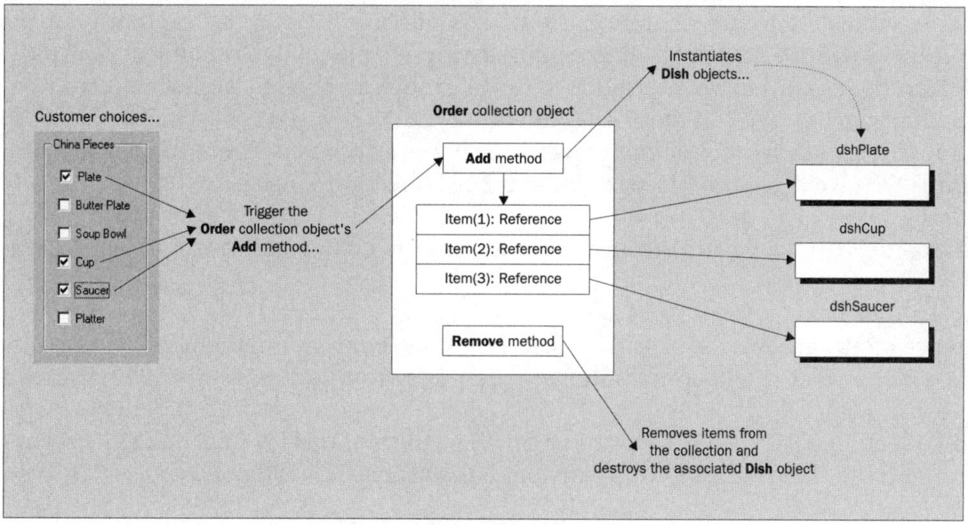

"The whole idea behind a collection object," I said, "is to make life easier. You saw last week that even though the use of the **Dish** object does simplify some of the coding in the **cmdCalculate** event procedure, working with and keeping track of six individual **Dish** objects, and trying to work with the various properties of those six **Dish** objects can be a real pain. The creation of the **Order** collection object, along with its methods, means that we can get it to do the work of creating and maintaining the **Dish** objects. And we'll integrate the **Order** collection object with the rest of the program so that it seamlessly creates, maintains and destroys the appropriate **Dish** objects at the right times."

"It kind of reminds me of working with individual controls before you introduced us to control arrays," Dave said.

"That's a good point, Dave," I said. "You should find working with a collection object easier than dealing with multiple **Dish** objects – although creating your first collection object requires a little more work up-front than a simple **Dish** object."

"Is that your way of saying that this won't be all that easy?" Rhonda asked.

"Collection objects do require a little more work in advance to get them ready," I said, "but the great thing about them is that once you create your first collection object, creating the second one is a piece of cake – one collection object won't vary much from any other."

"How's that?" Kate asked.

"Each collection object will usually have **`Add`**, **`Count`**, **`Item`** and **`Remove`** methods," I said. "Internally, a collection object – such as the **`Order`** collection object – consists of a collection, whose items are references to the actual objects – such as the **`Dish`** objects – that the collection will work with. In this essential respect, one collection object doesn't vary much from the next: they're all used to refer to groups of objects, and act as an intermediary so that we can work effectively with that group of objects. The basic things we'll do with the **`Order`** collection object – such as adding and removing items – are also the things that we'd want to do with most other collection objects."

"What exactly will we be adding and removing in the **`Order`** collection object?" Chuck asked.

"References to **`Dish`** objects," I said. "The whole idea behind creating a collection object called **`Order`** is that it will contain items which refer to **`Dish`** objects – and nothing else."

"Can a collection object have methods other than the standard **`Add`**, **`Count`**, **`Item`** and **`Remove`** methods that we saw in the system collections?" Dorothy asked.

"Yes, it can," I confirmed. "For example, the **`Order`** collection object will have a **`TotalPrice`** method that will allow us to access the total price of all the **`Dish`** objects referenced by the collection."

"I guess I'll have to see this before I fully understand it," he said. "Will you be creating a collection object for the Student Grades project that we've been using for the last few weeks?"

"You bet, Chuck," I said. "I think everyone's had an easier time learning about objects by following the Student Grades demo. Let's start getting our hands dirty and do that now."

The Student Grades Project – the Sequel

"Before we see how using a collection object can improve it, let's review where we are with the Student Grades project at the moment," I said, displaying the project's form on the classroom projector:

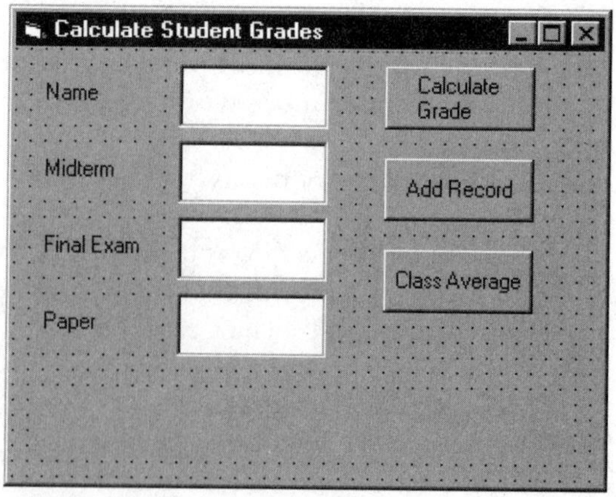

"Two weeks ago," I said, "we created code in the **Click** event procedure of the project's **cmdCalculate** command button, which made an instance of the **Student** object, based on the **Student** class module, setting the object's **Name**, **MidTerm**, **FinalExam**, and **TermPaper** properties. The code then calculated the individual student's average grade and assigned it to the **Average** property."

I paused to let them take this in.

"Last week," I continued, "we coded the **cmdAddRecord** button's **Click** event procedure. This executes the **AddRecord** method of the **Student** object, resulting in a record of the student's grades and average being written to the **Grades.txt** file. Let me display the code for the **cmdAddRecord** button on the classroom projector, because I think you may be able to see where a **Course** collection object may come in handy:"

```
Private Sub cmdAddRecord_Click()

m_stuNew.AddRecord

m_intRunningTotal = m_intRunningTotal +
        ↳m_stuNew.Average
m_intRunningCount = m_intRunningCount + 1

txtName.Text = ""
txtMidterm.Text = ""
txtFinalExam.Text = ""
txtTermPaper.Text = ""
txtName.SetFocus
lblFinalGrade.Caption = ""

Set m_stuNew = Nothing

End Sub
```

"Now let me show you the code currently in the Class Average command button," I said. "That code could really benefit from a collection object of **Students**:"

```
Private Sub cmdClassAverage_Click()

MsgBox "The Final Class average is " &
        ↳m_intRunningTotal / m_intRunningCount

End Sub
```

"Now here's a question for you," I said. "What do both of these event procedures have in common?"

"Both of them are using the module-level variables **m_intRunningCount** and **m_intRunningTotal**," Dave said. "The **Click** event procedure of **cmdAddRecord** is updating the values of those variables, and the **Click** event procedure of **cmdClassAverage** is using them to calculate an overall class average grade."

"That's excellent, Dave," I said. "The area where a collection object may come in handy is in this section of code..."

```
m_intRunningTotal = m_intRunningTotal +
        ↳m_stuNew.Average
m_intRunningCount = m_intRunningCount + 1
```

"...where we maintain the running total and the running count of the students whose scores have been calculated by our program. What we're really doing here is calculating the average of every **Student** object that's been instantiated within our program – doesn't that sound like a perfect job for running a **For...Each** statement against each item in a collection?"

"I guess so," Ward said. "But there isn't all that much code devoted to updating and maintaining those variables. Should we really complicate things by creating a collection to manage the **Student** objects?"

"We shouldn't measure the payback of a collection object solely by the number of lines of code it eliminates," I said, "but also by how much it simplifies the program – both in terms of writing it initially, and of understanding it later. Implementing a **Course** collection object here will make calculating the overall class average as simple as executing a method of the collection object. This has the advantage of simplifying the program by reducing the number of variables we need to keep our hands on, and by encapsulating the class average functionality inside an object: remember that in object-oriented programming we always try and encapsulate behavior in the object where it's best suited."

"I think I'm starting to see where you're going with this," Rhonda said. "Where do we begin?"

"Let's start by creating the **Course** collection's class," I said. "We need to build a class that the **Course** collection object can be instantiated from."

Creating a Collection Object in the Student Grades Project

"Here's a summary of the steps that we'll take in creating the collection object:"

Steps in Creating a Collection Object

Add a new class module to the project

Name the class, forming the name (in some – but not all – cases) by using the plural form of the objects that will be stored as items in the collection (e.g. a Horses collection that stores references to multiple instances of a Horse object)

Declare a collection in the General Declarations section of the class module

Code the collection object's Add method

Code its Count method

Code the Item method

Code the Remove method

Code the NewEnum method

Adjust the NewEnum method's attributes

Code any additional properties or methods

"Don't worry if you're puzzled by some of these at the moment," I reassured the class. "I guarantee that every item on the list will make perfect sense to you by the end of today's session. If they don't, I'll eat my hat!"

I then began the process of creating the `Course` collection object by creating a new class module for the Student Grades project.

> **If you're working through the Student Grades project with me – and you are, aren't you? – then you should make these changes as I introduce them.**

Creating the Collection Class

I selected Project | Add Class Module from the Visual Basic menu bar and double-clicked on the Class Module icon on the New tab of the resulting Add Class Module window. A new class module appeared in the IDE, and I brought up its properties window by pressing *F4*. Next, I changed the class module's **`Name`** property from **`Class1`** to **`Course`**:

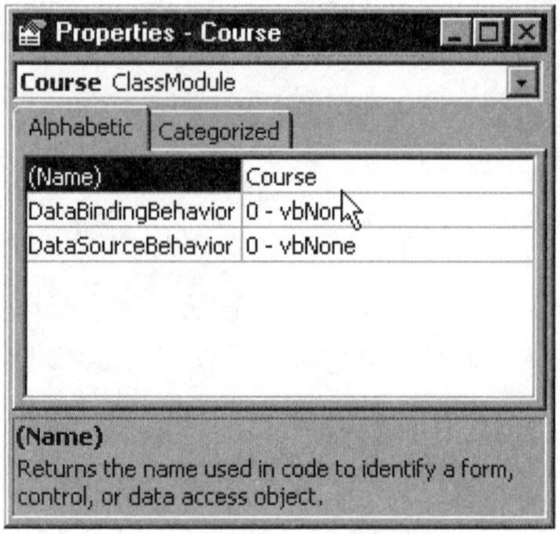

"It's funny," Rhonda said, "but somehow I expected that there would be some property of the class module you would set to designate this class module as a collection object – but there isn't, is there?"

"No, there isn't, Rhonda," I answered, "it's the code that goes inside of the collection object that characterizes it as a collection object – nothing else."

"Didn't you imply in the list of steps you showed us just now that it's a good idea to name the collection object using the plural of the objects it will hold?" Melissa asked. "**`Course`** isn't the plural of **`Student`**."

"You've found me out, Melissa," I answered. "That **is** the normal convention, and ordinarily I would have named this collection object **`Students`**. However, whenever I teach collection objects, I find that the learning process is easier if I give the collection object a unique name. When you're having to concentrate on learning about collection objects, it helps if we can avoid the confusion of needing to always be thinking about the difference between the word **`Student`** and **`Students`**."

"OK, if it's going to make it easier to follow, then I'm all for it!" she answered.

I then saved the **Course** class module in the **\VBFiles\Practice** directory with the name **Course.cls**, and brought up the Project Explorer window:

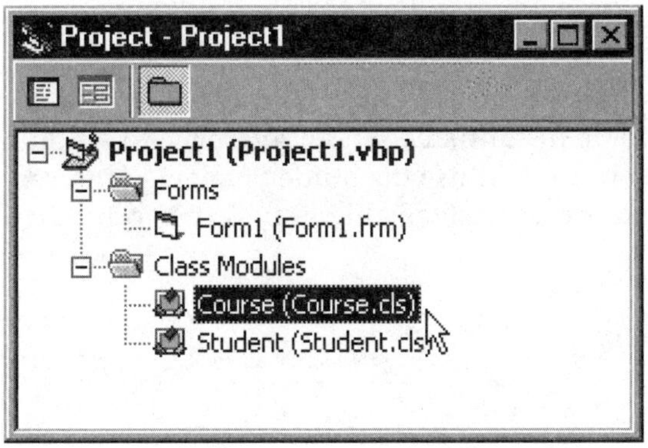

"As you can see," I said, "we now have two class modules in the project. Let's begin the detailed work by coding the **Course** collection object."

Coding the Class Module

I then added the following two lines of code to the General Declarations section of the **Course** class module:

```
Option Explicit

Private m_colCourse As New Collection
Private m_ClassAverage As Single
```

"This first line of code," I said, "is the crucial line of code in the collection object – this is the declaration of **m_colCourse** as a collection which, as you can see, is **Private** to the class module. This is the collection that'll actually be used inside the **Course** collection object to hold references to the individual **Student** objects that are created when the program runs:"

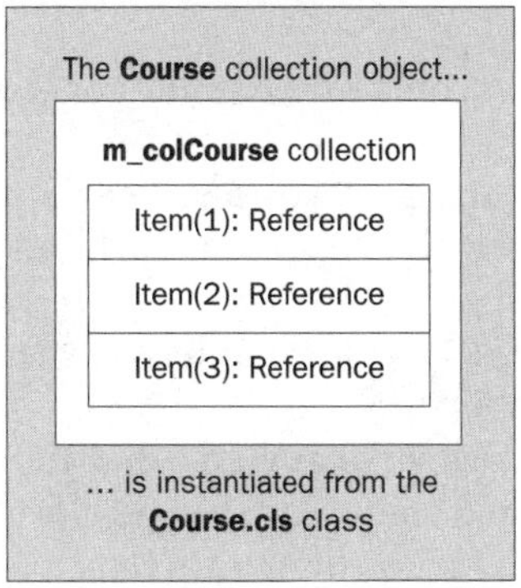

"As I mentioned earlier today, we'll be coding **Add**, **Count**, **Item** and **Remove** methods for this collection object. These methods will allow the rest of the program to interact with the **m_colCourse** collection – declared as **Private** – that actually stores the references to the **Student** objects. Again, we're using object-oriented principles to expose the inside of the **Course** collection object to the outside world, in a controlled and consistent way."

I waited a moment, then added some more detail about the **Add** method:

"When the user of our **Course** collection object executes its **Add** method, a **Student** object will be instantiated, and a reference to it added to the **m_colCourse** collection. This reference will use the student's name (entered in the text box on the form) as its key – this means that we'll be able to find this individual item in the collection again when we need to:"

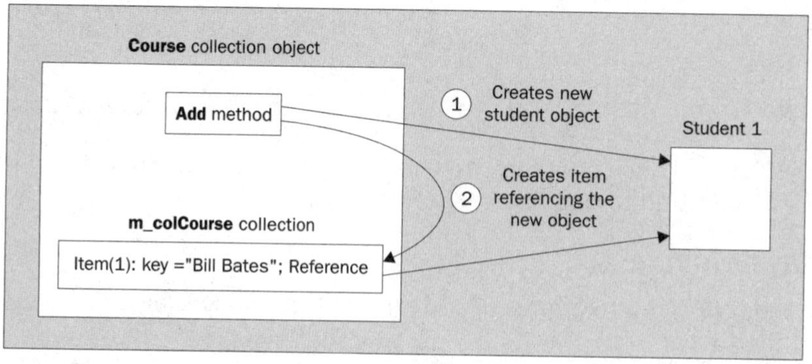

"We'll code the **Add** method so that the very act of executing it will instantiate a new **Student** object and perform the rest of the processing shown in the diagram. Likewise, when the user of our object executes its **Remove** method, a **Student** object reference will be removed from the collection, and the object that the reference points to will be destroyed too."

"What's the second line of code for?" Kathy asked.

"We'll be creating a **ClassAverage** property for the collection object," I said. "This is the declaration for the **Private** variable holding its value:"

```
Private m_ClassAverage As Single
```

"So," I said, "we've sketched what the **Course** collection object's **Add** and **Remove** methods will do. At this stage, just let me say this about the other methods: the **Count** method will let us see how many items there are in the **m_colCourse** collection; and the **Item** method will allow us to extract a reference to a **Student** object from **m_colCourse** collection – we can then use the reference to interact with that individual object. We'll talk about all of these methods in more detail when we create and use them."

"Will the **Course** collection object have any methods besides **Add**, **Count**, **Item** and **Remove**?" Steve asked.

"No, Steve," I said. "That's all it needs for our purposes. Remember, though, that we **can** create extra methods for a collection if we need to. It just so happens that for this collection the 'standard' set of methods will do everything that we want."

"I don't see declarations for any of the properties of the **Student** object," Kevin said. "Shouldn't we declare variables for the **Name**, **MidTerm**, **FinalExam**, **TermPaper** and **Average** properties?"

"No, we don't need to declare variables for any of the properties of the **Student** object here," I replied.

"If we don't declare the properties of the **Student** object here in the **Course** class module," Kathy asked, "then how can we create a collection of **Student** objects?"

The Course Collection Object and the Student Objects

"The **Student** object's properties have already been declared within the **Student** class module," I said. "There's no need to 'reinvent the wheel' by declaring the **Student** object all over again within our collection object. All we need to do, to use the **Student** object from within the **Course** collection object (or to use any object from within another object, for that matter) – is to declare an instance of the **Student** object – this will refer to the **Student** class module to create the individual **Student** object: all of the definitions for the **Student** object are in the **Student.cls** class module, and the **Course** object can use those to create new **Student** objects. We'll do that shortly within the **Add** method of the **Course** class module."

"Does that mean," Dave asked, "that we'll no longer be declaring an instance of the **Student** object within the **Click** event procedure of the **cmdCalculate** button on the Student Grades project's main form?"

"You have the idea, Dave," I said. "The **Student** object will no longer be instantiated directly within the code of the **Student** form. Whenever the **Student** object is created from now on, it'll be created from within the **Course** collection."

"So that means," Dave continued, "that we'll be declaring the **Course** collection object instead? And that we'll then use the **Course** collection to create the **Student** objects?"

"That's right, Dave," I said. "And we'll apply this principle in the China Shop program as well: we'll no longer have to code six different object variable declarations – just one, for the **Order** collection. In a similar way, here in the Student Grades project, we'll declare an instance of the **Course** collection object instead of the **Student** object."

"Let me give you a run-through of the process," I said. "We'll start by declaring an instance of the **Course** collection object in the General Declarations section of the Student Grades project's main form. When the user clicks on the Calculate Grade button, we'll execute the **Course** collection's **Add** method, which will add a **Student** object to the **Course** object. Then, when the user clicks on the Add Record button, we'll execute the **Item** method of the **Course** collection to access the **AddRecord** method of the **Student** object: this will add a record containing the student's information to the **Grades.txt** file. Finally, when the user clicks on the Class Average command button, we'll execute the **Count** method and run the **For...Each** statement against the collection object to calculate an overall class average."

"Did you say the **AddRecord** method of the **Student** object?" Kate asked. "You mean we'll still be able to execute the **Student** object's methods even though we're accessing them via a collection?"

"That's right, Kate," I said. "There's no need to reinvent the wheel by coding an **AddRecord** method of the **Course** collection. In conjunction with the **Item** method of the **Course** collection object, we'll be able to execute the **AddRecord** method of the **Student** object."

"Let's get started with the creation of the **Course** collection object," I said. "Nothing will help you to understand this better than seeing it in action. Our first step is to code the **Course** collection object's **Initialize** and **Terminate** event procedures."

Coding the Course Class's Initialize and Terminate Procedures

I then added the following line of code to the **Course** class module's **Initialize** procedure...

```
Private Sub Class_Initialize()

Debug.Print "The Course object has been born..."

End Sub
```

...and this code in the **Course** class module's **Terminate** event procedure:

```
Private Sub Class_Terminate()

Debug.Print "The Course object has died..."

End Sub
```

"I'm glad we're using these **Debug** statements again," said Steve. "They really come in handy in seeing what's going on when the program runs."

"I agree, Steve," I said.

"What's next?" Ward asked.

"Next," I said, "we need to turn our attention towards building up the methods that will give our **Course** collection object its functionality – the methods that will actually let it do the job we want it to do."

Building the Course Collection Object's Methods

"The first thing to do is create the **Add** method for the **Course** collection object," I said. "The purpose of the **Add** method is to instantiate a **Student** object, and add a reference to that **Student** object as an item of the **Course** collection object's **Private** collection – **m_colCourse**."

Coding the Add Method

"OK," I went on, "here's the code for the **Add** method..."

I then keyed this next complete chunk of code into the **Course** class module's General Declarations section:

```
Public Sub Add(ByVal strName As String,
        ↳ByVal intMidTerm As Integer,
        ↳ByVal intFinalExam As Integer,
        ↳ByVal intTermPaper As Integer)

Dim objStudent As New Student

objStudent.Name = strName
objStudent.MidTerm = intMidTerm
objStudent.FinalExam = intFinalExam
objStudent.TermPaper = intTermPaper
```

```
m_colCourse.Add objStudent, strName

Set objStudent = Nothing

End Sub
```

"Notice," I said, "the **Add** method's procedure header:"

```
Public Sub Add(ByVal strName As String,
        ↳ByVal intMidTerm As Integer,
        ↳ByVal intFinalExam As Integer,
        ↳ByVal intTermPaper As Integer)
```

"We've coded it with four arguments: **strName**, **intMidTerm**, **intFinalExam**, and **intTermPaper**."

"Those four arguments refer to the attributes that describe the **Student** object," Valerie declared.

"That's right, Valerie," I said. "Here's the reason for that. Three things are happening in the **Add** method of the **Course** collection object: first, an instance of the **Student** object is being created. Secondly, its **Name**, **MidTerm**, **FinalExam** and **TermPaper** properties are being assigned values as defined in the **Add** method; and lastly, the **Student** object is being added as an item to the **m_colCourse** collection within the **Course** collection object."

"That makes sense," Dave said. "In the old version of the code, the **Student** object was instantiated within the **Click** event procedure of **cmdCalculate**. Now that event procedure will be executing the **Add** method of the **Course** collection object, and passing values for these four arguments to it."

"Exactly, Dave," I said. "This next line of code declares an instance of the **Student** object..."

```
Dim objStudent As New Student
```

"...and then we assign the value of the four passed arguments to the **Student** object's four properties:"

```
objStudent.Name = strName
objStudent.Midterm = intMidTerm
objStudent.FinalExam = intFinalExam
objStudent.TermPaper = intTermPaper
```

"This next line of code is vitally important," I said:

```
m_colCourse.Add objStudent, strName
```

"Now that the **Student** object has been instantiated, we need to add a reference to it to the **m_colCourse** collection, and we do that with this line of code, using the name of the student whose grades we're entering in this iteration, passed to the **Add** method as the **key** to the item."

"Key?" Rhonda said. "Does that mean that we'll be able to use the student's name to retrieve the object from the collection object later on?"

"That's excellent, Rhonda," I said. "Because we add a reference to the **Student** object as an item in the **m_colCourse** collection (with the student's name as the key), we'll be able to retrieve a reference to that particular **Student** object later, just as long as we know the student's name. We'll add code to do exactly that in the collection object's **Item** method."

"You've used the term reference several times," Blaine said. "What's the difference between adding the actual **Student** object to the **m_colCourse** collection, and adding a reference to the collection that points at the object?"

"That's a good question, Blaine," I said. "As you may recall, the **Student** object itself isn't actually stored as an item in the collection – the **Student** object is just too big to fit into the collection. Instead, the address of the **Student** object in our program's memory is stored as an item in the collection. Storage-wise, it makes sense to store the address of the object instead of the object itself."

"So when you speak of a reference to an object," Kate said, "you really mean the memory address of the object?"

"That's right, Kate," I said. "And the important thing to remember is this: if you know how to get at the reference to that object's address, you can always locate that object and work with it. That's what we achieve by creating the key for each item: all we have to remember is the student's name, and Visual Basic can use that to find the relevant reference and, through that, the relevant **Student** object that's stored elsewhere in memory."

"What about that last line of code?" Mary asked, "the one where you set the value of the **objStudent** object variable to **Nothing**..."

```
Set objStudent = Nothing
```

"...if you set **objStudent** to **Nothing**, aren't you destroying the **Student** object? Won't we need the information contained in the **Student** object later on in the program?"

"Setting the **objStudent** object Variable to **Nothing**," I said, "**doesn't** destroy the **Student** object. All we're doing is destroying the object variable itself."

"But didn't you say last week that when all references to an object go away, the object dies?" Dave queried.

"That's right, Dave," I said. "When all references to an object are destroyed, the object itself dies. However, even after we set **objStudent** to **Nothing**, there's still a reference to the **Student** object somewhere. Can anyone tell me where that is?"

"I think I can," Melissa said. "A reference to each **Student** object's address is stored as an item in the **m_colCourse** collection! And since the **m_colCourse** collection was declared as a module-level collection, it will exist as long as the **Course** object exists."

"I couldn't have said it better myself," I said. "Let me try to illustrate this concept of the **Student** object and its references with a series of charts I've drawn. This first chart illustrates the **Course** collection object when it's first initialized. It contains the empty **m_colCourse** collection, which doesn't yet have any references in it to any **Student** objects. In fact, at this point, no instances of the **Student** object have been created:"

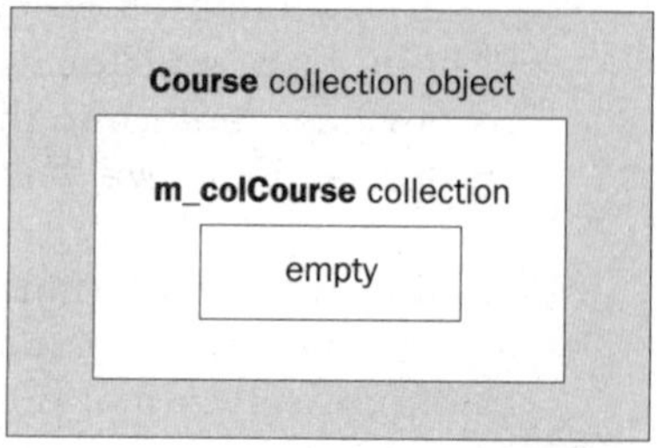

"This next chart," I said, "illustrates the **Course** collection object just after we've executed the line of code in the **Add** method that instantiates a **Student** object. Notice that there's just one pointer to the **Student** object at the moment – the one maintained by the **objStudent** object variable:"

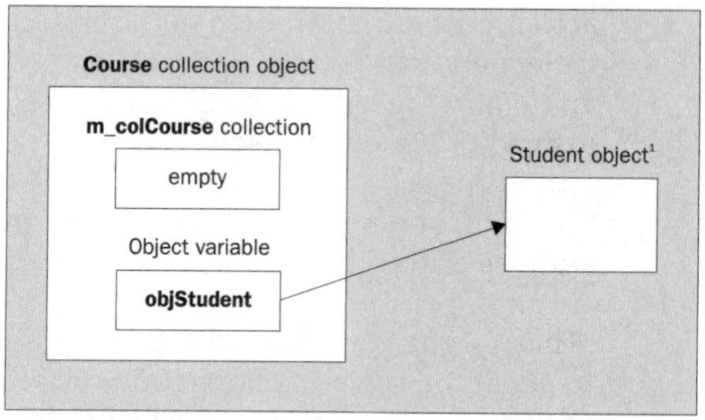

"Now, this next chart," I continued, "illustrates the **Course** collection object just after the line creating an item in the **m_colCourse** collection has been executed – this item is the collection's reference to the instantiated **Student** object:

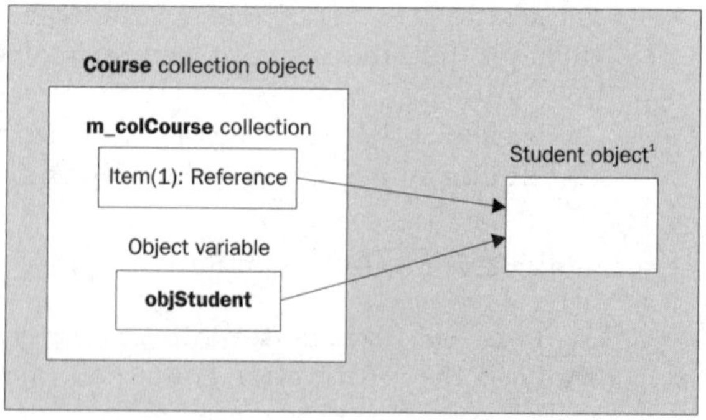

"Notice that there are now two references to the **Student** object in the **Course** collection object – the original pointer from the object variable that we used to instantiate the **Student** object, and the reference to the **Student** object that's been added to the **m_colCourse** collection."

"Finally," I said, "this next chart illustrates the **Course** collection object after the temporary **objStudent** object variable has been set to **Nothing** and the **Course** collection's **Add** method has finished. We have one reference to the **Student** object, maintained as an item in the **m_colCourse Collection** that lives inside the **Course** collection object. This reference is 'permanent', in the sense that it will stay in the collection until we remove it, or the related **Student** object is destroyed, or we close the program:"

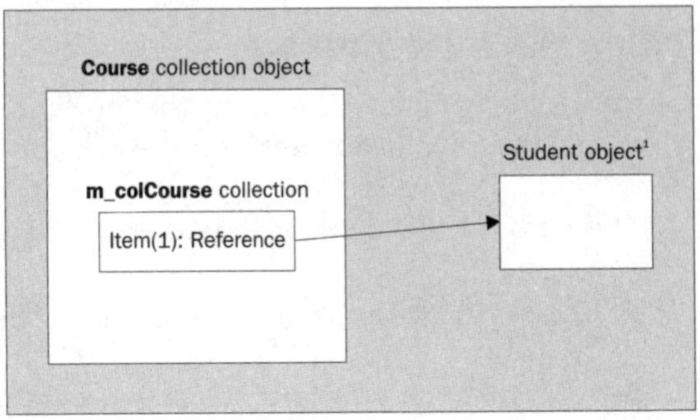

"I think I can see what's going on, now," Bob said. "I presume that as we continue to calculate more student grades, the number of **Student** objects added as items to the collection object will continue to grow?"

"That's right, Bob," I said. "This is the picture after we've calculated the grades for three students:"

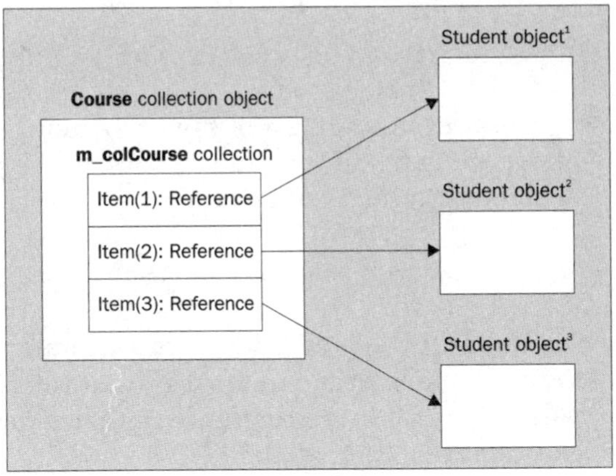

"This is the **Course** collection object after three students have been graded," I said. "The **m_colCourse** collection object now contains, as **Items**, references to three different **Student** objects."

"OK," Rhonda said, "I think I understand that the **Course** collection object will maintain references to the **Student** object via the **m_colCourse** collection. But how exactly can we subsequently retrieve information about the **Student** objects we've created?"

"We'll take care of that by writing an **Item** method of the collection object," I replied.

Coding the Item Method

"Provided we know the key – the student's name – of the **Student** object whose information we need, retrieving it will be surprisingly easy."

I then added this code to the **Course** class module to create the **Item** method:

```
Public Function Item(ByVal strStudentName As String) As Student

Set Item = m_colCourse.Item(strStudentName)

End Function
```

"This **Item** method of the collection object," I said, "is actually a function that accepts a single argument called **strStudentName** and returns a reference to the **Student** object."

"Is that reference what the **As Student** part means in the function header?" Ward asked.

"That's right, Ward," I said:

```
Public Function Item(ByVal strStudentName As String) As Student
```

"The **As Student** part of this statement," I explained, "is effectively saying 'pass a reference to a **Student** object back to the program that calls this function'. The next bit of code is concerned with finding the correct **Student** object reference to pass:"

```
Set Item = m_colCourse.Item(strStudentName)
```

"Here, the **Item** method uses the argument that's passed to it – **strStudentName** – to locate the item in **m_colCourse** that refers to a **Student** object with the matching key value. This returns a reference to that **Student** object – an address – back to the code that executed the **Item** method."

"So the program executing the **Item** method of the **Course** collection object is given the address of the relevant **Student** object, is that correct?" Tom asked.

"That's right, Tom," I said, "and once the program has the address, it has access to the properties of the **Student** object."

"I saw an example of the **Item** method in Visual Basic Help," Dave said, "where the argument passed to it was declared as a **Variant** – yet you declared it as a **String** data type. Why is that?"

"You could code the **Item** method of a collection object," I explained, "so that it can return a reference to the object using either the key of the collection, or the numeric position of that item in the collection."

"In other words," Kevin said, "if we wanted to, we could locate the **Student** object using either their name – say, 'Amanda Smith' – or the position of that **Student** object's **Item** reference in the collection, such as number 1."

"Exactly right, Kevin," I said. "Here in the Student Grades project, we won't be bothering with the numeric positions of the items in the collection. We'll just be locating them via the student's name – that's why I declared the argument as a **String** data type."

Coding the Remove Method

"Here's the code for the **Remove** method of the **Course** collection object," I said. "It's similar to the **Item** method in that it accepts a single argument – **strStudentName**. I'll add it to the **Course** collection class module now:"

```
Public Sub Remove(ByVal strStudentName As String)

m_colCourse.Remove strStudentName

End Sub
```

"All we're doing here," I said, "is executing the **Remove** method of the **m_colCourse** collection, using the **strStudentName** argument that we pass to the **Course** collection object."

"We don't actually execute the **Remove** method in the Student Grades project, do we?" Steve asked.

"No, we don't, Steve," I answered. "But it's a method that should be incorporated into any collection objects you build – it's good programming practice to build our objects with the features that programmers will expect to find in them. And we *will* be using a **Remove** method in the China Shop's **Package** collection object, so it's all good practice for that."

Coding the Count Method

"Here's the code for the **Count** method of the **Course** collection object," I said. "Like the **Item** method, the **Count** method is actually a function, which returns the **Count** property of the **m_colCourse** collection. We'll invoke this method whenever we want to extract the current value of the **m_colCourse** collection's **Count** property. That value will be equal to the number of **Student** object references stored as items in the collection. Let me add the code now:"

```
Public Function Count() As Long

Count = m_colCourse.Count

End Function
```

"The collection object is beginning to make more and more sense to me," Kate said. "I can see that we're really just hiding the details of the **Student** object from the program using it."

"That's right, Kate," I said, "Unfortunately, no sooner do you say that this is all beginning to make sense, than I'm about to show you something that, at first sight, will probably seem a bit weird – for now, though, you'll need to take it on faith."

"What's that?" Bob said.

"Part of the functionality of a collection that we want to build into our collection object is the ability to use a **For...Each** statement," I said, "just like the one's we've used with the other types of Visual Basic collections. It's essential that we're able to loop through the items in a collection – remember, this all contributes to our using the collection to manage the multiple objects in our programs. However, unlike the pre-defined system collections, which have this looping ability built-in, we need to code from scratch that ability into any collections we make for ourselves."

"How do we do that?" asked Valerie.

"We need to implement a special method of the collection object called the **NewEnum** method," I replied. "Let me show you."

Coding the NewEnum Method

To create the **NewEnum** method that would give our collection 'loopability', I entered the following code into the **Course** class module:

```
Public Function NewEnum() As IUnknown

Set NewEnum = m_colCourse.[_NewEnum]

End Function
```

"The **NewEnum** method," I said, "is what turns on our ability to use the **For...Each** statement within the course collection object."

"This code is a little on the cryptic side, isn't it? Dave said. "What the heck is **IUnknown**?"

"**IUnknown** is something called an **interface** that each Visual Basic object possesses," I said. "The **IUnknown** interface is designed to allow objects to communicate with one another, and what we're doing here is creating something called an enumerator – which is very similar to a loop control variable: it's like the **intCounter** variable you'd define in a **For...Next** loop to track how many times we've been round a loop. Details of the **IUnknown** interface are really beyond the scope of this course, but the important thing to note here is that if you forget to code this **NewEnum** method in your collection object, you won't be able to use the **For...Each** statement to loop through the items in its collection!"

"Why the square brackets around the word **NewEnum**?" Melissa asked.

"Because the word **NewEnum** begins with an underscore," I replied. "The brackets stop Visual Basic from tripping over the underscore when it comes to run the code."

"Is this all we need to do to make the **For...Each** statement work?" Dave asked.

"There's one more thing we need to do, Dave" I said. "We need to set an attribute of the **NewEnum** method so that Visual Basic can use it in the way that it expects to use the **IUnknown** code. "

"How do we do that?" Dorothy asked.

"First, select Tools | Procedure Attributes from the Visual Basic menu bar," I explained:

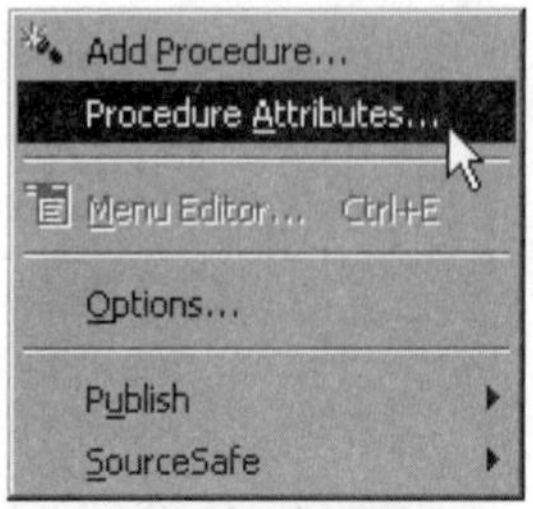

"Then select the Advanced button..."

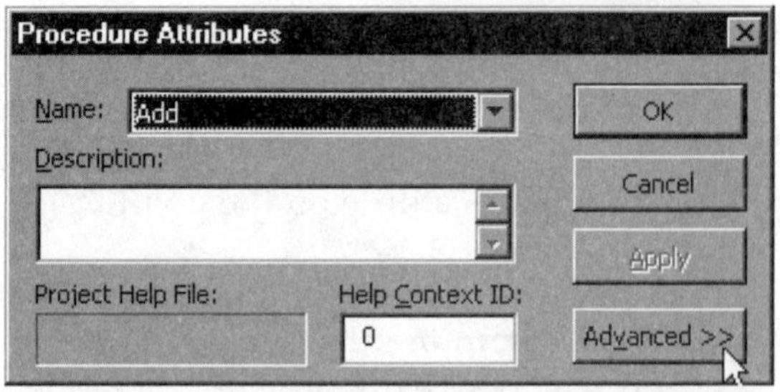

"...and the NewEnum method in the drop-down Name list box:"

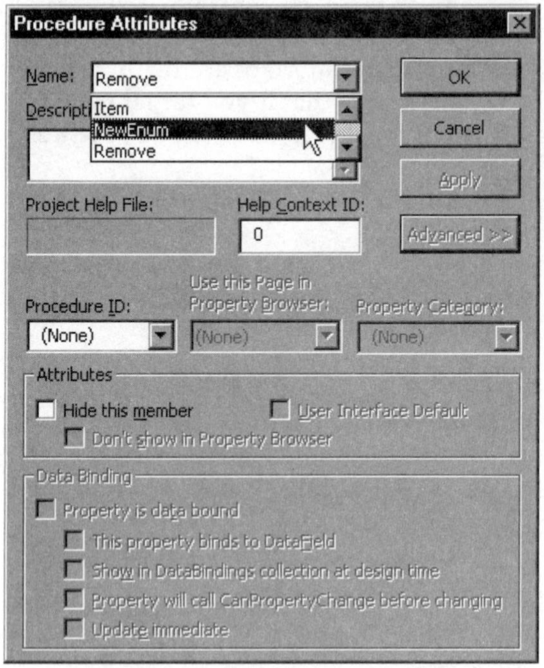

"Next, check the Hide this member check box in the pane's Attributes section:"

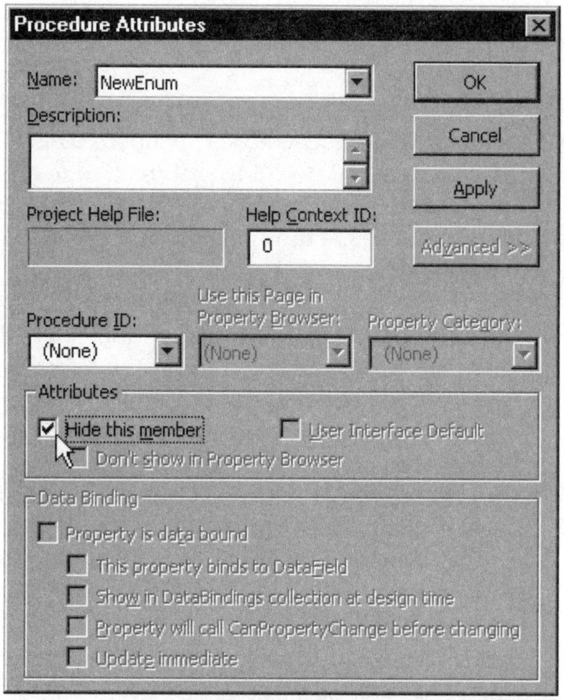

"And, finally, specify -4 as the Procedure ID for the NewEnum method by typing it into the box:"

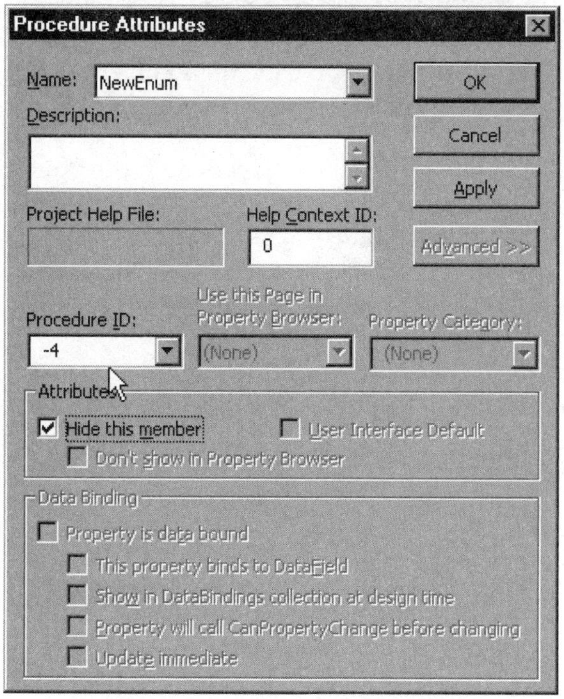

"I was doing pretty well following you until you got to the -4 part," Rhonda said. "What's going on there?"

"When we execute the **For...Each** statement of a collection object," I said, "Visual Basic looks for a method whose Procedure ID is -4 to implement that functionality. It's a small thing to do – but if you forget to change the Procedure ID for your **NewEnum** method, the **For...Each** statement won't work. Incidentally, we use the number 4 for reasons that are beyond the scope of this book. Just treat it as a rule – it comes with using the architecture that Visual Basic objects are based on."

"Suppose you forget to check on the Hide this member box in the Procedure Attributes window," Kathy asked. "Would the **For...Each** loop still work?"

"Yes," I said, "but the **NewEnum** method would also be made visible to the user of the **Course** object: they'd be able to refer to this procedure in code – something we really don't want. Remember that this method is created purely to allow us to loop through the items in our self-created collection. We want to conceal the complexity of the interior of the object as much as possible, and just reveal a simple interface to the people who use our objects. For those reasons, we hide this method."

Next, we needed to look at the Course object's **ClassAverage** property:

The ClassAverage Property

"We have just one more piece of the puzzle to complete in terms of the collection object," I said, "and that's to code the **Property Get** procedure for the **ClassAverage** property. Here's the code."

I entered the following code into the **Course** class module:

```
Property Get ClassAverage() As Single

Dim objStudent As Student
Dim intRunningTotal As Integer

For Each objStudent In m_colCourse
    intRunningTotal = intRunningTotal + objStudent.Average
Next

ClassAverage = intRunningTotal / m_colCourse.Count

End Property
```

"This code is pretty interesting," I said. "We're using a **For...Each** statement to loop through each item in the **m_colCourse** collection. The first thing we do is declare a variable to use while looping through the collection:"

```
Dim objStudent As Student
```

"This is followed by a variable that we'll use to keep a running total of the student's averages:"

```
Dim intRunningTotal As Integer
```

"This next line of code starts the **For...Each** loop:"

```
For Each objStudent In m_colCoursee
```

"We use this to obtain a reference to a **Student** object, retrieving the value of that **Student** object's **Average** property, and then adding it to the value of the variable **intRunningTotal**:"

```
intRunningTotal = intRunningTotal + objStudent.Average
```

"When we're done looping through the **Student** objects in the **m_colCourse** collection, we divide the value of **intRunningTotal** by the value of the **Course** object's **Count** property, and assign the result to the **ClassAverage** property:"

```
ClassAverage = intRunningTotal / m_colCourse.Count
```

"In a little while, you'll see that all we'll do to calculate the overall class average is to retrieve the value of this property using the **cmdClassAverage** button's **Click** event procedure."

"This code really is fascinating," Ward said. "I'm beginning to see the value of objects, particularly collection objects, although I welcome the practice we'll get when we code this in the China Shop project."

"That completes the coding of the **Course** collection object," I said, "now it's time to see how to implement the **Course** collection object in the Student Grades project."

Using the Course Object in the Student Grades Demo

"That's all there is to it," I said. "We've worked through the steps I outlined a few minutes ago:"

Steps in Creating a Collection Object

Add a new class module to the project

Name the class, forming the name (in some – but not all – cases) by using the plural form of the objects that will be stored as items in the collection (e.g. a Horses collection that stores references to multiple instances of a Horse object)

Declare a collection in the General Declarations section of the class module

Code the collection object's Add method

Code its Count method

Code the Item method

Code the Remove method

Code the NewEnum method

Adjust the NewEnum method's attributes

Code any additional properties or methods

"And the great thing about this is that you could take that same collection object class module, and, with very little modification, turn it into a collection object class for another application."

"I see that now," Dave said. "That could be very powerful."

"Let's begin the modifications to the Student Grades project by adding a line of code to the General Declarations section of the main form."

I modified the code in the General Declarations section of the form of the Student Grades project's main form to look like this – we're replacing all of the existing code:

```
Option Explicit

Private m_objCourse As New Course
```

"This new line of code is a declaration of our new **Course** collection object," I said. "Not only have we added that declaration, but notice that we have also removed the declaration of the **Student** object we had there previously. We no longer need it – all **Student** objects will be created by way of the **Course** collection object."

"It looks like we have also eliminated the two module level variables, **m_intRunningTotal** and **m_intRunningCount**," Tom said.

"That's right, Tom," I answered, "we no longer need either of those variables – the **Course** collection object's **ClassAverage** property will be doing that work for us."

"Now let's modify the code in the **cmdCalculate** command button," I said.

The Calculate Grade Button

"When the Calculate Grade button is clicked, it will execute the **Course** object's **Add** method, triggering the creation of a new instance of the **Student** object, and passing the contents of the four text boxes to the method as arguments: these arguments will be used to set the values of the **Student** object's properties."

I amended the code of the **cmdCalculate** button's **Click** event procedure to look like the next listing (again, we've left the four **If...Then** loops that check if the user's entered some data out of this listing for clarity – these are replaced here by the ellipsis):

```
Private Sub cmdCalculate_Click()

...

m_objCourse.Add txtName.Text, txtMidTerm.Text,
          ➥txtFinalExam.Text, txtTermPaper.Text
```

> **The line above replaces the existing** `Set m_stuNew = New Student` **line**

> **You also need to delete the four lines starting** `m_stuNew`**...**

```
lblFinalGrade.Caption =
    ➥"The grade for " & txtName.Text & " is " &
    ➥m_objCourse.Item(txtName.Text).Average &
    ➥". Click on the 'Add Record' button to save the record."

End Sub
```

"As I mentioned earlier," I said, "in this event procedure we're creating an instance of the **Student** object using the **Course** collection object's **Add** method. Notice that we pass the **Add** method four arguments, which are passed as the **Text** properties of the form's four text boxes:"

```
m_objCourse.Add txtName.Text, txtMidTerm.Text,
            ↳txtFinalExam.Text, txtMidterm.Text
```

"When the **Add** method is triggered in the **Course** object," I said, "an instance of the **Student** object is created, and a reference to that object is added as an item in the **m_colCourse** collection. Remember, this reference uses the student's name as a key to the item."

"This portion of code," I continued…

```
m_objCourse.Item(txtName.Text).Average &
```

"…executes the **Course** object's **Item** method to retrieve the value of the **Average** property for the **Student** object that we just created. Notice, we're using the student's name from the **txtName** text box as the key to retrieving the item. Once retrieved, that value is concatenated to the **Caption** property of the **lblFinalGrade** label."

"I'm still trying to fathom how this **Item** method works," Mary said. "It sure does look to me as though the **Course** collection object has an **Average** property – yet it's really a property of the **Student** object, isn't it?"

"That's right, Mary," I said. "The **Average** property we're referring to here belongs to the **Student** object we reference, and whose name is equal to the value of the argument passed to the **Item** method."

I displayed the code for the **Item** method of the **Course** class module on the classroom projector:

```
Public Function Item(ByVal strStudentname As String) As Student

Set Item = m_colCourse.Item(strStudentname)

End Function
```

"The **Course** object's **Item** method," I went on, "is a function, and what it's returning to the **cmdCalculate** button's **Click** event is a reference to a specific **Student** object in the **m_colCourse** collection."

"With 'reference' meaning a memory address?" Mary queried.

"That's right, Mary," I agreed, "an address for a particular **Student** object in the **m_colCourse** collection. Once we have an address to that **Student** object, we can use it to execute any of the methods of the **Student** object, or retrieve or update its properties."

"Here's an illustration," I said. "Let's pretend that the name of the **Student** object passed as an argument to the **Item** method of the **Course** collection object is 'Jane Doe'. The **Item** method returns a reference to that object, let's say this address in memory happens to be '123':"

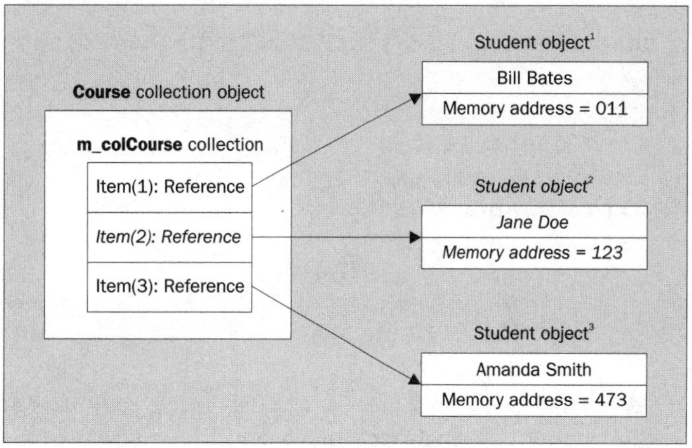

"When that address is returned to the **cmdCalculate** button's **Click** event procedure," I said, "Visual Basic interprets this line of code..."

```
m_objCourse.Item(txtName.Text).Average
```

"...in this way:"

```
123.Average
```

"**123** is the address of the **Student** object dedicated to Jane Doe. Visual Basic then automatically executes the **Property Get** procedure for that object's **Average** property, retrieves the property value, and concatenates it to the **lblFinalGrade** label."

"I think that helps," Dorothy said. "Perhaps running the program in Step mode will help even more?"

"We'll do that in just a few minutes," I said, "but first I'd like to code the **Click** event procedures for the Student Grades program's **cmdAddRecord** and **cmdClassAverage** command buttons."

The Add Record Button

I modified the code in the **Click** event procedure of the **cmdAddRecord** button to look like this:

```
Private Sub cmdAddRecord_Click()

m_objCourse.Item(txtName.Text).AddRecord

txtName.Text = ""
txtMidterm.Text = ""
txtFinalExam.Text = ""
txtTermPaper.Text = ""
txtName.SetFocus
lblFinalGrade.Caption = ""

End Sub
```

"What we're doing here," I said, "is using the **Course** object's **Item** method to return a reference to a **Student** object, which we again retrieve using the student's name as the key. Then we execute the **AddRecord** method of that **Student** object."

"I'm beginning to get more comfortable with this **Item** method," Blaine said.

"There's no doubt that it's confusing at first," I said. "Let's take a look at the code in the **Click** event procedure of **cmdClassAverage** now."

The Class Average Button

I then modified the code in the **cmdClassAverage** button's **Click** event procedure so that it matched this next listing:

```
Private Sub cmdClassAverage_Click()

MsgBox "The Final Class average is " & m_objCourse.ClassAverage

End Sub
```

"As you can see," I said, "we've reduced the number of lines of code again."

"There's just one more thing we need to do," I continued, "and that's to perform a little housekeeping. We declared the **Course** object variable **m_objCourse** in the General Declarations section of the form, so we really should set that object variable to nothing when the form unloads."

To achieve this, I added the next line of code to the form's **`Query Unload`** event procedure:

```
Private Sub Form_QueryUnload(Cancel As Integer, UnloadMode As Integer)

Set m_objCourse = Nothing

End Sub
```

There were no further questions, so I told the class that it would be a good idea to follow Dorothy's suggestion of running the program in Step mode. I started the program by pressing the *F8* function key, entered the information for a fictitious student, and then clicked on the Calculate Grade command button:

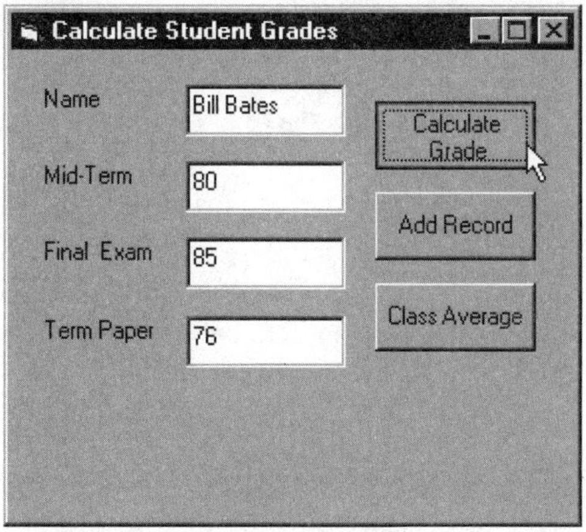
Calculate Student Grades
Name
Bill Bates
Calculate Grade
Mid-Term
80
Add Record
Final Exam
85
Term Paper
76
Class Average

We immediately saw the button's **`Click`** event procedure highlighted in the Code window, and I stepped through the program line by line by pressing the *F8* key.

"In Step mode," I said, "the line of code highlighted in yellow is the line of code that is about to be executed, and this line of code..."

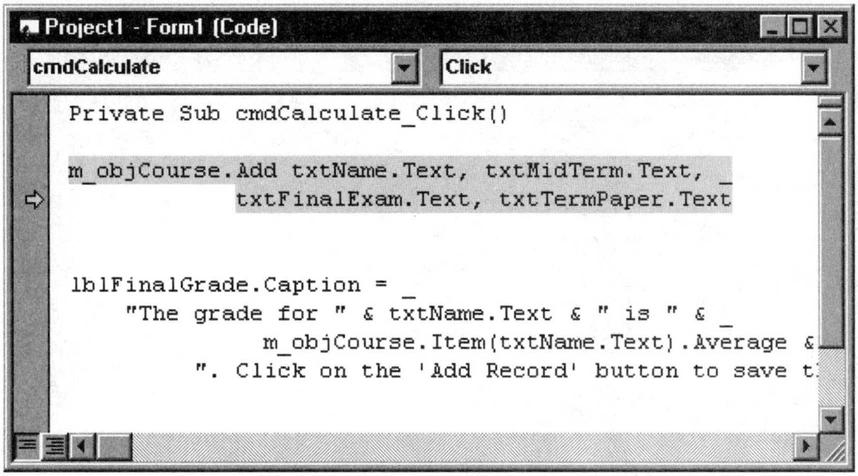
Project1 - Form1 (Code)
cmdCalculate
Click
Private Sub cmdCalculate_Click()
m_objCourse.Add txtName.Text, txtMidTerm.Text, _
txtFinalExam.Text, txtTermPaper.Text
lblFinalGrade.Caption = _
"The grade for " & txtName.Text & " is " & _
m_objCourse.Item(txtName.Text).Average &
". Click on the 'Add Record' button to save t

"...will trigger the **Add** method of the **Course** collection object..."

I pressed *F8* again:

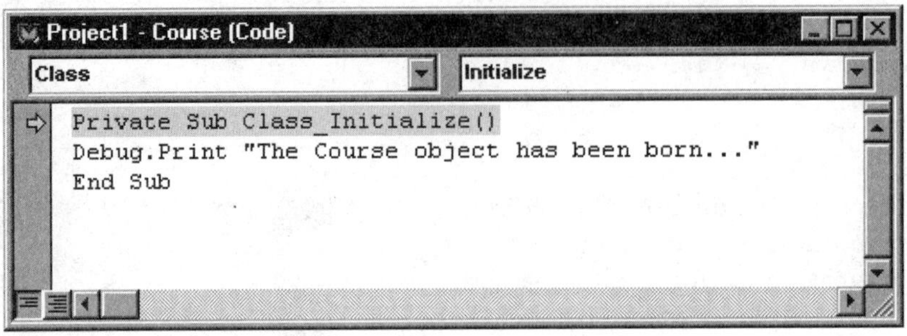
Project1 - Course (Code)
Class
Initialize
Private Sub Class_Initialize()
Debug.Print "The Course object has been born..."
End Sub

"As you can see," I said, "the **Initialize** event procedure of the **Course** collection object has just been triggered."

"That's a little surprising to me," said Kate. "Shouldn't it have been triggered before now? After all, we declared the **Course** object variable in the General Declarations section of the form, didn't we?"

"You're right, Kate," I said, "we did declare the **Course** object's object variable in the General Declarations section of the form, but the **Course** object isn't actually instantiated *until the first reference is made to it* – either by triggering one of its property procedures, or by executing one of its methods."

I then pressed *F8* again, and we all watched as the **Course** collection object's **Add** method began to execute:

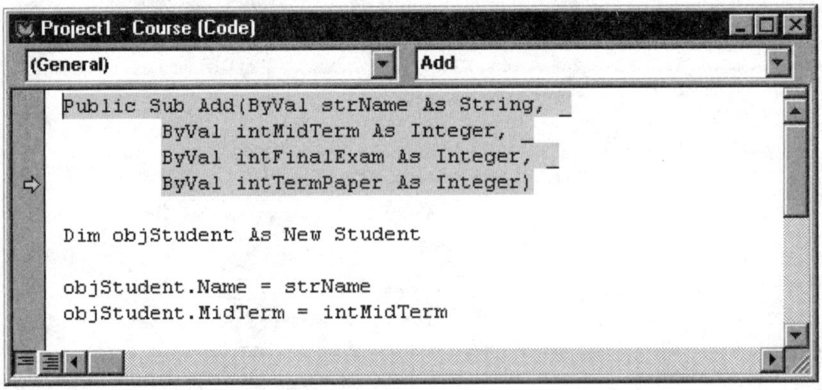
Project1 - Course (Code)
(General)
Add
Public Sub Add(ByVal strName As String, _
ByVal intMidTerm As Integer, _
ByVal intFinalExam As Integer, _
ByVal intTermPaper As Integer)
Dim objStudent As New Student
objStudent.Name = strName
objStudent.MidTerm = intMidTerm

I pressed *F8* again, and Visual Basic skipped over the **Dim** statement for the **objStudent** object variable. I waited a moment to allow everyone to focus on the line of code that was about to be executed...

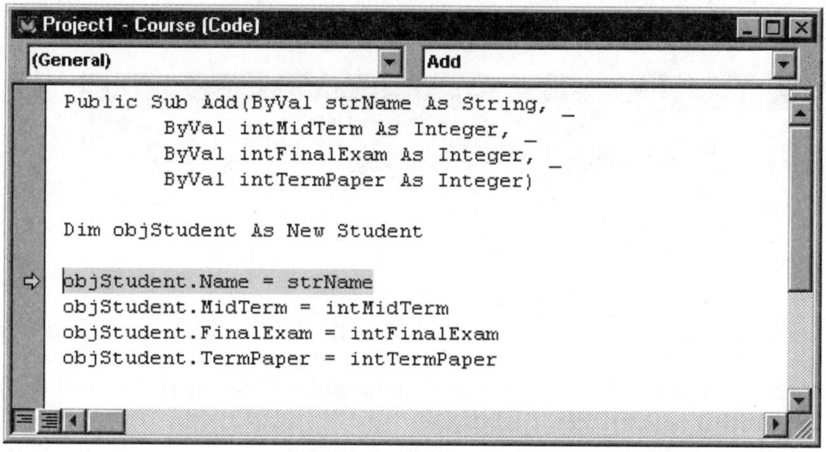
Project1 - Course (Code)
(General)
Add
Public Sub Add(ByVal strName As String, _
ByVal intMidTerm As Integer, _
ByVal intFinalExam As Integer, _
ByVal intTermPaper As Integer)
Dim objStudent As New Student
objStudent.Name = strName
objStudent.MidTerm = intMidTerm
objStudent.FinalExam = intFinalExam
objStudent.TermPaper = intTermPaper

"In Step mode," I said, "Visual Basic appears to jump over variable declaration statements. But let me assure you that Visual Basic has just declared an object variable for the **Student** object, and that VB is now about to set the **Student** object's **Name** property. When that line of code is executed, an instance of the **Student** object will be instantiated within the **Course** collection object."

I pressed *F8* again, with this result:

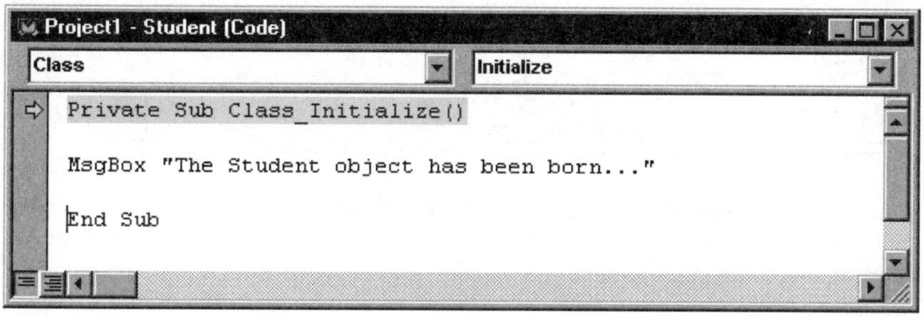
Project1 - Student (Code)
Class
Initialize
Private Sub Class_Initialize()
MsgBox "The Student object has been born..."
End Sub

"As was the case with the **Course** object just a moment ago," I said, "the first reference to one of its methods or properties causes the **Student** object to be created."

"That's really amazing," Dorothy said. "So the **Course** object has actually spawned a **Student** object..."

"That's exactly the idea of a collection object, Dorothy," I said, "we have the collection object do all of the hard work!"

I continued to press the *F8* function key, stepping through the code line by line, and we saw the **`Property Let`** procedure for the **`Student`** object's **`Name`** property execute:

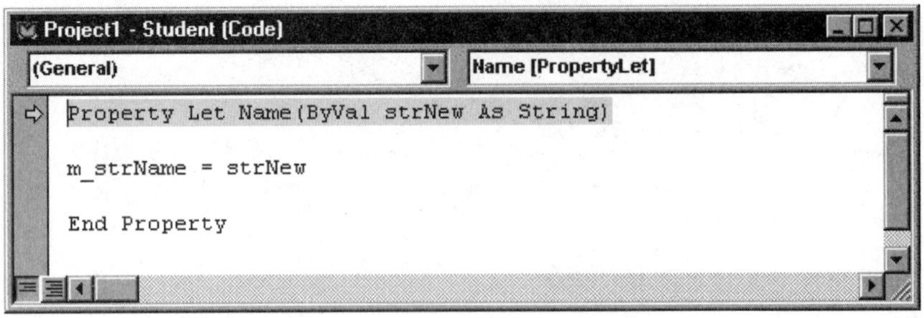
Project1 - Student (Code)
(General)
Name [PropertyLet]
Property Let Name(ByVal strNew As String)
m_strName = strNew
End Property

Then it was back to the **`cmdCalculate`** button's **`Click`** event procedure to set the **`Student`** object's **`MidTerm`** property...

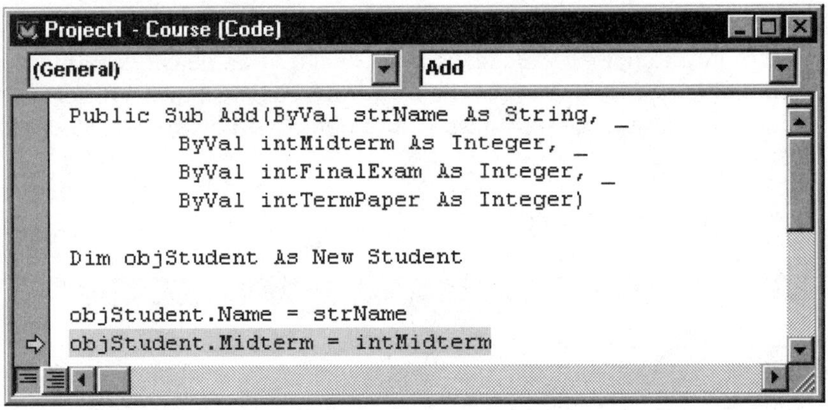
Project1 - Course (Code)
(General)
Add
Public Sub Add(ByVal strName As String, _
ByVal intMidterm As Integer, _
ByVal intFinalExam As Integer, _
ByVal intTermPaper As Integer)
Dim objStudent As New Student
objStudent.Name = strName
objStudent.Midterm = intMidterm

...followed by the **`Property Let`** procedure for the **`MidTerm`** property:

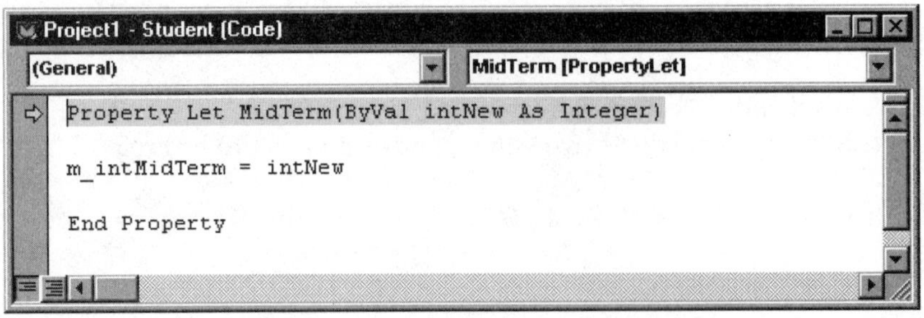
Project1 - Student (Code)
(General)
MidTerm [PropertyLet]
Property Let MidTerm(ByVal intNew As Integer)
m_intMidTerm = intNew
End Property

Then it was time to go back again to the **cmdCalculate** button's **Click** event procedure to set the **FinalExam** property:

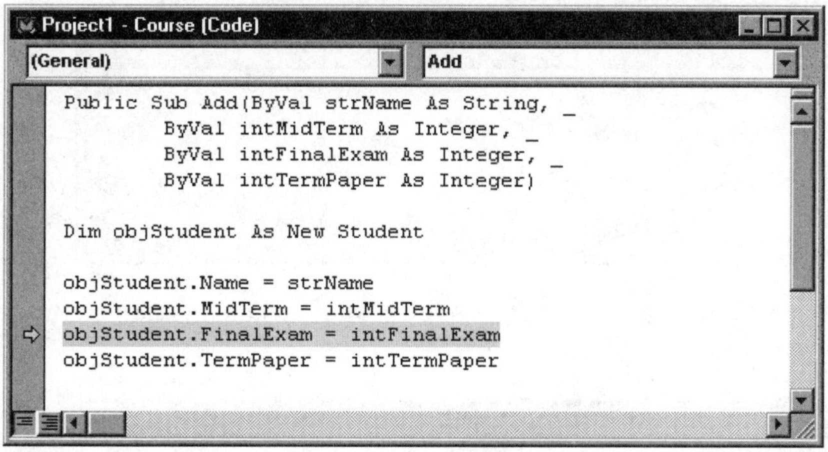
Project1 - Course (Code)
(General)
Add
Public Sub Add(ByVal strName As String, _
ByVal intMidTerm As Integer, _
ByVal intFinalExam As Integer, _
ByVal intTermPaper As Integer)
Dim objStudent As New Student
objStudent.Name = strName
objStudent.MidTerm = intMidTerm
objStudent.FinalExam = intFinalExam
objStudent.TermPaper = intTermPaper

Now for the **Property Let** procedure for the **Student** object's **FinalExam** property:

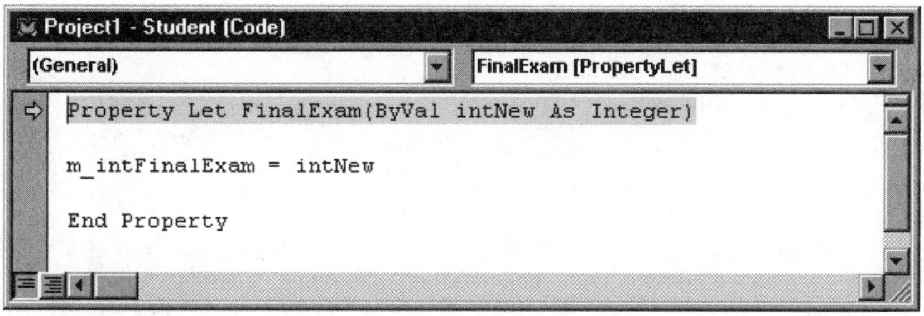
Project1 - Student (Code)
(General)
FinalExam [PropertyLet]
Property Let FinalExam(ByVal intNew As Integer)
m_intFinalExam = intNew
End Property

Then back, once again, to the **cmdCalculate Click** event procedure...

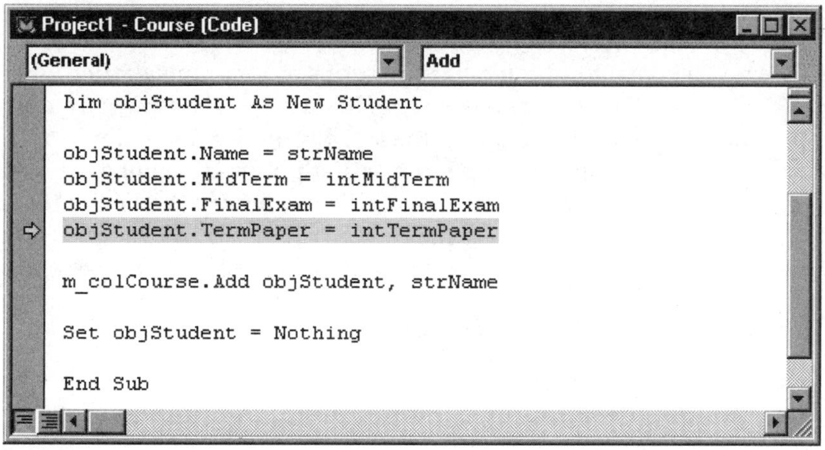
Project1 - Course (Code)
(General)
Add
Dim objStudent As New Student
objStudent.Name = strName
objStudent.MidTerm = intMidTerm
objStudent.FinalExam = intFinalExam
objStudent.TermPaper = intTermPaper
m_colCourse.Add objStudent, strName
Set objStudent = Nothing
End Sub

...followed by the **Property Let** for the **TermPaper** property:

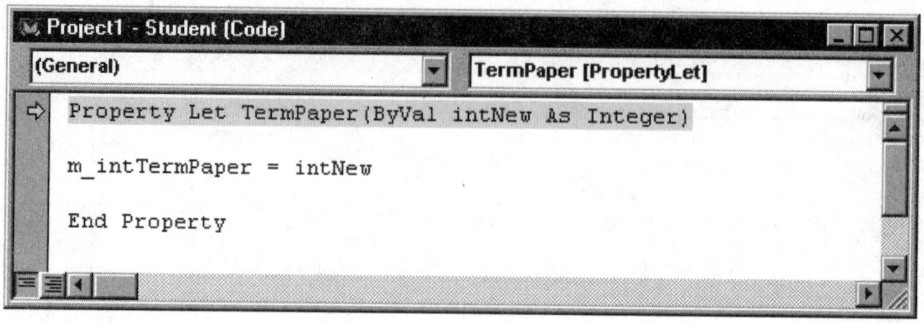
Project1 - Student (Code)
(General)
TermPaper [PropertyLet]
Property Let TermPaper(ByVal intNew As Integer)
m_intTermPaper = intNew
End Property

And – surprise! – back to the **cmdCalculate** code again to execute the **Add** method of the **m_colCourse** collection:

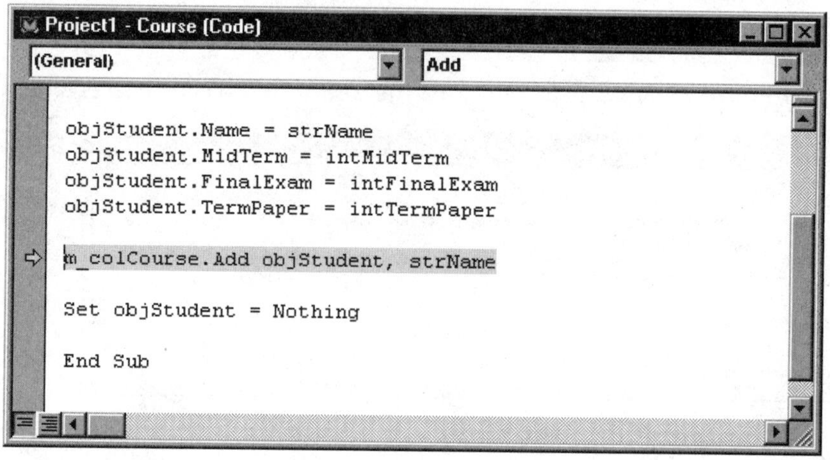
Project1 - Course (Code)
(General)
Add
objStudent.Name = strName
objStudent.MidTerm = intMidTerm
objStudent.FinalExam = intFinalExam
objStudent.TermPaper = intTermPaper
m_colCourse.Add objStudent, strName
Set objStudent = Nothing
End Sub

This line," I said, "is the one that actually creates the item in **m_colCourse** that references the **Student** object we've just created. Remember the series of diagrams earlier where we showed the relationship between the **Course** collection object and the **Student** objects as they get created? This line does that by executing the **m_colCourse** collection's **Add** method, passing it two arguments: a memory reference that points to the new **Student** object, and the name of the student to use as the key value to identify the new item in the collection."

The next line sets the object variable reference to the **Student** object to **Nothing**:

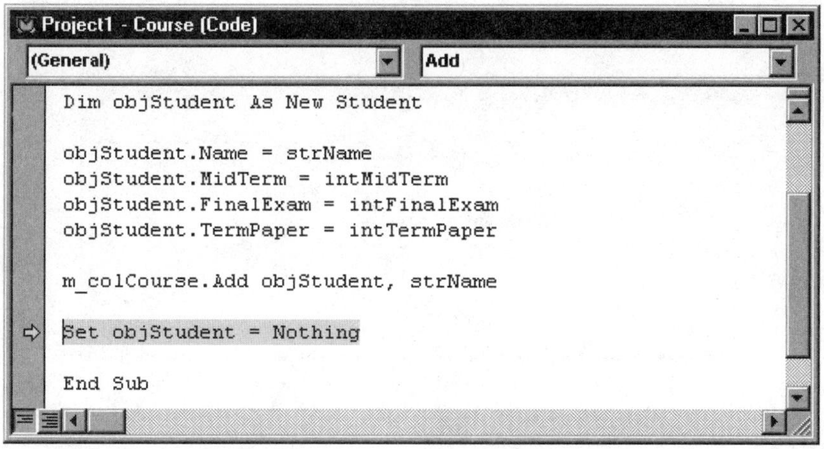

Then it was back to **cmdCalculate**'s **Click** event procedure to display the student's average grade on the form:

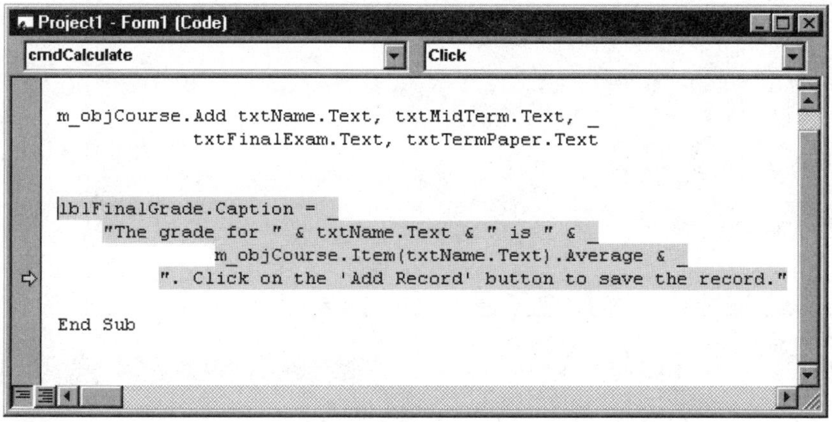

Project1 - Form1 (Code)
cmdCalculate
Click
m_objCourse.Add txtName.Text, txtMidTerm.Text, _
txtFinalExam.Text, txtTermPaper.Text
lblFinalGrade.Caption = _
"The grade for " & txtName.Text & " is " & _
m_objCourse.Item(txtName.Text).Average & _
". Click on the 'Add Record' button to save the record."
End Sub

"This line of code," I said, "executes the **Course** object's **Item** method. This returns a reference – an address – for the **Student** object that has the name that matches the **Text** property of the **txtName** text box. Once we have that reference, we then retrieve that object's **Average** property and display it in the **Caption** of the **lblFinalGrade** label control."

I pressed *F8* once more and we watched as the **Course** collection object's **Item** method was executed...

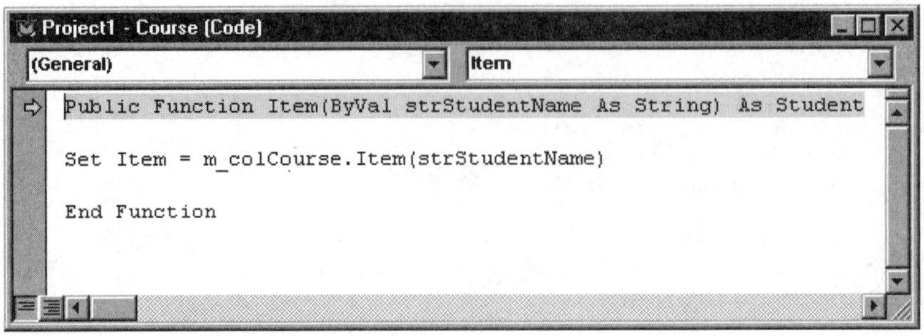
Project1 - Course (Code)
(General)
Item
Public Function Item(ByVal strStudentName As String) As Student
Set Item = m_colCourse.Item(strStudentName)
End Function

...followed immediately by the **Property Get** procedure of the **Student** object's **Average** property:

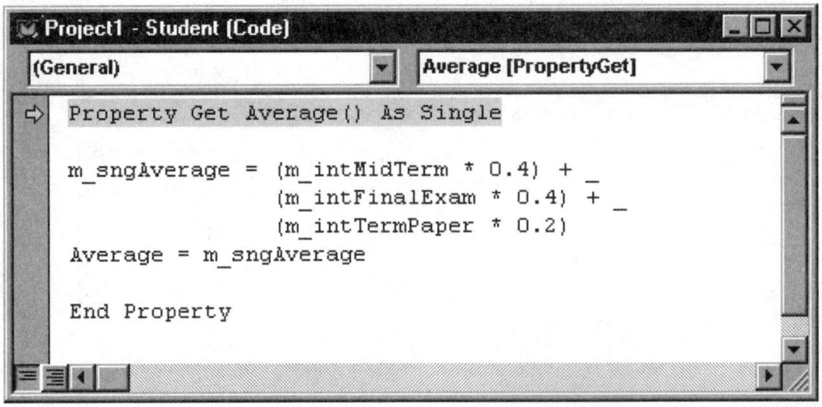
Project1 - Student (Code)
(General)
Average [PropertyGet]
Property Get Average() As Single
m_sngAverage = (m_intMidTerm * 0.4) + _
(m_intFinalExam * 0.4) + _
(m_intTermPaper * 0.2)
Average = m_sngAverage
End Property

After the **Average** property's **Property Get** procedure had concluded, the grade average for our fictitious student was displayed on the form:

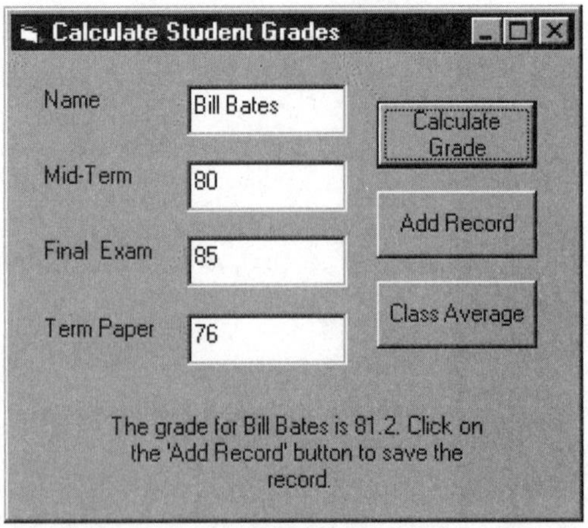
Calculate Student Grades
Name
Bill Bates
Calculate Grade
Mid-Term
80
Add Record
Final Exam
85
Term Paper
76
Class Average
The grade for Bill Bates is 81.2. Click on the 'Add Record' button to save the record.

"Let's check the Immediate window now to see what the status of our objects are," I said:

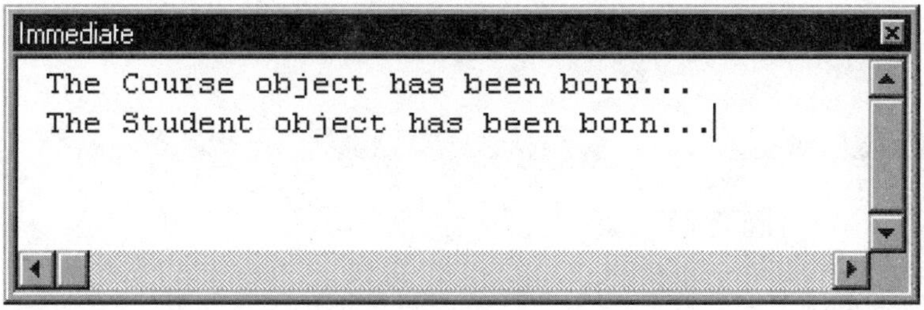

"As you can see," I said, "currently we have one instance of the **Course** collection object instantiated – exactly what we would expect: we'll never have more than one instance of the **Course** collection object 'alive' at one time. We also have just one **Student** object instantiated, since we've only entered the information for one student."

"Let's add this record to the **Grades.txt** file now," I said, and clicked on the Add Record command button, continuing by pressing the *F8* key to step through each line of code.

"This line of code," I said, "executes the **Course** object's **Item** method, this time within the **Click** event procedure of **cmdAddRecord**:"

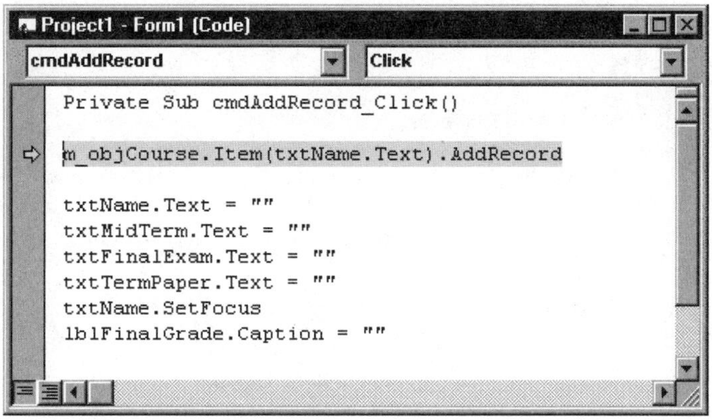

Project1 - Form1 (Code)
cmdAddRecord
Click
Private Sub cmdAddRecord_Click()
m_objCourse.Item(txtName.Text).AddRecord
txtName.Text = ""
txtMidTerm.Text = ""
txtFinalExam.Text = ""
txtTermPaper.Text = ""
txtName.SetFocus
lblFinalGrade.Caption = ""

"Here, the **Item** method returns a reference to the **Student** object with a name matching the value of **txtName**'s **Text** property by passing that value to the **Item** method as the **strStudentName** argument..."

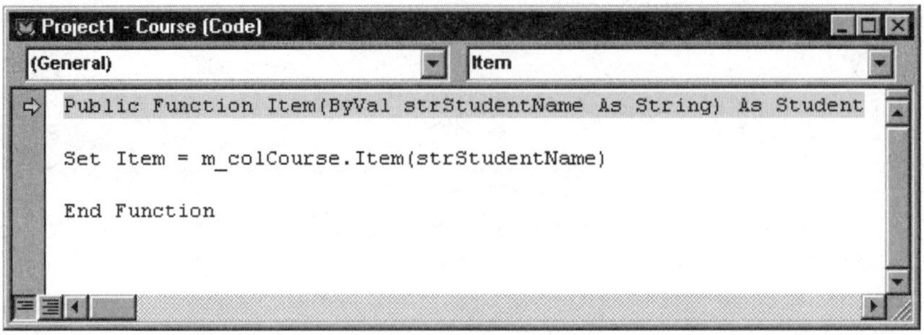

"...and then the **Student** object's **AddRecord** method is executed, using the property values from the **Student** object to write the student's details:"

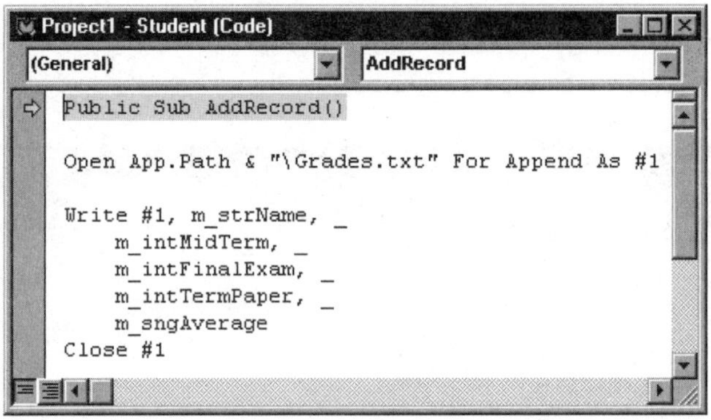

"I notice," Dave said, "that you still have code in the **Student** object's **AddRecord** method which is raising the **AddSuccessful** event, but we're no longer reacting to that event on the demo project's main form."

"That's right, Dave," I said. "Because the main form is now instantiating an instance of the **Course** object, rather than creating a **Student** object, the main form no longer has direct access to any of the **Student** object's properties, methods, and events. Since it's the **Student** object that is raising the **AddSuccessful** event, there's no way to get to it directly from the main form."

"Is there any way," Blaine asked, "that we can still react to that **AddSuccessful** event – as we did before – and produce a message box saying that the student's record has been added successfully to the **Grades.txt** file?"

"Yes, there is, Blaine," I answered. "We could declare the **Student** object **WithEvents** within the **Course** object, which would then give the **Course** object access to the **AddSuccessful** event procedure. We could then place the code for our message box in the **AddSuccessful** event procedure. In fact, if we wanted, we could declare an event in the **Course** object, and then raise that to signal back to the main form. To do this, we'd also need to declare the **Course** object **WithEvents** within the main form – it's a bit circuitous, but it can be done!"

"Now, let's click on the Class Average command button," I said. "Bear in mind that, at this point, we have one **Course** collection object instantiated, containing a reference to one **Student** object – Bill Bates' object."

I clicked on the Class Average button, with this result:

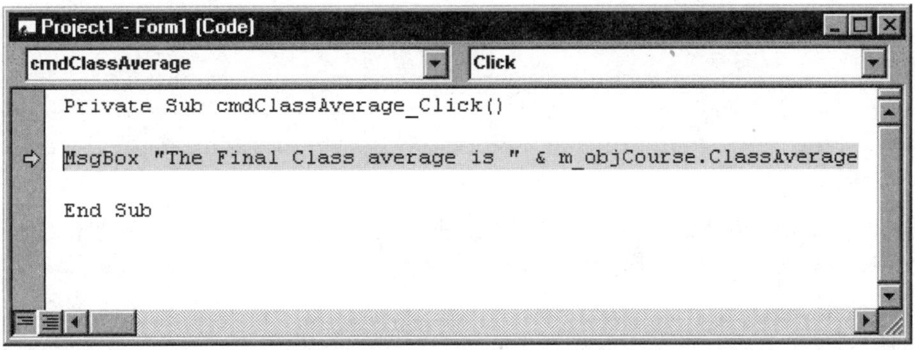
Project1 - Form1 (Code)
cmdClassAverage
Click
Private Sub cmdClassAverage_Click()
MsgBox "The Final Class average is " & m_objCourse.ClassAverage
End Sub

"When this line of code is executed and invokes the **ClassAverage** property," I said, "it will trigger the **ClassAverage**'s **Property Get** procedure:

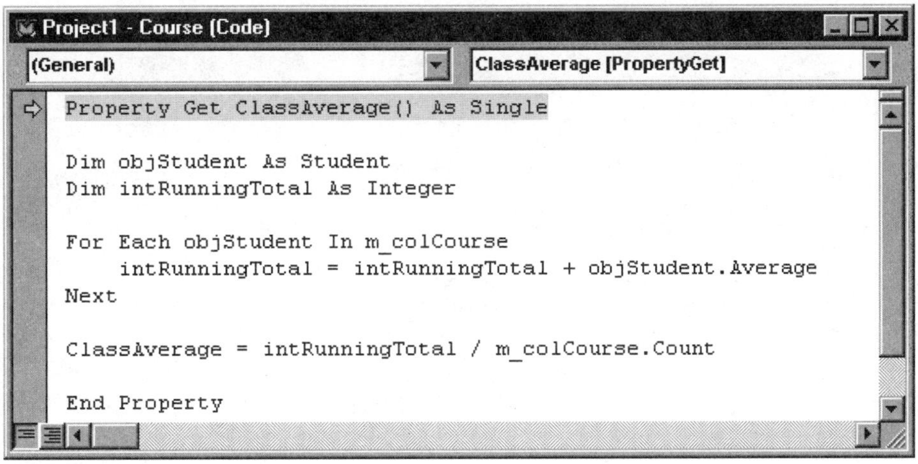
Project1 - Course (Code)
(General)
ClassAverage [PropertyGet]
Property Get ClassAverage() As Single
Dim objStudent As Student
Dim intRunningTotal As Integer
For Each objStudent In m_colCourse
intRunningTotal = intRunningTotal + objStudent.Average
Next
ClassAverage = intRunningTotal / m_colCourse.Count
End Property

"Here's where the hidden **NewEnum** method we coded just a few minutes ago comes into play," I said. "When the **For...Each** statement is executed..."

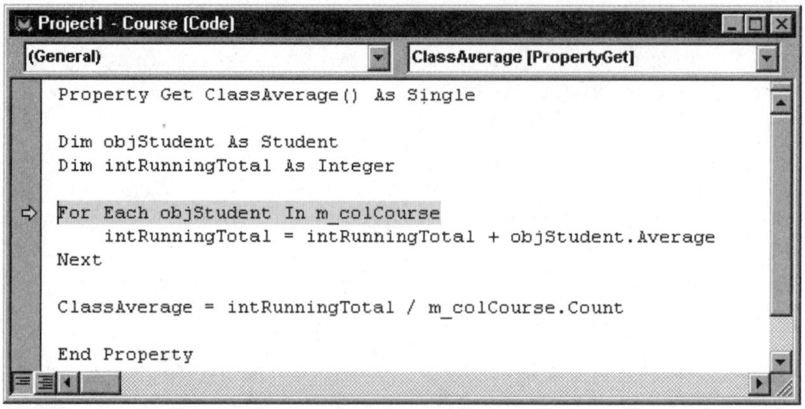
Project1 - Course (Code)
(General)
ClassAverage [PropertyGet]
Property Get ClassAverage() As Single
Dim objStudent As Student
Dim intRunningTotal As Integer
For Each objStudent In m_colCourse
intRunningTotal = intRunningTotal + objStudent.Average
Next
ClassAverage = intRunningTotal / m_colCourse.Count
End Property

"The **For...Each** loop structure triggers the **NewEnum** method of the **Course** collection object – remember, the reason we created that method was precisely to allow us to loop through all the items in the collection. We don't see the **NewEnum** method run in Step mode – it's invisible to us."

"Because we checked the Hide this member check box on the Procedure Attributes window for the **NewEnum** method?" Blain suggested.

"Exactly," I replied, "but it's actually facilitating our loop through the items in the **m_colCourse** collection. The **For...Each** statement loops through each item in the collection object – where each item contains the address of a **Student** object. The body of the loop is then executed once for each item in the **m_colCourse** collection. Notice that within the body of the loop, we're accessing the **Average** property referenced via the **Student** object variable:"

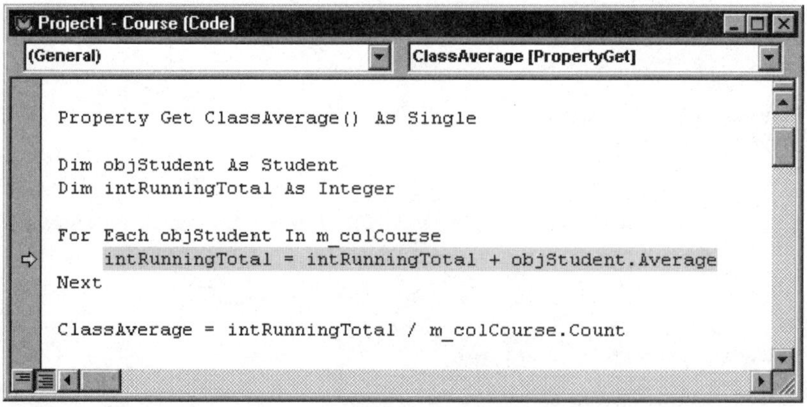
Project1 - Course (Code)
(General)
ClassAverage [PropertyGet]
Property Get ClassAverage() As Single
Dim objStudent As Student
Dim intRunningTotal As Integer
For Each objStudent In m_colCourse
intRunningTotal = intRunningTotal + objStudent.Average
Next
ClassAverage = intRunningTotal / m_colCourse.Count

"...which in turn triggers the individual **Student** object's **Average** method..."

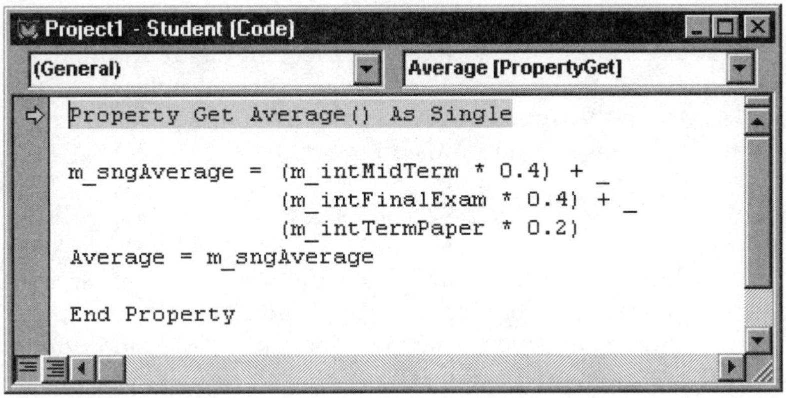
Project1 - Student (Code)
(General)
Average [PropertyGet]
Property Get Average() As Single
m_sngAverage = (m_intMidTerm * 0.4) + _
(m_intFinalExam * 0.4) + _
(m_intTermPaper * 0.2)
Average = m_sngAverage
End Property

"The value of the **Student** object's **Average** property is then added to the value of the variable **intRunningTotal**," I said. "After that, this next line of code is executed:"

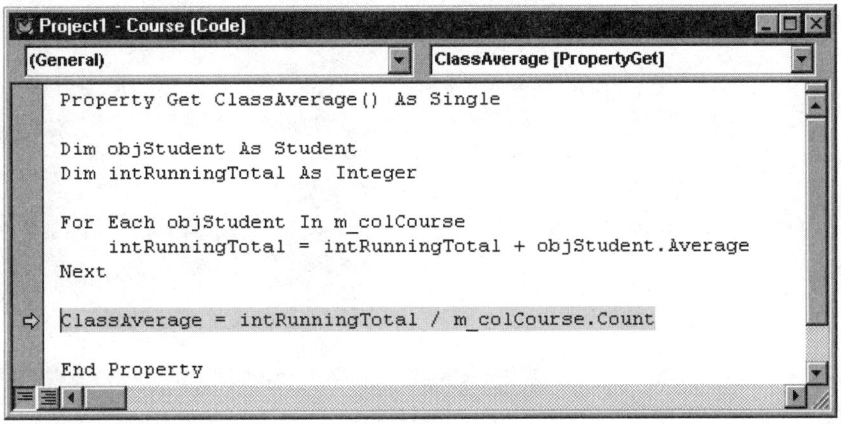
Project1 - Course (Code)
(General)
ClassAverage [PropertyGet]
Property Get ClassAverage() As Single
Dim objStudent As Student
Dim intRunningTotal As Integer
For Each objStudent In m_colCourse
intRunningTotal = intRunningTotal + objStudent.Average
Next
ClassAverage = intRunningTotal / m_colCourse.Count
End Property

"...which assigns the result of the division of **intRunningTotal** by the **Count** property of **m_colCourse** to the **ClassAverage** property. Finally, this message box is displayed showing the overall class average:"

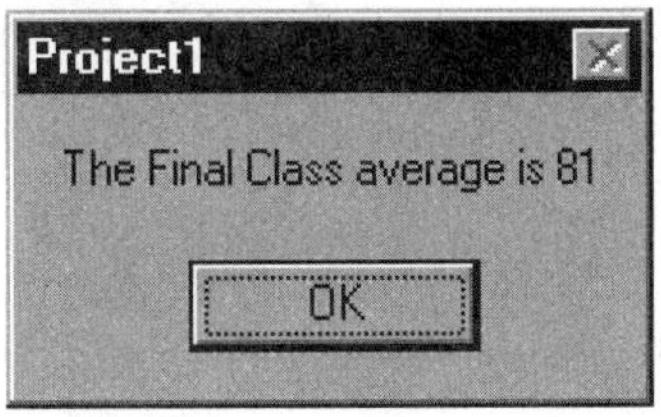
Project1
The Final Class average is 81
OK

"I think you can see," I said, "that there's quite a bit going on behind the scenes here. Just about any time you execute a method of the **Course** collection object you wind up executing either a property or method procedure within the **Student** object. You could say that working with the **Course** object has a **cascading** effect on the **Student** object: that's the way we've designed it to be. By building the **Course** collection object, we've taken the responsibility of implementing the **Student** object away from the programmer – which should in the long run make things easier on them."

"Suppose we enter another student?" Rhonda asked. "Do we have to change anything?"

"That's the beauty of a collection object," I said. "The code that we've written works just as well with thousands of students as it does with a single student. If we enter the information for another student, the **Course** collection object will instantiate a second **Student** object, and add a reference to it as an item in the **m_colCourse** collection. Let's add one more student and see what happens."

I then clicked on the run button to exit Step mode, entered the information for a second fictitious student, and clicked on the Calculate Grade button...

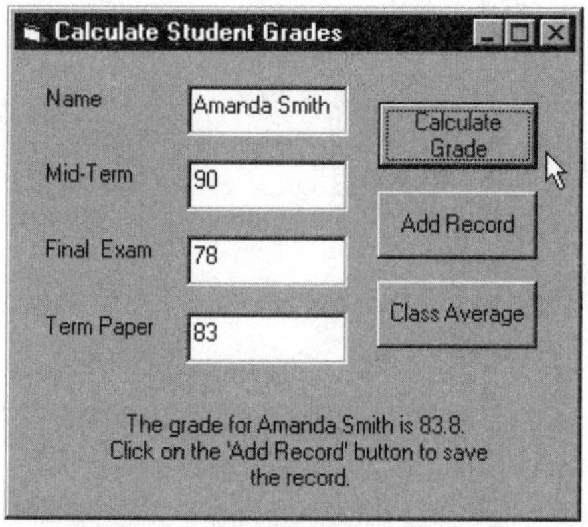

"We now have two instantiated **Student** objects," I said. "Let's look in the Immediate window..."

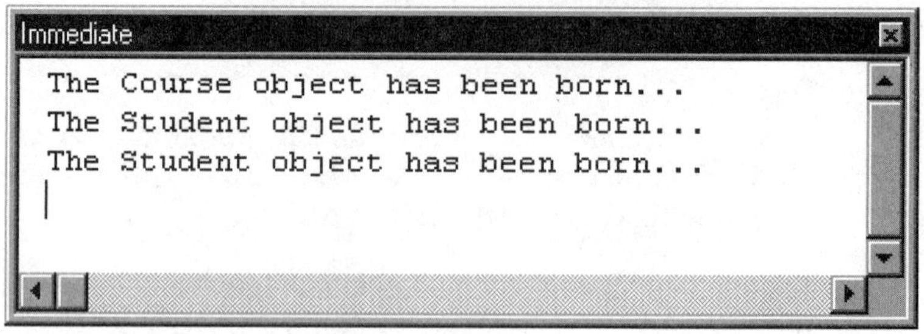

I then clicked on the Add Record command button, followed by the Class Average button, with this result:

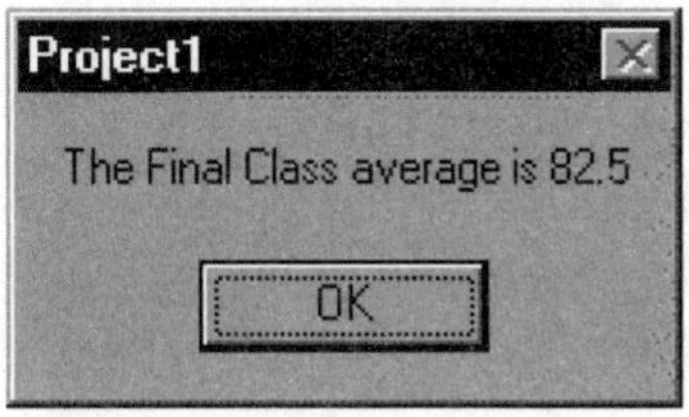
Project1
The Final Class average is 82.5
OK

"As you can see," I said, "our demo program works just as well with two **Students** as it does with one. Let's see what happens if we close the form now."

I then closed the form, and displayed the Immediate window on the classroom projector:

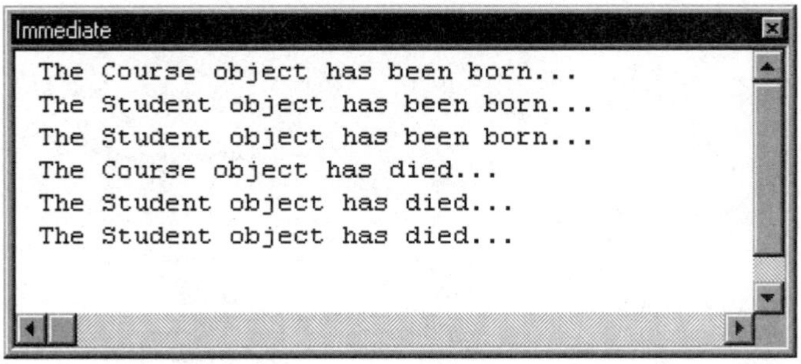
Immediate
The Course object has been born...
The Student object has been born...
The Student object has been born...
The Course object has died...
The Student object has died...
The Student object has died...

"Let me explain the chronology of our object again here," I said. "First, we instantiated the **Course** object. When we calculate the grades for the first student, a **Student** object is added to the **Course** collection object, followed by a second **Student** object when the second student's information was entered. When we closed the form, we set the **Course** collection object to nothing, triggering its **Terminate** event procedure. When the **m_colCourse** collection of the **Course** collection object was destroyed, each one of the **Student** objects, whose address was stored as an item in that collection, lost its one and only reference – and when there are no longer any references to an object, Visual Basic destroys it."

I looked around the classroom for signs of confusion, and I was pleasantly surprised not to see a great deal of it. Now it was time for my students to turn their attention to creating a collection object for the China Shop project.

"Now it's your turn to create a collection object," I said. "But first, it's been a long morning, and I'd like you to be fresh before we tackle that task – let's take a fifteen minute break first."

Back to the China Shop Project

"So far," I said, when the class returned, "we've seen how to create a collection object, how to build the properties and methods that it needs, and how to use it in conjunction with the multiple objects that we want to manage. Now we're going to put this into action in the China Shop program."

Creating the Order Collection Object

"The first thing we'll do is create an **`Order`** collection object that will help us instantiate and manage the **`Dish`** objects:

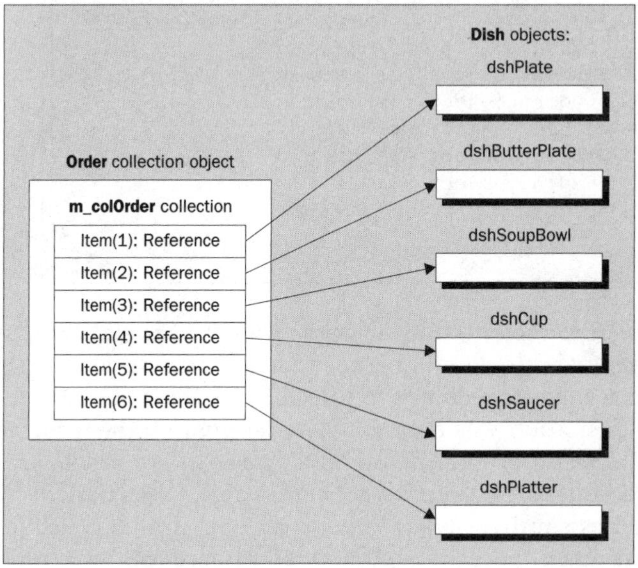

"We'll begin by creating the basic class module that the **`Order`** collection object will be instantiated from."

So saying, I handed out the first exercise for the class to complete:

Exercise - Creating the Order Collection Class

In this exercise, you'll create the **`Order`** collection object of the China Shop program.

1. Open up the China Shop project in Visual Basic.
2. Select Project | Add class module from the Visual Basic Menu Bar.

3. When the **Add Class Module** dialog box appears, double-click **Class Module** on the **New** tab and the new class module's code window will appear in the IDE.

4. Bring up the Properties window for the class by pressing *F4*. Change the **`Name`** property of the class from **`Class1`** to **`Order`** (Yes, I'm aware that we should be naming the class **`Dishes`** to stick with the naming convention I outlined earlier – but remember that we're using the name **`Order`** here to avoid confusion in the classroom):

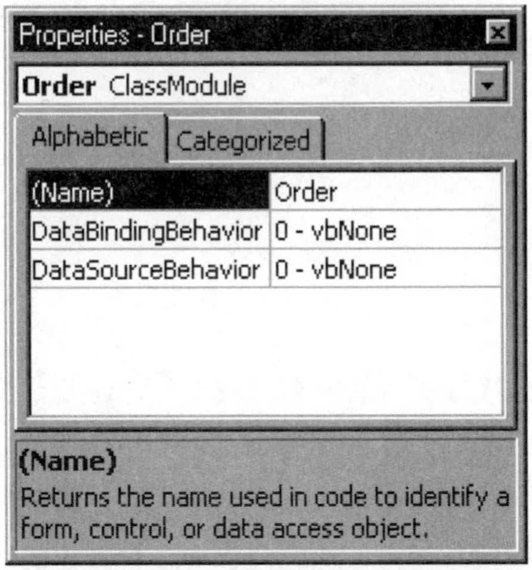

5. Click on the 'save' icon and save this class, with the name **`Order.cls`**, in your **`\VBFiles\China`** folder:

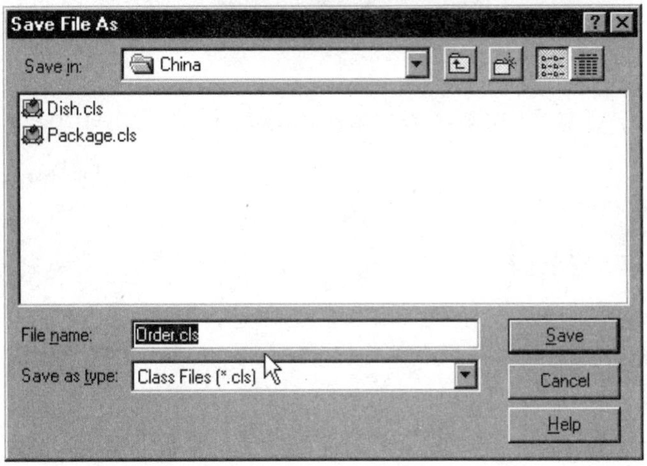

6. Save the China Shop project.

7. Bring up the Project Explorer window. You should now have two forms and three class modules in your project:

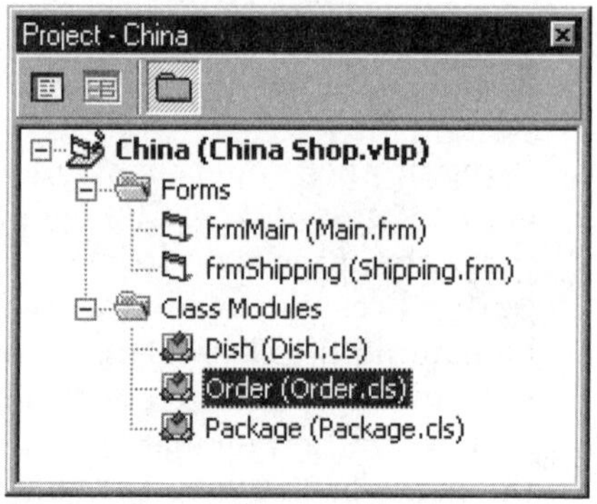

Creating the Order Object's Private Variables

"Now that we've got the class module for the **Order** collection object established," I said, "we need to fill it up with code. Here's the first exercise that will help do that:"

Exercise - Creating Private Variables in the Order Class Module

In this exercise, you'll declare the **Private** variables inside the **Order** class module:

1. Continue working with the China Shop project's **Order** class module.
2. Add the following code to the General Declarations section of the class:

```
Option Explicit

Private m_colOrder As New Collection
Private m_intDiscount As Integer
```

3. Save the China Shop project.

Discussion

Valerie said: "I understand why we declare **m_colOrder** here – it's essential – but what's the purpose of the **m_intDiscount** variable?"

"Well", I explained, "that has to do with the discount that the China Shop offers to customers who select a complete place setting. We'll use the value in this variable to determine whether or not a discount should be applied to the customer's price quotation. We'll see how this works in just a little bit."

The Initialize and Terminate Event Procedures

"What we'll do now," I continued, "is quickly code the **Initialize** and **Terminate** event procedures so that they can provide us with information while the program is running. Here's an exercise that covers this angle:"

Exercise - Coding the Initialize and Terminate Event Procedures

In this exercise, you'll code the **Initialize** and **Terminate** event procedures for the **Order** object. Placing code in these event procedures isn't strictly necessary for the proper operation of the China Shop program, but it is a good idea to add these diagnostic lines when you're coding your first few class modules – they can help you keep track of what's going on. In other programs, you can use the **Initialize** event to code any important pre-processing that you want performed before the user starts interacting with your object.

1. Continue working with the **Order** class.

2. Add the following code to the **Initialize** event procedure:

```
Private Sub Class_Initialize()

Debug.Print "The Order object has been born..."

End Sub
```

3. Now key the following code into the **Terminate** event procedure:

```
Private Sub Class_Terminate()

Debug.Print "The Order object has died..."

End Sub
```

4. Save the China Shop project.

Discussion

"All we're doing here," I said, "is using the Immediate window to let us know when an **Order** object has been created, and when it dies. As I've mentioned during the class, code like this is a great aid in understanding how your program is operating – and when you compile your project into an executable, all debug statements are automatically excluded."

Coding the Order Class's Methods

"OK," I went on, "now it's time to code up the methods that the **Order** class will implement. There are six of them: **Add**, **Item**, **Remove**, **Count**, **NewEnum**, and **TotalPrice**. These methods encapsulate the functionality that we need to create **Dish** objects via the **Order** collection, and to work with those objects."

The Add Method

To get them to create the **Add** method, I handed out the following exercise for the class to work through:

Exercise - Creating the Order Class's Add Method

1. Continue working with the **Order** class of the China Shop project.

2. Create the **Add** method of the **Order** class by adding the following code to the class module's General Declarations section:

```
Public Sub Add(ByVal strDishBrand As String,
        ➥ByVal strDishItem As String,
        ➥ByVal intDishQuantity As Integer)

Dim objDish As New Dish

objDish.Brand = strDishBrand
objDish.Item = strDishItem
objDish.Quantity = intDishQuantity

m_colOrder.Add objDish, strDishBrand & strDishItem

If strDishItem = "Plate" Or strDishItem = "Butter Plate" Or
            ➥strDishItem = "Soup Bowl" Or strDishItem = "Cup" Or
            ➥strDishItem = "Saucer" Then
            m_intDiscount = m_intDiscount + 1
End If

Set objDish = Nothing

End Sub
```

3. Save the China Shop project.

Discussion

"This code," Steve said, "looks very similar to the code for the **Add** method of the **Course** collection object we worked on in the Student Grades project. Don't you think?"

"That's right, Steve," I said. "Most collection objects implement pretty much the same **interface**."

"By *interface*, what do you mean, exactly?" asked Dave.

"The interface is like the reception desk, across which the object deals with the outside world," I said. "It's across this desk that the object presents information about what's inside of it so that we can work on it. We present our requirements at the front desk and tell the receptionist what it is we want from inside the organization. The agents inside the organization then go about their business behind the scenes and present us with the information we want: we don't have to know about the internal workings of the office – all we want is the information we seek. The interface is the standard way of asking for that information, and the standard way of the response being given to us. I think you'll find that the rest of the methods of the **Order** collection object are also similar to those of the **Course** collection object. There will be some differences – the **Order** collection object is instantiating **Dish** objects, not **Student** objects – but the process is essentially the same."

I paused before moving on to the specifics of the code to hand.

"Let's take a look at the **Add** method's procedure header first. The **Add** method of the **Order** object instantiates a **Dish** object and then adds a reference to that **Dish** object as an item to the **m_colOrder** collection. Therefore the **Add** method needs information about the **Dish** object to be instantiated – and this information is passed to it via three arguments – **strDishBrand**, **strDishItem** and **intQuantity**:"

```
Public Sub Add(ByVal strDishBrand As String,
        ↳ByVal strDishItem As String,
        ↳ByVal intQuantity As Integer)
```

"Next," I said, "comes the declaration for the **Dish** object variable:"

```
Dim objDish As New Dish
```

"At the moment, in the main form of the China Shop project, the six **Dish** objects are being declared directly – but that will change shortly," I explained. "Next, these next three lines of code take the values of the three passed arguments – a china piece's brand, type, and quantity – and assign them to the **Brand**, **Item** and **Quantity** properties of the **Dish** object:"

```
objDish.Brand = strDishBrand
objDish.Item = strDishItem
objDish.Quantity = intQuantity
```

"The next line of code adds a reference (or address) to the newly instantiated **Dish** object to the **m_colOrder** collection as an item, using the combination of brand and item as the key value that identifies that item:"

```
m_colOrder.Add objDish, strDishBrand & strDishItem
```

"That ensures," I went on, "that we will be able to get to that **Dish** object later, provided we know its brand and item – 'item' here being the *type* of china piece, such as a plate or cup."

"I must say that I'm amazed at the way I've been able to follow this code so far," Melissa said, "I think our work with the Student Grades project helped out immensely. But this next section of code is confusing me. I don't think we did anything similar to this in the Student Grades project, did we?"

"No, we didn't, Melissa," I said, "This is the section of code that determines if the **Order** object has references to all of the **Dish** objects that comprise a complete place setting – that is, whether the customer has chosen a full set of china pieces from the selection options on the form. As you may recall, a complete place setting is made up of a plate, butter plate, soup bowl, cup and saucer. What we're doing here is checking to see if the **Dish** object we just created has an **Item** property equal to any one of those five..."

```
If strDishItem = "Plate" Or strDishItem = "Butter Plate" Or
           ↳strDishItem = "Soup Bowl" Or strDishItem = "Cup" Or
           ↳strDishItem = "Saucer" Then
```

"If it does, then we increment the value of the variable **m_intDiscount** by 1:"

```
           m_intDiscount = m_intDiscount + 1
End If
```

"Later on, when the time comes to calculate the price of the customer's sales quotation, we'll see that, if the value of **m_intDiscount** is 5, that means we have **Dish** objects for each one of those **Item** names in the **m_colOrder** collection: this means that the customer has selected a complete place setting. We'll then display a discounted price for the sales quotation."

"Sounds nifty," Ward said.

"Thanks, Ward," I replied. "It also means that we'll be able to remove the logic for the complete place setting calculation from the **cmdCalculate** button's **Click** event procedure: the code in that event procedure will be greatly streamlined."

"When will the **Add** method of the **Order** collection object be executed?" Kate asked.

"That's a good question, Kate," I said. "The **Add** method will be executed whenever the customer selects an item of china, and it'll also be executed whenever the user changes their selected brand of china."

"I can understand executing the **Add** method when the user selects an item," Tom said, "but why execute it when the user changes their selected brand? Can't we use the **Item** method of the collection object to change the **Item** property of the **Dish** objects in the collection?"

"Yes, we could do that, Tom," I said. "We'll be writing the **Item** method for the **Order** collection object shortly: there you'll see that the **Text** property of **lstBrands**, in combination with the **Caption** property of a selected china piece, is used as the key to locating an item in the **m_colOrder** collection. Locating an item in the collection, therefore, and then finding the **Dish** object to which it refers, is straightforward."

"And once we've done that, changing the **Brand** property of that **Dish** objects wouldn't present any difficulties, either," Ward observed. "What's the problem, then?"

"I think I can see a problem," Melissa declared. "The user can change the selected brand of china, but each item in the **m_colOrder** collection will still have the old brand name as part of its **key** – in fact, we're not allowed to change the key for an item in a collection – so if we change the brand, we won't be able to locate any of the items again!"

"I'm afraid I still don't understand," Rhonda said. "Can you spell it out to me why we wouldn't be able to locate the items?"

"The key to the **m_colOrder** collection," I said, "is the combination of the **Dish** item's brand and the name of the selected piece of china. You may recall, that I explained to you in Lesson Two, that Visual Basic doesn't let you change the key of an item in a collection."

"Gee, that feels like years ago!" Rhonda declared. "I'd forgotten about that."

"You'll pick it up with practice," I assured her. "Since we need to know the key of an item in order to find it in the **m_colOrder** collection, this means that any time the user changes any one of the those two values – brand or item – we need to do the following: first, remove **every** item from the collection, and second, add each item back using the new brand and item name as the key to the replacement item."

"I think I understand now," Rhonda said. "This is similar to what I learned about changing the key to a record in a database – you can't. If the value of the key needs to change, you need to delete the record, then add it back with the new key."

"That's the idea," I said.

The Item Method

"OK," I resumed, "what we need to do next is create the **Order** collection class's **Item** method."

Here's the exercise:

Exercise - Creating the Order Class's Item Method

1. Continue working with the **Order** class.

2. Create the **Order** class's **Item** method by adding the following code to the **Order** class module:

```
Public Function Item(ByVal strDishBrand As String,
      ↳strDishItem As String) As Dish

Set Item = m_colOrder.Item(strDishBrand & strDishItem)

End Function
```

3. Save the China Shop project.

Discussion

"This code is virtually identical to the code we saw in the **Course** collection **Item** method," I said, "with the exception that this **Item** method requires two arguments to locate an item in the **m_colOrder** collection – **Brand** and **Item**. Once the item is located, the reference – or address to the **Dish** object – is passed back to the program executing the **Item** method."

The Remove Method

No one had any problems with the last exercise, so we moved to the next exercise – coding the **`Order`** collection object's **`Remove`** method:

Exercise - Creating the Remove Method for the Order Class

1. Continue working with the **Order** class.

2. Create the **`Remove`** method of the **`Order`** class by keying this code into the **`Order`** class module:

```
Public Sub Remove(ByVal strDishBrand As String,
        ↳ByVal strDishItem As String)

m_colOrder.Remove strDishBrand & strDishItem

If strDishItem = "Plate" Or strDishItem = "Butter Plate" Or
            ↳strDishItem = "Soup Bowl" Or strDishItem = "Cup" Or
            ↳strDishItem = "Saucer" Then
            m_intDiscount = m_intDiscount - 1
End If

End Sub
```

3. Save the China Shop project.

Discussion

"When will this method be executed?" Kevin asked.

"The **`Remove`** method," I said, "will be executed whenever the user un-checks an item of china on the China Shop form, and also – as we discussed earlier – whenever the user changes the brand selection."

"There's that code again!" Rhonda said, "I mean, the bit referring to the **`m_intDiscount`** variable – although this time we're subtracting 1 from its value."

"That's exactly right, Rhonda," I said. "We use the value of **`m_intDiscount`** to determine if the customer's selections comprise a complete place setting. If the value of **`m_intDiscount`** is five, that means that all five of the items comprising a complete place setting have been selected. If the customer un-checks an item, and it's one of these five items, we subtract one from the value of **`m_intDiscount`**."

The Count Method

"OK," I said, "time to move on to the next stage. In this exercise, you'll code the **Count** method for the **Order** collection class."

Here's the exercise I handed out:

Exercise - Creating the Order Class's Count Method

1. Continue working with the **Order** class.
2. Create the **Count** method of the **Order** class by adding the following code to the **Order** class module:

```
Public Function Count() As Long

Count = m_colOrder.Count

End Function
```

3. Save the China Shop project.

Discussion

"All we're doing here," I said, "is returning the value of the **Count** property of the **m_colOrder** collection to the program that executes this method. We'll use the **Count** property in the **Click** event procedure of **cmdClassAverage**."

The NewEnum Method

"Now," I said, "for the next exercise. In this one, you'll create the **NewEnum** method, which is necessary to enable the **For...Each** statement capability within the **Order** object."

Exercise - Creating the Order Class's NewEnum Method

1. Carry on working with the **Order** Class.
2. Create the **NewEnum** method of the **Order** class by adding the following code to the **Order** class module:

```
Public Function NewEnum() As IUnknown

Set NewEnum = m_colOrder.[_NewEnum]

End Function
```

3. Select Tools | Procedure Attributes | Advanced, and change the Procedure ID of the **NewEnum** method to –4. At the same time, check on the Hide this member check box:

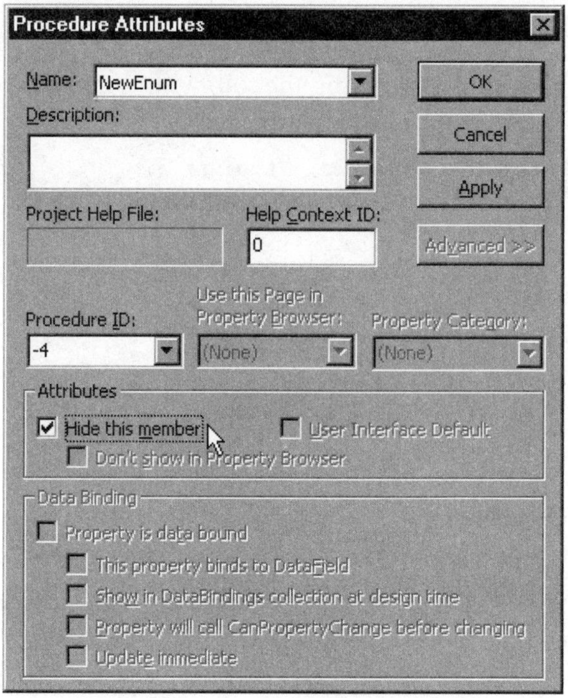

4. Save the China Shop project.

Discussion

I'm not sure if fatigue was setting in, but a number of students made some minor typographical errors while completing this exercise – several of them forgot to place brackets around the word **NewEnum**, and one student forgot the leading underscore.

The TotalPrice Method

"Now it's time to code one of the most important methods of the **Order** collection class – the **TotalPrice** method," I said. "This is the code that will actually calculate the customer's price quotation."

Exercise - Creating the Order Class's TotalPrice Method

1. Once again, work with the China Shop project's **Order** class.

2. Create the **TotalPrice** method by typing the following code into the **Order** class module:

```
Public Function TotalPrice(strBrand As String,
      ↳intQuantity As Integer) As Currency

Dim objTotal as Dish
Dim curPlatterPrice As Currency

If m_colOrder.Count = 0 Then
    TotalPrice = 0
    Exit Function
End If

For Each objTotal In m_colOrder
    TotalPrice = TotalPrice + (objTotal.Price * objTotal.Quantity)
    If objTotal.Item = "Platter" Then
        curPlatterPrice = objTotal.Price
    End If
Next

If m_intDiscount = 5 Then
    MsgBox "Price includes a Complete Place Setting Discount"
    Set objTotal = New Dish
    objTotal.Item = "Complete Place Setting"
    objTotal.Brand = strBrand
    TotalPrice = (objTotal.Price * intQuantity) + curPlatterPrice
End If

Set objTotal = Nothing

End Function
```

3. Save the China Shop project.

Discussion

"The code in the **TotalPrice** method," I said, "would be pretty simple, except for two things. First, Joe Bullina offers a price discount for a complete place setting, and secondly, the restriction on the number of platters that a customer can purchase. Both of these exceptions impact the calculation of the customer's total price, and you should bear both of these exceptions in mind as we go through this code. First, let's take a look at the function header. In order to calculate the sales quotation for a complete place setting, this function requires the brand and quantity of the customer's selection. This is reflected by the two arguments in the header:"

```
Public Function TotalPrice(strBrand As String,
      ↳intQuantity As Integer) As Currency
```

"This first variable declaration..."

```
Dim objTotal as Dish
```

"...is for an object variable called **objTotal** that we'll use in conjunction with the **For...Each** statement to loop through the items in the **m_colOrder** collection. The next variable..."

```
Dim curPlatterPrice As Currency
```

"...is used in the calculation of the complete place setting price."

I waited a moment before continuing.

"This next section of code shouldn't ever really execute," I said. "The code on the main form of the China Shop program won't execute the **TotalPrice** method unless the customer has made valid selections. However, you should make your objects as 'bullet-proof' as possible. Remember, you can't always count on the programmer using your objects working with them correctly, so it's best to include code like this whenever possible. What we're doing here is checking the **m_colOrder** collection's **Count** property. If it's **zero**, we know there are no items in the collection, which means that no items of china have been selected on the form. In that case, we just exit the function:"

```
If m_colOrder.Count = 0 Then
    TotalPrice = 0
    Exit Function
End If
```

"This next section of code," I said, "uses a **For...Each** statement to loop through the items in the **m_colOrder** collection, each of which references a **Dish** object. Once we have the reference to the **Dish** object, we take the value of its **Price** property, multiply it by its **Quantity** property, and then add that to the value of the **TotalPrice** function name:"

```
For Each objTotal In m_colOrder
    TotalPrice = TotalPrice + (objTotal.Price * objTotal.Quantity)
```

"If the item of the **Dish** object is a platter," Blaine asked, "should we be multiplying its **Price** property by its **Quantity** property – isn't the customer limited to just a single platter?"

"That's true, Blaine," I said, "but in the **Property Let** procedure for the **Quantity** property of the **Dish** object, we automatically assign a value of one, if the item is a platter."

"That's right," Blaine answered, "I entirely forgot about that."

"Your point about the platter is a good one" I said, "We'll see in a minute that for the calculation of the complete place setting discount price, we need to know the quantity that the user has selected, and we also need to know if the collection contains a platter. That's why we have this line of code..."

```
    If objTotal.Item = "Platter" Then
```

"...which checks to see if any of the items in the **m_colOrder** collection is a platter. If it is, then we take its **Price** property, and assign it to the variable **curPlatterPrice**:"

```
        curPlatterPrice = objTotal.Price
End If
Next
```

"When the **For...Each** loop has concluded," I said, "we now have a total price equal to the subtotal prices of each item in the collection. And, if it weren't for the complete place setting discount, our work would be done now. Before we pass the total price back to the program invoking the **TotalPrice** method, we need to see if we are dealing with a complete place setting. That's what this section of code does:"

```
If m_intDiscount = 5 Then
```

This line of code checks the value of **m_intDiscount**. If it's equal to five, that means that we have five items in the **m_colOrder**, and these five items comprise a complete place setting. We then display a message box to the user informing them that they're going to receive a discount:"

```
    MsgBox "Price includes a Complete Place Setting Discount"
```

"Then we create a new instance of a **Dish** object," I said.

"Why do we need to create a **Dish** object here?" Chuck asked.

"This is a little programming trick," I said. "We'll use the **Dish** object to calculate the complete place setting price."

"What do you mean?" Linda asked.

"Well," I said, "you could open the **Prices.txt** file, read the records, and determine the complete place setting price that way," I said, "but we can perform the same function quickly and easily by using the **Dish** object. Here's how: all we need to do is create an instance of a **Dish** object:"

```
Set objTotal = New Dish
```

"Then we set its **Item** property to **Complete Place Setting**..."

```
objTotal.Item = "Complete Place Setting"
```

"... set the **Brand** property equal to the value of the **strBrand** argument:"

```
objTotal.Brand = strBrand
```

"Next, we multiply the **Price** property of the newly created **Dish** object by the value of the argument **intQuantity**, and then add the price of a platter if there is one in the collection:"

```
TotalPrice = (objTotal.Price * intQuantity) + curPlatterPrice
End If
```

"Finally," I said, "we perform our normal housekeeping, setting our object variable to **Nothing**:"

```
Set objTotal = Nothing
```

"I can't wait to see this in action," Rhonda said. "Are we done coding the **Order** collection object?"

"Yes, we are," I said. "Now we need to turn our attention to modifying the code on the main form of the China Shop in order to utilize the **Order** collection object."

Modifying frmMain

"The first thing to do is set up the necessary variable declarations in the China Shop's **frmMain** form. Here's an exercise to do that:"

Exercise - Modifying the General Declarations Section of frmMain

1. Select **frmMain** in the Project Explorer window and open it up in design view.
2. Modify the General Declarations section of **frmMain** so that it looks like the next code listing. New code is highlighted. You need to delete every reference to the individual **Dish** object variables – the six lines beginning **Private With Events** – that you had in there before:

```
Option Explicit

Private m_lngBackColor As Long
Private m_blnDateDisplay As Boolean
Private m_colDishPrice As New Collection
Public Quantity as Integer

Private m_objOrder As New Order
Private m_strOldBrand As String
```

3. Save the China Shop project.

Discussion

"What's going on with that **m_strOldBrand** variable?" asked Rhonda.

"A few minutes ago," I continued, "I mentioned that whenever the customer changes their selection for the brand of china they want in their sales quotation, we need to remove every **Dish** object from the **Order** collection object, and then add each **Dish** object back with the new brand. However, we have a little problem: we'll know that the user has changed their selected brand when they click on the **lstBrands** list box. The problem is that when they do that, we only know the new brand selection – we don't know what was selected in the list box before they changed their brand selection."

"Which means," Dave added, "that there's no way to delete the items in the collection objects –without the old brand name, we can't locate them."

"That's excellent, Dave," I said, "and that's where this variable comes in handy. What we'll do is store the currently selected brand name in this variable. That way, when we need to execute the **Remove** method of the collection object, we can use its value as an argument. Then we'll be able to remove the **Dish** objects, using the old brand of china to locate them in the **m_colOrder** collection."

The chkChinaItem Click Event Procedure

There were no more questions and so I distributed another exercise for the class to complete:

Exercise - Modifying the Click Event Procedure of chkChinaItem

In this exercise, you'll code the **Click** event procedure of the **chkChinaItems** control array:

1. Continue working with **frmMain**.
2. Replace the code in the **Click** event procedure of **chkChinaItem** – yes, all of it! – with this code:

```
Private Sub chkChinaItem_Click(Index As Integer)

If chkChinaItem(Index).Value = 1 Then
    m_objOrder.Add lstBrands.Text, chkChinaItem(Index).Caption,
      ↳frmMain.Quantity
Else
    m_objOrder.Remove lstBrands.Text, chkChinaItem(Index).Caption
End If

End Sub
```

3. Save the China Shop project.

Discussion

"This code is pretty straightforward," I said. "What we're doing here is either adding an item to the collection object, or removing one. What determines which path we take is whether the customer has checked or unchecked an item on the form which we can determine by interrogating the **Value** property of the check box that triggered this **Click** event:"

```
If chkChinaItem(Index).Value = 1 Then
```

"If the customer has selected an piece of china, then we add an item – a **Dish** object – to the **Order** collection object using its **Add** method, making sure to pass the three required arguments: the brand, stored in the **Text** property of **lstBrands**, the item name, stored in the **Caption** property of the check box, and the quantity, stored in the **Quantity** custom form property:"

```
m_objOrder.Add lstBrands.Text, chkChinaItem(Index).Caption,
frmMain.Quantity
```

"Executing the **Add** method of the **Order** collection object," I said, "results in the creation of a **Dish** object, and the addition of an item to the **m_colOrder** collection that refers to that **Dish** object."

"What about if the user has unchecked an item on the form?" Melissa asked.

"In that case," I replied, "we execute the **Remove** method of the **Order** object."

```
m_objOrder.Remove lstBrands, chkChinaItem(Index).Caption
```

"This passes the two required arguments, brand and item, which are the key values that let us identify items in **m_colOrder**."

"What about that **m_strOldBrand** variable?" Rhonda said. "Didn't you say we needed to pass that to the collection object's **Remove** method?"

"That's only when the brand changes," I said. "In this instance, the **Click** event procedure of **chkChinaItem** is triggered when the user either checks or unchecks a check box. The brand name we need in order to find an item in the **m_colOrder** collection is the value from the **Text** property of **lstBrands**. But hang on, we're about to put that variable – **m_strOldBrand** – to use in the next exercise."

The lstBrands Click Event Procedure

In this exercise, you'll code the **Click** event procedure of **lstBrands**:

Exercise - Modifying the Click Event Procedure of lstBrands

1. Continue working with **frmMain**.
2. Modify the code in the **Click** event procedure of **lstBrands** so that it matches this listing:

```
Private Sub lstBrands_Click()

Dim chkObject As CheckBox

If lstBrands.ListIndex = -1 Then Exit Sub

If App.Path = "\" Then
    imgChina.Picture = LoadPicture(App.Path & lstBrands.Text & ".gif")
Else
    imgChina.Picture = LoadPicture(App.Path & "\" & lstBrands.Text
      ⇘ & ".gif")
End If

For Each chkObject In chkChinaItem
   If chkObject.Value = 1 Then
      m_objOrder.Remove m_strOldBrand, chkObject.Caption
      m_objOrder.Add lstBrands.Text, chkObject.Caption,
        ⇘frmMain.Quantity
   End If
Next

m_strOldBrand = lstBrands.Text

End Sub
```

3. Save the China Shop project.

Discussion

"As I mentioned earlier," I said, "if the user changes their selected brand of china, we need to first remove every item from the **m_colOrder** collection, and then add each one back with the new brand name as part of the key. Let's take a look at the code now. After declaring the object variable which we'll use in a **For...Each** statement that loops through all the check boxes in the **chkChinaItem** control array..."

```
Dim chkObject As CheckBox
```

"...we then check to ensure that an item has been selected in the list box. If one hasn't been selected, we exit the event procedure immediately:"

```
If lstBrands.ListIndex = -1 Then Exit Sub
```

"I know we went over this in our Intro course," Rhonda said, "but why do we need to check for this again?"

"It's possible to trigger the `Click` event procedure of the list box," I said, "without an item actually being selected by the customer – for instance, the code we have for our Reset command button will trigger this `Click` event procedure. So, we need to confirm that an item in the list box has actually been selected before we continue: if no item is selected, then the list box's `ListIndex` property will be equal to `-1`."

"With this next section of code," I continued, "we load up a image of the china brand onto an image control. We determine the `.gif` file to be loaded by ascertaining the customer's selection in the list box:"

```
If App.Path = "\" Then
    imgChina.Picture = LoadPicture(App.Path & lstBrands.Text & ".gif")
Else
    imgChina.Picture = LoadPicture(App.Path & "\" & lstBrands.Text &
".gif")
End If
```

"...This next section of code uses a `For...Each` statement to loop through each check box in the `chkChinaItem` control array:"

```
For Each chkObject In chkChinaItem
```

"This is looking at each individual check box to see if the customer has previously selected it. We do this by looking for a `Value` property equal to `1`:"

```
    If chkObject.Value = 1 Then
```

"If the check box was previously checked, we must remove its corresponding item from the `Order` collection object, using the value of the `m_strOldBrand` variable and the check box's `Caption` as arguments to pass to the `Remove` method:"

```
        m_objOrder.Remove m_strOldBrand, chkObject.Caption
```

"Once we remove the item from the **m_colOrder** collection of the **Order** collection object," I went on, "we need to create a new **Dish** object for each selected check box. We do that by executing the **Add** method of the **Order** object. We need to pass this some arguments, and to do this we use the brand currently selected in the list box, the **Caption** property from the check box, and the value of the **Quantity** custom form property:"

```
    m_objOrder.Add lstBrands.Text, chkObject.Caption,
      ↳frmMain.Quantity
End If
Next
```

"I've been following you so far," Ward said, "but I'm not sure what's going on with the next line of code:"

```
m_strOldBrand = lstBrands.Text
```

"Well," I explained, "the **m_strOldBrand** variable was created to store the currently selected brand," I said. "That means that when the customer selects another brand of china, we always know what the previous selection was. That's what this line of code is doing – assigning the newly-selected brand to the **m_strOldBrand** variable so that we can use it the next time the customer changes their choice of brand."

I waited a moment, because I could see that Kate was formulating a query.

"My only question," said Kate, "is this: where does the **initial** value of **m_strOldBrand** come from? Won't this event procedure be run the first time the user clicks on the list box – and surely it will find the value of **m_strOldBrand** to be empty? Will the program crash if we execute the **Order** collection object's **Remove** method and pass it an empty argument for the brand? "

"That's very well anticipated, Kate," I said. "You're right – if the user clicks on the list box without first having selected either a quantity or any items, then the value of **m_strOldBrand** will be null. However, since no check boxes are selected, the **Remove** method won't actually be executed. Another possibility is that the user first selects an item of china, which results in an item being added to the **m_colOrder** collection of the **Order** object. However, the item will be added with a null brand name. This means that if the user clicks on the list box to change the brand name, the **Remove** method is also being executed with a null brand name – and that's fine, because the value of the brand name in the key to the item will actually be null too! So you see, the program won't bomb at all."

'I see, that makes sense," Kate replied.

"OK, folks – time for the next exercise."

The optQuantity Click Event Procedure

"We need to make sure that we update the **Order** collection – and its associated **Dish** objects – if the customer changes their mind about the quantity of china they want to buy. In this exercise, you'll modify the code in the **optQuantity** option button array's **Click** event procedure to modify the **Quantity** property of any existing **Dish** objects referenced by the **Order** collection object."

Here's the exercise:

Exercise - Modifying the optQuantity Button's Click Event Procedure

1. Continue working with **frmMain**.
2. Modify the code in the **optQuantity** control array's **Click** event procedure to match the code shown below:

```
Private Sub optQuantity_Click(Index As Integer)

frmMain.Quantity = Index

Dim chkObject As CheckBox

For Each chkObject In chkChinaItem

  If chkObject.Value = 1 Then
    m_objOrder.Item(lstBrands.Text, chkObject.Caption).Quantity
      ↳= frmMain.Quantity
  End If

Next

End Sub
```

3. Save the China Shop project away as usual.

Discussion

"In this code," I said, "we're using the **Item** method of the **Order** collection object to retrieve a reference to each **Dish** object in the **m_colOrder** collection, and then modifying the **Quantity** property of each one."

"It would have been great if we could have used this technique to change the brand name," said Dave.

"That *would* have been a little cleaner," I said. "In the event of a change to the **Quantity** property of the **Dish** objects, things are a bit simpler, since the quantity is not part of the key value of the item in **m_colOrder**."

The QueryUnload Event Procedure

"Now, let's move on. In this next exercise, you'll modify the **Query_Unload** event procedure of **frmMain** to destroy the reference to the collection object when the form is unloaded.

Exercise - Modifying frmMain's Query_Unload Event Procedure

1. Continue working with **frmMain**.
2. Modify the code in the **Query_Unload** event procedure of **frmMain** as follows:

```
Private Sub Form_QueryUnload(Cancel As Integer, UnloadMode As Integer)

Set m_objOrder = Nothing

End Sub
```

3. Save the China Shop project.

Discussion

"This code," I said, "will erase the **m_objOrder** object variable – the program's reference to our collection object – when the main form of the China Shop is unloaded. Cleaning up the object variable effectively deletes the **m_colOrder** collection – which in turn destroys the individual **Dish** objects that were spawned from it. This will ensure that we keep the computer's memory as clean as possible."

"Now," I continued, "we have just two more exercises to complete – we're nearly done implementing the **Order** collection."

The cmdReset Button's Click Event Procedure

I handed out today's penultimate exercise, which is concerned with modifying the **cmdReset** button's **Click** event procedure – we need to make sure that we clean up all objects on the form when this is pressed.

Exercise - Modifying the cmdReset Button's Click Event Procedure

1. Open up the China Shop's **frmMain** in design view.

2. Modify the code in the **Click** event procedure of **cmdReset** so that it's the same as the next listing. All you're doing here is moving the line of code that sets the **ListIndex** property to -1 to the end of the event procedure:

```
Private Sub cmdReset_Click()

Dim chkObject As CheckBox
Dim optObject As OptionButton

For Each chkObject In chkChinaItem
    chkObject.Value = 0
Next

For Each optObject In optQuantity
    optObject.Value = False
Next

chkCompletePlaceSetting.Value = 0
lblPrice.Visible = False
imgChina.Picture = LoadPicture()

lstBrands.ListIndex = -1

End Sub
```

3. Save the China Shop project.

Discussion

"Why the change in the location of that line of code?" asked Ward.

"We had a small problem with the existing code as it stood before we made this little change," I said. "Let me explain: clicking the Reset command button unchecks each of the check boxes, which results in their **Click** event procedures being executed. Part of that process was to execute the collection object's **Remove** method. The way we had this event procedure coded before, the list box had been unselected, and so the **Remove** method was being passed a null argument for the brand. What we've done here is move the line of code that unselects the list box item to the end of the procedure: as a result, the **Remove** method will now be executed with a valid argument for the brand name."

"Time now for our last exercise," I said as I handed it out. "Here, we'll amend the **cmdCalculate** button's **Click** event procedure. And with the completion of this exercise, we'll have finished object-orienting the China Shop program."Here's that last exercise:

Exercise - Modifying the Click Event Procedure of cmdCalculate

1. Continue working with **frmMain**.

2. Modify the **cmdCalculate** button's **Click** event procedure code so that it looks like this next listing. We're replacing big chunks of code with smaller blocks that do the job more efficiently, using the object architecture that we've set up in the lesson so far:

```
Private Sub cmdCalculate_Click()

Dim curTotalPrice As Currency
```

> **Note that we've deleted all of the other variable declarations that were here, as well as the line that points to the old error handling routine.**

```
'Has the customer selected a brand of china?
If lstBrands.Text = "" Then
   MsgBox "You must select a China brand"
   Exit Sub
End If

'Has the customer selected one or more china items?
If chkChinaItem(0).Value = 0 And
     ↳chkChinaItem(1).Value = 0 And
     ↳chkChinaItem(2).Value = 0 And
     ↳chkChinaItem(3).Value = 0 And
     ↳chkChinaItem(4).Value = 0 And
     ↳chkChinaItem(5).Value = 0 Then
  MsgBox "You must select one or more china items"
  Exit Sub
End If
```

```
'Has the customer selected a quantity?
If optQuantity(8).Value = False And
      ↳optQuantity(4).Value = False And
      ↳optQuantity(2).Value = False And
      ↳optQuantity(1).Value = False Then
   MsgBox "You must select a quantity"
   Exit Sub
End If

'If the customer has selected a platter
'warn them that there is only 1 permitted per sales
'quotation

If chkChinaItem(5).Value = 1 And frmMain.Quantity > 1 Then
   MsgBox "Customer is limited to 1 Platter per order" &
        ↳vbCrLf & "Adjusting price accordingly"
End If

'All the pieces are here, let's calculate a price.

'Calculate subtotal prices by item

curTotalPrice = m_objOrder.TotalPrice(lstBrands.Text,
   ↳frmMain.Quantity)
```

> **!** The line of code highlighted above replaces the section of code that starts with `curPlatePrice =` ... and which ends with the `End If` line.

```
'If the price is greater than 0, display the price and
'make the label visible
If curTotalPrice > 0 Then
   lblPrice.Caption = "The price of your order is " &
        ↳Format(curTotalPrice, "$##,###.00")
   lblPrice.Visible = True
End If
```

> **!** We've deleted the old error handling code here.

```
End Sub
```

3. Save the China Shop project.

4. Run the program and select the Mikasa brand of china. Now select the Plate, Butter Plate and Soup Bowl Items, and a quantity of 2. Click on the Calculate button. The price displayed should be $90.

5. Change the brand from Mikasa to Corelle, and click on the Calculate button. The price should change to $14. Add a Platter to the selection, and click on the Calculate button. The price displayed after you've negotiated the informative message box should be $19.

6. Change the brand from Corelle to Faberware and click on the Calculate button. The price should change to $49. Now click on the Complete Place Setting check box and click on the Calculate button. The price should change to $55. Uncheck the Platter and click on the Calculate button. The Price should change to $42. Change the quantity from 2 to 1 and click on the Calculate button one more time. The price displayed in the label should change to $21.

Discussion

"It's sobering to think," I said, "that all of the logic to calculate the price quotation that we had at the start of this course has been reduced to this single line of code:"

```
curTotalPrice = m_objOrder.TotalPrice(lstBrands.Text,
   ↳frmMain.Quantity)
```

"But that's exactly what's happened. We've encapsulated all of the logic for the calculation of the sales quotation into the **Dish** and **Order** collection objects."

"This is really great," Ward said.

"I'm afraid I have a problem," Rhonda said. "I just ran my version of the program, and when I clicked on the Calculate button, I got an error telling me that the object doesn't support this property or method..."

"Does your error look like this," I said, as I displayed the following screenshot on the classroom projector:

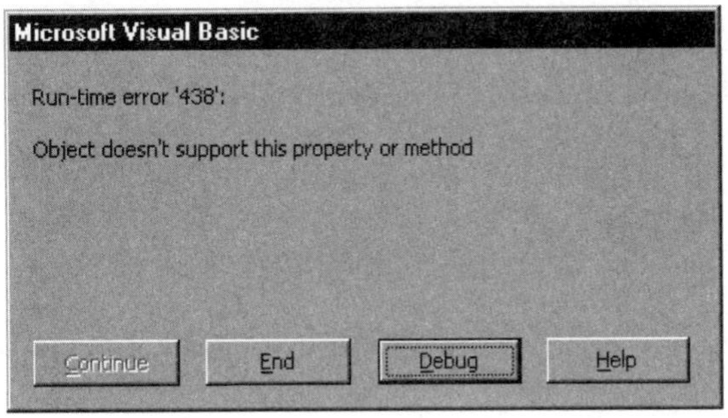

"That's the one," Rhonda confirmed. "Did you make the same mistake as me?"

"Well, Rhonda," I said, "this is a common occurrence. This is the error message you receive when you attempt to assign a value to a non-existent property, or when you try to execute a method of an object that doesn't exist. It also occurs if you forget to change the Procedure ID of the **`NewEnum`** method to **`-4`**."

A quick walk to Rhonda's PC revealed that the problem was the Procedure ID of the **`NewEnum`** method – something she corrected in no time. Once we fixed this, her code worked fine.

In the meantime, while I was working with Rhonda, I noticed that everyone in the class was busily experimenting with their own copies of the China Shop program. They were really having a great time with it.

At first, I suggested that we run my copy of the China Shop program in Step mode, but I soon realized that most of the class wouldn't be paying attention anyway. We only had about ten minutes left in our session, and so I suggested that they take the remainder of the class to enjoy the fruits of their labors.

Ten minutes later I dismissed class for the day.

"We'll be working with the **`Dish`** and **`Order`** objects again in future lessons," I said. "But next week we'll take a short break from them, and learn how we can work with objects outside of the Visual Basic environment – using things like Word and Excel."

Chapter Summary

In this chapter we learned about Visual Basic collection objects, and coded the `Order` collection object, which saw us complete the core object-orientation of the China Shop project. You've seen that we can use collections to manage and manipulate large numbers of similar objects much more easily than would otherwise be possible.

Once again, our Student Grades demo program gave sterling service as a test-bed where we could put theory into practice before applying it to the China Shop program.

We saw:

- What **collection objects** are
- How collection objects help us manage large groups of other objects
- How to create a **class module** for a collection object
- How to code the methods and properties that embody the collection object's functionality

In the China Shop, the collection that we built has made our code even more streamlined that it already was. By the end, we saw that our entire price calculation was being performed by just one line of code.

The key changes we made to the China Shop project were these:

- We created an `Order` collection object in the China Shop program, and coded its methods
- We modified the China Shop Program to utilize the `Order` collection object

Next week, we'll be looking at an exciting and powerful feature of Visual Basic: its ability to utilize the internal functionality of other programs – such as Word and Excel – by using ActiveX components. These components let us get at the internal objects, properties and methods of these applications, and allow us to use them in our own Visual Basic programs. I think you'll really like next week's lesson.

Learn to Program Objects with Visual Basic
Bullina's
China

Chapter 8
Excel and Word – by Remote Control!

This week's class concentrates on using some of most exciting features of the Windows environment to really perk up your applications. I want to show you how to use the objects contained in the **ActiveX components** that other Windows applications, such as Word and Excel, have made available to you. Essentially, an ActiveX component is a small package of code that encapsulates a bit of functionality – such as the functionality to edit an Excel spreadsheet or a Word document. ActiveX components give you access to this functionality by letting you run it from inside your Visual Basic program. This means, for example, that you could use the China shop to create Word documents that print customers' price quotations, or update an Excel spreadsheet with sales data when a customer makes a purchase.

By the end of this chapter you'll have seen how to apply ActiveX components in a Visual Basic project and will be ready for next week's work, when we'll build objects from the China Shop into ActiveX components of our own.

Here's a quick preview of the topics we'll discuss today:

- Exactly what is an ActiveX component?
- Preparatory steps to include ActiveX components in your projects
- Using ActiveX components in your programs
- Using Word and Excel to generate code for your programs
- Embodying Excel and Word functionality in Visual Basic programs

Once again, we'll be using the Student Grades demo to prototype our understanding of a lot of these features. However, we'll also be changing the China Shop program in the following ways:

- We'll add the necessary ActiveX architecture to open Word from within the China Shop program and prepare a really professional-looking sales quotation

- We'll add a button to the China Shop main form to print this sales quotation
- We'll give the program the ability to use the printer-control technology of Word to print this sales quotation on Joe Bullina's laser printer

By the time you're done, you'll have a swish, object-oriented version of the China Shop program.

Putting on the Ritz

It was now mid-March, and I was glad to be waking up and driving into the University in the daylight each Saturday morning! My eighth lesson was going to be a sizzler – I just knew it. Using the ActiveX components of Word and Excel within a Visual Basic application can be real fun, and the output you get from your programs suddenly looks very professional. By the time they reach this stage in the course, most students agree that any amount of climbing would've justified the view from the top! Since we had the added bonus of having the China Shop program to apply the ActiveX technology to, I knew this lesson would be great.

ActiveX Components

"Hi there!" I said to the students, as I entered the classroom. "I think you're going to enjoy the next few hours. We've spent the last three weeks creating and using objects of our own, but in today's class, we're going to learn how to use some objects that the Windows' programmers at Microsoft have made available to us from Word and Excel – and use them in our own Visual Basic programs."

"Do you mean that the Windows programmers have provided class modules that we can use to create objects in our Visual Basic programs?" Peter enquired.

"Not quite," I replied. "Microsoft doesn't ship class modules with packages like Word or Excel, but they have **exposed** the functionality for those objects that's contained in those class modules. This functionality is stored in compiled programs known as **ActiveX components**."

!

> You'll often hear the word *exposed* in object-oriented programming circles. It means that an object shows – exposes – its properties and methods to other programs, making them available for the programmer to use, but not allowing the programmer to get under the hood with a screwdriver and wrench and change anything inside the component itself. ActiveX components are already compiled and ready-to-use, so the source code is no longer there to be modified. This is actually the great strength of the ActiveX design.

"I'm a little puzzled about exactly which objects you are talking about," Rhonda told me.

"The object-oriented design process we've gone through here is the same as the one that's been followed by Microsoft in later versions of their software," I said. "For instance, the Microsoft Office suite has been designed around objects. Word contains a `Document` object, and Excel contains `Workbook`, `Worksheet` and `Chart` objects. And those are just a few of the objects contained within those products."

"Are you saying," Kathy asked, "that we can instantiate a Word `Document` object within our own Visual Basic program?"

"Exactly, Kathy," I said. "We're able to use Word's objects by interacting with the interface that they expose to us – their properties and methods. This means that we can borrow the functionality that's already been programmed into Word's objects and use it within a Visual Basic program – so we don't have to write code from scratch to do a job that's already been coded in the Word objects!"

"I think Kathy's a little ahead of me here," Rhonda confessed." Could you explain what exactly you mean?"

"Sure," I said. "We're saying that we can create and amend a Word document – be it a letter, a table or a color poster – from inside a Visual Basic program. In fact, with enough VB code, you could probably write an entire novel if you wanted!"

"Like all Windows programs," I continued, "Word is object-oriented. Its objects are compiled-up into packages called ActiveX components that can be used separately from Word itself. For instance, later today we'll be writing code to generate a sales quotation for the China Shop program and route it to a printer. We'll use the functionality in Word to do this."

"Couldn't we use the `Printer` object you showed us in the Intro course?" asked Ward.

"Yes, we could," I replied. "But you may remember that using the `Printer` object is a no-frills affair. It'd be tough to produce a very attractive report with it."

"Producing a sales quotation is part of the enhanced China Shop project's Requirements Statement, isn't it?" Kevin asked. "Will using the functionality of Word allow us to make a much more professional-looking job of it?"

"That's correct, Kevin," I said. "Because Word was written using objects, we'll be able to tap into their functionality and create a really nice-looking sales quotation. Advanced features of Word, like mail-merging, spell-checking, and printing, will be accessible to us from within Visual Basic."

"Wow!" Dorothy said, obviously seeing the potential. "That's an incredible lot of power!"

"It sure is," I concluded.

> **We'll use Microsoft Word to create and print the sales quotation in this book, but there are other alternatives. Some versions of Visual Basic come supplied with third party report writers - such as *Crystal Reports* - which you can use to design and print reports, and other versions have a *Data Report Designer* which can do the same thing.**

"By the way," Blaine observed, "you said you'd give us two examples of using ActiveX components in our programs. I'm just guessing here, but was Excel going to be the other example? I'd love to be able to use some of those Excel spreadsheet features in my own programs: will we be able to do that?"

"You're getting the idea, Blaine," I told him. "We'll be using some of the ActiveX components of Excel today as well. Any objects that are packaged into an ActiveX component are available for use within your Visual Basic program."

"Getting back to something else you said earlier," Melissa said, "did you say that we'll be able to create ActiveX components of our own? Could we package our `Dish` and `Order` objects in an ActiveX component for other Visual Basic programs to use?"

"That's an excellent question, Melissa," I said. "We'll actually be doing that in next week's lesson. And once we've done that, not only will other Visual Basic programs be able to use the `Dish` and `Order` objects, but *any* Windows program that can work with ActiveX objects will be able to access them through their exposed methods and properties."

Lou said: "Can't a programmer just obtain a copy of the `Dish` and `Order` class modules and include them in their own Visual Basic project if they want to use them?"

"Yes, that's possible, Lou," I said. "But there are two major problems with that. Firstly, the programmer using the class module can see, and *modify*, all of the code in that class module. An ActiveX component, on the other hand, holds a *compiled* version of the class module, and it can't have its internal code altered in any way by the person who's using it."

"But why wouldn't you want them to change your class modules?" Linda asked. "Authorship?"

"Ha-ha, no! Not even I'm *that* vain!" I replied, laughing.

There were some chuckles from around the room.

"No," I went on. "It has to do with our second problem: duplication of class modules. Most programmers prefer to work with their own copies of a class module. In a large organization, there can be hundreds – even thousands – of copies of the same class module contained in many projects. If each one's been tweaked in some way, you end up with a situation where even a single programmer may have many different copies of the *same* module. If, for some reason, something about the object needs to be changed – let's say a new property needs to be added, or a method needs updating – each programmer using the module would have to get the latest version, include it in their project, and then recompile the program."

"I see," said Ward. "And for a class module used in many programs, that can be a daunting task – right?"

"Right!" I replied. "With an ActiveX component you don't have this headache – ActiveX components can be distributed in such a way that every programmer in the organization uses the same copy."

"I can see that's a real advantage," Dave said. "If I were to compile my objects into an ActiveX component, I could just put a single copy of the component out on the company's network: any programmer wanting to use it could just access that copy of the component."

"That's the way," I went on. "This means that if an object in the component needs to be changed, the component is recompiled and redistributed: in most cases, the programs using that component won't notice any difference. You see, when you use an object in an ActiveX component, your program uses it at *run time* – the component doesn't need to be compiled into your program."

"So, if an object in the ActiveX component changes, your program will see the latest version of that object at run time?" Mark suggested. "Regardless of what version it used the last time it ran?"

"Exactly," I told him. "As long as the object has not changed in a way that clashes with the program using the component, the program needn't be recompiled."

"But how does the ActiveX component become available for us to use in the first place?" Tom said.

"ActiveX components are usually installed as part of the installation process of the software package," I answered. "That's how the ActiveX components for Microsoft Office are installed."

"So, using ActiveX components is basically a great way to avoid reinventing the wheel," Dorothy concluded. "Are they hard to use?"

Using ActiveX Components

"The mechanics of including an ActiveX component in your program isn't difficult," I replied. "You must remember, though, that you need to be familiar with the objects contained within the component in order to use them properly. If you don't know anything about the contents of the component, trying to utilize any of them in your Visual Basic program is like trying to fly an airplane with no flight training – a very frustrating experience, at the least!"

"When we work with ActiveX components," Rhonda said, "won't we be writing Visual Basic code to manipulate the objects contained within them? What can be so difficult? We know Visual Basic code already."

"That's certainly true, Rhonda," I said, "by now we know Visual Basic code pretty well. What makes working with ActiveX components challenging is knowing the names of the objects to manipulate, as well as the names of all their properties and methods. An ActiveX component is compiled, so you can't look inside it: most likely, the names of the objects contained by the component will be totally foreign to you. For instance, Word exposes many objects in its ActiveX components, which together consist of hundreds of properties and methods – none of which you'll ever have worked with before."

"This sounds like a losing proposition," Blaine said, with a sigh. "How can we use the objects within an ActiveX component, then?"

"The most obvious answer," I said, "is to obtain documentation on the objects contained within the component from the person or vendor who supplied it to us in the first place. This documentation is sometimes free, or it may be sold in the form of a **Software Developers Kit**."

"Is there anything else you can do, short of paying money to the vendor?" Kevin asked. "I don't necessarily want to invest in an entire software developers kit, just to incorporate some enhanced functionality into one of my programs. You would think that with the component installed on your PC, you should be able to get some information about it."

"There are other possibilities, Kevin," I said. "You might find you already have some documentation about using the ActiveX component and may not know it. For instance, a few months ago, I found that my email package included information on its ActiveX components in its Help files."

"Isn't there a legal issue here?" asked Kevin. "I mean – using someone else's components for your own ends seems a bit cavalier."

"That's certainly an important thing to take account of in the wider world of business," I replied. "But with components from the Microsoft's Office suite, there isn't a problem: anyone who can run a Word or Excel component from a program you've sold them must already have Word and Excel installed on their own machines. Installing licensed copies of Word and Excel on your machine gives you full and legal access to all the ActiveX components and functionality that these programs expose to you."

"Sounds good," said Kevin.

"I just checked the Word Help file," Kate put in, "and I don't see any information in there on using its objects in a Visual Basic program."

"There's nothing in Word's Help file about that," I agreed, "But we're actually very lucky with Word and Excel. We can take a short cut and use their **Macro Recorders** to help us understand its objects and write code that manipulates them."

The Macro Recorder

"What's a macro?" asked Rhonda.

"A macro is a chunk of code that contains the necessary instructions to perform a task," I replied. "In this context, it's really a 'batch file', containing the batch of instructions to do the job we want. Word and Excel are very clever, in that they have a Macro Recorder that automatically writes this code for us, based on a series of manual actions that we perform in Word or Excel. In a moment, we'll run Excel and perform the tasks we want to do in our program, whilst we record our actions using the Macro Recorder: the recorder will watch what we do and write the code to duplicate it. In many cases, we can just copy and paste the generated code directly into our Visual Basic Code window. Then, with a few minor changes, it's ready to duplicate the actions we performed, but this time from within Visual Basic!"

"So the Macro Recorder writes the code for us," Melissa murmured. "Professor, I can feel myself becoming redundant, here!"

"Don't worry, Melissa," I replied, laughing. "The robots aren't taking over just yet! The Macro Recorder only writes very short bits of code to carry out simple actions. However, the code it writes does automatically contain all the names of the objects inside the ActiveX components that are used to carry out those actions – plus their methods and properties."

"So we don't have to know them ourselves," Ward concluded. "That's a help."

"It sure is," I said. "The Macro Language of the Office 97 Suite is VBA, short for **Visual Basic for Applications**. When you record a macro in Word or Excel, and then examine it using the Macro Editor, what you'll see is VBA code. VBA is essentially the same as the code portion of Visual Basic. I think you'll find it reassuringly familiar."

"Even though the code will be recognizable," Dave interjected, "I guess that since the generated macro code is manipulating Word or Excel objects, there'll be a bit of a learning curve to negotiate?"

"Yes, Dave," I answered, "that's true, but both Word and Excel have a built in Visual Basic Editor that looks very similar to the IDE of Visual Basic. I think you'll get the hang of it quite quickly. The only real tasks are learning to recognize the various objects named in the code, and understanding what they do."

"A few minutes ago," Mary pointed out, "you said we could just copy and paste the recorded macro from Word or Excel into the Visual Basic Code window and run the code, with just a few minor modifications. Is it really that easy?"

"Well," I said, "working with ActiveX components from applications other than Word or Excel can be tricky if you try to do it without any documentation. But for Word and Excel, the process is much simpler – the Macro Recorder really helps, and you can find quite a bit of support, too, either in the Visual Basic Help files, or out on the Microsoft web site."

I showed them the URL:

http://www.microsoft.com/com/

"What I'd like to do now," I said, "is to continue working with the Student Grades demo project we've been following, and show you how we can incorporate Word and Excel ActiveX components within that program."

Finding Available ActiveX Components

"Before we can use an ActiveX component," I continued, "we must first identify the ActiveX components that are available for us to use on our PCs. The most common way that an ActiveX component gets installed on a PC is when the corresponding software package is installed there. The installation of an ActiveX component is a two part process – the component is copied to a directory on the PC, and an entry is made in the PC's Windows Registry to let the operating system know that the component is present."

"How can we see the components that are installed on our PC?" Linda asked. "Do we use the Object Browser?"

"That's a good guess," I said. "But the Object Browser only includes information on components that are already selected for use in your Project. To see all of the available ActiveX components, you need to add a reference to its **type library**."

"What's a type library?" Melissa asked.

"A type library, among other things" I said, "provides Visual Basic with the information about objects that you see in the Object Browser. A component, once selected in your project's References window, will have its objects appear in the Object Browser."

"Let me show you this by loading up the version of the Student Grades demo we finished with last week..."

Adding a Type Library Reference

I selected Project | References from the menu bar...

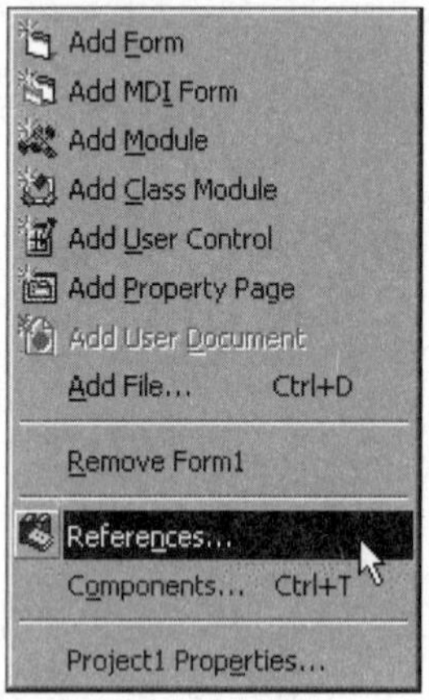

The following screen shot appeared on the classroom projector:

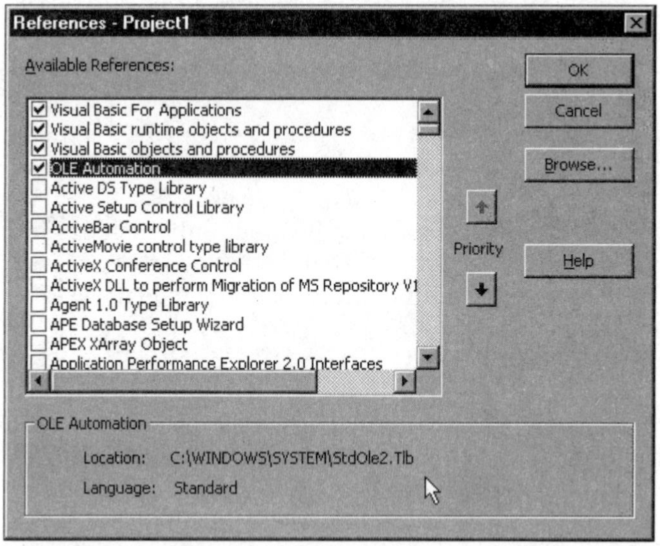

"This is the Visual Basic References window," I said. "Any ActiveX component that has a type library will usually appear here."

"Is it possible for a component to be installed on the PC and not have it show up in the References window?" Dave asked.

"Yes it is, Dave," I said. "That's what the Browse button is for – you can search for the component by clicking on the Browse button..."

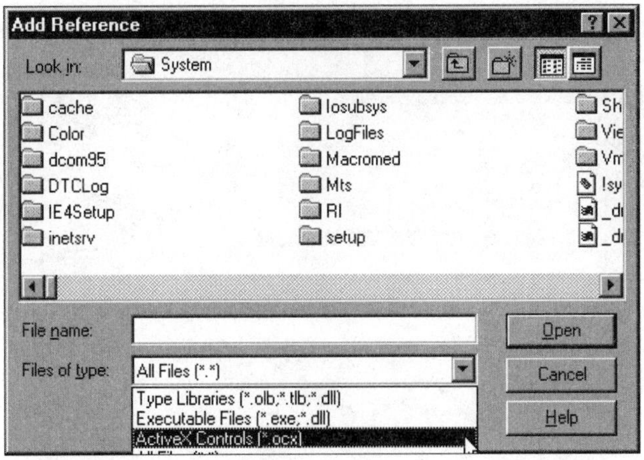

"...and searching for it by selecting one of the file types that you see here."

"What file type should we select?" Chuck asked.

"Any of the three types of files you see here," I said, "may contain an ActiveX component. If you have reason to believe that a folder contains an ActiveX component, navigate to it, and then select any valid file type within it. If the file you select does **not** contain an ActiveX component, you'll receive a message telling you that the file can't be added as a reference:"

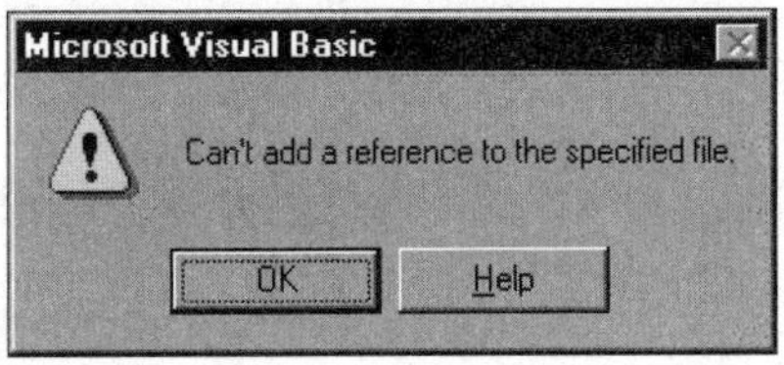

Selecting an ActiveX Component

"Fortunately," I said, "most ActiveX components available for use in our Visual Basic programs will appear in the References window. Let's select the Object Library for Microsoft Excel."

I scrolled down through the list box and selected the reference for the Microsoft Excel 8.0 Object Library in the References window. A checkmark appeared:

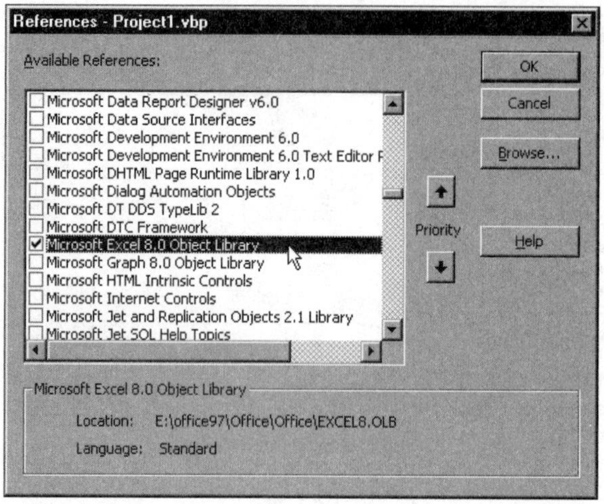

> **The list of references you see in this window on your own machine may be different from what you see here in the screenshot. Don't worry – different versions of Office will show different references: so long as you can find one that's similar to what you see here, you should be OK.**

"Notice that this reference is pointing to a file on my PC's hard drive called `Excel8.olb`," I said. "That's the name of the type library for the collection of Excel 97 objects supplied with Office 97. Let's find the reference to the Word 97 type library too:"

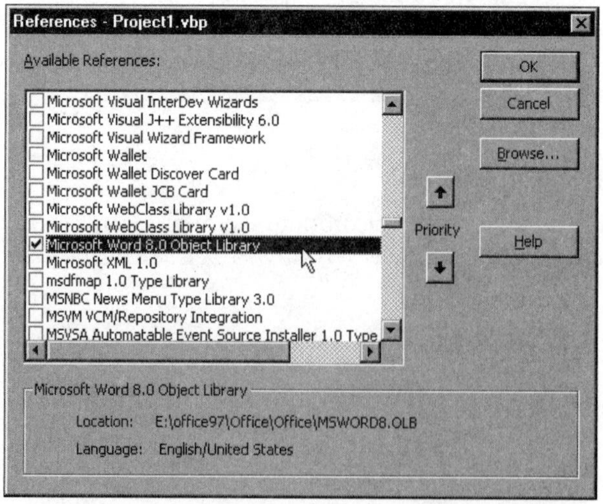

"Again," I said, "notice that the reference is pointing to a file on my PC's hard drive – this time to a file called **MSWord8.olb**. Not surprisingly, this is the type library for the collection of objects contained in Word 97. If we now select this reference, and then click on the OK button, we'll add a reference to both the Excel and the Word Object Libraries to the Student Grades demo program."

I clicked on the OK button, and the References window closed.

"Let's open up the References window once again," I said, "We should see both the Excel and the Word Object Libraries as selected references in our Student Demo project..."

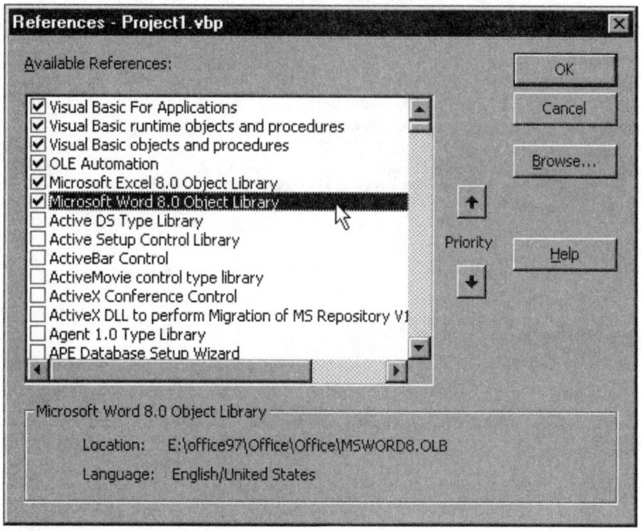

"Selected references always appear at the top of the list when we open up the References window," I added.

"So what has selecting the ActiveX component in the References window done for us?" Rhonda asked. "Can we use the objects contained in Word and Excel ActiveX components within the Student Grades program now?"

"Yes, Rhonda," I said, "adding those references to the Excel and Word Object Libraries lets us use the objects contained within those ActiveX components. Of course, it would be a great idea to have some familiarity with those objects before we try using them, and that's where the Object Browser can come in very handy. Once you add a Reference to an ActiveX component in the References window, the objects contained within that ActiveX component can then be seen in the Object Browser. Let's take a look..."

I then opened up the Object Browser by selecting View | Object Browser from the Visual Basic menu bar:

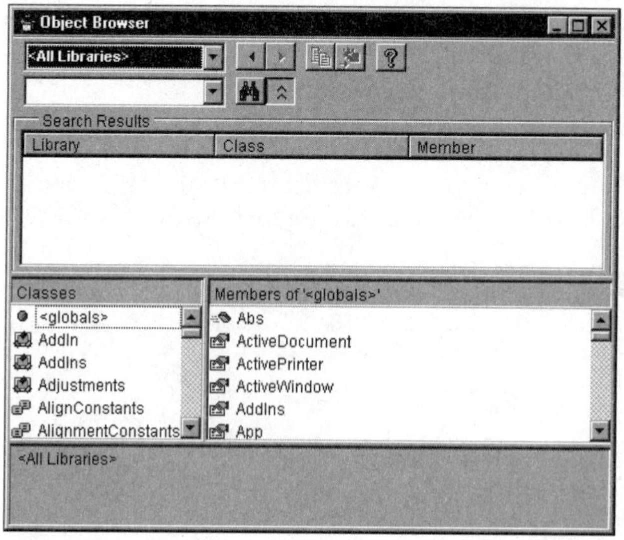

"By default," I said, "the Object Browser displays the objects for all the libraries selected in our project."

"The ones ticked in the Reference window?" suggested Rhonda.

"Exactly. If we now select Excel in the Library list box..."

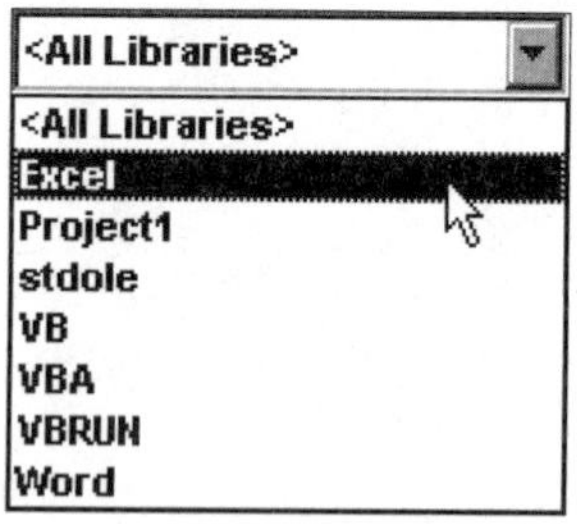

"...we'll be able to see all of the classes that are exposed in the Excel Object Library. As you can see, there are quite a few of them, beginning with the AddIn object..."

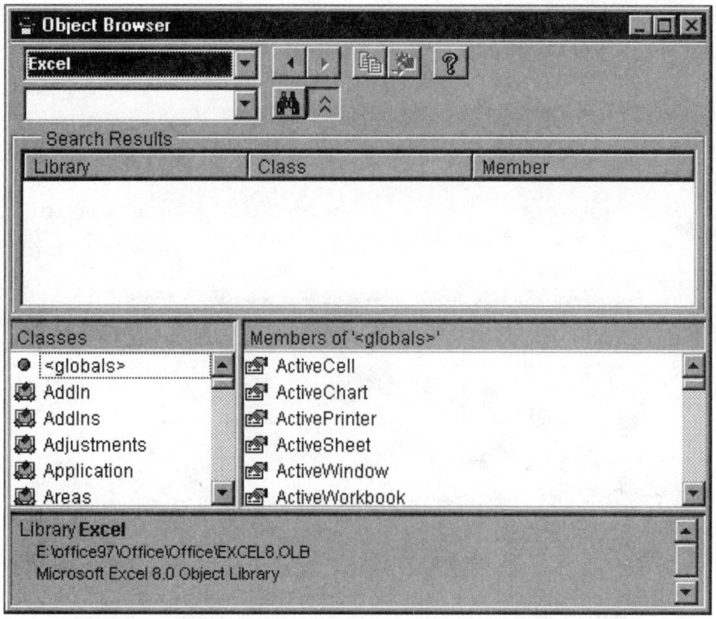

"Do the Classes that we see here in the left hand pane represent all of objects that we can work with in our Visual Basic program?" Valerie asked.

"That's an excellent question Valerie," I said. "And the answer's no, they don't. In an ActiveX component, some objects can only be created by other objects in that component. We call that type of object a **dependent object**. By default, dependent objects are not shown in the Object Browser. If you want to see dependent objects in the Object Browser, right click your mouse anywhere on the form other than the Search Text list box – you'll get a pop-up menu. From this, select Show Hidden Members:"

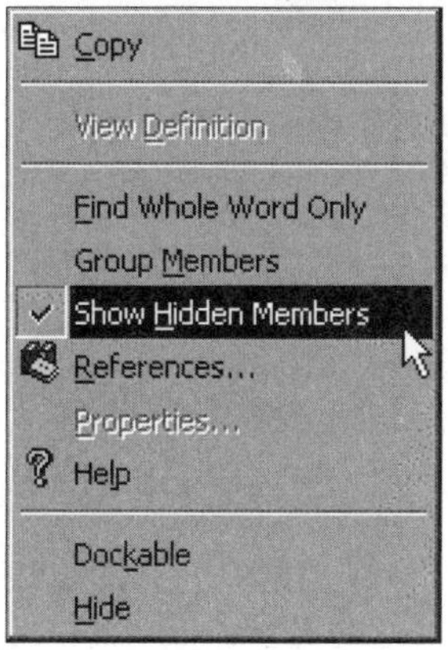

"Doing this will display the dependent objects in the ActiveX component. Let's search for one of those dependent objects now."

I typed Button into the Find Text list box and clicked the 'binoculars' icon to search for the `Button` object's class.

"The Button object is a dependent object – notice also that the dependent objects are all grayed:"

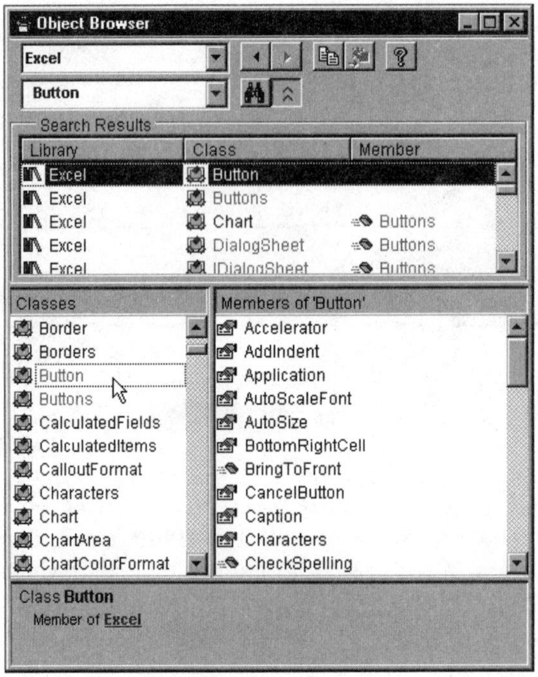

"This is all beginning to sound a little complicated to me," Rhonda said. "Will the Object Browser give us all the information so that we can work with the objects in Excel or Word's Object Libraries?"

"Unfortunately not," I said. "While the Object Browser can tell us the objects contained within the ActiveX component, and the properties and methods of each, it doesn't tell us how to use them. Without documentation, you're pretty much on your own unless you're lucky enough to be able to record a macro, and that's what I want to show you now. Let's work with Excel first."

ActiveX and an Excel Macro

As I started up Microsoft Excel 97, the default workbook Book1 appeared...

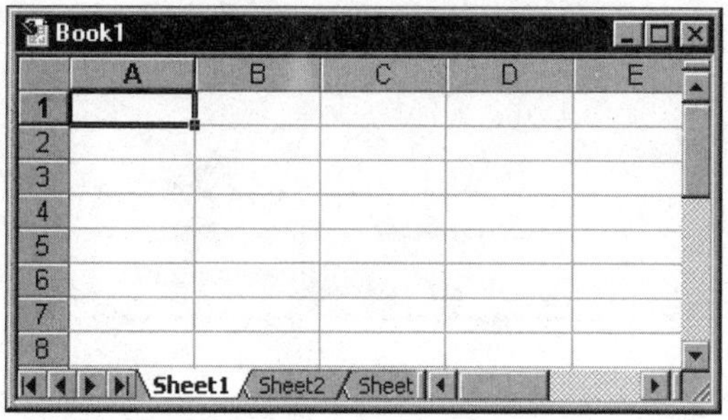

"What I want to do," I said, "is record a macro that captures the actions I take when I enter the scores for a student's mid-term, final exam, and term paper grades into cells A1, A2 and A3 respectively. I'll also enter the relative percentages that each grade contributes to the student's final grade in cells B1, B2 and B3, respectively. To record the macro, we just need to select Tools | Macro | Record New Macro from the Excel menu bar ..."

"...and the Record Macro window will appear. At this point we need to specify a name for the macro, and a description. Let's call the macro StudentDemo:"

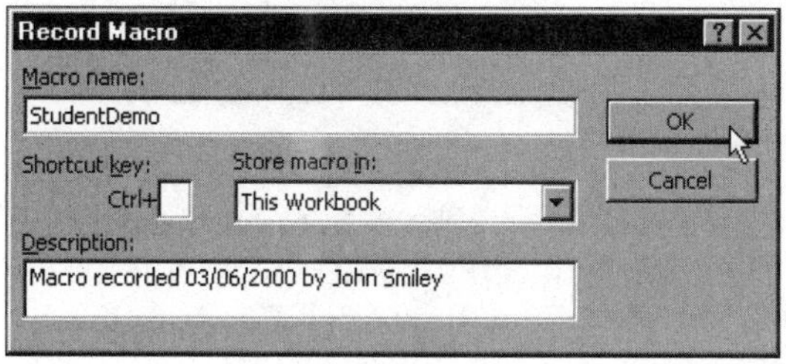

I then clicked on the OK button. The Stop Recording form appeared, indicating that the recording of the Macro had started and that I now had the option of stopping it:

"Now," I said, "we can start entering the data into the workbook..."

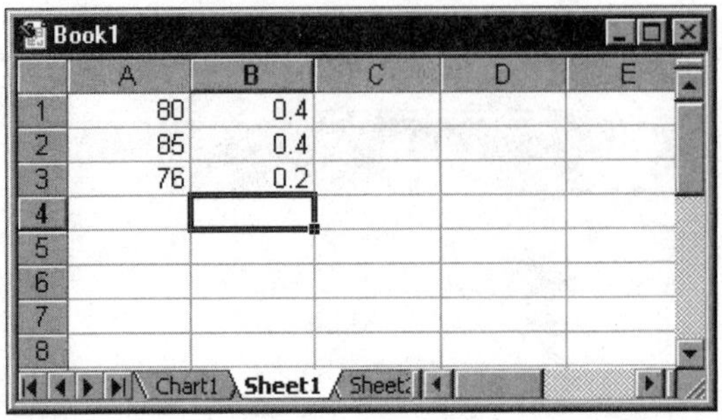

"While this macro is being recorded," I said, "the recorder is watching us behind the scenes, generating VBA code that we can use in the Student Grades demo project. As soon as we're done recording the macro, we'll take a look at it. We're about to complete the most crucial part of the macro, and that's the Excel formula that I'm going to enter into cell B4."

I entered this formula into cell B4:

=(A1*B1)+(A2*B2)+(A3*B3)

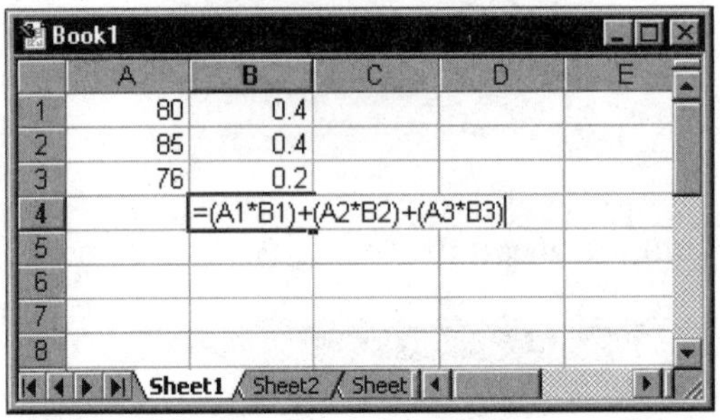

"I know that many of you are familiar with Excel formulae," I said, "but for those of you who aren't, what I'm telling Excel to do here is to take the value in cell A1, multiply it by the value in cell B1, take the value in cell A2 and multiply it by the value in cell B2, take the value in cell A3 and multiply it by the value in cell B3, and finally, to add all three of those multiplications together, and place the result in cell B4."

I then hit the enter key: sure enough, the value 81.2 appeared in cell B4.

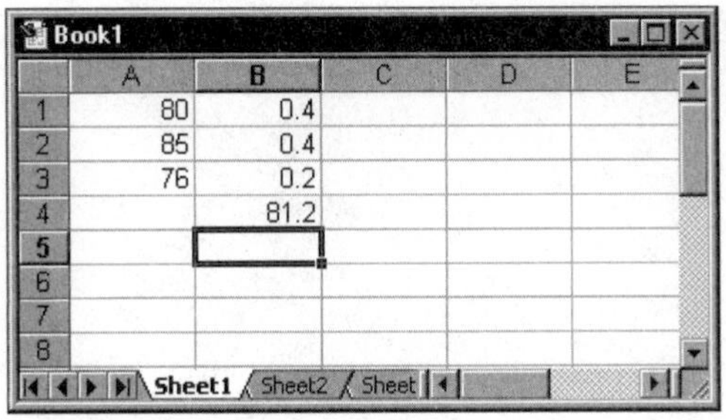

"If we now click on the 'stop' button, we'll terminate the macro recording," I said:

"Can we see the macro code now?" Linda asked.

"Yes, we can," I said. "If we select Tools | Macro | Macros from the Excel menu bar, the Macro window will appear. If we select the StudentDemo macro..."

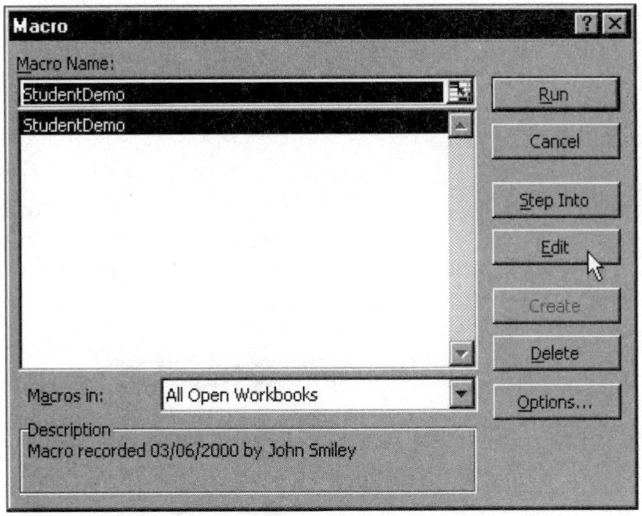

"...and then click on the Edit button, we'll be able to have a look at the VBA code for the macro that the Macro Recorder has kindly generated for us..."

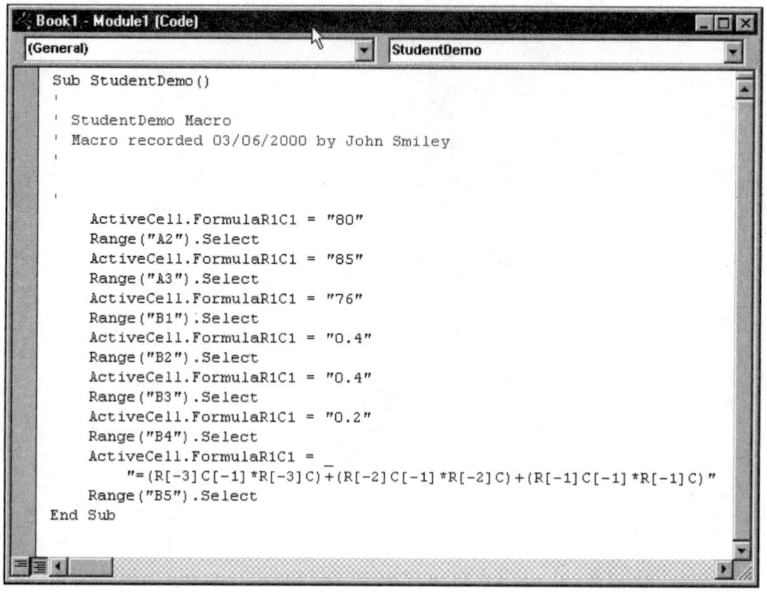
Book1 - Module1 (Code)
(General)
StudentDemo
Sub StudentDemo()
'
' StudentDemo Macro
' Macro recorded 03/06/2000 by John Smiley
'
'
ActiveCell.FormulaR1C1 = "80"
Range("A2").Select
ActiveCell.FormulaR1C1 = "85"
Range("A3").Select
ActiveCell.FormulaR1C1 = "76"
Range("B1").Select
ActiveCell.FormulaR1C1 = "0.4"
Range("B2").Select
ActiveCell.FormulaR1C1 = "0.4"
Range("B3").Select
ActiveCell.FormulaR1C1 = "0.2"
Range("B4").Select
ActiveCell.FormulaR1C1 = _
"=(R[-3]C[-1]*R[-3]C)+(R[-2]C[-1]*R[-2]C)+(R[-1]C[-1]*R[-1]C)"
Range("B5").Select
End Sub

"If you take a good look at this code," I said, "you'll see that it's really nothing more than a Visual Basic subprocedure, and that its header matches the name we gave to the macro when we told Excel to record it. Notice that there's also a Visual Basic line continuation character automatically inserted into the code, to aid readability."

"What do **`Range`**, **`ActiveCell`**, and **`FormulaR1C1`** refer to?" Bob asked.

"Those are some of Excel's object, property, and method names," I said. "We'll touch upon those in a few minutes. First, though, I want to use this macro code in the **`Click`** event procedure of a Visual Basic command button," I said. "Let's add a new command button to the Student Grades demo form, naming it **`cmdExcel`** and captioning it Excel..."

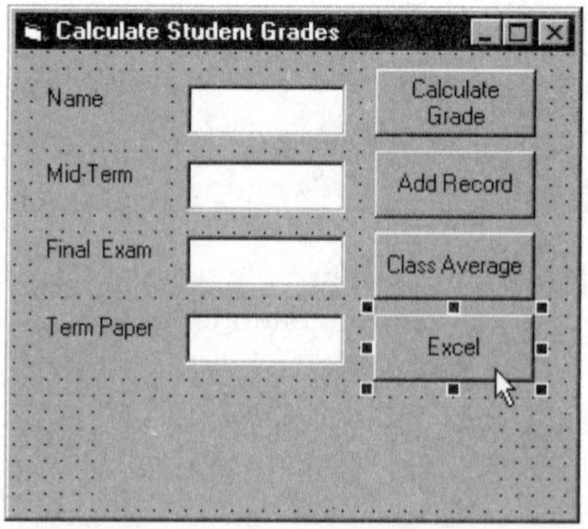
Calculate Student Grades
Name
Mid-Term
Final Exam
Term Paper
Calculate Grade
Add Record
Class Average
Excel

"Now let's copy the body of the code from the Excel macro we just created," I said, "and paste it into the `Click` event procedure of the `cmdExcel` command button:"

```
Private Sub cmdExcel_Click()

ActiveCell.FormulaR1C1 = "80"
Range("A2").Select
ActiveCell.FormulaR1C1 = "85"
Range("A3").Select
ActiveCell.FormulaR1C1 = "76"
Range("B1").Select
ActiveCell.FormulaR1C1 = "0.4"
Range("B2").Select
ActiveCell.FormulaR1C1 = "0.4"
Range("B3").Select
ActiveCell.FormulaR1C1 = "0.2"
Range("B4").Select
ActiveCell.FormulaR1C1 = _
 "=(R[-3]C[-1]*R[-3]C)+(R[-2]C[-1]*R[-2]C)+(R[-1]C[-1]*R[-1]C)"
Range("B5").Select

End Sub
```

If you didn't follow exactly the sequence of actions that I took while the Macro Recorder was capturing what I was doing, then the generated code from the macro might look slightly different to what you see here. Again, don't worry – so long as you performed the essential actions, things will be fine.

"Is this code going to run as it is?" Dave asked. "You said that you could copy and paste the macro code into Visual Basic, but didn't you also say you'd need to modify it slightly first?"

"You're right, Dave," I said "just copying and pasting the macro code into a Visual Basic event procedure is not good enough. If that's all we do, the program will bomb. Take a look..."

I then ran the program, and clicked on the Excel command button, with this result:

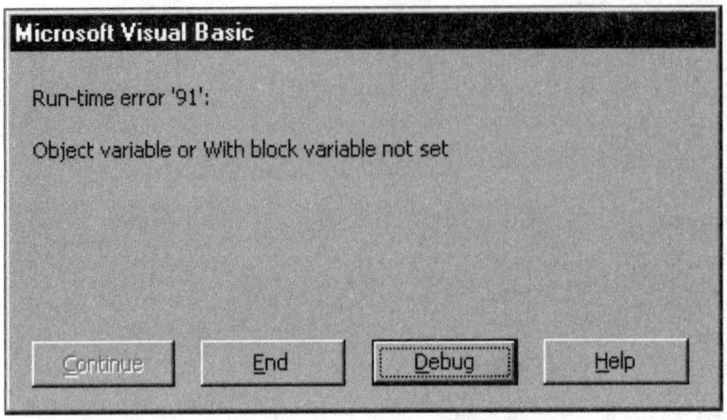
Microsoft Visual Basic
Run-time error '91':
Object variable or With block variable not set
Continue
End
Debug
Help

"Oops!" said Kathy. "What does this error message indicate?"

I clicked on the Debug button, and this line of code was highlighted:

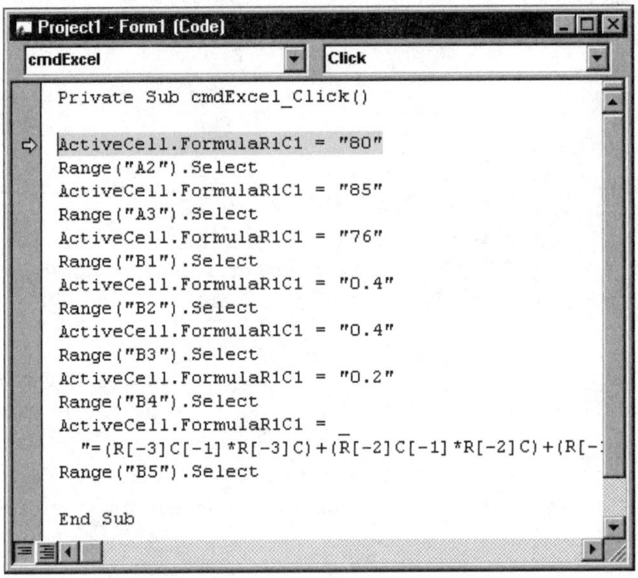
Project1 - Form1 (Code)
cmdExcel
Click
Private Sub cmdExcel_Click()
ActiveCell.FormulaR1C1 = "80"
Range("A2").Select
ActiveCell.FormulaR1C1 = "85"
Range("A3").Select
ActiveCell.FormulaR1C1 = "76"
Range("B1").Select
ActiveCell.FormulaR1C1 = "0.4"
Range("B2").Select
ActiveCell.FormulaR1C1 = "0.4"
Range("B3").Select
ActiveCell.FormulaR1C1 = "0.2"
Range("B4").Select
ActiveCell.FormulaR1C1 = _
"=(R[-3]C[-1]*R[-3]C)+(R[-2]C[-1]*R[-2]C)+(R[-
Range("B5").Select
End Sub

"Visual Basic is telling us," I said, "that it doesn't know what to make of the word **ActiveCell**. Visual Basic doesn't know if it's an object, a property or a method..."

"Isn't **ActiveCell** a property contained within the Excel ActiveX component?" Dorothy asked. "We set a reference to the Excel Object Library before we copied this code into the **Click** event procedure – so why the error message?"

"You're right, Dorothy," I said, "we did set a reference to the Excel Object Library, but we didn't specify *which object* in the ActiveX component we were going to use. Last week, when we wanted to create an instance of a `Student` object in the Student Grades demo program, not only did we need to include the `Student` class module in our project, we needed to declare an instance of the `Student` object in our code."

"Oh, I see now," Dorothy said. "We need to declare an instance of an Excel object."

"You're on the right track, Dorothy," I said, "except there's no Excel object. The top-level object we need to declare is the `Application` object."

"What exactly does that mean?" Lou asked. "**Top-level object**?"

"The `Application` object occupies the top of the application hierarchy," I answered. "Put simply, it's the first element of the dot notation we use to work with the properties of the ActiveX component. Don't confuse it with the `App` object we discussed in Lesson Three: here, today, the `Application` object represents the application that the ActiveX component belongs to, **not** our VB application. What we must do here, is declare an instance of Excel's `Application` object – in fact, as it turns out, `ActiveCell` is a property of Excel's `Application` object."

"So what do we have to do to declare an instance of the `Application` object?" Steve asked.

"I'll show you," I said.

I modified the code in the `Click` event procedure of `cmdExcel` to look like the next listing (modified code is highlighted):

```
Private Sub cmdExcel_Click()

Dim xlApp As Excel.Application
Dim xlBook As Excel.Workbook
Dim xlSheet As Excel.Worksheet

Set xlApp = New Excel.Application
Set xlBook = xlapp.Workbooks.Add
Set xlSheet = xlBook.Worksheets.Add

With xlApp
.Visible = True
```

For the next block of code, all you need to do is add a period (.) to the start of each line as shown:

```
.ActiveCell.FormulaR1C1 = "80"
.Range("A2").Select
.ActiveCell.FormulaR1C1 = "85"
.Range("A3").Select
.ActiveCell.FormulaR1C1 = "76"
.Range("B1").Select
.ActiveCell.FormulaR1C1 = "0.4"
.Range("B2").Select
.ActiveCell.FormulaR1C1 = "0.4"
.Range("B3").Select
.ActiveCell.FormulaR1C1 = "0.2"
.Range("B4").Select
.ActiveCell.FormulaR1C1 =
    ↳"=(R[-3]C[-1]*R[-3]C)+(R[-2]C[-1]*R[-2]C)+(R[-1]C[-1]*R[-1]C)"
```

Now add the next line:

```
End With
```

```
End Sub
```

"We've made several changes to the code," I said, "but the core of it – from the macro – has remained unaltered. The first thing we did was to declare the object variable that refers to the Excel objects:

```
Dim xlApp As Excel.Application
```

"There are also two other objects crucial for the code to work," I added, "the **`Workbook`** and the **`Worksheet`**. Remember, Excel needs to have an instance of both of these to run anything:"

```
Dim xlBook As Excel.Workbook
Dim xlSheet As Excel.Worksheet
```

"Once we've established these, this next line instantiates the **`Excel.Application`** object..."

```
Set xlApp = New Excel.Application
```

"...and the following line executes the **`Add`** method of the **`Excel.WorkBooks`** object collection to create an instance of a new workbook:"

```
Set xlBook = xlapp.Workbooks.Add
```

"This is the same principle as we used in the last lesson when we were instantiating objects from our **Course** and **Order** collections: here, we're using the **WorkBooks** collection's built-in **Add** method to create a new workbook. And the next bit of code is similar, in that it executes the **Excel.WorkSheets** collection's **Add** method to create a new instance of a worksheet:"

```
Set xlSheet = xlBook.Worksheets.Add
```

"So, these are collection objects?" Kate asked. "Like the **Course** collection or the **Order** collection?"

"That's right, Kate," I answered.

"An Excel workbook can contain more than one worksheet, can't it?" Dorothy queried. "How do we define the number of worksheet objects that we want?"

"Well, the default value is 1, but you could specify more via the **Application** object's **SheetsInNewWorkbook** property," I replied.

"I have a really basic question here," Ward said. "How did you know to do this? I mean, declare these three object variables, and instantiate each one?"

"Quite honestly, Ward," I said smiling, "the first time I did it, I looked up the syntax in Visual Basic Help. For whatever reason, virtually all of the examples you will find in Visual Basic Help pertaining to using ActiveX components cite the **Excel** object as an example. You'll see in a few minutes, when we use some of the ActiveX components of Word, that we won't get nearly as much assistance from Visual Basic Help – I confess, it was a colleague of mine who helped me with the object declarations for Word!"

"What's the purpose of the **With** and **End With** statements in this code," Rhonda asked, "and what are those dots in front of the macro code you pasted?"

The With...End With Structure

"The Visual Basic **With** and **End With** statements," I said, "allow you to execute a series of statements that all relate to a single object without having to repeat the object variable name for each and every statement. For instance, in this code, the dot tells Visual Basic that each property and method name refers to the Excel **Application** object which we've referred to using the **xlApp** object variable."

"So using the **With...End With** structure eliminates the need to preface each line of code with **xlApp**?" Valerie said.

"Exactly," I answered.

"Why did you set the **Visible** property of the **Application** object to **True**?" Melissa asked. "What will that do?"

"Normally," I answered, "when an object in an ActiveX component is being used by your Visual Basic program, there's no need for its interface to be visible to the user. However, when we're developing an application, it's good to see what's going on behind the scenes – to make sure everything's working OK. Setting the **Visible** property of the **Application** object to **True** will allow us to see the worksheet in action:"

```
.Visible = True
```

"This next section of code," I said, "assigns the student's grades to the appropriate cells in the worksheet. By default, the active cell of a new worksheet is cell A1, so this line of code will place the value 80 into cell A1, using the **FormulaR1C1** method of that **ActiveCell** object:"

```
.ActiveCell.FormulaR1C1 = "80"
```

"And this line of code changes the active cell to cell A2, using the **Select** method of the **Range** object:"

```
.Range("A2").Select
```

"Remember, all of this was written for us by the Macro Recorder, so don't worry too much about these property names," I said. "This next piece of code repeats the process of assigning values for the student's grades into cells A2 and A3, and the appropriate percentages for each grade in cells B1, B2 and B3..."

```
.ActiveCell.FormulaR1C1 = "85"
.Range("A3").Select
.ActiveCell.FormulaR1C1 = "76"
.Range("B1").Select
.ActiveCell.FormulaR1C1 = "0.4"
.Range("B2").Select
.ActiveCell.FormulaR1C1 = "0.4"
.Range("B3").Select
.ActiveCell.FormulaR1C1 = "0.2"
```

"And this line of code," I continued, "changes the active cell to cell B4:"

```
.Range("B4").Select
```

"After that, we insert the formula in cell B4: this calculates the student's average based on the entries in cells A1, A2 and A3, and stores the result in cell B4:"

```
.ActiveCell.FormulaR1C1 =
    ↳"=(R[-3]C[-1]*R[-3]C)+(R[-2]C[-1]*R[-2]C)+(R[-1]C[-1]*R[-1]C)"
```

"Notice that values are provided for the offsets – by **row**, **R**, and **column**, **C** – of the relevant cells they come from," I pointed out. "That's what the property name **FormulaR1C1** means. It reminds the user that the **ActiveCell** is considered to be **row 1**, **column 1**, and that to access values from other cells we must provide a plus or minus offset for those cells."

"In some cases, a column offset doesn't seem to be given," observed Ward.

"Yes, that's because the default offset is zero, and we're accessing the percentage values from the column directly above our active cell – B4," I told him. "Like I say, don't worry too much about it. The Excel Macro Recorder wrote this code for us – what I'm really interested in covering are the essential principles."

"Shouldn't we be closing Excel after we've done with it?" Dave asked.

"We will eventually, Dave," I said, "but let's wait until we're sure everything is flowing properly before we do that. Let's run the program now."

I ran the Student Grades demo and clicked on the Excel command button. Excel started up, and a workbook and worksheet appeared. As if by magic, numbers started appearing…

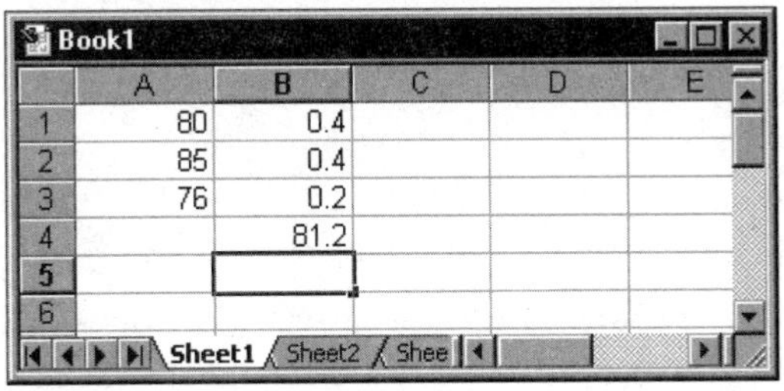

Book1
A
B
C
D
E
1 80 0.4
2 85 0.4
3 76 0.2
4 81.2
5
6
Sheet1
Sheet2
Shee

"I must say, I'm impressed by this," Blaine said, "But this worksheet isn't very flexible, is it? It will always come up with the answer 81.2."

"You're right, Blaine," I said, "and we can fix that. Let's modify our code to obtain the value for the three grade components from the text boxes on the form..."

I closed Excel, and modified the code in the **Click** event procedure of **cmdExcel** as shown by the code listing below. Modified code is highlighted, of course:

```
Private Sub cmdExcel_Click()

Dim xlApp As Excel.Application
Dim xlBook As Excel.Workbook
Dim xlSheet As Excel.Worksheet

Set xlApp = New Excel.Application
Set xlBook = xlApp.Workbooks.Add
Set xlSheet = xlBook.Worksheets.Add

With xlApp
  .Visible = True
  .ActiveCell.FormulaR1C1 = txtMidTerm.Text
  .Range("A2").Select
  .ActiveCell.FormulaR1C1 = txtFinalExam.Text
  .Range("A3").Select
  .ActiveCell.FormulaR1C1 = txtTermPaper.Text
  .Range("B1").Select
  .ActiveCell.FormulaR1C1 = "0.4"
  .Range("B2").Select
  .ActiveCell.FormulaR1C1 = "0.4"
  .Range("B3").Select
  .ActiveCell.FormulaR1C1 = "0.2"
  .Range("B4").Select
  .ActiveCell.FormulaR1C1 =
  ↳"=(R[-3]C[-1]*R[-3]C)+(R[-2]C[-1]*R[-2]C)+(R[-1]C[-1]*R[-1]C)"
End With

End Sub
```

"As you can see," I said, "we're now entering values into the worksheet using the **Text** properties of the three text boxes on the form that hold the individual student's grades. Let's see what happens..."

I ran the program and entered the values for a fictitious student:

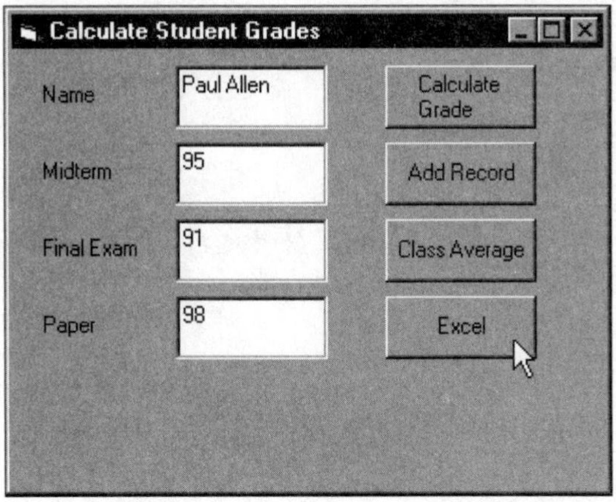

Then I clicked on the Excel command button. After a few seconds, this Excel worksheet was displayed on the classroom projector:

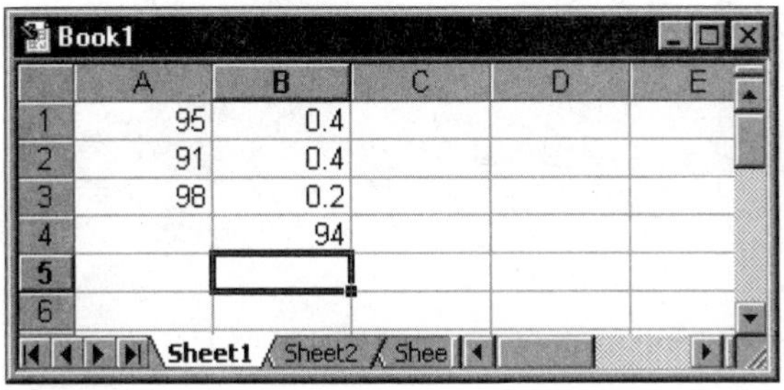

"That's better," Ward said.

"Now that *is* flexible!" Kate said. "This time, we've used the values we put in the three text boxes of the form as values in the formula calculation in the Excel worksheet."

"Is there any way we can return the result in cell B4 back to our Visual Basic program?" Kathy asked.

"You bet, Kathy," I said. "All we need to do is add the following line to our procedure…"

I added this code to the **Click** event procedure of **cmdExcel** (modified code is highlighted, and code omitted for clarity is represented by an ellipsis):

```
Private Sub cmdExcel_Click()

Dim xlApp As Excel.Application
Dim xlBook As Excel.Workbook
Dim xlSheet As Excel.Worksheet

Set xlApp = New Excel.Application
Set xlBook = xlApp.Workbooks.Add
Set xlSheet = xlBook.Worksheets.Add

With xlApp

  ...

  .Range("B4").Select
  .ActiveCell.FormulaR1C1 =
     ↳"=(R[-3]C[-1]*R[-3]C)+(R[-2]C[-1]*R[-2]C)+(R[-1]C[-1]*R[-1]C)"
  .Range("B4").Select

  MsgBox "The student's grade is " &
       ↳.ActiveCell.Value
End With

End Sub
```

"All we're doing here," I said, "is making sure that the active cell is set to cell B4..."

```
.Range("B4").Select
```

"...and then displaying the **Value** property of the active cell in a message box..."

```
MsgBox "The student's grade is " &
      ↳.ActiveCell.Value
```

"Let's run the program now and see how it behaves," I said.

I ran the program, once again entering the values for a fictitious student in the text boxes, and clicked on the Excel command button. This time, not only was the Excel worksheet displayed, but this message box too:

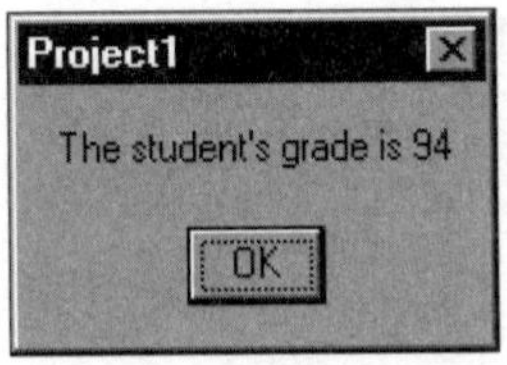
Project1
The student's grade is 94
OK

> **The message box will be hidden behind the Excel worksheet – minimize Excel, and you'll see it.**

"As you can see," I continued, "not only can we provide values from our Visual Basic program for use as values in the cells of an Excel worksheet, we can also obtain cell values from it, too."

"This is really fabulous," Valerie said. "I had no idea we could do something like this from within Visual Basic. I can't wait to see how many applications on my PC expose their objects via ActiveX components."

"I think you'll be pleasantly surprised to find that quite a few of them do," I said. "*All* Microsoft products do, and quite a few non-Microsoft applications, as well."

"Did you say that you were going to show us how to close Excel from within Visual Basic?" Dave asked. "The way the code is written now, Excel is visible and left open when the event procedure ends. I'm sure we don't want that."

"You're absolutely right, Dave," I said. "We don't want to make it the responsibility of the user to close Excel. If they forget to close it – and it's not visible, remember – the user won't even know the application is running – and that could be a severe performance drain."

I then changed the code in the `Click` event procedure of `cmdExcel` to look like this (modified code is again highlighted and omitted code represented by an ellipsis):

```
Private Sub cmdExcel_Click()

Dim xlApp As Excel.Application
Dim xlBook As Excel.Workbook
Dim xlSheet As Excel.Worksheet

Set xlApp = New Excel.Application
Set xlBook = xlApp.Workbooks.Add
```

```
Set xlSheet = xlBook.Worksheets.Add

With xlApp

...

End With

xlBook.Close savechanges:=False
xlApp.Quit

Set xlApp = Nothing
Set xlBook = Nothing
Set xlSheet = Nothing

End Sub
```

"We've added some code to close the workbook object, and quit the application," I explained.

"Will we run the Student Grades, now?" Valerie asked.

"Not just yet," I told her. "Let's just remove this line of code, as well..."

```
.Visible = True
```

"This is the line that made Excel visible while this code was running," I explained, "and we've finished with that, now, since we know everything's working OK inside the spreadsheet when we run the program."

"I can see we're executing the **`Close`** method of the **`Workbook`** object," Blaine said, "and then executing the quit method of the **`Application`** object. But what does the **`Close`** method's **`savechanges`** argument do?"

"We're closing the workbook and then quitting the application," I said. "However, when we execute the **`Close`** method of the workbook, the same thing happens in code as would happen if the user were closing a workbook they'd just been working on – Excel wants to know if it should save the changes made to the workbook."

"Will a prompt appear?" Kevin asked.

"No, Kevin," I said, "the user won't see a prompt – but if we don't provide Excel with a value of **False** for the **savechanges** argument, the workbook won't close – and the Excel application will remain active. We need to pass the **Close** method the **savechanges** argument with a value of **False** to close Excel without saving the changes made to the workbook:"

```
xlBook.Close savechanges:=False
```

"Finally," I said, "this line of code quits the Excel application..."

```
xlApp.Quit
```

"...and these lines of code set the three object variables we used to **Nothing** – which, as we know by now, is always a good idea:"

```
Set xlApp = Nothing
Set xlBook = Nothing
Set xlSheet = Nothing
```

"Let's see how well this code works," I said. "Excel will fire up in the background when the Excel button is pressed, accept the values for the student's grades from the text boxes on the form, use our formula to calculate the student's grade, and then return the result back to our program in a message box."

I ran the program. Once again, I entered information for a student and clicked on the Excel command button. A few seconds later, a message box with the student's grade appeared:

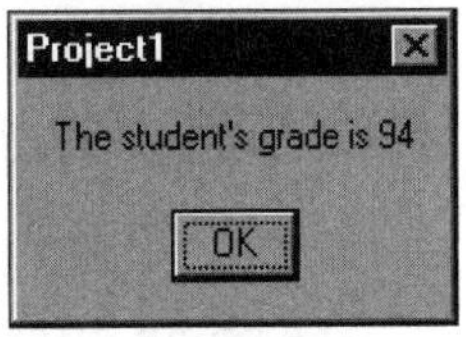
Project1
The student's grade is 94
OK

"That worked like a charm," Rhonda said, displaying the confidence of an ActiveX component professional. "I think I'm really beginning to get the hang of this. What's next? Can we start working on the China Shop project yet?"

"Not just yet," I said. "In the China Shop, we'll use Word's ActiveX component to create a sales quotation, but I think it would be a good idea if we also use the Student Grades demo project to work with Word before we use it in the China Shop project."

Using Word from Visual Basic

"This will be interesting," I said. "Word's objects are just a bit more challenging than Excel's."

"Will we be using the same technique with Word to record a macro?" Valerie asked.

"Yes, we will," I answered. "Let's put a new command button on our form, first, though. Call it `cmdWord` and caption it Word:"

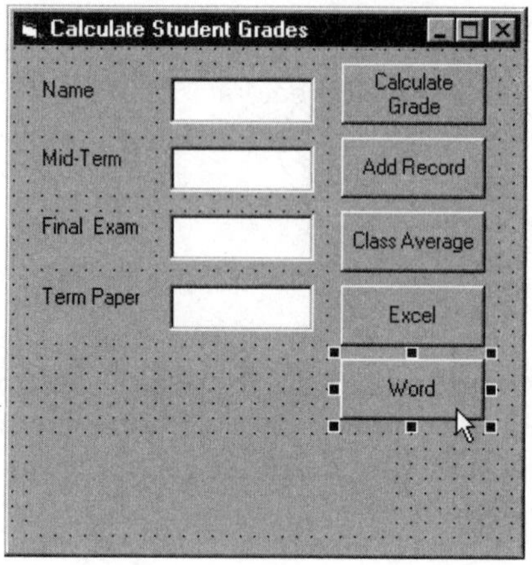

Next, I started Word 97 on my instructor's PC.

> **Again, don't worry if you're not running exactly the same mix of Windows/Office versions as I am.**

"Remember, we've already made a reference to the Microsoft Word type library in the Student Grades project," I told them. "Let's begin our study of interacting with Word by recording a macro to report the student's grades."

I selected Tools | Macro | Record New Macro from the Word menu bar. On the Record Macro form, I entered a name of StudentDemo for the macro and a short description...

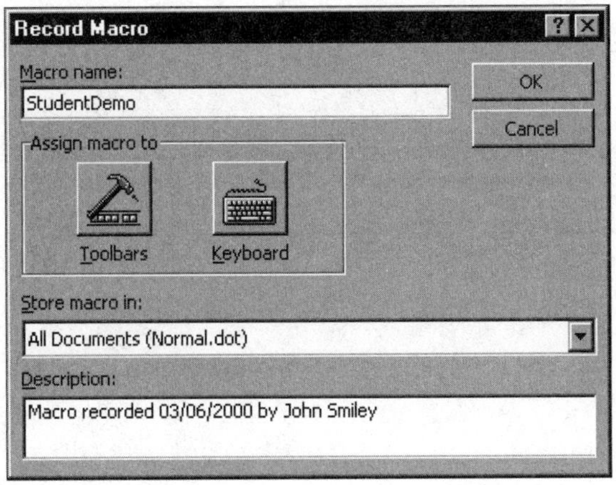

...and clicked on the OK button.

"As we did when we recorded the Excel macro," I said, "what we're interested in doing here is having Word record the basics of what we want our Visual Basic program to do: the Macro Recorder will generate the code to perform those actions, and we can then get a good idea of the properties and methods that are being executed behind the scenes of Word to achieve our aim. In this instance, let's enter the grade data for two fictitious students, and a summary line for the overall class average."

Recording the Macro

I then typed the following document while Word recorded the macro:

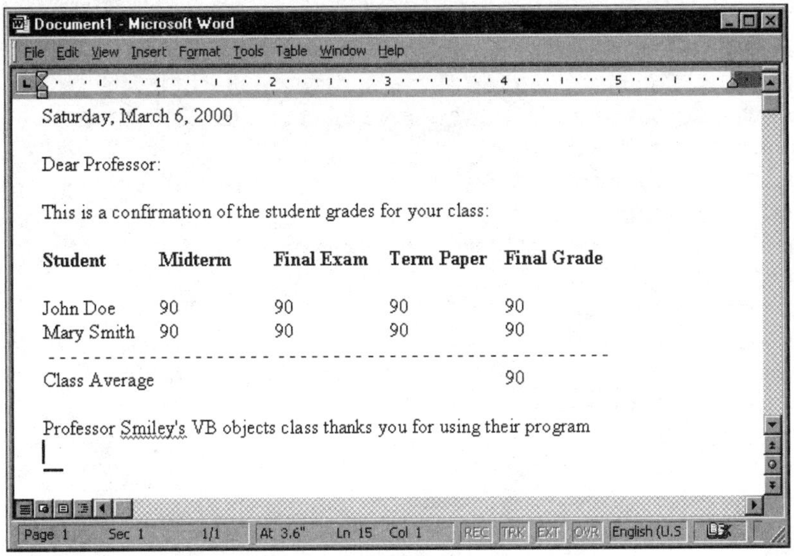

> ! The date was inserted by selecting **Insert | Date and Time** from the menu bar, and the table columns were created by tabbing across to the relevant positions. This, of course, is very important in determining the final structure of the VBA code that the Macro Recorder generates for you. The Macro Recorder copies *exactly* what you do while typing the report.

As I finished typing, I stopped the recording of the macro.

Modifying the Code

I opened up the Word macro editor and copied and pasted the code from the Word macro into the new `cmdWord` command button's `Click` event procedure:

> ! We've included a text file that contains the exact text of this macro on the CD. You can find it in the `For Chapter 08\Additional Examples\Student Grades Demo` folder, and it's called `Student Grades Code.txt`. If you copy and paste the text from this file into the Student Grades project instead of recording your own macro, your code will exactly match that shown on the following pages. If you record your own macro, the chances are that your code will look slightly different from mine, as the Macro Recorder records the exact actions you take when you're typing up the Word document. It's not a problem if your code doesn't exactly match mine, but it will be easier to follow my explanations if we're all working with identical code:

```
Private Sub cmdWord_Click()

 Selection.ParagraphFormat.TabStops.ClearAll
 ActiveDocument.DefaultTabStop = InchesToPoints(1)
 Selection.InsertDateTime DateTimeFormat:="dddd, MMMM dd, yyyy",
     ↳InsertAsField:=True
 Selection.TypeParagraph
 Selection.TypeParagraph
 Selection.TypeText Text:="Dear Professor:"
 Selection.TypeParagraph
 Selection.TypeParagraph
 Selection.TypeText Text:=
     ↳"This is a confirmation of the student grades for your class:"
 Selection.TypeParagraph
 Selection.TypeParagraph
 Selection.Font.Bold = wdToggle
 Selection.TypeText Text:="Student"
```

```
Selection.Font.Bold = wdToggle
Selection.TypeText Text:=vbTab
Selection.Font.Bold = wdToggle
Selection.TypeText Text:="Midterm"
Selection.Font.Bold = wdToggle
Selection.TypeText Text:=vbTab
Selection.Font.Bold = wdToggle
Selection.TypeText Text:="Final Exam"
Selection.Font.Bold = wdToggle
Selection.TypeText Text:=vbTab
Selection.Font.Bold = wdToggle
Selection.TypeText Text:="Term Paper"
Selection.Font.Bold = wdToggle
Selection.TypeText Text:=vbTab
Selection.Font.Bold = wdToggle
Selection.TypeText Text:="Final Grade"
Selection.Font.Bold = wdToggle
Selection.TypeParagraph
Selection.TypeParagraph
Selection.TypeText Text:="John Doe" & vbTab & "90" & vbTab &
  ↪"90" & vbTab & "90" & vbTab & "90"
Selection.TypeParagraph
Selection.TypeText Text:="Mary Smith" & vbTab & "90" & vbTab &
  ↪"90" & vbTab & "90" & vbTab & "90"
Selection.TypeParagraph
Selection.TypeText Text:=
  ↪" - - - - - - - - - - - - - - - - - - - - "
Selection.TypeText Text:=" - - - - - - - - - - - - - - - - "
Selection.TypeParagraph
Selection.TypeText Text:="Class Average" & vbTab & vbTab &
  ↪vbTab & vbTab & "90"
Selection.TypeParagraph
Selection.TypeParagraph
Selection.TypeText Text:=
     ↪"Professor Smiley's VB objects Class thanks you for using the"
Selection.TypeText Text:="ir program"

End Sub
```

I gave everyone a minute or two to look the code over, and then I said: "There's a lot more code in this macro than there was in our Excel macro – but in terms of Word's methods and properties, there are just a few of the same ones being executed over and over again."

"I presume," Steve said, "that we won't be able to run this code purely as it stands – we'll need to modify it a bit to make it run, right?"

"That's correct, Steve," I said. "We'll need to declare some Word object variables, execute some **Set** statements, and use **With...End With** statements – the same kind of things we did with the Excel macro and code earlier."

I then modified the code in the **cmdWord** button's **Click** event procedure to match the next listing. The modified code is highlighted, and note that the procedures inside the **With...End With** structure must all be preceded by a period. Furthermore, remember that if you recorded your own macro, the details of the code may be slightly different from my version:

```
Private Sub cmdWord_Click()

Dim wdApp As Word.Application
Dim wdDoc As Word.Document

Set wdApp = New Word.Application
Set wdDoc = wdApp.Documents.Add

With wdApp

.Visible = True
```

All you need to do with the next chunk of code is add the leading period to each line as indicated:

```
.Selection.ParagraphFormat.TabStops.ClearAll
.ActiveDocument.DefaultTabStop = InchesToPoints(1)
.Selection.InsertDateTime DateTimeFormat:="dddd, MMMM dd, yyyy",
   ↳InsertAsField:=True
.Selection.TypeParagraph
.Selection.TypeParagraph
.Selection.TypeText Text:="Dear Professor:"
.Selection.TypeParagraph
.Selection.TypeParagraph
.Selection.TypeText Text:=
   ↳"This is a confirmation of the student grades for your class:"
.Selection.TypeParagraph
.Selection.TypeParagraph
```

```
.Selection.Font.Bold = wdToggle  'Bold on
.Selection.TypeText Text:="Student"
.Selection.Font.Bold = wdToggle  "Bold off
.Selection.TypeText Text:=vbTab

.Selection.Font.Bold = wdToggle  'Bold on
.Selection.TypeText Text:="Mid Term"
.Selection.Font.Bold = wdToggle  'Bold off
.Selection.TypeText Text:=vbTab

.Selection.Font.Bold = wdToggle  'Bold on
.Selection.TypeText Text:="Final Exam"
.Selection.Font.Bold = wdToggle  'Bold off
.Selection.TypeText Text:=vbTab

.Selection.Font.Bold = wdToggle  'Bold on
.Selection.TypeText Text:="Term Paper"
.Selection.Font.Bold = wdToggle  'Bold off
.Selection.TypeText Text:=vbTab

.Selection.Font.Bold = wdToggle  'Bold on
.Selection.TypeText Text:="Final Grade"
.Selection.Font.Bold = wdToggle  'Bold off

.Selection.TypeParagraph
.Selection.TypeParagraph
.Selection.TypeText Text:="John Doe" & vbTab & "90" & vbTab &
   ↳"90" & vbTab & "90" & vbTab & "90"
.Selection.TypeParagraph
.Selection.TypeText Text:="Mary Smith" & vbTab & "90" & vbTab &
   ↳"90" & vbTab & "90" & vbTab & "90"
.Selection.TypeParagraph
.Selection.TypeText Text:=
   ↳" - - - - - - - - - - - - - - - - - - - - - "
.Selection.TypeText Text:=" - - - - - - - - - - - - - - - - "
.Selection.TypeParagraph
.Selection.TypeText Text:="Class Average" & vbTab & vbTab &
   ↳vbTab & vbTab & "90"
.Selection.TypeParagraph
.Selection.TypeParagraph
.Selection.TypeText Text:=
   ↳"Professor Smiley's VB objects Class thanks you for using the"
.Selection.TypeText Text:="ir program"
```

Now add these next few lines:

```
'.ActiveWindow.Close savechanges:=False
End With
```

```
'wdApp.Application.Quit
'Set wdDoc = Nothing
'Set wdApp = Nothing
```

```
End Sub
```

"Not surprisingly," I said, "the objects that we need to work with in Word are different from those we used with Excel – although we do start out in a similar way, by declaring an object variable for Word's top-level `Application` object:"

```
Dim wdApp As Word.Application
```

"Unlike Excel, which makes us declare a `Workbook` and `WorkSheet` object, Word just requires a `Document` object:"

```
Dim wdDoc As Word.Document
```

"After that, we instantiate the Word `Application` object using the `Set` statement…"

```
Set wdApp = New Word.Application
```

"…and then, like we did in the Excel code, we use the `Add` method of the `Documents` collection to create an instance of a `Document` object. The text we're writing will reside in the `Document` object:"

```
Set wdDoc = wdApp.Documents.Add
```

"The rest of the code," I said, "is basically the VBA code that we copied out of our Word macro, sandwiched between a `With` and `End With` statement. As before, we start out by setting the `Visible` property of the Word application to `True`, so that we can see what's going on as we test the program:"

```
With wdApp

.Visible = True
```

"As I said, from this point on, it's really just the recorded macro doing all the work. Some of the Word methods and properties that we see in action bear a comment or two. Most of them are methods of the **Selection** object. You can think of the **Selection** object as the **Insertion Point** in a Word document – the place where the cursor is, and where anything that we key will be entered in the document. Bearing that in mind, look at this next line of code – it uses the **ClearAll** method of the **TabStops** object to clear all the tab stops in the document:"

```
.Selection.ParagraphFormat.TabStops.ClearAll
```

"That action is followed by a line of code that uses the **DefaultTabStop** property of the **ActiveDocument** object to set tabs one inch apart throughout the document:"

```
.ActiveDocument.DefaultTabStop = InchesToPoints(1)
```

"This next line is another interesting one – it inserts the current date and time into the document..."

```
.Selection.InsertDateTime DateTimeFormat:="dddd, MMMM dd, yyyy",
    ↳InsertAsField:=True
```

"Remember, the output on our prototype report was Saturday, March 6, 1999," I said: "the option we selected from Insert | Date and Time. This VBA code represents that format to the **InsertDateTime** method of the **Selection** object."

"Which the Macro Recorder wrote for us!" Ward added. "Neat!"

> **Bear in mind that different versions of Word have different date display formats – you may need to adjust this line of code accordingly.**

"Next, we've got these two lines that use the **TypeParagraph** method of the **Selection** object to insert a paragraph marker – effectively a new line – into the document:"

```
.Selection.TypeParagraph
.Selection.TypeParagraph
```

"From our standpoint," I said, "the **TypeText** method of the **Selection** object is probably the most important. The **TypeText** method, which accepts a single argument called **Text**, enters text into the document. Its' really the workhorse of our code:"

```
.Selection.TypeText Text:="Dear Professor:"
.Selection.TypeParagraph
.Selection.TypeParagraph
.Selection.TypeText Text:=
   ↳"This is a confirmation of the student grades for your class:"
.Selection.TypeParagraph
.Selection.TypeParagraph
```

"We can toggle the **Bold** attribute on and off," I said, "by assigning the value **wdToggle** to the **Font** object's **Bold** property:"

```
.Selection.Font.Bold = wdToggle
```

"There's nothing new in the rest of the code until we get to this next line:"

```
.Selection.TypeText Text:="John Doe" & vbTab & "90" & vbTab &
   ↳"90" & vbTab & "90" & vbTab & "90"
```

"Here, we concatenate the **vbTab** intrinsic constant – representing a tab character – onto our string literals for John Doe's name and grades. This concatenated string is passed as an argument to the **Selection** object's **TypeText** method."

"As was the case with the Excel code," I continued, "we need to close Word by executing the **Close** method of the **Application** object's **ActiveWindow** property. Notice that we pass a value of **False** as the **savechanges** argument, just as we did in Excel:"

```
'.ActiveWindow.Close savechanges:=False
End With
```

"For the moment," I said, "I've commented this line of code out so that it won't execute. That way, we can see the document when we run our code. Finally, we need to quit the Word application by executing the **Quit** method of the **Application** object..."

```
'wdApp.Application.Quit
```

"...and then set our two object variables to nothing..."

```
'Set wdDoc = Nothing
'Set wdApp = Nothing
```

"Again," I concluded, " I've commented out these lines of code out temporarily – that way, the Word document will stay open so that we can see it."

Running the Modified Code

I ran the program and clicked on the Word button. A few seconds later, Word appeared on the classroom projector, and the letter to our fictitious professor was automatically typed in for us. For whatever reason, the ActiveX Word demonstration elicited more interest than the Excel demonstration had:

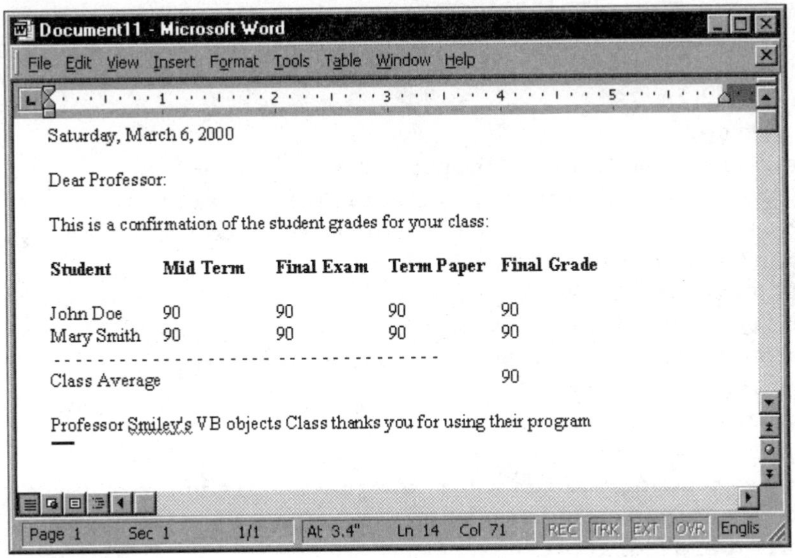

"This is fantastic," Kate said. "You can't believe how this capability is going to make my life easier at work. I can't wait to apply what I've learned here. Are we going to start on the China Shop code now?"

"Not yet, Kate," I said. "This code's still pretty inflexible – we need to make it a bit more adaptable before we can transfer these principles over to the China Shop."

"That's right," Bob said. "The code we have now will always generate the same document."

"What I'd like to do now," I said, "is modify this code so that it prints information from the `Student` objects in the `Course` collection – a process that'll be good practice for when we generate a sales quotation in the China Shop program."

Making the Code more Flexible

I modified the code in the `Click` event procedure of `cmdWord` to look like the next listing (as usual, modified code is highlighted, and 'omitted-for-clarity' code is represented by the ellipses):

```
Private Sub cmdWord_Click()

Dim objStudent As Student
Dim wdApp As Word.Application
Dim wdDoc As Word.Document

Set wdApp = New Word.Application
Set wdDoc = wdApp.Documents.Add

With wdApp
.Visible = True
.Selection.ParagraphFormat.TabStops.ClearAll
.ActiveDocument.DefaultTabStop = InchesToPoints(1)
.Selection.InsertDateTime DateTimeFormat:="dddd, MMMM dd, yyyy",
  ➥InsertAsField:=True
.Selection.TypeParagraph
.Selection.TypeParagraph
.Selection.TypeText Text:="Dear Professor:"
.Selection.TypeParagraph
.Selection.TypeParagraph
.Selection.TypeText Text:=
  ➥"This is a confirmation of the student grades for your class:"
.Selection.TypeParagraph
.Selection.TypeParagraph

...

.Selection.Font.Bold = wdToggle 'Bold on
.Selection.TypeText Text:="Student"
.Selection.Font.Bold = wdToggle 'Bold off
.Selection.TypeText Text:=vbTab

...

.Selection.Font.Bold = wdToggle 'Bold on
.Selection.TypeText Text:="Final Grade"
.Selection.Font.Bold = wdToggle 'Bold off

.Selection.TypeParagraph
.Selection.TypeParagraph
```

> **This where the real changes come – you're replacing the lines that wrote out the details for John doe and Mary Smith (the section beginning with the line reading** `.Selection.TypeText Text:="John Doe"`**… and ending with the line reading** `.Selection.TypeText Text:="Class Average" & vbTab & vbTab & vbTab & vbTab & "90"`**). Replace this whole section with the lines shown below, which use the information stored about each student in the properties of their dedicated** `Student` **object:**

```
'Loop through the item in the Course object
For Each objStudent In m_objCourse
 .Selection.TypeText Text:=objStudent.Name
 .Selection.TypeText Text:=vbTab
 .Selection.TypeText Text:=Str(objStudent.MidTerm)
 .Selection.TypeText Text:=vbTab
 .Selection.TypeText Text:=Str(objStudent.FinalExam)
 .Selection.TypeText Text:=vbTab
 .Selection.TypeText Text:=Str(objStudent.TermPaper)
 .Selection.TypeText Text:=vbTab
 .Selection.TypeText Text:=Str(objStudent.Average)
 .Selection.TypeParagraph
Next

.Selection.TypeText Text:=String(120, "-")

.Selection.TypeParagraph
.Selection.TypeText Text:="Class Average" & vbTab & vbTab &
   ↳vbTab & vbTab & m_objCourse.ClassAverage
```

```
.Selection.TypeParagraph
.Selection.TypeParagraph
.Selection.TypeText Text:=
   ↳"Professor Smiley's VB objects Class thanks you for using the"
.Selection.TypeText Text:="ir program!"
```

> **Add this chunk:**

```
'Print the Professor's Report
'.Application.PrintOut FileName:="", Range:=wdPrintAllDocument,
   ↳'Item:= wdPrintDocumentContent, Copies:=1, Pages:="",
```

```
        ↳'PageType:=wdPrintAllPages, Collate:=True,
        ↳'Background:=False, PrintToFile:=False

'.ActiveWindow.Close savechanges:=False

End With

'wdApp.Application.Quit

Set objStudent = Nothing
'Set wdDoc = Nothing
'Set wdApp = Nothing

End Sub
```

> ! **You can find the full text of this modified code in the** `Student Grades Code2.txt` **file on the CD. Look in the** `For Chapter 08\Additional Examples\Student Grades Demo` **folder.**

"Before I explain the code," I said, "let's run the program to see its new functionality."

I ran the program, added information for two fictitious students, added their records to the **`Grades.txt`** file with the Add Record button, and clicked on the Word button. A few seconds later, the following screen shot was displayed:

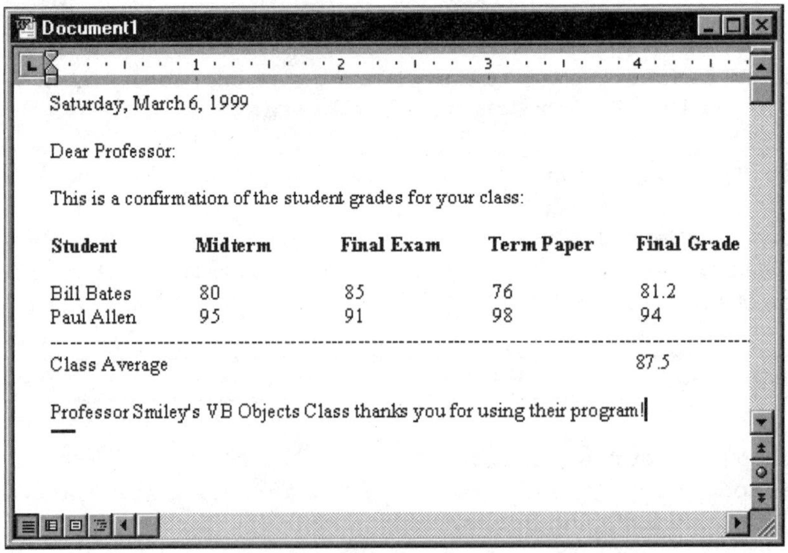

"That's just amazing," Rhonda said. "I never imagined such a thing was possible. You've generated a Word document by examining the **Student** objects in the **Course** collection. Can you explain the changes in the code that made that possible?"

"Sure, Rhonda," I said.

Explaining the Word Code

"The first thing we did was to declare a **Student** object variable that we'll use to 'loop' through the **Student** items in the **Course** collection object..."

```
Dim objStudent As Student
```

"The next few lines of code haven't changed," I said. "We declare the **Application** and **Document** objects, then set the **Visible** property of the **Application** object to **True** so that we can see what's going on..."

```
Dim wdApp As Word.Application
Dim wdDoc As Word.Document

Set wdApp = New Word.Application
Set wdDoc = wdApp.Documents.Add

With wdApp
.Visible = True
```

"...then set the tab stops to one inch apart...

```
.Selection.ParagraphFormat.TabStops.ClearAll
.ActiveDocument.DefaultTabStop = InchesToPoints(1)
```

"...insert the current date into the document..."

```
.Selection.InsertDateTime DateTimeFormat:="dddd, MMMM dd, yyyy",
   ↳InsertAsField:=True
```

"...then the Professor's salutation ..."

```
.Selection.TypeParagraph
.Selection.TypeParagraph
.Selection.TypeText Text:="Dear Professor:"
.Selection.TypeParagraph
.Selection.TypeParagraph
```

```
.Selection.TypeText Text:=
   ↳"This is a confirmation of the student grades for your class:"
.Selection.TypeParagraph
.Selection.TypeParagraph
```

"...then the headings for the student's name, mid-term, final exam, term paper and final grade:"

```
.Selection.Font.Bold = wdToggle 'Bold on
.Selection.TypeText Text:="Student"
.Selection.Font.Bold = wdToggle 'Bold off
.Selection.TypeText Text:=vbTab

.Selection.Font.Bold = wdToggle 'Bold on
.Selection.TypeText Text:="Mid-term"
.Selection.Font.Bold = wdToggle 'Bold off
.Selection.TypeText Text:=vbTab

.Selection.Font.Bold = wdToggle 'Bold on
.Selection.TypeText Text:="Final Exam"
.Selection.Font.Bold = wdToggle 'Bold off
.Selection.TypeText Text:=vbTab

.Selection.Font.Bold = wdToggle 'Bold on
.Selection.TypeText Text:="Term Paper"
.Selection.Font.Bold = wdToggle 'Bold off
.Selection.TypeText Text:=vbTab

.Selection.Font.Bold = wdToggle 'Bold on
.Selection.TypeText Text:="Final Grade"
.Selection.Font.Bold = wdToggle 'Bold off
.Selection.TypeText Text:=vbTab

.Selection.TypeParagraph
.Selection.TypeParagraph
```

"This next section of code," I said, "is where the dramatic changes have occurred. We use a **For...Each** statement to loop through each **Student** object that has a reference in the **Course** collection object. Once we obtain a reference to the **Student** object, we use the properties of the **Student** object as arguments to the **TypeText** method of the **Selection** object: our code uses this to display the student's information as a line of text in the document. We do this for each and every **Student** object in the **Course** collection object:"

```
'Loop through the item in the Course object
For Each objStudent In m_objCourse
 .Selection.TypeText Text:=objStudent.Name
 .Selection.TypeText Text:=vbTab
 .Selection.TypeText Text:=Str(objStudent.MidTerm)
 .Selection.TypeText Text:=vbTab
 .Selection.TypeText Text:=Str(objStudent.FinalExam)
 .Selection.TypeText Text:=vbTab
 .Selection.TypeText Text:=Str(objStudent.TermPaper)
 .Selection.TypeText Text:=vbTab
 .Selection.TypeText Text:=Str(objStudent.Average)
 .Selection.TypeParagraph
Next
```

"This next line of code has changed from the original too, hasn't it?" Melissa asked:

```
.Selection.TypeText Text:=String(120, "-")
```

"Yes, it has, Melissa," I answered. "For readability purposes, we're now passing a string of 120 dashes as the **`Text`** argument of **`TypeText`** by using the Visual Basic **`String`** function." I paused to let them see this. "After the dashes, it's time to insert the overall class average into the document, by executing the **`ClassAverage`** property of the **`Course`** collection object, and assigning it to the **`Text`** argument of the **`TypeText`** method:"

```
.Selection.TypeParagraph
.Selection.TypeText Text:="Class Average" & vbTab & vbTab &
   ↳vbTab & vbTab & m_objCourse.ClassAverage
```

"That **`ClassAverage`** property of the **`Course`** collection object comes in quite handy here," I added. "We then insert a thank you statement to the Professor..."

```
.Selection.TypeParagraph
.Selection.TypeParagraph
.Selection.TypeText Text:=
   ↳"Professor Smiley's VB objects Class thanks you for using the"
.Selection.TypeText Text:="ir program"
```

"This section of code uses the **`Printout`** method of the **`Application`** object to print the document to the default printer. For now, I've commented this code out so it won't execute for the moment, but when you run the program yourself, you'll see that the document will be printed..."

```
'Print the Professor's Report
'.Application.PrintOut FileName:="", Range:=wdPrintAllDocument,
   ↳' Item:= wdPrintDocumentContent, Copies:=1, Pages:="",
      ↳'PageType:=wdPrintAllPages, Collate:=True,
      ↳Background:=False, PrintToFile:=False
```

"Finally," I concluded, "we close the active window and close the application – again, these lines are commented for the time being..."

```
'.ActiveWindow.Close savechanges:=False
End With

'wdApp.Application.Quit
```

"Lastly, we set all of our object variables to **Nothing**..."

```
Set objStudent = Nothing
'Set wdDoc = Nothing
'Set wdApp = Nothing
```

"Using ActiveX components in your program," I summarized, "can open up new worlds to you. What we've done here today has been a quick survey of using the ActiveX components of two very popular Windows applications – but there are hundreds of others out there. There's no limit to what you can do within your Visual Basic program using objects from other applications – provided that those objects are exposed as a component."

It had been a long morning, and so, prior to beginning our work on the China Shop program modifications, I suggested that we take a break.

Back to the China Shop

After the break, it was time to modify the China Shop program to print a sales quotation using the Word ActiveX component.

Printing the Sales Quotation

"The remainder of today's class," I said, "will be spent modifying the China Shop program so that we can print a sales quotation for the customer. The first thing we need to do is add a reference for the Word 8.0 Object Library to the project."

I handed out this exercise for the class to complete to achieve this aim.

Exercise - Adding a Reference to the Word Object Library

In this exercise, you'll add a reference to the Microsoft Word 8.0 Object Library in the China Shop program.

1. Load up the China Shop project.

2. Select Project | References from the Visual Basic menu bar, and find and select the Microsoft Word 8.0 Object Library:

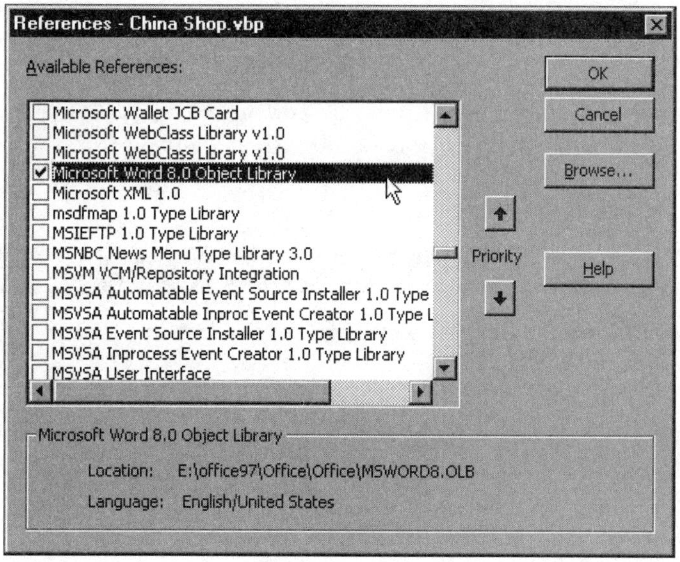

> **Don't forget: you're library list may differ slightly from mine – select the nearest equivalent that you can find.**

3. Click on the OK button to add the reference.

4. Save the China Shop project.

Discussion

"Before we actually start working with the Word ActiveX component in our code," I said, "we need to slightly modify the `TotalPrice` method of the `Order` collection object, since we'll now be executing that method in the code that prints the sales quotation."

Modifying the Order Object's TotalPrice Method

If you recall, the current version of the code displays a message box when the items in the **Order** collection object represent a complete place setting. We don't want that message displayed to the customer twice – once when their price is displayed on the China Shop form and once when the sales quotation is printed. For that reason, we'll be adding an optional argument to the **TotalPrice** method in this next exercise: this will ensure that we can let the method know whether or not we want that message box to be displayed."

"Won't modifying the **TotalPrice** method cause the code we created last week to crash?" Valerie asked.

"That's a good question, Valerie," I said. "Whenever you make a modification to an object, you need to consider how that change will impact programs already using it. However, adding an optional argument to a method is pretty safe – any code already in existence will be passing all the *required* arguments anyway. Adding an optional argument to an object's method doesn't require changes to any code already executing that method."

I circulated the next exercise for the class to complete:

Exercise - Modifying the TotalPrice Method

In this exercise, you'll modify the **TotalPrice** method of the **Order** collection object to accept an optional argument.

1. Select the **Order** class module in the Project Explorer window.
2. Modify the code in the **TotalPrice** method of the **Order** class to look like the next listing by changing the highlighted code. We'll talk through the new code in a moment:

```
Public Function TotalPrice(strBrand As String,
   ↳intQuantity As Integer,
   ↳Optional blnMessage As Variant) As Currency

Dim objTotal As Dish
Dim curPlatterPrice As Currency

If IsMissing(blnMessage) Then
 blnMessage = True
End If
```

```
If m_colOrder.Count = 0 Then
 TotalPrice = 0
 Exit Function
End If

For Each objTotal In m_colOrder
 TotalPrice = TotalPrice + (objTotal.Price * objTotal.Quantity)
 If objTotal.Item = "Platter" Then
 curPlatterPrice = objTotal.Price
 End If
Next

If m_intDiscount = 5 Then
 If blnMessage = True Then
 MsgBox "Price includes a Complete Place Setting Discount"
 End If
 Set objTotal = New Dish
 objTotal.Item = "Complete Place Setting"
 objTotal.Brand = strBrand
 TotalPrice = (objTotal.Price * intQuantity) + curPlatterPrice
End If

Set objTotal = Nothing

End Function
```

3. Save the China Shop project.

Discussion

"What we've done here," I said, "is modify the `TotalPrice` method to accept an **optional argument** called `blnMessage`..."

```
Public Function TotalPrice(strBrand As String,
   ↳intQuantity As Integer,
   ↳Optional blnMessage As Variant) As Currency
```

"We discussed creating procedures with optional arguments in our Intro class," I said. "Optional arguments must appear at the end of the argument string, **after** any required arguments have been declared."

"I gather from the name of the argument," Dorothy said, "that **blnMessage** is a **Boolean** argument. Why did you declare it as a **Variant**?"

"There's a Visual Basic function called **IsMissing**," I said, "that can be used to determine if an optional argument has been passed to a procedure. Unfortunately, **IsMissing** only works if the argument has been declared as a **Variant** – so that's why we've done that here in this way – for convenience."

"Can you explain what the **IsMissing** function is doing here?" Kevin asked.

"I'd be glad to, Kevin," I said. "The **IsMissing** function is used to determine if an optional argument has been passed to your procedure. There are other ways we could determine this, but using the **IsMissing** function is probably the simplest. **IsMissing** accepts a single **Variant** argument – the name of the optional argument that you want to check for. If the optional argument *hasn't* been supplied – in other words, it's **missing** – the **IsMissing** function returns a **True** value. If the optional argument *has* been supplied, **IsMissing** returns a **False** value. In our modified code, if the optional **blnMessage** argument *hasn't* been supplied, we assume that the programmer wants the message box displayed, so we set the value of **blnMessage** to **True** ourselves:"

```
If IsMissing(blnMessage) Then
 blnMessage = True
End If
```

"Now what happens?" Rhonda asked. "We have a value for the argument, but what do we do with it?"

"Just a few lines of code further on," I explained, "after we've calculated the total price of the customer's order, our method determines if the order is a complete place setting by checking to see if the value of **m_intDiscount** is equal to 5. If the order represents a complete place setting, *and* if the value of **blnMessage** is **True**, then we display the message box to the customer:"

```
If m_intDiscount = 5 Then
 If blnMessage = True Then
 MsgBox "Price includes a Complete Place Setting Discount"
 End If
```

"So what you're saying," Kevin said, "is that when the **Click** event procedure of the Calculate command button is executed for a complete place setting, the customer will see a message box. However, when the same code is executed to print their sales quotation, the message box *won't* be displayed."

"That's right, Kevin," I replied.

"What's next on the agenda?" Lou asked. "Is it time to modify the China Shop form yet?"

"Not quite yet, Lou," I answered. "First, we're going to give the program access to a `Discount` property in the `Order` collection object."

Adding the Discount Property Access

"If the customer has selected a complete place setting, we want to alert them on their printed sales quotation that their total price reflects a complete place setting discount. That's why we're adding the `Discount` property access to the `Order` collection's class – it will let us code for this functionality."

With that, I handed out the next exercise for the class to complete:

Exercise - Adding a Discount Procedure to the Order Class

In this exercise, you'll create a `Property Get` procedure that gives the program access to the `Order` collection's `m_intDiscount` variable – which is currently `Private` to the object.

1. Continue working with the China Shop project's `Order` class.

2. Create the `Discount` property of the `Order` class by adding the following code to the `Order` class module: there's no need to declare the `m_intDiscount` variable – it's already in the General Declarations section of the class module:

```
Property Get Discount() As Boolean

If m_intDiscount = .5 Then
 Discount = True
Else
 Discount = False
End If

End Property
```

3. Save the China Shop project.

Discussion

"You'll see shortly," I said, "that adding the **Discount** property to the **Order** collection object will really make our work easier when the time comes to print the sales quotation. Let me explain what's going on in the **Property Get** procedure. First off, we declare the **Discount** property as a **Boolean** data type – that is, a property that returns either a **True** or **False** value:"

```
Property Get Discount() As Boolean
```

"We already have a module-level variable declared called **m_intDiscount**," I said, "which we use in the **TotalPrice** method to determine whether the items the customer has selected represent a complete place setting. We can check the value of this variable to determine if the **Discount** property should be set to **True** or **False**. If the value of **m_intDiscount** is equal to five..."

```
If m_intDiscount = 5 Then
```

"...that means that the items the customer has selected represent a complete place setting, and we set the **Discount** property to **True**..."

```
 Discount = True
```

"...otherwise, we set it to **False**:"

```
Else
 Discount = False
```

"OK," Rhonda said, "that makes sense to me. And the reason we didn't code a **Property Let** for the **Discount** property is that it's read-only, is that right?"

"That's right, Rhonda," I answered.

"I can't wait to see how all of this turns out," Steve said. "Do we need to make any more changes to the **Order** collection object?"

"No, Steve," I replied. "That's the last of the changes required to the **Order** collection object. All of the remaining exercises we'll complete today will be made to the China Shop form itself."

Modifying the China Shop's Main Form

"Our next step is to integrate this new functionality with the interface that the customer sees – the **Main** form. First, let's place a new command button on the form."

Adding the I'll Take It Command Button

"We'll caption this new button I'll Take It. When the customer clicks it, it will print his or her sales quotation. This command button will be invisible until the customer has calculated their price quotation. When they do that, the I'll Take It button will spring into view, giving them the option to accept the quotation and print it off."

I handed out another exercise for the class to complete:

Exercise - Adding the (invisible) I'll Take It Button

In this exercise, you'll place a new command button called **cmdIllTakeIt** on the **Main** form of the China Shop project:

1. Using the Project Explorer window, select **frmMain**.
2. Place a new command button on the form, change its **Name** property to **cmdIllTakeIt**, its **Caption** property to I'll Take It, and its **Visible** property to **False**. Position the command button roughly according to the screenshot:

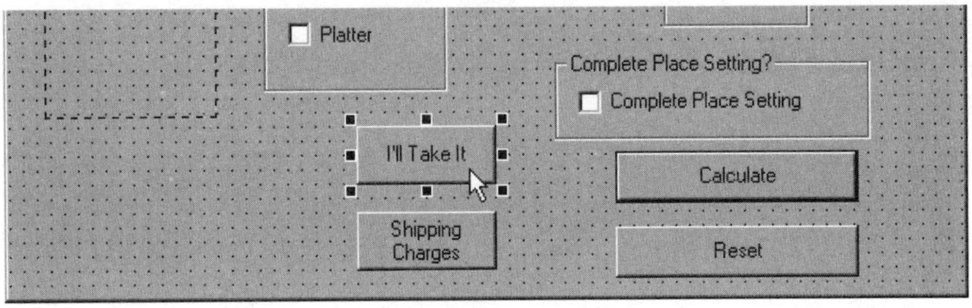

3. Save the China Shop project.

Discussion

"I'm beginning to see where we're going with this," Ward said. "When the customer clicks on the Calculate button, we'll make the I'll Take It command button visible. If the customer decides to purchase the china, they click on the button, and we'll print a sales quotation for them."

"Right on the mark, Ward," I said.

"Why are we making the I'll Take It button invisible?" Mary asked.

"Just to avoid confusion," I answered. "We don't want the button visible until a price is displayed. Let's add the code that makes the new button visible now."

Making the I'll Take It Button visible

"To make the new button visible, we need to add some code to the **cmdCalculate** command button," I explained. "Here's the exercise with that code:"

Exercise - Modifying cmdCalculate to Display the I'll Take It Button

In this exercise, you'll modify the code in the **Click** event procedure of **cmdCalculate** to display the I'll take It button:

1. Continue working with **frmMain** of the China Shop project.
2. Modify the code in the **Click** event procedure of **cmdCalculate** so that it looks like this (modified code is highlighted, omitted code is replaced by an ellipsis):

```
Private Sub cmdCalculate_Click()

Dim curTotalPrice As Currency

'Has the customer selected a brand of china?
If lstBrands.Text = "" Then
 MsgBox "You must select a China brand"
 Exit Sub
End If

...

'If the price is greater than 0, display the price and
'make the label visible
If curTotalPrice > 0 Then
 lblPrice.Caption = "The price of your order is " &
    ↳Format(curTotalPrice, "$##,###.00")
 lblPrice.Visible = True
 cmdIllTakeIt.Visible = True
End If

End Sub
```

3. Save the China Shop project.

4. If you wish, you can run the program now, make a selection of china and then click on the Calculate button – the I'll Take It button should become visible. However, clicking on it will do nothing for the moment – we haven't written that code yet.

Discussion

"As you can see," I said, "there's just a single line of new code in this event procedure: it sets the `Visible` property of the `cmdIllTakeIt` command button to `True` if a valid price has been calculated:"

```
cmdIllTakeIt.Visible = True
```

"Not surprisingly," I continued, "now that we've written code to make the I'll Take It command button visible, we now need to write code to make it *invisible* again when the customer clicks on the Reset button."

I distributed a further exercise:

Exercise – Modifying cmdReset to Hide the I'll Take It Button

In this exercise, you'll modify the code in the `Click` event procedure of `cmdReset` to make the I'll Take It command button invisible.

1. Continue working with `frmMain` of the China Shop project.

2. Modify the code in the `Click` event procedure of `cmdReset` as follows (modified code is highlighted, and an ellipsis replaces the omitted code in the familiar fashion):

```
Private Sub cmdReset_Click()

Dim chkobject As CheckBox
Dim optobject As OptionButton

...

chkCompletePlaceSetting.Value = 0
lblPrice.Visible = False
imgChina.Picture = LoadPicture()
```

```
lstBrands.ListIndex = -1

cmdIllTakeIt.Visible = False

End Sub
```

3. Save the China Shop project.

4. If you want, you can try running the program now: make a selection of china, and then click on the Calculate button – the I'll Take It command button should become visible. Now click on the Reset command button – the I'll Take It command button should disappear.

Discussion

"Again," I said, "this exercise involved adding just a single line of code to the event procedure – this time to make the I'll Take It command button invisible."

"Is it time to write the code to print the sales quotation?" Kate asked in anticipation.

"Yes, Kate," I said smiling. "Let's do that now."

Printing the Price Quotation

I then handed out the final exercise of the day:

Exercise - Creating the Code to Print the Price Quotation

In this exercise, you'll add the code to the `Click` event procedure of `cmdIllTakeIt` button. This code uses the ActiveX component supplied by Microsoft Word to print the price quotation.

1. Continue working with `frmMain`.

2. Key the following code into `cmdIlltakeIt`'s `Click` event procedure:

> **If you have any trouble keying this code block, you can find a text file that contains it on the CD. Look for `Print the Price.txt` file in the `For Chapter 08\China Shop Code` folder.**

```
Private Sub cmdIllTakeIt_Click()

Dim objDish As Dish
Dim wdApp As Word.Application
Dim wdDoc As Word.Document
Dim strCaptionSave As String
Dim strColorSave As Long

strCaptionSave = lblPrice.Caption
strColorSave = lblPrice.BackColor

lblPrice.Caption = "Printing sales quotation now..."
lblPrice.BackColor = vbRed

Set wdApp = New Word.Application
Set wdDoc = wdApp.Documents.Add

With wdApp
.Visible = True
.Selection.ParagraphFormat.TabStops.ClearAll
.ActiveDocument.DefaultTabStop = InchesToPoints(1)
.Selection.InsertDateTime DateTimeFormat:=
   ➥"dddd, MMMM dd, yyyy", InsertAsField:=True
.Selection.TypeParagraph
.Selection.TypeParagraph
.Selection.TypeText Text:="Dear Sir or Madam:"
.Selection.TypeParagraph
.Selection.TypeParagraph
.Selection.TypeText Text:=
   ➥"This is to confirm your order of the following "
.Selection.Font.Bold = wdToggle  'Bold on
.Selection.TypeText Text:=lstBrands.Text
.Selection.Font.Bold = wdToggle  'Bold off
.Selection.TypeText Text:=" items:"
.Selection.TypeParagraph
.Selection.TypeParagraph

.Selection.Font.Bold = wdToggle  'Bold on
.Selection.TypeText Text:="Item"
.Selection.Font.Bold = wdToggle  'Bold off
.Selection.TypeText Text:=vbTab
.Selection.Font.Bold = wdToggle  'Bold on
```

```
.Selection.TypeText Text:="Quantity"
.Selection.Font.Bold = wdToggle 'Bold off
.Selection.TypeText Text:=vbTab
.Selection.Font.Bold = wdToggle 'Bold on
.Selection.TypeText Text:="Unit Price"
.Selection.Font.Bold = wdToggle 'Bold off
.Selection.TypeText Text:=vbTab
.Selection.Font.Bold = wdToggle 'Bold on
.Selection.TypeText Text:="Total Price"
.Selection.Font.Bold = wdToggle 'Bold off
.Selection.TypeText Text:=vbTab
.Selection.TypeParagraph
.Selection.TypeParagraph

'Loop through the items in the Order Collecton
For Each objDish In m_objOrder
 .Selection.TypeText Text:=objDish.Item
 .Selection.TypeText Text:=vbTab
 .Selection.TypeText Text:=Str(objDish.Quantity)
 .Selection.TypeText Text:=vbTab
 .Selection.TypeText Text:="$"
 .Selection.TypeText Text:=Str(objDish.Price)
 .Selection.TypeText Text:=vbTab
 .Selection.TypeText Text:="$"
 .Selection.TypeText Text:=Str(objDish.Quantity * objDish.Price)
 .Selection.TypeParagraph
Next

.Selection.TypeText Text:=String(80, "-")

.Selection.TypeParagraph
.Selection.TypeText Text:=vbTab & vbTab & vbTab & "$" &
   ↳m_objOrder.TotalPrice(lstBrands.Text, frmMain.Quantity, False)

.Selection.TypeParagraph
.Selection.TypeParagraph
.Selection.TypeText Text:="The total price of your sales quotation is "
.Selection.Font.Bold = wdToggle 'Bold on
.Selection.TypeText Text:="$"
.Selection.TypeText Text:=
   ↳Str(m_objOrder.TotalPrice(lstBrands.Text,
   ↳frmMain.Quantity, False))
```

```
.Selection.Font.Bold = wdToggle 'Bold off
.Selection.TypeText Text:="."

If m_objOrder.Discount = True Then
 .Selection.TypeText Text:="(This price includes a
   ➥Complete Place Setting Discount.)"
End If

.Selection.TypeParagraph
.Selection.TypeParagraph
.Selection.TypeText Text:="Thank you for your business!"
.Selection.TypeParagraph
.Selection.TypeParagraph
.Selection.TypeParagraph
.Selection.Font.Name = "Script"
.Selection.Font.Size = 22
.Selection.TypeText Text:="Joe Bullina"

'Print the sales quotation
'.Application.PrintOut FileName:="", Range:=wdPrintAllDocument,
   ➥Item:= wdPrintDocumentContent, Copies:=1, Pages:="",
   ➥PageType:=wdPrintAllPages, Collate:=True,
   ➥Background:=False, PrintToFile:=False
 '.ActiveWindow.Close savechanges:=False
End With

'wdApp.Application.Quit

Set objDish = Nothing
'Set wdDoc = Nothing
'Set wdApp = Nothing

lblPrice.Caption = strCaptionSave
lblPrice.BackColor = strColorSave

End Sub
```

3. Save the China Shop project.

4. Run the program now, and select the Mikasa brand of china. Select, as items, the Plate, Butter Plate and Soup Bowl, and specify a quantity of 2. Now click on the Calculate button. The price displayed should be $90, and the I'll Take It command button should become visible. Click on the I'll Take It button. You should see Word start up, and display a sales quotation that looks like this screenshot:

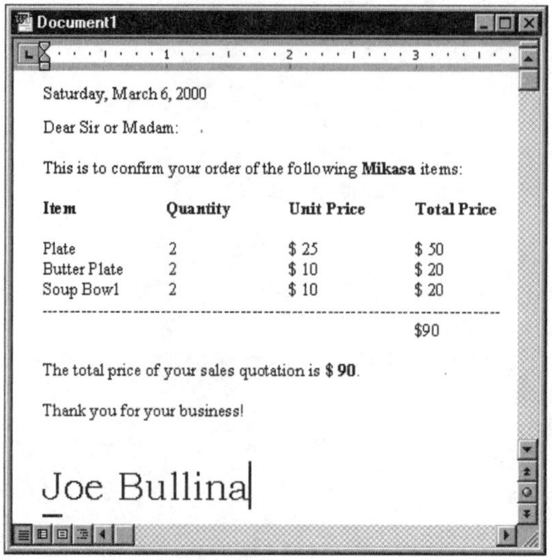

Saturday, March 6, 2000

Dear Sir or Madam:

This is to confirm your order of the following **Mikasa** items:

Item	Quantity	Unit Price	Total Price
Plate	2	$ 25	$ 50
Butter Plate	2	$ 10	$ 20
Soup Bowl	2	$ 10	$ 20
			$90

The total price of your sales quotation is **$ 90**.

Thank you for your business!

Joe Bullina

5. For now, manually close Word.

6. Click on the Reset button – your selections should be reset, and the I'll Take It command button should disappear.

7. Now select Faberware as the brand and click on the Complete Place Setting check box. All of the china items should be selected for you.

8. Click on the Platter as well, and select a Quantity of 2. Click on the Calculate button, and a price of $55 should be displayed. Click on the I'll Take It command button. Word should start up, and display a sales quotation like this:

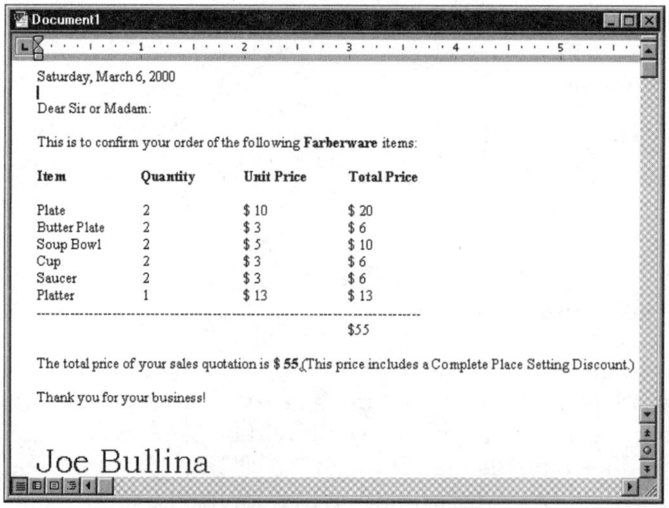

Saturday, March 6, 2000

Dear Sir or Madam:

This is to confirm your order of the following **Farberware** items:

Item	Quantity	Unit Price	Total Price
Plate	2	$ 10	$ 20
Butter Plate	2	$ 3	$ 6
Soup Bowl	2	$ 5	$ 10
Cup	2	$ 3	$ 6
Saucer	2	$ 3	$ 6
Platter	1	$ 13	$ 13
			$55

The total price of your sales quotation is **$ 55**.(This price includes a Complete Place Setting Discount.)

Thank you for your business!

Joe Bullina

9. If you're content that the program is working properly, and you'd like to print the sales quotation, remove the comment characters from the code, and either delete the line of code that sets the `Visible` property of the Word application to `True`, or comment it out. Then run the program again, and print your sales quotation. Congratulations! The China Shop program modifications are complete.

> **If you're running this code against Word 2000 you should leave the `Visible = True` commented out to avoid an error message.**

Discussion

The classroom was a hive of activity. The printer was whirring steadily as people printed off sample sales quotations. There were a few glitches, of course, but it seemed like as many of the students were helping each other out with their problems as were seeking my help. I could see that this aspect of the program had really caught their imaginations. Ward was already experimenting with different fonts for Joe Bullina's name, and Rhonda was trying some alternative layouts. I urged them to keep their copies of the original project, and save any modified versions under different names.

"Wow, this is so cool!" Rhonda declared. "Admittedly, the structure of the code for the Word ActiveX component is very lengthy and quite complicated, but since I know a fair amount about Word, there's still something intuitive about it: almost everything you change has an immediate effect on the output you get on the screen."

"Very true, Rhonda," I replied. "With a working chunk of code like this, you usually find that you can twiddle around with the various property calls and soon get a good grip on how they work. You'll find this code similar to the code we used in the Student Grades demo project," I said.

> **For a full reference guide to the Word objects, methods, and properties that are exposed via the ActiveX components, we recommend that you refer to Wrox Press's *Word 2000 VBA Programmer's Reference* (ISBN = 1-861002-55-6). For Excel, we recommend the same company's *Excel 2000 VBA Programmer's Reference* (ISBN = 1-861002-54-8). These books have comprehensive coverage of Word and Excel's object models, showing you in detail all the facilities that you can use in Word and Excel by using project references and dot notation in your Visual Basic programs.**

"Did you write this code from scratch?" Rhonda asked, "or record a macro?"

"I recorded a macro to build the basic portion of the document," I said, "and then modified it – just like we did with the Student Grades demo project."

"Couldn't we have done that, too?" asked Ward.

"Sure, we could've, Ward," I assured him, "but a downside to what the Word Macro Recorder does, is that it slavishly copies *every one* of your actions whilst recording the macro – even if those changes don't have a permanent effect on the document."

"How do you mean?" asked Ward.

"Well, if you write something and then delete it while recording the macro," I said, "the Macro Recorder will record the entire sequence of steps to first write and then delete the text in the VBA code it generates for you. It's not very intelligent about thing like that."

Melissa cheered: "Hurray! One up for the humans!"

"That's right, Melissa," I told her, smiling. "There's hope for we Visual Basic programmers yet! The reality is that if we'd all recorded our own macros, we'd almost certainly have ended up with dozens of different pieces of Visual Basic code, all of which printed the same report, but went about it slightly differently. They wouldn't have been very easy to summarize."

"So, why don't you sum up your code for us?" Kevin suggested.

"That's a good idea," I told him, shutting the blind to stop the early afternoon sunlight from shining on the monitor screens. "Time's getting on, and I get the impression you're all eager to go away and start playing with ActiveX components."

"So, what's the code doing?" Rhonda asked. "Explain it to me, so I can play more imaginatively."

"Well, the first thing we do," I said, "is declare all of the variables we'll be using in the event procedure. The first variable, `objDish`, is an object variable that we'll be using in a `For ...Each` statement later to loop through the `Dish` objects in the `Order` collection:"

```
Dim objDish As Dish
```

"The next two declarations are the object variables for the Word `Application` and `Document` objects:"

```
Dim wdApp As Word.Application
Dim wdDoc As Word.Document
```

"I don't know if you noticed," I said, "but after I clicked on the I'll Take It command button, and when the sales quotation was being printed, we displayed a message in red using the **Caption** property of the label **lblPrice**, indicating that the customer's sales quotation was now being printed."

"That's a nice touch," Melissa observed.

"It's always a good idea to let the user of your program know what's going on," I said. "Since we changed both the **Caption** and the **BackColor** property of the label control, we need a way to change those properties back to their original values, and so for that reason, we declared two variables to save their original values in:"

```
Dim strCaptionSave As String
Dim strColorSave As Long
```

"These two lines of code save the original values of **Caption** and **Backcolor** of **lblPrice**, so that they can be reset when we've finished..."

```
strCaptionSave = lblPrice.Caption
strColorSave = lblPrice.BackColor
```

"...and these two lines display the message to the user:"

```
lblPrice.Caption = "Printing sales quotation now..."
lblPrice.BackColor = vbRed
```

"The next two lines of code," I continued, "instantiate the Word **Application** object, followed by the Word **Document** object:"

```
Set wdApp = New Word.Application
Set wdDoc = wdApp.Documents.Add
```

"This next section," I said, "we've seen before. All we're doing is setting the **Visible** property of the **Application** object to **True**..."

```
With wdApp
.Visible = True
```

"...clearing the current tab stops, and then setting tab stops one inch apart:"

```
.Selection.ParagraphFormat.TabStops.ClearAll
.ActiveDocument.DefaultTabStop = InchesToPoints(1)
```

"Now, this line of code inserts the current date and time into the document..."

```
.Selection.InsertDateTime DateTimeFormat:="dddd, MMMM dd, yyyy",
   ↳InsertAsField:=True
```

"...followed by this section which inserts the salutation to the customer into the document..."

```
.Selection.TypeParagraph
.Selection.TypeParagraph
.Selection.TypeText Text:="Dear Sir or Madam:"
.Selection.TypeParagraph
.Selection.TypeParagraph
.Selection.TypeText Text:="This is to confirm your order of the
following "
```

"This next line of code," I said, "toggles the **`Bold`** attribute **`on`**..."

```
.Selection.Font.Bold = wdToggle 'Bold on
```

"...and then we insert the brand of china, using the **`Text`** property of the **`lstBrands`** list box to confirm the brand of china ordered by the customer..."

```
.Selection.TypeText Text:=lstBrands.Text
.Selection.Font.Bold = wdToggle 'Bold off
.Selection.TypeText Text:=" items:"
.Selection.TypeParagraph
.Selection.TypeParagraph
```

"The next sections insert the headings for item – the china piece itself..."

```
.Selection.Font.Bold = wdToggle 'Bold on
.Selection.TypeText Text:="Item"
.Selection.Font.Bold = wdToggle 'Bold off
.Selection.TypeText Text:=vbTab
```

"...quantity..."

```
.Selection.Font.Bold = wdToggle 'Bold on
.Selection.TypeText Text:="Quantity"
.Selection.Font.Bold = wdToggle 'Bold off
.Selection.TypeText Text:=vbTab
```

"...price..."

```
.Selection.Font.Bold = wdToggle  'Bold on
.Selection.TypeText Text:="Unit Price"
.Selection.Font.Bold = wdToggle  'Bold off
.Selection.TypeText Text:=vbTab
```

"...and total price:"

```
.Selection.Font.Bold = wdToggle  'Bold on
.Selection.TypeText Text:="Total Price"
.Selection.Font.Bold = wdToggle  'Bold off
.Selection.TypeText Text:=vbTab
.Selection.TypeParagraph
.Selection.TypeParagraph
```

"This next section of code," I said, "is the crucial section in this event procedure. We use a `For...Each` statement to loop through each `Dish` Item in the `Order` collection object:"

```
For Each objDish In m_objOrder
```

"Each loop returns a reference that we then use to assign to the `Text` argument of the `Selection` object's `TypeText` property:"

```
  .Selection.TypeText Text:=objDish.Item
  .Selection.TypeText Text:=vbTab
  .Selection.TypeText Text:=Str(objDish.Quantity)
  .Selection.TypeText Text:=vbTab
  .Selection.TypeText Text:="$"
  .Selection.TypeText Text:=Str(objDish.Price)
  .Selection.TypeText Text:=vbTab
  .Selection.TypeText Text:="$"
  .Selection.TypeText Text:=Str(objDish.Quantity * objDish.Price)
  .Selection.TypeParagraph
Next
```

"We then print our string of dashes:"

```
.Selection.TypeText Text:=String(80, "-")
```

"This next section," I said, "executes the modified `TotalPrice` method, passing it three arguments – the brand of china, the quantity selected by the customer, and a value of `False` for the `blnMessage` argument – we don't want a message box displayed while the sales quotation is being printed:"

```
.Selection.TypeParagraph
.Selection.TypeText Text:=vbTab & vbTab & vbTab & "$" &
   ↳m_objOrder.TotalPrice(lstBrands.Text, frmMain.Quantity, False)
```

"We then display a nicely formatted summary, once again executing the **`TotalPrice`** method of the **`Order`** object..."

```
.Selection.TypeParagraph
.Selection.TypeParagraph
.Selection.TypeText Text:="The total price of your sales quotation is "
.Selection.Font.Bold = wdToggle  'Bold on
.Selection.TypeText Text:="$"
.Selection.TypeText Text:=
   ↳Str(m_objOrder.TotalPrice(lstBrands.Text,
   ↳frmMain.Quantity, False))
.Selection.Font.Bold = wdToggle  'Bold off
.Selection.TypeText Text:="."
```

"Some of you," I continued, "may have been wondering when we would use the **`Discount`** property of the **`Order`** object we created earlier. Here it is – we use it in an **`If`** statement to determine if we should tell the customer that the quoted price reflects a price discount:"

```
If m_objOrder.Discount = True Then
 .Selection.TypeText Text:="(This price includes a
   ↳Complete Place Setting Discount.)"
End If
```

"We then thank the customer for their business, and sign Joe Bullina's name using a 22-point Script font:"

```
.Selection.TypeParagraph
.Selection.TypeParagraph
.Selection.TypeText Text:="Thank you for your business!"
.Selection.TypeParagraph
.Selection.TypeParagraph
.Selection.TypeParagraph
.Selection.Font.Name = "Script"
.Selection.Font.Size = 22
.Selection.TypeText Text:="Joe Bullina"
```

"Now its time to print the sales quotation using the **Application** object's **PrintOut** method:"

```
'Print the sales quotation
'.Application.PrintOut FileName:="", Range:=wdPrintAllDocument,
   ↳Item:= wdPrintDocumentContent, Copies:=1, Pages:="",
   ↳PageType:=wdPrintAllPages, Collate:=True,
   ↳Background:=False, PrintToFile:=False
 .ActiveWindow.Close savechanges:=False
```

"Then we close the active window, and specify a value of **False** for **Savechanges**:"

```
.ActiveWindow.Close savechanges:=False
End With
```

"Next, we close the Word application itself..."

```
wdApp.Application.Quit
```

"...and set all of our object variables to **Nothing**:"

```
Set objDish = Nothing
Set wdDoc = Nothing
Set wdApp = Nothing
```

"Finally," I said, "it's time to restore the values of the **Caption** and **BackColor** properties of **lblPrice**:"

```
lblPrice.Caption = strCaptionSave
lblPrice.BackColor = strColorSave
```

"Absolutely fantastic," Ward said, "If a knowledge of using ActiveX components in a Visual Basic program doesn't get me promoted to senior Visual Basic programmer at work, nothing will!"

"You had indicated at the end of the exercise," Rhonda said, "that the China Shop program is now completed. Is that true? When will we be delivering the program to Joe?"

"We'll do that two weeks from today," I answered. "Even though the China Shop program is done, we still have some more to learn. Next week, I'll show you how to create your own ActiveX components based on the objects you've created for the China Shop. And guess what? You'll not only be able to use them within a Visual Basic program, but within Word and Excel as well!"

"I truly cannot wait!" Rhonda told me, saving her China Shop project onto a floppy disc and slipping it into her handbag. I could see she was going to have a busy weekend with her ActiveX components.

With that, I dismissed class for the day, content in the knowledge that what they'd learned today would set them off on a voyage of discovery about how they could make use of components from other programs.

Chapter Summary

This week's lesson showed you the power of using ActiveX components. You've seen how to use the Macro Recorder and modify the VBA code that it outputs so you can apply it to your programming tasks. Now you're ready to build the objects from the China Shop into ActiveX components of your own.

Here's a quick rundown of today's work:

- We now have a clearly defined understanding of what an ActiveX component is
- You saw how to include the type libraries in your projects
- You used ActiveX components
- You got a taste of using the Word and Excel object libraries
- You used the Macro Recorders of Word and Excel, and saw both their power and their limitations

Most importantly, you made the following changes to the China Shop program:

- You added the necessary code to open Word from within the China Shop program and prepare a sales quotation
- You created a smart button on the China Shop main form that became visible only when we wanted it to
- You gave the program the ability to use the printer-control technology of Word to print out the sales quotation

You've object-oriented the China Shop program: well done!

In next week's lesson, we'll see how to create our own ActiveX components: this will show us the principles of exposing the objects, methods, and properties of our own programs to the greater world outside.

Learn to Program Objects with Visual Basic
Bullina's China

Chapter 9
Creating Your Own ActiveX Components

Last week, you saw how to use the objects that the Word and Excel applications make available for you in ActiveX components. In this lesson, you'll see how we can compile **our own** objects into ActiveX components. You'll also see that we can use them in other Visual Basic programs – and even within other Windows applications, like Microsoft Word or Excel. This will extend your knowledge of the interchangeability and sharing of functionality that's such an important part of the world of software development.

In this lesson's practical work, we won't be making any permanent changes to either the Student Grades demo or the China Shop program, but we will see how we can use objects from either of them in other applications.

In particular, today's lesson covers:

- What is an ActiveX component?
- Types of ActiveX component
- Compiling an ActiveX component

In particular, we'll be doing the following:

- Compiling the **Student** class from the Student Grades demo into ActiveX components
- Using the **Student** object's ActiveX components in a **Standard.EXE** project and in Excel
- Compiling the **Package** class from the China Shop project into an ActiveX component
- Using the ActiveX **Package** component inside a **Standard.EXE** project and in Excel

By doing all this, we'll see how we can use the architecture of our **`Student`** and **`Package`** objects in an entirely separate context from the original programs they were created for. Learning this will reinforce the power of objects and components being used in other programs, and show that you don't need to write every part of your own programs: if you can find the right component, you can just plug it in!

Have Objects, Will Travel

"In last week's class," I said, as I began our penultimate session on Visual Basic Objects, "we learned how to use objects from other Windows applications in our Visual Basic programs. These objects were revealed to us in the form of ActiveX components, ActiveX being a standardized technology that lets us share the functionality of other people's programs – and vice-versa. You'll recall that it's also possible to package the objects we create into ActiveX components of our own. That way, not only can other Visual Basic programs employ our objects, but other Windows applications such as Word and Excel can use them, too."

"What do we need to do to make our objects available like this?" Chuck asked. "I take it you're not talking about simply making a class module available to another application?"

"No, Chuck, I'm not," I said. "We discussed last week the potential problems of making a class module available to other programmers: it's an open invitation for them to modify it. Plus, if something about the object needs to be changed, it's up to us to ensure the updated class module gets delivered to everyone using the old one. It's so much easier to compile our class modules into an ActiveX component, and then make that component available to anyone who needs it."

"So, do we make an object library, like the ones we used last week?" suggested Valerie.

"No, our own Visual Basic ActiveX components aren't packaged in an object library like they are with Word and Excel," I replied. "Instead, they're compiled into a file – either an **`ActiveX.DLL`** file, or an **`ActiveX.EXE`** file."

"Are those the only two types of ActiveX components?" Blaine asked.

"Good question, Blaine," I said. "In Visual Basic, you can actually create **four** types of ActiveX components."

I showed them on the screen:

ActiveX DLL

ActiveX EXE

ActiveX Documents

ActiveX Controls

"However," I said, "in this course, we'll only be learning how to create `ActiveX.DLL`s and `ActiveX.EXE`s. ActiveX documents will be covered in a new course the University will be running shortly called **Visual Basic Web Programming**. ActiveX **controls** also require a separate course of their own to do them justice."

"When you say that `ActiveX.DLL`s and `ActiveX.EXE`s are **compiled**," Bob asked, "do you mean the same type of compilation that's performed on a `Standard.EXE` project when we compile it into a stand-alone executable file?"

"Well, the process is the same," I replied. "When it's compiled, our VB code is turned into binary code that can be run on any PC (and therefore doesn't need the Visual Basic IDE to be able to run it) – but the aim is different. When you compile a `Standard.EXE` project, you're creating a complete, 'runnable' application for a user that does the whole job for them."

"Whereas a programmer can exploit both `ActiveX.DLL`s and `ActiveX.EXE`s in building their own applications," Melissa observed.

"Absolutely," I said. "These types of components are separate, autonomous chunks of functionality that you can combine in different ways to assemble different applications. That's their great strength."

"I've heard the terms **in-process** and **out-of-process** when people talk about ActiveX components," Mary said. "Are those terms relevant to what we're going to be doing here today?"

Out-Of-Process and In-Process Components

"Yes, they are," I assured her. "In Windows, programs are allocated space in the computer's memory in which to run. This dedicated space is known as a **process**. As you know, other programs – called **clients** – utilize the objects (and therefore the functionality) that the ActiveX component exposes – the question is, where do these ActiveX components execute in memory? Do they execute in the process space of the client program that's using them, or in their own process space? As it turns out, Visual Basic allows you to compile an ActiveX component that operates either way. `ActiveX.DLL` components execute in the client's program's process – or memory space – and are therefore known as **in-process components**. In contrast, `ActiveX.EXE` components execute in their own process, separate from their client's process, and are known as **out-of-process components**."

"It sounds to me," Dave said, "like those are fundamental differences. Is one type of component more efficient than the other?"

"You've raised an excellent question, Dave," I said. "When a client program employs an ActiveX component, it uses it to create new instances of the objects that it exposes. The client therefore needs to communicate with the component during the course of its execution. A client program that uses an `ActiveX.EXE` component communicates with the component using something called **cross-process** or **out-of-process** communication – also known as **marshalling**. In this situation, the client program needs to be constantly communicating between two different processes – obviously a performance overhead. On the other hand, if the ActiveX component is in the same process as the program using it – in other words, the client's using an `ActiveX.DLL` component – then communication between the two of them does not need to cross process boundaries – this is called **in-process** communication."

"It sounds like cross-process communication isn't as efficient as in-process communication," Kate said.

"You're right, Kate," I said. "In-process communication is a bit like opening your refrigerator and taking out a ready-made sandwich. Out-of-process communication is like finding the refrigerator bare and having to make a trip to the grocery store down the road to purchase a loaf. With an `ActiveX.DLL`, communication between the client and the component is done within the same process – so it's faster. This means that objects are created more quickly, and that the code behind properties and methods are accessed sooner."

"So `ActiveX.DLL`'s are the way to go," Valerie said. "Why would you ever create an `ActiveX.EXE`?"

"There can be a disadvantage in using **`ActiveX.DLL`** components," I replied. "In addition to using the client's process space, **`ActiveX.DLL`**'s also use the client's **thread of execution**, which can lead to bottlenecks. **`ActiveX.EXE`**'s utilize their **own** thread of execution."

"I thought I was doing OK with this discussion until now," Rhonda said. "What's a thread of execution?"

"I'll simplify this a little bit," I said. "When a program executes under Windows, each program gets its own thread of execution – remember our discussion about multitasking from the Intro course? A thread of execution is very much like a lane on a highway. In order to execute an instruction, the line of code is placed on the program's thread, and Windows takes over and executes it. Ordinarily, one program is not aware of another program's thread of execution: nor does it need to be – each program acts autonomously, has it's own dedicated lane to drive along, and, in theory anyway, neither one can block the other."

"So far so good," Rhonda answered.

"Here's where we run into a problem with **`ActiveX.DLL`**s," I said. "**`ActiveX.EXE`**s run in their own process, and because of that, they get to use their own thread of execution. The client program and the **`ActiveX.EXE`** are executing their instructions in their own threads. However, because an **`ActiveX.DLL`** runs in the same process as the client program, it also uses the client program's thread of execution. The client program and the **`ActiveX.DLL`** are both in the same lane on the highway."

"Is that a big deal?" Bob asked.

"It can be," I said. "For instance, let's say that the client program executes a method of one of the objects in the ActiveX component. If that object is running in-process – in other words, it's an **`ActiveX.DLL`** – the client program's thread of execution will be used to execute the code in the method. So while the method is being executed, no other program instructions in the client program can be executed. For a method that takes a long time to finish, this can be a significant performance problem."

"I see," Dave said. "So there are advantages and disadvantages with the two types of ActiveX components."

"That's exactly right, Dave," I said. "Out-of-process ActiveX components execute in a separate process which causes marshalling to occur and can slow down performance. But on the other hand, **`ActiveX.EXE`**'s are executed using their own thread of execution, which allows the client program to continue executing while the ActiveX component goes about its business."

"That's what I thought," said Dave.

"And just to complicate the picture even more," I went on, "in some instances the ActiveX component may not even be on the same PC as the client program using it – perhaps not even in the same country – so the marshalling has to occur across one or more networks!"

"So what's the bottom line?" Dorothy asked. "Should we use the in-process or out-of-process option?"

"The Microsoft recommendation is to go with an in-process component – an **ActiveX.DLL** – unless there's an overwhelming reason to do otherwise," I said. "Unless you have really time-consuming methods, an in-process component should produce the faster program."

More on the Student Demo

"OK," I said, "Why don't we take the **Student** class module from the Student Grades demo project that we've built over the last few weeks, and compile it into an ActiveX component? Let's start by compiling it into an **ActiveX.DLL**, and then into an **ActiveX.EXE**. We'll compare the speeds of each type of component within a Visual Basic project, and then use one of them in Word or Excel."

"Sounds great to me," Peter said. "What do we need to do first?"

"First," I said, "we create a new Visual Basic project – but instead of selecting a new **Standard.EXE** project, as we're used to doing, we'll specify a Visual Basic **ActiveX.DLL** project instead."

I started up Visual Basic, and when the New Project window appeared, I double-clicked on the icon for an ActiveX DLL:

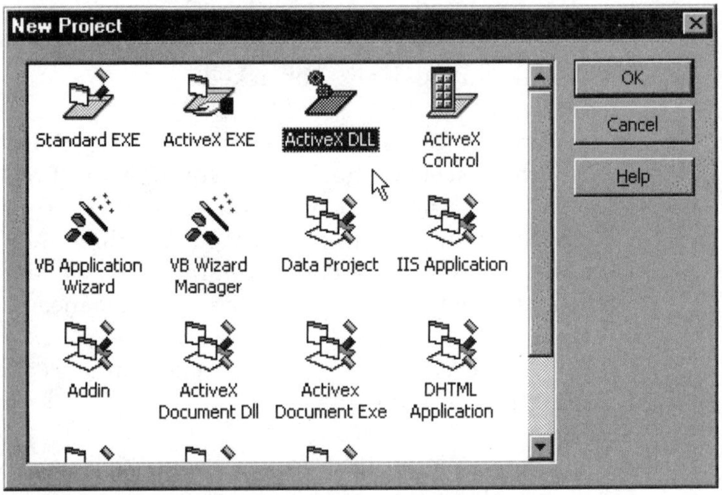

An empty class module appeared in the Visual Basic IDE.

> **!** **If you're using the Working Model Edition of Visual Basic (supplied with the *Learn to Program with Visual Basic 6* book) you won't have all of these options on your screen. But don't worry, you can download and install the components we create in this chapter from our web site – we'll point you towards them as we go through the chapter.**

"Although both `ActiveX.DLL`s and `ActiveX.EXE`s can have forms," I said, "by default, both types start up with just a single class module for us to type code into. What we'll do now is add the `Student` class module to this `ActiveX.DLL` project, and then we'll compile the project into a DLL."

"Before you get too far ahead of me," Rhonda said, "I have a question. I don't see the `ActiveX.DLL` project type in my New Project window. In fact, the only project type I see is the `Standard.EXE` type. Am I doing something wrong?"

"No, Rhonda," I answered, "The ability to create `ActiveX.DLL`s and `ActiveX.EXE`s is limited to the **Visual Basic Professional** or **Enterprise Editions**. My PC is the only one in the classroom running the Enterprise Edition – so I'll be the only one able to create these types of projects today. The student PCs here in the classroom are running the **Working Model Edition** – so although you were able to build class modules, you won't be able to compile them into an ActiveX component on your machines. I'll mail the completed programs to you as we finish them – that way, you can have a play around with them yourselves."

Turning back to the screen, I said: "We won't be needing this default class module. We already have the `Student` class module that we'll be including in this ActiveX component. Let's get rid of the default class module..."

I closed the empty class module that Visual Basic had created for me, brought up the project's Project Explorer window, selected the default `Class1` class module with my mouse, and then right-clicked on it. This was the result:

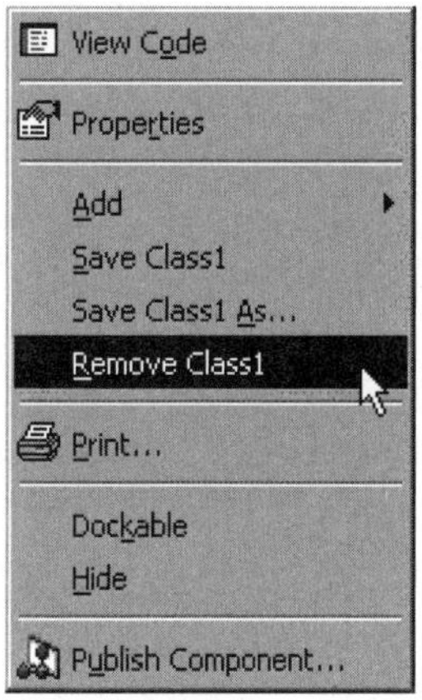

I clicked on Remove Class1. Visual basic prompted me with a message box asking me whether I wanted to save it. I opted for No, of course.

"Now that we've removed the default class module," I continued, "all we need to do is select Project | Add Class Module from the Visual Basic menu bar and, when the Add Class Module window appears, select the Existing tab…"

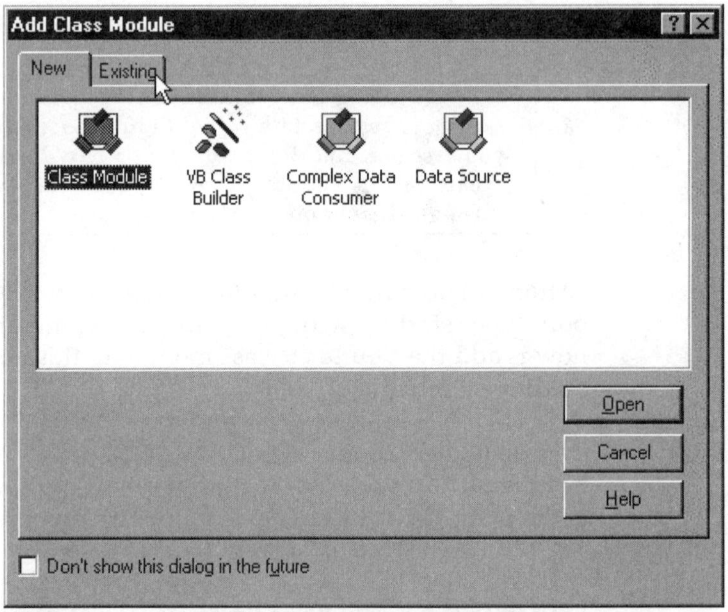

"Now," I continued, "we need to find the existing **Student** class module in the **\VBFiles\Practice** folder and include it in this **ActiveX.DLL** project by double-clicking on it:"

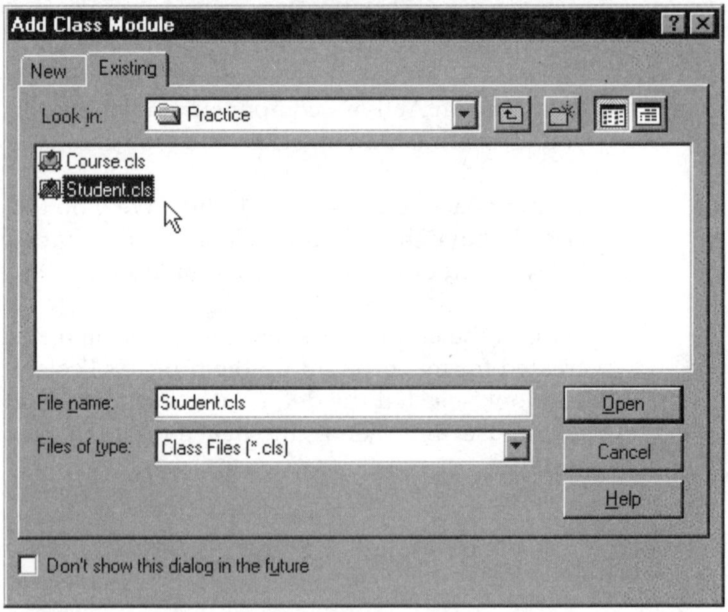

"Once we've done that," I said, "we should look in the Project Explorer window and ensure that the **Student** class module is included in the project. We should see just the **Student** class module, and nothing else..."

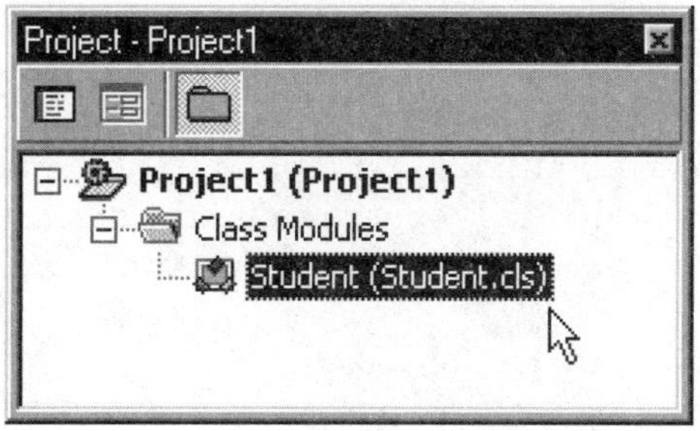

"Believe it or not," I said, "at this point, our **ActiveX.DLL** component is basically complete – we'd already done the hard work of creating the class module in the original Student Grades project."

"Are we ready to compile the component now?" Melissa asked.

"Not quite, Melissa," I said. "Before we compile the component, there's a property of the class module that we need to give some thought to – and it's a property that we didn't need to worry about at all when we were working with the class module from within a **Standard.EXE** project. What I'm talking about is the **Instancing** property."

The Instancing Property

"This property influences how the component that we're going to compile is allowed to create objects using the **Student** class."

To demonstrate, I used the Project Explorer window to select the **Student** class module in the **ActiveX.DLL** project that we had open. Then I right-clicked my mouse on it and brought up the Properties window for the **Student** class module:

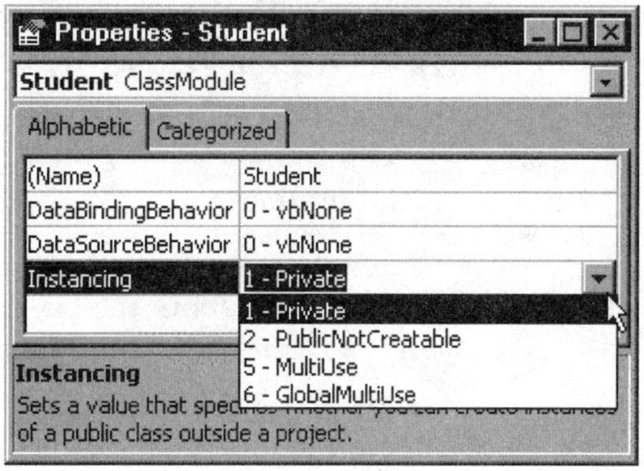

"As I said," I explained, " the **Instancing** property has something to do with the act of creating an instance of an **Student** object. In fact, the **Instancing** property of a class module determines the way that objects created from the class module in the component can be used."

"I don't remember seeing the **Instancing** property in the Properties windows of the class modules we built in the last few weeks," Kate said.

"You're right, Kate," I replied. "The **Instancing** property of the class module doesn't appear in the Properties window of class modules contained in **Standard.EXE** projects – only within **ActiveX.DLL** or **ActiveX.EXE** projects."

"Why's that?" Bob asked.

"By default," I replied, "the **Instancing** property of a class module within a **Standard.EXE** project is set to **Private** – so since there's only one choice for the property, Visual Basic doesn't bother to display the property in the Properties window."

"So, what exactly does **Private** mean in this context?" Valerie asked.

"**Private** means that no instances of the object defined in the class module can be created outside of the project containing the class module," I said.

"So that would mean that no **Dish** objects can be created outside of the China Shop project," Dave said, "since it's within the China Shop project that the **Dish** class module resides."

"That's it, Dave," I said. "And if you think about it, it makes perfect sense. After all, we don't want instances of the **Dish** object to be creatable outside of the project containing the **Dish** class module. ActiveX components are a different story, however. An ActiveX component is **meant** to share its objects with other programs, sometimes with several programs simultaneously. This means that we have a number of different possible values for the **Instancing** property of class modules contained in ActiveX projects. Here's a table of those possible values:"

Value	Explanation
1	**Private**. Other applications aren't allowed access to type library information about the class, and cannot create instances of it. Private objects are only for use within your component.
2	**PublicNotCreatable**. Other applications can use objects of this class only if your component creates the objects first. Other applications cannot use the **CreateObject** function or the **New** operator to create objects from the class.
3	**SingleUse**. Allows other applications to create objects from the class, but every object of this class that a client creates starts a new instance of your component. **Not allowed in ActiveX.DLL projects.**

Value	Explanation
4	`GlobalSingleUse`. Similar to `SingleUse`, except that properties and methods of the class can be invoked as if they were simply global functions. **Not allowed in `ActiveX.DLL` projects.**
5	`MultiUse`. Allows other applications to create objects from the class. One instance of your component can provide any number of objects created in this fashion.
6	`GlobalMultiUse`. Similar to `MultiUse`, with one addition: properties and methods of the class can be invoked as if they were simply global functions. It's not necessary to explicitly create an instance of the class first, because one will automatically be created.

"As you can see," I said, "there are six possible values for the `Instancing` property of class modules contained within an `ActiveX.DLL` or `ActiveX.EXE` project. Take note that `SingleUse` and `GlobalSingleUse` are **not** permitted for `ActiveX.DLL` projects."

"Can you explain these settings a little more for us, please?" asked Lou.

"Sure thing, Lou," I said.

Private

"Let's start with `Private`," I said. "This means that objects can be created from the class module only within the ActiveX component itself."

"Didn't you say a minute ago," Peter said, "that the idea behind ActiveX components is to share its objects with client programs? If you set the `Instancing` property of a class module within an ActiveX component to `Private`, aren't you defeating that purpose? Why would you choose `Private` anyway?"

"There are cases," I said, "where the designer of a component will want some objects in the component to be `Private` – that is, totally hidden from the client program using the component, but available to other objects within the component. For instance, I'm sure that there are objects within the Word or Excel object libraries that we cannot access – however, since they're `Private`, we have no way of knowing what they are!"

"That makes sense," Dorothy said. "Now what about `PublicNotCreatable`?"

PublicNotCreatable

"A class module with a **`PublicNotCreatable Instance`** property," I said, "tells the operating system that the methods and properties of the object are available to a client – but only if the ActiveX component creates the object first. An example of this kind of object is the Word **`Document`** object. We first had to execute the **`Add`** method of the **`Documents`** collection before accessing the properties and methods of the specific **`Document`** object."

"I can see reasons for that," Melissa said. "Would the **`Dish`** object be an example of this type of class module?"

"That's an excellent observation, Melissa," I said. "If we were to fully implement the China Shop objects in an ActiveX component, most likely we would set the **`Instancing`** property of **`Dish`** object to **`PublicNotCreatable`**, to ensure that when a **`Dish`** object was created it was only created by the **`Add`** method of the **`Order`** collection object."

"What about the **`SingleUse`** property?" Kevin asked.

SingleUse

"**`SingleUse`**," I said, "is only available for **`ActiveX.EXE`** components, which, as you'll recall, run in their own process. Every time a request is made to instantiate an object from a class module whose **`Instancing`** property is set to **`SingleUse`**, a new instance of the ActiveX component will be created."

"Wow," Tom said, "does that mean several instances of the same **`ActiveX.EXE`** may be running at the same time?"

"That's right, Tom," I said. "Each time a client program creates an object from a class whose **`Instancing`** property is set to **`SingleUse`** it will cause another instance of the **`ActiveX.EXE`** to be started."

"Is that a good idea?" asked Kathy, dubiously. "Why would you want to do that?"

"Rather than having one component providing services to many client programs at once," I explained, "each client program using a **`SingleUse`** object in a ActiveX component will be serviced by their very own copy of the component."

"Right," Ward said. "That's much more efficient from each program's point of view."

"But surely," said Dave, "wouldn't having several versions of your component running at the same time have a detrimental effect on the memory resources of your PC?"

"Very true, Dave," I replied. "I see you're really getting a feel for the design decisions that go into creating ActiveX components. There are many variables to consider – and, as is the case in other areas of Visual Basic, there may not be a 'universal best answer'. By the way, last week the Word application we created from within the China Shop program was defined with an **`Instancing`** property of **`SingleUse`** – if we'd declared another instance of the Word application from within our program, we would have started another instance of Word."

"I didn't realize that," Blaine said. "How is **`SingleUse`** different from **`GlobalSingleUse`**?"

GlobalSingleUse

"All of the global **`Instancing`** properties," I said, "let the client program refer to the properties and methods of the object created from this class module as if they are global functions."

"What does that mean?" Lou asked.

"Referring to a property or a method as if it's a global function," I answered, "means that you can reference the property or method without prefacing each one with the name of the object it belongs to. You've been using global functions throughout this *and* the Intro course. The Visual Basic functions – for instance, **`Left`** and **`Right`** – are global functions. That means that a class module declared with either of the two global **`Instancing`** properties will allow us to use its properties and methods in code as if they were part of the intrinsic Visual Basic command set. Provided, of course, we first set a reference to the ActiveX component."

"I'm still a little confused about this," Rhonda admitted. "Can you give us an example?"

"Yes, I can," I said. "If Microsoft had declared the Word **`Application`** object with a global **`Instancing`** property, it would have meant that last week, after setting a reference to the Word object library, we could have coded the methods and properties of the **`Application`** object without declaring an **`Application`** object variable first."

"It sounds like declaring a class module with a global **`Instancing`** attribute can really make coding much easier for a programmer," Ward said.

"It can," I said, "and many component designers declare their class modules using a global **`Instancing`** property for just that reason. But if you're going to do this, there's something you need to keep in mind: you have to name the properties and methods of your class module in such a way that they **do not** conflict with the names of any other global properties and methods."

"You'd need to know what the properties and methods are called, if you're going to be able to give your own functions unique names, though," Dorothy observed. "Can we find a list of them someplace?"

"You can check them by opening up the Object Browser," I answered, "and searching through the globals name space..."

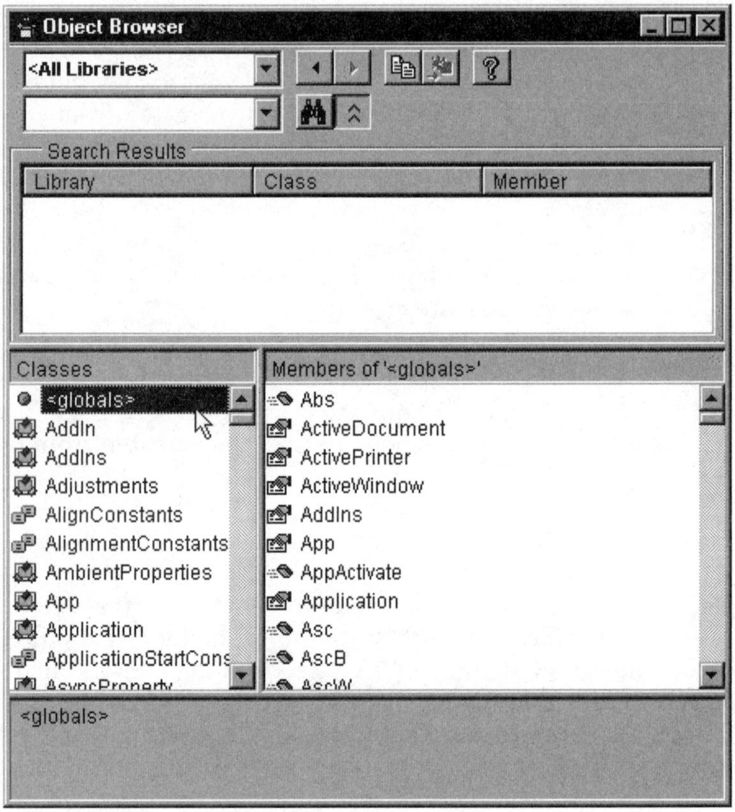

"What's the globals name space?" Kevin asked.

"Every Visual Basic project," I said, "has a globals name space that contains a list of objects and modules that don't first require a declaration before their properties and methods can be used within the project. Anything that has its name in that space can be referenced directly."

"The members of the globals name space look like the Visual Basic commands that we've been using all along," Rhonda said as she scrolled around the Members of <globals> window.

"That's right, Rhonda," I said, "many of them are. Commands like `InStr`, `Left` and `MsgBox` are all contained in the globals name space. The designers of Visual Basic didn't want to force programmers to create an instance of the underlying object before being able to use these commands. We can provide the same courtesy to the programmers using our ActiveX components by setting the `Instancing` property of the class modules to either `GlobalSingleUse` or `GlobalMultiUse`."

"This is beginning to make sense to me," Rhonda said. "Am I right in thinking that **MultiUse** means that only one instance of the ActiveX component will ever be running at a given time?"

GlobalMultiUse & MultiUse

"That's right, Rhonda," I said. "Only one copy of the component will exist, and it can be used by more than one application at a time – hence the name **MultiUse**. **GlobalMultiUse** means virtually the same thing – only one instance of the ActiveX component will ever run at once, plus the users of the component don't have to explicitly declare an object before being able to use its properties and methods – as long as they've included a reference to it's object library in their project, of course!"

"What kind of **Instancing** property will we be choosing for the **Student** class module of the demo project?" Dorothy asked.

"Let's start by choosing **MultiUse**," I said, and clicked on the **Instancing** box to see the drop-down list:

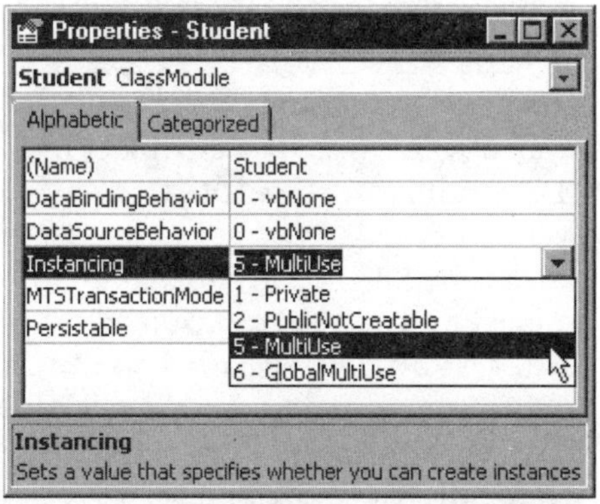

"Next we'll compile it and see how to use it in a Visual Basic project," I said. "But before we do that, let's give the project a name..."

I brought up the Project Explorer window once more, right-clicked on the project, and then clicked on the Project1 Properties... option in the resulting pop-up menu. This screen appeared:

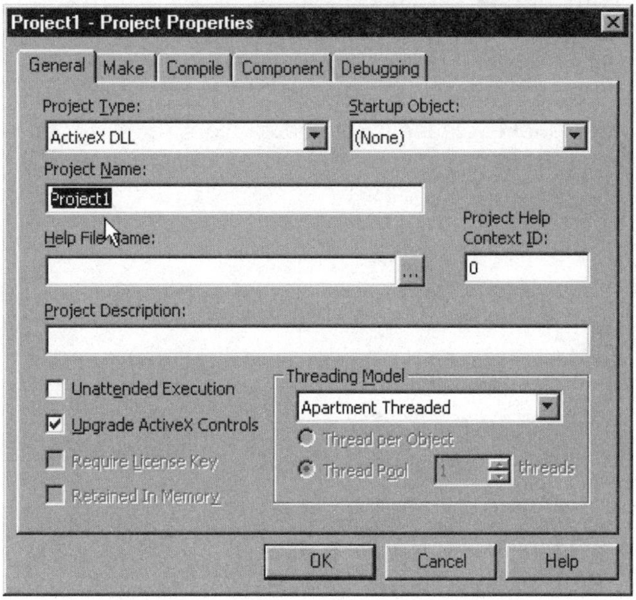

Selecting the Project Name box, I changed the name of the project from Project1 to AcademicSupport, and then clicked on OK.

The name listed in the Project Explorer window changed:

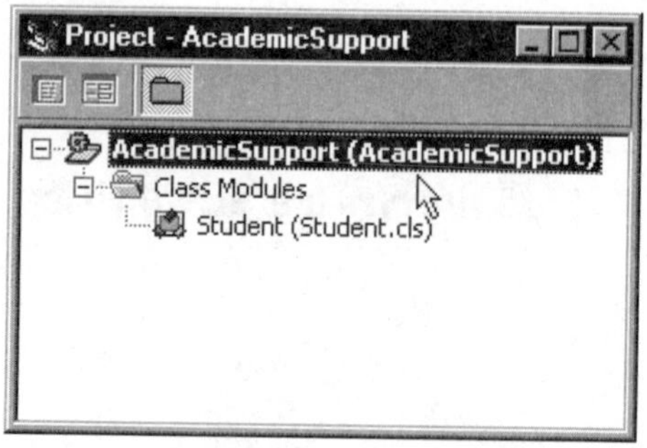

> **The name that you give your ActiveX project is very important, because that's the name you'll see listed in the References window when you go looking to add your component to a `Standard.EXE` project.**

"I also want to save our project in a separate folder within the **`Practice`** directory," I said. "Let's call it **`ActiveXDLL`**."

I used the File | Save Project menu options to save the project as **`AcademicSupport.vbp`** in a new folder called **`\VBFILES\Practice\ActiveXDLL`**. Then – **and this important** – I right-clicked on the **`Student`** class module in the Project Explorer and used the pop-up menu's Save Student.cls As... option to save the new copy of the class module in the new **`ActiveXDLL`** folder.

"Now I can compile our project," I said, as I selected File | Make AcademicSupport.dll from the Visual Basic menu bar:

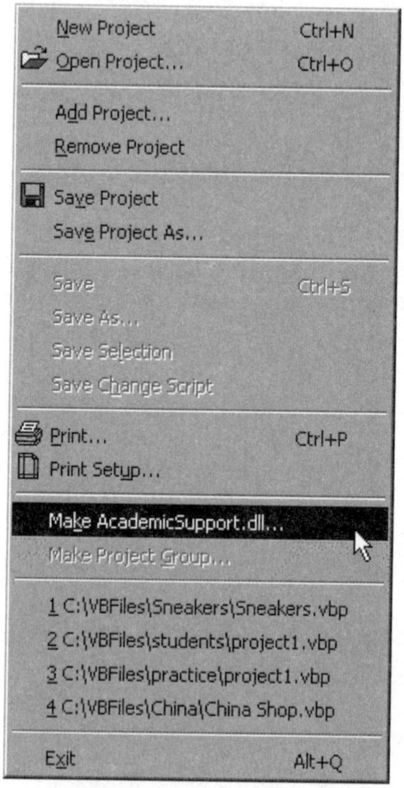

"Let's make sure that we save the compiled DLL into the **\VBFILES\Practice\ActiveXDLL** folder that we just created:"

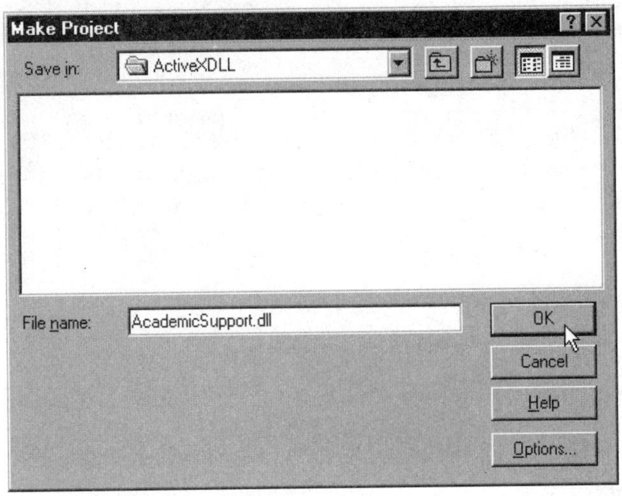

I clicked on the OK command button and after a few seconds the project had been compiled into a DLL.

"Is there any special place where the ActiveX component should be saved?" Dave asked. "Such as the **Windows** directory?"

"The compilation process will create a file with an extension of **.dll**," I said, "and that file can be saved anywhere on your hard drive. **However**..."

I put the following information point on the screen:

> **!** **When the ActiveX component is compiled, Visual Basic automatically adds an entry to the Windows Registry pointing to the corresponding `.dll` file on your hard drive. Without this, you won't be able to use it, because you can't make a reference to it in the References window. It's not so important to place the component in a particular location as it is to make sure that once you compile it into a `.dll` file, you don't move that file.**

> **You should make a backup copy of your Windows Registry periodically, just to ensure that all the entries on it are recoverable in the event of a disk failure or some other unforeseen problem. I covered backing up the Registry in Chapter 15 of *Learn to Program with Visual Basic 6.***

"The fact that the compilation process adds an entry to the Windows Registry is a very important thing to understand," I said, "and it's why I can't simply compile these components and mail them across to you. Even if I did, you still wouldn't be able to run them."

"So, do we just sit and watch?" Valerie asked.

"You'll be glad to know," I replied, "that although you haven't be able to make the `AcademicSupport.dll` file yourselves, I've used another feature of the Enterprise Edition of Visual Basic called the **Packaging and Deployment Wizard** to create a Setup file for inserting our ActiveX components onto your system. This automatically puts an entry into the Windows Registry at the same time as it puts the component onto your hard drive. At the end of the Lesson, I'll mail the Setup files across to you, and you can take them home and play around with them, to convince yourselves that they work."

> **These files can be downloaded from the Active Path website by going to** `www.activepath.com` **and following the links for this book.**

"The ActiveX component has been compiled," I said. "It's now ready for us to use."

"Is there any way to test it first?" Ward asked. "In fact, how *do* you test an ActiveX component?"

Testing the ActiveX.DLL Component

"We've several choices," I said. "We could close this `ActiveX.DLL` project and start a new `Standard.EXE` project, setting a reference to the new ActiveX component, and testing it like that, but I prefer to start a second session of Visual Basic – that way, we can have our `ActiveX.DLL` project open at the same time as we're testing the component in the other Visual Basic window."

"I didn't know we could do that," Mary said.

"You can run as many Visual Basic sessions as you like simultaneously," I said. "As you may recall, I showed you this in Lesson Three, when we talked about preventing multiple copies of the China Shop program from running at once. Sometimes the ability to run two instances of Visual Basic at the same time can come in quite handy – particularly here, as it allows us to test our component in one Visual Basic window, and make changes to the ActiveX component and recompile it in the other."

"Won't that be confusing?" asked Ward.

"Well," I replied, "it might be a good idea to move the various windows and toolbars on one of the versions about into a different order, so that you can tell them apart. You can grab the top of any of the windows that make up the Visual Basic IDE and rearrange them as you wish."

I gave them a moment or two to do this, then started a second Visual Basic session of my own, selected a new **Standard.EXE** project from the New Project window. I saved the project as **Test.vbp** and then placed a single command button on the form:

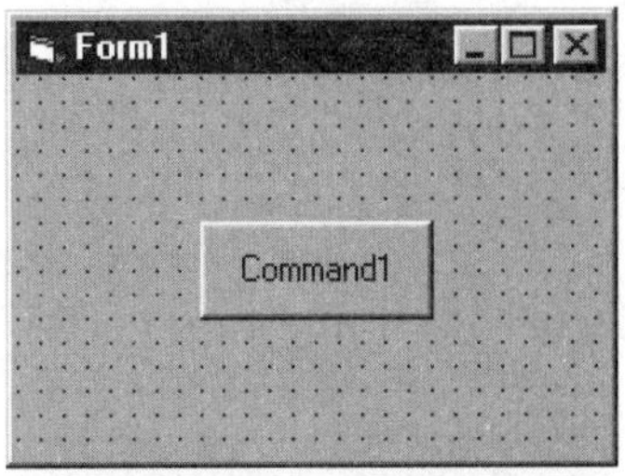

"To use the **Student** object in the ActiveX component we just compiled," I said, "all we need to do is find it in the References window, select it and then click on the OK button. Notice the AcademicSupport component near the top of the References window..."

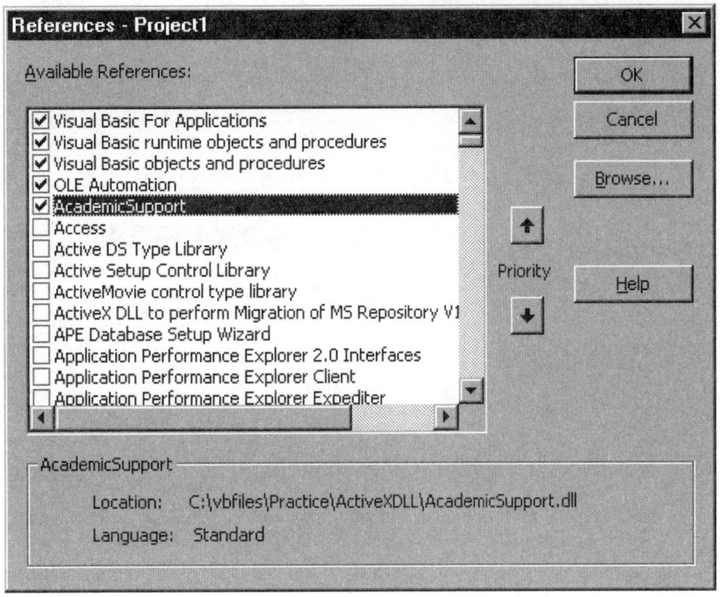

"Check out its Location at the bottom of the window as well," I suggested. "The directory we created earlier is listed as the home of this component's `.dll` file."

> **If you run through the compilation process several times and store the resulting DLL in different locations, you'll end up with multiple same-name references in the References window. We'll cover removing unwanted references in Chapter 10.**

"I know you told us that our component would appear here," Peter said, "but I must confess, I still find it all pretty amazing. How did the reference to our component get here again?"

"When we compiled the **`ActiveX.DLL`**," I said, "Visual Basic automatically created a Windows Registry entry for the DLL – and that's what you're seeing here. Now for even more magic: if we select the AcademicSupport **`ActiveX.DLL`** component, and then click on the OK button, we should be able to see this component in the Object Browser."

I clicked on OK, and then brought up the Object Browser and typed the name of our component into the Library list box, and then clicked on Student in the Classes box:

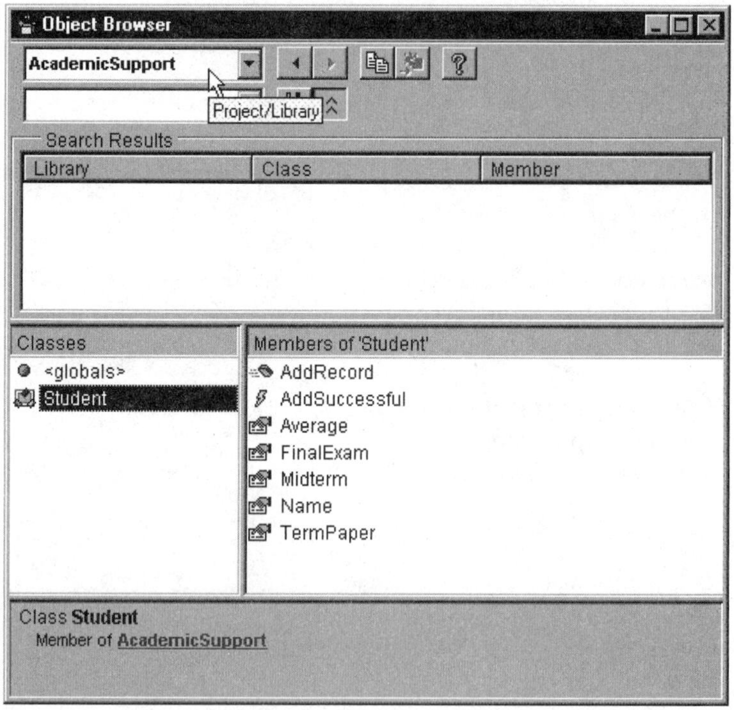

"There's the Visual Basic Object Browser," I said. "Notice how the **Student** class in the component is visible in the Classes window, along with its method, its event, and its five properties – all shown in the Members of 'Student' window."

"This is really beginning to make sense to me," Valerie said. "Now that we've included the component in our **Test** project, will we be able to use the **Student** object in our project, even though we haven't manually added the **Student** class module to the **Test** project?"

"That's right, Valerie," I said. "Using the **AcademicSupport** ActiveX component has eliminated the need to include the **Student** class module in the **Test** project. All we need to do to use the **Student** object now is to declare an instance of the **Student** object, set the values of the **MidTerm**, **FinalExam** and **TermPaper** properties, and then return the value of the **Average** property. Watch this..."

I typed the following code block into the command button's **Click** event procedure:

```
Private Sub Command1_Click()

Dim objStudent As New Student

objStudent.MidTerm = 80
objStudent.FinalExam = 100
objStudent.TermPaper = 90

MsgBox "The Student's Average is " & objStudent.Average

End Sub
```

"Let's run the **Test** program now," I said.

I did that, and when I clicked on the command button this message box appeared:

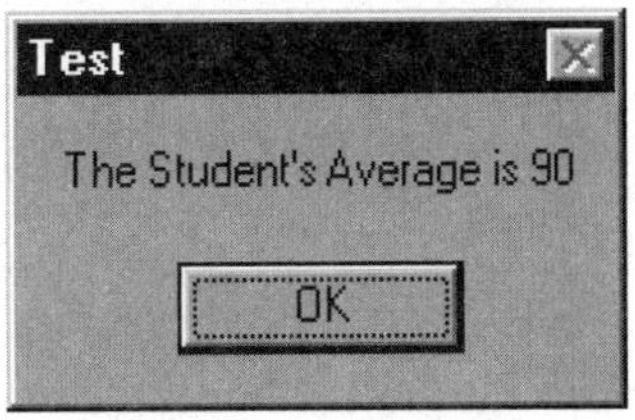

"So what we've done here," Kate said, "is incorporate the functionality of the **Student** class module in our project using the ActiveX component, *without* including the actual class module itself."

"Exactly, Kate," I said. "And the advantage of using the ActiveX component over the class module is that if a change is made to the ActiveX component, we don't need to do a thing to our **Test** project to pull in the latest version, provided the change isn't major. The program will automatically use the latest version of the component."

"I'm convinced!" Kevin said. "Let me ask this question: some objects I've seen in the Object Browser have descriptions for their methods and properties. Is there any way to do that with the components that we create?"

"That's a great question, Kevin," I said. "We can, but we'll need to go back to our ActiveX project, make some changes to the `Student` class module, and then recompile the `ActiveX.DLL`..."

I switched back to the Visual Basic session containing the `ActiveX.DLL` project and opened up the Code window for the `Student` class module.

"To have a description for the object show up in the Object Browser," I continued, "we need to open up the Procedure Attributes window and enter a description for each one of the methods or properties that appears in your class module. Let me demonstrate by adding a description for the `Average` property of the `Student` object."

I selected Tools | Procedure Attributes from the Visual Basic menu bar...

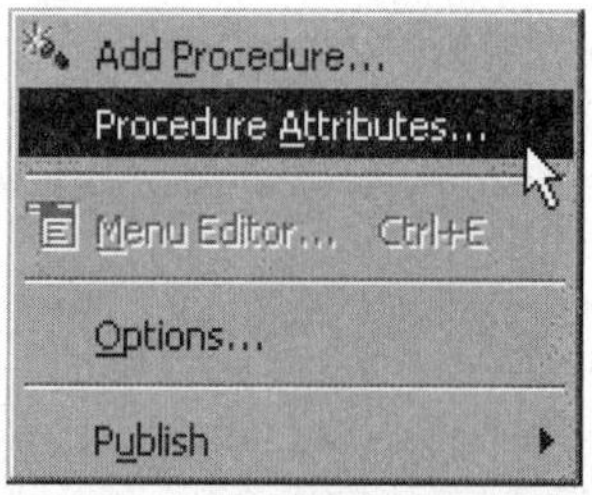

I then wrote the brief description of the `Average` property shown in the Description box here, and clicked on the OK button:

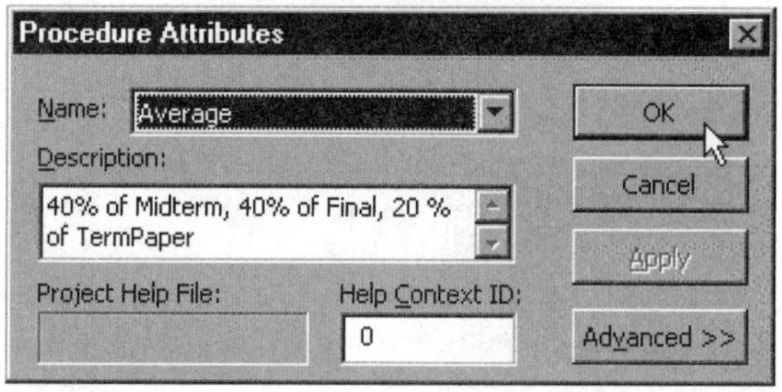

"If we open up the Object Browser from within our `ActiveX.DLL` project," I said, "we'll see the change to the `Average` description in the Object Browser immediately. But we mustn't forget that we need to recompile our component for the description of the `Average` property to show up in the Object Browser of any project using the component."

I recompiled the component (you might find that you have to close the `Test` project to allow the recompile to work), saving the recompiled version in place of the original one in the `ActiveXDLL` folder, and then switched back to the `Test` project.

"Let's bring up the Object Browser for the **Test** project," I went on. "We should see that the **Average** property now has a description:"

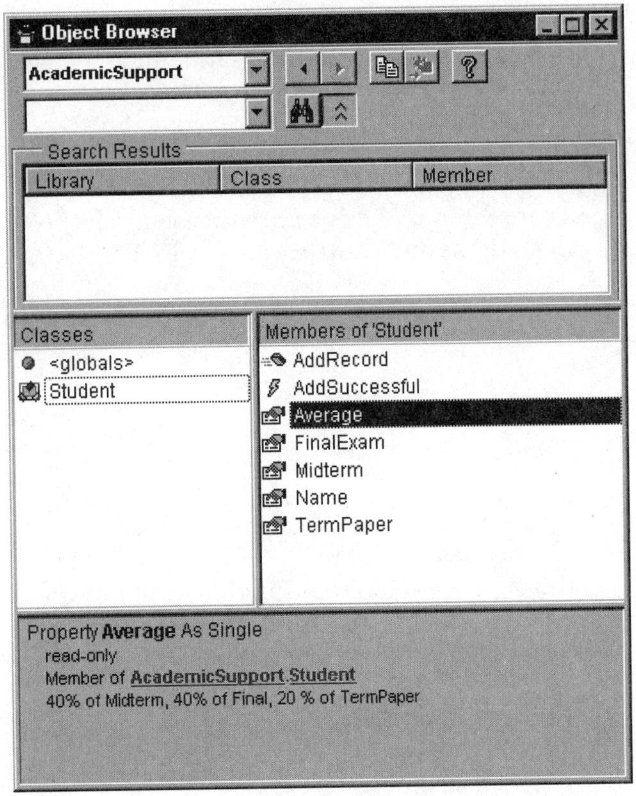

"There it is at the bottom of the window," I said. "Providing descriptions for the properties and methods of your objects will make you very popular with those who use your components!"

Everyone agreed that this was a good idea.

"What I'd like to do now," I said, "is show you how changing the **Student** class module's **Instancing** property in the **ActiveX.DLL** project to a global **Instancing** property can make life easier still on the programmers who use our component."

I shut down the **Test** project and switched back to the **ActiveX.DLL** program in design view.

"Let's select the **Student** class module in the Project Explorer window," I said, "and change its **Instancing** property from **MultiUse** to **GlobalMultiUse** – remember, the global **Instancing** properties mean that the user of our component will not need to declare an instance of our object before they can refer to it's methods and properties in their code:"

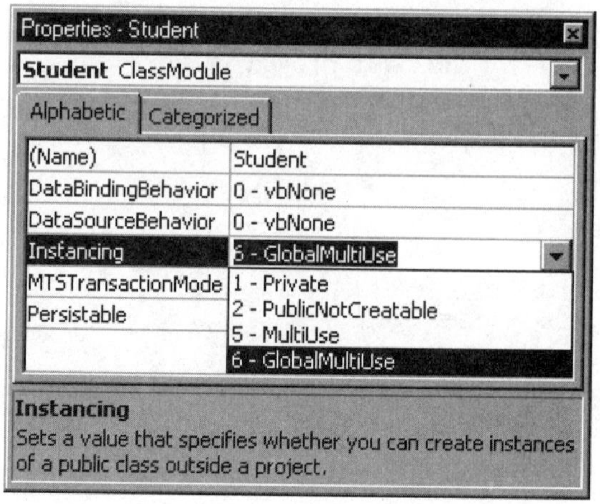

"Let's recompile the DLL now," I said.

I did so, once again replacing the existing version of the DLL in the **ActiveXDLL** folder. Switching back to the **Test** project, I modified the code in the **Click** event procedure of the command button to look like this:

```
Private Sub Command1_Click()

MidTerm = 80
FinalExam = 100
TermPaper = 90

MsgBox "The Student's Average is " & Average

End Sub
```

"Notice how I've removed the declaration of the **Student** object variable," I said. "Also, I'm now referencing the properties of the **Student** object directly, without prefacing them with the **Student** object variable name."

I ran the **Test** program and clicked on the command button – with this result:

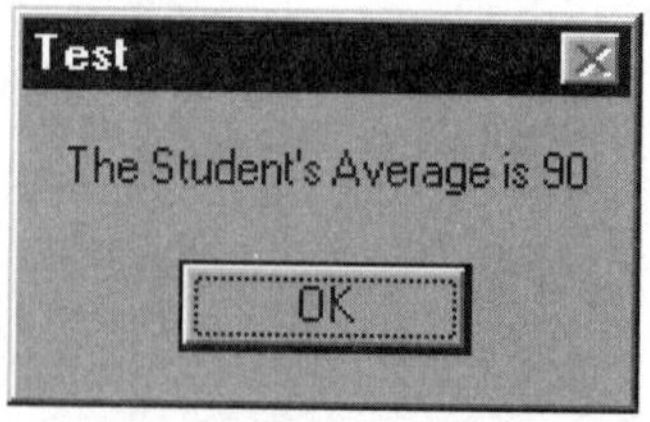

"Assigning a global **Instancing** property to the **Student** class module," I said, "didn't impact the behavior of the object – but it did make coding the properties of the object a little less tedious."

"It's a lot less clear that we're using properties of an object, though, isn't it?" Dave observed.

"Yes, that's true," I agreed. "You have to weigh up the advantages of quick coding against the possibility of making the code harder to follow. Even if implicitly declaring and referencing an object variable for the underlying object can be tedious, it can make values like the **Average** property of that object a lot easier to understand."

I paused.

"What about compiling an **ActiveX.EXE** component?" Dorothy said. "I know you went over the differences between the two component types, but are there any major differences in creating them?"

ActiveX.EXE Components

"Creating an **ActiveX.EXE** component," I said, "is very similar to creating an **ActiveX.DLL** component. Remember that the real difference between them is the way that they run – the **ActiveX.EXE** we're about to create will run 'out-of-process', whereas the **ActiveX.DLL** that we just worked with runs 'in-process'. Let's look at the **ActiveX.EXE** component now."

"We start," I went on, "by creating a new **ActiveX.EXE** project from the New Project window:"

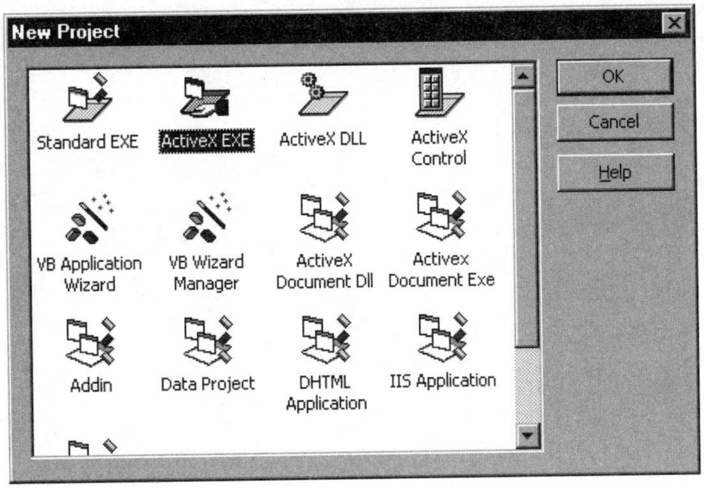

"As with the previous **ActiveX.DLL** project," I said, "when we select a new **ActiveX.EXE** project, Visual Basic loads up a default class module – **Class1** – into the IDE. As we did with the **ActiveX.DLL** project, we'll remove the default class module, and then add our own **Student** class module to this project. After that, we'll update the **Instancing** property of the class module and compile the **ActiveX.EXE**."

I removed the default **Class1**class module, opting not to save it, and selected Project | Add class module from the Visual Basic menu bar. The Add Class Module window appeared, and I selected the Existing tab and added the **Student** class module to the project.

"Let's check the Visual Basic Project Explorer," I said, "to make sure that we have just a single class module in our project:"

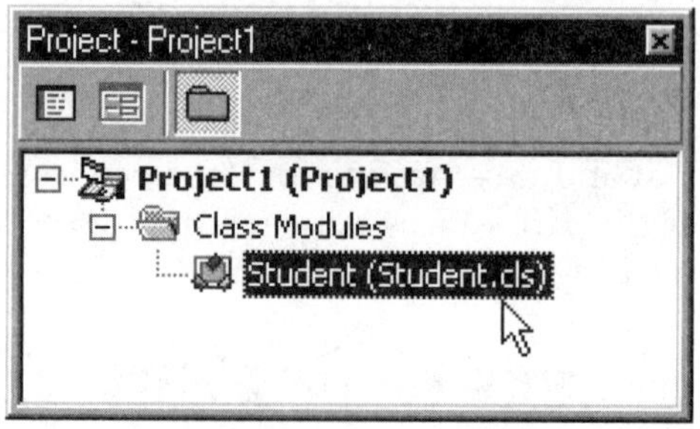

"Setting the **Instancing** property of the **Student** class module is something we have to do in an **ActiveX.EXE** project, also," I said. "The only difference is that with an **ActiveX.EXE** project we have two choices available to us that we didn't have with an **ActiveX.DLL** project: **SingleUse** and **GlobalSingleUse** are now available – let's choose **SingleUse**."

"Er, this may seem a dumb question," Rhonda said, "but why do we chose **SingleUse**?"

"**SingleUse** is the most appropriate, since we're only going to access this component from our one **Test** project," I explained. "Remember, **SingleUse** means that only one application can access our component at any one time, and that separate instances of the component are made if more than one application wants to gain access to the exposed properties and methods within it. This option wasn't available for the **ActiveX.DLL**s we just compiled, but I'm using it here, now, for that reason."

Rhonda seemed happy with that, so I went ahead and selected **SingleUse** for our **Instancing** property from the Properties window:

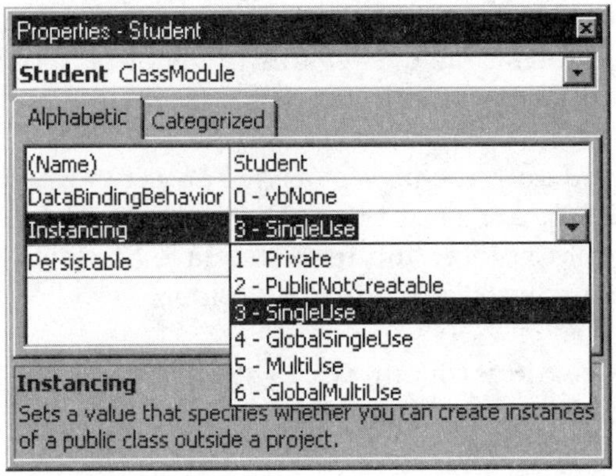

"Now we need to change the project name," I said, "from its default value of Project1 to something a little more meaningful. Remember, it's the project name that determines the name of the ActiveX component that appears in the References window. We named the **ActiveX.DLL** version of this component AcademicSupport – let's name this project AcademicSupportE, using the letter E on the end to differentiate it."

I brought up the Project Explorer, and right-clicked on the project to bring up its Properties window. Then I renamed the project from Project1 to AcademicSupportE...

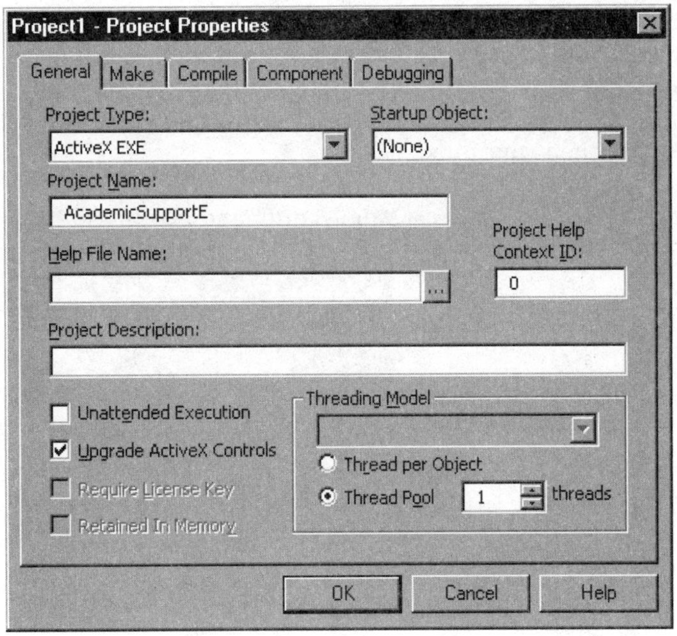

And clicked on the OK button.

"Now that we've set the **Instancing** property of the class module," I said, "and named the project, it's time to save this project in a separate folder within the **Practice** directory called **ActiveXEXE**."

I saved both the project as **AcademicSupportE.vbp** in a new folder called **\VBFILES\Practice\ActiveXEXE**. Then I right-clicked on the **Student** class module in Project Explorer and used the Save Student.cls As... option to save a new copy of the class module in the **ActiveXEXE** folder.

"As we did with our **ActiveX.DLL** project," I said, "let's now compile it into an **ActiveX.EXE**."

I selected File I Make AcademicSupportE.EXE from the Visual Basic menu bar, and specified the directory **\VBFiles\Practice\ActiveXEXE** as the location for the compiled program. A few seconds later, our **ActiveX.EXE** type component – called **AcademicSupportE.EXE** – was compiled and saved.

"Now what?" Rhonda said.

"Now we test the component," I said. "Does everyone remember how we were able to test our **ActiveX.DLL** component by running two sessions of Visual Basic? We can do that again here with our **ActiveX.EXE** component, too. Let's open up another copy of Visual Basic and start a brand new **Standard.EXE** project, and then save it as **Test2.vbp**" I did that, and then continued:

"Once again, we'll place a single command button on the form:"

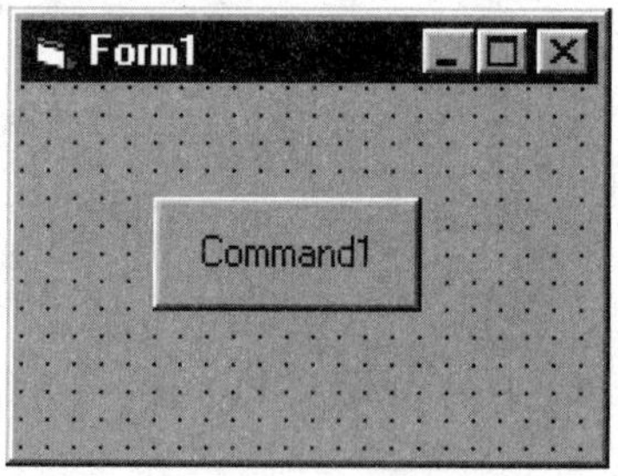

"Let's take a look at the References window," I said, as I selected Project | References from the Visual Basic menu bar, "and see if we can find our **ActiveX.EXE** component:"

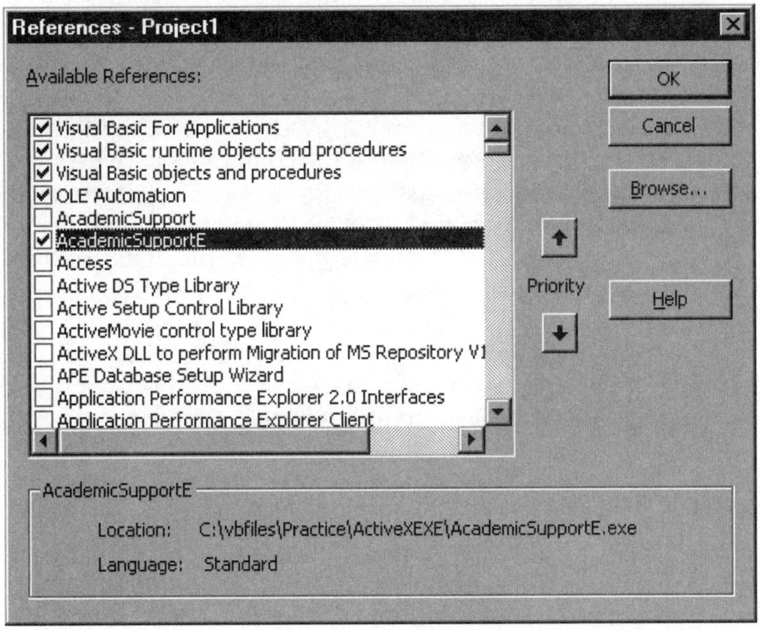

"As you can see," I continued, "both our **ActiveX.DLL** component and our **ActiveX.EXE** component are registered on my instructor's PC. Let's select the **ActiveX.EXE** component, AcademicSupportE, in the References window."

I did that, clicked on OK, and then added the following code to the command button's **Click** event procedure:

```
Private Sub Command1_Click()

Dim objStudent As New Student

objStudent.MidTerm = 80
objStudent.FinalExam = 100
objStudent.TermPaper = 90

MsgBox "The Student's Average is " & objStudent.Average

End Sub
```

I ran the program and clicked on the command button. This was the result:

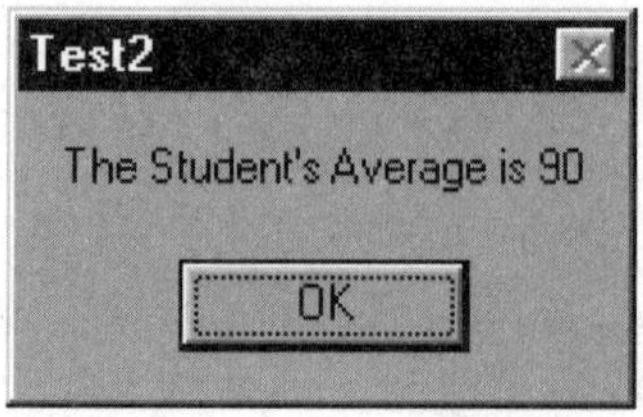

"As you can see," I said, "this code is identical to what we used to work with our **ActiveX.DLL** component. To the programmer using the components, there's no difference – the results are the same. But as we discussed earlier, there may be performance issues in choosing the **ActiveX.DLL** versus the **ActiveX.EXE** – in the long run, you should create both types of components, and test them to see which one gives the better performance in your particular environment."

"I can't tell you how exciting this technology is for me," Ward said. "I can really use ActiveX components back at work. I can envision working with ActiveX components being a lot easier than incorporating class modules into my projects."

"That's the whole idea, Ward," I said – "building components that can be easily used by other programmers."

"Did you say earlier that we'd also be able to compile our own components and then use them in Word or Excel?" Kate asked. "That's definitely something that I'd be interested in learning."

Excel and Word

"Yes, Kate," I answered. "The ActiveX components that we just created – both **ActiveX.DLL** and **ActiveX.EXE** – can be used in Word and Excel: in fact, they can be used within any Windows program that supports ActiveX. Let's take one of the ActiveX components we just compiled and use it in Excel. What we'll do is create a worksheet, enter some values for **Student** grades, and then use the **Average** property of the **Student** object exposed by our ActiveX component to calculate the student's average. Watch this."

I started up Excel, and, in the default worksheet, entered the text as shown, and the values 80, 100 and 90 in cells B1 through B3 respectively:

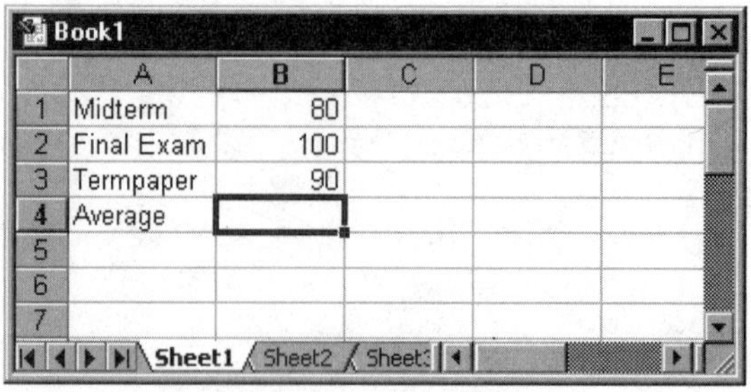

"To use an ActiveX component within Excel," I said, "we need to delve just a little bit into the world of VBA – that's **Visual Basic for Applications**."

"Do you mean there's a way to use Visual Basic within Excel?" Kathy asked.

"That's right, Kathy," I said. "All of the Office products have a Visual Basic editor available for us to use. If we select Tools | Macro | Visual Basic Editor from the Excel menu bar..."

"...the Excel Visual Basic editor will appear. As you can see, it looks similar to the Visual Basic IDE. It's from within this Visual Basic environment that we tell Excel that we want to use an ActiveX component in conjunction with Excel. We do that by selecting Tools | References from the menu bar..."

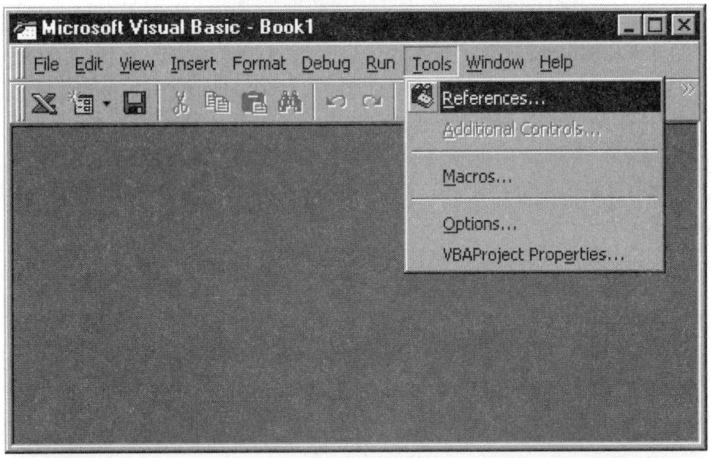

"...and the References window appears:"

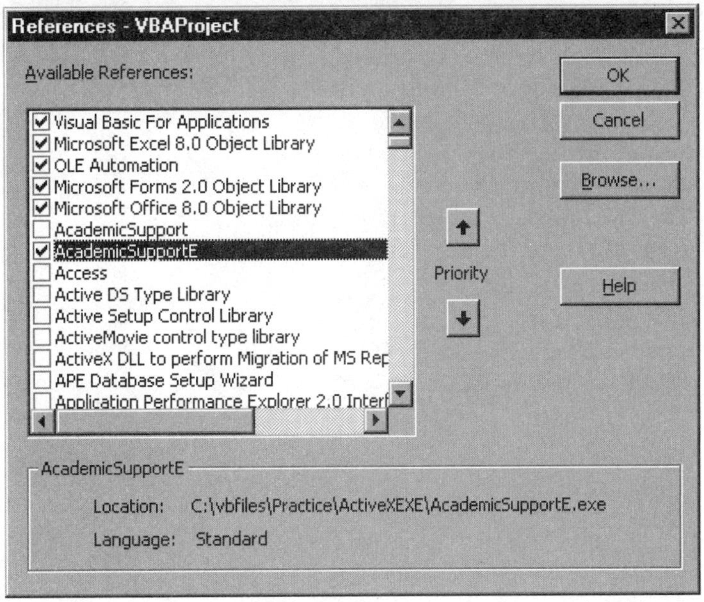

"This is familiar," Bob commented. "It looks just like the Visual Basic References window."

"It's nearly identical, Bob," I confirmed. "In fact, except for the title bar reading VBA Project, you'd think you were working within the Visual Basic IDE. Let's select the AcademicSupportE ActiveX component for inclusion in the VBA module that we're about to write.."

"Is that like a Visual Basic module?" Linda asked.

"That's right, Linda," I confirmed. "To utilize our ActiveX component from within Excel, we need to write a procedure and place it in an Excel VBA module. But this shouldn't confuse you – the code we recorded last week in the Word and Excel macros was saved in the form of a VBA module. We now need to add a new module, although Excel VBA uses the term 'Insert' instead of 'Add' in its menu options."

I then selected Insert | Module from the Excel VBA menu bar...

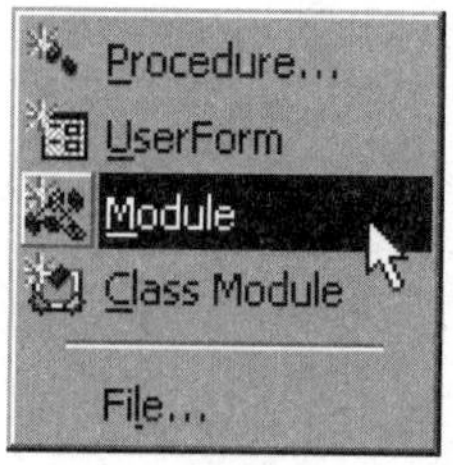
Procedure...
UserForm
Module
Class Module
File...

"This opens up a Module window," I continued. "It's here that we type the code that will utilize our ActiveX component. We've already set a reference to the component, so to work with its properties and methods we just need to make an instance of the **Student** object. Then we'll use the properties and methods of the Excel **Worksheet** object to assign values to the **Student** object's properties. Like this..."

I entered the following code into the Module window:

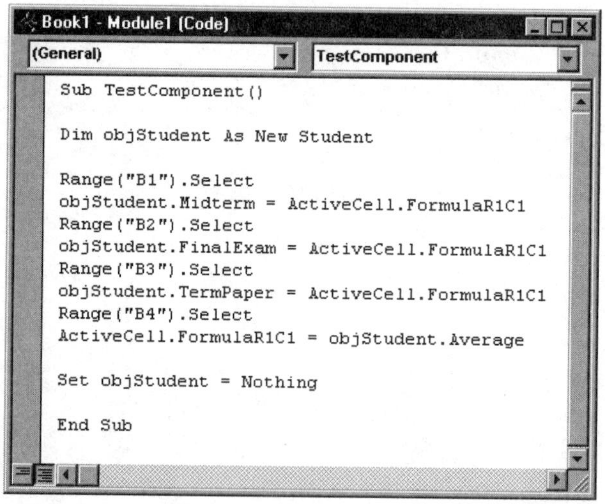
Book1 - Module1 (Code)
(General)
TestComponent
Sub TestComponent()
Dim objStudent As New Student
Range("B1").Select
objStudent.Midterm = ActiveCell.FormulaR1C1
Range("B2").Select
objStudent.FinalExam = ActiveCell.FormulaR1C1
Range("B3").Select
objStudent.TermPaper = ActiveCell.FormulaR1C1
Range("B4").Select
ActiveCell.FormulaR1C1 = objStudent.Average
Set objStudent = Nothing
End Sub

"Notice," I said, "that we've incorporated the code into a subprocedure called **TestComponent**. You'll see shortly that the name of this procedure will be displayed in the available list of macros when we close the Visual Basic editor."

"This code looks familiar," Kathy said. "It's like the code we saw last week when we were using the Excel component from within our VB programs, isn't it?"

"That's right, Kathy," I said. "Working with Excel's objects from within Excel is no different than working with them from within Visual Basic. What we're doing here is taking the values in cells B1, B2 and B3, assigning them to the **Student** object's **MidTerm**, **FinalExam** and **TermPaper** properties, and then retrieving the value of the **Student** object's **Average** property, and placing it in cell B4."

I waited to see if there were any questions before moving on.

"I just mentioned," I continued, "that when we close the Visual Basic editor, we'll see **TestComponent** listed as a macro in the Macros window. We can also run this procedure from within the Visual Basic editor by clicking on the run button on the toolbar in the Module window."

I did just that and switched back to the worksheet. It had changed to look like this:

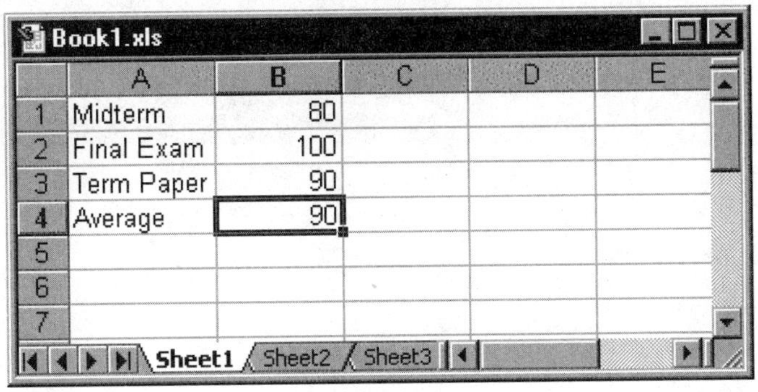

"The student's average of 90 has been calculated and placed in cell B4," I said.

"That's really great," Rhonda added. "And you say there's a way to run this code from within Excel itself, so that the user doesn't need to open up the Visual Basic editor?"

"That's right, Rhonda," I said, "The procedure we just created will appear to the user in a list of available macros. Let's close the Visual Basic editor now by selecting Close and Return to Microsoft Excel from the Visual Basic menu bar..."

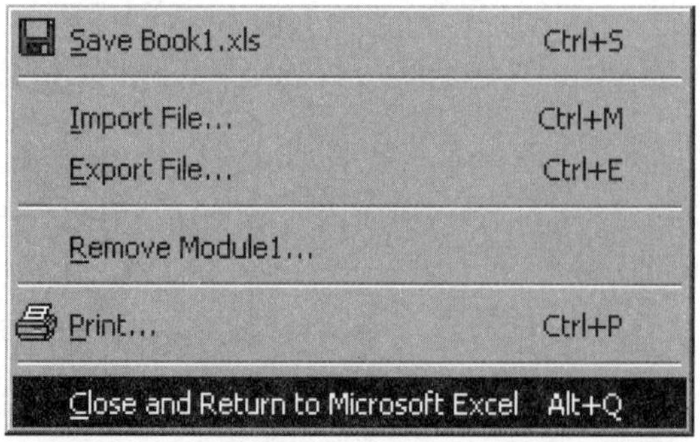

"...enter some new values for the mid-term, final exam, and term paper grades into cells B1, B2 and B3, and clear out cell B4..."

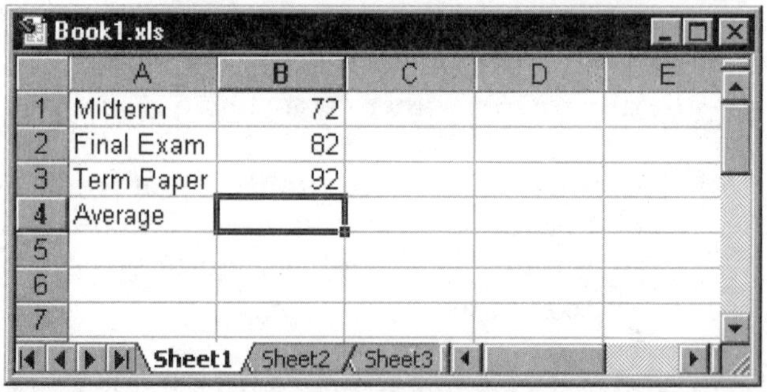

"Now, we'll select Tools | Macro | Macros from the Excel menu bar:"

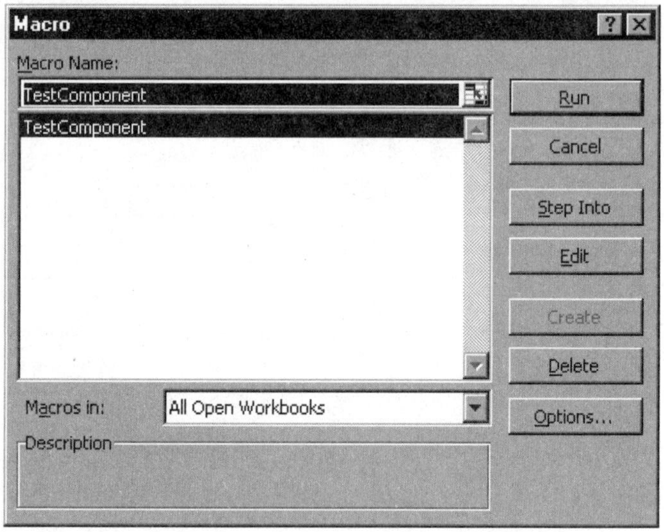

"There's the **TestComponent** subprocedure we just coded a minute ago. To execute the code within it, all we need to do is select it and then click on the run button..."

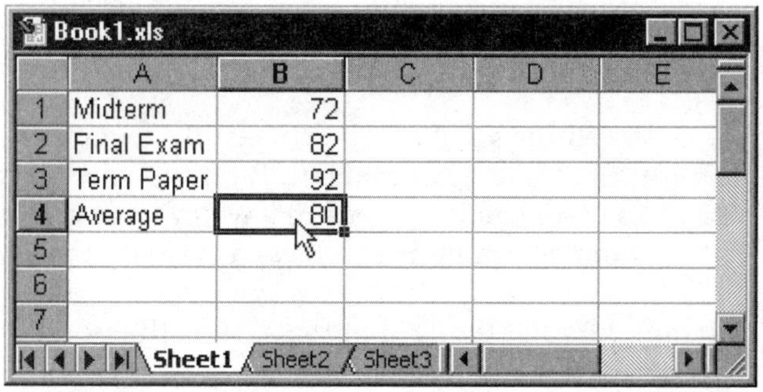

"There's the student's final grade in cell B4," I said.

"This is absolutely incredible," Ward said, "This means that objects that we create in Visual Basic are truly portable to other Windows applications."

"That's right, Ward," I said, "that's the whole idea. And we can incorporate them into Word as well – although I'll leave you to do that on your own."

"I'd like everyone to take a fifteen minute break now," I said. "When we come back, we'll go through a series of exercises where we'll create an ActiveX component embodying the **Package** object that we created several weeks ago: then we'll use the component from within the China Shop project."

Back to the China Shop

Fifteen minutes later we resumed class.

"How will we be able to complete these exercises if we don't have a version of Visual Basic that allows us to create components?" Kate asked.

"Unfortunately," I said, "you won't be able to. But I know that many of you have the Visual Basic Professional or Enterprise Editions available to you outside of class. I'll be completing the exercises for you on the classroom projector – so you'll still derive a benefit from that: at the end of class, I'll mail you the setup files to install the ActiveX components we've been working with today on your own hard-drives, so that even those of you without access to a means of compiling the components can convince yourselves that what we've done today really does work."

"I'm anxious to see you compile a China Shop ActiveX component," Peter said, "even if we can't do it ourselves I'll be taking detailed notes, I assure you. Where do we start?"

"The first thing we need to do," I said, "is modify the **Package** class module slightly before compiling it into a component. Right now, it contains a reference to **frmMain** in its **Initialize** event procedure – we need to remove that, since there's no guarantee that the user of our component will have a form by that name in their project."

"Hmm, I hadn't thought of that," Dorothy pondered. "What's the reference to **frmMain** doing?"

"When the **Package** class **Initialize** procedure executes," I said, "it looks for the **Shipping.txt** file and, if it can't find it, it displays an error message and then unloads the form to shut down the project. We can't be doing that within our component."

"Will we still be checking for a missing **Shipping.txt** file?" Dave asked.

"Yes we will, Dave," I said, "but we'll handle that problem a little differently. We'll be 'raising' an error back to the program that's using our component, and it will then be up to that program to deal with the error."

I then distributed this exercise to the class, and together we proceeded to complete it on my machine:

Exercise - Using the Package Class Module in an ActiveX Component

In this exercise, you'll modify the **Package** class module to eliminate the reference to **frmMain**.

1. Load up the China Shop project.
2. Using the Project Explorer, select the **Package** class module.
3. Modify the **Initialize** procedure of the **Package** class module to look like this next listing (modified code is highlighted, as you'd expect by now!):

```
Private Sub Class_Initialize()

On Error GoTo ICanHandleThis

Dim strState As String
Dim curPrice As Currency

If App.Path = "\" Then
 Open App.Path & "SHIPPING.TXT" For Input As #1
Else
 Open App.Path & "\SHIPPING.TXT" For Input As #1
End If

Do While Not EOF(1)
 Input #1, strState, curPrice
 m_colShippingCharges.Add Item:=curPrice, Key:=strState
Loop
Close #1

Exit Sub

ICanHandleThis:
Select Case Err.Number
 Case 53
 Err.Raise Number:=vbObjectError + 512 + 1,
   ↳Description:="PACKAGE COMPONENT - SHIPPING.TXT not found"
 Exit Sub
 Case Else
 Err.Raise Number:=vbObjectError + 512 + 2,
   ↳Description:="PACKAGE COMPONENT - UNKNOWN ERROR ENCOUNTERED"
 Exit Sub
End Select

End Sub
```

4. Click on File | Save As on the toolbar and save the project in the `\VBFiles\China` directory.

Discussion

"What's going on here?" Rhonda asked. "I don't believe I've seen that syntax before. What does **Err.Raise** do?"

```
Err.Raise Number:=vbObjectError + 512 + 1,
   ↳Description:="PACKAGE COMPONENT - SHIPPING.TXT not found"
```

"The built-in **Err** object's **Raise** method," I said, "is used to tell the program using our component that an error has occurred within the component, and that the program using it should handle it. If the **Shipping.txt** file wasn't found in the previous version of the **Initialize** procedure, we displayed a message box informing the user of that fact, and then unloaded the China Shop project's main form. However, as the designers of this component, we've no way of knowing exactly how the programmer is going to use it – it could be from within a **Standard.EXE** project, an Excel worksheet, even from within another component. To cater for all of these different eventualities, we're raising an error to the program that's using our component, and letting that program decide how to handle it. That means that the program should have an enabled error handler that's set up to detect the error codes we'll generate out of the component."

"So..." said Dave tentatively, "we're making up an error number of our own and passing it back to the program that's using our component?"

"Yes indeed, Dave," I said. "And we need to ensure that the number we invent to identify the error to the program that's using the component isn't already being reserved for use by Visual Basic itself. To do that, Microsoft recommends that we take the value of the Intrinsic Visual Basic Constant **vbobjectError**, whose value is **-2147221504**, and add a number to it. If we've got several codes that we want to use, we can add 1 for the first error code we generate, 2 for the second, and so forth. Microsoft further recommends that you add 512 to this combination, since the valid range of system type errors runs from 0 to 512. This convoluted activity will ensure that the number identifying our error is unique and distinctive in Visual Basic. As a result, we use this line of code to generate a unique error number..."

```
Err.Raise Number:=vbobjectError + 512 + 1,
```

"...followed by a pretty self-explanatory description, including the name of the component from which the error originated:"

```
↳Description:="PACKAGE COMPONENT - SHIPPING.TXT not found"
```

"It's then up to the program using our component to deal with this error in an error handler. I'll be showing you how to do that in just a few moments."

"Couldn't we just use the **`Raise`** method of the **`Err`** object to raise an error number?" Dave asked. "This seems a bit circuitous."

"That's a good point, Dave," I said. "Sure, we could code a statement like this..."

```
Err.Raise 40000
```

"Microsoft suggest this method as a way to raise an error number that's most likely not being used by any other component in your project, and it's fairly easy for you to keep track of."

I distributed this next exercise. Again, the students couldn't go through it on their machines, but they could follow what I was doing on mine, via the classroom projector:

Exercise - Creating an ActiveX.DLL Project

In this exercise, follow along with me while I create and compile an **`ActiveX.DLL`** project.

1. Start a new Visual Basic project. Select the ActiveX DLL type from the New tab of the New Project window.

2. Remove the default class module that Visual Basic adds to a new **`ActiveX.DLL`** project by selecting it in the Project Explorer window, right-clicking on Class1, and then selecting the Remove Class1 option. You're asked if I want to save the class module before removing it from the project – answer No, of course!

3. Now it's time to add the **`Package`** class module to our **`ActiveX.DLL`** project. Select Project | Add Class Module from the Visual Basic menu bar, click on the Existing tab and then find and select the **`Package`** class module in the **`\VBFiles\China`** folder:

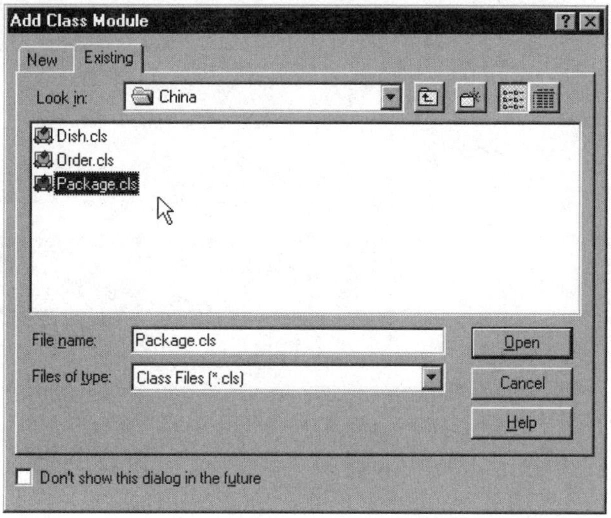

4. Now select the **Package** class in your **ActiveX.DLL** project using the Project Explorer, and bring up its Properties window. Change its **Instancing** property from **Private** to **MultiUse**:

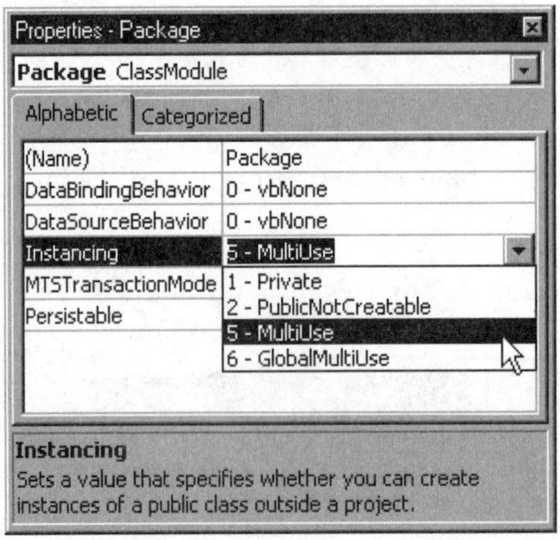

5. Now bring up the Properties window for the project and change its name from Project1 to ChinaShopPackage…

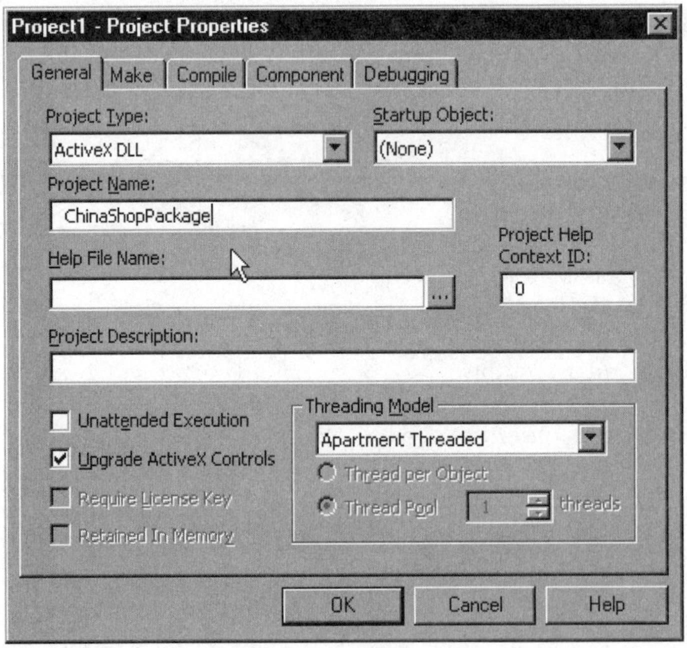

6. ...and click on OK.

7. Compile your component by selecting File | Make ChinaShopPackage.dll from the Visual Basic menu bar. Specify a location of `\VBFiles\China` for the DLL.

8. Click on the save icon on the toolbar and save the project as `PackageObjectDLL.vbp` in the `\VBFiles\China` directory.

Discussion

"That's it," I said, triumphantly . "We've now compiled an ActiveX component based on the `Package` object of the China Shop project. As you've seen throughout the course of today's class, compiling the component is the easy part – all the hard work is done with the creation of the class itself. What I'd like to do now is show you how we can use this within a `Standard.EXE` type project."

"Could we also have added the other class modules in the China Shop project to this component?" Valerie asked.

"That's an excellent question, Valerie," I replied, "and the answer's 'yes'. In fact, if we were going to be using components in the delivered China Shop project, we would add every class module to the component."

With that, I distributed this exercise for the class to look over.

Exercise - Using the ChinaShopPackage Component in a Standard.EXE Project

In this exercise, I'll create a `Standard.EXE` project to use the `ChinaShopPackage` component I just compiled.

1. Start a new `Standard.EXE` project, and add a command button to the default form.

2. Select Project | References from the Visual Basic menu bar, and then select the ChinaShopPackage DLL as a reference.

3. Add the following code to the `Click` event procedure of the command button.

```
Private Sub Command1_Click()

Dim objPackage As New ChinaShopPackage.Package
objPackage.State = "New Jersey"
MsgBox "Charges are $" & objPackage.Charges

Set objPackage = Nothing
End Sub
```

4. Save the **Standard.EXE** project as **TestComponent** and the form as **Form1**, both in the China Shop directory.

5. Run the program and click on the command button. You should see the following message box displayed:

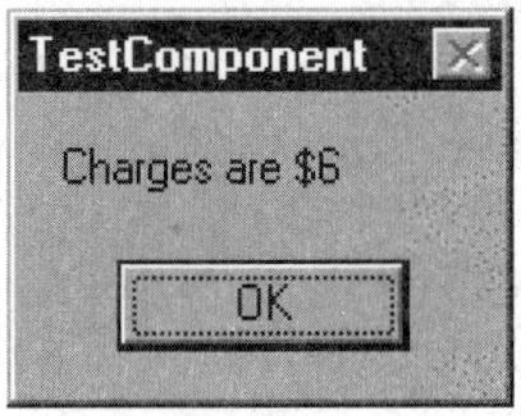

Now let's see what happens if we instantiate the **Package** object, and its **Initialize** procedure can't find the **Shipping.txt** file.

6. Stop the program, and use Windows Explorer to rename the file **Shipping.txt** to **Shipping.old**.

7. Run the program again and click on the command button. You should see an error message like this:

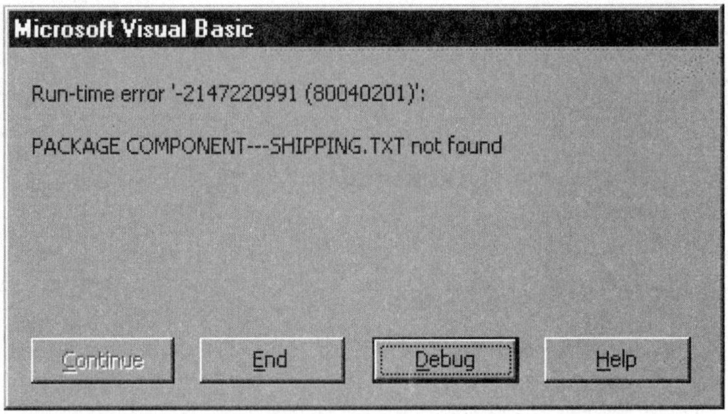

8. Now let's add an error handler to the **Click** event procedure to more gracefully handle this error. Modify the code in the **Click** event procedure of the command button to look like this – with modified code highlighted, as always:

```
Private Sub Command1_Click()

On Error GoTo ICanHandleThis

Dim objPackage As New ChinaShopPackage.Package
objPackage.State = "New Jersey"
MsgBox "Charges are $" & objPackage.Charges

Set objPackage = Nothing

Exit Sub

ICanHandleThis:
Select Case Err.Number
 Case -2147220991 'File not found
 MsgBox "A file required by the " &
    ↳"China Shop program " & vbCrLf &
    ↳"is missing. Please ensure that " & vbCrLf &
    ↳"SHIPPING.TXT is in " & vbCrLf &
    ↳"the China Shop directory " & vbCrLf &
    ↳"on the computer's hard drive"
 Unload Me
 Exit Sub
 Case Else
 MsgBox "Unexpected error has occurred" & vbCrLf &
    ↳"Contact a member of staff"
 Unload Me
 Exit Sub
End Select

End Sub
```

9. Run the program and click on the command button. You should see a message box that looks like this:

> ! You may need to check your settings for error trapping on the General tab of the **Tools | Options** menu. Your error-trapping options will need to be set to either **Break in Class Module** (the default) or **Break on Unhandled Errors.**

10. Use Windows Explorer to change the name of `Shipping.old` back to `Shipping.txt`.

Discussion

"We've demonstrated several things here," I said. "Firstly, we've seen how easy it is to use the `ChinaShopPackage` component in a `Standard.EXE` project. Secondly, we've seen the effect of the `Err` object's `Raise` method. When we renamed the `Shipping.txt` file to `Shipping.old`, the code in the `Initialize` procedure of the `Package` class passed an error back to the program that instantiated the object. Initially, since we hadn't coded an error handler, our program bombed – although it did tell us the error number and the error description. To handle the error more gracefully, we added code to detect the error number – in this case `-2147220991` – and respond accordingly:"

```
Select Case Err.Number
 Case -2147220991 'File not found
```

"I have only one question," Kate asked, "and that's how a programmer using our component would know they have to lookout for this error code?"

"Documentation," I said. "We'd need to provide a list of error codes generated by our component for any programmers who were using it."

I distributed the final exercise of the day before saying a few words about it.

"We've just one more exercise to complete today," I said. "I want to show you how to use our ActiveX component from within Microsoft Excel."

Exercise - Using the ChinaShopPackage Component in Excel

In this exercise, you'll use the `ChinaShopPackage` component from within Excel, and use the component's `Package` object to display a list of shipping charges for each state.

1. Start up Excel and specify that you want to work with a new worksheet.

2. Save the worksheet as `Book1` in the `\VBFiles\China` directory.

3. Starting in cell A4, and working through to cell A55, enter the names of the fifty one states found in the `Shipping.txt` file (open `Shipping.txt` in notepad if you need to see them all):

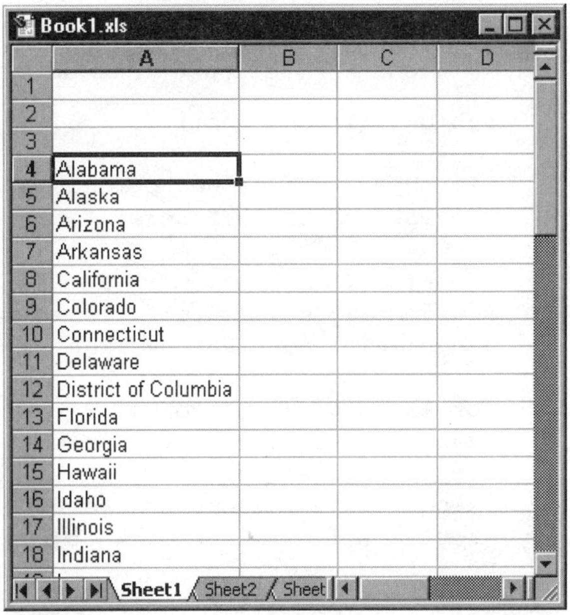

4. Open the Visual Basic editor in Excel by selecting Tools | Macro | Visual Basic Editor.

5. When the Visual Basic editor appears, select Tools | References from the menu bar, and then find and select the reference to the ChinaShopPackage ActiveX component we created in the previous exercise:

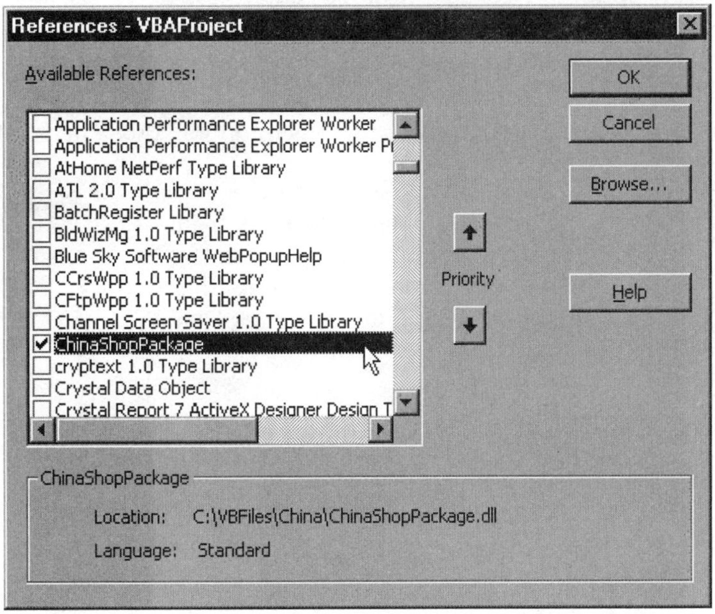

6. Now select Insert | Module from Excel's Visual Basic menu bar, and enter the following code into the module:

```
Sub ShippingCharges()

Dim objPackage As New ChinaShopPackage.Package
Dim intCounter As Integer

Range("A1").Select
ActiveCell.FormulaR1C1 = "Bullina China Shop Shipping Charges"
Range("A1").Font.Bold = True

For intCounter = 4 To 54
 Range("A" & intCounter).Select
 objPackage.State = ActiveCell.FormulaR1C1
 Range("B" & intCounter).Select
 ActiveCell.FormulaR1C1 = objPackage.Charges
Next intCounter

Set objPackage = Nothing

End Sub
```

7. Close the editor by selecting File | Close and Return to Microsoft Excel from the menu bar.

8. Select Tools | Macro | Macros from the Excel menu bar, select ShippingCharges from the available list of macros, and then click Run:

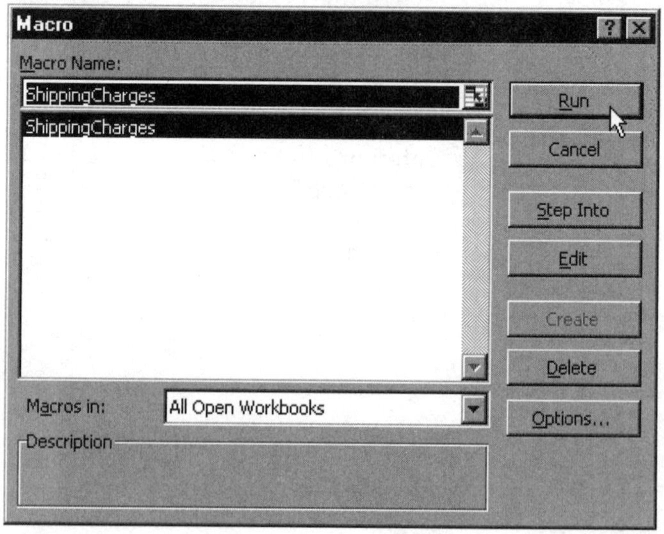

9. The charges for each state should be calculated, and your worksheet should now look like this:

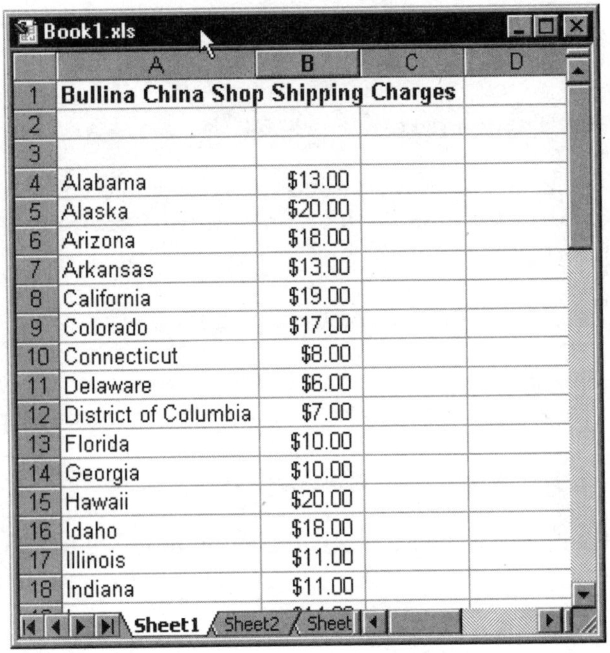
Book1.xls
A
B
C
D
1 Bullina China Shop Shipping Charges
2
3
4 Alabama $13.00
5 Alaska $20.00
6 Arizona $18.00
7 Arkansas $13.00
8 California $19.00
9 Colorado $17.00
10 Connecticut $8.00
11 Delaware $6.00
12 District of Columbia $7.00
13 Florida $10.00
14 Georgia $10.00
15 Hawaii $20.00
16 Idaho $18.00
17 Illinois $11.00
18 Indiana $11.00
Sheet1
Sheet2

Discussion

"What we're doing here," I said, "is instantiating a **`Package`** object, and, starting with cell A4, using the name of the state found in column A to set the value of the **`State`** property of the **`Package`** object. Then we're retrieving the value of the **`Charges`** property and inserting it into column B. We do this for each row of data, starting from row 4 and working our way through to row 54. We *start* by declaring an instance of the **`ChinaShopPackage`** component's **`Package`** object:"

```
Dim objPackage As New ChinaShopPackage.Package
```

"This is the variable we use to keep track of the current row number..."

```
Dim intcounter As Integer
```

"...and these three lines of code display a heading for our worksheet:"

```
Range("A1").Select
ActiveCell.FormulaR1C1 = "Bullina China Shop Shipping Charges"
Range("A1").Font.Bold = True
```

"This next line of code," I continued, "initializes a **For...Next** loop that initializes the value of **intCounter** and sets its upper limit:"

```
For intcounter = 5 To 54
```

"...and then uses the **intCounter** variable value to designate the value for **Range**. The first time through the loop, the value of **Range** is "**A5**', the second time through "**A6**", and so forth:"

```
Range("A" & intcounter).Select
```

"Once the value for **Range** is determined – which will be the name of the state that's in that cell – we assign the value of that cell to the **State** property of the **Package** object:"

```
objPackage.State = ActiveCell.FormulaR1C1
```

"Then we set the **Range** value again to move to column B..."

```
Range("B" & intcounter).Select
```

"...and assign the current value of the **Package** object's **Charges** property to that cell. This process is repeated for each cell in column A:"

```
ActiveCell.FormulaR1C1 = objPackage.Charges
Next intcounter
```

"Finally," I said, "as you're used to by now, we set the object variable to **Nothing** once we've finished:"

```
Set objPackage = Nothing
```

"All clear?" I asked, and everyone nodded. We had come to the end of the lesson.

"What will we be doing next week?" Melissa asked. "Should we head right over to the China Shop?"

"We'll meet here first, Melissa," I said. "Next week is the final week of our course, and at this point, we're actually finished with the China Shop project. We won't be making any more changes to it. However, next week I'll be handling any questions that you might have, and I also want to give you the opportunity to finish your own versions of the China Shop project. After that, you're all invited to accompany me to Joe Bullina's China Shop to deliver the finished product – if pattern holds true, he'll be throwing quite a party for us!"

There was just one last thing to do.

"If you look on the classroom network drive," I said, highlighting the drive on my screen in Windows Explorer, "you'll see I've put a series of 'install' programs there for you: these will allow those of you without access to a Professional or Enterprise edition of Visual Basic to run the ActiveX components you've watched me build today on your own machines."

> **You can find these files yourself on the Active Path web site: just go to** `www.activepath.com` **and follow the links for this book.**

"Feel free to take a copy," I said. "Although those of you with only the Working Model Edition perhaps ought to think about moving up in the world and getting yourselves a copy of Professional or Enterprise Edition Visual Basic. You're not learners any more!"

With that, I dismissed class for the day.

Chapter Summary

In this chapter, you learned how to compile your classes into ActiveX components – both **`ActiveX.DLL`**s and **`ActiveX.EXE`**s – and to use your own created components within other Visual Basic projects and within Microsoft's Office programs.

By now, you've seen:

- What an ActiveX component is
- What the types of ActiveX components are, and how to work with two of them in detail
- How to compile ActiveX components

In particular, we've looked at:

- Compiling the **Student** class from the Student Grades demo into **ActiveX.DLL** and **ActiveX.EXE** components
- Using the **Student** object **ActiveX.DLL** component in a **Standard.EXE** project
- Using the **Student** object **ActiveX.EXE** component in a **Standard.EXE** project and in Excel
- Compiling the **Package** class from the China Shop project into an **ActiveX.DLL** component
- Using the **ActiveX.DLL** component (which exposes the **Package** object) inside another **Standard.EXE** project, and within an Excel spreadsheet

We did all this without the support of the original programs we created these objects for, proving that we have created genuinely portable, independent objects. This is the critical feature of the ActiveX technology – allowing us to share functionality easily between programs.

Join us next week for our finale, when we'll see how to manage our components efficiently in the References window, and how to unregister unwanted components. And, of course, we'll deliver the finished product and reflect on what we've done.

Learn to Program Objects with Visual Basic
Bullina's
China

Chapter 10

Troubleshooting, Testing, and a Ticker-tape Parade

The concluding lesson of the Objects course is always a short one: all the hard work has been done, and everyone has the chance to wind down and get final clarification on anything that's still troubling them. There's definitely a relaxed, 'end of term' feel about this final class.

In this chapter, we'll address some of the issues that fall out of using components in our programs, and we'll test and deliver the modified China Shop program. There's important material here on ensuring that different versions of our programs are compatible with previous versions, too.

Specifically, we'll see:

- How to manage our project's components more tidily
- How to make sure that newer versions are compatible with earlier versions
- Some tips on testing
- The delivery of the new program

This lesson is a comfortable ride, so come along with us and enjoy the scenery.

The Final Frontier

Walking through the door of the classroom, I felt a palpable sense of anticipation: today would be a big day for us – the day we'd deliver the modified China Shop Program to Joe Bullina and his staff at the China Shop.

After wishing everyone a hearty "good morning!" I began the final class by asking if there were any questions about what we'd covered during the rest of the course. Most of the students were busy making last-minute adjustments to their China Shop projects, but Ward took me up on my offer.

"As you may have gathered from my enthusiastic reaction to ActiveX components," he said, "I think they're just great. I was experimenting with creating some of my own at work this past week, and I've got two questions. The first is about how to remove a component from the Visual Basic References list once we've compiled it, and the second question...well, that's a little bit more involved, and it deals with compiling different versions of the same ActiveX component. I ran into trouble when I attempted this during the week."

"OK," I said, "I think I know what you mean – these are quite common issues when people first start using components to add extra power and flexibility to their programs. Let's tackle your first question, about un-registering ActiveX components, and then we'll come back and look at the problem you're having compiling subsequent versions of the program."

Unregistering ActiveX Components

"Now," I went on, "the ActiveX components that you see in the Visual Basic Reference window all have an entry recorded in the **Windows Registry**."

"Which Reference window are you talking about?"Linda asked, "I'm not quite sure I know what you mean."

"Let me show you, Linda," I answered, as I fired up Visual Basic and started a new `Standard.EXE` project. "If I select Project | References from the Visual Basic menu bar, the References window appears:"

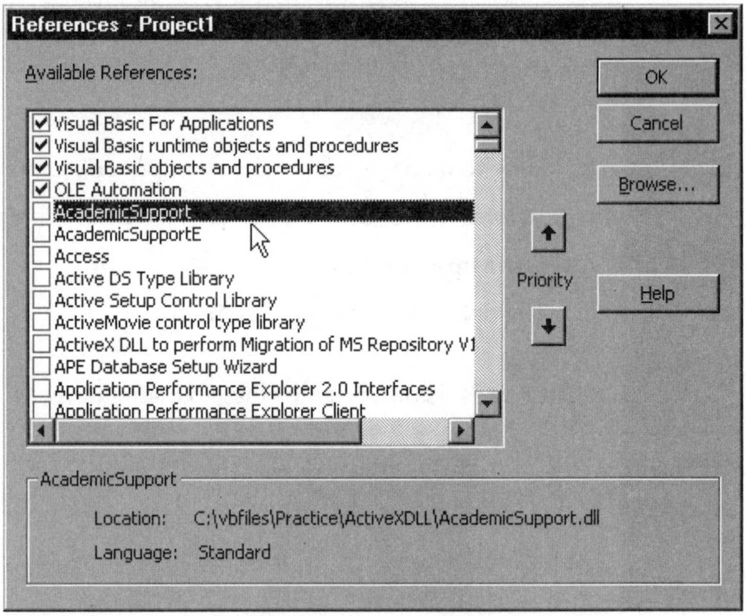

"Notice that the two ActiveX components we compiled last week are listed in the References window – AcademicSupport, and AcademicSupportE."

"I see what you mean now," Linda said. "I guess I never thought about deleting those entries."

"Ward's question is an interesting one," I continued. "When you're developing ActiveX components, the list in this Reference window can quickly become cluttered."

"How does that Windows Registry entry get created to start with?" Chuck asked.

"When you use Visual Basic to compile an ActiveX component," I said, "an entry for that component is automatically added to the Windows Registry for you. However, that's not the only way an entry for a component can be added to the Registry: they can also be made when a software package is installed – that's how the Word and Excel Object Libraries we worked with a few weeks back got added to the Registry. Furthermore, Registry entries can also be made manually by executing a program called **`REGSVR32.EXE`** – this program is bundled with the Windows operating system itself, so it's just sitting there, waiting for you to use it. However, the two ActiveX components that we compiled last week, and which you can see in the Reference window here, both had their entries added to the Registry by Visual Basic as part of their compilation process."

"Can we just delete the **`ActiveX.DLL`** or **`ActiveX.EXE`** file from its folder to get rid of the entry in the Registry?" Kathy asked. "And will that remove the component from the References window, too?"

"Unfortunately, no," I said. "Deleting the **`ActiveX.DLL`** or **`ActiveX.EXE`** file doesn't remove the Registry entry – nor does it remove it from the Visual Basic References window. Worse yet, once the DLL or EXE file is removed, it makes it more difficult to erase the entry in the Windows Registry and to get rid of it in the References window."

"So what can we do?" Steve asked. "Is there a way to get rid of the components from within Visual Basic itself?"

"No, there isn't, Steve," I replied. "Fortunately, however, there **are** other ways to delete the entries for an ActiveX component. Not surprisingly, the technique we use varies, depending upon whether the ActiveX component is a DLL or an EXE. If the ActiveX component is a DLL, we execute the **`REGSVR32`** program with a **`/U`** option to un-register the component: we run this from Windows' Start | Run window."

"And if the ActiveX component is an EXE?" enquired Rhonda.

"For **ActiveX.EXE** files we type the name of the **ActiveX.EXE** file in the Start | Run window," I told her, "and use an **unregserver** argument to un-register the component. Let me demonstrate both of these methods now by deleting the Registry entries for the **AcademicSupport** components we created last week – both the **AcademicSupport.DLL** and the **AcademicSupportE.EXE** files."

Unregistering an ActiveX DLL Component

"Let's start," I resumed, "by un-registering our **ActiveX.DLL** component. To do that, all we need to do is run the **REGSVR32** program, supply it with the name of the DLL we want to un-register, and specify the **/u** argument – which stands for **unregister**."

To illustrate this, I closed the Visual Basic References window, clicked on the Windows Start button and selected Run. I typed the following statement into the Open box of the Run window that opened:

regsvr32 c:/vbfiles/practice/activexdll/academicsupport.dll /u

Like this:

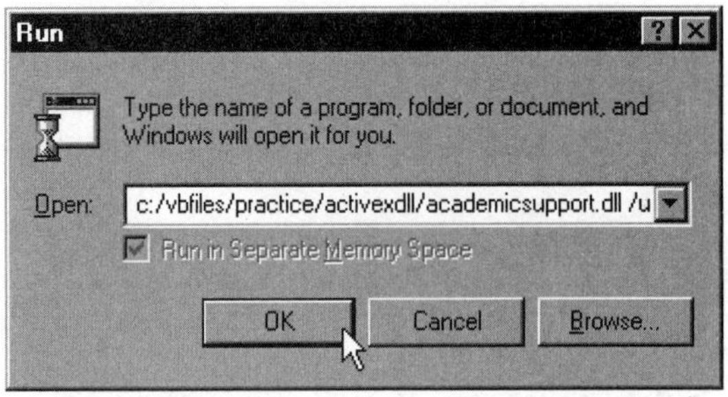

> **Caution: note that the text box in this window is too small to show the whole statement – you need to type the whole thing as shown *above* the screenshot.**

"Do we have to provide the full path name of the DLL to the **REGSVR32** program?" asked Peter.

"Well, Peter," I replied, "that depends on whether the DLL was compiled and saved in a directory that is part of the PC's default search path. For instance, the **\Windows** and **\Windows\System** directories are automatically searched when you type an entry into the Run window – any DLL that's compiled and saved in those directories will be found without specifying the directory name. The ActiveX component DLL that we compiled last week, however, was stored in a directory that **isn't** part of the PC's default path: that means that to un-register the component, we should provide the full path in the Run window."

I waited a moment to see if there were any other questions. There weren't.

"If I click on the OK button," I continued, "we'll receive a confirmation message indicating that the our **ActiveX.DLL** component has been successfully unregistered – in other words, the entry for the DLL has been removed from the Windows Registry. By the way, don't be thrown off by the fact that the message box uses the term 'Server' instead of 'component' – that's a carry-over from earlier versions of Visual Basic:"

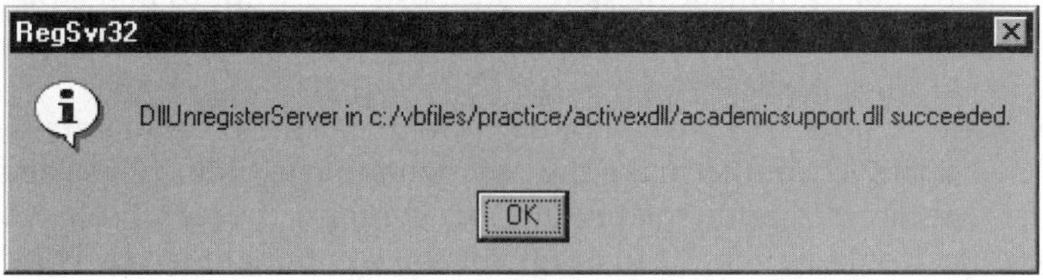

"Now let's check the References window in Visual Basic," I said, "and verify that the entry for the component is really gone."

I selected Project | References from the Visual Basic menu bar to view the References window:

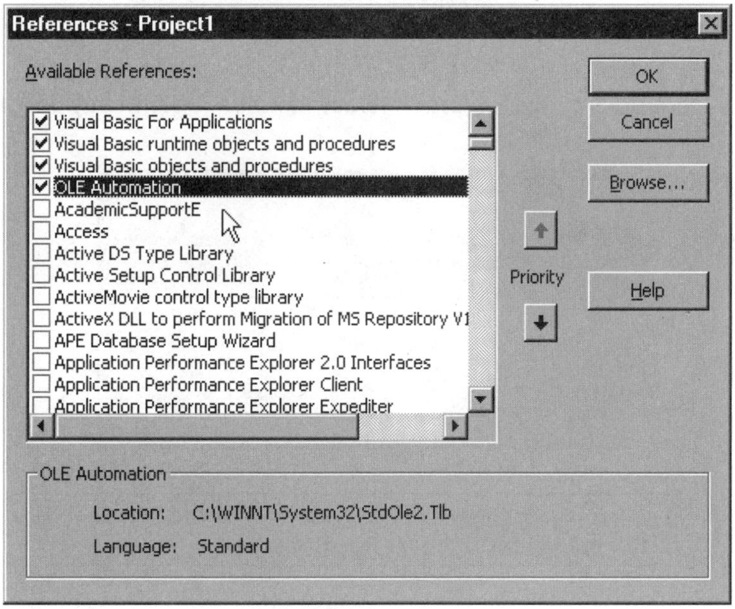

"As you can see," I said, "AcademicSupport is no longer listed in the References window – and its entry in the Windows Registry has been removed."

"Does un-registering an ActiveX component like this also remove the file from the our PC's hard drive?" Mary asked.

"No, it doesn't, Mary," I told her. "The ActiveX component's file is still physically on the user's PC at this point: we can remove it if we want, or leave it there in the event we choose to re-register it in the future."

"I was just about to ask about that!" Kate said. "Suppose you want to make the component available as a Reference again? That's possible, huh?"

"Most definitely, Kate," I said. "All we've done is unregister the component – we haven't physically removed it. If we want to make the component available for use again, we have two options. First, we can recompile the project that contains the **`ActiveX.DLL`** again: if we do that, Visual Basic will automatically register the component in the Windows Registry for us. Second, we can *manually* register the ActiveX component ourselves by running **`REGSVR32`** again, but this time **without** the **`/u`** option. Let me show you."

I closed the Visual Basic References window, clicked on the Start | Run button again, and typed the following statement into the Run window:

regsvr32 c:/vbfiles/practice/activexdll/academicsupport.dll

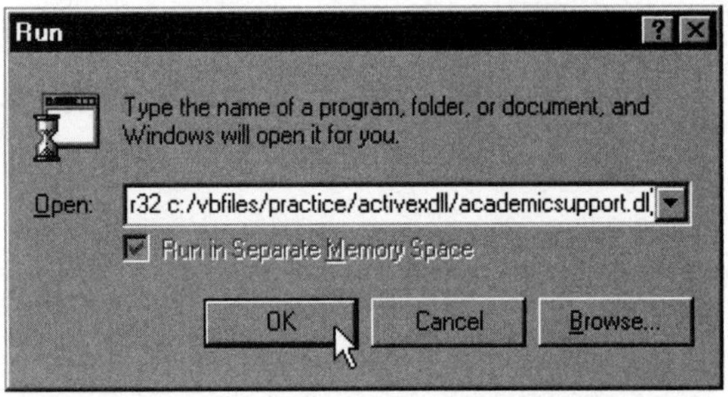

> **Once again, note that the text box in the screenshot is too small to display the full statement that you need to type.**

"As long as the DLL can be found at the location we specify," I said, "**`REGSVR32`** can be used to register the component manually."

I clicked on the OK button, and this message box appeared:

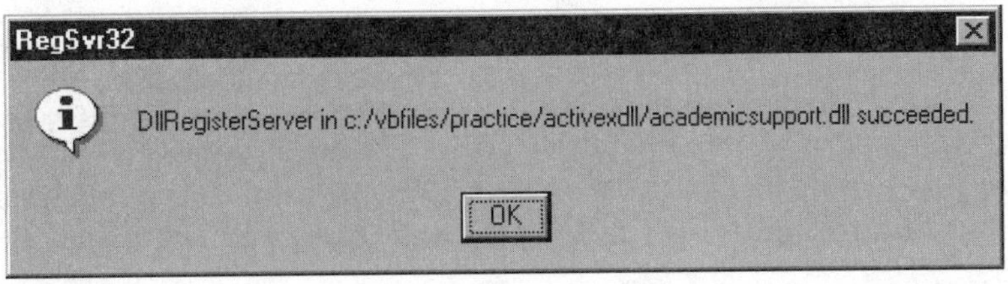

"Again," I said, "this message is telling us that the ActiveX component has been successfully registered. If we now check the Visual Basic References window again, we should find that the reference for our **ActiveX.DLL** component has been restored."

I brought up the References window once more:

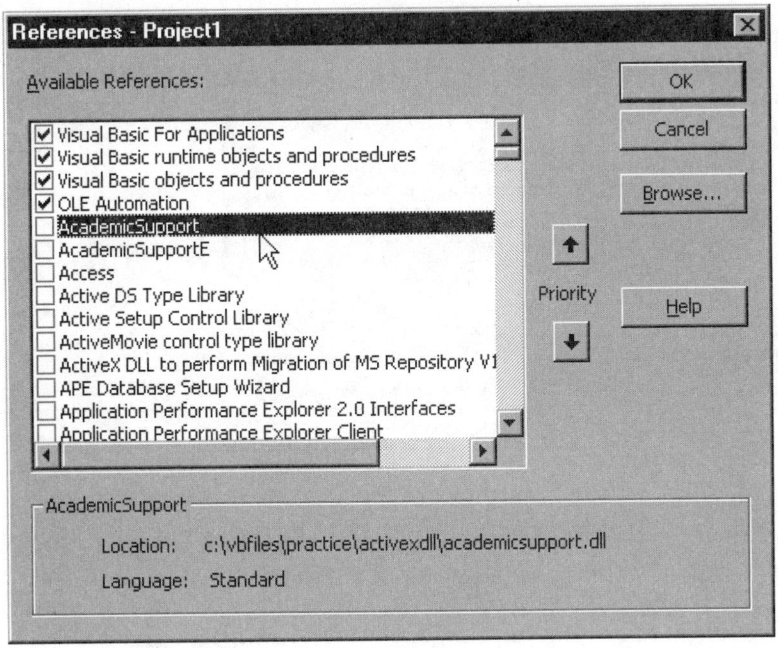

"Cool," said Kevin.

I un-registered the **ActiveX.DLL** component once more by running **REGSVR32** again. That left us with just the other component we created last week to remove from the Windows Registry – the **ActiveX.EXE** component.

"Now," I continued, "let's turn our attention to the **ActiveX.EXE** component."

Unregistering an ActiveX EXE Component

"Do we need to follow a different process to unregister an **ActiveX.EXE**?" Kathy asked.

"Yes, Kathy," I said, "we do. I frequently receive questions from frustrated programmers who're trying to use **REGSVR32** to un-register **ActiveX.EXE** components – but that simply won't work. To unregister an **ActiveX.EXE** component, you have to type the name of the component in the Start | Run window and append an **unregserver** argument to it. Let me show you how..."

I closed the Visual Basic References window, clicked on the Start | Run button, and keyed the following statement into the window:

c:\vbfiles\practice\activexexe\academicsupporte.exe /unregserver

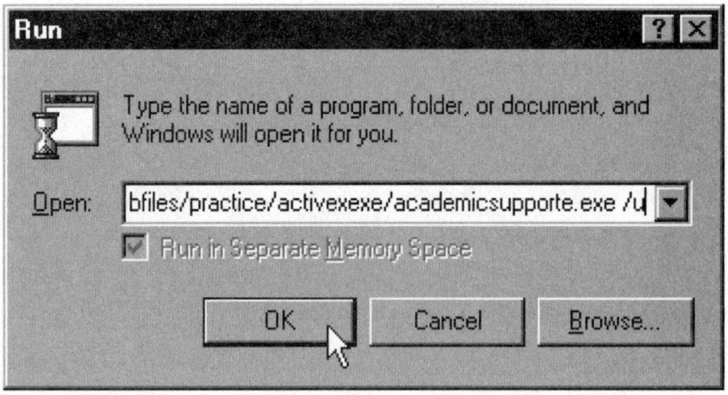

Again, take care to enter the full statement.

"If I click on the OK button now," I continued, "the **ActiveX.EXE**'s entry in the Windows Registry will be removed, and the component will be un-registered. As was the case when we un-registered our **ActiveX.DLL** a moment ago, the **ActiveX.EXE** file remains on the PC – all we're doing here is removing its entry from the Windows Registry."

"Did I miss something?" Valerie said. "I didn't notice any confirmation message appear when you clicked on the OK button."

"Good observation, Valerie," I said. "When we un-register an **ActiveX.EXE** component, no confirmation message is displayed. To check that the process worked, let's have a look at the Visual Basic References window again."

One more time, I selected Project | References from the Visual Basic menu bar:

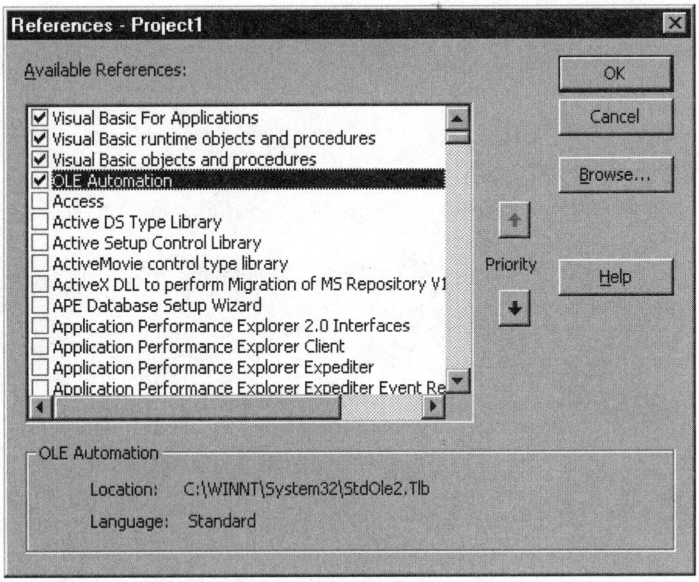

"As you can see," I said, "the entry for the **ActiveX.EXE** component is gone – in fact, at the moment, we have no ActiveX components of our own registered on this PC at all."

"Is there a way to manually register an **ActiveX.EXE** component," Blaine asked, "the same as we did for the **ActiveX.DLL** component a few minutes ago?"

"Yes, there is, Blaine," I confirmed. "As with our **ActiveX.DLL** component, we have two choices. First, we can either recompile the **ActiveX.EXE** component, in which case Visual Basic will automatically register the component for us; or second, we can manually register the ActiveX component ourselves just by typing the name of the component at the command line, like this..."

I shut the Visual Basic References window, clicked on the Start | Run button, and typed another statement into the now-familiar Run window:

c:\vbfiles\practice\activexexe\academicsupporte.exe

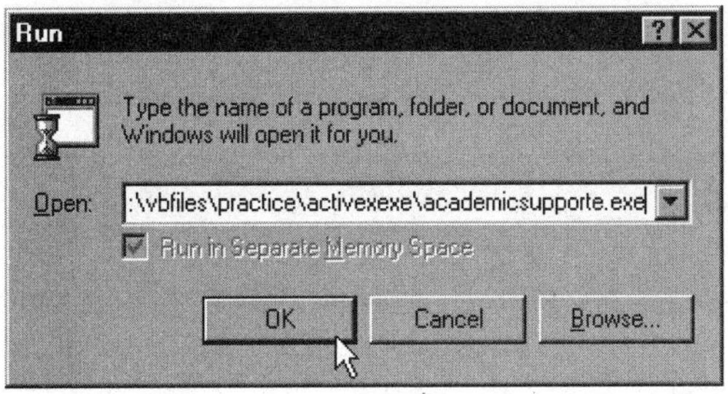

> **The usual warning about the size of the text box applies here, too.**

"Let's check the Visual Basic References window again," I said. "We'd expect to see a reference for our **`ActiveX.EXE`** component in there once more:"

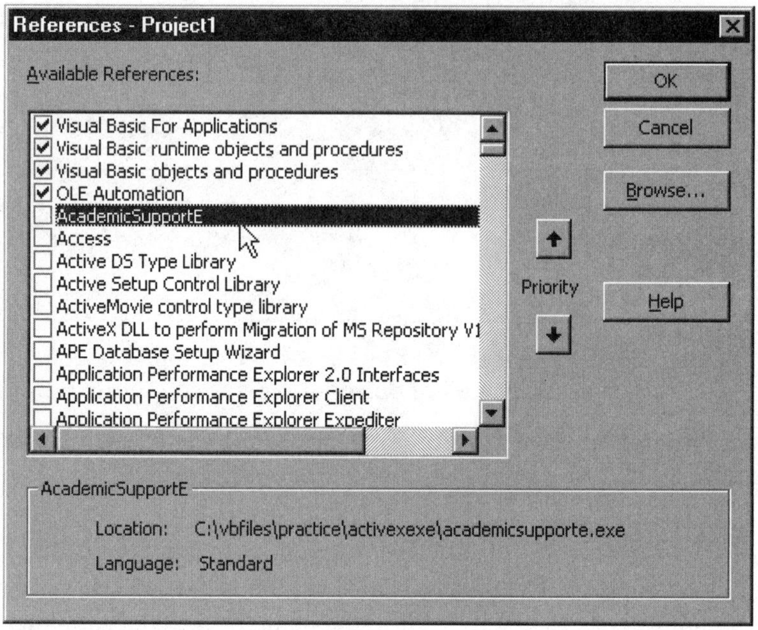

"There it is," I said.

"I'm glad Ward asked that question," Rhonda said. "Seeing this has really clarified this component registration business for me."

"There's just one extra point I'd like to make," I said, displaying the following information point on the screen:

> **You can use the references window to make a note of the path of any component you want to un-register – the filename of the component appears at the bottom of the window.**

"This can come in very handy," I said, "especially if you've made multiple copies of the same component in different locations on your directory tree – each with their own registry entry."

"How likely is that?" Rhonda queried.

"Pretty likely," I replied. "Since, during the development of a component, you may want to retain the previous versions whenever you make modifications – in fact, I'd recommend such an approach."

"Thanks for taking care of my first query," said Ward. "Now, can you solve my other conundrum for me? It's been aggravating me all week!"

"What's the problem, exactly, Ward?" I asked.

Version Compatibility

"As soon as I got into work on Monday," Ward explained, "I compiled several of my classes into an **`ActiveX.EXE`** component. I then used that component in a **`Standard.EXE`** project of mine, and it worked like a charm. A few hours later, I made a couple of very minor changes to one of the class modules in my component and recompiled it. When I ran the **`Standard.EXE`** project that I'd added the component to, I got an error message saying that the program couldn't create an instance of my object. I wasn't quite sure what to make of that, and when I opened up the **`Standard.EXE`** project and went to the Visual Basic References window, I saw the word 'Missing' next to my component. Now I was more confused than ever – I *knew* the component was still on the PC. Not knowing what to do, I just unselected the component in the References window, re-selected it, and recompiled the **`Standard.EXE`** program. Then I ran the program, this time with no problems. I'm not exaggerating when I say I probably went through this scenario close to twenty times over the course of the week – and it was driving me nuts! It seemed that every time I recompiled the component – even if I made absolutely no changes to the component's underlying class modules – the **`Standard.EXE`** program using it bombed. Can you tell me what's happening, and how I can avoid it? "

"I think I know what the trouble is, Ward," I said. "But first, so everyone else can understand the frustration you were going through last week, let me try to simulate your problem here in the classroom. First, let's open up the **`ActiveX.EXE`** project we created last week."

I opened up the **ActiveX.EXE** project from last week – **AcademicSupportE** – and brought up the project's Properties window by selecting Project | AcademicSupportE Properties.

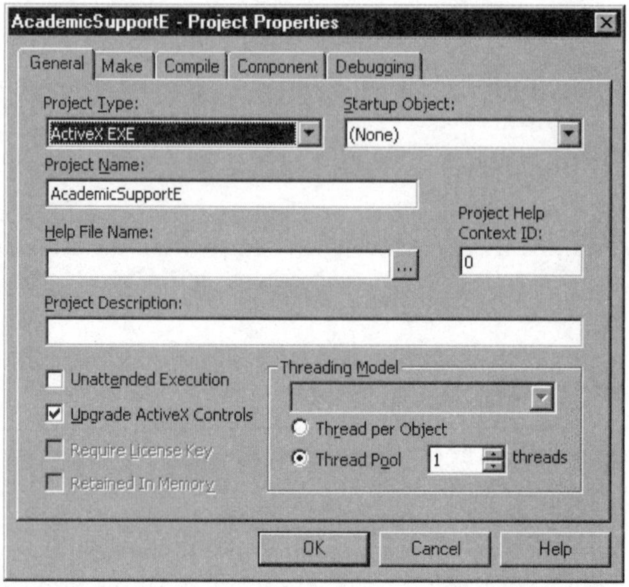

"There are some features of an ActiveX project's Properties window that I didn't discuss last week," I said, "because they're a little beyond the scope of this introductory look at Visual Basic objects. However, I will discuss the one which think I may have been responsible for Ward's problems with his ActiveX project: it's possible that either you or someone at work may have been experimenting with the Component tab of the Properties window:"

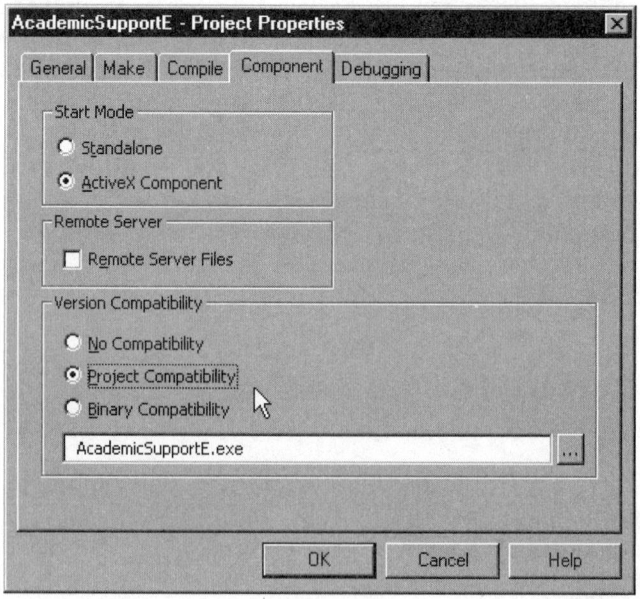

"Specifically, I think we need to look at the Version Compatibility section – down at the bottom of the Component tab."

"I'm sure that I've never seen this Component tab," Ward said, "but I can't vouch for some of the programmers I work with. You know how programmers are – they love to experiment!"

"What does **Version Compatibility** mean, anyway?" asked Blaine. "How could it have caused Ward's problem?"

"Version compatibility," I continued, "is Visual Basic's attempt to ensure that successive versions of ActiveX components are **backward-compatible**."

"Another new term!" exclaimed Rhonda. "What does that one mean?

"If a new version of an ActiveX component **is** backward-compatible," I explained, "it won't create any problems for a program that was written using the old version of the component. We're aiming to ensure that the program can work just as well with the new version as it did with the old one. "

"I'm not sure I'm following this," Kevin said. "Can you give us an example?"

"Sure thing, Kevin," I said. "Let's say we have a program that uses an ActiveX component, instantiates an object from it, and then executes one of the object's methods to perform some kind of action. Now, let's say that, two months later, the designer of the object changes the method so that it now does something different, and places the new version of the component out on the network. All of a sudden, the programs using the component start misbehaving."

"Right," Ward concluded. "The programs are making calls to methods that no longer act as they're expected to by the programs using them."

"Correct," I replied. "In this instance, we would say that the designer of the object had created a new version of the component which was **not** backward-compatible – it won't work with old versions of the programs, because they expect it to do something other than what it now does."

I looked around the classroom – so far so good.

"That's one extreme," I went on. "Now let me give you an example of a change that **is** backward-compatible. The designer adds another method to perform the desired new functionality, to the component, instead of modifying the existing method. He then puts his modified component out on the network, and, in this instance, the change has absolutely no impact on any programs using the old version. All of the original methods are still in the new version of the component, and so calls to them still execute as before."

"So, it has *more* functionality, but the existing functionality hasn't been changed," Rhonda observed.

"Exactly," I replied. "As an aside, Ward, maybe you should check up on the standards that your company has for version compatibility. If you don't have **any**, then maybe you can steer them in the right direction. After all, programmers can waste phenomenal amounts of time trying to sort out issues like this when all that's required is a simple standard that everyone is told about and has to adhere to – I speak from painful experience! When you work in a team, it's essential that you foster the right kind of attitude to group co-operation."

"OK," Ward said, "I'll do that. I see the difference between backward-compatible and non-backward-compatible now. But what does the Version Compatibility section of the Component tab have to do with this?"

"When an ActiveX component is first compiled," I explained, "a special marker called a **Globally Unique IDentifier** – or **GUID** – is placed in the header portion of the component. A GUID is a unique number, randomly generated, and it's used to identify a specific ActiveX component. The component's GUID is **also** recorded in the Windows Registry alongside the name of the component."

"So," said Rhonda, "when a programmer sets a reference to an ActiveX component in a **`Standard.EXE`** project, the component's GUID is stored with the project **and** in the Windows Registry. How does that help?"

"Since ActiveX components are accessed at run time," I explained, "the first thing the program using them does is check that the GUID contained in the header of the ActiveX component it's opening is the same as the GUID that it's expecting: if they don't match, the program crashes with the error message that Ward saw all week long."

"So..." said Mary, "you're saying that Ward's **`Standard.EXE`** program fell over because the ActiveX component's GUID didn't match the one the program was looking for?"

"That's right, Mary," I said. "It wasn't until Ward re-added the reference – thus getting access to the component with the latest GUID – that he could run his program successfully."

"How did the GUID of Ward's ActiveX component change?" Peter asked. "Does it change every time you recompile the component?"

"Good question, Peter," I said. "The answer is...maybe – depending upon the option selected for Version Compatibility on the Component tab. There are three options in all – No Compatibility, Project Compatibility, and Binary Compatibility:"

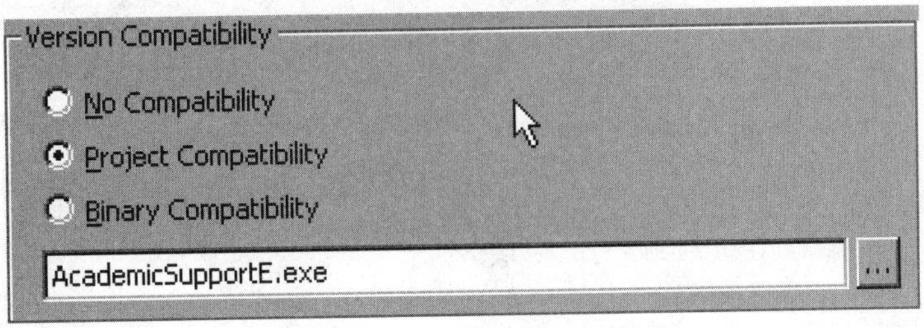

"With No Compatibility set – which is what I think may have been set on Ward's PC – then every time the ActiveX component is compiled, the GUID changes, causing any program using it to crash. With Project Compatibility, the GUID remains the same unless Visual Basic detects that a change has been made within the component that would render it **not** backward-compatible. In that case, the GUID changes. Finally, there's Binary Compatibility. Binary Compatibility is the same as Project Compatibility, except that a prompt informs you, after compiling the component, that it is no longer backward-compatible. Visual Basic then gives you the opportunity to override the change in the GUID."

"It seems to me that Project Compatibility is the best of all possible worlds," Valerie said. "Visual Basic only updates the GUID when necessary."

"I agree with you, Valerie," I said, "and so does Microsoft – that's why Project Compatibility is the default Version Compatibility option. During the course of the week, it's possible that Ward may have made changes to his component that would have updated the GUID even with Project Compatibility selected – but I suspect that he may have had the No Compatibility option selected."

"Can you show us what happens when the GUID changes?" Bob asked.

"No problem, Bob," I said. "Last week we compiled the `ActiveX.EXE` component. Now let's create a project to use it, and then recompile the component with the No Compatibility option selected and see what happens."

I opened up another copy of Visual Basic to run alongside the one I already had open, created a new **Standard.EXE** project, added a single command button on its form, and then selected the **AcademicSupportE** component from the References window:

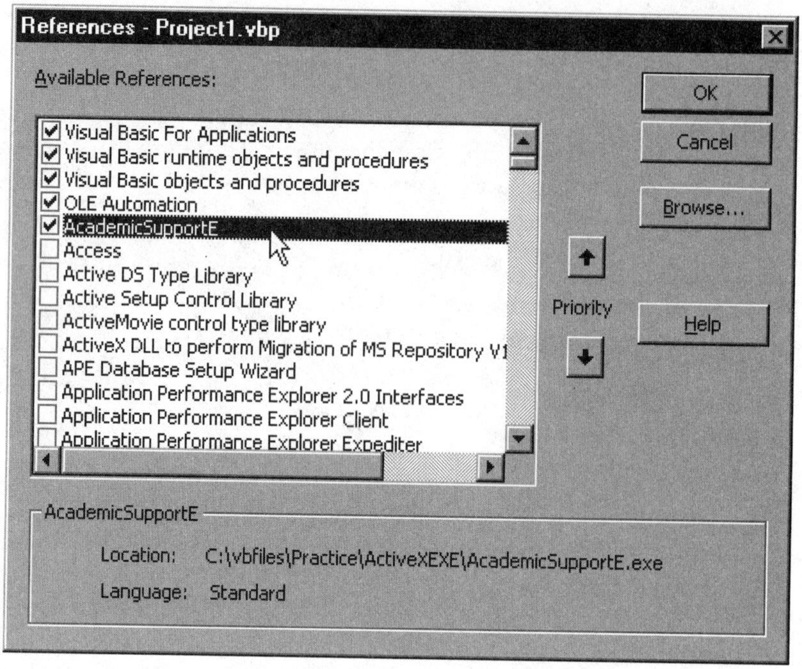

"Now I'll add some code to the command button's **Click** event procedure," I said. Here's that code:

```
Private Sub Command1_Click()

Dim objStudent As New Student

objStudent.MidTerm = 40
objStudent.FinalExam = 60
objStudent.TermPaper = 90

Msgbox "The Student's average is " & objStudent.Average

End Sub
```

"This code is an old friend of ours now," I said. "All we're doing is creating an instance of the **Student** object from our ActiveX component, setting the value of three of its properties, and then displaying the value of the **Average** property in a message box."

I ran the program and clicked on the command button, with this result:

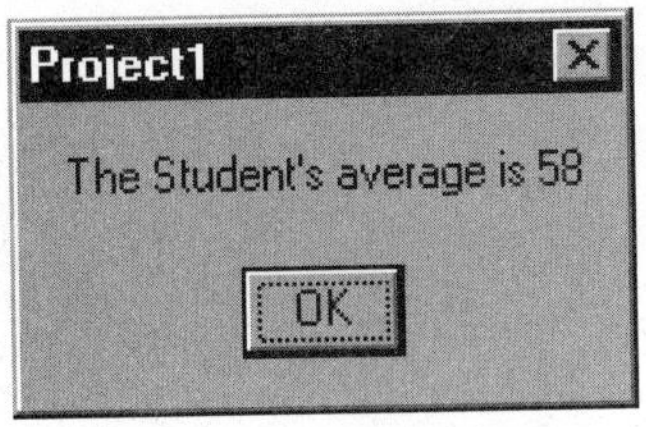

"This code runs with no problem," I said. "Now let's watch what happens if we recompile our ActiveX component after first selecting No Compatibility in the Component tab's Version Compatibility section. Bear in mind that we haven't changed a single thing about the component..."

I saved the **Standard.EXE** project as **Test.vbp** in the **Practice** directory and then closed it. Next, I switched to a Visual Basic session running the **AcademicSupportE** project and brought up its Properties window, where I selected No Compatibility on the Component tab...

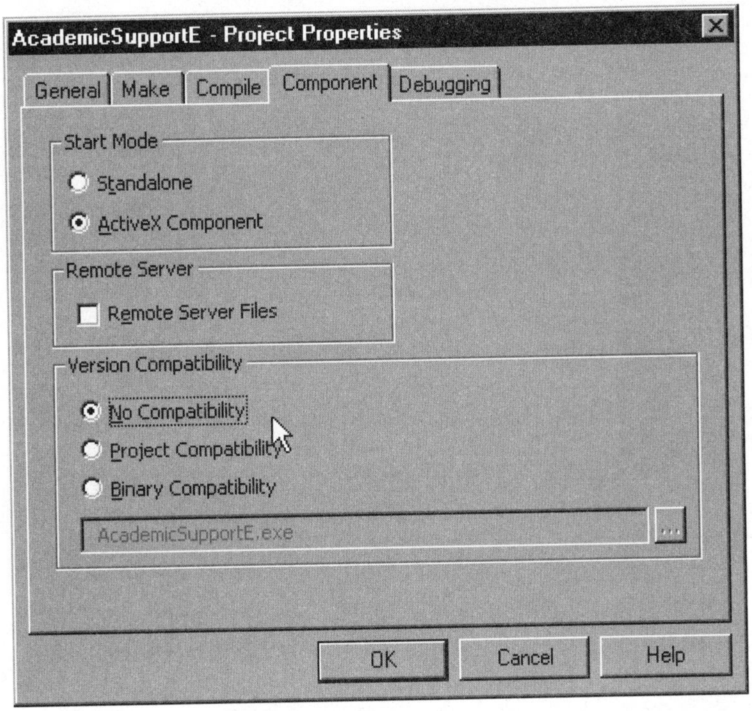

...and clicked on the OK button.

"Next," I continued, "we'll recompile the component over the previous version by compiling it to the existing **AcademicSupportE.exe** file in the **\VBFiles\Practice\ActiveXEXE** folder." I did that, and then went on: "Now let's run our **Test** project again and see what happens."

I then loaded up the **Test** project in its own Visual Basic session, ran it, and clicked on its command button. This was the result:

"This error message," I said, "tells us that our project can't find the correct version of the ActiveX component it's looking for..."

I clicked on the OK button, stopped the program, and brought up the References window:

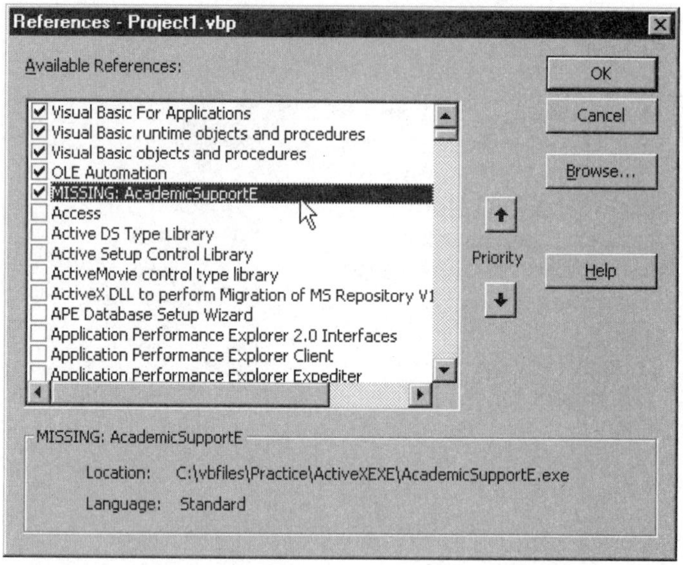

"What happened?" Rhonda said. "Visual Basic is saying that the **AcademicSupportE** component is Missing – but we didn't remove it. It **is** weird."

"It's pretty misleading, isn't it?" I said. "The ActiveX component **is** there – it's just that the GUID our **Test** project is looking for doesn't exist on the PC. When we recompiled the ActiveX component with the No Compatibility Option selected, the GUID changed."

"What do we do now?" asked Lou, looking forlorn.

"All we need to do," I reassured him, "is to unselect the component in the References window, click on the OK button, and then reopen the References window again. We should find that the Missing tag has disappeared, and we'll be able to select the current version of the **AcademicSupportE** component."

I did that, and then clicked on the OK button:

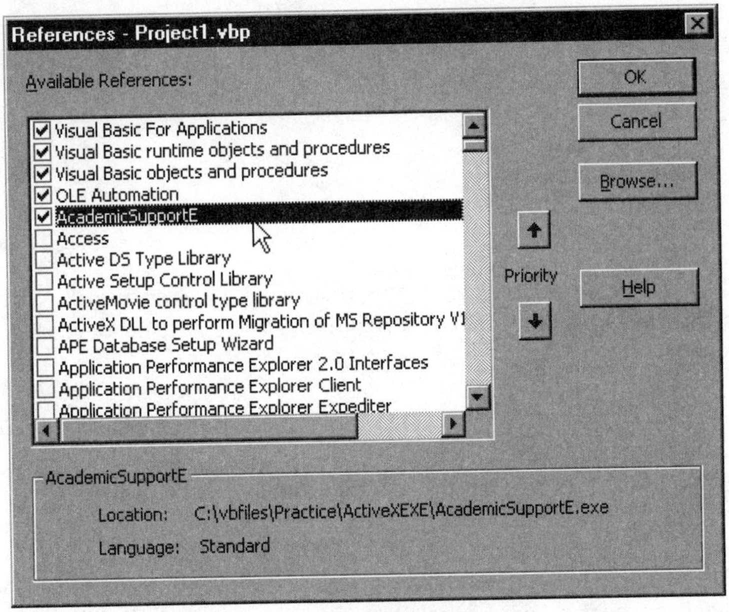

"Now," I continued, "if we run the **Test** program and click on the command button, the program will run just fine. Let's do just that..."

I did so, with this result:

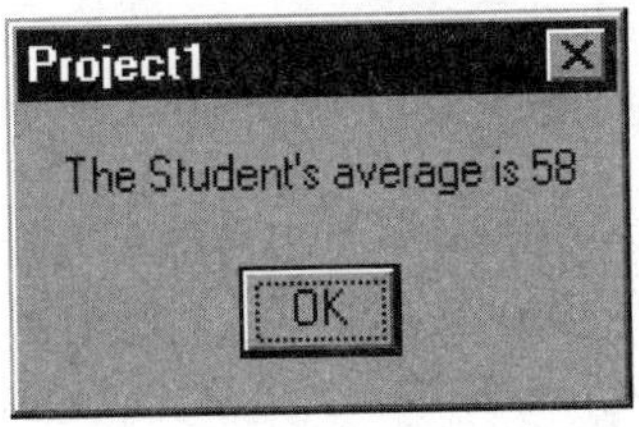

"What about that error message Ward said he got?" Kate said, "the one about not being able to create an object? We didn't see that here, did we?"

"No, that's correct," I said. "That's the error message you'll get if a compiled program – rather than one run directly from the Visual Basic IDE – can't find an ActiveX component with the correct GUID. Let me show you..."

I compiled the **Test** project into an executable file called **Test.exe**, shut down the **Test** project, recompiled our ActiveX component in the **AcademicSupportE** project – thus generating a new GUID.

"If we now run the **Test.exe** project," I said, as I double-clicked on it in Windows Explorer, "and then click on the command button that appears on the form, we should receive the error message that Ward saw all week long."

I did so, and the following message box was generated:

"That's the error message I was receiving, sure enough!" Ward confirmed. "Wow, was that a nightmare! So you think my problems were caused because of the Version Compatibility option?"

"I think so, Ward," I said, "At any rate, no harm was done – other than the week of frustration you suffered!"

I glanced at the clock – we'd been working for well over an hour.

"If there are no other questions," I said, pausing to see if the were any, "I declare the teaching part of our Visual Basic objects course officially ended. I want to thank you all for your attention and participation throughout the course – I've really enjoyed meeting with all of you these last ten weeks. All that remains is for us to take care of a few administrative details – and then it's off to the China Shop to deliver and install the program!"

"What administrative details are those?" Melissa asked.

Testing...

"Last semester," I said, "when we delivered the original version of the China Shop program to Joe's Bullina's China Shop, we had a little dilemma on our hands. All nineteen of us had worked on the China Shop program – but there was only one PC at the store. At Joe's insistence, we all voted for our three favorite programs – and the one that received the most first place votes was the one that actually got installed on Joe's machine, and is running to this day in the China Shop."

"Are we going to do that today, too?" asked Tom.

"I think it's a good idea," I said, "and it seemed to work out well last semester. What I'd like to ask everyone to do is to take a few moments to perform a final test of your neighbor's program, and see if you can find any problems. When you're sure that it's working properly, come to the front of the classroom and pick up a ballot – then take a quick walk around the classroom and vote for your top three versions of the China Shop program. The project that receives the most first place votes will be the program that we'll install on both the PCs at the China Shop today. As I did in last semester's class, I'm removing my own version of the project from the voting, and Rhonda, whose project was the one chosen last semester, has also withdrawn her project from consideration. Remember everyone, this is your project – one of you deserves to have the place of honor in the China Shop."

"Speaking of testing our own version of the program," Dorothy said, "can you give us any tips on testing our programs?"

"The object-oriented version of the China Shop program shouldn't be much more difficult to test than the original version," I said. "Outwardly, except for the new `Shipping` form, not much has changed, although I'm sure you would all agree that it's a very different program **internally**. At a minimum, you need to ensure that the program calculates the customer's sales quotation properly, and to do that, you should have some kind of price matrix already calculated so that you know what the correct prices are for a variety of customer selections. In particular, you want to pay special attention to any selection involving a complete place setting and a platter. "

"Anything else?" Kevin asked.

"Yes. Don't forget that Joe Bullina's main aim in having us update this program in the first place was to give him and his staff an easy way to calculate shipping charges for mail order purchases. That's vitally important. Beyond that, ensure that all of the functionality identified in the requirements statement is present and working – including printing the sales quotation for the customer."

"I would think that most of the real bugs in the program should have been discovered by now," Kevin said.

"I'm not sure we can say that with one hundred percent certainty, Kevin" I replied. "I know that we've gone through a lot of the functionality of the program in class – but we haven't covered every possible customer selection or even every possible shipping charge. It's conceivable that there may be bugs in the program – although like you, somehow I doubt that there's anything major."

> **!** **Programmers seldom come to their first jobs understanding how important testing is, or that it requires a methodical approach. In the real world, you should always draw up a rigorous testing regime that thoroughly checks out your program.**

"I originally thought," Ward said, "that the chances for a bug of some kind slipping through would be greater with this version of the program than with the previous one – after all, we now have two forms instead of one. But after seeing how the use of objects made coding this version so much *easier*, if anything, I think this version of the program should be cleaner than the previous one."

"You're probably right, Ward," I said. "Object-orienting the program has made it easier to follow, and more elegant too – and don't forget that all of this work should make modifying it in the future much easier, too!"

I then asked the class to spend the next fifteen minutes giving their projects one final check, playfully – but respectfully – reviewing their fellow classmate's projects, and voting for their three favorites.

Fifteen minutes later, as I collected their ballots and tallied the totals, I asked each student to give me a diskette containing their own copy of the object-oriented China Shop project. Then I gave everyone a printed set of directions to the Bullina China Shop, and sent them on their way.

"Class is dismissed," I said, "I hope you see all of you at the China Shop – and please drive safely."

I called Dave aside – he'd volunteered to coordinate the installation of the objects version of the China Shop program at the Bullina China Shop. I handed Dave the diskette containing the project that had received the most first place votes, and asked him to install the enhanced version of the program at the China Shop. "You'll get there before me," I said. "You know how I drive – real slow."

"I'll be glad to do the installation for you," he said, "see you there!"

Delivering the China Shop Program

As I began to gather my things together, I watched the students leave the classroom, and I have to confess I felt a little melancholy – endings and partings are invariably sad. Just then, my cell phone rang – one of my clients calling from Seattle seeking some advice about a Visual Basic program they were writing. Knowing that the delivery and installation of the enhanced China Shop Program was in Dave's capable hands, I spent the next half hour working on the phone with him – so it was about two hours later when I finally arrived at the Bullina China Shop – quite obviously the last one to get there.

A Ticker-tape Parade

Late afternoon business at the China Shop was brisk – the newly expanded parking lot was jammed. As I walked through the door, a beautiful sight met my eyes. Just as he'd done at the conclusion of the Introductory class, Joe Bullina had arranged a celebration party: the China shop was full of balloons and streamers, and a sumptuous buffet table of food had been set up in one corner.

Through the crowd of chattering people, Joe Bullina caught my eye.

"John," he said, "you and your students have done it again – the new enhanced program is just great – even better than the original, I think – we all love it! We've spent the last hour trying it out – and that printed sales quotation is a great touch. By the way, have a sandwich!" I took the proffered pastrami on rye.

Amidst the hullabaloo and excitement, I glanced toward the middle of the China Shop showroom, and there on a kiosk in the middle of the sales floor was a computer (with a brand new laser printer attached) running the enhanced China Shop program. Kate was seated at the PC, training the sales staff.

I wandered over and caught Kate's eye. She had just gotten up from her seat and was now watching Midge, the China Shop's head sales clerk, put the program through its paces.

"I'm delighted that the class voted to install my version of the China Shop project," she said, "thanks for all your help!"

"You did a great job with the program, Kate," I said, "I would say that your Visual Basic future is very bright."

Joe Bullina waved to an elderly couple who were nibbling at some pizza, encouraging them to come over to the desk.

"I don't know whether you remember these folks from last year," Joe said, "but this is the couple who received the first sales quotation from the original China Shop program. For good luck, I invited them back here today to be the first customers to try out the new version of the program."

"Hi," I said, "I believe you're Rita and Gil – aren't you?"

"You have a good memory," Gil said, "that's quite right."

"Last year," said Rita, "Gil bought me china for our anniversary. Today, Gil has promised to buy me new china for my next birthday – 82 years young on June 7th."

"Congratulations!" Joe said.

As Midge and Kate vacated the area around the kiosk, Joe Bullina pulled up two chairs. Gil sat down beside Rita and the two of them began to use the modified China Shop program. Kate and the rest of the students from our class watched them as they put the modified program through its paces. Gil seemed to know exactly what he wanted and, after making a selection of china...

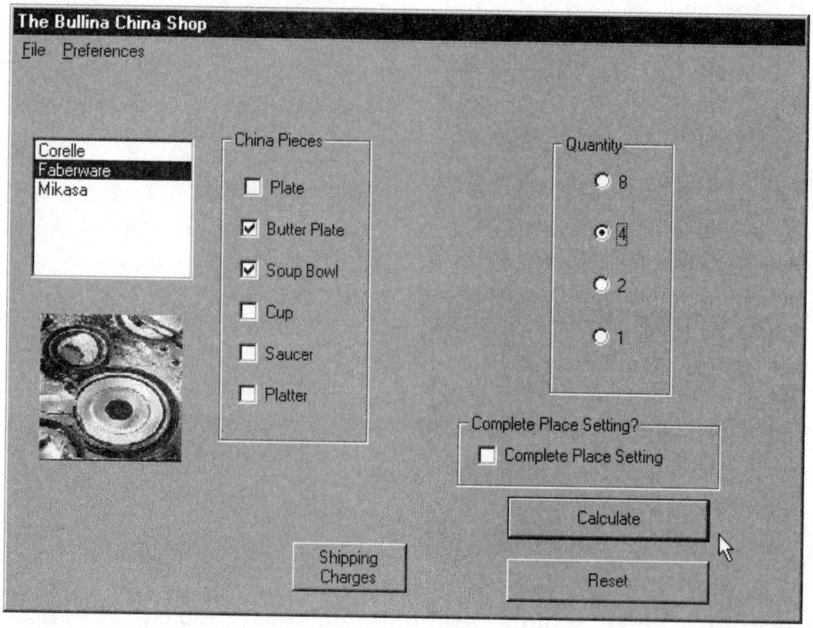

… and clicking the Calculate command button, the two of them were greeted with an unfamiliar I'll Take It command button in addition to the displayed price of $32:

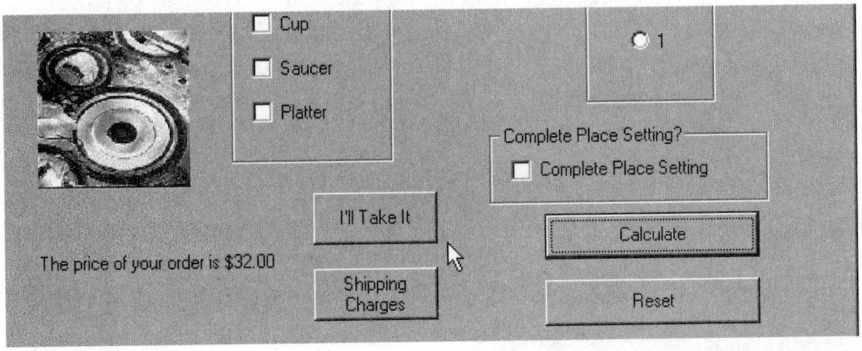

I overheard Gil tell Rita that "the price looks good to me," but before they clicked on the I'll Take It button, the two of them decided to check the shipping charges to Colorado. Gil clicked on the Shipping Charges button and then clicked on the state of Colorado in the list box:

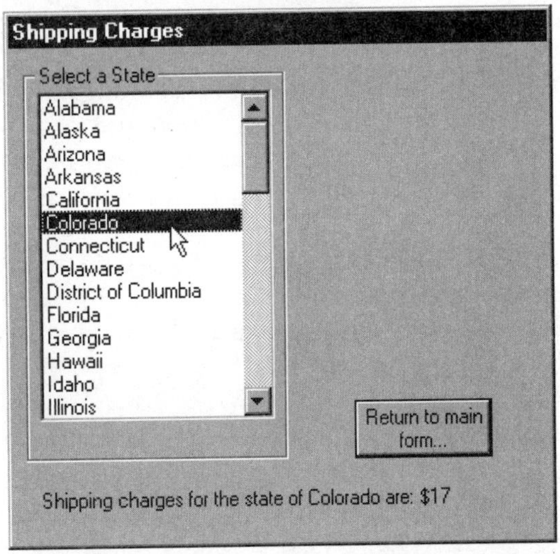

I heard Rita say that she thought $17 to ship china to Colorado was reasonable. She took control of the mouse and, after clicking on the Return to main form… button, she clicked on I'll Take It, and…

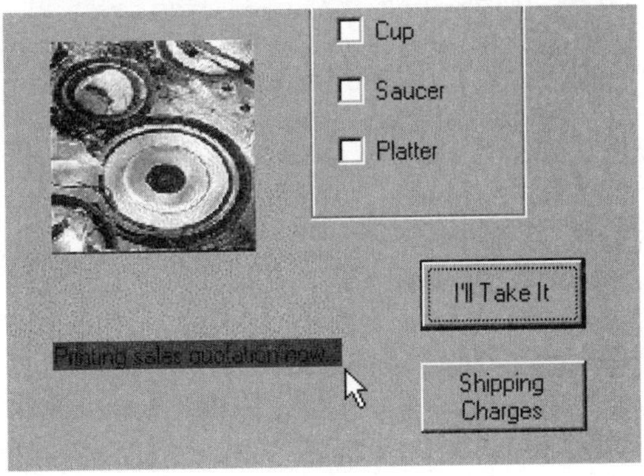

They both noticed the message that the sales quotation was printing, and waited for the printout to come off on the attached laser printer. After a few seconds, Rita reached over to the laser printer, picked up the sales quotation and, arm in arm, she and Gil strolled to the sales counter at the front of the store to pay for their china, and to arrange shipping it to Colorado. As Gil passed by me, he gave me a big wink and said "Works great!"

As Rita and Gil stood at the counter, I addressed my assembled class:

"The modified program works as requested," I told them. "Rita and Gil used the program to make selections of china on the main form of the China Shop program, were able to receive a quotation of shipping charges to a destination state of their choice and, finally, after making a decision to purchase the china, they printed a sales quotation. The two of them are on their way, and Joe had made his sale."

I turned to Joe Bullina.

"As we did last semester, Joe," I said, "pairs of students have volunteered to be on site to make observations and assist you and your staff with any problems that might come up – they'll also be showing your sales staff how to update the shipping charges in the `Shipping.txt` file."

"It's always great to have your students here," Joe said. "And after seeing the great work you've done on this project, I'm sure I'll have more work for your next class – that fellow who called me a few weeks ago from Seattle gave me a few ideas about web-enabling the China Shop!"

"Maybe we can tackle that issue in my upcoming Visual Basic Web Development course," I said. "I expect that some of these students will be in that class too, and I'm sure they would be more than willing to develop something along those lines. Joe, on behalf of all the students in my class I want to thank you for a wonderful learning opportunity. I'm sure we'll be in touch."

Turning to the class, I said: "I've got to take off now. Everyone please be mindful of your technical support coverage schedules, and if you have any problems, you all know where to find me. I hope to see you all in a few weeks."

Summary

Congratulations! You've completed the class, and completed and implemented the object-oriented version of the China Shop project. I hope you felt the excitement of delivering and installing the China Shop project as much as the students in my class did, because you were a very welcome part of it. But don't let this be the end of your learning experience with objects, or with Visual Basic.

We've come a long way together in the past ten weeks, and I hope you've started to appreciate the power, elegance, and logic of the object-oriented approach. I won't pretend that there isn't still a whole lot to learn if you're going to take your object-oriented programming career further – there is! Object-oriented programming is a large and complex subject – that's why there are so many specialist books out there covering object-oriented theory, analysis, design, and coding in detail.

What this book has aimed to do is to give you the big picture – a sketch of the world of objects that will let you navigate through the landscape in an informed way. You can think of this book as the large-scale map that shows you the main features of the countryside. Now it's down to you to tie up your boots, strap on your backpack, and explore each mountain, river and small town with an understanding of where they fit into the bigger picture. Don't forget to stop once in a while for refreshment!

At this point, you should feel confident enough to tackle a variety of programs, including projects that have object-oriented implications. I hope that by following along with my Visual Basic objects programming class, you've seen that the world of object-oriented programming need not be as daunting as it's sometimes made out to be, and how real-world object-oriented applications are developed. That's not to say that all projects go as smoothly as this one did, and neither does every client meet us on delivery day with sandwiches, balloons and streamers. You can expect your share of mistakes, misinterpretations, and misunderstanding along the way. But it's invariably exciting and, if you love it as much as I do, it'll always be fun.

As I close, I just want to give you a few words of advice:

First, remember that in programming, there's rarely a single "correct" solution. There really is more than one way to paint a picture.

Secondly, always be your own best friend. Inevitably, while trying to work through a solution, there will be frustrating moments. Never doubt yourself, and never get 'down' on yourself.

And finally, remember that there is always more to learn. The world of programming is an endless series of free learning seminars. All you need to do is open up a manual, read a help file, surf the Internet, or pick up a Visual Basic book, and you are well on your way. You can never know it all, let alone master it all – but try and move in that direction.

I wish you good luck, and I hope to see you in a future class of mine.

Professor Smiley

Learn to Program Objects with Visual Basic
Bullina's
China

Appendix A
Student Biographies

On the evening of the first class I took home the biographies that the eighteen students had written about themselves. I'm always interested to know the mix of abilities and backgrounds of my students.

They turned out to be a varied bunch, who fell roughly into five categories:

Some of the students were looking to have a new skill-set to use if their current job fell through:

Linda wrote that she loved her Network Administration job, but was glad to have something to 'fall back' on in the future. She hoped that this course would give her a solid foundation in the object-orientation methodology of Visual Basic.

Dave reported that his job as a mid-level manager was still very much in jeopardy, and that he thought it was just a matter of time before he received 'bad news'. I knew that with his obviously outstanding abilities in Visual Basic he wouldn't have any trouble securing another job – particularly with this class under his belt too!

Mary, a statistical analyst for a railroad that was currently undergoing a merger, was also fearful for her job. She wrote that she hoped that this class in Visual Basic, along with the Introductory class, would enable her to obtain a new position if the worst did happen. I felt that after she heard the success stories from some other members of the class, her demeanor would perk up a bit.

There were those who wanted to improve their current status at work:

Peter wrote that he continued to enjoy his job as a COBOL programmer, and expressed hopes that after completing this class his company would finally let him tackle a Visual Basic project.

Kathy, a Microsoft Access programmer, reported that she was now working on a Visual Basic project at work – something she'd wanted to do for some time.

Kate happily reported that she was also writing Visual Basic programs back at the office. Kate, unlike Kathy, had no prior programming experience, so this was quite an accomplishment. Working in a small office, Kate had taken advantage of her boss's offer to pay for a Visual Basic programming class, and in the few weeks between the end of the Introductory class and the beginning of this one, she had already designed, programmed and implemented a Visual Basic project! Needless to say, she was elated over the chance to do some more, and wrote that she was looking forward to 'object-orienting' her program.

A few students wanted to use the skills they could gain on the course to help start a new career:

Valerie was a stay at home mom looking to do some Visual Basic programming part time. Based on her performance in the introductory class, this class would make that desire achievable.

Blaine wrote that his greatest fears had been realized over the semester break – he had finally lost his job as a mainframe programmer. But, due in no small part to the Introductory Visual Basic course and the China Shop project, he had already been offered a new job, and would be starting work a week from Monday!

We had two younger students, plus those that wanted to study for their own general interests:

Chuck wrote that he'd built a Visual Basic program for his mother's law firm over the semester break. He was joined by his friend Rachel. Together, they were the youngest students in the Introductory Visual Basic class – both 16 years of age.

Rachel was a new student – both a friend and classmate of Chuck's. Chuck had told her how much he had enjoyed the introductory class. She wrote that she had done a lot of programming in C and C++, and had worked with Chuck on his Visual Basic programs during the Introductory class.

Lou wrote that his illness, which would one day totally disable him and leave him wheel chair bound, was slowly but gradually progressing. He added that he held high hopes for genetic research, and despite his worsening symptoms, reported that he had been able to write a Visual Basic program for his local florist during the semester break.

Rhonda reported that she had fulfilled her latest life's desire in the introductory class – to be able to keep up with her grandchildren! Not surprisingly, she told the class that she had taken her grandchildren to the China Shop to show them the program their grandmother wrote!

That left six students who wanted to use visual basic within their workplace to both generally enhance procedures and speed up their work, or to use for a specific application:

Ward, with his typically dry humor, wrote that, for a 78 year old senior citizen, he thought he was doing pretty well just getting up in the morning! That was a gross understatement; he made wonderful contributions to the Introductory class.

Kevin, new to the class, wrote that he had a Ph.D. in Microbiology, and that he was interested in using Visual Basic as a tool in his research.

Tom, also new to the class, wrote that he was both a civil engineer and an architect for a major construction firm in the Philadelphia area, and that he was interested in using Visual Basic to interface with a Computer Aided Design package he used for his job.

Melissa wrote that she was a physician currently doing research with a large pharmaceutical company, and that she was interested in using Visual Basic to assist her in genetic research.

Steve indicated that he had quite profitably used the Visual Basic techniques he learned in the Introductory class in his own computer consulting firm. He had invited everyone in the class to examining the brand new four-wheeled fruits of his Visual Basic labors in the parking lot after class!

Bob, a commercial plumber by trade, wrote that during the semester break he had written a Visual Basic program to automate his process of bidding on large construction jobs. According to Bob, the program had already saved him more money than the tuition for the Introductory Visual Basic course. He was definitely a happy camper!

That covered everyone, I was pleased to think that my class reflected a range of people who all had much to gain from this course.

Learn to Program Objects with Visual Basic

Learn to Program Objects with Visual Basic
Learn to Program Objects with Visual Basic
Learn to Program Objects with Visual Basic

Learn to Program Objects with Visual Basic
Learn to Program Objects with Visual Basic
Learn to Program Objects with Visual Basic
Learn to Program Objects with Visual Basic
Learn to Program Objects with Visual Basic

Appendix B

Installing the China Shop Project

We've included the code for the existing China Shop project (the one that was built in John Smiley's first book) on the CD that comes bundled in the back of *this* book.

If you haven't already got the completed version of the China Shop program from *Learn to Program with Visual Basic 6* on your PC, you'll need to copy the relevant files from the CD before you can start work on enhancing it. (If you *do* already have a completed China Shop application on your machine, you can continue working with it.)

The following steps explain how to get a working version of the China Shop program up and running on your PC.

Creating the Folders

1. Create a folder on your PC's hard drive called **`VBFiles`**. Note that all the references in the pre-built code supplied on the CD expect this folder to be on the PC's **`C:`** drive, so if you create the **`VBFiles`** folder elsewhere, you'll have to change the code accordingly.

2. Within the **`VBFiles`** folder, create a sub-folder called **`China`**. All of the China Shop's files will live in this **`C:\VBFiles\China`** folder. Your folder setup should look like this in Windows Explorer:

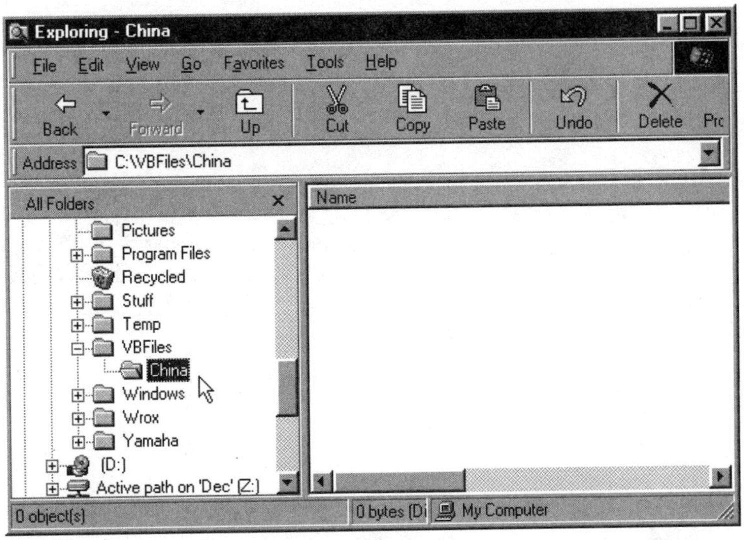

Copying the Files

1. Open up the CD in Windows Explorer, navigate to the `For Chapter 1` folder, and select all of the files that you find there:

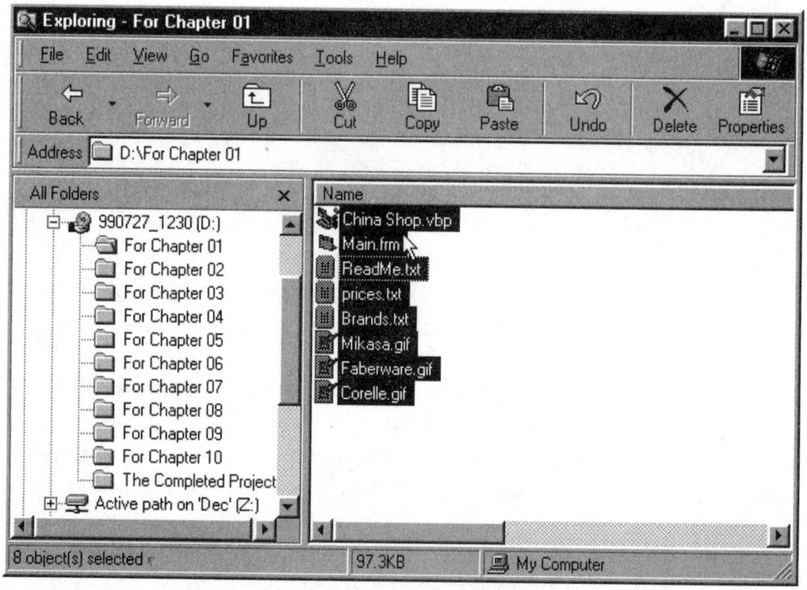

2. Drag these files across and drop them in the `C:\VBFiles\China` folder.

3. Next, make sure you've selected all the files in the `C:\VBFiles\China` directory, and then right click on the multiple selection. From the pop-up menu which appears...

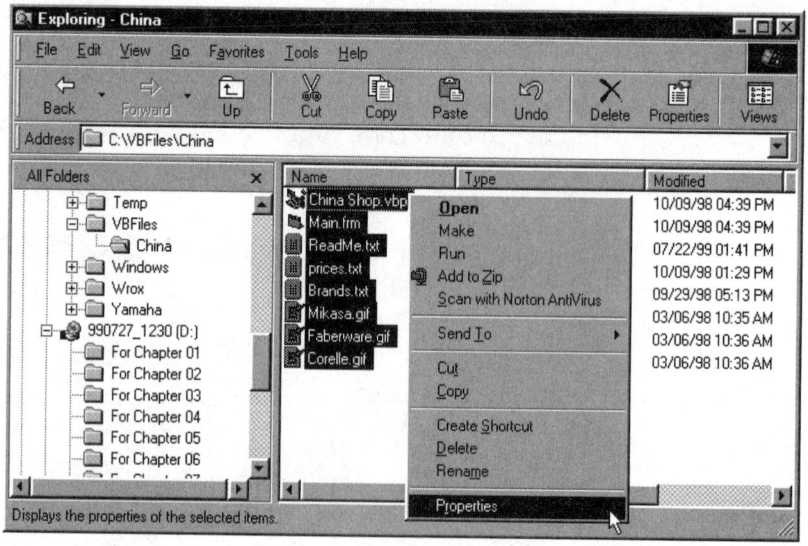

4. ...select the Properties option.

5. Now make sure that the Read-only attribute box is **unchecked**, as shown here:

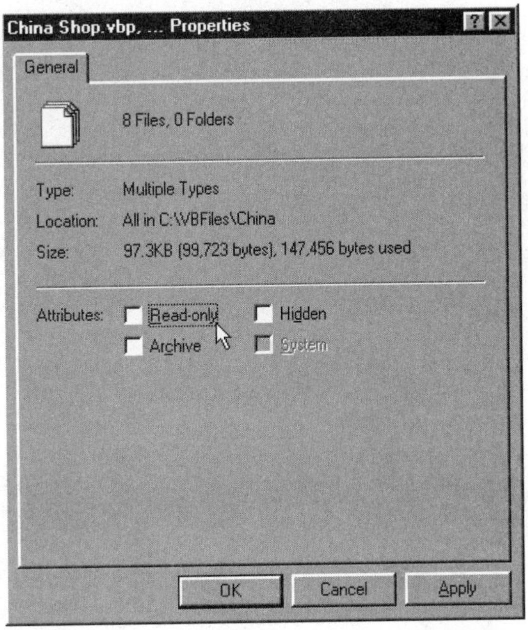

6. Click on the OK button, and the files for the initial version of the China Shop will be ready for you to use and update. You can now double-click on the **`China Shop.vbp`** file and the project will open up in design view in Visual Basic (assuming you have VB installed on your machine!)

This is what the files you've copied do: **`China Shop.vbp`** and **`Main.frm`** are the project file and single form file for the existing program; **`ReadMe.txt`** is information-only; **`Prices.txt`** and **`Brands.txt`** contain price and inventory information that the program uses; and the three **`.gif`** files are used to display images of china pieces on the project's user interface.

Using the Supplied Versions of the Modified Code

The other folders on the CD contain the modified China Shop code at various stages of development through this book. Thus, the **`For Chapter 5`** folder contains the code as it appears at the end of Chapter 4, ready for input to Chapter 5, and so on. In addition, we've included any significant portions of code for the other example projects that we create in the book.

If you need to replace your own code at any time, you can simply copy the relevant version from the appropriate folder on the CD and set the files' attributes so that they are not Read-only – just like you did in the steps described above. However, we really really really do urge that you only use these built files as a last resort – building your skills and learning properly depend on practice and experience. Good luck!

Learn to Program Objects with Visual Basic
Bullina's China

Appendix C

The Systems Development Life Cycle

> **It takes less time to do a thing right than explain why you did it wrong.**
>
> *Henry Wadsworth Longfellow, Poet (1807-1882)*

The Systems Development Life Cycle (**SDLC**), was developed because, historically, many computer systems were being delivered which did not satisfy user requirements, and because those few projects that *did* satisfy user requirements were being developed over-budget or over time. The SDLC is a methodology that has been constructed to ensure that systems are designed and implemented in a methodical, logical and step-by-step approach. There are six steps, known as **phases**, in the SDLC:

- The Preliminary Investigation Phase
- The Analysis Phase
- The Design Phase
- The Development Phase
- The Implementation Phase
- The Maintenance Phase

Each phase of the SDLC creates a tangible product or **deliverable**. An important component of the SDLC is that at each phase, a conscious decision is made to continue development of the project, or to drop it. In the past, projects developed without the guidance of the SDLC were continued well after 'common sense' dictated that it made no sense to proceed further. The deliverables act as milestones against which we can judge the progress and continuing viability of the project.

> **You might be inclined to skip portions of what the SDLC calls for, but remember that the value of the process is that it forces you to follow a standardized methodology for developing programs and systems. Skipping parts of the SDLC can be a big mistake, whereas adhering to it ensures that you give the project the greatest chance for success.**

To understand the structure and working of the SDLC, we'll examine each phase in turn.

Phase 1: The Preliminary Investigation

The **Preliminary Investigation Phase** may begin with a phone call from a customer, a memorandum from a Vice President to the director of Systems Development, a letter from a customer to discuss a perceived problem or deficiency, or a request for something new in an existing system.

The purpose of the **Preliminary Investigation** is not to develop a system, but to verify that a problem or deficiency really exists, or to pass judgment on the new requirement. This phase is typically very short, usually not more than a day or two for a big project, and in some instances it can be as little as two hours!

The end result, or deliverable, from the Preliminary Investigation phase is either a willingness to proceed further, or the decision to 'call it quits'. There are three factors, typically called **constraints**, which result in a 'go' or 'no-go' decision:

- **Technical**. The project can't be completed with the technology currently in existence. This constraint is typified by Leonardo da Vinci's inability to build a helicopter even though he is credited with designing one in the 16th century. Technological constraints made the construction of the helicopter impossible.
- **Time**. The project can be completed, but not in time to satisfy the user's requirements. This is a frequent reason for the abandonment of the project after the Preliminary Investigation phase.
- **Budgetary**. The project can be completed, and completed on time to satisfy the user's requirements, but the cost is prohibitive.

It could be an individual constraint, or any combination of the three that prevents a project from being developed any further.

When an agreement has been made to continue with the project, the second phase of the SDLC is implemented – The **Analysis Phase**.

Phase 2: Analysis

In the **Analysis Phase**, (sometimes called the **Data Gathering Phase**) we study the problem, deficiency or new requirement in detail. Depending upon the size of the project being undertaken, this phase could be as short as the Preliminary Investigation, or it could take months.

While some developers would make the case that we have gathered enough information in Phase 1 of the SDLC to begin programming, the SDLC dictates that phase 2 should be completed before any actual writing of the program begins. It is surprising to find out how much additional information can be gleaned from spending just a little more time with the user.

At the end of phase 2, the **Requirements Statement** should be in development: this provides details about what the program should do. It can easily form the basis of a contract between the customer and the developer. The Requirements Statement should list all of the major details of the program.

Phase 3: Design

The exceptional (or foolish) programmer might begin coding without a good design. Programmers who do so may find themselves going back to modify pieces of code they've already written as they move through the project. With a good design, the likelihood of this happening will be reduced dramatically. The end result is a program that will behave in the way it was intended, and will generally have with a shorter overall program development time.

Design in the SDLC encompasses many different elements. Here is a list of the different components that are 'designed' in this phase:

- Input
- Output
- Processing
- Files

By the end of the design phase, we would hope to have a formal Requirements Statement for the program, and a rough sketch of what the user interface will look like.

Most programs are designed by first determining the output of the program. The reasoning here is that if you know what the output of the program should be, you can determine the input needed to produce that output more easily. Once you know both the output *from*, and the input *to* the program, you can then determine what processing needs to be performed to convert the input to output. You will also be in a position to consider what information needs to be saved, and in what sort of file.

While doing the Output and Input designs, more information will be available to add to the Requirements Statement. It is also possible that a first screen design will take shape and at the end of these designs, and a sketch made of what the screen will look like.

At this stage of the SDLC it isn't necessary to discuss the 'how' of what the program will do, just to get the requirements down on paper.

Phase 4: Development

The **Development Phase** is in many ways the most exciting time of the SDLC. During this phase, computer hardware is purchased and the software is developed. That means that we actually start coding the program.

In the Development phase, examination and re-examination of the Requirements Statement is needed to ensure that it is being followed to the letter. Any deviations would usually have to be approved either by the project leader or by the customer.

The Development phase can be split into two sections, that of **Prototyping** and **Production Ready Application Creation**. Prototyping is the stage of the Development phase that produces a pseudo-complete application, which for all intents and purposes appears to be fully functional.

Developers use this stage to demo the application to the customer as another check that the final software solution answers the problem posed. When they are given the OK from the customer, the final version code is written into this shell to complete the phase.

Phase 5: Implementation

In the **Implementation Phase,** the project reaches fruition. After the Development phase of the SDLC is complete, the system is implemented. Any hardware that has been purchased will be delivered and installed. Software, which was designed in phase 3, and programmed in phase 4 of the SDLC, will be installed on any PCs that require it. Any people that will be using the program will also be trained during this phase of the SDLC.

During the Implementation phase, both the hardware and the software is tested. Although the programmer will find and fix many problems, almost invariably, the user will uncover problems that the developer has been unable to simulate. This leads on to the sixth and final stage.

Phase 6: Audit and Maintenance

Phase 6 of the SDLC is the **Audit and Maintenance Phase**. In this phase someone (usually the client, but sometimes a third party such as an auditor) studies the implemented system to ensure that it actually fulfills the Requirements Statement. Most important, the system should have solved the problem or deficiency, or satisfied the desire that was identified in phase 1 of the SDLC - the Preliminary Investigation.

More than a few programs and systems have been fully developed that, for one reason or another, simply never met the original requirements. The Maintenance portion of this phase deals with any changes that need to be made to the system.

Changes are sometimes the result of the system not completely fulfilling its original requirements, but they could also be the result of customer satisfaction. Sometimes the customer is so happy with what they have got that they want more. Changes can also be forced upon the system because of governmental regulations, such as changing tax laws, while at other times changes come about due to alterations in the business rules of the customer.

Summary

To recap, we have six phases in the SDLC. They form the plan of taking a customer's requirement and turning it into the finished application.

Learn to Program Objects with Visual Basic

Index

A

B

C

D

E

F

G

H

I

K

L

M

P

Q

R

S

Learn to Program Objects with Visual Basic

Y2K 'You can Be an Author, too' Shock

John Smiley, internationally acclaimed author, programmer, teacher, and all-around nice guy, never seems to be far away from the media. Some may argue it comes with the job. Unfortunately, the kind of coverage he's recently experienced since embarking upon his writing career has been less than helpful.

Experts and skeptics alike all agree that there's nothing wrong with his writing. And while the media have been unable to unearth anything unsavory, nonetheless his name just seems to keep coming up.

Earlier this year, Smiley was cleared of any culpability in the East Coast VB riots. An appeal against the summer's teaching quotas successfully overturned the previous verdict that one programming teacher should not have in excess of 30,000 students, which Mr. Smiley (known as Professor Smiley to his loving fans) most definitely has, even before you count the cable TV audience.

As a response to the appeal, rivals have launched an inquiry by the Monopolies Commission, with the claim that Professor Smiley has no right to take over the entire programming education arena by himself, and has ordered the publishing house Active Path to do more to foster the teaching careers of others. John Smiley himself has yet to release a statement, but his press officer did state that Smiley did not feel that the move would lose him any students. Mr. Smiley's stance has always been that he wanted to reach as many people as possible and teach them all to program. If more authors can reach more people, Mr. Smiley will, apparently, be delighted.

In an exclusive story, Active Path have revealed that Smiley wannabes now have the chance to break into the market for themselves. Their spokeswoman, **Sarah Inston**, told us:

"If you think you could be the next John Smiley, and you have a deep knowledge of programming, probably some teaching experience, and the desire to communicate with a beginner audience, please contact me via `authors@ActivePath.com`. We're particularly keen to hear from people who want to teach Java, web technologies, databases, and Visual Basic. Please contact us and tell us about your ideas. We always listen."

Learn to Program Objects with Visual Basic
Bullina's
China

Forthcoming Titles from Active Path

We are continuing to expand our output to teach you the programming skills that you need.

Our next publications are:

Learn to Program Websites with HTML

– a comprehensive guide to getting started on the web

Learn to Program on the Web with Visual Basic (by John Smiley)

– how to web-enable your Visual Basic programs

Learn to Program Successful Visual Basic Applications

– the detailed steps in developing a project from start to finish: everything from budgeting and planning, through to testing and maintenance

Learn to Program Objects with Visual Basic

Learn To Program Objects with Visual Basic 6 - Registration Card

Name ______________________

Address ______________________

____

____

____

City__________ State/Region __________

Country__________ Postcode/Zip __________

E-mail ______________________

Occupation ______________________

How did you hear about this book? ______________________

☐ Book review (name) ______________________

☐ Advertisement (name) ______________________

☐ Recommendation ______________________

☐ Catalog ______________________

☐ Other ______________________

Where did you buy this book? ______________________

☐ Bookstore (name) __________ City__________

☐ Computer Store (name) ______________________

☐ Mail Order ______________________

☐ Other ______________________

What influenced you in the purchase of this book?

☐ Cover Design

☐ Contents

☐ Other (please specify) ______________________

How did you rate the overall contents of this book?

☐ Excellent ☐ Good

☐ Average ☐ Poor

What did you find most useful about this book? ______________________

What did you find least useful about this book? ______________________

Please add any additional comments. ______________________

What other subjects will you buy a computer book on soon? ______________________

What is the best computer book you have used this year? ______________________

Note: This information will only be used to keep you updated about new Active Path titles and will not be used for any other purpose or passed to any other third party.